HUMAN DIGNITY IN INTERNATIONAL LAW

Over the past two centuries, the concept of human dignity has moved from the fringes to the centre of the international legal system. This book is the first detailed historical, theoretical and legal investigation of human dignity as a normative value, the intellectual sources that shaped its legal recognition, and the main legal instruments used to give it expression in international law. Ginevra Le Moli addresses the broad historical and philosophical developments relating to the legal expression of dignity and the doctrinal geography of human dignity in international law, with a focus on international humanitarian law, international human rights law and international criminal law. The book fills a major lacuna in the literature by providing a comprehensive account of dignity within international law that draws on an extensive documentary and archival basis and a vast body of decisions of international judicial and quasi-judicial bodies

Ginevra Le Moli is Assistant Professor of International Law at the Grotius Centre for International Legal Studies, Leiden University, and a Fellow of the Cambridge Centre for Environment, Energy and Natural Resources Governance (C-EENRG), University of Cambridge.

ASIL STUDIES IN INTERNATIONAL LEGAL THEORY

The purpose of the ASIL Studies in International Legal Theory series is to clarify and improve the theoretical foundations of international law. Too often the progressive development and implementation of international law has foundered on confusion about first principles. This series raises the level of public and scholarly discussion about the structure and purposes of the world legal order and how best to achieve global justice through law.

This series grows out of the International Legal Theory project of the American Society of International Law. The ASIL Studies in International Legal Theory series deepens this conversation by publishing scholarly monographs and edited volumes of essays considering subjects in international legal theory.

Books in the Series

Human Dignity in International Law
Ginevra Le Moli

Tipping Points in International Law: Commitment and Critique
Edited by Jean d'Aspremont and John Haskell

Ethical Leadership in International Organizations: Concepts, Narratives, Judgment, and Assessment
Edited by Maria Varaki and Guilherme Vasconcelos Vilaca

International Law as Behavior
Edited by Harlan Grant Cohen and Timothy Meyer

Space and Fates of International Law: Between Leibniz and Hobbes
Ekaterina Yahyaoui Krivenko

Why Punish Perpetrators of Mass Atrocities?: Purposes of Punishment in International Criminal Law
Edited by Florian Jeßberger and Julia Geneuss

The Challenge of Inter-Legality
Edited by Jan Klabbers and Gianluigi Palombella

The Nature of International Law
Miodrag A. Jovanović

Reexamining Customary International Law
Edited by Brian D. Lepard

Theoretical Boundaries of Armed Conflict and Human Rights
Edited by Jens David Ohlin

Human Rights in Emergencies
Edited by Evan J. Criddle

The Theory of Self-Determination
Edited by Fernando R. Tesón

Negotiating State and Non-State Law: Global and Local Legal Pluralism
Edited by Michael A. Helfand

Jus Post Bellum and Transitional Justice
Edited by Larry May and Elizabeth Edenberg

Normative Pluralism and International Law: Exploring Global Governance
Edited by Jan Klabbers and Touko Piipaerinen

The Future of International Law: Global Government
Joel P. Trachtman

Morality, Jus Post Bellum, and International Law
Edited by Larry May and Andrew T. Forcehimes

Global Justice and International Economic Law: Opportunities and Prospects
Edited by Chios Carmody, Frank J. Garcia, and John Linarelli

Parochialism, Cosmopolitanism, and the Foundations of International Law
Edited by M. N. S. Sellers

The Role of Ethics in International Law
Edited by Donald Earl Childress III

The New Global Law
Rafael Domingo

Customary International Law: A New Theory with Practical Applications
Brian D. Lepard

International Criminal Law and Philosophy
Edited by Larry May and Zachary Hoskins

Whither the West?: Concepts on International Law in Europe and the United States
Edited by Chiara Giorgetti and Guglielmo Verdirame

Human Dignity in International Law

GINEVRA LE MOLI
Leiden University

CAMBRIDGE
UNIVERSITY PRESS

CAMBRIDGE
UNIVERSITY PRESS

Shaftesbury Road, Cambridge CB2 8EA, United Kingdom

One Liberty Plaza, 20th Floor, New York, NY 10006, USA

477 Williamstown Road, Port Melbourne, VIC 3207, Australia

314–321, 3rd Floor, Plot 3, Splendor Forum, Jasola District Centre, New Delhi – 110025, India

103 Penang Road, #05–06/07, Visioncrest Commercial, Singapore 238467

Cambridge University Press is part of Cambridge University Press & Assessment, a department of the University of Cambridge.

We share the University's mission to contribute to society through the pursuit of education, learning and research at the highest international levels of excellence.

www.cambridge.org
Information on this title: www.cambridge.org/9781009045711

DOI: 10.1017/9781009042765

First published 2021
First paperback edition 2026

A catalogue record for this publication is available from the British Library

ISBN 978-1-316-51762-8 Hardback
ISBN 978-1-009-04571-1 Paperback

To my Family

Contents

Figures

Acknowledgements

This book is the culmination of many years of research, which started out as a doctoral project in 2015. The guidance I received from my PhD supervisors made the long journey a unique and wonderful experience. The thesis was written under the direction of Professor Andrea Bianchi. I am deeply grateful for his wisdom, sensibility, availability and precious comments. He believed in my idea since the beginning and supported me in finding the road of human dignity and translating its language into international law. Professor Andrew Clapham acted as the second reader of the thesis and encouraged me with enthusiasm from the beginning of my research. His inputs have been vital in shaping this text. I would also like to thank Professor Sarah Nouwen for her support during my stay in Cambridge and for having accepted to be part of my doctoral jury. Her detailed and insightful comments on the dissertation and during the defence have been extremely useful to refine the text for publication.

I am also grateful to all the professors I have had the privilege of meeting and collaborating with over the years. I am especially grateful to Professors Paola Gaeta, Marcelo Kohen and Makane Mbengue, for the many conversations on the fundamental principles of international law and for their encouragement throughout my studies as well as in my first steps as an assistant professor. I also would like to thank Professors Gian Luca Burci, Vincent Chetail, Nico Krisch and Fuad Zarbiyev, part of the faculty members of the Graduate Institute, as well as Professors Sarah Cleveland and Shaheed Fatima for their support. I must express an equal sense of gratitude to the wonderful staff of the Lauterpacht Centre for International law, University of Cambridge, for making the last six months of my PhD journey so intellectually stimulating. In particular, thanks to Professor Eyal Benvenisti for his warm welcome and for having shared with me his views on my research.

Through the several years spent in Geneva, a 'Geneva Family' of friends formed, to whom I owe a great debt of gratitude. A PhD is supposed to be a lonely and gruelling experience, but having them around made it a brilliant one (only the silent Lac Léman holds memory of long walks and conversations on the masters of philosophy, history and law). This family is now extending to my new intellectual homes in Leiden and Cambridge.

And for having taught me the meaning of *humanity*, I owe thanks to my family. To their positive energy, to my mother's courage and enthusiasm, to my father's unique sense of humour and imagination, to my sister Lucrezia's friendship and special soul, and to Amedeo, who left us too early but still inhabits a world within this world. I hope at least half of your perseverance and sense of curiosity, on or off stage, found expression in the pages of this manuscript. Lastly, I am grateful to Jorge, for his heart, energy and vision, spiced with constant support.

A heartfelt thank you for being part of my story. Grazie.

Table of Instruments

INTERNATIONAL

International Conventions

Agreement for the Prosecution and Punishment of Major War Criminals of the European Axis, and Establishing the Charter of the International Military Tribunal (IMT), annex (1951) 82 UNTS 279

C107 ILO Convention No. 107 Indigenous and Tribal Populations Convention, 1957 (entered into force, 2 June 1959)

C111 ILO Convention No. 111 Discrimination (Employment and Occupation) Convention, 1958 (entered into force, 15 June 1960)

C122 ILO Convention No. 122 Employment Policy Convention, 1964 (No. 122). Convention concerning Employment Policy (entered into force, 15 July 1966)

C155 ILO Convention No. 155 Concerning Occupational Safety and Health and the Working Environment, 1331 UNTS 279, 1 August 1983 (entered into force, 22 June 1981)

Charter of the IMT, Nuremberg, 8 August 1945

Charter of the United Nations, 1 UNTS XVI, 26 June 1945 (entered into force, 24 October 1945)

Constitution of the ILO, originally adopted on 11 April 1919 and subsequently amended in 1922, 1945, 1946, 1953, 1962 and 1972

Constitution of the United Nations Educational, Scientific and Cultural Organization (UNESCO), 16 November 1945, 3 Bevans 1311

Convention (II) for the Amelioration of the Condition of the Wounded, Sick, and Shipwrecked Members of Armed Forces at Sea, 12 August 1949, 6 UST 3217, 75 UNTS 85

Convention (III) Relative to the Treatment of Prisoners of War, 12 August 1949, 6 UST 3316, 75 UNTS 135
Convention (IV) Relative to the Protection of Civilian Persons in Time of War, TIAS No. 3365, 75 UNTS 287, 12 August 1949 (entered into force, 21 October 1950)
Convention (IV) Respecting the Laws and Customs of War on Land and Regulations, The Hague, 18 October 1907 (entered into force, 26 January 1910)
Convention against Torture and Other Cruel, Inhuman or Degrading Treatment or Punishment, GA Res. 39/46 (1984), 10 December 1984 (entered into force, 26 June 1987)
Convention for the Amelioration of the Condition of the Wounded and Sick in Armies in the Field, 1906
Convention for the Amelioration of the Condition of the Wounded and Sick in Armies in the Field, 27 July 1929, 47 Stat. 2074, TS No. 847
Convention for the Amelioration of the Condition of the Wounded in Armies in the Field, Geneva, 22 August 1864
Convention (I) for the Amelioration of the Condition of the Wounded and Sick in Armed Forces in the Field, 12 August 1949, Art. 63, 6 UST 3114, 75 UNTS 31
Convention for the Protection of Cultural Property in the Event of Armed Conflict, 249 UNTS 216, 14 May 1954 (entered into force, 7 August 1956)
Convention for the Suppression of the Traffic in Persons and of the Exploitation of the Prostitution of Others, GA Res. 317(IV), 2 December 1949 (entered into force, 25 July 1951)
Convention for the Suppression of Unlawful Acts against the Safety of Maritime Navigation, with Related Protocol, UNTS 1678, I–29004 (adopted 10 March 1988, entered into force, 1 March 1992)
Convention on Biological Diversity of 1992, 5 June 1992, 31 ILM 818
Convention on Cluster Munitions, Dublin, 30 May 2008 (entered into force, 1 August 2010)
Convention on the Non-Applicability of Statutory Limitations to War Crimes and Crimes against Humanity, GA Res. 2391, 26 November 1968 (entered into force, 11 November 1970)
Convention on the Prevention and Punishment of the Crime of Genocide, GA Res. 260 (III) A, 9 December 1948 (entered into force, 12 January 1951)
Convention on the Prohibition of the Development, Production and Stockpiling of Bacteriological and Toxin Weapons and on Their Destruction, 10 April 1972 (entered into force, 26 March 1975)

Convention on the Prohibition of the Development, Production, Stockpiling and Use of Chemical Weapons and on Their Destruction, 3 September 1992 (entered into force, 29 April 1997)

Convention on the Rights of Persons with Disabilities, 24 January 2007, A/RES/61/106

Convention on the Rights of the Child, GA Res. 44/25 (1989), 20 November 1989 (entered into force, 2 September 1990)

Convention on the Safety of United Nations and Associated Personnel, GA Res. 49/49 (1994), 9 December 1994 (entered into force, 15 January 1999)

Convention Relating to the Status of Refugees, 28 July 1951, United Nations, Treaty Series, vol. 189, p. 137

Convention relative to the Treatment of Prisoners of War, 27 July 1929, 47 Stat. 2021, TS No. 846

Convention revising the General Act of Berlin, 26 February 1885, and of the General Act and the Declaration of Brussels, 2 July 1890, signed at Saint-Germain-en-Laye, 10 September 1919 (1922) LNTSer 19, 8 LNTS 27

Convention to Suppress the Slave Trade and Slavery, 25 September 1926, 60 LNTS 253 (entered into force, 9 March 1927)

Covenant of the League of Nations, 28 April 1919

International Convention on the Elimination of All Forms of Racial Discrimination, GA Res. 2106 (XX), 660 UNTS 195, 21 December 1965 (entered into force, 4 January 1969)

International Convention on the Protection of the Rights of all Migrant Workers and Members of Their Families, GA Res. 45/158, 18 December 1990 (entered into force, 1 July 2003)

International Covenant on Civil and Political Rights (adopted 16 December 1966, entered into force, 23 March 1976) 999 UNTS 171 (ICCPR)

International Covenant on Civil and Political Rights, GA Res. 2200a (XXI), 999 UNTS 171, 16 December 1966 (entered into force, 23 March 1976)

International Covenant on Economic, Social and Cultural Rights, (adopted 16 December 1966, entered into force, 3 January 1976) 993 UNTS 3 (ICESCR)

International Covenant on Economic, Social and Cultural Rights, GA Res. 2200a (XXI), 16 December 1966 (entered into force, 3 January 1976)

Limitation of Employment of Force for Recovery of Contract Debts (Hague, II), Convention signed at The Hague October 18, 1907, 36 Stat. 2241, Treaty Series 537

Protocol Additional to the Geneva Conventions of 12 August 1949, and Relating to the Protection of Victims of International Armed Conflicts, 1125 UNTS 3, 8 June 1977 (entered into force, 7 December 1978)

Protocol Additional to the Geneva Conventions of 12 August 1949, and Relating to the Protection of Victims of Non-International Armed Conflicts, 1125 UNTS 609, 8 June 1977 (entered into force, 7 December 1978)
Protocol against the Smuggling of Migrants by Land, Sea and Air, Supplementing the UN Convention against Transnational Organized Crime, GA Res. 55/25, 15 November 2000 (entered into force, 28 January 2004)
Rome Statute of the International Criminal Court, 2187 UNTS 90, 17 July 1998 (entered into force, 1 July 2002)
Statute of the International Court of Justice, 3 Bevans 1179, 26 June 1945 (entered into force, 24 October 1945)
Statutes of the International Red Cross and Red Crescent Movement (adopted by the 25th International Conference of the Red Cross at Geneva in 1986, amended in 1995 and 2006)
Supplementary Convention on the Abolition of Slavery, the Slave Trade and Institutions and Practices Similar to Slavery of 1956 (the Supplementary Convention), United Nations Treaty Series, vol. 226, p. 3 (entered into force, 30 April 1957)
Treaty between Great Britain, Germany, Austria, France, Italy, Russia, and Turkey for the Settlement of Affairs in the East, Berlin, 13 July 1878, 153 CTS 171 (Treaty of Berlin)
Treaty between the United States of America, Belgium, the British Empire, China, France, Italy, Japan, the Netherlands, and Portugal, Washington, 6 February 1922, Treaty Series No. 724
Treaty between the USA and the Other American Republics on the Protection of Artistic and Scientific Institutions and Historic Monuments (Roerich Pact), 15 April 1935, 167 LNTS 289 (entered into force, 26 August 1935)
Treaty for the Suppression of the African Slave-trade, 20 December 1841, signed by Austria, Great Britain, France (which did not ratify it), Prussia and Russia for the Suppression of the African Slave-trade, 73 CTS 32 [Quintuple Treaty]
Treaty of Amity and Commerce, adopted on 10 September 1785
Treaty of Versailles (1919), 2 Bevans 235
UN Convention against Transnational Organized Crime, GA Res. 55/383, 15 November 2000 (entered into force, 29 September 2003)
UN Convention on the Law of the Sea, GA Res. 48/263, 1833 UNTS 396, 10 December 1982 (entered into force, 14 November 1994)
UNESCO Convention against Discrimination in Education, 14 December 1960 (entered into force, 22 May 1962)

Other International Instruments and Documents

United Nations

UN SECURITY COUNCIL

Statute of the International Tribunal for Rwanda, Annex to S/RES/955, 8 November 1994

Statute of the International Tribunal for the Prosecution of Persons Responsible for Serious Violations of International Humanitarian Law Committed in the Territory of the Former Yugoslavia since 1991, Annex to Security Council S/RES/827, 25 May 1993

UN GENERAL ASSEMBLY

UNGA Res 95(I) (11 December 1946) Affirmation of the Principles of International Law recognized by the Charter of the Nuremberg Tribunal

UNGA Res. 217(III) (10 December 1948), Universal Declaration of Human Rights

UNGA Res 1514 (XV) (14 December 1960)

UNGA Res 1904 (XVIII) (20 November 1963) (Declaration on the Elimination of All Forms of Racial Discrimination) UN Doc A/RES/1904(XVIII)

UNGA Res 36/55 (25 November 1981) UN Doc A/RES/36/55

UNGA Res 1514 (XV) (14 December 1960) United Nations Declaration on the Granting of Independence to Colonial Countries and Peoples

UNGA Res 2103 A (XX) (20 December 1965) UN Doc A/RES/2103A(XX)

UNGA Res 2166 (XXI) (5 December 1966) UN Doc A/RES/2166(XXI)

UNGA Res 2167 (XXI) (5 December 1966) UN Doc A/RES/2167(XXI)

UNGA Res 2181 (XXI) (12 December 1966) UN Doc A/RES/2181(XXI)

UNGA Res 2222 (XXI) (19 December 1966) (outer space) UN Doc A/RES/2222(XXI)

UNGA Res 2340 (XXII) (18 December 1967) (sea-bed) UN Doc A/RES/2340 (XXII)

UNGA Res 2263 (XXII) (7 November 1967) UN Doc A/RES2263(XXII)

UNGA Res. 2542 (XXIV) (11 December 1969) Declaration on Social Progress and Development

UNGA Res. 2856 (XXVI) (20 December 1971) Declaration on the Rights of Mentally Retarded Persons of UNGA Res. 34/169, Code of Conduct for Law Enforcement Officials of 17 December 1979

UNGA Res. A/RES/3318(XXIX) (14 December 1974) Declaration on the Protection of Women and Children in Emergency and Armed Conflict

UNGA Res. 3348 (XXIX) (17 December 1974) Universal Declaration on the Eradication of Hunger and Malnutrition, 16 November 1974;

UNGA Res. 3384 (XXX) (10 November 1975) Declaration on the Use of Scientific and Technological Progress in the Interests of Peace and for the Benefit of Mankind

UNGA Res. 3447 (XXX) (9 December 1975) Declaration on the Rights of Disabled Persons

UNGA Res. 3452 (XXX) (9 December 1975) Declaration on the Protection of All Persons from Being Subjected to Torture and Other Cruel, Inhuman or Degrading Treatment or Punishment

UNGA Res 34/146 (17 December 1979) (International Convention against the Taking of Hostages) UN Doc A/RES/34/146

UNGA Res 34/46 (23 November 1979) UN Doc A/RES/34/46

UNGA Res. 34/169 (17 December 1979) Code of Conduct for Law Enforcement Officials

UNGA Res 34/180 (18 December 1979) UN Doc A/RES/34/180 (adoption of the Convention on the Elimination of All Forms of Discrimination against Women)

UNGA Res. A/RES/36/55 (25 November 1981) Declaration on the Elimination of All Forms of Intolerance and of Discrimination Based on Religion or Belief

UNGA Res. 39/11 (12 November 1984) Declaration on the Right of Peoples to Peace

UNGA Res. 43/173 (9 December 1988) Body of Principles for the Protection of All Persons under Any Form of Detention or Imprisonment

UNGA Res. 45/110 (14 December 1990) United Nations Standard Minimum Rules for Non-custodial Measures (The Tokyo Rules)

UNGA Res. 45/111 (14 December 1990) Basic Principles for the Treatment of Prisoners

UNGA Res. 45/113 (14 December 1990) United Nations Rules for the Protection of Juveniles Deprived of their Liberty

UNGA Res. 46/91 (16 December 1991) United Nations Principles for Older Persons

UNGA Res. 46/119 (17 December 1991) Principles for the Protection of Persons with Mental Illness and the Improvement of Mental Health Care

UNGA Res. 47/133 (18 December 1992) Declaration on the Protection of All Persons from Enforced Disappearance
UNGA Res 48/132 (20 December 1993) UN Doc A/RES/48/132
UNGA Res. 48/96 (4 March 1994) Standard Rules on the Equalization of Opportunities for Persons with Disabilities, A/RES/48/96
UNGA Res. S–26/2 (27 June 2001) Declaration of Commitment on HIV/AIDS, of Persons Living with and Affected by HIV/AIDS
UNGA Res 61/295 (2 October 2007) UN Doc A/RES/61/295 (UN Declaration on the Rights of Indigenous Peoples)
UNGA Res 62/160 (18 December 2007) UN Doc A/RES/62/160
UNGA Res. 62/211 (19 December 2007) UN Doc A/RES/62/211 ('Towards Global Partnership')
UNGA Res. 64/223 (21 December 2009) UN Doc A/RES/64/223 ('Towards Global Partnership')

CESCR (ECOSOC)

General Comment No 4: The Right to Adequate Housing (Art 11(1) of the Covenant) (13 December 1991) UN Doc E/1992/23
General Comment No 12: The Right to Adequate Food (Art 11), E/C.12/1999/5 (12 May 1999)
General Comment No 13 (Twenty-first session, 1999): The Right to Education (Art 13 of the Covenant), E/C.12/1999/10
General Comment No 14: The Right to the Highest Attainable Standard of Health (Art 12), E/C.12/2000/4 (11 August 2000)
General Comment No. 18: Obligations of Actors Other than State Parties, HRI/GEN/1/Rev.9 (Vol I) 243 (24 November 2005)
General Comment No 21: Right of Everyone to Take Part in Cultural Life (Art 15, Para 1a of the Covenant on Economic, Social and Cultural Rights), E/C.12/GC/21 (21 December 2009)

UN Treaty Bodies

CAT

General Comment No. 3 (2012), Implementation of article 14 by States parties, CAT/C/GC/3 (13 December 2012)

HRC

General Comment No. 7: Article 7 (Prohibition of torture or cruel, inhuman or degrading treatment or punishment) [General comment No. 7 has been replaced by general comment No. 20], Sixteenth session (30 May 1982)
General Comment No. 9: Article 10 (Humane treatment of persons deprived of their liberty) [General comment No. 9 has been replaced by general comment No. 21], Sixteenth session (30 July 1982)
General Comment No. 15: The position of aliens under the Covenant, Twenty-seventh session (30 September 1986), CCPR
General Comment No. 16: Article 17 (Right to privacy), Thirty-second session (28 September 1988)
General Comment No. 20: Article 7 (Prohibition of torture, or other cruel, inhuman or degrading treatment or punishment), Forty-fourth session (30 September 1992)
General Comment No. 21: Article 10 (Humane treatment of persons deprived of their liberty) Forty-fourth session (13 March 1993)
General Comment No. 24: Issues relating to Reservations made upon Ratification or Accession to the Covenant or the Optional Protocols thereto, or in relation to Declarations under Article 41 of the Covenant, CCPR/C/21/Rev.1/Add.6 (11 November 1994)
General Comment No. 28: Article 3 (The equality of rights between men and women) (Replaces general comment No. 4), CCPR/C/21/Rev.1/Add.10 (29 March 2000)
General Comment No. 29: Article 4 (Derogations during a State of Emergency), CCPR/C/21/Rev.1/Add.11 (31 August 2001)
General Comment No. 31: The Nature of the General Legal Obligation Imposed on States Parties to the [International] Covenant [on Civil and Political Rights], CCPR/C/21/Rev.1/Add.13 (29 March 2004)
General Comment No. 36: Article 6 of the ICCPR, on the right to life, CCPR/C/GC/36 (3 September 2019)

CEDAW

General Recommendation No. 19: Violence against women, Eleventh session (1992).
General Recommendation No. 21: Equality in marriage and family relations, Thirteenth session (1994)

General Recommendation No. 23: Political and public life, Sixteenth session (1997)
General Recommendation No. 24: Article 12 of the Convention (women and health), Twentieth session (1999)
General Recommendation No. 25: Article 4, paragraph 1, of the Convention (temporary special measures), Thirtieth session (2004)
General Recommendation No. 27: Older women and protection of their human rights (16 December 2010)
Joint General Recommendation No. 31 of the CEDAW/General Comment No. 18 of the CRC on harmful practices, CEDAW/C/GC/31-CRC/C/GC/18 (14 November 2014)
General Recommendation No. 32: Gender-related dimensions of refugee status, asylum, nationality and statelessness of women (14 November 2014)
General Recommendation No. 33: Women's access to justice (3 August 2015)
General Recommendation No. 34: Rights of rural women (7 March 2016)
General Recommendation No. 35: Gender-based violence against women, updating general recommendation No. 19 (26 July 2017)
General Recommendation No. 36: Right of girls and women to education (27 November 2017)

CERD

General Recommendation No. 13: Training of law enforcement, officials in the protection of human rights, Forty-second session (1993)
General Recommendation No. 21: Right to self-determination, Forty-eighth session (1996)
General Recommendation No. 22: Article 5 of the Convention on refugees and displaced persons, Forty-ninth session (1996)
General Recommendation No. 30: Discrimination against non-citizens, Sixty-fifth session (2005)
General Recommendation No. 31: Prevention of racial discrimination in the administration and functioning of the criminal justice system, Sixty-fifth session (2005)
General Recommendation No. 32: The meaning and scope of special measures in the International Convention on the Elimination of All Forms Racial Discrimination (24 September 2009)
General Recommendation No. 35: Combating racist hate speech (26 September 2013)

CESCR

General Comment No. 5: Persons with disabilities, Eleventh session (1994)

General Comment No. 4: The right to adequate housing (art. 11 (1) of the Covenant), Sixth session (1991)

General Comment No. 6: The economic, social and cultural rights of older persons, Thirteenth Session (1995)

General Comment No. 12: The right to adequate food (art. 11), Twenty-first session (1999)

General Comment No. 13: The right to education (art. 13 of the Covenant), Twenty-first Session (1999)

General Comment No. 14: The right to the highest attainable standard of health (art. 12 of the International Covenant on Economic, Social and Cultural Rights), E/C.12/2000/4 (2000)

General Comment No. 15: The right to water (arts. 11 and 12 of the International Covenant on Economic, Social and Cultural Rights), E/C.12/2002/11 (20 January 2003)

General Comment No. 16: The equal right of men and women to the enjoyment of all economic, social and cultural rights (art. 3 of the International Covenant on Economic, Social and Cultural Rights), E/C.12/2005/4 (11 August 2005)

General Comment No. 17: The right of everyone to benefit from the protection of the moral and material interests resulting from any scientific, literary or artistic production of which he or she is the author (art. 15, para. 1 (c), of the Covenant), E/C.12/GC/17 (12 January 2006)

General Comment No. 18: The right to work, E/C.12/GC/18 (6 February 2006)

General Comment No. 19: The right to social security (art. 9), E/C.12/GC/19 (4 February 2008)

General Comment No. 20: Non-discrimination in economic, social and cultural rights (art. 2, para. 2, of the International Covenant on Economic, Social and Cultural Rights), E/C.12/GC/20 (2 July 2009)

General Comment No. 21: Right of everyone to take part in cultural life (art. 15, para. 1 (a), of the International Covenant on Economic, Social and Cultural Rights), E/C.12/GC/21 (21 December 2009)

General Comment No. 22: The right to sexual and reproductive health (art. 12 of the International Covenant on Economic, Social and Cultural Rights), E/C.12/GC/22 (2 May 2016)

General Comment No. 24: State obligations under the International Covenant on Economic, Social and Cultural Rights in the context of business activities, E/C.12/GC/24 (10 August 2017)

CMW

General Comment No. 2 on the rights of migrant workers in an irregular situation and members of their families, CMW/C/GC/2 (28 August 2013)

CRC

General Comment No. 1, Article 29 (1): The Aims of Education, CRC/GC/2001/1 (17 April 2001)
General Comment No. 4: Adolescent health and development in the context of the Convention on the Rights of the Child, CRC/GC/2003/4 (1 July 2003)
General Comment No. 6: Treatment of Unaccompanied and Separated Children Outside their Country of Origin CRC/GC/2005/6 (1 September 2005)
General Comment No. 7: Implementing child rights in early childhood, CRC/C/GC/7/Rev.1 (20 September 2006)
General Comment No. 8: The right of the child to protection from corporal punishment and other cruel or degrading forms of punishment (arts. 19; 28, para. 2 and 37, inter alia), CRC/C/GC/8 (2 March 2007)
General Comment No. 9: The rights of children with disabilities, CRC/C/GC/9 (27 February 2007)
General Comment No. 10: Children's rights in juvenile justice, CRC/C/GC/10 (25 April 2007)
General Comment No. 11: Indigenous children and their rights under the Convention, CRC/C/GC/11 (12 February 2009)
General Comment No. 13: The right of the child to freedom from all forms of violence, CRC/C/GC/13 (18 April 2011)
General Comment No. 14: The right of the child to have his or her best interests taken as a primary consideration (art. 3, para. 1), CRC/C/GC/14 (29 May 2013)
General Comment No. 16: State obligations regarding the impact of the business sector on children's rights, CRC/C/GC/16 (17 April 2013)
General Comment No. 20: The implementation of the rights of the child during adolescence, CRC/C/GC/20 (6 December 2016)

International Labor Organization

International Labour Conference, 26th, The Declaration of Philadelphia, 1944

International Law Commission

Articles on Responsibility of States for Internationally Wrongful Acts, commentary, YILC, 2001

Draft Articles on State Responsibility adopted by the ILC on first reading, January 1997, Doc. No. A/CN.4/L. 528/Add. 2

Draft Code of Crimes against the Peace and Security of Mankind (Responsibility of States) provides for the same distinction, Report of the International Law Commission on the Work of its Forty-eighth Session, II (2) YbILC 1996, 17

Lauterpacht, H, First Report on the Law of Treaties, II YbILC 1953, 154– 156, para. 4

Fitzmaurice, G, Second Report, YbILC 1957, Vol. II

Fitzmaurice, G, Third Report, draft article 18(2) and commentary, YbILC 1958, Vol. II

Fitzmaurice, G, Fourth Report, draft articles 18 and 20 and commentaries, YbILC 1959, Vol. II

Waldock, H, Second Report on the Law of Treaties, II YbILC 1963

Riphagen, W, Sixth Report, A/CN.4/389 and Corr.1& Corr.2, YILC 1985, vol. II, Part One

Ago, R, Second Report on State Responsibility, Doc. A/CN.4/233, YILC 1970, vol. II

Ago, R, Fifth Report on State Responsibility, II(1) YbILC 1976

Arangio–Ruiz, G, Fourth report on State Responsibility, A/CN.4/444 and Add. 1–3, YbILC 1992, vol. II, Part Two

Report of the ILC on the Work of its Forty–Eighth Session, Doc. No. A/51/10, II(2) YbILC 1996 32

Crawford, J, Third Report on State Responsibility, A/CN.4/507, 2000

Crawford, J, Fourth Report on State Responsibility, A/CN.4/517 and Add. 1, 2001

Galicki, Z, Second Report of the Special Rapporteur on the Obligation to Extradite or Prosecute (aut dedere aut judicare), 59th session of the ILC (2007), A/CN.4/585

Other Documents

'Final Act of the Havana Meeting of the American Institute of International Law' [1917] 11(2) *AJIL* 47–53

Basic Principles on the Role of Lawyers Adopted by the Eighth United Nations Congress on the Prevention of Crime and the Treatment of Offenders, Havana, Cuba, 27 August to 7 September 1990

Capotorti, F, 'Study of the Rights of Persons Belonging to Ethnic, Religious and Linguistic Minorities, Sub-Commission on Prevention of Discrimination and Protection of Minorities', U.N. ESCOR, 30th Sess., U.N. Doc. EJCN.41Sub. 2/3841 REV. 1 (1979)

Commission on the Responsibility of the Authors of the War and on Enforcement of Penalities, Report Presented to the Preliminary Peace Conference, 29 March 1919, reprinted in [1920] 14(1) AJIL

Declaration and Action Plan of the III World Conference against Racism, Racial Discrimination, Xenophobia, Durban, 31 August – 8 September 2001, A/CONF.189/12

Declaration by United Nations, done 1 January 1942, entered into force 1 January 1942, 204 LNTS 381

Declaration of Rights, see 'A Declaration of Rights', Bishops of the National Catholic Walfare Conference (USA), June 1946

Declaration of the International Rights of Man, 12 October 1929, Institute of International Law, the original is in French, but an English version was published many years later: Institut de droit international, 'Declaration of International Rights of Man', 35 *AJIL* 663

Declaration on Race and Racial Prejudice, adopted and proclaimed by the General Conference of the United Nations Educational, Scientific and Cultural Organization at its twentieth session, on 27 November 1978

Declaration on Race and Racial Prejudice, UNESCO, 27 November 1978

Declaration Relative to the Universal Abolition of the Slave Trade, 8 February 1815, Consolidated Treaty Series, vol. 63, No. 473. Final Act of the Congress of Vienna, ACT, No. XV

Declaration Renouncing the Use, in Time of War, of Explosive Projectiles under 400 Grammes Weight, St Petersburg, 29 November/ 11 December 1868

Forty-ninth session (1996), General Recommendation XXII on article 5 of the Convention on refugees and displaced persons, CERD

Global Compact for Safe, Orderly and Regular Migration, Resolution adopted by the General Assembly on 19 December 2018, A/RES/73/195, 11 January 2019

Guidelines for Action on Children in the Criminal Justice System Recommended by Economic and Social Council resolution 1997/30 of 21 July 1997

Guidelines on the Role of Prosecutors Adopted by the Eighth United Nations Congress on the Prevention of Crime and the Treatment of Offenders, Havana, Cuba, 27 August to 7 September 1990

ICRC, 'Autonomous weapon systems: Technical, military, legal and humanitarian aspects', Expert meeting, Geneva, Switzerland, 26–28 March 2014 (ICRC 2014)

ICRC, Commentary on the First Geneva Convention: Convention (I) for the Amelioration of the Condition of the Wounded and Sick in Armed Forces in the Field, 2nd edition, 2016, or (in brief) as ICRC, Commentary on the First Geneva Convention, 2016

ILO Tripartite Declaration of Principles Concerning Multinational Enterprises and Social Policy (1977)

Inter-American Council of Jurists, Recommendaciones e Informes, Documentos Officiales, 1945–1947, Organization of American States, 1948, p. 18–19

Joint general recommendation No. 31 of the Committee on the Elimination of Discrimination against Women/General Comment No. 18 of the UN CRC on harmful practices, CEDAW/C/GC/31–CRC/C/GC/18, (14 November 2014)

Joint Inspection Unit, UN Corporate Partnerships, The Role and Functioning of the Global Compact, UN Doc. JIU/REP/2010/9 (2010)

Lauterpacht, H, Human Rights, the Charter of the United Nations, and the International Bill of the Rights of Man, – Preliminary Report, E/CN.4/89, International Law Association Conference (43rd, 1948)

League of Nations, Nansen International Office for Refugees, A.19.1933, Report of the Governing Body, 1, 5

League of Nations, Ten Years of World Cooperation (Secretariat of the League of Nations 1930), 269

Office of the US Chief of Counsel for Prosecution of Axis Criminality, *Nazi Conspiracy and Aggression*, Opinion and Judgment (US Government Printing Office 1946)

Project of an International Declaration Concerning the Laws and Customs of War, Brussels (27 August 1874)

Report of the Director-General (Part I) to the International Labour Conference, 'The ILO and human rights', 52nd Session, Report presented by the ILO to the International Conference on Human Rights (1968)

Sixty-fifth Session (2005), General Recommendation No. 30 (XXX) on discrimination against non-citizens, General recommendation No. 34 adopted by the Committee Racial discrimination against people of African descent, CERD/C/GC/34 (3 October 2011)

Standard Minimum Rules for the Treatment of Prisoners, adopted by the First United Nations Congress on the Prevention of Crime and the Treatment of

Offenders, held at Geneva in 1955, and approved by the Economic and Social Council by its resolutions 663 C (XXIV) of 31 July 1957 and 2076 (LXII) of 13 May 1977 (Part II)
Study of Discrimination in the Matter of Religious Rights and Practices, UN (N.Y.) 1960, E/CN.4/Sub.2/200/Rev.1
TEEB (The Economics of Ecosystems and Biodiversity), *Mainstreaming the Economics of Nature: A Synthesis of the Approach, Conclusions and Recommendations of TEEB*, 2010
The American Jewish Committee, 'Declaration of Human Rights' (October 1944)
The League and the Minorities Treaties, *Bulletin of International News*, Vol. 5, No. 18 (16 March 1929)
Third Decade to Combat Racism and Racial Discrimination and its Program of Action since 1993, A/RES/48/91
UN Guiding Principles on Business and Human Rights, Implementing the United Nations 'Protect, Respect and Remedy' Framework, Human Rights Council (16 June 2011)
UN Norms on the Responsibilities of Transnational Corporations and Other Business Enterprises with regard to Human Rights, adopted by the UN Sub–Commission on the Promotion and Protection of Human Rights, ECOSOC, Commentary to the Norms on the Responsibilities of Transnational Corporations and Other Business Enterprises with regard to Human Rights, UN Doc. E/CN.4/Sub.2/2003/38/Rev.2 (26 August 2003)
UNESCO, International Declaration on Human Genetic Data (22 July 2003)
UNESCO, Universal Declaration on Bioethics and Human Rights (19 October 2005)
UNESCO, Universal Declaration on Cultural Diversity (2 November 2001);
UNESCO, Universal Declaration on the Human Genome and Human Rights (11 November 1997)
Vienna Declaration and Programme of Action, A/CONF.157/23, (12 July 1993);
Vienna Declaration on the Right to Development of 1986, A/RES/41/128 (4 December 1986)

REGIONAL

African Union

ACHPR, Guidelines for National Periodic Reports, 1989

AU Convention for the Protection and Assistance of Internally Displaced Persons in Africa, Kampala, 23 October 2009 (not yet entered into force)
AU Convention on Preventing and Combating Corruption, Maputo, 11 July 2003 (entered into force, 4 August 2006)
Bamako Convention on the Ban of the Import into Africa and the Control of Transboundary Movement and Management of Hazardous Wastes within Africa, Bamako, 30 January 1991 (entered into force, 22 April 1998)
Convention of the OAU for the Elimination of Mercenarism in Africa, Libreville, 3 July 1977 (entered into force, 22 April 1985)
Guidelines on the Conditions of Arrest, Police Custody and Pre-trial Detention in Africa (April 2015)
Ouagadougou Declaration and Plan of Action on Accelerating Prisons and Penal Reforms in Africa (2003)
Principles and Guidelines on Human and Peoples' Rights while Countering Terrorism in Africa, adopted by the African Commission on Human and Peoples' Rights during its 56th Ordinary Session in Banjul, Gambia (21 April to 7 May 2015)
Principles and Guidelines on the Implementation of Economic, Social and Cultural Rights in the African Charter on Human and Peoples' Rights, African Commission on Human and Peoples' Rights, adopted by the Commission at its 48th Ordinary Session held from 10 to 24 November 2010 in Banjul, The Gambia
Protocol to the African Charter on Human and Peoples' Rights on the Rights of Women in Africa – Maputo Protocol, 11 July 2003
African Charter on Human and Peoples' Rights, adopted 27 June 1981, O.A.U. Doc. CAB/LEG/67 /3/Rev. 5 (Banjul Charter)
African Charter on the Rights and Welfare of the Child, 1 July 1990

Asia

Association of Southeast Asian Nations (ASEAN), ASEAN Human Rights Declaration, 18 November 2012

Council of Europe

Council of Europe

Council of Europe Convention on Action against Trafficking in Human Beings, Warsaw, 16 May 2005 (entered into force, 1 February 2008)

Council of Europe Criminal Law Convention on Corruption, Strasbourg, 4 November 1998 (entered into force, 1 July 2002)
European Convention for the Protection of Human Rights and Fundamental Freedoms, as Amended by Protocols No. 11 and 14, Rome, 4 November 1950 (entered into force with Protocol 14, 1 June 2010)
European Convention for the Protection of Human Rights and Fundamental Freedoms, First Protocol, 20 March 1952 (entered into force, 1 November 1998)
European Social Charter of the Council of Europe, as Revised on 3 May 1996 (entered into force, 1 July 1999)

European Union

Recommendation CM/Rec(2016)6 of the Committee of Ministers to member States on research on biological materials of human origin (Adopted by the Committee of Ministers on 11 May 2016 at the 1256th meeting of the Ministers' Deputies)
Convention on Action against Trafficking in Human Beings, Council of Europe Treaty Series – No. 197, Warsaw, 16 May 2005
Council of Europe Treaty Series – No. 195 Additional Protocol to the Convention on Human Rights and Biomedicine, concerning Biomedical Research, Strasbourg, 25 January 2005
Council of Europe Treaty Series – No. 203 Additional Protocol to the Convention on Human Rights and Biomedicine, concerning Genetic Testing for Health Purposes, Strasbourg, 27 November 2008
European Social Charter (ESC), and Revised Social Charter, European Treaty Series – No. 163, Strasbourg, 3 May 1996
European Treaty Series – No. 168, Additional Protocol to the Convention for the Protection of Human Rights and Dignity of the Human Being with regard to the Application of Biology and Medicine, on the Prohibition of Cloning Human Beings, Paris, 12 January 1998
European Treaty Series – No. 186 Additional Protocol to the Convention on Human Rights and Biomedicine concerning Transplantation of Organs and Tissues of Human Origin, Strasbourg, 24 January 2002
Explanations Relating to the Charter of Fundamental Rights, 14 December 2007, Official Journal of the European Union, C 303/17, (2007/C 303/02)
Guidelines, Recommendation Rec(2006)4 of the Committee of Ministers to member states on research on biological materials of human origin and its

Explanatory Memorandum (Adopted by the Committee of Ministers on 15 March 2006 at the 958th meeting of the Ministers' Deputies);

European Treaty Series – No. 164, Convention for the Protection of Human Rights and Dignity of the Human Being with regard to the Application of Biology and Medicine: Convention on Human Rights and Biomedicine, Oviedo, 4 April 1997

Protocol No. 13 to the Convention for the Protection of Human Rights and Fundamental Freedoms, concerning the abolition of the death penalty in all circumstances, ETS No.187, 3 May 2002 (entry into force, 1 July 2003)

Charter of Fundamental Rights of the European Union, 26 October 2012, 2012/C 326/02

League of Arab States

Arab Charter on Human Rights (Revised), 12 Int'l Hum. Rts. Rep. 893 (2005), 22 May 2004 (entered into force, 15 March 2008)

Cairo Declaration of Human Rights in Islam (OIC,1990)

Organization of American States

Additional Protocol to the American Convention on Human Rights in the Area of Economic, Social and Cultural Rights 'Protocol of San Salvador', OAS Treaty Series No. 69, 17 November 1988

American Convention on Human Rights, adopted at the Inter-American Specialized Conference on Human Rights, San José, Costa Rica, 22 November 1969

American Declaration of the Rights and Duties of Man, OAS, 2 May 1948

American Declaration on the Rights of Indigenous Peoples, AG/RES.2888 (XLVI-O/16)

Inter-American Convention against Corruption, 29 March 1996 (entered into force, 6 March 1997)

Inter-American Convention on Forced Disappearance of Persons, OAS, 9 June 1994

Inter-American Convention on the Elimination of All Forms of Discrimination against Persons with Disabilities, OAS, 7 June 1999, AG/RES. 1608 (XXIX-O/99)

Inter-American Convention on the Prevention, Punishment, and Eradication of Violence against Women, Adopted at Belém do Pará, Brasil, on 9 June 1994, at the twenty-fourth regular session of the General Assembly

Inter-American Convention to Prevent and Punish Torture, OAS Treaty Series, No. 67, 9 December 1985 (entered into force, 28 February 1987)
Statute of The Inter-American Commission on Human Rights, approved by Resolution N° 447 taken by the General Assembly of the OAS at its ninth regular session, held in La Paz, Bolivia, 1 October 1979

Organisation for Economic Cooperation and Development

OECD Convention on Combating Bribery of Foreign Public Officials in International Business Transactions, 21 November 1997 (entered into force, 15 February 1999)

STATEMENTS

Address given by Winston Churchill, The Council of Europe, Strasbourg, 17 August 1949
Address to the UN General Assembly by President George W. Bush, 14 September 2005
E Rodriguez Larreta, 'Inter-American Solidarity: Safeguarding the Democratic Ideal: Note from Uruguayan Foreign Minister to Secretary of State', Bulletin, 25 November 1945
Intervention du 28 janvier 1919 à la Conférence de la paix à Paris, Président du Conseil italien, M. Vittorio-Emanuele Orlando, in *La prassi italiana di diritto internazionale. Terza serie* (1919–1925) (vol. IV, Rome, 1995)
President Franklin D. Roosevelt, 1941 State of the Union Address 'The Four Freedoms', 87 Congressional Record (6 January 1941), Part I
I Gandhi, 'Man and Environment', Statement by Indira Gandhi (Prime Minister of India) to the Plenary Session of the UN Conference on the Human Environment, Stockholm, 14 June 1972
Address by the Secretary-General of the United Nations at the Opening of the World Conference on Human Rights, 14 June 1993, A/CONF.157/22, p. 3

VATICAN DOCUMENTS

Diuturnum Illud, Encyclical Letter of Pope Leo XIII (1981)
Gaudium et Spes, Vatican Council II (1965)
Pius XI, Encyclical Letter 'Mit Brennender Sorge', 14 March 1937
Pope John Paul II, *Centesimus Annus* (1991)

Pope John XXIII, *Pacem in Terris* (1963)
Pope Paul VI, *Populorum Progressio* (1967)
Pope Pius XI, *Quadragesimo Anno* (1931)
Lettre de S. Em. Le Cardinal Pacelli, 1937, in Semaines sociales de France, *La Personne humaine en péril*, (Clermont-Ferrand 1937)
Pope Francis, *Encyclical Letter Laudato Si'* (2015)

PROCEEDINGS

International

ILO

ILO, Conference of the International Labour Organization, New York and Washington DC, Record of Proceedings (Montreal) (1941)
Thomas, A., 'Le Bureau International du Travail', *Speech*, 5 November 1920 (ABIT, CAT/2/20/10)
Thomas, A, *Speech*, 15 February 1923 (ABIT, CAT/2/23/3) (Comité National d' Etudes sociales et politiques, Paris)
Thomas, A, *Speech*, 7 December 1924 (ABIT, CAT 2/24/5) (Belgrade)
Thomas, A, *Speech*, 27 October 1926 (ABIT, CAT/2/26/8) (Cambridge)
Thomas, A, *Speech on Disarmament*, 21 November 1921 (ABIT, CAT/2/21/5) (Geneva)

PCIJ

PCIJ, Advisory Committee Jurists: Proces-Verbaux of the Proceedings of the Committee, 16 June–24 July 1920, p. 11

ILC

ILC, I YbILC 1963, 76, para. 28 (685th Meeting), Statement by Mr Tunkin
ILC, I YbILC 1963, 62– 78 (683rd–686th Meetings)
ILC, I (1) YbILC 1966, 36– 41 (828th Meeting)
ILC, I YbILC 1996, 26, para. 26 (2436th Meeting), Statement by Mr Villagrán Kramer

Regional

Inter-American Juridical Committee, *The Dumbarton Oaks Proposals: Preliminary Comments and Recommendations of the Inter-American Juridical Committee* (Pan American Union, 1944)

The Foundations of International Order (proceedings of the Catholic Congress on International Peace, The Hague, 1938)

TRAVAUX PRÉPARATOIRES

Archives and Document Collections

Charles Malik Collection, Library of Congress, Manuscript Reading Room, Washington, DC

United Nations Archives, New York City

Official Records of the General Assembly, 1947–1980

Summary Records of the Commission on Human Rights, 1949–1974

Summary Records of the Economic and Social Council, 1967–1970

Summary Records of the Sixth Committee, 1972

Summary Records of the Social Committee of the Economic and Social Council, 1966–1967

Summary Records of the Sub-Commission on the Prevention of Discrimination and the Protection of Minorities, 1966–1970

Summary Records of the Third Committee, 1948–1980

Verbatim Records of the General Assembly Plenary, 1960

International Instruments

UN Charter

Draft Preamble to the Charter of the United Nations Proposed by the Union of South Africa, 26 April 1945, UNCIO, vol. 3

Preamble to the Charter of the United Nations Submitted by the South African Delegation in Revision of Draft of 26 April 1945, 3 May 1945, UNCIO, vol. 3

Fifth Meeting of Committee I/1, 14 May 1945, UN Conference on International Organization [UNCIO], vol. 6

Sixth Meeting of Committee I/1, 14 May 1945, UNCIO, vol. 6
Report of Rapporteur, Subcommittee I/1/A, to Committee I/1, 1 June 1945, UNCIO, vol. 6
Tenth Meeting of Committee I/1, 2 June 1945, UNCIO, vol. 6
Report of Rapporteur, Subcommittee I/1/A, Section 3, to Committee I/1, 5 June 1945, UNCIO, vol. 6
Thirteenth Meeting of Committee I/1, 5 June 1945, UNCIO, vol. 6
Report of Rapporteur, Subcommittee I/1/A, Section 3, to Committee I/1, 5 June 1945, UNCIO, vol. 6
Report of Rapporteur of Committee 1 to Commission I, 9 June 1945, UNCIO, vol. 6
Fourteenth Meeting of Committee I/1, 7 June 1945, UNCIO, vol. 6
Fifteenth Meeting of Committee I/1, 11 June 1945, UNCIO, vol. 6
First Session of Commission I, 14 June 1945, UNCIO, vol. 6
Summary Report of Eleventh Meeting of Steering Committee, 23 June 1945, UNCIO, vol. 5
Summary Report of Forty-First Meeting, 25 June 1945, UNCIO, vol. 17
Final Plenary Session, 26 June 1945, UNCIO, vol. 1
Statement of Uruguayan Delegation on Its Position with Reference to Chapters I and II as Considered by Committee I/1, 15 June 1945, UNCIO, vol. 6

UNESCO

Conference for the establishment of the UNESCO, Institute of Civil Engineers, London, 1–16 November 1945, ECO/CONF/29
'General Conference, First Session' (PDF). UNESDOC database. UNESCO House, Paris, from 20 November to 10 December 1946. UNESCO/C/30 [1 C/Resolutions] Item 14, p. 73: UNESCO, 1947
Huxley, J, *UNESCO: Its Purpose and Its Philosophy* (Preparatory Commission of UNESCO 1946)
National Archives, Paris 382AP134, 'Delegation francaise', 1 November 1945, UN Conference for the establishment of an educational and cultural organization (ECO/CONF) was convened in London from 1–16 November 1945

UDHR

A/C.3/339, 'Projet de la Declaration internationale des droits de l'homme: France: Amendements', p. 1

Drafts: E/CN.4/AC.l/3, Humphrey; E/CN.4/AC.l/W.2/Rev.l and Rev.2, Cassin

E/CN.4/11, Draft of a Resolution for the General Assembly Submitted by the Representative of India, 31 January 1947, p. 1

E/CN.4/147, Statement by Mr. René Cassin, Representative of France, on the Implementation of Human Rights, 16 June 1948

National Archives, Paris 382AP63, Cassin to Laugier, 1 September 1942

Verbatim Records/Meetings

382AP/128, dossier 3, 'Discours de René Cassin, Délégué de la France à l'Assemblée Générale des Nations Unies à Paris', 9 December 1948

Human Rights Commission, First Session, Summary Records, E/CN.4/SR.7, E/CN.4/SR.8 and E/CN.4/SR.9

Human Rights Commission, Second Session, E/CN.4/SR.34

Hundred and Sixty-Fifth Meeting of the Third Committee, 30 November 1948, A/C.3/SR.165

Hundred and Twenty-Seventh Meeting of the Third Committee, 9 November 1948, A/C.3/SR.127

Hundred and Twenty-Third Meeting of the Third Committee, 5 November 1948, A/C.3/SR.123 and A/C.3/264

Memorandum by the Division of Human Rights, E/CN.4/31, Yugoslav proposal, p. 35

Official Records of the General Assembly, Third Session, 1948

Recapitulation of Amendments to Article 1 of the Draft Declaration (E/800), A/C.3/243

Report of the First Session of the Drafting Committee to the Second Session of the Commission (E/CN.4/21/Annex F/p. 73)

Summary Record of the Ninety-Sixth Meeting [of the Third Committee], A/C.3/SR.96, p. 101

Thirty-Seventh Meeting of the Commission on Human Rights, 13 December 1947, E/CN.4/SR.37

Verbatim Record of the Hundred and Eightieth Meeting of the General Assembly, A/PV. 180

Verbatim Record of the Hundred and Eighty-First Meeting of the General Assembly, 10 December 1948, A/PV.181

Verbatim Records of the First Session of the Human Rights Commission, *The More Important Speeches and Interventions of Charles Malik* (Papers of Charles Habib 'Malik, Library of Congress, Manuscript Division)

Caribbean Commission

U.S. National Archives, RG 59/ 150/ 70/ UD 07D 68 – Box 39 (Caribbean Commission series)
U.S. National Archives, RG/ 59/ 150/ 70/ 28/ 6 – Box 40

Genocide Convention

A/C.6/177, 30 October 1947, Sixth Committee on the Legal Questions, Draft Convention on the Crime of Genocide, Resolution of the National Assembly of Panama
A/C.6/84, 25 November 1946, 22nd Meeting, Sixth Committee on the Legal Questions
A/C.6/91, 28 November 1946, 23rd Meeting, Sixth Committee on the Legal Questions
A/PV.123, 21 November 1947, General Assembly Hall
E/SR.218, General Statements on Draft Convention on the Crime of Genocide, 218th Meeting of ECOSOC, Palais de Nations, Geneva, 26 August 1948

Four Geneva Conventions of 1949

1946

Preliminary Conference of National Red Cross Societies for the Study of Conventions and Various Problems Relating to the Red Cross (Geneva, July 26 – August 3, 1946) [Preliminary Conference 1946]
Summary report on the work of the Preliminary Conference 1946, I – Convention Relative to the Treatment of Prisoners of War

1947

Proceedings of the Meeting for the study of Treaty Stipulations relative to the spiritual and intellectual needs of prisoners of war and civilian internees (Geneva, 3 and 4 March 1947), Convention relative to Prisoners of War, Art. 2 and 4, 27

Commission of government experts for the study of Conventions for the protection of war victims (Geneva, 14 to 26 April 1947): Preliminary documents submitted by the ICRC [Preliminary Documents Commission 1947]

Conference of Governmental Experts for the Study of Conventions Protecting Victims of War (Geneva, 14–26 April 1947) [Conference Governmental Experts 1947]: Program, committee reports, document No. 3

Report on the work of the Conference of Governmental Experts for the Study of Conventions Protecting Victims of War (Geneva, 14–26 April 1947), Report of the Third Committee

Joint Commission responsible for examining the texts of the draft Conventions to be submitted to the XVIIth International Conference of the Red Cross (Geneva, 15–16 September 1947)

1948

XVIIth International Conference of the Red Cross, Stockholm, August 1948: Documents B.III, Resolution 1

Summary of the proceedings of the sub-commissions of the Legal Commission [of the] XVII International Conference of the Red Cross, Stockholm, August 1948

1949

Revised and new Draft Conventions for the protection of war victims: Remarks and proposals submitted by the ICRC: Document for the consideration of governments invited by the Swiss Federal Council to attend the Diplomatic Conference at Geneva (21 April 1949)

Diplomatic Conference of Geneva (21 April to 12 August 1949: Geneva) [Diplomatic Conference 1949]

Diplomatic Conference 1949, stenograms of Commission I, volume II, 24th meeting of 31 May 1949

Diplomatic Conference 1949, stenograms of Commission I, Volume III, 30th meeting of 21 June 1949

Diplomatic Conference 1949, stenograms of Commission I, volume III, 35th meeting of 1 July 1949

Diplomatic Conference 1949, stenograms of Commission II, Volume I, 9th meeting of 5 May 1949

Diplomatic Conference 1949, stenograms of Commission II, volume II, 19th meeting of 14 June 1949
Diplomatic Conference 1949, stenograms of Commission II, volume II, 20th meeting of 16 June 1949
Diplomatic Conference 1949, stenograms of Commission III, volume I, 10th meeting of 6 May 1949
Diplomatic Conference 1949, stenograms of Commission III, Volume II, 23rd meeting of 25 May 1949
Diplomatic Conference 1949, stenograms of Commission III, Volume II, 24th meeting of 27 May 1949

Refugee Convention and Related Documents

Gustave Ador to League Secretary-General Eric Drummond 20 February 1921, Reprinted as League Council Document 11/111/69/10598, 2
Jean Gout to Drummond 11 April 1921. Reprinted in C. 126.M.72.1921 VII. 3 The French position was formed in part through substantial lobbying from the ICRC
Letter from Baker to Lodge, 17 August 1921, NBKR 4/450
Noel-Baker Archives (NBKR) 4.450 'Memorandum on the Possible Action of the League in Connection with Russian Refugees', 3–4
Rapport de M. Slavic concenant son activité a Paris du 1 au 8 Mai 1921, LNA R1713/12606
Report from Brig. General C. B. Thomson, 21 April 1921 League of Nations Archive, Geneva (LNA) R1713/12381
Russian Refugees – Note by the Secretary-General, LNA R1713/15001
The Refugee Convention, 1951, *The Travaux Préparatoires Analysed with a Commentary by Dr Paul Weis* (UNHCR 1990)
United Kingdom Public Records Office, FO371 6867/N5827/38/38, 17 May 1921
Wrangel to Drummond, 17 June 1921, C. 126.M.72.1921 VII. 29

Declaration on Promotion of World Peace and Cooperation

'Zhou Enlai's Report on the Asian-African Conference, Made at the Meeting of the Standing Committee of the National People's Congress', 13 May 1955

Abdoh, D, 'The Bandung Conference. An Appreciation', Tehran: British Foreign Office, Tehran Embassy, 3 May 1955, 1–2, National Archives UK, Kew, FO 371/116984, 1071/55/55, D2231/336

Casey, RG, Asian-African Conference: Cabinet Submission No. 373, c. May 1955, 3, 4, National Archives of Australia, A1838/2

Final Communiqué of the Asian-African Conference, Bandung, 24 April 1955, p. 9

Final Communiqué, Article C–1, as reproduced in Kahin, The Asian-African Conference, 80

Hassan, F, *Collected Documents of the Asian-African Conference*, 18–24 April 1955 [Centre for the Study of Asian-African and Developing Countries]

Loveday, HM, 'ROK Reaction to Bandung Conference', 3, Seoul: Department of External Affairs, Australia, Seoul Delegation, 4 May 1955, 1, National Archives of Australia, A1838/2, 851/19/1, Memorandum No. 127, Seoul Ref. 9/8. 55

Mahmoud Aboul Fath, Letter to Bandung Delegates, 13 April 1955, Charles Malik Collection, Box 130, File 7, Correspondence – Asian-African Conference, April 1955

Malik, C, 'A.B.C Sunday Radio Program Transcript. Guest of Honour Charles Malik', Australian Broadcasting Corporation, 5 May 1955, 1, National Archives of Australia, A1838/278, 3002/1 Pr 5

Malik, C, 'Talk Given by Dr. Charles Malik at Luncheon', Canberra: Department of External Affairs, Australia, 28 April 1955, 2, National Archives of Australia, A1838/278, 3002/1 Pr 5, File No. 156/3/3

ICC Statute

Preparatory Committee on the Establishment of an International Criminal Court, 16 March–3 April 1998, Report of the Inter-Sessional Meeting from 19 to 30 January in Zutphen, Netherlands, UN Doc. A/AC.249/1998/L.13, 4 February 1998

Preparatory Committee on the Establishment of an International Criminal Court, Report of the Informal Group on Procedural Questions, Fair Trial and rights of the Accused, 27 August 1996

Preparatory Committee on the Establishment of an International Criminal Court, Rules of Procedure: Working Paper submitted by Argentina, 13 August 1996

Report of the International Law Commission on the work of its forty-sixth session, 2 May–22 July 1994, General Assembly, Forty-ninth Session Supplement No. 10 (A/49/10)

Report Preparatory Committee on the Establishment of an International Criminal Court, 4–15 August 1997, UN Doc. A/AC.249/1997/L.8/Rev.1, 14 August 1997

United Nations Diplomatic Conference of Plenipotentiaries on the Establishment of an International Criminal Court, Committee of the Whole Working Group on Procedural Matters, Report of the Working Group on Procedural Matters: Addendum, 4 July 1998

United Nations Diplomatic Conference of Plenipotentiaries on the Establishment of an International Criminal Court, Committee of the Whole Working Group on Procedural Matters, Report of the Working Group on Procedural Matters: Addendum, 9 July 1998

United Nations Diplomatic Conference of Plenipotentiaries on the Establishment of an International Criminal Court, Rome, 15 June–17 July 1998, Official Records, Vol. III

Regional Instruments

American Declaration on the Rights and Duties of Man

Comité Jurídico Interamericano, Informe anexo al Anteproyecto de Declaración de los derechos y deberes internacionales del hombre, Rio de Janeiro, 31 December 1945

Novena Conferencia Internacional Americana, Actas y Documentos (Ministerio de Relaciones Exteriores de Colombia, Bogotá, 1953)

European Convention on Human Rights (1950)

Council of Europe, Collected Edition of the 'Travaux Préparatoires' of the European Convention on Human Rights, Vols. 1–2 (Martinus Nijhoff, The Hague, 1975)

Council of Europe, Collected Edition of the 'Travaux Préparatoires' of the European Convention on Human Rights, Vol. 4 (Martinus Nijhoff, The Hague, 1977)

Council of Europe, Collected Edition of the 'Travaux Préparatoires' of the European Convention on Human Rights, Vol. 5 (Martinus Nijhoff, The Hague, 1979)

GP/ M/9: Minutes of a meeting of the General Purposes Committee held on Wednesday, 17th March, 1948, at the House of Commons, CAC, Sandys Papers, box 9/ 1/ 2

Letter addressed by Mr Paul Henri Spaak, President of the Consultative Assembly to Mr Gustave Rasmussen, Chairman of the Committee of Ministers, 10 November 1949, Doc. AS/CP/PV (1) 2/5, A 514, II TP 298–301

Letter addressed on 18 November 1949 by the Secretary General to the Ministers for Foreign Affairs of the Member States, Ref. D 26/2/49, II TP 302–305

Report [of the Committee on Legal and Administrative Questions], 5 September 1949, Doc. AS (1) 77, I TP 216–239, at p. 216

Report of the Sitting [of the Consultative Assembly], 7 September 1949, I TP 258–295, at p. 268

Report presented by Mr P. H. Teitgen, 5 September 1949, Doc. A 290, I TP 192–213

Table of Cases

INTERNATIONAL

International Court of Justice and Permanent Court of International Justice

Admissibility of Hearings by the Committee on South West Africa (Advisory Opinion) [1956] ICJ Rep 23

Ahmadou Sadio Diallo (Guinea v. *DRC*) (Merits) [2010] ICJ Rep 639

Application of the Convention on the Prevention and Punishment of the Crime of Genocide (*Bosnia and Herzegovina* v. *Serbia and Montenegro*) [2007] ICJ Rep 43

Armed Activities on the Territory of the Congo (New Application: 2002) (*Democratic Republic of the Congo* v. *Rwanda*) [2006] ICJ Rep 3

Arrest Warrant of 11 April 2000 (*Democratic Republic of the Congo* v. *Belgium*) [2002] ICJ Rep 3

Barcelona Traction, Light and Power Company, Limited (*Belgium* v. *Spain*) [1970] ICJ Rep 3

Case Concerning Armed Activities on the Territory of the Congo (*DRC* v. *Uganda*) [19 December 2005] ICJ Rep 168

Case Concerning the Application of the Convention on the Prevention and Punishment of the Crime of Genocide (*Bosnia and Herzegovina* v. *Yugoslavia*) [1996] ICJ Rep 595

Certain Criminal Proceedings in France (*Republic of the Congo* v. *France*) (Provisional Measures) [2003] ICJ Rep 102

Corfu Channel case (*UK* v. *Albania*) (Merits) [1949] ICJ Rep 4

Difference Relating to Immunity from Legal Process of a Special Rapporteur of the Commission on Human Rights (Advisory Opinion) [1999] ICJ Rep 62

East Timor (*Portugal* v. *Australia*) (Jurisdiction, Judgment) [1995] ICJ Rep 90

International Status of South West Africa (Advisory Opinion) [1950] ICJ Rep 128
Jurisdictional Immunities of the State (*Germany* v. *Italy*) (Greece Intervening), Judgment [2012] ICJ Rep 99
Legal Consequences for States of the Continued Presence of South Africa in Namibia (South West Africa) Notwithstanding Security Council Resolution 276 (1970), Advisory Opinion of 21 June 1971, ICJ Rep 16
Legal Consequences of the Construction of a Wall in the Occupied Palestinian Territory (Advisory Opinion) [2004] ICJ Rep 136
Legal Consequences of the Separation of the Chagos Archipelago from Mauritius in 1965 (Advisory Opinion) [25 February 2019] ICJ Rep 95
Legality of the Threat or Use of Nuclear Weapons (Advisory Opinion) [1996] ICJ Rep 226
Military and Paramilitary Activities in and against Nicaragua (*Nicaragua* v. *USA*) (Merits) [27 June 1986] ICJ Rep 14
Questions Relating to the Obligation to Prosecute or Extradite (*Belgium* v. *Senegal*) (Merits) [20 July 2012] ICJ Rep 422
Reservations to the Convention on the Prevention and Punishment of the Crime of Genocide (Advisory Opinion) [1951] ICJ Rep 15
South West Africa –Voting Procedure (Advisory Opinion) [1955] ICJ Rep 67
South West Africa Cases, Second Phase [1966] ICJ Rep 6
United States Diplomatic and Consular Staff in Tehran (*USA* v. *Iran*) [1980] ICJ Rep 3, p. 42
Voting Procedure on Questions relating to Reports and Petitions concerning the Territory of South West Africa (Advisory Opinion) [1955] ICJ Rep 67
Western Sahara (Advisory Opinion) [1975] ICJ Rep 68

International Criminal Court

Arrest Warrant for Al Bashir, 4 March 2009, Pre-Trial Chamber I, ICC-02/05–01/09, ICC
Arrest Warrant for Kony, as Amended on 27 September 2005, 27 September 2005, Pre-Trial Chamber II, ICC-02/04–01/05, ICC
Arrest Warrant for Lukwiya, 8 July 2005, Pre-Trial Chamber II, ICC-02/04, ICC
Arrest Warrant for Odhiambo, 8 July 2005, Pre-Trial Chamber II, ICC-02/04, ICC
Arrest Warrant for Ongwen, 8 July 2005, Pre-Trial Chamber II, ICC-02/04, ICC

Arrest Warrant for Otti, 8 July 2005, Pre-Trial Chamber II, ICC-02/04, ICC
Decision on the Prosecution's Application for a Warrant of Arrest against Omar Hassan Ahmad Al Bashir, 4 March 2009, Pre-Trial Chamber I, ICC-02/05–01/09, ICC
Decision on the Prosecutor's Application Pursuant to Article 58 as to Gaddafi, Gaddafi and Alsenussi, 27 June 2011, Pre-Trial Chamber I, ICC-01/11, ICC
Decision Pursuant to Article 15 of the Rome Statute on the Authorization of an Investigation into the Situation in the Republic of Kenya, 31 March 2010, Pre-Trial Chamber II, ICC-01/09, ICC
Prosecutor v. *Mbarushimana*, ICC-01/04–01/10, 16 December 2011, ICC
Prosecutor v. *Mudacumara*, ICC-01/04–01/12, Decision on the Prosecutor's Application under Article 58, 13 July 2011, ICC
Prosecutor v. *Muthaura et al.*, ICC-01/09–02/11, 23 January 2012, ICC (PTC)
Prosecutor v. *Bemba*, Decision on the Charges of the Prosecutor, 15 June 2009, Pre-Trial Chamber II, ICC-01/05–01/08–424, ICC
Prosecutor v. *Germain Katanga*, T. Ch. II, Judgment pursuant to Article 74 of the Statute, ICC-01/04–01/07–3436, 07 March 2014
Prosecutor v. *Katanga and Chui*, Closing Statements, 23 May 2012, Trial Chamber II, ICC-01/04–01/07-T, ICC
Prosecutor v. *Katanga and Chui*, Decision on the Confirmation of Charges, 30 September 2008, Pre-Trial Chamber I, ICC-01/04–01/07, ICC
Prosecutor v. *Lubanga Dyilo,* Decision Establishing the Principles and Procedures to Be Applied to Reparations, 7 August 2012, Trial Chamber I, ICC-01/04–01/06, ICC
Prosecutor v. *Lubanga Dyilo*, Decision on the Confirmation of Charges, 29 January 2007, Appeals Chamber, ICC-01/04–01/06–803, ICC
Prosecutor v. *Lubanga Dyilo*, Judgment Pursuant to Article 74 of the Statute, 14 March 2012, Trial Chamber I, ICC-01/04–01/06–2842, ICC
Second Decision on the Prosecution's Application for a Warrant of Arrest against Al Bashir, 12 July 2010, Pre-Trial Chamber I, ICC-02/05–01/09, ICC
Situation in Democratic Republic of the Congo, Judgement on the Prosecutor's Application for Extraordinary Review of Decision Denying Leave to Appeal, 13 July 2006, Appeals Chamber, ICC-01/04, ICC

International Criminal Tribunal for the former Yugoslavia

Prosecutor v. *Aleksovski*, Appels Chamber Judgement [24 June 2000] IT–95–14/1–A, Appeals Chamber, ICTY

Prosecutor v. *Aleksovski*, ICTY, Trial Judgement [25 June 1999] IT–95–14/ 1–T, Trial Chamber, ICTY
Prosecutor v. *Blagojević and Jokić*, IT-02–60-A, 9 May 2007, ICTY
Prosecutor v. *Blagojević and Jokić*, IT-02–60-T, 17 January 2005, ICTY
Prosecutor v. *Blaškić*, IT-95–14-A, 29 July 2004, ICTY
Prosecutor v. *Blaškić*, IT-95–14-T, 3 March 2000, ICTY
Prosecutor v. *Brđanin*, IT-99–36-A, 3 April 2007, ICTY
Prosecutor v. *Brđanin*, IT-99–36-T, 1 September 2004, ICTY
Prosecutor v. *Brđanin*, No. IT-99–36-T, 1 September 2004, ICTY
Prosecutor v. *Delalić*, IT-96–21-A, 20 February 2001, ICTY
Prosecutor v. *Delalić*, IT-96–21-T, 16 November 1998, ICTY
Prosecutor v. *Erdemović*, IT-96–22, 7 October 1997, ICTY
Prosecutor v. *Furundžija*, IT-95–17/1-A, 21 July 2000, ICTY
Prosecutor v. *Furundžija*, IT-95–17/1-T, 10 December 1998, ICTY
Prosecutor v. *Gotovina*, IT-06–90-T, 15 April 2011, ICTY
Prosecutor v. *Hadžihasanović*, IT-01–47-T, 15 March 2006, ICTY
Prosecutor v. *Haradinaj et al.*, IT-04–84-A, 19 July 2010, ICTY
Prosecutor v. *Haradinaj et al.*, IT-04-84bis-T, 29 November 2012, ICTY
Prosecutor v. *Jelisic*, IT-95–10-T, 14 December 1999, ICTY
Prosecutor v. *Jokić*, IT-01–42/1-S, 18 March 2004, ICTY
Prosecutor v. *Karadžić and Mladić*, Review of the Indictments Pursuant to Rule 61 of the Rules of Procedure and Evidence, Cases Nos. IT-95–5-R61 and IT-95–18-R61, 11 July 1996, ICTY
Prosecutor v. *Karadžić*, Preliminary Motion on Lack of Jurisdiction Concerning Omission Liability, IT -95–05/J8-Pt, 25 March 2009, ICTY
Prosecutor v. *Kordić, Čerkez*, IT-95–14/2-A, 17 December 2004, ICTY
Prosecutor v. *Kordić, Čerkez*, IT-95–14/2-T, 26 February 2001, ICTY
Prosecutor v. *Krajišnik*, IT-00–39-T, 27 September 2006, ICTY
Prosecutor v. *Krnojelac*, IT-97–25-A, 17 September 2003, ICTY
Prosecutor v. *Krnojelac*, IT-97–25-T, 15 March 2002, ICTY
Prosecutor v. *Krstić*, IT-98–33-A, 19 April 2004, ICTY
Prosecutor v. *Krstić*, IT-98–33-T, 2 August 2001, ICTY
Prosecutor v. *Kunarac, Kovac and Vukovic*, IT-96–23-A, 12 June 2002, ICTY
Prosecutor v. *Kunarac, Kovac and Vukovic*, IT-96–23-T, 22 February 2001, ICTY
Prosecutor v. *Kupreškić*, Brief of the Defendants on Legal Trial Issues, IT-95–16-T, 19 November 1998, ICTY
Prosecutor v. *Kupreškić*, IT-95–16-A, 23 October 2001, ICTY
Prosecutor v. *Kupreškić*, IT-95–16-T, 14 January 2000, ICTY
Prosecutor v. *Kvočka*, IT-98–30/1-T, 2 November 2001, ICTY

Prosecutor v. *Lukić and Lukić*, No. IT- 98–32/1-T, 20 July 2009, ICTY
Prosecutor v. *Martić*, IT-95–11-A, 8 October 2008, ICTY
Prosecutor v. *Martić*, IT–95–11–R61, 8 March 1996, ICTY
Prosecutor v. *Milošević*, IT-02–54-T, Decision on Motion for Judgment of Acquittal, 16 June 2004, ICTY
Prosecutor v. *Mucić et al.*, IT-96–21, 16 November 1998, ICTY
Prosecutor v. *Muvunyi*, ICTR-2000-55A-T, 12 September 2006, ICTR
Prosecutor v. *Naletilić & Martinović*, IT-98–34-T, 31 March 2003, ICTY
Prosecutor v. *Naletilić*, IT-98–34-A, 3 May 2006, ICTY
Prosecutor v. *Nicolić*, Review of Indictment Pursuant to Rule 61 on the Rules of Procedure and Evidence, IT-94–2-R61, 20 October 1995, ICTY
Prosecutor v. *Perišić*, IT-04–81-T, 6 September 2011, ICTY
Prosecutor v. *Sikirica et al.*, IT–95–8–I, Judgment on Defence Motions to Acquit, 3 September 2001, ICTY
Prosecutor v. *Simić*, IT-95–9, 17 October 2003, ICTY
Prosecutor v. *Stakić*, IT-97–24-A, 22 March 2006, ICTY
Prosecutor v. *Stakić*, IT-97–24-T, 31 July 2003, ICTY
Prosecutor v. *Stanišić and Simatović*, IT-03–69, 30 May 2013, ICTY
Prosecutor v. *Stanišić and Župljanin*, IT-08–91-T, 27 March 2013, ICTY
Prosecutor v. *Strugar*, IT-01–42-T, 31 January 2005, ICTY
Prosecutor v. *Tadić*, Decision on the Defence Motion for Interlocutory Appeal on Jurisdiction, IT-94–1-Ar72, 2 October 1995, ICTY
Prosecutor v. *Tadić*, IT-94–1-A, 15 July 1999, ICTY
Prosecutor v. *Tadić*, IT-94–1-T, 7 May 1997, ICTY
Prosecutor v. *Tolimir*, IT-05–88/2-T, 12 December 2012, ICTY
Prosecutor v. *Vasiljevic*, IT-98–32-T, 29 November 2002, ICTY

International Criminal Tribunal for Rwanda

Prosecutor v. *Akayesu*, ICTR-96–4-T, 2 September 1998, ICTR
Prosecutor v. *Bagilishema*, ICTR-95-1a-T, 7 June 2001, ICTR
Prosecutor v. *Bagilishema*, ICTR–95–1A–T, Judgment, 7 June 2001, ICTR
Prosecutor v. *Bagosora et al.*, No. ICTR-98–41-T, 18 December 2008, ICTR
Prosecutor v. *Bikindi*, ICTR-01–72, 2 December 2008, ICTR
Prosecutor v. *Bisengimana*, ICTR-00–60-T, 13 April 2006, ICTR
Prosecutor v. *Kajelijeli*, ICTR-98- 44A-A, 1 December 2003, ICTR
Prosecutor v. *Kamuhanda*, ICTR-95-54a-T, 22 January 2004, ICTR
Prosecutor v. *Kayishema and Ruzindana*, ICTR-95–1-T, 21 May 1999, ICTR
Prosecutor v. *Munyakazi*, ICTR-97-36a-T, 5 July 2010, ICTR

Prosecutor v. *Musema*, ICTR-96–13-T, 27 January 2000, ICTR
Prosecutor v. *Musema*, ICTR–96–13–T, Judgment, 27 January 2000, ICTR
Prosecutor v. *Nahimana et al.*, ICTR-99–52, 3 December 2003, ICTR
Prosecutor v. *Ndindabahizi*, ICTR-2001–71-I, 15 July 2004, ICTR
Prosecutor v. *Niyitegeka*, ICTR-96–14-A, 9 July 2004, ICTR
Prosecutor v. *Ntakirutimana*, ICTR-96–10-A & ICTR-96–17-A, 13 December 2004, ICTR
Prosecutor v. *Ntakirutimana*, ICTR-96–10-T & ICTR-96–17-T, 21 February 2003, ICTR
Prosecutor v. *Rutaganda*, ICTR-96–3-T, 6 December 1999, ICTR
Prosecutor v. *Rutaganira*, ICTR-95-1 c-T, 14 March 2005, ICTR
Prosecutor v. *Semanza*, ICTR-97–20-T, 15 May 2003, ICTR

International Military Tribunal at Nuremberg

Trials of the Major War Criminals before the International Military Tribunal (IMT), vol. I, Library of Congress Call Number KZ1176.T748 1947
Krupp case (1948), US Military Tribunal at Nuremberg, Annual Digest of Public International Law Cases (now ILR), vol. 15, 1948, p. 622
United States v. *List et al.* (The Hostage Case), in 11 Trials of War Criminals before the Nuremberg Military Tribunals under Control Council Law No. 10 759 (Washington: GPO 1950)
Nuremberg Trial Proceedings Vol. 1, Indictment: Count Three, War crimes, (Charter, Article 6, especially 6 (b)), under title '(A) Murder and Ill–Treatment of Civilian Populations of or In Occupied Territory and on the High Seas'
Nuremberg Trial Proceedings Volume 22, Two Hundred and Sixteenth Day, Saturday, 31 August 1946
Nuremberg Trial Proceedings Volume 17, One Hundred and Sixty-Third Day, Tuesday, 25 June 1946
France et al. v. *Goering et al.* (1946) 22 IMT 203, pp. 497–498

Cases before Internationalized Tribunals (Special Court for Sierra Leone)

Prosecutor v. *Kallon and Kamara*, Decision on Challenge to Jurisdiction: Lomé Accord Amnesty, SPCL [13 March 2004] SCSL–04–15–PT–060–I

Subsequent Nuremberg Proceedings under Control Council Law Number 10

United States of America v. *Altstoetter et al.* (Justice Trial), III TWC 954, NMT
United States of America v. *Brandt et al.* (Medical Trial), II TWC 171, NMT
United States of America v. *Flick et al.* (Notes on the Case), IX TWC 1, NMT
United States of America v. *Flick et al.* (Opinion and Judgment), VI TWC 1187, NMT
United States of America v. *Greifelt et al. (RuSHA Case)*, V TWC 88, NMT
United States of America v. *Krauch et al. (IG Farben)*, VIII TWC 1081, NMT
United States of America v. *Krupp et al.*, IX TWC 1327, NMT
United States of America v. *List et al. (Hostage Case)*, XI TWC 1230, NMT

Communications before Human Rights Committee

A.H.G. and M.R. v. *Canada*, Communication No. 2091/2011, CCPR/C/113/D/2091/2011, 5 June 2015
A.S. v. *Nepal*, Communication No. 2077/2011, CCPR/C/115/D/2077/2011, 4 January 2016
Abdelkader Boudjemai v. *Algeria*, Communication No. 2283/2013, CCPR/C/121/D/2283/2013, 1 December 2017
Abdilafir Abubakar Ali and Mayul Ali Mohamad v. *Denmark*, Communication No. 2409/2014, CCPR/C/116/D/2409/2014, Annex III
Ahmet Hudaybergenov v. *Turkmenistan*, para. 7.3; and Communication No. 2223/2012, *Japparow* v. *Turkmenistan*, Views adopted on 29 October 2015
Aminov v. *Turkmenistan*, CCPR/C/117/D/2220/2012
Bennet v. *Jamaica*, Communication No. 590/1994, Views adopted on 25 March 1999; *Simpson* v. *Jamaica*, Communications No. 695/1993, Views adopted on 31 October 2001
Berzig v. *Algeria*, Communication No. 1781/2008, Views adopted on 31 October 2011
Bozbey v. *Turkmenistan*, Communication No. 1530/2006, Views adopted on 27 October 2010
Chhedulal Tharu and others v. *Nepal*, Communication No. 2038/2011, CCPR/C/114/D/2038/2011, 21 October 2015
Djebrouni v. *Algeria*, Communication No. 1781/2008, Views adopted on 31 October 2011
Dovran Bahramovich Matyakubov v. *Turkmenistan*, Communication No. 2224/2012, CCPR/C/117/D/2224/2012, 26 September 2016

Dzhakishev Mukhtar v. *Kazakhstan*, Communication No. 2304/2013, CCPR/C/115/D/2304/2013, 9 December 2015

Egor Bobrov v. *Belarus*, Views adopted by the Committee under article 5 (4) of the Optional Protocol, concerning communication No. 2181/2012, CCPR/C/122/D/2181/2012, 12 November 2018

Gorji-Dinka v. *Cameroon*, Communication No. 1134/2002, Views adopted on 17 March 2005

Kayum Ortikov v. *Uzbekistan*, Communication No. 2317/2013, CCPR/C/118/D/2317/2013, 27 January 2017

Lounis Khelifati v. *Algeria*, CCPR/C/120/D/2267/2013, Communication No. 2267/2013, 21 September 2017

Mahmud Hudaybergenov v. *Turkmenistan*, Communication No. 2221/2012, CCPR/C/115/D/2221/2012, 22 December 2015

Malika El Boathi v. *Algeria*, CCPR/C/119/D/2259/2013, Communication No. 2259/2013

Matkarim Aminov v. *Turkmenistan*, Communication No. 2220/2012, CCPR/C/117/D/2220/2012, 27 September 2016

Mevlida Iščić v. *Bosnia and Herzegovina*, Communication No. 2028/2011, CCPR/C/113/D/2028/2011, 20 August 2015, para 4 (emphasis added); *Nura Hamulić and Halima Hodžić* v. *Bosnia and Herzegovina*, Communication No. 2022/2011, 20 August 2015, CCPR/C/113/D/2022/2011

Mevlida Iščić v. *Bosnia and Herzegovina*, Communication No. 2028/2011, CCPR/C/113/D/2028/2011, 20 August 2015

Mohamed Rabbae, A.B.S and N.A. v. *The Netherlands*, Communication No. 2124/2011, CCPR/C/117/D/2124/2011, 29 March 2017

Mwamba v. *Zambia*, Communication No. 1520/2006, Views adopted on 10 March 2010

Nura Hamulić and Halima Hodžić v. *Bosnia and Herzegovina*, Communication No. 2022/2011, 20 August 2015, CCPR/C/113/D/2022/2011

Rafik Belamrania v. *Algeria*, Communication No. 2157/2012, CCPR/C/118/D/2157/2012

Rouba Alhaj Ali v. *Morocco*, Communication No. 682/2015, CAT/C/58/D/682/2015, 13 September 2016

Shadurdy Uchetov v. *Turkmenistan*, Communication No. 2226/2012, CCPR/C/117/D/2226/2012, 26 September 2016, 26 September 2016

Shaw v. *Jamaica*, Communication No. 704/1996, Views adopted on 2 April 1998; *McLeod* v. *Jamaica*, Communication No. 734/1997, Views adopted on 31 March 1998; *Mezine* v. *Algeria*, Communication No. 1779/2008, Views adopted on 25 October 2012

Sunnet Japparow v. *Turkmenistan*, Communication No. 2223/2012, CCPR/C/115/D/2223/2012, 17 December 2015
X v. *Sri Lanka*, Communication No. 2256/2013, CCPR/C/120/D/2256/2013, 22 August 2017
Yuba Kumari Katwal (represented by counsel, Track Impunity Always–TRIAL) v. *Nepal*, Communication No. 2000/2010, Views adopted by the Committee at its 113th session, CCPR/C/113/D/2000/2010, 5 May 2015
Zafar Abdullayev (represented by counsel) v. *Turkmenistan*, Communication No. 2218/2012, CCPR/C/113/D/2218/2012, 19 May 2015
Zarzi v. *Algeria*, Communication No. 1780/2008, Views adopted on 22 March 2011 and *Guezout and Rakik* v. *Algeria*, Communication No. 1753/2008, Views adopted on 19 July 2012
Zhaslan Suleimenov v. *Kazakhstan*, Communication No. 2146/2012, CCPR/C/119/D/2146/2012, 12 May 2017

REGIONAL

African Commission on Human and Peoples' Rights

Amnesty International v. *Zambia*, Communication 212/98, ACHPR, Communication 212/98, 5 May 1999
Amnesty International v. *Zambia*, Communication 212/98, African Commission on Human and Peoples' Rights, 5 May 1999
Centre for Minority Rights Development and Minority Rights Group International on behalf of Endorois Welfare Council v. *Kenya* ('*Endorois*') Communication 276/2003, ACHPR, 25 November 2009
Darfur Relief and Documentation Centre v. *Sudan*, Communication 310/05, ACHPR, 25 November 2009
Egyptian Initiative for Personal Rights and INTERIGHTS v. *Egypt*, Communication 323/06, African Commission on Human and Peoples' Rights, 12 October 2013
Eyob B. Asemie v. *the Kingdom of Lesotho*, Communication 435/12, ACHPR, 13 February 2015
Huri – Laws v. *Nigeria*, Communication 25/98, ACHPR, 6 November 2000
J.E Zitha & P.J.L.Zitha (represented by Prof. Dr. Liesbeth Zegveld) v. *Mozambique*, Communication 361/08, African Commission on Human and Peoples' Rights, 1 April 2011
John K. Modise v. *Botswana*, Communication 97/93_14AR, ACHPR, 06 November 2000

Luke Munyandu Tembani and Benjamin John Freeth (represented by Norman Tjombe) v. *Angola and Thirteen Others*, Communication 409/12, ACHPR, 30 April 2014

Malawi Africa Association, Amnesty International, Ms Sarr Diop, Union interafricaine des droits de l'Homme and RADDHO, Collectif des veuves et ayants–Droit, Association mauritanienne des droits de l'Homme v. *Mauritania*, Communications 54/91–61/91–96/93–98/93–164/97_196/97–210/98, ACHPR, 11 May 2000

Media Rights Agenda v. *Nigeria*, Communication 224/98, African Commission on Human and Peoples' Rights, 6 November 2000

Purohit and Moore v. *Gambia (The)*, Communication 241/01, ACHPR, 29 May 2003

Social and Economic Rights Action Center (SERAC) and Center for Economic and Social Rights (CESR) v. *Nigeria*, Communication 155/96, ACHPR, 27 October 2001

Sudan Human Rights Organisation & Centre on Housing Rights and Evictions (COHRE) v. *Sudan*, Communications 279/03–296/05, ACHPR, 27 May 2009

Zimbabwe Lawyers for Human Rights & Associated Newspapers of Zimbabwe/Republic of Zimbabwe, Communication 284/03, ACHPR, 3 April 2009

Zimbabwe Lawyers for Human Rights and the Institute for Human Rights and Development in Africa v. *Zimbabwe*, Communication 293/04, ACHPR, 22 May 2008

Council of Europe

European Commission of Human Rights

Austria v. *Italy*, Application No. 788/60, [1961] *YECHR* 4 EurComm'nHR

Crutzescu v. *Germany*, Application No. 8247/78, Unreported Admissibility Decision of 4 July 1979 (on file with the author), ECommHR

Cyprus v. *Turkey*, Application Nos. 9780/74 and 6950/75 (Report of the Commission 10 July 1976), ECommHR

'Greek Case', Application Nos. 3321/67, 3322/67, 3323/67, 3344/67, Report Adopted on 15 April 1970, Yearbook of the European Convention on Human Rights, Vol. 12 (1972), ECommHR

Tanko v. *Finland*, Application No. 23634/94, Admissibility Decision of 19 May 1994, ECommHR

European Court of Human Rights

Section Chamber

A.A. v. *Greece*, Application No. 12186/08, 22 July 2010
Akkum and Others v. *Turkey*, Application No. 21894/93, ECtHR, 24 March 2005
Aksoy v. *Turkey*, Application No. 21987/93, 18 December 1996, ECtHR
Alimov v. *Turkey*, Application No. 14344/13, ECtHR, 6 September 2016
Ananyev and Others v. *Russia*, Application Nos. 42525/07 and 60800/08, 10 January 2012
Bitiyeva and X v. *Russia*, Application Nos. 57953/00 and 37392/03, ECtHR, 21 June 2007
Bonura v. *Italy*, Application No. 57360/00, ECtHR, 30 May 2002
Case of Mcdonald v. *The United Kingdom*, 4241/12, Judgment (Merits and Just Satisfaction), Court (Fourth Section), 20 May 2014
Case of Medžlis Islamske Zajednice Brčko and Others v. *Bosnia And Herzegovina*, Application No. 17224/11, 27 June 2017
Chember v. *Russia*, Application No. 7188/03, ECtHR, 3 July 2008
Dordević v. *Croatia*, Application No. 41526/10, ECtHR, 24 July 2012
Evans v. *United Kingdom*, Application No. 6339/05, Judgment of 10 April 2007
Frerot v. *France*, Application No. 70204/01, ECtHR, 12 June 2007
Głowacki v. *Poland*, Application No. 1608/08, ECtHR, 20 October 2012
Gorobet v. *Moldova*, Application No. 30951/10, ECtHR, 11 October 2011
Ilhan v. *Turkey*, Application No. 22277/93, ECtHR, 27 June 2000
Ireland v. *United Kingdom*, Application No. 5310/71, ECtHR, 18 January 1978
Iwanczuk v. *Poland*, Application No. 25196/94, ECtHR, 15 November 2001
Jalloh v. *Germany*, Application No. 54810/00, ECtHR, 11 July 2006
Khudoyorov v. *Russia*, Application No. 6847/02, ECtHR, 8 November 2005
Kurt v. *Turkey*, Application No. 24276/94, ECtHR, 25 May 1998
Labita v. *Italy*, Application No. 26772/95, ECtHR, 6 April 2000
Lorse and Others v. *The Netherlands*, Application No. 52750/99, ECtHR, 4 February 2003
M.S. v. *UK*, Application No. 24527/08, ECtHR, 3 May 2012
McGlinchey and Others v. *United Kingdom*, Application No. 50390/99, ECtHR, 29 April 2003
Melnitis v. *Latvia*, Application No. 30779/05, ECtHR, 28 February 2012
Peers v. *Greece*, Application No. 28524/95, ECtHR, 19 April 2001
Perinçek v. *Switzerland*, Application No. 27510/08, ECtHR, 15 October 2015

PETA Deutschland v. *Germany*, Application No. 43481/09, ECtHR, 8 November 2012
Pretty v. *United Kingdom*, ECtHR 427, 29 April 2002
Rahimi v. *Greece*, Application No. 8687/08, ECtHR, 5 April 2011
Rantsev v. *Cyprus and Russia*, Application No. 25965/04, ECtHR, 7 January 2010
Siliadin v. *France*, Application No. 73316/01, ECtHR, 26 July 2005
Soulas and Others v. *France*, Application No. 15948/03, 10 July 2008
Svinarenko and Slyadnev v. *Russia*, Application Nos. 32541/08 and 4431/08, ECtHR, 17 July 2014
Valašinas v. *Lithuania*, Application No. 44558/98, ECHR 2001–VIII
Van der Ven v. *The Netherlands*, Application No. 50901/99, ECtHR, 4 February 2003
Vasyukov v. *Russia*, Application No. 2974/05, ECtHR, 5 April 2011
Vereinigung Bildender Künstler v. *Austria*, 68354/01, Judgment, First Section, 25 January 2007, Final 25 April 2007
Wiktorko v. *Poland*, 14612/02, ECHR, 31 March 2009
X v. *Germany*, Application No. 7705/ 76, ECtHR, 5 July 1977
Yaroslav Belousov v. *Russia*, Application No. 2653/13, ECtHR, 4 October 2016

Grand Chamber

Blokhin v. *Russia* [GC], Application No. 47152/06, 23 March 2016
Bouyid v. *Belgium* [GC], Application No. 23380/09, ECtHR, 28 September 2015
Christine Goodwin v. *the United Kingdom* [GC], Application No. 28957/95, ECtHR 2002–VI
D.H. and Others v. *Czech Republic* [GC], Application No. 57325/00, 13 November 2007
Dubská and Krejzová v. *The Czech Republic* [GC], Application Nos. 28859/11 and 28473/12, 15 November 2016
El-Masri v. *'The former Yugoslav Republic of Macedonia'* [GC], Application No. 39630/09, ECtHR, 13 December 2012
Khamtokhu and Aksenchik v. *Russia* [GC], Application Nos. 60367/08 and 961/11, Judgment, 24 January 2017
Khlaifia and others v. *Italy* [GC], Application No. 16483/12, 15 December 2016
Kudła v. *Poland* [GC], Application No. 30210/96, ECtHR, 26 October 2000
Leyla Şahin v. *Turkey* [GC], Application No. 44774/98, ECtHR, 10 November 2005

Lopes De Sousa Fernandes v. *Portugal* [GC], Application No. 56080/13, 19 December 2017
M.S.S. v. *Belgium and Greece* [GC], Application No. 30696/09, ECtHR, 21 January 2011
Mozer v. *The Republic of Moldova and Russia* [GC], Application No. 11138/10, 23 February 2016
Muršić v. *Croatia* [GC], Application No. 7334/13, 20 October 2016
Nachova and Others v. *Bulgaria* [GC], Application Nos. 43577/98 and 43579/98, ECtHR, 6 July 2005
Paradiso and Campanelli v. *Italy* [GC], Application No. 25358/12, 24 January 2017
Parrillo v. *Italy case* [GC], Application No. 46470/11, ECHR, 2015
Regner v. *The Czech Republic* [GC], Application No. 35289/11, 19 September 2017
Rooman v. *Belgium* [GC], Application No. 18052/11, 31 January 2019
S.A.S. v. *France* [GC], Application No. 43835/11, Judgment (Merits and Just Satisfaction), 1 July 2014
Selmouni v. *France* [GC], Application No. 25803/94, ECtHR, 28 July 1999
Simeonovi v. *Bulgaria* [GC], Application No. 21980/04, 12 May 2017
Timishev v. *Russia* [GC], Application Nos. 55762/00 and 55974/00, ECtHR 2005-XII
Vinter and Others v. *the United Kingdom* [GC], Application Nos. 66069/09, 130/10 and 3896/10, 9 July 2013

Inter-American Court of Human Rights

Advisory Opinion No. 14, on *International Responsibility for the Promulgation and Enforcement of Laws in Violation of the American Convention on Human Rights*, 9 December 1994
Advisory Opinion No. 16, on *The Right to Information on Consular Assistance in the Framework of the Guarantees of the Due Process of* Law, 1 October 1999
Advisory Opinion No. 17, on *The Juridical Status and Human Rights of the Child*, 28 August 2002
Advisory Opinion on Juridical Condition and Rights of the Undocumented Migrants, 2003, OC–18/03
Aguirre v. *Peru* (Barrios Altos Case), Judgment of 3 September 2001, IACtHR Report (Ser. C) No. 83 (2001)
Baena Ricardo et al. v. *Panama*, Judgment of 2 February 2001

Bámaca Velásquez case, Judgment of 25 November 2000, Series C No. 70
Cantoral Benavides case, Judgment of 18 August 2000, Series C No. 69
Cantos v. *Argentina*, Judgment of 7 September 2001
Case of Rodríguez Vera et al. (the Disappeared from the Palace of Justice) v. *Colombia*, Judgment of 14 November 2014 (Preliminary objections, merits, reparations and costs)
Case of Artavia Murillo et al. ('In Vitro Fertilization') v. *Costa Rica*, Judgment of 28 November 2012 (Preliminary objections, merits, reparations and costs)
Case of Atala Riffo and daughters v. *Chile*, Judgment of 24 February 2012
Case of Baldeón García v. *Peru*, Merits, reparations and costs, Judgment of 6 April 2006, Series C No. 147
Case of Bulacio, Judgment of 18 September 2003, Series C No. 100
Case of Caesar, Judgment of 11 March 2005, Series C No. 123
Case of De la Cruz Flores, Judgment of 18 November 2004, Series C No. 115
Case of Fermín Ramírez, Judgment of 20 June 2005, Series C No. 126
Case of García Asto and Ramírez Rojas, Judgment of 25 November 2005, Series C No. 137
Case of Gelman v. *Uruguay*, Merits and reparations, Judgment of 24 February 2011, Series C No. 221
Case of J. v. *Peru*, Preliminary objection, merits, reparations and costs, Judgment of 27 November 2013, Series C No. 275
Case of Kimel v. *Argentina*, Judgment of 2 May 2008 (Merits, Reparations and Costs)
Case of López Álvarez, Judgment of 1 February 2006, Series C No. 141
Case of Lori Berenson-Mejía v. *Peru*, Judgment of 25 November 2004 (Merits, Reparations and Costs)
Case of Maritza Urrutia v. *Guatemala*, Judgment of 27 November 2003 (Merits, Reparations and Costs)
Case of Maritza Urrutia, Judgment of 27 November 2003, Series C No. 103
Case of Plan de Sánchez Massacre v. *Guatemala*, 29 April 2004
Case of Raxcacó Reyes, Judgment of 15 September 2005, Series C No. 133
Case of Ricardo Canese v. *Paraguay*, Merits, Reparations and Costs, Judgment of 31 August 2004, Series C No. 111
Case of Rodríguez Vera et al. (The Disappeared from the Palace of Justice) v. *Colombia*, Judgment of 14 November 2014 (Preliminary objections, merits, reparations and costs)
Case of Rosendo-Cantú and other v. *Mexico*, Preliminary Objection, Merits, Reparations and Costs, Judgment of 31 August 2010. Series C No. 216
Case of the 'Street Children' (Villagrán Morales et al.) v. *Guatemala*, Merits, Judgment of 19 November 1999, Series C No. 63

Case of the 'Street Children' (Villagran–Morales v. *Guatemala)* [1999] (Merits) Series C No 77, IACtHR
Case of the Barrios Family v. *Venezuela*, Judgment of 24 November 2011 (Merits, Reparations and Costs)
Case of the Gómez-Paquiyauri Brothers v. *Peru*, Judgment of 8 July 2004 (Merits, Reparations and Costs)
Case of the Ituango Massacres v. *Colombia*, Judgment of July 1, 2006 (Preliminary Objections, Merits, Reparations and Costs)
Case of the Mayagna (Sumo) Awas Tingni Community v. *Nicaragua*, 31 August 2001 (Merits, Reparations and Costs)
Case of the Miguel Castro-Castro Prison v. *Peru*, Judgment of 25 November 2006 (Merits, Reparations and Costs)
Case of the Pueblo Bello Massacre, Judgment of 31 January 2006. Series C No. 140
Case of The Río Negro Massacres v. *Guatemala*, Judgment of 4 September 2012 (Preliminary objection, merits, reparations and costs)
Case of The Río Negro Massacres v. *Guatemala*, Judgment of 4 September 2012 (Preliminary objection, merits, reparations and costs)
Case of Yvon Neptune v. *Haiti*, Merits, reparations and costs, Judgment of 6 May 2008, Series C No. 180
Fairén Garbi and Solís Corrales case, Judgment of 15 March 1989, Series C No. 6
Fernández Ortega et al. v. *Mexico*, 30 August 2010 (Preliminary Objections, Merits, Reparations and Costs)
Five Pensioners v. *Peru*, Judgment of 28 February 2003
Ituango Massacres v. *Colombia*, Judgment (Preliminary Objections, Merits, Reparations and Costs), 1 July 2006
Juan Humberto Sánchez case, Judgment of 7 June 2003, Series C No. 99
Juridical Status and Human Rights of the Child, Advisory Opinion OC–17/02, 28 August, 2002, Series A No. 17
Loayza Tamayo v. *Peru*, Judgment, 17 September 1997 (ser. C), N. 33 (1997)
Manuel Cepeda Vargas v. *Colombia*, Judgment of 26 May 2010 (Preliminary Objections, Merits, Reparations and costs)
Plan De Sánchez Massacre v. *Guatemala*, Reparations, Judgment of 19 November 2004, IACtHR Report (Ser. C) No. 116 (2004), IACtHR
Rosendo Cantú et al. v. *Mexico*, Judgment 31 August 2010 (Preliminary Objections, Merits, Reparations and Costs)
Velásquez Rodríguez v. *Honduras*, 29 July 1988
Velásquez v. *Guatemala*, Judgment (Merits) of 25 November 2000, Case No. 91/129, IACtHR Report (Ser. C) No. 70 (2000)

Yakye Axa Indigenous Community v. *Paraguay*, Merits, Reparations and Costs, Judgment of 17 June 2005, Series C No. 125

NATIONAL TRIBUNALS

Canada

Supreme Court of Canada, Reference Re ss. 193 and 195.1(1)(c) of the Criminal Code (Man.), [1990] 1 S.C.R. 1123, 4 W.W.R. 481

Reference re Secession of Quebec, Supreme Court of Canada, 20 August 1998, 2 SCR 217

France

Conseil D'Etat, *Dwarf–Throwing Case*, Ville d'Aix–en–Provence, [1996] Dalloz 177

Gaddafi case, Court of Cassation, Criminal Chamber, Appeal No 00–87215, Decision No 64, (2001) 125 ILR 490, 13 March 2001

Israel

Attorney General of the Government of Israel v. *Adolf Eichmann*, District Court of Jerusalem, judgment of 12 December 1961, 36 ILR (1968); 5 and Supreme Court of Israel, judgment of 29 May 1962, 36 ILR (1968), 277

Italy

Ferrini v. *Federal Republic of Germany*, Decision No. 5044/2004 (Rivista di diritto internazionale, Vol. 87, 2004, p. 539; International Law Reports (ILR), Vol. 128, p. 658

Ferrini v. *Germany*, Appeal decision, Cass No 5044/04, ILDC 19 (IT 2004), 11 March 2004, Italy, Supreme Court of Cassation

Germany v. *Milde*, Court of Cassation (First Criminal Section) (Italy), No. 1072/ 2009, ILDC 1224 (2009)

Germany v. *Milde* (Max Josef), Appeal judgment, Case no 1072/2009, (2009) 92 Riv Dir Int 618, ILDC 1224 (IT 2009), 13 January 2009, Italy, Supreme Court of Cassation, 1st Criminal Section

Switzerland

A. c. Ministère public de la Confédération, B. et C. A, Tribunal pénal fédéral, Cour des plaintes, décision du 25 juillet 2012 (no de dossier : BB.2011.140)

United Kingdom

Exchange v. *McFaddon*, 11 U.S. 116 (1812)
Marble Islands v. *I Congreso del Partido*, House of Lords, 16 July 1981 [1983] 1 AC 244
Regina v. *Bartle and the Commissioner of Police for the Metropolis and Others Ex Parte Pinochet Regina* v. *Evans and Another and the Commissioner of Police for the Metropolis and Others Ex Parte Pinochet* (On Appeal from a Divisional Court of the Queen's Bench Division), House of Lord, 24 March 1999
The Parlement Belge (1879) LR4PD 129
The Parlement Belge CA (1880) LR 5 PD 197

Abbreviations

ACHPR	African Charter on Human and Peoples' Rights
ACHR	American Convention on Human Rights
ACommHPR	African Commission on Human and Peoples' Rights
ACtHPR	African Court on Human and Peoples' Rights
AP	additional protocol
ASEAN	Association of Southeast Asian Nations
AWS	autonomous weapons systems
BIT	bilateral investment treaty
CAT	Convention Against Torture and Other Cruel, Inhuman or Degrading Treatment or Punishment is commonly known as the United Nations Convention against Torture (UNCAT)
CCW	Convention on Prohibitions or Restrictions on the Use of Certain Conventional Weapons which may be Deemed to be Excessively Injurious or to Have Indiscriminate Effects
CED	Committee on Enforced Disappearances
CEDAW	Convention on the Elimination of all forms of Discrimination Against Women
CERD	Convention on the Elimination of Racial Discrimination
CESCR	Committee on Economic, Social and Cultural Rights
CHR	Commission on Human Rights
CJEU	Court of Justice of the European Union
CMW	Committee on Migrant Workers
CRC	Committee on the Rights of the Child
CRPD	Convention on the Rights of Persons with Disabilities
ECHR	European Convention on Human Rights
ECOSOC	UN Economic and Social Council
ECtHR	European Court of Human Rights

EGE	European Group on Ethics in Science and New Technologies to the European Commission
GA	General Assembly
GC	general comment
GC/s	Geneva Convention/s
GR	general recommendation
HRC	Human Rights Committee
HRL	Human Rights Law
IACs	international armed conflicts
IACommHR	Inter-American Commission on Human Rights
IACtHR	Inter-American Court of Human Rights
IBC	International Bioethics Committee (UNESCO)
ICC	International Criminal Court
ICCPR	International Covenant on Civil and Political Rights
ICERD	International Convention on Elimination of all forms of Racial Discrimination
ICESCR	International Covenant on Economic, Social and Cultural Rights
ICJ	International Court of Justice
ICL	International Criminal Law
ICRC	International Committee of the Red Cross
ICTR	International Criminal Tribunal for Rwanda
ICTY	International Criminal Tribunal for the former Yugoslavia
IGOs	intergovernmental organizations
IHL	international humanitarian law
IHRL	international human rights law
ILC	International Law Commission
ILO	International Labour Organization
IMT	International Military Tribunal
IRO	International Refugee Organization
ISIL	Islamic State in Iraq and the Levant
LARs	lethal autonomous robots
NGO	non-governmental organization
NIACs	non-international armed conflicts
NSAs	non-state actors
OAS	Organization of American States
OAU	Organization of African Unity
PACE	Parliamentary Assembly of the Council of Europe
PCIJ	Permanent Court of International Justice
POW	prisoner of war

SC	Security Council
SCSL	Special Court for Sierra Leone
UDHR	Universal Declaration of Human Rights
UNESCO	United Nations Educational, Scientific and Cultural Organization
UNHCR	United Nations High Commissioner for Refugees
VCLT	Vienna Convention on the Law of Treaties
WHO	World Health Organization
WMA	World Medical Association

Introduction

DIGNITY AS A CONCEPTUAL BATTLEFRONT

On 14 February 1878, a Belgian vessel, en route from Ostend to Dover, ran into a storm and, as it approached Dover Bay, collided with the British steam-tug *Daring*. The ship, fittingly called *Parlement Belge*, was owned by the King of the Belgians, and it carried, in addition to mail, also passengers, merchandise and the King's royal pennon. Soon after the incident, the owners of the *Daring* instituted proceedings before the Admiralty Division of the UK High Court against Belgium on grounds of negligence and faulty navigation. The Belgian Attorney General took on the defence of the case and claimed sovereign immunity. The Admiralty Judge, Sir Robert Phillimore, overruled the objection and allowed the warrant to proceed.[1] On appeal, the Court of Appeal reversed the decision, on the ground that the *Parlement Belge* was, by virtue of the law of nations, immune from the jurisdiction of UK courts, as it was the public property of a foreign State. The relevant passage is worth-noting:

> as a consequence of the absolute independence of every sovereign authority, and of the international comity which induces every sovereign state to respect the independence and *dignity of every other sovereign state*, each and every one declines to exercise by means of its courts any of its territorial jurisdiction over the person of any sovereign or ambassador of any other state.[2]

This case is significant because it was the first time the question of immunities of government ships other than warships was brought before the Court of Appeal in England. In the court's reasoning resonates the findings of an earlier

[1] *The Parlement Belge* (1879) LR4PD 129.

[2] *The Parlement Belge*, CA (1880) LR 5 PD 197, at 214–215. This case provides a detailed review of the legal authorities connecting sovereignty to dignity, including Blackstone, Vattel, Wheaton and others.

case, the *Schooner Exchange*, heard by the US Supreme Court in 1812.[3] The relevance of these precedents is well known in the common law tradition. As noted in an early writing of Rosalyn Higgins, who would years later become the President of the International Court of Justice, the *Parlement Belge* case is one of the 'most celebrated authorities' in favour of the absolute theory of immunity followed and confirmed for a long time by the English Courts.[4] Immunity was the logic corollary of sovereignty, itself understood as arising from the *dignity* owed by each State to every other State. Dignity was a shield ingrained as deep in the heart of international law as this body of law permitted, namely in the very concept of sovereignty.

And yet, a hundred years later, such dignity is hardly recognizable. From a shield protecting the legal position of States, dignity has been turned into a sword to cut through it in pursuit of higher values, which, in turn, are now at the very core of international law. On 24 March 1999, the majority of the members of the UK House of Lords converged in the conclusion that the UN Convention against Torture (CAT) had introduced a conventional exception to immunity from foreign criminal jurisdiction *ratione materiae*. It thus famously held that the former Chilean dictator Augusto Pinochet was not entitled to immunity in respect of charges of torture and conspiracy to commit torture for conduct falling under the UN CAT, in force in the UK from 8 December 1988 onwards.[5] In the words of Lord Justice Millet,

> the fundamental human rights of individuals, *deriving from the inherent dignity of the human person*, had become a commonplace of international law. Article 55 of the Charter of the United Nations was taken to impose an obligation on all states to promote universal respect for and observance of human rights and fundamental freedoms. The trend was *clear*. [...] The way in which a state treated its own citizens within its own borders had become a matter of legitimate concern to the international community. [...] By the

[3] The *Exchange* v. *McFaddon*, 11 U.S. 116 (1812), at 123, 'in the present case [...] the commander of the national vessel exercises a part of his sovereign power; and in such a case no consent to submit to the ordinary judicial tribunals of the country can be implied [...] it cannot be implied where the law of nations is unchanged – nor where the implication is destructive of the independence, the equality, and *dignity* of the sovereign'.

[4] R Higgins, 'Recent Developments in the Law of Sovereign Immunity in the United Kingdom' [1977] 71(3) *AJIL* 423–437, 423.

[5] Convention against Torture and Other Cruel, Inhuman or Degrading Treatment or Punishment, 10 December 1984, UNTS Treaty Series, vol. 1465, p. 85, entry into force 26 June 1987 [CAT]. UK signed the CAT on 15 March 1985, entry into force in UK 8 December 1988.

time Senator Pinochet seized power, the international community had renounced the use of torture as an instrument of state policy.[6]

The regime of Pinochet was known for appalling acts of violence, such as torture, murder and the enforced disappearance of individuals, committed in Chile and elsewhere between 1974 and 1990. In 1999, even though the reasoning of the various members of the House of Lords shows profound differences of opinion, the majority agreed that the immunity to which Pinochet was entitled as a former head of State could not attach to acts of torture.[7] The legal contribution of this decision, that is, the denial of immunity from criminal prosecutions of former heads of State for violations of the prohibition of torture in a State Party to the CAT, may appear as narrowly circumscribed. But its symbolic value is much deeper: the old conception of dignity as a shield was turned on its head and became the very sword through which a new conception was brought to a very specific and practical bearing.

The Pinochet case before the UK House of Lords is but one symbolically remarkable manifestation of a profound and fundamental trend that, by the late 1990s, was fully consolidated. It is a truism today to state that 'humanity' underpins much of international law, or that international law has been 'humanized' or, still, that dignity plays an important role within international law. More complex is to ascertain what conceptions of dignity have found expression in international law, when, through which specific legal concepts, and with what implications. The purpose of this study is to provide answers to these more granular questions, both theoretically and technically, through a study of the corpus of international legal theory and practice in the last one and a half centuries. These answers are, of necessity, tentative because they are the result of an interpretive exercise based on a substantial but unavoidably selective set of materials. Going back to the two cases briefly outlined in the previous paragraphs, although they are certainly different, they share a common feature. In their reasoning, the same concept is used in diametrically opposed meanings: *dignity* is associated with two distinct purposes. In the nineteenth century, *sovereign dignity* rules international legal affairs largely unchallenged. Only a minority voice introduces some dissonance, referring to the *dignity of the human being* to challenge the slave trade and subsequently

6 Judgment – *Regina* v. *Bartle and the Commissioner of Police for the Metropolis and Others Ex Parte Pinochet Regina* v. *Evans and Another and the Commissioner of Police for the Metropolis and Others Ex Parte Pinochet* (On Appeal from a Divisional Court of the Queen's Bench Division), House of Lord, 24 March 1999, Opinions of the Lords of Appeal for Judgment in the Cause, Lord Millet, 90.

7 *Ibid.*, Lord Hutton, 166e. For an analysis of the implications of this decision see A Bianchi, 'Immunity v. Human Rights: The Pinochet Case' [1999] 10 *EJIL* 237–277.

slavery itself or to call for restraints in the conduct of hostilities. Over time, this voice will become more and more assertive. The history of the twentieth century is that of the gravest encroachments on human dignity and, as a result, also of the greatest achievements in its international legal recognition. To borrow the words of the French luminary René Cassin, it is the very 'protest of humanity'[8] that will vindicate the legal recognition of human dignity in hard law. In the immediate aftermath of the Second World War, *human dignity* will be seen as the antidote of *sovereign dignity*. The dignity of the *human person* is placed above the writ of any individual State, curtailing State sovereignty and the legal implications of *sovereign dignity*. Yet, what is remarkable is the choice of the concept of 'dignity', out of so many other concepts, to assert the normative claim of a value against another. Even more remarkable is the fact that dignity has been progressively and, in many ways, sequentially at the root of State sovereignty and of the efforts to defend – against that sovereignty – the dignity of human beings.

Cassin's words were proffered in a highly symbolic context. On 9 December 1948, the UN General Assembly was gathered in the *grande salle* of Palais de Chaillot in Paris. Only a few steps away, in 1940, Hitler had surveyed his new conquest. Eight years later, Cassin rose before the Assembly to offer his concluding remarks. What the delegates gathered in Paris were about to vote upon was, as Cassin put it:

> the most vigorous, the most essential protest of humanity against the atrocities and the oppression which millions of human beings suffered through the centuries and in particular during and after the two world wars.[9]

Late at night, the Universal Declaration of Human Rights was put to the final vote. The Declaration crystallized the protection of human dignity in its very text, and it became the moral manifesto of the twentieth century, a refusal to condone what had just happened. Forty-eight countries voted in favour of the text; eight abstained. The just war had been won, and the wartime Alliance had voted on the first international instrument aiming at representing the basis of just peace.

This is where this research finds its territory. In its process of international legal recognition, human dignity came to nuance, then influence and, ultimately, fundamentally transform the very architecture of international law. This study examines when, where and how this development occurred and with

[8] 382AP/128, dossier 3, 'Discours de René Cassin, Délégué de la France à l'Assemblée Générale des Nations Unies à Paris', 9 December 1948.

[9] *Ibid.*

what implications. It explores the long and sinuous road followed by human dignity in international law. In a lapse of time of about a century and a half, important historical changes brought human dignity to the centre of international law and upset the rules governing relations between States, and, above all, between States and individuals. Human dignity entered international law by nuancing, reinterpreting and reformulating roles and principles that appeared to be immutable, transforming the architecture of international law from within. These changes occurred both at a slow or at a fast pace, in a peaceful or a tragic manner.

From sovereign to human dignity, the concept of dignity underlies the normative claims of two competing views of international law. From this perspective, this study explores the conceptual battlefront opened by the concept of human dignity. At the root of the modern conception of sovereignty lies the ancient idea of *dignitas* in its institutionalized expression of sovereignty. Dignitas conveyed a social stratification or, in other words, the different social importance attributed to classes or castes or strata of individuals.[10] A term such as State 'dignitaries', as a synonym of high-rank State officials, still recalls the ancient use of *dignitas* and its links to social stratification. And it is against that stratification that the concept of dignity came to be used, in the Christian tradition, to affirm that all human beings are the holders of an inherent dignity, given to them by God.[11] The second conception of dignity thus challenges the distinction and/or the powers conferred by *dignitas*. This radically different understanding of dignity can, in turn, be conceptualized under two broad strands: first, a religious perspective, which looks at the concept as connected to the divine or to a metaphysical account;[12] second, what could be called a set of 'secular' accounts that have enabled the development of human rights.[13] Both the religious and the secularized conceptions of human dignity entail significant limitations not only for the powers conferred by 'sovereign dignity' but, potentially, for its very recognition. The concept of human dignity assumes, in its entry into international law, a restraining role and, in a broader sense, a function of control over the first conception of *dignitas*, as applied to sovereigns and officials. Thus, what was originally an

10 H Spiegelberg, 'Human Dignity: A Challenge to Contemporary Philosophy' in *Steppingstones toward an Ethics for Fellow Existers* (Martinus Nijhoff 1986), 175–198.

11 C Starck, 'Religious and Philosophical Background of Human Dignity and its Place in Modern Constitutions' in D Kretzmer and E Klein (eds), *The Concept of Human Dignity in Human Rights Discourse* (Brill 2002), 180.

12 A Barak, *Human Dignity: The Constitutional Value and the Constitutional Right* (Cambridge University Press 2015).

13 S Moyn, *Christian Human Rights* (UPenn 2015).

analogy, once applied to human nature, developed into a limit to sovereign dignity. Human dignity, first in its religious and then in its secularized conceptions, was thus turned into a platform against sovereign dignity, a platform that would in time conquer, through a range of legal instruments, vast swathes of international law where sovereign dignity previously rule unchallenged.

This study provides a historical and legal investigation of human dignity as a normative value, the intellectual sources that drove and shaped its legal recognition, and the main legal instruments used to express it in international law. The analysis identifies the main vehicles through which human dignity finds expression across different fields of international law and the functions it performs. The historical dimension of the project unveils the roots of human dignity and situates it within the broader secularization process. Human dignity first entered the field of international law as a religious concept in the second half of the nineteenth century. It then underwent a transformation into a secularized concept, as a condition for its generalization after the Second World War. In both cases, however, it performed the function of placing limits to an older concept of dignity, which is still ingrained today in the very principle of sovereignty, with its many expressions. The study aims to provide a detailed topography of this tension in its complex legal manifestations across international law. However, the use of dignity as a platform has not come to an end with its extension to human dignity. As it will be shown in the last chapter of this study, an analogy can be made between, on the one hand, the use of human dignity to restrain sovereign dignity and, on the other hand, the growing references to the dignity of nature to put limits on the 'species exceptionalism' implied in a conception of international law based on human dignity. Indeed, the very assertion of human dignity to protect the individual against the powers of the State may in fact also lay the foundations for an over-exploitation of nature. This study sheds light on the first conceptual battlefront, namely that of human against sovereign dignity, but in unveiling the underlying logic at play in such conceptual antagonism, it discerns a no less important one that may unfold through this century, that between human dignity and the intrinsic value of nature.[14]

STRUCTURE OF THE STUDY

Valued human traits, such as intelligence, charm or strength, define us both in our own eyes and in those of others, setting a foundation for differential

[14] G Le Moli, 'Three Circles of Dignity' [2019] 11 *JHRP* 1–13.

concerns in family, society and work.[15] And yet, from a legal standpoint, such diversity does not provide grounds for a different treatment at the most basic level, as we are always due the same respect merely as persons. Our humanity, it is said, provides us with a status that deserves recognition from others. It seems, however, unclear what grounds this status. It is the idea of human dignity, it is argued, which sets the outer boundaries of what we may do to one another, applies to the same extent to every human being, and is rooted in our most distinctive human capabilities. It also provides the foundation for a set of individual human rights – which we possess by virtue of our humanity.[16]

This normative and secularized claim can explain why human dignity deserves recognition from a conceptual standpoint. But it does not tell us why it prevailed at specific points in history (the last century and a half), in specific contexts (international legal circles and, particularly, the circles that we associate today with international humanitarian law, human rights law, and criminal law), and with specific legal results (the recognition of principles, obligations, rights and even crimes). Thus, rather than starting from the assumption that human dignity demands recognition and looking for the implications of this statement, the aim of the study is to reconstruct when, where and how human dignity moved from a normative claim to a set of actionable legal concepts in international law and, later on, to an overall foundation of international law. This book therefore aims to understand the roots of the idea of dignity and, subsequently, reconceptualize it within the language of international law. To do so, it proceeds by induction, seeking to extract answers to the questions of *when, where and how* from a wide body of practice spanning one and a half centuries. From these answers, the study derives *implications* for the overall fabric of international law, and it projects such implications for a potential new conceptual battlefront, which is only identified but not fully investigated.

These more specific questions are necessary to render the broader research question, that is, the determination of the place of human dignity in international law, manageable. Indeed, human dignity is as pervasive as it is difficult to pin down in any concrete sense and, yet, this what this study attempts to do. Rather than a single answer, the investigation has led to several answers to each more specific question, which are brought together under a single analytical framework introduced in Chapter 1 and further developed

15 A Sangiovanni, *Humanity without Dignity: Moral Equality, Respect, and Human Rights* (Harvard University Press 2017), 1; see also J Waldron, *Dignity, Rank and Rights*, M Dan-Cohen (ed.) (Oxford University Press 2012).

16 See, for instance, G Vlastos, 'Justice and Equality' in J Waldron (ed.), *Theories of Rights* (Oxford University Press 1984), 141–176. See also Sangiovanni, *supra* n 15.

in subsequent chapters. In exploring, *when* human dignity transitioned from a normative claim to an actionable legal form, the book identifies different constitutive stages, understood as processes of progressive permeation of human dignity into the fabric of international law. These constitutive stages are analysed *where* they more clearly and powerfully permeated and indeed transformed international law, namely in the areas we call today international humanitarian law, international human rights law, and international criminal law. The analysis of these three areas seeks to induct patterns in the legal recognition of human dignity to understand *how* this process unfolded and through which legal instruments human dignity was given expression. Finally, the study pulls the different threads unwound in examining these more specific questions and offers a combined interpretation of the place of human dignity in international law. This analysis is organized in seven chapters.

Chapter 1 is devoted to the clarification of the methodological structure. It characterizes the analytical framework developed to study the place of human dignity in international law and, more specifically, it introduces its four main components: (i) the definition of the concept of dignity and of the main analytical distinctions used in the study; (ii) the characterization of the processes of progressive recognition of human dignity in international law, which are referred to in this study as 'constitutive stages'; (iii) an analytical cartography of different legal instruments, understood as specific ways of formulating a norm (principles, rights, obligations, crimes), on which the analysis of the legal expression of human dignity in international law is subsequently conducted; and (iv) the main overall narrative and argument regarding the place of human dignity in international law developed in the study. This framework is an attempt at integrating three broader methodologies for the study of human dignity in international law, namely a historical or dynamic account of constitutive stages, a technical or positivist examination of legal instruments, and a conceptual analysis of dignity as a concept and of its overall place in international law. Components (i) to (iv) are each developed in one or more chapters of the study.

Chapter 2 focuses on the concept of dignity. It characterizes the two main competing conceptions subsequently analysed in the book, *sovereign* and *human* dignity. It begins by exploring the *intellectual origins* of the concept of dignity – with its religious and philosophical strands. Within human dignity, particular emphasis is laid on the Christian and Kantian (secularized) conceptions of human dignity due to their distinctive historical influence on the shaping of international law. The methodological approaches used here are therefore historical and philosophical in nature. On this basis, the first component of the analytical framework is built, namely the conceptual categories of dignity that will, subsequently, be used to explore how dignity has found expression in international law. These two conceptions are a static component of the analytical framework that will be immersed in a dynamic perspective in Chapter 3. This conceptual clarification exercise is, however, necessary in order to trace the roots of the legal concept and to dispel one major challenge in providing an account of dignity in law, which is the tendency to see it everywhere.

Chapter 3 relies on these conceptions of dignity to examine the historical processes through which human dignity found expression in international law, narrating *when*, *why* and, most importantly, *which* conceptions of human dignity permeated international law. The primary objective of Chapter 3 is not to examine the emergence of human dignity in the international legal discourse in an exhaustive manner or to uncover its expressions in the various areas of law – which is analysed in detail in the following chapters of the book – but to demonstrate that those distinct conceptions of the past (sovereign and human dignity, the latter in its Christian and secularized strands) have permeated debates at the origins of international law, sometimes blending with – and blurring – each other. The concept of human dignity has been legally formalized in discernible historical stages, through the work of diplomats, scholars and humanitarian aid workers. More specifically, the study identifies three different *constitutive stages* in this formalization process in international law, specifically: (i) a first constitutive stage, spanning from 1850 until 1949 (when the main area of expression of human dignity is international humanitarian law); (ii) a second constitutive stage, from 1919 until 1966 (with rise of international human rights law); and (iii) a third constitutive stage, running from 1899 until 1998 (with the emergence and slow consolidation not only of international crimes but also of international criminal tribunals). These three constitutive stages of dignity are distinct but closely intertwined. The chronology of each of them is sufficiently distinct and recognizable and, very importantly, they each give expression to human dignity through different language and, specifically, by means of different legal instruments. The specificities of each process and area are discussed in separate chapters (Chapters 4–6), which discuss in detail the types of instruments most widely relied in each area to give expression to human dignity. Yet, the analysis in Chapters 4–6 relies on the combined application of the three components of the analytical framework (conceptions of dignity, constitutive stages, and legal instruments) and it reaches partial conclusions regarding the implications of human dignity for that specific area.

The emergence of international humanitarian law is viewed as the first constitutive stage. It begins in the second half of the nineteenth century, with human dignity's symbolic entrance into the fabric of international law with the adoption and entry into force of the Hague Law (Martens Clause, 1899 and 1907 Conventions).[17] The process to impose legal restraints on the conduct of hostilities preceded the Martens Clause and the actual consolidation of this stage was only completed in the aftermath of the Second World War with the watershed represented by the adoption of the Four Geneva Conventions in 1949[18] and, subsequently, the two Additional Protocols of 1977.[19] Thus, the historical processes referred to in this study as constitutive stages extend over long periods of time, with a range of different legal manifestations which are singled out as key milestones.

The same applies to the origins and span of the second constitutive stage, characterized by the rise of international human rights law. Its first expressions in the 1920s (which echoed developments in connection with slave trade and slavery in the nineteenth century) and later in 1945 (with the UN Charter and the UNESCO Constitution[20]) must be considered in the light of the decisive adoption of the Universal Declaration on Human Rights, in 1948,[21] and the adoption of the Convention against Genocide[22] later that year. But it is difficult to consider these entry points, however important, as sufficient for the consolidation of human dignity in the form of human 'rights'. In earnest, such consolidation cannot be said to have been completed until the adoption of the two human rights Covenants in 1966, the International Covenant on Civil and Political Rights

[17] The Hague Conventions of 1899 (II) and 1907 (IV) respecting the Laws and Customs of War on Land.

[18] Convention (I) for the Amelioration of the Condition of the Wounded and Sick in Armed Forces in the Field, 12 August 1949, Art. 63, 6 UST 3114, 75 UNTS 31; Convention (II) for the Amelioration of the Condition of the Wounded, Sick and Shipwrecked Members of Armed Forces at Sea, 12 August 1949, 6 UST 3217, 75 UNTS 85; Convention (III) Relative to the Treatment of Prisoners of War, 12 August 1949, 6 UST 3316, 75 UNTS 135; Convention (IV) Relative to the Protection of Civilian Persons in Time of War, 12 August 1949, 6 UST 3516, 75 UNTS 287.

[19] Protocol Additional to the Geneva Conventions of 12 August 1949, and Relating to the Protection of Victims of International Armed Conflicts, 1125 UNTS 3, 8 June 1977 (entered into force 7 December 1978); Protocol Additional to the Geneva Conventions of 12 August 1949, and Relating to the Protection of Victims of Non-International Armed Conflicts, 1125 UNTS 609, 8 June 1977 (entered into force 7 December 1978).

[20] Charter of the United Nations, 24 October 1945, 1 UNTS XVI (UN Charter); UNESCO Constitution, 16 November 1945, 3 Bevans 1311.

[21] Universal Declaration of Human Rights, 10 December 1948, 217 A (III).

[22] Convention on the Prevention and Punishment of the Crime of Genocide, GA Res. 260 (III) A, 9 December 1948 (entered into force 12 January 1951).

(ICCPR)[23] and International Covenant on Economic, Social and Cultural Rights (ICESCR).[24]

The evolution of international criminal law embodies the third and last constitutive stage of human dignity. Its first manifestations coincide with the adoption and entry into force of the Hague Law (1899 and 1907) and the largely symbolic, in retrospect, Article 227 of the 1919 Treaty of Versailles,[25] under which the German Kaiser was to be brought to justice, although that did not happen. In 1945, with the Nuremberg Statute,[26] human dignity is unequivocally enshrined in legal form, both in the definition of international crimes, including 'against humanity', and in the necessary corollary of an international prosecution of such crimes. The institutional and legal criminal framework of the 1990s, however, provides a more solid basis for the consolidation of human dignity through international criminal law, vesting it with an actionable nature. Indeed, aside from the expansion of conflict-specific *ex post facto* international tribunals, the conclusion in 1998 of the Rome Statute establishing a general International Criminal Court,[27] defining both crimes and institutional processes for the prosecution, consolidates the incremental approach prevailing until then in international criminal law.

The broad brush or 'macro' picture described in the foregoing paragraphs is derived from what could be called 'micro' foundations. To clarify *when* and *where* human dignity made its entrance in international law (and not only when scholars start – or started – to refer to it), the analysis conducted in this study rests on the detailed examination of a vast body of legal documents, their *travaux préparatoires*, the notes of the drafters, their biographies, and the exchanges of letters among colleagues. This part of the research sought to distil by a process of induction: (a) the main legal and political processes through which human dignity (more specifically, certain historical conceptions of this value) came to be enshrined in international legal instruments relating to humanitarian law, international human rights, international criminal law, international refugee and migration law, bioethics, and self-determination; (b) the most influential figures (such as Albert Thomas,

23 International Covenant on Civil and Political Rights (adopted 16 December 1966, entered into force 23 March 1976) 999 UNTS 171 (ICCPR).

24 International Covenant on Economic, Social and Cultural Rights (adopted 16 December 1966, entered into force 3 January 1976) 993 UNTS 3 (ICESCR).

25 Treaty of Versailles (1919), 2 Bevans 235.

26 United Nations, Charter of the International Military Tribunal – Annex to the Agreement for the prosecution and punishment of the major war criminals of the European Axis, 8 August 1945.

27 Rome Statute of the International Criminal Court, A/CONF. 183.9 (17 July 1998, entered into force 1 July 2002).

Fridtjof Nansen, Eglantyne Jebb, Raphael Lemkin, Henri Laugier, Charles Malik, Peng Chun Chang, René Cassin, Eleanor Roosevelt, John Peters Humphrey), and their own intellectual traditions and influences (e.g. Christian political thinkers, Confucianism, socialism and trade unionism).

The investigation of this vast body of documentary traces also offers a basis to understand *why* human dignity came to be enshrined in legal form and, indeed, in a certain legal form. By emphasizing the negotiation and drafting process behind treaties and international instruments, the study attempted to bring to life political and historical realities as a major driver of the recognition of human dignity in international law. As this is a story of the development of international *norms* and international *law* in relation to human dignity, legal standards evolved in sometimes historically contingent conditions that only later turned to be authoritative sources of law. At times, these conditions may give the impression of randomness; yet, on closer inspection, some patterns remain discernible, adding nuance to the picture and emphasizing the historicity in the human dignity narratives.

The historical and conceptual analysis so far described places in perspective the more technical analysis conducted on a partly overlapping documentary basis focusing on treaties, soft-law instruments, case-law, and commentary. Such analysis aims to identify the specific legal instruments through which human dignity was given expression in different bodies of international law. As noted earlier, Chapters 4–6 examine this question, respectively, in the context of international humanitarian law, international human rights law, and international criminal law. A conceptual cartography of four main legal instruments (principle, obligation, right, crime) is used to conduct this legal analysis. This cartography is not intended, nor can it purport, to engage or settle with a vast body of legal theory seeking to clarify what exactly is the meaning of the terms 'principle', 'obligation', 'right', 'crime', or whether other 'instruments' could be included in the 'class' or 'set'. Rather, consistently with the overall methodology followed in this book, this cartography is a result of a pattern induction effort from the documentary sources surveyed. Its purpose is to reduce the daunting complexity found in the references to 'dignity' or other cognate terms such as 'humanity' or 'elementary considerations of humanity' in such documentary sources to a limited number of legally relevant categories.

Indeed, in examining traces and patterns of human dignity in international law, in order to later assess the frame–language of dignity (examined in more detail in Chapters 4–6), the study considers different terminological variations of the concept. Even when not expressly referred to as such, human dignity is in fact a reference point in a variety of different legal formulations able to convey and carry out the same meaning of dignity. By looking analytically at such formulations – which, in Fregean terminology, are said to express a sense and denote or refer to its reference[28] – it will be evident that each (i) tells us how (and how many times) the concept of human dignity is instantiated; (ii) holds the same truth–value, expressing the same fact; (iii) has a meaning that is the 'mode of presentation' or cognitive content associated with the expression in virtue of which the reference is picked out. I will therefore consider the numerous legal manifestations of 'humanity', as a qualification of dignity of the *human being*. Such standards will be viewed under its two sets of meanings: first, as referred to the human race, or to those attributes that make us, as human beings, distinctive; second, as referred to a virtue – acting with humanity.[29] But this treatment of a wide variety of references has no discernible legal value. It is therefore only a step in the process of identification of legal expressions of human dignity. Such expression must be formulated in a limited number of legal categories, that is, principles, rights, obligations, and crimes, in order to make sense of how human dignity has transitioned from a normative claim to actionable legal form in international law. Such translation into recognizable legal categories is also useful to assess whether human dignity is manifested through a specific and predominant technique in a given context (e.g. the use of 'principles' in international humanitarian law, of 'rights' in international human rights law, of 'crimes' in international criminal law, and 'obligations' throughout), and which functions it performs.

For consistency, Chapters 4–6 follow a common division addressing, in turn, the main legal instruments through which it is given expression and its implications for the broader question of the place of human dignity in international law.

In the concluding Chapter 7, the study pulls all the threads from the previous chapters and highlights the main outcome of the study. As anticipated in the opening of this introduction, the study develops a broader historical narrative on the role of human dignity in international law. This analysis runs in parallel with the more strictly juridical one throughout the entire research. The narrative of *when, where and how* human dignity entered, expanded and transformed international law from within can be seen as an illustration of the theory of secularization, according to which contemporary political and legal concepts are in fact religious concepts that have been

[28] G Frege, 'Über Sinn und Bedeutung, Zeitschrift für Philosophie und philosophische Kritik', NF 100, 1892, S. 25–50 (see also, 'On Sense and Reference' in AP Martinich and D Sosa (eds), *Analytic Philosophy: An Anthology* (Blackwell 2001), 7–18.

[29] Chapters 3, 4, 5 and 6 will include a clarification of the meaning and functions of the formulation adopted and examined.

stripped from their more idiosyncratic religious dimensions (secularized).[30] The study shows that the concept of human dignity made its first appearance in legal history in a religious form, and later in a more secularized way, as a reaction to and limit upon the classical conception of *sovereign dignity*, enshrined in State sovereignty. This origin is at the root of and is still manifested in the various legal formulations of human dignity in different areas of law. To explain human dignity, to seek its religious roots, to see its evolution and its many legal manifestations, ultimately demonstrates that international law was historically shaped, despite the multi-cultural context in which it unfolded, by secularization process akin to that of many domestic legal systems. On the basis of the finer-grained analysis conducted in previous chapters, Chapter 7 adopts this macro view and discusses the secularization argument in the light of the transformative function of human dignity in international law.

[30] JC Monod, *La querelle de la secularisation, de Hegel à Blumenberg* (Librarie Philosophique J. Vrin 2002); JC Monod, 'What's New in Our Current "International Secularism"?' [2012] 25 (1) *LJIL* 67–72.

1

Analytical Framework

1.1 INTRODUCTION

This chapter aims to clarify the methodological structure of this study. It characterizes the analytical framework developed to examine the place of human dignity in international law. In particular, it introduces its four main structural foundations: (i) the definition of the concept of dignity and of the analytical distinctions used (Section 1.2); (ii) the characterization of the processes of progressive recognition of human dignity in international law, which are referred to as 'constitutive stages' (Section 1.3); (iii) an analytical cartography of different legal instruments, understood as specific ways of formulating a norm (principles, rights, obligations, crimes), on which the analysis of the legal expression of human dignity in international law is subsequently conducted (Section 1.4); and (iv) the main overall narrative and argument related to the place of human dignity in international law (Section 1.5). This framework also combines three broader methodologies for the study of human dignity in international law, namely a historical or dynamic account of constitutive stages, a technical or positivist examination of legal instruments and a conceptual analysis of dignity as a concept and of its place in international law. All the four components, from (i) to (iv), are developed in one or more chapters of the book.[1]

1.2 TWO CIRCLES OF DIGNITY[2]

1.2.1 *Framing the Debate*

In human rights practice, references to 'dignity' are as pervasive as they are difficult to pin down. 'Dignity' is used widely and often contradictorily. It

[1] In particular, the first component will be expanded in Chapter 2; the second, in Chapter 3; the third, in Chapters 4–6; and the last, in Chapter 7.

[2] This section relies on G Le Moli, 'Three Circles of Dignity' [2019] 11(1) *JHRP* 258–264.

underlies not only the privileged legal treatment afforded to States as a result of their sovereignty but also the claims to strip States and State officials of the manifestations of such sovereignty (e.g. immunities). It also grounds the overriding character of human rights and social development while at the same time adding legitimacy to the fight against anthropocentrism and the protection of nature for its own sake. These and other uses of the term 'dignity' have become a common feature of human rights practice, and we barely pay any attention to them, even when they are contradictory.

What is remarkable is the choice of the concept of 'dignity', out of so many other concepts, to assert the normative claim of a group or an entity – I shall use the term 'circle' – against another. Even more remarkable is the fact that dignity has been progressively, and in many ways sequentially, at the root of State sovereignty and of the efforts to defend – against that sovereignty – the dignity of human beings.[3] Thus, in spite of its ambiguous and rhetorical uses, it is not a concept that can be easily dismissed. It performs a foundational function. From 'sovereignty' to 'human dignity', the concept of dignity underlies the normative claims of two competing circles.

I relied on the distinction between these two circles of dignity to organize the review of a vast body of work on dignity, including academic writings as well as a number of other discursive materials that have contributed to the clarification of the contours of the concept of dignity. Charting and organizing the different uses of the term appears useful to avoid not only the abuse of this concept but also the 'dilution' that may result from casual and unconsidered reference to it. More fundamentally, this research will explore the conceptual battlefront opened by the concept of human dignity to protect the individual against the powers of the State.

1.2.2 *Dignitas or 'Sovereign' Dignity*

Understanding exactly what the concept of dignity means or refers to, and its practical implications, requires pondering its many facets. Two main ideas of dignity have emerged over time. On the one hand, dignity was the basis of rank, status and, ultimately, through the dignity of kings, 'sovereignty'. On the other hand, dignity was emphasized as an attribute of human beings.[4] These

[3] O Schachter, 'Human Dignity as a Normative Concept' [1983] 77 *AJIL* 848; JP Théron, 'Dignité et libertés. Propos sur une jurisprudence contestable' in *Pouvoir et liberté. Etudes offertes à Jacques Mourgeon* (Bruylant 1998), 305; D Feldman, 'Human Dignity as a Legal Value: Part I' [1999] *PL* 682, 697.

[4] R Debes (ed.), *Dignity. A History* (Oxford University Press 2017); K Bayertz, 'Menschenwürde' in HG Sandkühler (ed.), *Enzyklopädie Philosophie. Band 1* (Meiner 1999), 824–826.

concepts are both different and interlocked in a sequential and rival manner, which means the use of the concept to assert the normative claim of one circle is largely dependent on the use of the concept by the other circle. Yet, at the same time, the two uses cannot be fully conciliated because they entertain a competing or rival relationship in that one concept developed to limit expansion of the other.

Sovereign dignity reflects the first and ancient meaning of dignity, and it is still used today mainly to express features of a high social standing.[5] According to this conception, examined in detail by Jeremy Waldron in his 'Dignity, Rank, and Rights' paper, dignity is to be attributed only to some human beings, whose legal status is defined in terms of honour, title, powers and responsibilities[6] – and granted to different degrees.[7] This meaning of dignity is expressed in dignities that are conferred on *dignitaries*, for example honours or titles, as an award for more or less 'decent' behaviours. The roots of this conceptualization of dignity are ancient. Commenting on the work of Cicero, Hubert Cancik notes that dignity 'denotes worthiness, the outer aspect of a person's social role which evokes respect and embodies the charisma and the esteem presiding in office, rank or personality'.[8]

This conception of dignity has three noteworthy features. The first is that dignity can, and typically does, attach to persons holding a specific position and hence to the institution. In this sense, one could use the expression 'institutional dignity' when an institution as an entity is a dignity bearer. In his introduction to *Understanding Human Dignity*, McCrudden argues that, in the present day, *dignitas* is generally attached to those appointed to a particular public office and applied to institutions and the State itself.[9] Samuel Moyn, in the same volume, calls this understanding of the concept 'corporatist' dignity.[10] By way of illustration, dignity would attach to

5 A Sangiovanni, *Humanity without Dignity: Moral Equality, Respect, and Human* Rights (Harvard University Press 2017), 16.

6 J Waldron, 'Dignity, Rank, and Rights. The 2009 Tanner Lectures at UC Berkeley' [2009] in NYU Public Law and Legal Research Paper Series, paper 151; J Waldron, 'Dignity, Rights and Responsibilities [2010] in NYU Public Law and Legal Research Paper Series, paper 242.

7 H Spiegelberg, 'Human Dignity: A Challenge to Contemporary Philosophy' in *Steppingstones toward an Ethics for Fellow Existers* (Martinus Nijhoff 1986), 175–198.

8 H Cancik, 'Dignity of Man and Persona in Stoic Anthropology: Some Remarks on Cicero, De Officiis I 105–107' in D Kretzmer and E Klein (eds), *The Concept of Human Dignity in Human Rights Discourse* (Brill 2002), 19.

9 C McCrudden, 'In Pursuit of Human Dignity: An Introduction to Current Debates' in C McCrudden (ed.), *Understanding Human Dignity* (Oxford University Press 2013), 1–58; C McCrudden, 'Human Dignity and Judicial Interpretation of Human Rights' [2008] 19(4) *EJIL* 655, 656–657.

10 S Moyn, 'The Secret History of Constitutional Dignity' in McCrudden, *Understanding Human Dignity*, *supra* n 9, 95–112.

institutions like Parliament or the Church, which corresponds to the eighteenth- and nineteenth-century meaning of dignity as distinction and status. For present purposes, it is important to note that, from a legal standpoint, this conception of *dignitas* attaches first and foremost to the State and to State officials, and it finds expression in a range of more specific legal concepts expressing the idea of sovereignty, such as the immunities of States and State officials. A judicial decision dating back to the late nineteenth century is evidence for this statement. In *The Parlement Belge*, an 1880 decision, the English Court of Appeals reasoned that:

> as a consequence of the absolute independence of every sovereign authority, and of the international comity which induces every sovereign state to respect the independence and *dignity of every other sovereign state*, each and every one declines to exercise by means of its courts any of its territorial jurisdiction over the person of any sovereign or ambassador of any other state.[11]

This conception was restated a century later by the House of Lords' 1981 decision in *Congreso del Partido*:

> to require a State to answer a claim based on such [commercial] transactions does not involve a challenge or inquiry into any act of sovereignty or governmental act of that State. It is, in accepted phrases, neither *a threat to the dignity of that State* nor any interference with its sovereign functions.[12]

At the root of the modern conception of sovereignty thus lies the ancient idea of *dignitas* in its institutional expression.

A second feature of this conception is the transient character of *dignitas*. The institutionalization of *dignitas* necessarily entails its detachment from the person holding the office and its conferral on the office itself. To continue with the example of the immunities of State officials, so-called functional immunities attach to State officials exercising acts of their office, which are immune because they are necessary to preserve the sovereignty of the State they represent. Even the so-called personal immunities, namely immunities attaching to the very State representative in their personal dealings and those of their family, are based on the idea of *ne impediatur legatio*, that is to allow the operation of a diplomatic representation of the foreign State by virtue of its own sovereignty. It must be noted, however, that whereas the *dignitas* of the individual is transient, that of the institution itself – the State – is permanent. Yet its scope may change in such a way that an action considered an

[11] *The Parlement Belge*, CA (1880) LR 5 PD 197, 214–215 (emphasis added).

[12] *Marble Islands* v. *I Congreso del Partido*, House of Lords, 16 July 1981 [1983] 1 AC 244, 262 (emphasis added).

encroachment on such *dignitas* at a given time may no longer be considered as such at a later time.

The third and perhaps most important feature of this conception is its exclusionary character. *Dignitas* is expressed by the syntagma 'relational dignity' since dignity is defined in relation to certain qualities.[13] It is therefore a concept that carries with it a social distinction and establishes an unequal treatment between those (or the institutions) who have rank and honour and those who do not. Both the qualities conferring a special treatment and the treatment may change over time, but the exclusionary character of the concept remains. And it is this feature that, by its very definition, draws a circle that leaves outside a wider circle of those not enjoying special treatment. A challenge to exclusionary treatment can take two forms: either the circle is extended to include those left outside or the scope of the treatment is limited. As discussed next, in both cases, the claim rests on the assertion of a competing form of dignity.

1.2.3 *Human Dignity*

The second conception of dignity challenges the distinction and/or the powers conferred by *dignitas*. It refers to a specific attribute of every human being *qua* human and does not defer to any social degrees. Thus, human dignity cannot be acquired or lost[14] – it is not transient – and it attaches to every human being – thus not exclusionary within the circle of human beings, but excluding other entities, for example legal persons. Its permanent and non-exclusionary features do not mean that this conception, with its many variations, is not rival. This is important because, as mentioned earlier, the different circles of dignity are interlocked in a way that can be characterized as sequential (dependent on one another) and rival (competing). The following paragraphs discuss three prisms through which human dignity has been characterized.

An initial distinction can be made between two broad families of conceptualization: first, a religious perspective, which looks at the concept as connected to the divine or to a metaphysical account; second, what could be called a set of 'secular' accounts that have enabled the development of human rights. The emergence and consolidation of human rights embodies not the triumph of one concept over the other but a more complex process of conceptual elaboration and generalization of a religious conception so as to make it more widely acceptable. The affirmation of human dignity in constitutional and international legal documents is indeed a product of a secular age. Yet the

13 Spiegelberg, *supra* n 7, 193.
14 *Ibid.*, 192.

development of the underlying concept of what a human being is stems from religious thought[15] and, primarily, Christian thought.[16] Authors studying the non-Christian foundations of human rights[17] have identified a range of concepts close to the idea of human dignity in other religious traditions, including Hinduism,[18] Buddhism[19] and Confucianism,[20] as well as in similar ideas in Ubuntu and Maori traditions.[21] Yet these ideas did not act as drivers of the legal elaboration of human rights in the aftermath of the Second World War and the process of adoption of the Universal Declaration of Human Rights (UDHR). This process has been analysed from a historical perspective by authors such as Mary Ann Glendon[22] and Samuel Moyn.[23] Their narratives differ, but they all converge on the broad frame within which the process unfolded – one whereby an initially Christian conception of human dignity was progressively stripped of its idiosyncratic features as a condition for its generalization through international instruments.

Aside from the aforementioned historical work on the role of the religious conception of human dignity in the early stages of international human rights law (IHRL), there have been initiatives either to ground human rights in a wider range of cultural and religious traditions, such as the compilation directed by the Swiss philosopher Jean Hersch under the aegis of the United Nations Educational, Scientific and Cultural Organization (UNESCO)[24] or,

[15] A Barak, *Human Dignity: The Constitutional Value and the Constitutional Right* (Cambridge University Press 2015).

[16] C Starck, 'Religious and Philosophical Background of Human Dignity and Its Place in Modern Constitutions' in Kretzmer and Klein (eds), *supra* n 8, 180.

[17] RS Manglapus, 'Human Rights Are Not a Western Discovery' [1978] 21(10) *Worldview* 4–6; J Donnelly, 'Human Rights and Human Dignity: An Analytic Critique of Non-Western Conceptions of Human Rights' [1982] 76(2) *AmPolSciRev* 303–316; Debes, *supra* n 4.

[18] J Braarvig, 'Hinduism: The Universal Self in a Class Society' in M Düwell et al. (eds), *The Cambridge Handbook of Human Dignity: Interdisciplinary Perspectives* (Cambridge University Press 2014), 163–169.

[19] J Braarvig, 'Buddhism: Inner Dignity and Absolute Altruism' in Düwell et al., *supra* n 18, 170–176.

[20] L An'xian, 'Human Dignity in the Traditional Chinese Confucianism' in Düwell et al., *supra* n 18, 177–181; MYK Lee, 'Universal Human Dignity: Some Reflections in the Asian Context' [2008] 3(1) *AsJCL* 1–33.

[21] T Metz, 'Dignity in the Ubuntu Tradition' in Düwell et al., *supra* n 18, 310–318; J Barrett, 'Dignatio and the Human Body' [2005] 21(4) *SAJHR* 525–546; PG Carozza, 'Human Dignity in Constitutional Adjudication' in T Ginsburg and R Dixon (eds), *Comparative Constitutional Law* (Edward Elgar 2011), 459–472.

[22] MA Glendon, *A World Made New. Eleanor Roosevelt and the Universal Declaration of Human Rights* (Random House Publishing Group 2001).

[23] S Moyn, *Christian Human Rights* (University of Pennsylvania Press 2015); S Moyn, *The Last Utopia: Human Rights in History* (Harvard University Press 2010).

[24] J Hersch, *Le droit d'etre un homme, Recueil de textes préparé sous la direction de Jeanne Hersch* (UNESCO 1968).

following a different route, to conceptualize the world order around a secularized goal of human dignity. Regarding the latter, one of the major intellectual initiatives was that of Myres McDougal and Harold Lasswell who, writing in 1959, sought to shape a framework centred on human dignity, offering analytical tools taken from the social sciences.[25] Significantly, they 'postulated' this goal in order to 'deliberately leav[e] everyone free to justify it in terms of his preferred theological or philosophical traditions'. In fact, they viewed the 'essential meaning of human dignity ... [as] ... a social process in which values are widely and not narrowly shared, and in which private choice, rather than coercion, is emphasized as the predominant modality of power'.[26] Their conception rested upon eight categories of values that human beings seek (power, enlightenment, wealth, well-being, skill, affection, respect and rectitude) and affirmed that a global order centred on human dignity should allow people to pursue them. Thus, international law was seen as a normative practice orientated towards establishing the conditions through which everyone can have dignity.

Both the religious and the secularized conceptions of human dignity entail significant limitations, not only on the powers conferred by 'sovereign dignity', but, potentially, on its very recognition. The religious variant, whether in its Christian form or in its wider (and subsequent) cultural rooting, does not question the basis of authority of the State but it entails limitations for the scope of the powers that States can claim over humans. This is a delicate balance indeed but, in the aftermath of the Second World War, those limitations appeared as the most urgent task to be accomplished. Yet the conception expounded by McDougal and Lasswell, as well as other conceptions that were developed earlier (such as the account of the French jurist and philosopher George Scelle[27]) and subsequently the more recent work (such as by Patrick Capps),[28] go a step further and imply that the entire world order, including the very justification for the special powers arising from State sovereignty, rest upon and are a function of human dignity. Here, both the powers that a State may exercise over its population and the very qualities that confer such power on States and State officials are made dependent on human dignity.

[25] MS McDougal and HD Lasswell, 'The Identification and Appraisal of Diverse Systems of Public Order' [1959] 53(1) *AJIL* 1–29; MS McDougal, HD Lasswell and L Chen, *Human Rights and World Public Order* (Yale University Press 1980); MS McDougal and HD Lasswell, *Jurisprudence for a Free Society: Studies in Law, Science and Policy* (Martinus Nijhoff 1992).

[26] McDougal and Lasswell, *The Identification and Appraisal of Diverse Systems*, *supra* n 25, 11.

[27] G Scelle, *Précis de droit des gens* (Sirey 1932).

[28] P Capps, *Human Dignity and the Foundations of International Law* (Hart 2009), 3.

The discussion regarding the generalization of human dignity, that is to strip it out of its idiosyncratic origins in Christian thought, runs parallel with another partially overlapping dichotomy between 'reductionist' and 'essentialist' approaches to human dignity. Reductionist approaches see human dignity as, at best, a redundant concept and, at worst, an empty vehicle that offers judges as well as others the possibility of advancing their own idiosyncratic views. By way of illustration, philosopher Ruth Macklin has claimed that dignity seems to mean nothing other than respect for autonomy, which is already a respected societal value. Therefore, dignity, as used in medical ethics, 'can be eliminated without any loss of content'.[29] Others see human dignity as a 'vacuous concept',[30] a 'floating signifier',[31] which is an 'impossibly vague'[32] subjective idea that changes 'radically with the time, place, and beholder',[33] masking 'a great deal of disagreement and sheer confusion'.[34] It is a noble sentiment that 'can have no place in an attempt at rational persuasion'[35] failing to 'provide a universalistic, principled basis for judicial decision-making in the human rights context'.[36] Because dignity, with its elusive nature, has no 'concrete meaning or consistent way of being defined', judges are tempted to 'introduce their own moral standards amid competing claims of rights each of which has a plausible case of human dignity violation'.[37] It then appears that, in the eyes of its critics, the principle is too hollow to fill the jurisprudence and practice that recall it.

By contrast, so-called essentialists have tried to assess dignity's features, finding a core to establish roots and meaning. For example, the philosopher William Parent noted that dignity is 'a negative moral right not to be regarded or treated with unjust personal disparagement',[38] whereas McCrudden advanced a 'minimum core' according to which 'every human being possesses an intrinsic worth[,] ... that this intrinsic worth should be recognized and

[29] R Macklin, 'Dignity Is a Useless Concept' [2013] 327(7429) *BMJ* 1419–1420.

[30] M Bagaric and J Allan, 'The Vacuous Concept of Dignity' [2006] 5(2) *JHR* 257–270.

[31] C Douzinas, *Human Rights and Empire: The Political Philosophy of Cosmopolitanism* (Routledge 2007), 8.

[32] McCrudden, *Human Dignity and Judicial Interpretation of Human Rights*, *supra* n 9, 723.

[33] S Pinker, 'The Stupidity of Dignity' [2008] 238(9) *The New Republic* 28–31.

[34] M Rosen, *Dignity: Its History and Meaning* (Harvard University Press 2012), 67.

[35] FA Hayek, *The Constitution of Liberty* (University of Chicago Press 1960), 6.

[36] McCrudden, *Human Dignity and Judicial Interpretation of Human Rights*, *supra* n 9, 655.

[37] Lee, *supra* n 20, 3; M Rosen, 'Dignity: The Case Against' in McCrudden, *Understanding Human Dignity*, *supra* n 9, 143–154.

[38] WA Parent, 'Constitutional Values and Human Dignity' in MJ Meyer and WA Parent (eds), *The Constitution of Rights: Human Dignity and American Values* (Cornell University Press 1992), 62.

respected by others, and [that] some forms of treatment by others are inconsistent with, or required by, respect for this intrinsic worth'.[39]

The implications of this dichotomy for the rival character of human dignity must be analysed at two levels. Reductionist approaches seem to deny the ability of human dignity to ground a competing claim, either because the genuine basis would be some other value (e.g. autonomy) or because an empty concept cannot provide such a basis. Yet on closer inspection, these two implications do not challenge the rival character of human dignity. References to the redundancy of dignity are a challenge to the signifier, not to the meaning (which may encompass autonomy or other values); conversely, references to the emptiness of the human dignity are a challenge to the meaning (which may encompass the subjective moral judgements of a judge or other official) not to the signifier. But neither challenges the possibility that asserting a socially recognized competing value (e.g. autonomy) by means of the concept of human dignity may serve to place limitations on the powers of another circle. Reductionists converge with essentialists on this key point. The main difference between them is that essentialists see a distinctive meaning in the concept of human dignity, which is neither redundant nor subjective or illegitimate. And it is this meaning that grounds the competing normative claim.

Several cross-cutting themes emerge from the religious/secular and reductionist/essentialist dichotomies, which can be treated as a third prism on the concept of human dignity. This prism mainly concerns the character, dimensions and implications of human dignity. The character of dignity relates to an examination of what dignity is. It appears as a basic question, answered in either narrow or broad ways. It is said, for instance, that dignity 'refers to' an intrinsic value[40] that therefore recalls why dignity is recognized, rather than what dignity is. As to what dignity is, legal commentators have provided different definitions, seeing 'human dignity' as a 'type of value;'[41] a 'need;'[42] a 'normative property;'[43]

39 McCrudden, *Human Dignity and Judicial Interpretation of Human Rights*, *supra* n 9, 679.

40 R Andorno, 'Human Dignity and Human Rights as a Common Ground for a Global Bioethics' [2009] 34(3) *JMedPhilos* 223–240, 233.

41 Rosen, *supra* n 34, 19–23.

42 D Shultziner and I Rabinovici, 'Human Dignity, Self-Worth, and Humiliation: A Comparative Legal–Psychological Approach Psychology' [2012] 18(1) *PubPoly&L* 105–143, 107.

43 D Birnbacher, 'Ambiguities in the Concept of Menschenwürde' in K Bayertz (ed.), *Sanctity of Life and Human Dignity* (Kluwer 1996), 118.

a 'potential';[44] or a 'process'.[45] Waldron has argued that dignity must be identified with a 'status'[46] – a perspective that others have criticized[47] or further explored.[48]

The dimensions of dignity analysed in legal circles in turn call for additional distinctions: some refer to different meanings;[49] to different directions taken by the protection of dignity;[50] or to dignity itself as having two dimensions. Andorno has defined dignity as having two natures, 'ontological' and 'ethical'.[51] Similarly, Maurer, studying the approach adopted by the European Court of Human Rights (ECtHR), has described the principle of human dignity as having a basic dimension ('fundamental') and a realizable or active dimension ('actioned').[52] Kass, instead, draws a distinction between the 'basic dignity of human beings' and the 'full dignity of being (actively) human – of human flourishing'.[53] These distinctions reflect the idea that dignity has a foundational core and an outer more flexible layer able to respond and adapt to different realities.

To understand the implications of human dignity, some scholars have focused on how it is violated and, conversely, how it is promoted. Scholars use the terms 'degradation' and 'humiliation'[54] to describe assaults on human dignity, seen as a form of 'denial of social recognition';[55] as a destruction of the capacity of self-direction;[56] or, in the bioethics field, as the deprivation of 'basic goods'.[57] Scholars who focus on promotion refer to empowerment and

44 A Pollmann, 'Embodied Self-Respect and the Fragility of Human Dignity: A Human Rights Approach' in P Kaufman et al. (eds), *Humiliation, Degradation, Dehumanization: Human Dignity Violated* (Springer 2010), 243–261.

45 N Lickiss, 'On Human Dignity: Fragments of an Exploration' in J Malpas and N Lickiss (eds), *Perspectives on Human Dignity: A Conversation* (Springer 2007), 27–42.

46 J Waldron, 'Is Dignity the Foundation of Human Rights?' [2013] NYU Public Law and Legal Research Paper, 374, 24–27.

47 M Rosen, 'Replies to Jeremy Waldron, Dignity Rank and Rights. The 2009 Tanner Lectures at UC Berkeley on Human Values' [2009].

48 CR Beitz, 'Human Dignity in the Theory of Human Rights: Nothing but a Phrase?' [2009] 41 (3) *PhilosPublicAff* 259–290, 283–288.

49 D Shultziner, 'Human Dignity – Functions and Meanings' in Malpas and Lickiss, *supra* n 45, 73–92.

50 C Dupré, 'Unlocking Human Dignity: Towards a Theory for the 21st Century' [2009] 3(2) *EHRLR* 190–205.

51 Andorno, *supra* n 40, 237.

52 B Maurer, *Le principe de respect de la dignité humaine et la Convention Europeéene des Droits de l'Homme* (La Documentation Française 1999), 50–58.

53 L Kass, 'Defending Human Dignity' in ED Pellegrino et al. (eds), *Human Dignity and Bioethics* (Notre Dame Press 2009), 299.

54 Shultziner, *supra* n 49, 73–92.

55 Shultziner and Rabinovici, *supra* n 42, 105–143.

56 Beitz, *supra* n 48, 289.

57 Birnbacher, *supra* n 43, 110.

constraint. By way of illustration, Deryck Beyleveld and Roger Brownsword have noted that human beings are 'recognized not only as having the capacity to make their own choices, but also as being entitled to enjoy the conditions in which they can flourish as self-determining authors of their own destinies'.[58] Human dignity as empowerment or as liberty is a function of human autonomy and is closely connected to modern human rights conceptions, which consider individuals to possess an inherent value which is the basis for their inalienable rights. But dignity may also entail constraints, which in turn require a delicate balance between respect for individual choice and limitations of such choice to avoid undignified situations. The balance is linked to a community's concept of civilized life. What a community considers to be the limits of dignity has a bearing on what can be negotiated – as it does, for instance, in the areas of human organ commerce or prostitution.[59]

The analysis of the character, dimensions and implications of human dignity provides a finer-grained cartography for the examination of how this concept may perform a rival function. If, as suggested by the literature on the implications of human dignity in the legal and social sphere, human dignity protection is implemented through agents' empowerment,[60] respect for individual freedom,[61] social justice[62] and respect for freedom of choice,[63] then the limitations placed on the State's exercise of sovereign prerogatives is closely circumscribed. Where such limitations may intervene is likely to concern the outer layer or dimension of human dignity, not its core. And, importantly, depending on whether dignity is seen as a value, a need, a normative property, a potential, a process or a status, there may be more or less room for encroaching on the core of human dignity.

In Chapter 2, I will follow this twofold nature and develop in more detail the analysis of the origin of the two circles of dignity, *sovereign* and *human*. In particular, human dignity will be viewed through two further distinct conceptual reflections about the idea of dignity: religious and philosophical. As we shall see, the modern meaning of dignity is first anticipated mostly at the time

58 D Beyleveld and R Brownsword, *Human Dignity in Bioethics and Biolaw* (Oxford University Press 2004), 64.

59 On prostitution, see Supreme Court of Canada, Reference Re ss. 193 and 195.1(1)(c) of the Criminal Code (Man.), [1990] 1 S.C.R. 1123, 4 W.W.R. 481. See also France, Conseil D'Etat, *Dwarf-Throwing Case*, Ville d'Aix-en-Provence, [1996] Dalloz 177.

60 Beyleveld and Brownsword, *supra* n 58, 218.

61 R Dworkin, *Life's Dominion: An Argument about Abortion, Euthanasia and Individual Freedom* (Vintage Books 1994), 239.

62 HC Kelman, 'The Conditions, Criteria, and Dialectics of Human Dignity – A Transnational Perspective' [1977] 21 *ISQ* 529–552.

63 McDougal, Lasswell and Chen, *Human Rights*, *supra* n 25, 467.

of the advent of Christianity and, later, in the history of thought, with Kant (1724–1804). This is the reason why the Christian and, among the secularized conceptions, the Kantian (and more universal) visions of dignity will be examined in more depth. These are not only circles but also *conceptions* in the broadest sense: as organized patterns of argument, each contextually situated, displaying a specific history and structured around a central theme, exposing many internal variations. I have therefore selected them for their central importance in our contemporary understanding of dignity.

1.3 THREE CONSTITUTIVE STAGES

The sovereign and human conceptions of thinking related to dignity just described remain in the texture of the contemporary idea of dignity. This conceptual clarification of dignity is in fact a condition to trace the roots of the *legal* expression of human dignity. To do so, it is necessary to clarify the process through which it entered into the law, how it turned into a legal concept and, more concretely, what conception (or tradition of thinking) those who discussed its relevance around the tables of international negotiations had in mind and defended. The clarification is, perhaps, also needed to enable us to see how far today's thinking about human dignity departs from the original spirit. Thus, the primary objective of the analysis that will be developed in Chapter 3 is not to examine the appearance of dignity in the international legal discourse in an exhaustive manner or to uncover its expressions in the various areas of law – which will be left to the following chapters of the study – but rather to demonstrate that those two distinct and theoretical conceptions of the past have permeated debates at the origins of international law, also often blending with each other.

The concept of human dignity has been formalized in separate but continuous historical legal stages, through the work of diplomats, scholars and humanitarian aid workers. The expression 'constitutive stage' most accurately refers to a legal consolidation of a historical-juridical development. Constitutive stage also reflects a normative crystallization of an international legal framework that will later evolve and expand over time.

The consolidation of human dignity into the law is the outcome of a lengthy process that involves social, philosophical, religious, political, as well as institutional components. To develop a periodization of dignity, however, calls for an assessment, within an historical path, of a certain level of legal recognition of human dignity. More specifically, there are three complementary criteria which represent the basis on which to build such periodization of dignity and verify the existence of a constitutive stage: first, a linguistic criterion, namely that human dignity shall be expressly mentioned as the basis and foundation of a legal document with a specific wording. This is also what I defined as an *entry point* of human dignity in international law, by identifying the moment at which human dignity first enters an international legal provision. However, this criterion is not sufficient in itself. To carry its full meaning, it must be supported by two further elements, namely the adoption of a legal framework which defines the province of dignity, the field in which human dignity is recalled (such as a declaration, statute or a convention) and the existence of one fully developed instrument (principle, right, crime or obligation), which corroborates the first and second factors. The existence of all three elements (linguistic criterion, legal framework and fully developed instrument) reflects the different passages of a process that gives evidence of a *crystallization* of human dignity in international law. This implies that dignity is reflected in an international legal source and expressed through a legal instrument. Human dignity is here capable of exercising an architectural function. The moment at which human dignity is fully spelt out in a specific legal framework, also through various instruments, is the actual final *consolidation* of human dignity and the completion of its constitutive stage. Thus, in this search and periodization, the identification of the *entry points* of human dignity – which can be multiple – and of its *crystallization* and final *consolidation* shows a chronological evolution of dignity and structure of the constitutive stage. All these three elements are not sufficient in themselves, but reinforce, clarify and validate each other the moment they all coexist. In this way, they enable us to trace, on the historical path, an entry point and a legal moment in which they crystallize and then consolidate a new constitutive stage of human dignity.

More specifically, we can identify three different *constitutive stages* in this formalization process of human dignity in international law. Whereas the emergence of international humanitarian law (IHL) represents the setting for its first constitutive stage, it consolidates as the foundation of the International Bill of Rights and, thus, international human rights law only in the 1960s. Lastly, the evolution and institutionalization of international criminal law (ICL) embody the third and last constitutive stage of human dignity. The historical process and reasons behind the consolidation of human dignity in the law and the three different stages will be elaborated in more detail in Chapter 3.

1.4 INSTRUMENTS

This study aims to provide a historical and legal analysis of human dignity as a normative value and of the main legal instruments used to express it in international law. In the previous section, I left open the question of the instruments that underlie this analysis and that define dignity's contours and manifestations in various areas of law. To understand the instruments' importance, as well as their differences, it may be helpful to first introduce some analytical distinctions.

Four main legal instruments are used to express human dignity and conform its conceptual structure in international law, namely 'principle', 'right', 'obligation' and 'crime'. A clarification of these instruments is an important step in the study of dignity's expressions and substantive features, which will be discussed in Chapters 4–6.

As a preliminary remark, however, I note that legal scholars have already discussed all these four elements that form the background conceptual criteria of this research and often viewed the elements in different ways depending on the perspectives adopted. To facilitate a useful comparison with these other views, distinctions that are recurrently implicit in these studies should first be made explicit to set the ground for a discussion of the four instruments.

Moreover, the main objective of this articulated study is to define the semantic field of human dignity, not in general language but, rather, in a particular language, that of law, and even more specifically, of international law. This enquiry therefore demands a particular attention to the vocabulary used in it. To understand the manifestations of dignity in international law, namely principle, right, obligation and crime, I found it necessary to construct a metalanguage to facilitate this exercise. The adoption of a new conceptual map makes the particularities of each instrument more evident. Despite the instruments' common traits, they present many distinct features. I note that the conceptual cartography that will be developed, inserts itself well into, and is therefore not inconsistent with, other conceptualizations expressed in international law, which will be referred to throughout this section. The other conceptualizations may, however, have different purposes and scopes and be only partially suited to this research.

The conceptual cartography can be organized around five main concepts presented in Figure 1.1.

At the top of the figure is shown the first and primary 'protected interest'. At its core is a widely accepted value or a social good that has acquired, through time and practice, legal recognition. Such value or social good has become a normative concept when associated with a normative use, by representing the *legal good* of a norm and its foundation.

The primary norm, called 'normative prescription', at the centre of Figure 1.1, can be described in its relation to the other four concepts. First, it preserves and guarantees, in legal terms, the protected interest. Second, it has a specific content and it is expressed by permissive or prescriptive rules: the

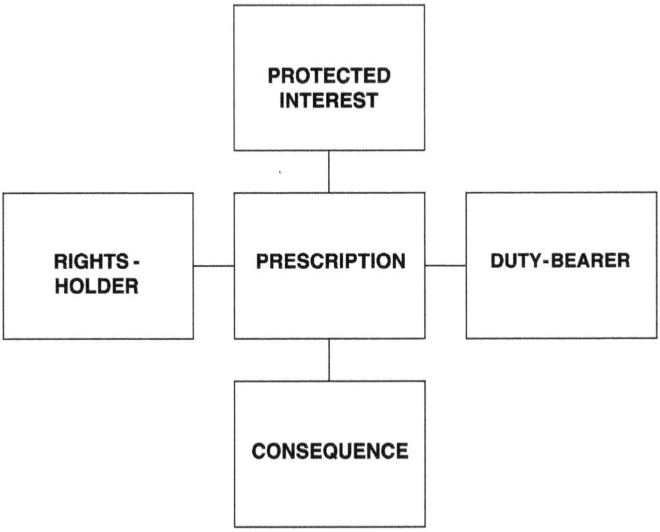

FIGURE 1.1 *Conceptual cartography of the instruments*

former allows or tolerates a specific conduct, while the latter prohibits or demands adoption (or not) of certain behaviours. Third, the primary norm can be directed to one or more 'right-holders' (States, non-state actors or individuals), as well as to one or many 'duty-bearers' (States, non-state actors or individuals). Last, if a primary norm of prescriptive nature is breached by a certain duty-bearer, this triggers specific effects and sanctions, attached to a given regime of responsibility. Every duty-bearer is subject to the primary norm that may eventually activate a system of international responsibility.

A 'primary' or 'triggering' norm may define in different ways a situation carrying legal effects. Typically, it will affirm a conduct to be followed with some degree of diligence (i.e. States shall (or shall not) do X). If this conduct is not performed accordingly, the norm will be deemed to be breached and will trigger effects defined by another set of norms that can be referred to as 'secondary' or 'reparation' norms (e.g. in case of breach, the following effects will apply). The nature of primary (triggering) and secondary norms inevitably changes according to the duty-bearer (State, international organizations, non-state actor or individual).

To understand the functioning of human dignity in international law means sensing and recognizing the centre of gravity of this conceptual framework. It can be preliminary argued that the centre is inevitably constituted by the protected interest. In itself, however, the protected interest does not say how it should be protected, who has a right or who bears a duty. It simply shows that a specific value, such as human dignity, or interest deserves protection. In this sense, once recognized as protected interest by a norm, the value acquires legal standing and relevance for the legal order. This map is a useful starting point and cartography to guide my reading and to describe and build assumptions related to my focus of analysis, namely human dignity. The following four subsections will define these instruments first by presenting how they are perceived in academic debates and subsequently refining their analysis through the aforementioned conceptual map, in order to better understand their relationship with human dignity.

1.4.1 *Principles*

For the purpose of this study, the instrument 'principle' can be examined from three perspectives, namely level of specificity, formulation and functions.

First, to position the instrument 'principle' among other instruments, the distinction based on the *degree* of generality and specificity of the norms implies using three categories (concepts, principles and rules).[64] Another way to understand this approach is to view concepts as guiding norms that are implemented by principles, which, in turn, are realized by rules.[65] The main difference between 'value' and 'principle' lies in the fact that, while a value has a social existence,[66] a principle postulates and transfers a value, which would otherwise remain unfulfilled, to a legal plan. When we use the word 'principles', in Virally's words, they 'remain synonymous of abstract legal rules, providing the basis for a legal regime capable of being applied to multiple concrete situations'.[67] They inform and conform the legal norms of any legal system,[68] playing an important role in international lawmaking, as

64 This distinction is taken from R Dworkin, *Taking Rights Seriously* (Harvard University Press 1977), 22 and recalled in an environmental setting by U Beyerlin, 'Different Types of Norms in International Environmental Law' in D Bodansky, J Brunnée and E Hey (eds), *The Oxford Handbook of International Environmental Law* (Oxford University Press 2007), 426–447.

65 See also PM Dupuy and JE Viñuales, *International Environmental Law* (Cambridge University Press 2018), 59.

66 A Peczenick, *On Law and Reason* (Springer 2008), 62. Some authors consider that, in this dimension of values, choices 'are the object of perceptions and inclinations not rationally justifiable', see G Zagrebelsky, *Intorno alla legge. Il diritto come dimensione del vivere comune* (Einaudi 2009), 63.

67 M Virally, *Le droit international en devenir* (Graduate Institute Publications 1990), 3 (my translation).

68 A Álvarez, *Exposé de motifs et Déclaration des grands principes du Droit international moderne* (2nd ed., Internationales 1938), 8–9 and 16–23, and 27 and 51; see, on the topic, B Cheng, *General Principles of Law as Applied by International Courts and Tribunals* (Stevens 1953).

well as in the application of international law.[69] Therefore, this first step is one of distillation. Principles must be contrasted with rules, which tend to express concrete requirements setting out the circumstances and conditions in which they are to apply.[70]

Second, an alternative prism through which to analyse principles is their *formulation*. They can be formulated in terms of permission or prescription, a cartography that is normally adopted in studies on deontic logic. A norm of law can be permissive 'in allowing individuals to establish their own legal relations with rights and duties, as in the creation of contracts'. Rules would thus be 'essentially tolerations' of a certain behaviour.[71] A norm of law can also be prescriptive, or duty-imposing, as it sets commands or prohibitions and punishes those who infringe its regulations.[72] A supplementary and further approach to principles is to view them through the prism of their *legal source* (treaty, custom or general principle of law).[73]

Third, an alternative and supplementary approach to the analysis of principles and concepts is to look at the *functions* they perform. Two functions can be distinguished: axiological and auxiliary. The first function is to represent and maintain the fundamental unity of the system of international law. It has a structural and *axiological* function, without which the legal order would dissolve itself into legal blocks.[74] Thus, I refer to *foundational or fundamental 'principles'* as general norms (i.e. norms that are specified and implemented through more specific 'rules') that define the basic overall approach taken with respect to a given question or area. Foundational principles are those upon which the international legal order was built. They are guiding principles of general content, and, in that way, they differ from the norms or rules of positive international law, as well as transcend them. As basic pillars of the

69 G Herczegh, *General Principles of Law and the International Legal Order* (Akadémiai Kiadó 1969), 90, 122 and 126; see also G Schwarzenberger, 'The Fundamental Principles of International Law' [1955] 87 *RCADI* 195–385; M Virally, 'Le rôle des "principes" dans le développement du Droit international' in *Recueil d'études de Droit international en hommage à Paul Guggenheim* (IUHEI 1968), XXI–901, 531–554.

70 See R Dworkin, 'The Model of Rules' [1967] 35 *UChiLRev* 14, 25; see also R Kolb, 'Principles as Sources of International law (With Special Reference to Good Faith)' [2006] 53(1) *NILR* 1–36, 9.

71 GH Von Wright, *Norm and Action: A Logical Enquiry* (Routledge 1963), 90.

72 M Shaw, *International Law* (8th ed., Cambridge University Press 2018), 1, who refers to the term 'coercive'.

73 See Beyerlin, *supra* n 64, 426–447.

74 See R Kolb, *Good Faith in International Law* (Bloomsbury 2017), 4–5; see Dupuy and Viñuales, *supra* n 65, 59–60, who refer to the principles' 'identity' and 'architectural' function. See also JE Viñuales, 'Cartographies imaginaires: Observations sur la portee juridique du concept de 'régime spécial' en droit international' [2013] 140 *JDI* (Clunet) 405.

international legal system (as of any legal system), those principles reflect the fundamental values of international society and the conscience of humankind.[75]

Principles also have an *auxiliary* function, mostly when they serve an interpretative role. Three subfunctions can be distinguished: interpretative, constitutive and rhetorical. First, through their auxiliary function, principles provide a tool for the interpretation of customary or conventional norms[76] and are used as a standard for the interpretation of discretionary powers of States. Principles guide the proper application of international rules and favour the evolution of the entire legal system.[77] Principles allow the judge to introduce some flexibility into the law to be applied and sometimes even to develop international law. The need for flexibility is characteristic of new areas into which international law expands.[78] Second, principles may influence the formation of conventional and customary rules of international law, and sometimes also of rules of internal law (legislation).[79] Lastly, principles may also serve a rhetorical auxiliary function when adopted as a tool with perlocutionary effect and to generate a specific reaction in the targeted audience[80] related to the level of gravity of a violation or point to the limits of legality.

If we consider now the instrument 'principle' in our *conceptual framework* it can be seen under different perspectives. First, it incorporates the meaning of the value it protects. Moreover, it directs not only the result but also the *modus agendi* expressed in a primary norm, which recognizes rights and imposes obligations and directs itself to one or more right-holders and is binding on one or more duty-bearers. A principle is capable of pushing the rules in given direction and must be taken into consideration in their drafting and application. For this reason, it is normally built and formulated in open terms and allows a balancing exercise with other principles and policies, in which it is not said to prevail.

75 GM Danilenko, *Law-Making in the International Community* (Martinus Nijhoff 1993), 7, 17, 175 and 186–187, and 215; J Wouters et al., 'The Influence of General Principles of Law' [2011] Leuven Working Paper No. 70, 3–4.

76 H Lauterpacht, *The Development of International Law by the International Court* (Stevens & Sons 1958), 158ff; W Friedmann, '*The Uses of 'General Principles' in the Development of International Law*' [1963] 57 *AJIL* 279–299, 286. It is open to debate as to whether true gaps exist in the legal order, see I Stribis, *La manifestation des lacunes en droit international* (Athènes 2009).

77 Virally, *supra* n 69, 543, 546–547 and 553–554.

78 In the context of international contracts, see P Weil, 'Principes généraux du droit et contrats d'Etat', *Essays in Honor of B. Goldman* (Litec 1982), 387ff; Kolb, *supra* n 74, 450–451.

79 See P Reuter, *Droit international public* (6th ed., PUF 1983), 119.

80 JL Austin, *How to Do Things with Words* (Clarendon Press 1962); JR Searle, *Speech Acts: An Essay in the Philosophy of Language* (Cambridge University Press 1969).

Therefore, the essence of this instrument is that a 'principle' constitutes an indispensable *medium* for bringing into the law a form of wealth derived from values and concepts. Any principle, however, functions through primary norms, setting the content of rights and obligations, and its operativity relies on dynamics not pre-established, which means that it is conditioned by the peculiarities of concrete cases. For this reason, the instrument 'principle' can be considered as the only instrument that relates to all the elements (and instruments) of our conceptual map and as their engine. It can be imagined as a circle (or square) around the entire framework, as pictured in Figure 1.2. Thus, the *centre of gravity* of the instrument principle is represented by the conceptual map seen as a whole. For this reason, it has been taken as the starting point in the analysis of the instruments.

Based on the characteristics of principles outlined earlier, this study argues that, within the legal system, the principle of human dignity has three main features: (i) it is a structural element and necessary foundational element of the international legal system; (ii) it carries a specific legal substance, which is to protect the human dignity of all individuals and to inject considerations of humanity concretized through a series of permissive and prescriptive norms in different areas of international law; (iii) it is an obligation-creating principle, which is directly derived from its legal substance and from its concretizations,

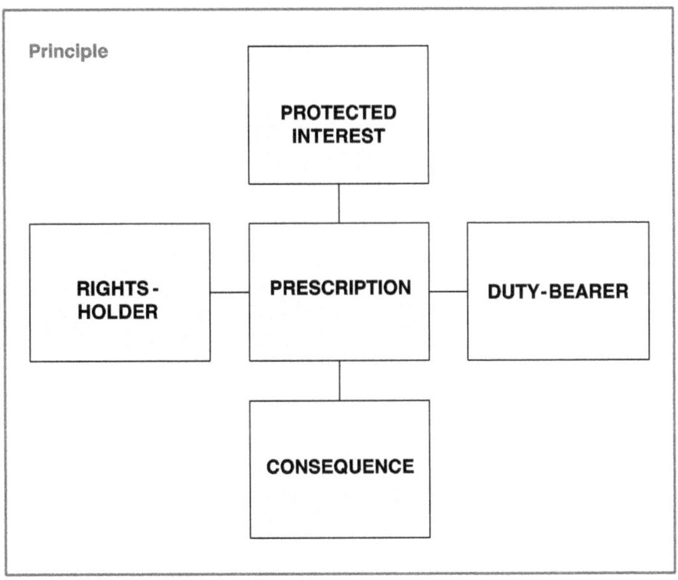

FIGURE 1.2 *Principle*

which serves two main functions: axiological and auxiliary. These features are examined and tested in Chapters 4–6.

1.4.2 *Rights*

Even if the importance of human rights in the international legal structure is now generally accepted,[81] the characterization of this legal instrument is still controversial.[82] Today, what is meant by a 'right' is itself the subject of intense debate.[83] For the purpose of this study, the instrument 'human right' can be examined by way of three considerations: the nature of human rights; the linkage rights – obligations in the interstate relationship; and the identification of right-holders and duty-bearers.

The nature of human rights is of particular relevance in this study; it will be a recurrent theme throughout the research. The concept and instrument of human rights is strictly combined with ethics and morality. Positive rights 'include those rights enshrined within a legal system, whether or not reflective of moral considerations'.[84] However, a moral right, which is not necessarily enforceable by law, may be seen as emanating from different sources, whether religion or the nature of humankind or the nature of society, and will depend upon the perception of whoever is seeking the existence of a specific right.[85] According to natural law theory, associated primarily with John Locke, explained in more detail in Chapter 2, rights exist as a result of a law higher than positive or human-made law, which provides universal principles governing all humanity.[86] Although it was abandoned in the nineteenth century, because of its non-empirical methodology, this theory was of immense

[81] See D Moeckli, S Shah and S Sivakumaran (eds), *International Human Rights Law* (3rd ed., Oxford University Press 2017); O de Schutter, *International Human Rights Law* (3rd ed., Cambridge University Press 2019); T Meron (ed.), *Human Rights in International Law* (Oxford University Press 1984); H Lauterpacht, *International Law and Human Rights* (Stevens & Sons 1950).

[82] See M Moskowitz, *The Policies and Dynamics of Human Rights* (Oceana 1968), 98–99, and McDougal, Lasswell and Chen, *Human Rights*, *supra* n 25, 63–68.

[83] See e.g. WN Hohfeld, 'Fundamental Legal Conceptions as Applied to Judicial Reasoning' [1913] 23 *YLJ* 16, and Dworkin, *supra* n 64; see also J Shestack, 'The Jurisprudence of Human Rights', in Meron, *supra* n 81, 69.

[84] Shaw, *supra* n 72, 210.

[85] See M Cranston, 'What Are Human Rights?' in W Laqueur and B Rubin (eds), *Human Rights Reader* (New American Library 1979), 17, 19.

[86] See Lauterpacht, *supra* n 81; R Tuck, *Natural Rights Theories* (Cambridge University Press 1979); J Finnis, *Natural Law and Natural Rights* (Oxford University Press 1980); and McDougal, Lasswell and Chen, *Human Rights*, *supra* n 25, 68–71.

value in the twentieth century in the establishment of human rights as universal principles. On the other hand, the positivist theory emphasized State authority and that rights emanate from the constitutional frame of a specific legal system.[87] Modern rights theories consider and cover a wide range of views, which clearly emphasizes the importance of coming to terms with the requirements of an evolving legal system that cannot be totally understood in terms of that system itself.[88]

Moreover, human rights entered international law relatively slowly. When looking at human rights sources today, it is important to view norms of customary international law, treaty law and general principles of law.[89] Some of these human rights norms have firmly become rules of *jus cogens*.[90] Human rights law is inherently non-synallagmatic,[91] and its provisions are *erga omnes*.[92] Hence, in human rights treaties, a State's interest to see the treaty obligations performed by the others is the implication of a 'contractual dimension', which is the source of a 'mutual right to enforcement'.[93]

Lastly, individuals as well as collective groups are the generally accepted rights-holders. Differently, together with States, also other entities may be bound to respect human rights obligations,[94] namely international

87 See D Lloyd, *Introduction to Jurisprudence* (4th ed., Stevens 1979), chapter 4; H Hart, *The Concept of Law* (Oxford University Press 1961); McDougal, Lasswell and Chen, *Human Rights, supra* n 25, 73–75.

88 See e.g. J Rawls, *A Theory of Justice* (Oxford University Press 1971); E Cahn, *The Sense of Injustice* (New York University Press 1949); R Nozick, *Anarchy, State and Utopia* (Oxford University Press 1974); and Dworkin, *supra* n 64.

89 N Rodley, 'International Human Rights Law' in M Evans (ed.), *International Law* (5th ed., Oxford University Press 2018), 789.

90 See also A Bianchi, 'Human Rights and the Magic of Jus Cogens' [2008] 19(3) *EJIL* 491.

91 B Simma, 'Sources of International Human Rights Law: Human Rights Treaties' in J D'Aspremont and S Besson (eds), *The Oxford Handbook of the Sources of International Law* (Oxford University Press 2017), 873.

92 They are opposable to the whole community of States or, in the case of treaties, States parties to the treaty. See UN HRC, General Comment No 31: The Nature of the General Legal Obligation Imposed on States Parties to the [International] Covenant [on Civil and Political Rights], 29 March 2004, CCPR/C/21/Rev.1/Add.13, para 2.

93 B Simma, *supra* n 91, 873–874. On this, see B Simma, 'Reservations to Human Rights Treaties —Some Recent Developments' in G Hafner, G Loibl, A Rest, L Sucharipa-Rehrmann and K Zemanek (eds), *Liber Amicorum Professor Ignaz Seidl–Hohenveldern* (Kluwer Law International 1998), 659–697.

94 A Clapham, *Human Rights Obligations of Non-state Actors* (Oxford University Press 2006); A Clapham, 'Non-State Actors' in Moeckli et al., *supra* n 81, chapter 28; N Rodley, 'Non-State Actors and Human Rights' in S Sheeran and N Rodley (eds), *Routledge Handbook of International Human Rights Law* (Routledge 2013), 523–544.

organizations,[95] transnational business enterprises, financial institutions[96] and armed non-state actors.[97]

If examined in our *conceptual framework*, however, the instrument human 'right' has two main and simple features: first, it is expressed through a *permissive* formulation by a primary norm, which protects a given interest or value; second, it identifies one or more *right-holders*, to which correspond one or more duty-bearers. Through the formulation prism of the instrument 'human rights', it can be seen that human rights provisions are expressed as *permissive* norms. Differently, obligations deriving from them fall in the category of *prescriptive* instruments. In fact, it is one question whether States are permitted to adjust their policies and regulation to better promote and protect human rights (what may be termed the 'permissive question'), and it is quite a different question as to whether States are obliged to do so as a matter of human rights law (what may be defined as the 'prescriptive question'). Last, a violation of the primary norm triggers a system of consequences that differ on the basis of the duty-bearer who triggered the regime. Figure 1.3 illustrates this frame.

The relationship between human dignity and the instrument 'right' will thus be studied at three levels. Human dignity appears not only as a *value* principle but also as the *object* and *source* of rights. The dual configuration of human dignity, as right in itself and as foundation of rights and source of other rights, will be developed in more detail in Chapter 5, and will be found as running transversely through different legal documents.

1.4.3 *Obligations*

Human dignity can be also manifested not only as a principle and as a right but also through an *obligation*. An obligation, as applied under civil law, is a legal tie (*vinculum iuris*), according to which one or more parties (obligants) have to perform or refrain from performing a specific conduct

95 See UN CESCR, General Comment No 18: Obligations of Actors Other than State Parties, 24 November 2005, HRI/GEN/1/Rev.9 (Vol I) 243; Rodley, *supra* n 89, 794–795; G Le Moli, 'Autonomy and Accountability of the UN in Peacekeeping Operations: The Case of the Central African Republic' [2017] 20 *UNYB* 213–238.

96 A Clapham, 'Non-State Actors' in Moeckli et al, *supra* n 81, 533. See for a different view, Rodley, *supra* n 89, 796–797.

97 See K Fortin, *The Accountability of Armed Groups under Human Rights Law* (Oxford University Press 2017). On the contrary, see L Moir, *The Law of Internal Armed Conflict* (Cambridge University Press 2002), 45.

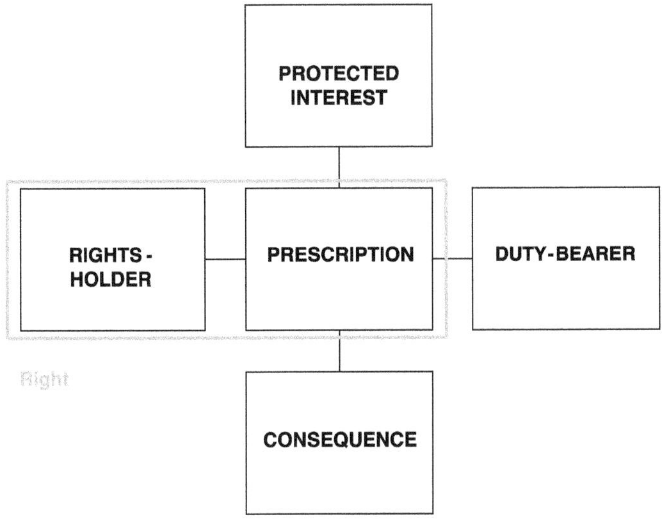

FIGURE 1.3 *Right*

(prestation).[98] Every obligation is thus composed of four essential elements, namely: (i) the duty-bearer or obligor, bound to fulfil the obligation; (ii) the right-holder or obligee, who is the obligant entitled to demand the fulfilment of the obligation; (iii) the subject matter, the prestation, which represents the performance to be exercised and relates to a specific protected value; (iv) the *vinculum juris* or legal bond, which is the cause that binds or connects the obligants to the prestation.[99] In particular, obligations in international law can be primarily identified according to (i) their protected value and types; (ii) their multiple duty-bearers (State, non-state actors and individuals); and (iii) the distinct, and at times concurrent, forms of international responsibility in the event a violation occurs.

Obligations may protect different values and, therefore, have different shapes and prescriptive formulations. Each typology also identifies a bilateral or multilateral number of duty-bearers. If obligations in Roman law used to arise out of contracts or delicts,[100] in international law, it is still

98 JL Baudouin, PG Jobin and N Vézina, *Les Obligations* (6th ed., Éditions Yvon Blais 2005), 19; R Zimmermann, *The Law of Obligations: Roman Foundations of the Civilian Tradition* (Oxford University Press 1996), 1–9; Justinian had first defined an obligation (obligatio) in his *Institutiones*, Book 3, section 13, see Justinian, *Institute*, Trans. John B. Moyle (Oxford University Press 1889), 132.

99 In Roman law, the execution of obligations was defined as a solution (*liberatio*), meaning dissolving, freeing. E Betti, *La struttura dell'obbligazione romana e il problema della sua genesi* (Giuffrè 1985), 32.

100 P Bonfante, *Corso di Diritto Romano*, vol. 4: Le obbligazioni (Giuffrè 1979), 10.

debated whether an analogy between contract law and public international law remains appropriate.[101] In this debate, important classifications have been put forward, such as the distinction between a treaty resembling legislation (*Vereinbarung*) and a treaty resembling a contract (*Vertrag*)[102] or between obligations *consenties* and obligations *assumées*.[103] With regard to non-reciprocal obligations, a further innovative categorization has been advanced between *interdependent*[104] and *absolute* obligations.[105] These categories concern obligations that are owed to a plurality of States,[106] either considered as a group (*erga omnes partes*) or the international community as a whole (*erga omnes*).[107] In international law, the concept of obligations *erga omnes* is closely related, or 'virtually coextensive',[108] to the legal concept of *jus cogens* norms.[109]

Thus, considering that an obligation may attach to a multiplicity of duty-bearers, the earlier distinctions add a relevant consideration to our conceptual

101 See G Schwarzenberger, *The Dynamics of International Law* (Milton 1976), 40, 48; PM Dupuy, 'L'obligation en droit international' [2000] 44 *Archives de philosophie du droit* 84–85.

102 H Triepel, *Volkerrecht und Landesrecht* (Hirschfeld 1899) who in turn relied on Bergbohm's earlier study published in 1887, K Bergbohm, *Vertrage und Gesetze als Quellen des Volkerrechts* (Dorpat1887), 79–81. See also T Gihl, *International Legislation. An Essay on Changes in International Law and in International legal Situations* (Oxford University Press 1937), 47–53.

103 See Dupuy, *supra* n 101, 218.

104 Obligations whose observance is conditioned upon performance by all other parties. PM Dupuy, 'Quarante ans de codification du droit de la responsabilité des etats: un bilan' [2003] 107 *RGDIP* 333; LA Sicilianos, 'The Classification of Obligations and the Multilateral Dimension of the Relations of International Responsibility' [2002] 13 *EJIL* 1133–1135; ILC, Articles on Responsibility of States for Internationally Wrongful Acts, commentary, YILC, 2001, vol. II, Part Two, 119 [ILC Draft Articles]. Crawford defines them as integral, see Third Report on State Responsibility, A/CN.4/507, 2000, para. 91 [Crawford, *Third Report*].

105 Multilateral obligations apply *regardless* of how and whether they are performed by other parties. Absolute obligations are also defined as '*internal*', see R Provost, 'Reciprocity in Human Rights and Humanitarian Law' [1994] 65 *BYIL* 133–134; '*self-existent*', see Fitzmaurice, *Second Report*, draft article 19 (1)(iv); or '*objective*' obligations, see *Ireland* v. *United Kingdom Case*, para 239; B Simma, 'From Bilateralism to Community Interest' [1994] 250 *RCADI* 364–369.

106 G Arangio-Ruiz, Fourth Report on State Responsibility, A/CN.4/444 and Add. 1–3, YbILC 1992, vol. II, Part Two, p. 44 [Arangio-Ruiz, *Fourth Report*].

107 Wyler and Papaux explain these as 'obligations assumées', since they are reciprocal in the recognition of values common to all States, E Wyler and A Papaux, 'Le mythe structurant de l'humanité: la communauté internationale vivante' in D Alland, V Chetail, O de Frouville and JE Viñuales (eds), *Unité et diversité du droit international/Unity and Diversity of International Law. Ecrits en l'honneur du Professeur Pierre-Marie Dupuy/Essays in Honour of Professor Pierre-Marie Dupuy* (Martinus Nijhoff 2014), 184.

108 Crawford, *Third Report*, para. 106(a); Crawford, *Fourth Report*, para. 49.

109 See A De Hoogh, *Obligations Erga Omnes and International Crimes* (Martinus Nijhoff 1996); M Ragazzi, *The Concept of International Obligations Erga Omnes* (Oxford University Press 1997); C Tams, *Enforcing Obligations Erga Omnes in International Law* (Cambridge University Press 2005).

map. In fact, they clarify that if some obligations imply that there may be a duty-bearer *without* the other party or parties being a duty-bearer(s) (i.e. *absolute* obligations), in other types of obligations, a duty-bearer's obligation corresponds and/or relates to the obligation of another duty-bearer (*bilateral* obligations and *interdependent* obligations). Depending on the duty-bearer (whether a State, a non-state actor or an individual), a failure to fulfil an obligation triggers a different regime of responsibility.

First, State responsibility is triggered when conduct attributable to a State constitutes a breach of its international obligations.[110] In essence, an internationally wrongful act stems from the non-conformity of the State's conduct when compared to the conduct that it ought to have adopted pursuant to a particular international obligation.[111] However, international law conceives separate forms of responsibility arising for the individual and the State under peremptory norms. The duality of responsibility is that by which the individual faces criminal and civil responsibility for violations of peremptory norms constituting *international crimes*, while the State faces responsibility for internationally wrongful acts deriving from the failure to fulfil obligations *erga omnes* arising from peremptory norms or through conduct attributable to the State in violation of a peremptory norm (so-called *aggravated responsibility*). Importantly, State responsibility is not itself criminal or civil in nature: as an 'undifferentiated regime', State responsibility knows no such distinction and conceives only of international responsibility.[112]

Conversely, international law does not address crimes of States.[113] The 1996 draft of the ILC Articles contained the renowned Article 19, which established the category of State 'crime'. Article 19 was ultimately considered inappropriate and omitted from the final version of 2001 since, in practice, there had been 'no development of penal consequences for States of breaches of these fundamental norms'.[114] As a result, State responsibility, as contemplated in the final version of the Articles, is concerned exclusively with internationally wrongful acts of a State, arising from attributable conduct in violation of its obligations under international law.[115]

110 Pursuant to the scheme embodied in Article 2 of the ILC Draft Articles.

111 See also F Latty, 'Actions and Omissions' in J Crawford, A Pellet and S Olleson (eds), *The Law of International Responsibility* (Oxford University Press 2010), 355–364; Y Nishimura, 'Source of the Obligation' in J Crawford, A Pellet and S Olleson (eds), *The Law of International Responsibility* (Oxford University Press 2010), 365–370.

112 J Crawford, 'The System of International Responsibility' in Crawford et al., *supra* n 111, 22.

113 J Crawford, 'International Crimes of States' in Crawford et al., *supra* n 111, 405–414.

114 ILC Draft Articles, 111–112, paras. 5–7 (Commentary to Chapter III). See also ILC, Fourth report on the content, forms and degrees of international responsibility (Part Two of the draft articles), Riphagen, *Sixth Report*, p. 11.

115 *Ibid.*, 26 (Articles 1–2).

In order to define the relationship between dignity and instrument obligation, it is necessary to clarify the meaning, the role and the functions of the specific instrument within the *conceptual framework* and, therefore, in its correlation with the five elements previously outlined. Through this lens, it can be seen that an obligation is characterized in the following four features, the linkages of which are portrayed in Figure 1.4.

First, the instrument preserves a *protected legal good* that can be of private nature, such as economic interests (e.g. protection of a private house, i.e. right to property), or of public nature (e.g. the protection from torture, i.e. the right not be tortured, or right to human dignity). The higher the protected value, the more extensive and strict is its protection.

Moreover, unlike the instrument 'right', an obligation derives from primary norms *prescriptive* in nature, commanding or prohibiting certain conducts. There are no *permissive* obligations. In particular, the obligation's prescriptive formulation can be expressed through two categories of obligations: it can be of *prohibitive* nature (negative obligations), placing a duty on the parties to refrain (*not to do*) from acting in a way that unjustifiably interferes with rights; and it establishes a *command* (positive obligations), which places a duty to take active steps (*to do*) in order to safeguard rights.

Furthermore, the concept and instrument of 'obligation' encompasses both the duty of the obligor (*duty-bearer*) to render prestation and the right of the obligee (*right-holder*) to receive a prestation. There can be a plurality of

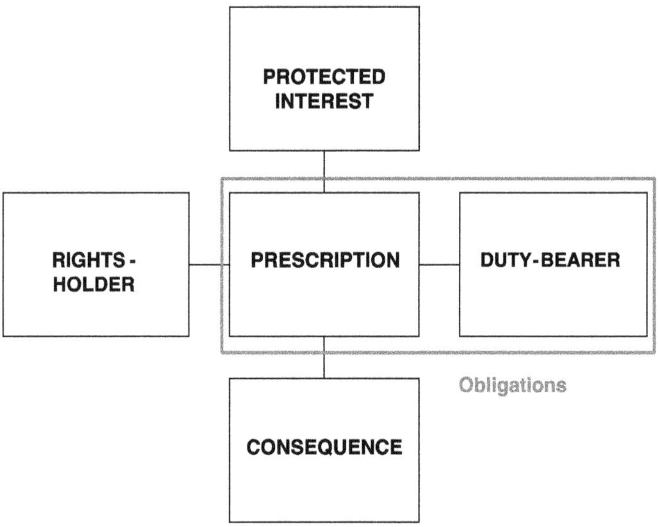

FIGURE 1.4 *Obligation*

different right-holders and duty-bearers, which are exposed to distinct regimes of liability in the case of a failure to fulfil such a duty.[116]

A last connotation refers to the specific effects of a violation of a primary norm. It must be primarily specified that these consequences are the *function of*, and depend on, two elements of the conceptual frame, namely the content of the primary norm and the type of duty-bearers. A failure to implement an obligation may trigger different regimes of responsibilities and sanctions, for States, international organizations and individuals. Therefore, it can be concluded that an obligation has a specific protected good and may have different contents, of prescriptive nature (command or prohibition), directed to a distinct duty-bearer. In case of a violation of a legal duty, in light of the primary norm, which is the source of the obligation's content and identifies the duty-bearer, international law sets specific effects and sanctions, which give rise to international responsibility.

It is now necessary to see how the conceptual frame can be refined in order to clarify the relationship between dignity and obligations. Preliminarily, the instrument 'obligation' has four fundamental characteristics: (i) it can protect a legal good, of a private or public nature, such as human dignity; (ii) it can have different contents (negative and positive) and forms (*consenties* and *assumée*); (iii) it can be directed to different duty-bearers; and (iv) a failure to fulfil its prescriptive order embodied in the primary norm triggers a different regime of sanctions in light of the duty-bearer bound to perform its mandate. These clear features will ground the analysis of human dignity that will be presented in Chapters 4–6.

1.4.4 *Crimes*

In simple terms, the instrument 'crime' defines what is an action or omission that constitutes an offence and is punishable by law. The definition of 'international crime' is quite controversial, and legal scholars have made several attempts to define its key characteristics.[117]

Before tracing its constitutive elements, however, it should be preliminarily noted that the development of a body of international criminal law that imposes responsibilities directly on individuals and prosecutes violations

116 See Zimmermann, *supra* n 98, 5, 7.

117 See for instance, A Cassese, *International Criminal Law* (3rd ed., Oxford University Press 2013), Part I; CM Bassiouni, 'International Crimes: The Ratione Materiae of International Criminal Law' in MC Bassiouni (ed.), *International Criminal Law. Vol. I: Sources, Subjects and Contents* (3rd ed., Martinus Nijhoff 2008), 129–203; G Werle, *Principles of International Criminal Law* (TMC Asser Press 2005).

through international mechanisms is relatively recent.[118] In light of this historical evolution, which will be detailed in Chapters 3 and 6 of this study, an international crime is today characterized by three main features: first, the violation of either international *customary* rules which protect fundamental values for the international community, or of *treaty* rules that clarify or develop such customary rules, and are applicable in the case at issue; second, the existence of a universal interest in repressing and prosecuting these crimes under international law, in the sense that, subject to certain conditions, alleged perpetrators may in principle be prosecuted and punished by any State, irrespective of any territorial or nationality link, provided that the suspect is on the territory of the State; third, if the perpetrator has acted in an official capacity, the State on whose behalf the perpetrator has acted is *barred* from claiming that he enjoys the immunity from jurisdiction of foreign States.[119] The debate and legal discourse surrounding the concept and definition of international crimes revolve around the importance given to these characteristics, which scholars use and present in different ways.[120] In accordance with the aforementioned general criteria for defining an international crime, core international crimes include war crimes, crimes against humanity, genocide and the crime of aggression.[121] They all find recognition in the Statute of the International Criminal Court[122] and will be further analysed in Chapter 6.

Moreover, for the purpose of this study, three specific features of the instrument 'crime' deserve a closer look.

First, to identify and understand the nature of a value or interest protected by the instrument crime is to explain and support why a given conduct may be

118 See MC Bassiouni, 'From Versailles to Rwanda in Seventy-Five Years: The Need to Establish an International Criminal Court' (1997) 10 *HHRJ* 11; P Gaeta, 'International Criminalization of Prohibited Conduct' in A Cassese (ed.), *The Oxford Companion to International Criminal Justice* (Oxford University Press 2009), 63.

119 P Gaeta, JE Viñuales, and S Zappalá, *Cassese's International Law* (3rd ed., Oxford University Press 2020), Chapter 19, section 19.1.

120 MC Bassiouni, 'The Sources and Content of International Criminal Law: A Theoretical Framework' in MC Bassiouni (ed.), *International Criminal Law* (Transnational Publishers Incorporated 1999), 3, 98; HH Jescheck, 'International Crimes' in R Bernhardt (ed.), *Encyclopaedia of Public International Law*, 2 (North Holland 1995), 1119, 1120; R Cryer, H Friman, D Robinson and E Wilmshurst, *An Introduction to International Criminal Law and Procedure* (Cambridge University Press 2007), 2.

121 According to Cassese, torture and some extreme forms of terrorism also fall within the (narrower) definition of international crimes, see Gaeta, JE Viñuales, and S Zappalá, *supra* n 119.

122 Rome Statute of the International Criminal Court, UN Doc. A/CONF. 183.9 (17 July 1998, entered into force 1 July 2002) [Rome Statute 1998].

prohibited by law and why any conduct against such prohibition may be punished.[123] The protected interest, or legal good, should direct the legislature in setting and formulating criminal conducts and the severity of the sanction as well as directing the interpretation of legal norms.[124] An international crime implies an offence to certain values deemed as important by the international community. This constitutes an essential element that distinguishes an international crime from other crimes[125] and is 'because of the importance of these [supra-national] values that the international community directly criminalizes them, *striking at the fabric of state in one of the most sacrosanct pillars of its sovereignty, the monopoly in criminal matters*'.[126] With respect to the content of these values, Cassese affirms that these are not values 'propounded by scholars or thought up by starry-eyed philosophers',[127] but rather are laid down, although sometimes not very directly, in international human rights instruments.[128] Thus, it is 'on account of the values they protect that these crimes are truly international'.[129]

Moreover, an international criminal offence is an act entailing the criminal liability of the perpetrator. International criminal law is a body of international law that imposes criminal responsibility directly upon the individual, the only duty-bearer.[130] As seen earlier, the idea of 'State's crimes' was ultimately left out by the ILC in the final text of 2001.[131]

123 See T Hörnle and M Kremnitzer, 'Human Dignity as a Protected Interest in Criminal Law' [2013] 44 *IsrLRev* 143–167.

124 See O Lagodny, 'Human Dignity and Its Impact on German Substantive Criminal Law and Criminal Procedure' [1999] 33 *IsrLRev* 575, 577.

125 Cassese, *supra* n 117, 20–23.

126 Gaeta, *supra* n 118, 66, emphasis added.

127 *Ibid.*

128 *Ibid.*; Werle, *supra* n 117, 31.

129 Gaeta, *supra* n 118, 66.

130 See B. Broomhall, *International Justice and the International Criminal Court: Between Sovereignty and the Rule of Law* (Oxford University Press 2003), 9–10. As the Nuremberg Tribunal clearly held, '[c]rimes against international law are committed by men, not by abstract entities, and only by punishing individuals who commit such crimes can the provisions of international law be enforced', Office of the US Chief of Counsel for Prosecution of Axis Criminality, *Nazi Conspiracy and Aggression*, Opinion and Judgment (US Government Printing Office 1946), 53.

131 See *supra* n 113. See also G Abi-Saab, 'The Uses of Article 19' [1999] 10 *EJIL* 350–351; see also Pellet, *Can a State Commit a Crime?*, 425; A Pellet, 'Can a State Commit a Crime? Definitely, Yes!' [1999] 10(2) *EJIL* 425–434, 426–427 and A Pellet, 'The New Draft Articles of the International Law Commission on the Responsibility of States for Internationally Wrongful Acts: A Requiem for States' Crime?' [2001] 32 *NethYIL* 55–79.

Lastly, if international law typically establishes the rights and responsibilities of States,[132] criminal law, conversely, is paradigmatically concerned with prohibitions addressed to individuals, violations of which are subject to a specific sanction by a State.[133]

Looking at the instrument 'crime' using the tools of our *conceptual map*, also in its relation with human dignity, requires wearing a different pair of lenses. In our cartography, the instrument 'crime' results from the combination of a specific primary norm and its relationship with a particular duty-bearer. Compared to the instrument 'obligation', a 'crime' has three peculiar features: first, its constitutive elements are described by a primary norm which protects only specific legal goods; second, the norm directs its prohibitive and prescriptive command to individuals, the only duty-bearers; third, a failure to respect the primary norm ultimately triggers the punitive regime of international criminal responsibility, which inherently differs from other regimes triggered by the breach of other international obligations.

These three features are shown in Figure 1.5.

Consequently, when we look at the relationship between human dignity and the instrument 'international crime', human dignity appears as the protected interest or legal good of specific international crimes. Although this consideration will be the object of further and more detailed examination in Chapter 6, this section enables us to conclude that the instrument 'international crime' associated with human dignity has three distinct features compared to other instruments previously seen: first, it protects the *legal value* through the formulation of a criminal conduct which constitutes an offence against it; second, it has direct binding force on *individuals*, the only duty-bearers; and third, it attaches a *criminal sanction* to a violation of the criminal norm. These three features will be the guiding characteristics of the instrument in the analysis that will be conducted mostly in Chapter 6 on the specific manifestations of human dignity in international criminal law.

[132] See R Jennings and A Watts (eds), *Oppenheim's International Law* (9th ed., Oxford University Press 2008), 5–7.

[133] G Williams, 'The Definition of Crime' [1955] 8 *CLP* 107; K Parlett, *The Individual in the International Legal System* (Cambridge University Press 2011), 229; R Portmann, *Legal Personality in International Law* (Cambridge University Press 2010), 162; A Bianchi, 'State Responsibility and Criminal Liability of Individuals' in Cassese, *supra* n 118, 22. Exploring the rationales of international punishment, see F Jeßberger and J Geneuss (eds), *Why Punish Perpetrators of Mass Atrocities?: Purposes of Punishment in International Criminal Law* (Cambridge University Press 2020).

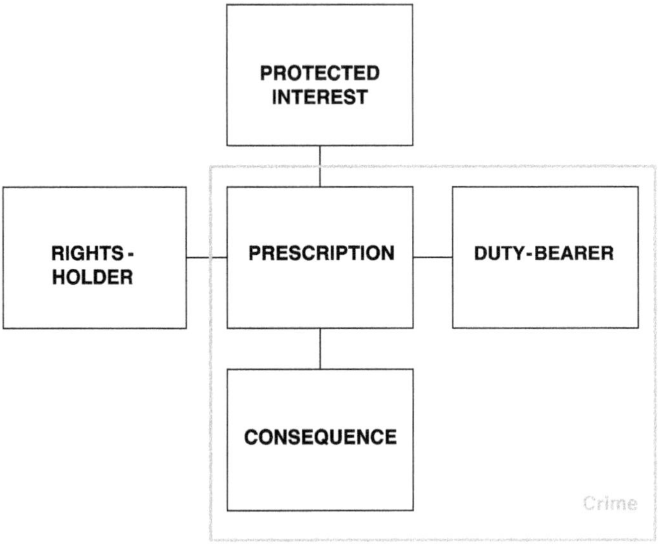

FIGURE 1.5 *Crime*

1.5 THE ARGUMENT

I intend to advance two levels of analysis, one legal and one historical narrative (as already anticipated in the Introduction), which will be developed in parallel throughout the following six chapters of the study. Once the three historical stages have been outlined, in Chapter 3, it will be necessary to examine, at a substantial level, the effects of these constitutive stages and how they relate to the four distinct instruments.

A first level of analysis, of a strictly juridical nature, requires an analysis aimed at helping to understand how the concept of human dignity has been formalized. This search calls for a clarification of the conceptual plan that I will try to follow in all chapters.

To maintain a focus on the scope of the study, I first need to set the specific *directions* in which I will look for manifestations of the concept. With the term 'directions', more specifically I want to convey that the language of dignity has found its own path in various legal frameworks, namely: IHL, IHRL and ICL. The reason for this choice will now be clarified. In fact, to better understand which legal forms have been adopted to realize in practice this formalization requires a careful examination of the juridical instruments through which the concept of human dignity has been expressed, and still is today. Each manifestation shows that human dignity appears in international legal reasoning through different legal guises or techniques. Therefore, in this respect, the instruments presented in Section 1.4 provide the basis to proceed with such analysis.

Most likely, each of the delineated constitutive stages will be paradigmatic of the manifestation of a specific instrument or of the combination of many. The research will follow the three historical stages which ground the decision to have *three* subsequent chapters (4–6) reflecting the consolidations of dignity in three different legal frameworks. This does not exclude, however, that contradictions may arise between the different uses, also on the basis of the specific historical stage in which the manifestation is situated. In this way, it will be evident that human dignity is present in international law, not only with the language of human *rights* but also with other instruments.

A second level of analysis follows a more historical-narrative approach, by tracing the intellectual history of the concept of dignity. This research plan, which will only be developed (and proven) through the research's net, as a *fil rouge* behind the legal argument, intends to advance two main considerations.

1.5.1 A *Narrative of Two Rival Circles of Dignity*

What first emerges from the conceptual examination of dignity and from its three constitutive stages is that (i) today we can still distinguish two circles of opposing dignities, sovereign and human; and that (ii) the second circle of human dignity developed a later date and in opposition to the first. As we have seen in Section 1.2, the two interlocking circles of dignity are rival in nature. I will now clarify this last assumption.

The classic and sovereign conception of dignity, and specifically that associated with the State, is traced in the past through, and remains today in, all manifestations of State sovereignty. For instance, sovereign dignity reappears when it is used today to support arguments associated with State immunities, with the principle of non-intervention in internal affairs or the status of ambassadorial staff serving their countries abroad. These are all corollaries of the principle of State sovereignty. The concept was by analogy adopted at the religious level to affirm that humans are the holders of a dignity, given to them by God. Religious imagery has long been based on a pre-existing social[134] and legal[135] imaginary. The hypothesis that the choice of the notion of *dignity*, as a human attribute, is an analogical derivative from the terminology

[134] See A Testart, *Des dons et des dieux. Anthropologie religieuse et sociologie comparative* (Errance 2006), 160.

[135] See HJ Berman, *Law and Revolution* (Harvard University Press 1983).

of sovereign dignity can also be legitimate. In this way, human dignity in the Christian sense made its historical entrance associated to the human being, who had a *special status* being created in the image of God. This concept will be increasingly refined over time, becoming less theological and assuming a *limiting function* of the first conception of sovereign (and State) dignity. The concept of human dignity assumes, in its entry into international law, a restraining role and, in a broader sense, a function of control over the first conception of State dignity. Therefore, what is originally an analogy, once applied to human nature, developed into a limit to the first conception.

This will be one of the lines of argumentation that will be found in the research and which I will try to show through the legal reconstruction described earlier. The analysis of the various legal frameworks will show how dignity manifested itself and influenced international law, as well as its development. Most likely, it will turn out that, in every legal framework, the influence of the concept of human dignity will imply a limit to the rights of the State or its sovereignty. Every instrumental tool of human dignity – and not just the subjective right, which may be the traditional association – will be used to contrast the two forms of dignity.

As will be shown in the analysis of the historical entrance of the concept in the first constitutive stage (in Chapter 3), human dignity, in a Christian sense, has found its way as a limit to the free decisional power of the State in times of conflict. The same happened when, starting from the abolition of slavery, up to, for instance, the protection of minorities and the development of peoples' right to self-determination, the protection of human dignity, at the foundation of the rights of every person, created a corresponding duty for each State to respect dignity, even against its own nationals. In ICL, the need to protect the individual's dignity was at the basis of the institution of the principle of individual criminal responsibility, which imposed limits on freedom to act. Also, the limits that are placed on the application of State immunities, specifically in the name of protection of dignity, are a further example of a limitation on freedom to act. Other instances of this contrast between the two circles of dignity (human dignity and sovereign dignity) will be explained and illustrated in more detail in Chapters 3–6 of this book, which will clarify how all these frameworks of international law have imposed limits on the first circle of sovereign dignity. In these four chapters I will not only develop the argument that there *are* limits but also identify *how* these limits have developed and *where* they have developed more. In this way, it should then also be clearer which tool has been more useful for the purpose of building boundaries to State sovereignty.

1.5.2 A *Narrative of Secularization*

A further consideration comes from looking at what kind of human dignity is adopted today in legal language. Here, a secularized use of dignity seems predominant, alongside an ever-present dignity in its Christian meaning (e.g. in the field of bioethics). Therefore, by examining in a more detailed way the process in which secularization took place historically, it seems that a circular process took shape. As anticipated, first, there was a detachment from the first classical conception of dignity, through an extension by analogy of the concept to express an inherent and religious value of each human being, given by God. The concept of dignity was later re-secularized when viewed as an adequate term to express a universal purpose. This process can be interpreted as an 'inverse secularization': a universal and secular concept of dignity entered again and opposed itself to a form of sovereign dignity still used today in relation to State sovereignty. Even when dignity becomes 'secular', it does not lose sight of the religious origins that enabled it to originally oppose sovereign dignity.

This level of analysis will try to prove that the concept of human dignity made its first appearance in legal history in a religious and later more secularized guise, as a reaction and limit to the first more classical conception of sovereign dignity and, thus, always in opposition to the concept of State sovereignty.

Moreover, clarifying that dignity has consolidated in international law enables conclusions on the historical relevance of the theory of secularization to be advanced. To explain human dignity, to seek its religious roots, to see its evolution and how it is manifested on a juridical level, ultimately enables us to demonstrate that the concept, originally rooted in religion, is today fully integrated in a secularization process. This intellectual history will be traced behind the various legal formulations of dignity that will be now discussed. Hence, this historical-narrative level of analysis provides a second (and last) reason that grounds the reasoning behind Chapters 4–6.

Each constitutive stage mostly reflects the injection of human dignity in a specific legal framework of international law and is therefore differently characterized. Whereas, at the chronological level, we see these consolidations of dignity in international law, there is not necessarily a clear-cut development in each historical stage. As previously noted, each phase may continue and overlap (or define a closure) with a previous stage or with subsequent ones. After assessing that, *historically*, human dignity has entered into international law in three constitutive stages, I intend to investigate *conceptually*, in three different chapters, how expressions of human dignity interrelate with each other and which one limits (or expands) the other. The conceptual analysis that will be developed in Chapter 2 is important to clarify that human dignity in international law, as an attribution of every human being, has Christian origins, has been secularized in order to be of universal application and finds itself in constant opposition with the first, more classical conception of sovereign dignity. To distinguish the stages in which human dignity has been introduced in the law is a historical exercise that is necessary to understand the transition from a theoretical idea to a juridical consecration. The two circles of dignity flow into the folds of the law and shape its provisions and interpretation. Therefore, for each of the three constitutive stages of human dignity, it is important to examine the different legal formulations in various related legal provinces. Chapters 4–6 will indeed show that specific legal instruments have been used to express human dignity in a particular context and demonstrate *how* such legal forms limit (or oppose) the sovereign conception of dignity and constitute the expression of a secularized religious idea.

2

Two Circles of Dignity

2.1 INTRODUCTION

To try to better understand *how* the concept of dignity made its entrance in international law requires clarification on *what* the concept exactly means or refers to. This chapter examines the intellectual origins of dignity, in its twofold nature, *sovereign* and *human* dignity – the latter, in its religious and philosophical strands. I defined them, in Chapter 1, as circles of dignity. Even though these conceptions may not be exhaustively presented, my final aim is to identify the central idea that animates each of them and to suggest that, over time, the concept of human dignity has undergone a metamorphosis, or a short circuit; it was used first to establish a hierarchical differentiation among human beings, and subsequently it developed into a concept adopted to express equality.[1] In Chapter 7, we will see how this metamorphosis is questioned today. Following the main argumentative narrative, this chapter provides the ground to understand how a religious and more secularized conception of dignity arose in history, namely as a reaction and in opposition to the first idea, that of the concept of sovereign dignity.

2.2 SOVEREIGN DIGNITY

The ancient concept of dignity is identifiable through the etymology of the term 'dignity' itself. The Latin for 'worthy', *dignus*, derives from 'dec-nos', with the Greek root *dek-*. The same root is also present in words such as *decet* (it's convenient), *decens* (decent) and *decorus* (decorum),[2] which share a common meaning.

[1] For a discussion on this short circuit, see U Vincenti, *Diritti e dignità umana* (Laterza 2009).
[2] See G Devoto, *Avviamento alla etimologia italiana. Dizionario etimologico* (Le Monnier 1967).

The first and ancient concept of dignitas was primarily linked to a kind of nobility or rank.[3] In the sovereign conception, dignity is adopted to primarily express three features of a high social standing.[4] First, dignity can imply the elevated nature of the personal status. A dignitary has a high position and will receive esteem commensurate with that role. In the Renaissance it was common to refer to the dignity of a prince or of a courtier, while today the dignity of a judge is a common image. Second, dignity can refer to the duties, attitudes and bearing of those who have a higher-ranking status. The dignity of a prince, for instance, would imply definitive virtues that derive from his role, and he can choose to act below his dignity, that is 'outside' or 'against' his dignity. This would imply that he has violated a role obligation or duty, or acted without virtue in some domain connected to his role, or failed to act in a way that is appropriate to his rank. Third, dignity can also be related to the higher worth of an office itself or of the acts conducted as its expression. Thus, someone who is 'worthy' of an office is *dignus* (in Latin) or *degno* (in Italian).

The status, of either the person or the office, is higher because it implies authority or power over others and because the role requires behaviours and qualities more demanding than lower-ranking positions, and also serving allegedly more worthy aims. Hence, acting 'with dignity' in this sense means acting in line with what is required by that rank or position. As a result of one's worthy act or virtue, they deserve to be highly valued.

The terms of sovereign dignity first arose in the crucible of late classical antiquity and later forged into our contemporary meaning in courtly settings in the Renaissance. In particular, in this context and conception, Aristotle's discussions in his *Nicomachean Ethics* of the 'great-souled man' (or *megalopsychos*) represent a source of important considerations. In the words of the philosopher, the great-souled man is one who maintains a measured behaviour towards wealth or influence and 'who thinks himself worthy of great things – and is indeed worthy of them'.[5] Among those 'great things', Aristotle

[3] See J Ober, 'Meritocratic and Civic Dignity in Greco-Roman Antiquity' in M Düwell, J Braarvig, R Brownsword, N van Steenbergen, D Mieth and D Düring (eds), *The Cambridge Handbook of Human Dignity: Interdisciplinary Perspectives* (Cambridge University Press 2014), 53; C Neuhäuser and R Stoecker, 'Human Dignity as Universal Nobility' in Düwell et al., *ibid.*, 298; see also J Waldron, *Dignity, Rank and Rights*, M Dan-Cohen (ed.) (Oxford University Press 2012).

[4] A Sangiovanni, *Humanity without Dignity: Moral Equality, Respect, and Human Rights* (Harvard University Press 2017), 16.

[5] For Aristotle, only men were capable of *megalopsychia*; see Aristotle, *Nicomachean Ethics*, Book IV, R Crisp (ed.) (Cambridge University Press 2000), 67.

affirms that there will be public honours worthy of the man's greatness, which will be the 'prize for the noblest achievements'.[6] Thus, the great-souled man is the *kalos kagathos*, or a man of dignity. Not surprisingly, the most well-known medieval Latin translation of Aristotle's *Nicomachean Ethics* is that of Robert Grosseteste, who translated the expression 'who deems himself worthy of great things' (or *megalon auton axioun*) as *qui magnis se ipsum dignificat*.[7]

The following sections present the evolution of the sovereign conception of dignity, namely its Stoic origins, its development in Renaissance humanism and its reflection in the first expressions of the concept of State sovereignty.

2.2.1 *The Stoics and Cicero*

The expression 'dignity of man' made its first appearance between the second and first century BCE in Stoic sources. It was most likely formulated first by Panaetius of Rhodes in 128 BCE in the lost 'peri tou Kathekontos', *On Appropriate Actions*, and by Marcus Tullius Cicero, who shared the Stoics' view in many of his speeches and treatises.[8] According to the Stoics, the original Latin term *dignitas hominis* was a synonym for worthiness, evoking elements of respect related to status, rank or personality, and inherent in the rational persona given by nature to all human beings.[9]

Cicero had the greatest influence on our modern understanding of dignity. Although the term *dignitas* appears in several of Cicero's writings and in Roman literature of the time,[10] only once in *De Officiis* does Cicero present the word *dignitas* as linked to humankind – thus not as rank or worth – despite quoting Panaetius several times.[11] In his *De Officiis*, classic themes on the greatness of man's soul are presented within a Stoic frame. The text was written in 44 BCE and was dedicated to Cicero's son. It was a moral

6 *Ibid.*, 68.

7 R Grosseteste, *Ethica Nicomachea*, Libri I–III ('recensio pura'), RA Gauthier (ed.), (Aristoteles Latinus 1972), Clavis 26.2.2 (M), 211.

8 See Cic. *Off.* 1.90; 2.76; see Cic. *Epistulae ad Atticum* 16:11.4; see Andrew R Dyck, *A Commentary on Cicero, De Officiis* (University of Michigan Press 1996), 18 ff.

9 H Cancik, 'Dignity of Man and Persona in Stoic Anthropology: Some Remarks on Cicero, *De Officiis* I 105–107' in D Kretzmer and E Klein (ed.), *The Concept of Human Dignity in Human Rights Discourse* (Brill 2002), 19.

10 O Sensen, 'Human Dignity in Historical Perspective: The Contemporary and Traditional Paradigms' [2011] 10 *EJPT* 71, 76.

11 Cancik, *supra* n 9, 22.

admonition for his life as a student in Athens and introduced him into the civic and political duties that his social standing (his *dignitatis*[12]) required of him.

In paragraph 1.30 (105–107) of the treatise,[13] Cicero sets forth Stoic principles and morals as follows: the human mind (*ratio*, reason) represents the central difference between human beings and is the ground of any moral decision (*honestum*) and behaviour (*decorum*).[14] This 'first *persona*' (mask, role) comes from nature, which acts as a positive normative force,[15] and is granted to all human beings, as a sign of excellence (*excellentia*, *praestantia*) above all living beings.[16] The dignity of man directly originates from his first persona. Individuality, instead, represents the second *persona*; the third comes from the historical context, which shapes the individual, while man's freedom is the fourth. Here, Cicero is anxious to mention what it takes to be worthy, or *dignus*, in a public role.[17]

These principles are calls to morality, as men have to keep their status, protect their personal dignity and control emotions and desire (*voluptas*).[18] Since human life is directed by logic, to live well is not to live as an animal looking for pleasures. Thus, Cicero calls for actions driven by moderation and respect (*verecundia*) and defines dignity as '*Dignitas est alicuius honesta er cultu er honore er verecundia digna auctoritas*' (dignity is someone's virtuous authority that makes him worthy to be honoured with regard and respect). This definition sees dignity as a concrete quality of a person: as an ornament (*decus*, *decorum*); as a quality of the body in terms of health, strength and swiftness;[19] as a charm (*venustas*) of both women and men.[20] It is a quality with a social and political dimension and a sign of status and respect, expressed as 'majesty' (*maiestas*) or 'greatness' (*amplitudo*),[21] which belongs to all Roman citizens, to the State and to the government, who all share a collective dignity.[22] Diminishing it (*maiestatem minuere*) would be a grave crime (*crimen laesae maiestatis*),[23] be

12 *Dignitatis* is used to delineate an elevated social standing throughout *De Officiis*, and *dignus* is used to identify those virtues, attitudes and bearing that make one worthy of that standing.

13 See Cic. *Off.* 1.30.105–107.

14 Cancik, *supra* n 9, 25.

15 See Cic. *Off.* 3.57; 3.5.23. Cicero even pictures a kind of *ius civile* for all men (quasi *ius civile*) (Cic. *Fin.* 3.19.64).

16 Cic. *Off.* 1.97.

17 *Ibid.*, 1.88.

18 *Ibid.*, 1.101.

19 Cic. *Inv.* 2.2; *De Or.* 3.155; *Livy* 45.40.4; Cic. *Fin.* 5.17.47: Tac. *Ann.* 11.16.8; 11.28.27; 12.51.22.

20 Cic. *Off.* 1.130; see Gellius 14.4.2; Cic. *Off.* 1.94; *Digesta* 26.22 (Ulpianus).

21 Cic. *Fin.* 5.17.47.

22 Cic. *Dom.* 1.4; *Epist. Fam.* 4.6.1; The Province of Sicilia (Cic. *Verr.* 2.2.45.111), the Senate (Cic. *Pis.* 64), the praetor (*Verr.* 2.3.38.87), the consul (Cic. *Agr.* 2.2.3; *Pis.* 24) and the augures (Cic. *Brutus* 1.1; *Livy* 10.7.12).

23 Cic. *De Or.* 2.64.

considered high treason and be punishable by exile or death.[24] What we have here is an identification of the duties, attitudes and bearing required of the man who is worthy of playing an elevated public role.

However, in particular, one passage might suggest a more universalist reading – a reading that might seem to bring Cicero closer to the understanding of dignity implicit in our modern conception of human rights.[25] He affirms that, because of the human *ratio*, individuals are similar to God (*cum deo similitudo*) and different from animals, 'who perceive nothing except pleasure and instincts'.[26] However, this view of man's superiority does not lead to any rights that the man has merely by virtue of his humanity. It simply says that our nature as rational and intelligent beings implies a duty to behave in line with and in accordance with our own nature. In the works of both Aristotle and Cicero, the concept of dignity was closely connected with the virtues, actions and duties of those who possess a high social standing.

2.2.2 *Renaissance Humanism*

The Aristotelian and Ciceronian ideas of decorum and worth of the human spirit strongly influenced the Renaissance perspective on human dignity. The Renaissance is firmly connected to the revival of classical culture, taking its guiding inspiration mainly from Cicero's *De Officiis*, informing a tradition known as 'Renaissance Humanism'.[27] Human dignity gained a richer content and the religious view of the sinner man in search of God's salvation was replaced by a humanistic view of the dynamic man, whose *ratio* forges his dignity.[28] The circumstances surrounding this shift are relevant.

Around 1195, Lotario dei Conti di Segni (Lothar of Segni), the future Pope Innocent III (1198–1216), wrote a treatise on the misery of the human condition titled *De Miseria Condicionis Humanae*, where in the prologue he writes about *dignitas humanae naturae* as an antithesis to *vilitas humane condicionis*.

24 G Rotondi, *Leges Publicae Populi Romani* (Società editrice libraria 1912), 339: *lex Varia de maiestate* (90 BCE, bellum soiale), 360: *Lex Cornelia de maiestate* (81 BCE); see Cic. *Epist. Fam.* 3.11.2; Tac. *Ann.* 1.72.

25 Sensen, *supra* n 10, 76; I Englard, 'Human Dignity: From Antiquity to Modern Israel's Constitutional Framework' [2000] 21 *CLR* 1905.

26 MT Cicero, *Cicero: On Duties* (Cambridge University Press 1991), 41, para 106.

27 P Steenbakkers, 'Human Dignity in Renaissance Humanism' in Düwell et al., *supra* n 3, 85–86.

28 Horst Dreier, GG *Grundgesetz Kommentar* (Band I 1996), 148; see also D Ullrich, 'Concurring Visions: Human Dignity in the Canadian Charter of Rights and Freedoms and the Basic Law of the Federal Republic of Germany' [2003] 3 *GJF* 1–103; C Ruiz Miguel, 'Human Dignity: History of an Idea' [2002] 50 *Jahrbuch des öffentlichen Rechts* 281, 288.

He was not able to complete a tract on human dignity before his death, as he had intended. In 1357, Giovanni Birel Limosino, Prior General of the Carthusians, asked Francesco Petrarca (Petrarch, 1304–74) to complete the project started by Lothar of Segni and produce a work on human dignity. The Petrarch declined, instead presenting his view on the issue in a dialogue titled 'Sadness and Misery' in *De Remediis utriusque fortunae* ('Remedies for Fortunes', 1354–1367). He writes, or rather reason personified writes, that writing about misery rather than happiness is easier for authors (Petrarch 1975). If moral philosophy tended to stress the negative face of Fortune (original sin and human wretchedness), Petrarch and other Renaissance authors rejected this view as not aligned with Genesis in which it is said that man was made in the image of God and is ruler of the Earth (1:26; 1:28). In his *De Viris Illustribus* ('On Illustrious Men', 1337), instead, Petrarch develops the concept of moral dignity and political dignity, as previously discussed by Cicero. He emphasizes that the human soul reflects God's image and man's power to forge his strength. This is the core of humanism, with man and his dignity placed at the centre. Each man derives his dignity from his rationality and from his power to build up his own world.

De excellentia ac praestantia hominis ('On the Excellence and Preeminence of Man', 1447) is a treatise commissioned by Alfonso of Aragon, King of Naples, to supply the volume that Lothar of Segni did not complete, and written by Bartolomeo Facio (or Faccio) in 1448. It describes man as made from God's image and having a divine nature stemming from the immortality of his mind and soul. Facio emphasizes that man can achieve happiness not from actions but only by contemplating God.

Alfonso of Aragon, most probably unsatisfied by Facio's work, asked Giannozzo Manetti (1369–1459), an erudite jurist from Florence, to provide him with another tract. In 1452, Manetti produced the work *De dignitate et excellentia hominis* ('On the Dignity and Excellence of Man', 1452),[29] composed of four volumes and devoted to the dignity and excellence of man. He demonstrates man's superiority by quoting Aristotle, the Bible, Cicero and Hermetism.[30]

If self-consciousness and nature are still the protagonists, the 'almighty Lord' is the master over all. The classical Stoic approach is Christianized, but with a similar outcome: the dignity of man lies in his body (*dignitas corporis*), the gifts of his mind[31] and in the honour (*honos*) of dominating the world.[32] It is

[29] G Manetti, *De dignitate et excellentia hominis* ('On the Dignity and Excellence of Man'), 1452 (ed. Antenore 2000); for a discussion, see Cancik, *supra* n 9, 28.

[30] See Manetti, *supra* n 29, 3.49.

[31] *Ibid.*, 4.71: *animi celsitudo ac sublimitas.*

[32] *Ibid.*, 1.50: *illi tantum honoris attribuit ut rerum omnium dominaretur.*

mainly in the tract's third volume that Manetti recognizes that active life and understanding, both a part of dignity and excellence, render man a superior creature and a mortal god. In the last part of the third volume, Manetti affirms that incarnation is the final demonstration of man's superiority.[33]

By the end of the fifteenth century, however, Marsilio Ficino (1433–99) enabled the development of an evolution in Renaissance philosophy, making available several Platonic documents, such as Plato's treatises, Plotinus and the *Corpus Hermeticum*, and producing several commentaries reviving Platonism, discussing man's power over nature and his great achievements in different areas, such as language, science and mathematics, as well as his freedom.[34] He focused on the relation between action and contemplation, stating that man becomes like God when his intellect connects with him (in *Theologia Platonica*).

Giovanni Pico della Mirandola (1463–94) was one of Ficino's pupils and highly influenced by Platonic philosophy. His most famous work is an introductory speech, an *Oration*, written in 1486, which he was not able to deliver as he was tried and exiled by the Inquisition. The *autographon* (manuscript) was published posthumously, with the title *Oration on the Dignity of Men*.[35] Pico discusses that God's creation granted man the freedom to act according to his own will. Thus, man's dignity derives from his own life course.[36] Dignity is an assignment; it cannot be claimed by all men but only by men with human traits.[37] Pico also adds that the men will 'make one spirit with God' if they will retreat into the centre of their own unity. Pico sees Ficino's view of man's unification with God through contemplation as part of 'a dynamic conception of human superiority',[38] where the creative power of man enriches the ascetic Stoic approach of human dignity. Pico thus extols humankind as being at the centre of the world and praises man's greatness and force.[39] The power to opt for different paths of development – 'thou art confined but no bounds' – as distinctive routes of dignity is where the originality of Pico's *Oration* lies. Only those who develop their intellect will be rewarded, while others will simply become lower human beings.

33 *Ibid.*, 97: para 59.

34 A Barak, *Human Dignity: The Constitutional Value and the Constitutional Right* (Cambridge University Press 2015), 24.

35 The first printing was reviewed by Pico's nephew, Gian Francesco Pico, and published in 1496, Bologna (Benedictus Hectoris, Hain 12–992). G Pico della Mirandola, *Oration on the Dignity of Men* (Regnery 1996).

36 Pico della Mirandola, *ibid.*, 6–8.

37 *Ibid.*, 6.

38 Steenbakkers, *supra* n 27, 91.

39 Pico, Heptaplus 1.IV: *De mundo humano, id est de homini natura*; IV 6.

Facio, Manetti and Pico undoubtedly carried out an innovative and sophisticated view of human dignity, connected to the human status and potential but, still, a result of God's creation. It is not clear, however, if the tradition from which the original idea of 'rights of men and citizens' developed is in any way connected to this work.[40]

Moreover, a clear expression of the developments of the Aristotelian and Ciceronian concepts of human dignity can be traced in other places. In the *Book of the Courtier* (1528), Baldassare Castiglione included stories on the typical exemplar of the courtly gentleman and lady.[41] In particular, Castiglione narrates how the courtier may protect his *dignità*, meant as worth and reputation in public events, dealing with inferiors or his prince or his superiors.[42] It is also worth remembering the metaphorical expressions of dignity used, mostly in debates around *paragoni*, or comparisons,[43] an important trope in the Renaissance discourse. This example also strengthens the pursued interpretation typical of this historical time. Through the *paragone*, or comparison, two aesthetic genres were combined and compared to assess which was of greater 'dignity'. For instance, in his *Trattato della Pittura* (1508),[44] Leonardo da Vinci recalls a classical *paragone* between painting and sculpture.[45] Leonardo writes that the dignity of the sculptor is connected with his capacity to create expression in art that is imperturbable and permanent. However, to prove the greater dignity of the painter, Leonardo mentions the physical strain and dishevelled appearance of the sculptor.[46] The painter, on the other hand, is graceful and aristocratic, dignified in bearing and station. The association of dignity with elevated status and the worth that comes from this status are here used to prove the higher value that painting should receive.

The sovereign conception of dignity also finds expression in the literature of the seventeenth century. In 1605, Francis Bacon published the *Advancement of Learning*, translated into Latin with the title *De Dignitate et Augmentis*

40 Cancik, *supra* n 9, 30, who observes that the authors Manetti and Ficino are not included in authors quoted in Pufendorf's *De Iure Naturae et Gentium*.

41 B Castiglione, *The Book of the Courtier*, C Singleton (trans.) (Norton 2002).

42 *Ibid.*, 74, II.10. For further examples, see also I.3, I.34 and II.11–13, 49. And for maintaining the dignity of the courtier in his relations with the prince, see IV.44–47. These considerations also arise in Books 2 and 3 of the Courtier, in which two characters have a classic querelle des femmes.

43 Sangiovanni, *supra* n 4, 21.

44 Around 1542, da Vinci's notes on the topic were first included in the *Codex Urbinas Latinus*.

45 L da Vinci, *Trattato Della Pittura* (Società tipografica de'classici italiani 1804), para 33. See also Castiglione, *supra* n 41, I.50–52 and I.45–47, and Leon Battista Alberti, *Della Pittura* (1435) and *De Statua* (1450).

46 Da Vinci, *ibid.*, para 32.

Scientiarum in 1623. Here *dignitas* is applied to an abstract entity – learning – and the natural translation of *dignitate* in the title would be 'worth' or 'value'. However, Bacon also writes, in the introduction of his piece 'Of Great Place': 'The rising into place is laborious, and by pains men come to greater pains; and it is sometimes base, and by indignities men come to dignities.' *Dignities* here are a matter of high social status – a synonym for 'place' – and the actions to reach that level are not 'dignified'. For Bacon, dignity has three different meanings: dignity as a value not limited to human beings, dignity as high status and dignity as behaviour with a specific respect-worthy nature – or indignity as behaviour lacking respect.[47] Also Pascal, in his *Pensées*, a collection of fragments on theology published posthumously in 1670, believes, like Pico, that man has a dignity superior to other creatures, but considers that all his '*dignity consists in thought*'.[48]

2.2.3 *Sovereign Dignity and 'State' Sovereignty*

By the end of the sixteenth and the beginning of the seventeenth centuries, scholastic discussions about *summa potestas*,[49] French treatises on sovereignty[50] and volumes on 'politics'[51] debated the concepts of State, statehood and the powers that States were entitled to have and exercise. The evolving nature of the concept of dignity and, as advanced in the introduction of this work, the development of a clash between human dignity and sovereign dignity show a specific unsettling irony: these two terms are ineluctably intertwined semantically, historically and discursively.

The term 'State' was increasingly employed to refer to a civil association, for example that of a *universitas* or community of people, under the authority of a monarch, and to describe the form of *union* underlying civil government. As Skinner notes, 'some writers preferred to speak of the *realm*, some even spoke

47 M Rosen, *Dignity: Its History and Meaning* (Harvard University Press 2012), 15.

48 B Pascal, *Pensées*, R Ariew (trans.) (Hackett 2004) n. 200H3 (emphasis added) [Pascal, *Pensées*] (emphasis added).

49 See AS Brett, *Liberty, Right and Nature: Individual Rights in Later Scholastic Thought* (Cambridge University Press 1997); H Höpfl, *Jesuit Political Thought: The Society of Jesus and the State, c.1540–1630* (Cambridge University Press 2004), 186–223.

50 Q Skinner, *The Foundations of Modern Political Thought* (Cambridge University Press 1978), Vol. II, 254–275.

51 See R de Mattei, *Il problema della 'ragion di stato' nell' età della controriforma* (Ricciardi 1979); G Borelli, *Ragion di stato e Leviatano* (Il Mulino 1993); as regards England, see G Baldwin, 'Reason of State and English Parliaments, 1610–42' [2004] 25 *HPT* 620–641; N Malcolm, *Reason of State, Propaganda, and the Thirty Years' War: An Unknown Translation by Thomas Hobbes* (Oxford University Press 2007), 30–73.

of the *nation*, while the terminology in most widespread use referred to the *body politic* generally with the implication that such bodies are incapable of action in the absence of a sovereign head to which they owe their direction and obedience'.[52]

A fairly simple process led to the term 'State' becoming the traditional expression in the lexicon, as it still is today. As Skinner clarifies, in the Renaissance, princes were advised to carefully read volumes on how rulers should act to maintain their state, that is, to uphold their higher *status* as princes. A well-known political thinker at the time, Machiavelli, in his opera *Il Principe*, gives a central role to the prince's ability to *mantenere lo stato*.[53] In 1640, this expression was translated as an emphasis on the capability of a prudent prince to act 'for the maintenance of his State' and 'take the surest courses he can to maintaine his life and State'.[54] Legal theorists, however, also argued that, to avoid a coup d'état and preserve their own status, rulers had to take due care of the welfare of the *corpus politicum*. At this time,[55] when writers started to describe the rulers' duty to maintain the States they governed, a transition occurred and the term 'State' was adopted to refer to the *body politic*. It was a slight 'linguistic slippage' that led to a central conceptual change.[56]

A few examples illustrate this development. First, Jean Bodin's *Six livres de la république* – translated by Richard Knollys as *The Six Bookes of a Commonweale* in 1606 – is paradigmatic.[57] In Book I, what is called in English 'the Citie or state' is defined.[58] Bodin states that 'it is neither the walls, neither the persons, that make the citie, but the union of the people under the same sovereignty of government'.[59]

52 Q Skinner, 'The Sovereign State: A Genealogy' in H Kalmo and Q Skinner (eds), *Sovereignty in Fragments* (Cambridge University Press 2010), 28.

53 JH Hexter, *The Vision of Politics on the Eve of the Reformation: More, Machiavelli, and Seyssel* (Basic Books 1973), 150–172.

54 N Machiavelli, *Nicholas Machiavel's Prince*, E Dacres (trans.) (1640) (David Nutt 1905), 139, 141, 169.

55 For a discussion on this transitional phase, see HC Mansfield, *Machiavelli's Virtue* (University of Chicago Press 1996), 281–294; A Harding, *Medieval Law and the Foundations of the State* (Oxford University Press 2002), 252–335; Skinner, *supra* n 50, Vol. II, 382–387.

56 Skinner, *supra* n 52, 28.

57 See JH Franklin, *Jean Bodin and the Rise of Absolutist Theory* (Cambridge University Press 1973); JH Franklin, 'Sovereignty and the Mixed Constitution: Bodin and His Critics' in JH Burns and M Goldie (eds), *The Cambridge History of Political Thought 1450–1700* (Cambridge University Press 1991), 298–328; Skinner, *supra* n 50, Vol. II, 284–301, 355–356.

58 J Bodin, *The Six Bookes of a Commonweale*, KD McRae (ed.) (Harvard University Press 1962), 1.2, 10.

59 *Ibid.*, 1.2, 10.

Interestingly, he also recognizes that people themselves can have sovereign powers, but he states his preference for a monarchy over all other forms of government. To institute a monarchy, he writes, is to constitute a form of public authority in which 'all the people in generall, and (as it were) in one bodie' swear 'faithfull alleageance to one soveraigne monarch' as head of State.[60] This strand of thinking about the State, known as 'absolutist theory',[61] was soon considered and transformed by two legal and political approaches in early seventeenth-century England which regarded the role of people in connection with States' powers in diametrically opposed ways. One arose out of debates about *suprema potestas* and was grounded on the premise that people are the original bearers of supreme power.[62] This strand, however, emphasized that, notwithstanding the original owner of the authority, the act of submitting to a ruler implies a 'quasi-alienation' of political rights.[63] Both Matthew Kellison's *Right and Jurisdiction of the Prelate*[64] and Machiavelli's *Il Principe* follow the same approach.

The opposite approach, the absolutist theory, was also included in another more influential strand, which constituted part of the doctrine of the divine right of kings. In *Patriarcha* (c. 1630),[65] Sir Robert Filmer condemns the belief in man's natural liberty,[66] stating that rulers receive their power directly from 'the ordination of God himself', not from the people. Thus, in his view, kings are the vicegerents of God on earth and thus are given the highest authority over the body of the State. References to this approach can be found in speeches of King James I about the extent of his sovereign rights[67] and in the works of Sir John Hayward, an English writer, lawyer and politician of this time.[68] Those who criticized the claim that temporal rulers have a right of

60 *Ibid.*, 1.8, 99.

61 G Poggi, *The Development of the Modern State: A Sociological Introduction* (Hutchinson 1978); A Vincent, *Theories of the State* (Oxford University Press 1987), 45–76; Skinner, *supra* n 52, 29.

62 Höpfl, *supra* n 49, 204–217, 224–230.

63 F Suárez, *De Civili Potestate* (III. 1–16) in *De Legibus*, L Pereña (ed.), (Corpus Hispanorum de Pace 1975) 3.4.2, 49: 'non est delegatio sed quasi alienatio'; Höpfl, *supra* n 49, 248–262.

64 J Sommerville, *Royalists and Patriots: Politics and Ideology in England 1603–1640* (2nd ed., Routledge 1999), 60–62.

65 J Sommerville (ed.), 'Introduction', in R Filmer, Sir, (ed.), *Patriarcha and Other Writings* (Cambridge University Press 1991), xxxii–iv, who demonstrates that the text of *Patriarcha* was concluded before 1631, though published in 1680.

66 *Ibid.*, 2.

67 King James VI and I, *Political Writings*, J Sommerville (ed.), (Cambridge University Press 1994), 143, 145, 147, 149; 247–253; Johann Sommerville, 'Absolutism and Royalism' in JH Burns and M Goldie (eds), *The Cambridge History of Political Thought 1450–1700* (Cambridge University Press 1991), 347–373; Sommerville, *supra* n 64, 107–110, 227–230.

68 Sommerville, *supra* n 64, 51–52, 68.

absolute control over ecclesiastical and civil affairs also pursued these arguments.[69] An anonymous tract from 1666, which is mainly a compilation of dynastic pretensions and religious differences, clarifies that alliances between princes, who differ in their dignity, are forged from and moved by asymmetrical power relationships.[70]

This language of dignity was also endorsed in papal bulls or sermons of the time. For instance, the Papal Bull of 1570 excommunicated Queen Elizabeth I from the Roman Catholic Church and stated 'we declare her to be deprived of her pretended title to the kingdom aforesaid, and of *all dominion, dignity and privilege whatsoever*'.[71]

In a 1659 sermon titled '*Sur l'éminente dignité des pauvres dans l'Église*' (On the eminent dignity of the poor in the Church), Bishop Bossuet, court preacher at the court of Louis XIV, assigned 'eminent dignity' to the poor, not to recognize them as having a status equal to (or even higher than) the nobility, but only to affirm a distinctive role within a hierarchy. Thus, dignity was expressed in different consistencies in each level of the social hierarchy.

This historical excursus demonstrates that the conception of sovereign dignity has been adopted in different contexts to reflect a hierarchical and aristocratic image of reality, as recognized even today.[72] The history of sovereign dignity clearly shows the roots of its three main features, described in Chapter 1 (Section 1.2.2). Sovereign dignity is to be conferred on *dignitaries* to different degrees by virtue of honour, title, powers and responsibilities.[73] Importantly, it is accorded to those appointed to a particular public office and applied to institutions and the State itself (the so-called 'institutional dignity').[74] As Cancik writes,

69 BP Levack, *The Civil Lawyers in England 1603–1641: A Political Study* (OUP 1973), 115–117, 187–188; Sommerville, *supra* n 64, 40–41; C Downing, *A Discourse of the State Ecclesiastic all of this Kingdome, in relation to the Civil* (2nd ed., William Turner, ed. Forrest 1634), the quoted version is taken from the extended text of the Downing's treatise, republished in 1634, 58, 68.

70 Anon., *Interets et maximes des Princes et des etats souverains* (Cologne, 1666), 5, which reads 'Si deux Princes Souverains, yssus d'un meme tige, & ayans leurs Etats voisins, sont inferieurs l'un a l'autre en dignitè & en puissance, on les verra de bonne intelligence entr'eux'; see also on this point, G Courtilz de Sandras, *Nouveaux interets des Princes de l'Europe* (Pierre Marteu 1686), 92; see on the topic, J Bartelson, *A Genealogy of Sovereignty* (Cambridge University Press 1995), 181.

71 *Regnans in Excelsis*. Pope Pius V. April 1570 (emphasis added).

72 H Spiegelberg, 'Human Dignity: A Challenge to Contemporary Philosophy' in *Steppingstones toward an Ethics for Fellow Existers* (Martinus Nijhoff 1986), 191.

73 See J Waldron, 'Dignity, Rank, and Rights. The 2009 Tanner Lectures at UC Berkeley' [2009] in NYU Public Law and Legal Research Paper Series, paper 151, 6; J Waldron, 'Dignity, Rights and Responsibilities [2010] in NYU Public Law and Legal Research Paper Series, paper 242, 10–83.

74 C McCrudden, 'Human Dignity and Judicial Interpretation of Human Rights' [2008] 19(4) *EJIL* 655, 656–657.

the term 'denotes worthiness, the outer aspect of a person's social role which evokes respect and embodies the charisma and the esteem presiding in office, rank or personality'.[75] Moreover, sovereign dignity is transient. As a quality, it is indeed subject to changes, increases and decreases – it can be earned or lost. Therefore, it does not have a universal or inalienable character. Lastly, due to its *relational* nature,[76] it is exclusionary, carrying a social distinction and establishing unequal treatment of those who have rank and honour and those who do not. Still today, these constitute the three main inherent and historical differences with the competing circle of human dignity, which will be examined in the following section.

2.3 HUMAN DIGNITY

Human dignity, differently from sovereign dignity, implies the very denial of a hierarchical order of dignities. It refers, specifically, to every human being *qua* human and does not imply any degrees. Thus, it cannot be acquired or lost.[77] This second concept was present in some classical Roman texts, particularly in those of Cicero, where *dignitas* referred also to the dignity of human beings as human, not dependent on any specific additional status.[78]

Drawing from its historical path, two main approaches have interpreted this conception: first, a religious perspective, looking at dignity as connected to the divine or supra-natural; second, a rigorous philosophical vision that has led to the secularization of the concept. The evolution in the understanding of the concept of human dignity is the result of these approaches in action. In particular, the modern meaning of human dignity arises, first, mostly during the advent of Christianity and, later, in the history of thought, with Kant (1724–1804). Both the religious and philosophical views of dignity (and herein, mostly the Kantian one) will be considered in turn in the subsequent sections.

2.3.1 *Religious Dignity*

The recent affirmation of human dignity in constitutional and international legal documents is a product of a relatively secular age. Yet, the development of the underlying concept of what a human being is closely parallels religious

75 Cancik, *supra* n 9, 19.
76 *Ibid.*, 193.
77 See Spiegelberg, *supra* n 72, 50 (emphasis added).
78 Cic. *De Off.*, I, p. 30 (105–106).

thought and, primarily, Christian thought.[79] As also noted in Chapter 1, a range of concepts close to the idea of human dignity are present in different religious traditions.

In this section, I focus on Judaism, Christianity and Islam, the central doctrines of which arose in the negotiations for and final adoption of international legal instruments, as will be described in more detail below in Chapter 3. These three monist religions all provided essential contributions to the development of the notion of human dignity as we know it in the international legal context today.[80] Importantly, human dignity presents three similar features in all three religions: (i) man's dignity derives from God and, thus, it is not inherent; (ii) man is in a hierarchical relationship with God and, because of the dignity that he receives from the divine, he enjoys a special status; (iii) all religious conceptions of dignity come with rights and duties. The following sections present these characteristics of dignity in each of these three religions.

2.3.1.1 Judaism

Jewish sacred texts embody not only Judaism's religious precepts but also the historical, cultural and social heritage of the Jewish people.[81] The term 'dignity' (*kavod* or *Kvod*) appears several times in the Hebrew Bible and in the Talmudic literature, where 'dignity' or 'the Dignity' (*ha-kavod*) is one of the official attributes of God.[82] The Hebrew Bible adopts the term to signify God's presence or substance, seeing God as the king of '*kavod*'. This creates a ladder of rights, where the Dignity of God (*Kvod ha-Makom*) has priority over the dignity of the community (*Kvod ha-Briot*) and is therefore superior to the individual's dignity (*Kvod-ha-Adam*). Two major issues arise from these considerations (and sources): first, the term *Kvod* stands for both dignity and the concept of *status*; second, some religious formulas may be in contrast or indifferent to the notion of human dignity, even though they may adopt its features.[83]

79 C Starck, 'The Religious and Philosophical Background of Human Dignity and its Place in Modern Constitutions' in Kretzmer and Klein, *supra* n 9, 182.

80 Barak, *supra* n 34, 19.

81 Y Lorberbaum, 'Human Dignity in the Jewish Tradition' in Düwell et al., *supra* n 3, 135–143.

82 King of Honor *Psalm* 24:17; Cloud of Honor *Exodus* 16:10; Tabernacle of Honor Jalkut Simoni 363. For Rabbinic use of Honour as a divine concept see: Tosefta Rosh Hashanah, 2:13 AdRN I II Ch 1., p. 1.

83 C Safrai, 'Human Dignity in Rabbinical Perspective' in Kretzmer and Klein, *supra* n 9, 100.

Several expressions are in fact linked to the term *Kvod*. In *primis*, '*Kvod-ha-Adam*', Hebrew for the expression 'human dignity', means that man's dignity derives from his being made in the image of God (*Tzelem Elohim* or *Imago Dei*).[84] However, no expression traced in rabbinical literature equates per se with the twentieth-century notion of dignity,[85] which only entered the Jewish Israeli culture in modern times under the influence of modern European thought.[86]

According to the Book of Genesis, human beings represent God in all his features, physical and mental.[87] More specifically, Jewish religious legal sources have examined the question of what constitutes 'His image' (*Tzelem Elohim*).[88] Maimonides, who rejects any concrete meaning of the Hebrew term *Tzelem Elohim*, identifies it with the 'intellectual apprehension'.[89] Interestingly, the biblical *Tzelem* theology transfers this nature into legal dimensions, when in Genesis 9:6 it is written 'Whoever sheds the blood of man, by man shall his blood be shed, for God made man in his own image'. This verse is at the core of the agreement between God and Noah after the flood, a covenant that 'structures the post-diluvian world',[90] and sets the basis for biblical criminal law. As Moshe Greenberg notes: 'That man was made in the image of God is expressive of the peculiar and supreme worth of a man. This view of the uniqueness and supremacy of human life has yet another consequence. It places life beyond the reach of other values.'[91] Therefore, the verse provides a concrete normative dimension to the value of life. Only the death penalty appears as commensurate punishment for those who take a life, as human life cannot be quantified.[92]

In addition, *Imago Dei* constitutes a denial of royal theology, since if all human beings are made in the image of God, no special relationship exists between the king (the authority) and God. Deuteronomy 17 places limitations upon a king's authority, setting up a mechanism of separation of powers.[93]

84 *Ibid.*, 101; D Shultziner, 'A Jewish Conception of Human Dignity: Philosophy and its Ethical Implications for Israeli Supreme Court Decisions' [2006] 34 *JReliEthi* 663.
85 *Ibid.*, 104.
86 Lorberbaum, *supra* n 81, 135.
87 See Genesis 1:26–27 and 5:1–3.
88 N Rakover, *Human Dignity in Jewish Law* (Library of Jewish Law 1998), 19.
89 M Maimonides, *The Guide of the Perplexed*, trans. Shlomo Pines, (University of Colorado Press 1963), 22; see also M Maimonides, *The Code of Maimonides, Book of Knowledge, The Laws of the Fundamental Principles of the Torah*, Chapter 4, Law 8.
90 Lorberbaum, *supra* n 81, 137.
91 See M Greenberg, *Some Postulates of Biblical Criminal Law* (Yehezkel Kaufmann Jubilee Volume 1960), 15–16.
92 Lorberbaum, *supra* n 81, 137.
93 *Ibid.*, 144–155.

The Jewish conception also adopts another expression of dignity, namely *Kvod ha-Briot* (or *Kevod ha-beryot*) – 'dignity of Creatures/People', and not the honour of human beings as such.[94] The expression sometimes signifies the intrinsic worth of every human being, but it is mostly referred to as an acquired political status (i.e. honour),[95] as in some halakhic rules (Bava Metzia 30a).[96] Some people objected to this concept, seeing it as a personal goal as 'jealousy, lust and honour (kavod) remove a person from the world'.[97] However, *Kvod*, as a special status, is sometimes opposed to *kavod* as honour due to God.[98] Man himself is a creature of God, and thus: 'All that God created in His world He created exclusively in His honour.'[99]

The common approach to the question of who are the creatures[100] is that it implies *all* the creatures – each and every person separately, whether or not they are Jewish.[101] Thus, *Kvod ha-Briot* is the dignity of the created. Humankind was created in God's image to rule over the other creations[102] and no man can renounce his dignity.[103]

Other terms are linked to the word *kavod*. *Kvod ha-Tsibur*, 'public dignity', is connected to a series of instructions to protect rights, dignity, interests and time of the community;[104] *Kvod ha-Nashim*, the 'dignity of women', appears only twice in rabbinical writings and both times in the context of burial rites. If women's dignity forbids showing their bodies in public,[105] they also must have burial rites that correspond.[106] *Kvod ha-Kala* refers to the 'dignity of the bride', who, on the day of her marriage, is the queen of the community and needs support to enter her new life.[107] *Kvod Aniym*, the 'dignity of the poor', is used in one text on funeral rites. The tradition of reducing funeral expenses, so that both rich and poor have equal funeral costs, it is attributed to Rabban Gamliel.[108] As Safrai points out, however, the concept of *kavod* in this context

94 Englard, *supra* n 25, 1906.
95 Lorberbaum, *supra* n 81, 135.
96 Safrai, *supra* n 83, 101.
97 Rebbi Eli'ezer ha-Kappar, Avot, 4:21.
98 See b. Kid 32b).
99 Mishnah, Pirke Avot 6:11.
100 D Kretzmer, 'Human Dignity in Israeli Jurisprudence' in Kretzmer and Klein, *supra* n 9, 161.
101 Rakover, *supra* n 88, 29.
102 Psalms 8:5; Mishna Avot 3:14. See Rakover, *supra* n 88, 18-22.
103 Rakover, *supra* n 88, 18.
104 See, for examples, *Babylonian Talmud* Yoma 70a; *Babylonian Talmud* Gittin 60a; *Babylonian Talmud* Megila 3b; *Babylonian Talmud* Megila 23a.
105 M. Moed Katan 3:8.
106 T. Nidda 9:16.
107 Safrai, *supra* n 83, 102.
108 T Nidda 9:16–17.

is closer to a social respect paid by members of the community to raise their own status instead of a human dignity concept per se.[109]

Kvod ha-Am, the 'dignity of the people', is similar to the notion of public dignity and is only used in the Tractate *Semachot*, in the context of mourning rites.[110] *Kvod ha-Shabbat* and *Kvod YomTov* – the 'dignity of the Sabbath and holy days' – are concepts mainly related to religious practice. For example, if mourning demands no washing of clothes, in honour of the Sabbath this is allowed on Thursday.[111] Human dignity is also of a particular relevance in the regulation of shame (*boshet*) in rabbinical literature.[112]

Thus, dignity appears to be applied to a variety of subjects, and includes social factors in society related to the poor, women, the community and the dead. However, Safrai notes that the notion of community is more connected to a concept of human sensitivity of the believers, rather than that of human dignity, and not all of the above expressions are important in the quest for human dignity.[113]

In conclusion, Judaism introduces the idea that man was created in the image of God (Genesis 1:27). Human dignity, the crowning value in human relations, has, however, been approached differently by two leading Mishnaic scholars. 'And you shall love your neighbour as yourself' (Leviticus 19:18), according to R. Akiva, is a major rule of the Torah. However, for Ben Azai, '[t]his is the book of the generations of Adam' (on the day God created man He did so in the image of God – Genesis 5:1), constitutes instead the more important rule (Sifra, Kedoshim, 4:10). Thus, if the first view is that the supreme value in human relations is love of one's fellow man, the second places equality of man at the core, since every man was created in the image of God.[114]

2.3.1.2 Christianity

Similarly, in Christianity, human dignity is theologically rooted in the biblical teaching present in Genesis (1:26). Christians believe that humankind is

109 Safrai, *supra* n 83, 102.

110 Semachot 4:9.

111 *Babylonian Talmud* Ta'nit 26b; for other examples, see M. Sukka 4:8; *Babylonian Talmud* Moed Katan 13b.

112 M. Baba Kama 8:1; T. Baba Kama 9:12; M. Ketubot 6:1; M. Arakhin 3:4 and parallels; Safrai, *supra* n 83, 105–107.

113 Safrai, *supra* n 83, 109.

114 As recalled also by Justice M. Elon in the case EA 2/84 *Moshe Neiman et al.* v. *Chairman of the Central Elections Committee for the Eleventh Knesset*, 8 IsrLR 83, 148 (1985); CrimA 3632/92 *Gabay* v. *State of Israel*; VCrimH 2145/92 *State of Israel* v. *Gueta*, IsrSC 46(5) 704, 716 (1992) (Heb.); CA 506/88 Yael Shefer (a Minor) by Her Mother and Natural Guardian, *Talila Shefer* v. *State of Israel*, 11 IsrLR 170, 204 (1993); see also Barak, *supra* n 34, 17–21.

created in the image of God (*Imago Dei*), as in Judaism, but revealed in Jesus of Nazareth and through him to humankind. Thus, the biblical notion of man's quality is enriched by the idea of Christ's ability, through incarnation and sacrifice, to restore to humankind the dignity lost through original sin.[115] Thus, since humankind is redeemed and recreated in Christ, people are called to esteem human dignity even more.[116] The Christian Church derives from here its mission to protect and defend human dignity and rights.[117]

I will now briefly present the evolution of the Christian conception of man's hierarchical relationship with God and the associated rights and duties at four different times: in the Middle Ages, which provided foundational understandings of the concept; in the nineteenth century, when dignity was mainly used in support of unequal treatment and against natural rights; in the twentieth century, when the Christian Church sees the advantages of bringing together human dignity and modern natural rights against totalitarianism and liberalism; and, lastly, in more recent decades.

Medieval attempts to define human dignity generally developed in combination with the analysis of biblical statements on the nature of the human being as the image (*imago*) and likeness (*similitudo*) of God (Genesis 1:26; Wisdom 2:23). Such analysis led to four different strands of interpretation.

First, some authors grounded such *similitudo* on the human *ratio*.[118] Trinitarian speculations also fuelled further reflections on the concept of 'person' and the nature of the human being. While Richard of Saint Victor talks about the 'incommunicable existence' of the intellectual nature of the person, emphasizing the *existens per se* (existing for oneself),[119] for Alexander of Hales (1185–1245) a person is a 'hypostasis distinguished

115 Englard, *supra* n 25, 1906.

116 D Hollenbach, 'Human Dignity in Catholic Thought' in Düwell et al., *supra* n 3, 252; John XXIII, 'Pacem in Terris' in DJ O'Brien and TA Shannon (eds), *Catholic Social Thought: The Documentary Heritage* (Orbis Books 1992), 131–162; Vatican Council II 1965, *Gaudium et Spes* (Pastoral Constitution on the Church in the Modern World), in W Abbott and J Gallagher (eds), *Documents of Vatican II* (America Press 1966), 199–308. No. 22; C Trinkaus, *In Our Image and Likeness: Humanity and Divinity in Italian Humanist Thought* (Notre Dam University Press 1995), 181–190; on the notions of likeness and image, which connote an 'in-between position of man', see N Rotenstreich, *Man and his Dignity* (Magnes Press, Hebrew University 1983), 23–31.

117 Hollenbach, *supra* n 116, 252.

118 Hugo of Saint Victor, *De Sacramentis*, I 6, 2; Monologion, 66, in Anselm of Canterbury, *The Major Works* (eds.) B Davies and GR Evans (Oxford University Press 1998); Soliloquia II, 1,1, in Augustinus, *Soliloquies – Augustine's Interior Dialogue* (trans. K Pfaffenroth and JE Rotelle, Hyde Park, NY: New City Press 2000).

119 Richard of Saint Victor, *De Trinitate* (J. Ribaillier 1958).

by a property pertinent to dignity' and is a moral being as that signifies 'the quality of dignity'.[120] Bonaventura says that personhood means possessing a *supereminens dignitas*, as does Albertus Magnus when he writes that persons are 'characterised by natural and moral dignity'.[121] Thomas Aquinas (c. 1224–74), described the individual as the most dignified (*dignissimus*) being, and able to govern himself (*dominium sui*) as he can imitate God through his ratio, self-knowledge and self-love.[122] Therefore, human dignity corresponds to the dignity of personhood.[123] Moreover, he argued that man's dignity cannot be separated from his relationship with God as part of the Trinity. This means that man's rationality enables him to distinguish himself from other creatures, but also forces him to imitate God through knowledge and love.[124]

Moreover, Bernard of Clairvaux (1090–1153) considered the quality of *freedom* as the central quality of every man.[125] In addition, Hildegard of Bingen, in line with the anthropocentrism of many medieval thinkers[126] and with sovereign readings of dignity, argued that man is endowed with dignity 'because he is more powerful than any other creature'.[127] Lastly, the rediscovery of Aristotle's writings prompted modernized considerations on the nature of human beings, introducing a view of the person as an *animal politicum*. Far from being a theological thesis, dignity here appears grounded in man's *social nature* – thus not in the supernatural – and *civitas* is regarded as an essential component of *humanitas*. For example, the Florentine Dominican Remigio dei Girolami considers that 'whoever is not a citizen, is not a human being' ('*si non est civis, non est homo*').[128] Thomas Aquinas, however, emphasizes sociability as anchored in human nature and the impetus towards knowledge and community life as

120 Alexander of Hales, *Glossa in quatuor sententiarum Petri Lombardi* (1223–1227), 3, 5, 20.

121 Albertus Magnus, *De Incarnatione*, 3, Art. 4, 'Opera Omnia' (Borgnet 1893), vol. 26 (Super I Sententiarum), 200.

122 Thomas Aquinas, *Summa Theologiae*, I, q. 93, Art. 4 (Editio Paulina, San Tommaso 1988).

123 Thomas Aquinas, *De Potentia*, q. 9, Art. 3; *Summa Theologiae*, I, q. 29, Art. 3.

124 DJ Merriell, *To the Image of The Trinity: A Study in the Development of Aquinas' Teaching* (Pontifical Institute of Mediaeval Studies 1990).

125 B of Clairvaux, *De Diligendo Deo*, II, 2, in 'Opera Omnia', in J Leclercq and H Rochais (eds), vol. 3 (Editiones Cistercienses, 1963), 165–203.

126 R Imbach, 'Human Dignity in the Middle Ages (Twelfth to Fourteenth Century)' in Düwell et al., *supra* n 3, 65.

127 H of Bingen, *Liber Divinorum operum*, I, 197 A Derolz and P Dronke (eds), (Turnhout: Brepols, Visio, 1, 1996).

128 R Dei Girolami, *De bono communi*, in *Memorie Domenicane* 16 (ed. E Pannella 1985), 123–168.

specifically human inclinations (*inclinationes*).[129] Aristotle's ideas also supported conceptions of natural *inequality*.[130]

However, only starting in the nineteenth century, can we trace some of the first modern Catholic understandings of human dignity and, more specifically, in the encyclicals of Pope Leo XIII (1810–1903). Dignity became central to nineteenth-century Catholic thought, and it was mostly developed against the alleged threat posed by socialism.[131] In particular, the Aquinian view of dignity and the creation of man in the image of God were key elements in this understanding and approach to dignity. Pope Leo XIII is best known for his encyclical *Rerum Novarum of* 1891,[132] which is considered one of the founding documents of modern social Catholicism. It discusses the relationship between labour and capital, placing the idea of the 'dignity of labour' within the Catholic conception of dignity, already developed by liberals and socialists. He regards all men as equal; in his view, there is here no difference between rich and poor, master and servant, ruler and ruled, 'for the same is Lord over all'. This is not by chance.[133] The Church in the nineteenth century was hardly a friend to either socialism or liberalism, often inveighing against the individualism of the rights of man proclaimed in the French Declaration and in the revolutions of 1848.[134] Pope Leo XIII had previously set out his perception of dignity's place in 1878 in his encyclical *Quod Apostolici Muneris*. His approach here showed that, if all members of society have dignity, their dignity lies in the fact that they fulfil the proper role for the hierarchical order to which they belong, since some are 'nobler than others'.[135] Far from egalitarianism, the social orders differ in 'dignity, rights and power'. Thus, the 'dignity of labour', as introduced by Leo, should not be seen as an assertion of equality but more as a need that labour should be given its place within a social order, where individuals are 'necessary to each other, and solicitous of the common good'.[136]

129 Thomas Aquinas, *Summa Theologiae*, I–II, q. 94, Art. 2; *Summa Theologiae*, II–II, q. 114, Art. 2.

130 Thomas Aquinas, *Summa Theologiae*, II–II, q. 57, Art. 3 ad 2; *Summa Theologiae*, q. 64, Art. 2.; *Summa contra gentiles*, III, c. 81.

131 McCrudden, *supra* n 74, 662.

132 Pope Leo XIII, *Rerum Novarum* (1891). See also CE Curran, *Catholic Social Teaching, 1891–Present* (Genova University Press 2002).

133 See P Misner, 'The Predecessors of 'Rerum Novarum' Within Catholicism' [1991] 49 *Review of Social Economy* 4, Centennial of 'Rerum Novarum' and Semicentennial of the Association, 444–464.

134 See, JD Cortés, *Essays on Catholicism, Liberalism, and Socialism, Considered in Their Fundamental Principles*, ed. W McDonald (Gill & Son 1879); See also JT McGreevy, 'Catholics, History, and Conscience' [2009] 54 *VLR* 609–612.

135 Pope Leo XIII, *Quod Apostolici Muneris* (1878), para 6.

136 *Ibid.* See also *Arcanum divinae sapientiae* (1880); *Diuturnum Illud*, Encyclical Letter of Pope Leo XIII, June 29, 1981, para 5, 12.

Once the anti-egalitarian character of Catholic thought about dignity is understood, the change that occurred around the middle of the twentieth century could be even more unappreciated.

The nineteenth-Century church had, as Sangiovanni notes, 'an ambivalent relationship with democracy (e.g., the widening of the franchise), religious freedom (e.g., the separation of church and state), and the natural liberal rights that had come to the fore in the wake of the American and French revolutions'.[137] Leo emphasized that all rights ultimately rest in Christ and in the Church, and not in the individual as such.[138]

When the situation of Catholics in Germany deteriorated after Hitler violated the 1933 *Reichskonkordat*, the Church began to consider modern natural rights as central to the fight against totalitarianism and liberalism. Thus, in the 1930s the Catholic Church started to recompose together human dignity and modern natural rights.[139] They could be used to protect the inviolability of the human person – as embedded in the community, society and Church, rather than standing isolated. In 1937, Pius XI declared, in his anti-Nazi encyclical of March 1937, *Mit brennender Sorge*,

> Man, as a person, possesses rights that he holds from God and which must remain, with regard to the collectivity, beyond the reach of anything that would tend to deny them, to abolish them, or to neglect them.[140]

This phrasing matched the anti-communist encyclical of the same month, *Divini redemptoris*.[141] Pius XI, barely two months before his death, also affirmed that 'Christian teaching alone gives full meaning to the demands of human rights and liberty because it alone gives worth and dignity to human personality'.[142] In 1937, year of the *Mit brennender Sorge*, Eugenio Pacelli, who was soon to become Pope Pius XII, wrote

137 See Sangiovanni, *supra* n 4, 29; See, e.g., JW O'Malley, *What Happened at Vatican II* (Harvard University Press 2010), Chapter 2.

138 See his *Diuturnum* (1881) on the foundations of civil power in the power of the Church.

139 S Moyn, 'Jacques Maritain, Christian New Order, and the Birth of Human Rights' in L Bonanate, R Papini and W Sweet (eds), *Intercultural Dialogue and Human Rights* (Council for Research in Values and Philosophy 2013), 55–77.

140 Pius XI, Encyclical Letter 'Mit Brennender Sorge,' 14 March 1937, G Passelecq and B Suchecky, *The Hidden Encyclical of Pius XI*, trans. S Rendall (Brace 1997), 105.

141 See X de Montclos, 'Le discours de Pie XI sur la défense des droits de la personne humaine' in *Achille Ratti pape Pie XI. Actes du colloque de Rome (15-18 mars 1989) organisé par l'École française de Rome en collaboration avec l'Université de Lille III* (École française de Rome 1996).

142 'Pope Bids Church to Guard Man's Rights' (13 October 1938), New York Times, 1. S Moyn, 'Personalism, Community and the Origins of Human Rights' in SL Hoffmann (ed.), *Human Rights in the Twentieth Century* (Cambridge University Press 2011), 93.

> A vast conspiracy threatens the inviolability of the human person that, in his sovereign wisdom and dignity, the Creator has honored with an incomparable dignity. … [I]f a society believed it could diminish the dignity of the human person in refusing all or some of the rights that come to it from God, it would miss its goal.[143]

For the fiftieth anniversary of *Rerum Novarum*, Pope Pius XII, in a radio message on 1 June 1941, stated: 'To protect the inviolable field of the rights of the human person and facilitate the fulfilment of his duties, should be the essential task of every public authority.'[144] Natural rights had become human rights grounded in the inviolable dignity of the individual as created in the image and likeness of God. From then on, and especially after Vatican II (in which the Church's ambiguity with respect to religious freedom was clarified in a liberal direction), the alliance between dignity, human life and human rights became the guide of modern Catholic ethics.

The Catholic Church has fought against secular views of human dignity in egalitarian terms. This has been visible with Pius XI[145] and with Pope John XXIII's encyclical *Pacem in Terris*[146] and in the central document *Gaudium et Spes* of the Second Vatican Council,[147] which crystallized the contemporary Catholic vision of the relationship between human dignity and human rights.

Also, Pope Paul VI and Pope John Paul II referred to dignity several times in their writings,[148] and the ground for the statement in *Gaudium et Spes* was, in the words of John Paul II's encyclical *Evangelium Vitae* (1995), the 'life which God gives man'. Such life differs from the life of all other living creatures, since every man, even if born out of the dust of the earth,[149] is an expression of God in the world, a sign of his presence, a trace of his glory.[150]

In short, the Church's reverence for human dignity – and therefore for human life, community and faith (and, more recently, for those human rights that protect each of these) – is based on the fact, if it is a fact, that man's rational and volitional capacities are manifestations of the special bond that

143 Lettre de S, 'Em. Le Cardinal Pacelli, 1937' in *La personne humaine en péril: sommaire des leçons de la XXIXe session des Semaines sociales de France, tenue à Clermont-Ferrand du 19 au 25 juillet* 1937 (Lyon, Chronique Social de France 1937), 5–8.

144 *The Individual Right Cannot in Any Way Be Suppressed*, Pope Pius XII, Broadcast from Rome, 1 June 1941.

145 Pope Pius XI, *Quadragesimo Anno* (1931).

146 Pope John XXIII, *Pacem in Terris* (1963).

147 *Gaudium et Spes*, Vatican Council II (1965); for an analysis, see Hollenbach, *supra* n 116, 252–257.

148 Pope Paul VI, *Populorum Progressio* (1967); Pope John Paul II, *Centesimus Annus* (1991).

149 See Gen 2:7, 3:19; Job 34:15; Ps 103:14; 104:29.

150 See Gen 1:26–27; Ps 8:6. See also Pope John Paul II, *Mulieris Dignitatem* (1988).

relates him to God, with whom he has in common an image and likeness shared by no other creature. Even today, the dignity of the human person is a central value among contemporary Christians, especially within the Catholic communion.

2.3.1.3 Islamic Dignity

The word 'Islam' (اسلام) derives from the root *sīn-lām-mīm*, which in Arabic means 'submission' (to the will of God), and from the Arabic word for peace, '*salam*' (سلام). 'Obey God and His Prophet' (Quran, 59th verse of chapter 4, *sūrat l-nisāa*), commands the Quran. In the Quran 'lies the supreme innovation introduced by Islam into the social structure of Arabia: the establishment of a novel political authority possessing legislative power'.[151] *Salam* can then be reached by submitting to God's will and living according to the precepts of the divine Islamic law – referred to as Sharia law.[152] To examine how the concept of dignity developed in Islam, this section examines the expressions of man's dignity, in his hierarchical relationship with God, also in light of the *scholastic jurisprudence* developed on the concept, and the associated rights and duties.

The Arabic expression for human dignity is *karamat-al-insan* and in the Quran many forms of the root *krm* ('to bestow honour upon' or 'to venerate', equivalent to *faddala*, meaning to 'give preference') are present in different contexts.[153]

In Sura 17, the word dignity appears in its basic meaning, where it is narrated that only Satan opposed the Allah's request to prostrate to Adam, sayings, 'Tell me, Lord, can I submit to this one whom Thou has honoured above me [*karramta aleyya*].' Here the word simply means 'to venerate' (Quran 17.62). However, the most explicit and clear affirmation of human dignity (*karamah*) is found in another part of the same Sura: 'We have honoured dignity on the children of Adam … and conferred upon them special favours above the greater part of Our creation' (Quran 17:70). Here, 'to honour' means that Allah provides everything necessary for a peaceful life ('*na'ma*' or 'life with ease', see Sura 89) and God is the only source of *karam*. Thus, dignity is not inherent in every human being but is a gift from the Prophet. Those privileged to receive *karam* from God are 'the most righteous

151 NJ Coulson, *The History of Islamic Law* (Edinburgh University Press 1964), 9.

152 *Sharia* is an Arabic word that literally means the 'way to be followed' and technically it stands for the regulation of people's lives in the best way for them, see MC Bassiouni and GM Badr, 'The Shari'a: Sources, Interpretation, and Rule Making' [2002] 1 *UCLA JINEL* 135.

153 M Maróth, 'Human Dignity in the Islamic World,' in Düwell et al., *supra* n 3, 155.

among you' (Quran 14,49). The 'most righteous' (*atqa*) can also be translated as the 'most pious' or 'God-fearing', as dignity is assigned on the basis of different levels of devotedness (expressed in the phrase al *takrim al-ilahi li-'l-insan*).[154]

A further concern is the meaning of *karam*, which the previous quotations indicate refer to a higher status, a special treatment and a life in security, in comfort and well-being. Human dignity is the outcome of Allah's dignifying action (*takrim*), which implies that each man acts as his deputy (*khalifat*) on Earth, fulfilling Islamic law obligations to in return receive rights (*huquq*) and a secure life. The main purpose of Sharia thus becomes to ensure and defend human dignity.[155]

Granting special spiritual and physical favours to humankind becomes evident when the text discusses manifestations of human dignity. First, when the Quran discusses the spiritual ranking of human beings as being above those of the angels, it would seem to suggest that knowledge and faith are relevant to the dignified spirit of man, who has been created 'in the best of forms' by God.[156] It is reported in a *hadith* that the Prophet stood one day before the Ka'bah, at the centre of Islam's most sacred mosque, Al-Masjid al-Haram in Mecca, and said: 'You are most pure and most dignified, but the One in whose hands Muhammad's life reposes, the sanctity and honour of a believer, his life and his property, is far greater in the eyes of God.'[157]

Second, the Quranic view of dignity of humankind is also related to the Muslim community (*ummah*), the honour of which is ranked by God (*al-'izzah*) as next to His own Self and His Messenger, Muhammad (Quran 63.8). The Muslim community is also designated as 'a community of moderation' (*ummatan wasatan*: Quran 2.143), devoted to the promotion of good and rejection of evil (Quran 3.110),[158] and committed to the vindication of truth and justice (Quran 3.103).[159] The Prophet is also quoted as having said: 'the best part of faith is to have beautiful manners'[160] and that 'I have been sent in order to perfect moral virtues (among you)'.[161]

154 *Ibid.*

155 Maróth, *supra* n 153, 159.

156 Quran 95.12; see also 2.30–32; 7.11; 38.75–76; 95.12; 64.3.

157 AA al-Khatib al-Tabrizi, *Mishkat al-Masabih*, ed. MN al-Din al-Albani (2nd ed., al-Maktab al-Islami, 1399/1979, vol. 2), hadith no. 2724.

158 See also Quran 9.71.

159 See also Muslim b. Hajjaj al-Nishapuri, *Mukhtasar Sahih Muslim*, ed. M Nasir al-Din al-Albani (2nd ed., Dar al-Maktab al-Islami, 1404/1984) 11, hadith 34. See also MH Kamali, *Freedom of Expression in Islam* (Islamic Texts Society 1997) 28–34.

160 Tabrizi, *Mishkat*, vol.1, hadith no. 46.

161 *Ibid.*, vol. 3, hadith no. 5097.

In essence, it appears that fundamental liberties in Islam rest in Allah and in the *ummah*, not in the human being, and individual entitlements can always be overridden for the sake of communal interests.[162] Importantly, the scholastic jurisprudence has related three distinct concepts to the broader conception of human dignity: first, *'ismah* (inviolability), second *adamiyyah* (humanity and personhood), and third, represented by the five (and later six) universal *maqasid* (goals and purposes) of Sharia, collectively known as *al-daruriyyat*. These are life, intellect, religion, family, property and honour, which represent the overriding purposes, priorities and values of Islam.[163] Universalist and communalist approaches interpret these concepts differently.

The Hanafi school of jurisprudence, which is followed by the majority of Muslims, is the promoter of the universalist perspective. The followers recognize *'ismah* for all human beings regardless of religion, gender, race and the like. Each individual has a dignity, and life, property and other connected rights are inviolable. Equal protection is, therefore, granted to everyone. The other leading schools, namely the Shafi'i, Maliki, Hanbali and the Shi'ah, tend to take a communalist position, which maintains that only by virtue of a specific commitment (*dhimmah*) to Islam can non-Muslims qualify for *'ismah*.[164] These schools argue that the injunction on fighting those who do not believe in the Quran and *hadith* is couched in a language that supersedes the grant of *'ismah* to non-Muslims.[165] Imam Abu Hanifah (d. 767), the leading advocate of the universalist position, identified a nexus between *adamiyyah* and *'ismah*, affirming that inviolability is inherent in being human.[166] The universalist position gained followers from other schools,[167] but the Hanafi school remained influential only until the early 20th century,

162 AB Sajoo, 'Islam and Human Rights: Congruence or Dichotomy?' [1990] 4 *TICLJ* 23–34.

163 On *daruriyyat*, see Mohammad Hashim Kamali, *Maqasid al-Shari'ah, the Objectives of Islamic Law*, vol. 38 (Islamic Studies 1999), 193–209; on *'ismah* see B Johansen, *Contingency in a Sacred Law: Legal and Ethical Norms in the Muslim Fiqh* (Brill 1999); R Senturk, 'Adamiyyah and 'Ismah: The Contested Relationship between Humanity and Human Rights in the Classical Islamic Law' [2002] 8 *TKIS* 39–70.

164 Imam al-Shafi'i (d. 820 CE), imam Ahmad Ibn Hanbal, (d.855), Malik (d.795) Daud al-Zahiri (d. 885) and in the Shi'ite scholars such as al-Tusi and (d.1274) and his contemporary 'Allamah al-Hilli.

165 Quran, 9:5 (a similar reference to the pagans of Makkah), and al-Anfal:8:39 (which allows fighting to put an end to oppression).

166 See *Abu al-Hassan Burhan al-Din al-Marghinani* (d. 593 H/1296C.E),*al-Hidayah Sharh Bidayat al-Mubtadi*, (ed. Muhammad Tamir, et al. Cairo: Dar al-Salam, 1420/2000, II) 852; R Senturk, 'Sociology of Rights: I Am Therefore I Have Rights: Human Rights in Islam Between Universalistic and Communalistic Perspectives' [2005] 2(1) *MWJHR*, Article 11.

167 See Senturk, *supra* n 166, 16.

when it suffered a steady decline and it appears conspicuously missing in the modern debate on human rights in the Islamic world.[168]

2.3.2 *Kantian and Post-Kantian Dignity*

As seen earlier, during the Renaissance, the Christian view of human dignity underwent a relevant transformation and a vision of the less transcendent man began to take shape, focused on his worldly activities, rather than on his relationship with God. A clear break with medieval and Christian thought did not occur.[169] In fact, the arguments of Renaissance authors are profoundly influenced by the Christian doctrine.[170] Yet, with the Renaissance 'the insistence on man and his dignity becomes more lasting, exclusive and ultimately more systematic than was the case during the previous centuries and also in classical antiquity'.[171] This new conception of man is mainly due to humanism, the initial and perhaps most important underlying current of thought in the Renaissance. Humanism celebrated the freedom, dynamism and versatility of man, his ability to change the world and to equal God in creative activity.[172] In addition to the new deification of man, there is the discovery of the individual and his talent.[173]

Overall, if we can talk about a more secular image of man,[174] although in humanist thought, the influence of the doctrine of the *Imago Dei* remains strong, as shown by the continuous references to the writings of the Fathers of the Church. Now God is in the background and interest is focused on the human being, who is considered a mortal god.[175] The work of Manetti, for instance, creates an original synthesis between the Christian image of men and the Renaissance image.[176] Indeed, in many of his works his perspective is

168 MH Kamali, *Human Dignity in Islam* (International Institute of Advanced Islamic Studies Malaysia 2007), 10.

169 See E Garin, 'Umanesimo e pensiero medioevale' in E Garin and M Ciliberto (eds), *Interpretazioni del Rinascimento* (Edizioni di Storia e Letteratura 2009), Pt. 1, 83–102; HC Baker, *The Image of Man. A Study of the Idea of Human Dignity in Classical Antiquity, the Middle Ages, and the Renaissance (1947)* (Harper 1961), 203.

170 Starck, *supra* n 79, 182.

171 See PO Kristeller, 'Human Dignity', transl. S Salvestroni, *Concetti rinascimentali dell'uomo e altri saggi* (Nuova Italia 1978), 9.

172 A Heller, *Renaissance Man* (Routledge & Kegan Paul 1967), 12 [Heller, *Renaissance Man*].

173 See J Burckhardt, *The Civilization of the Renaissance in Italy (1860)* (Penguin Books 1990); E Cassirer, *Dall'Umanesimo all'Illuminismo* (La Nuova Italia 1995).

174 See Kristeller, *supra* n 171, 4.

175 See G Gentile, *Il pensiero italiano del Rinascimento* (1940) (3rd ed., Le Lettere 2003), 112.

176 See Trinkaus, *supra* n 116.

anticipatory of the reflections of Pico della Mirandola.[177] The work of the humanist Ficino firmly fits in the process of secularization that characterizes the Renaissance and can be defined a sort of philosophical reinterpretation of Christianity.[178] Thus, as Arieli clearly affirms, the

> expression 'the inherent dignity of man' . . . defines the ontological status of man which derives ultimately from the fundamental conceptions of the West created by the fusion of Jewish-Christian monotheism with those derived from classical and humanistic conceptions of man.[179]

The humanists built a vision of dignity, combining the classical Roman thinking and a more dogmatic theology in two ways. First, by arguing that humankind was given dignity because man is made in the *image of God*, and different from other species,[180] which can be viewed as a manifestation of sovereign religious dignity. Second, after Thomas Aquinas,[181] and along the lines of the vision developed by Saint Augustine of Hippo, humanists such as Pico della Mirandola consider that the *similitudo* at the basis of the *Imago Dei* derives from human *reason*.[182] In Pico's thoughts, human dignity is no longer a gift, as it was for the previous conception, but one conquest, the final goal of a journey in which each individual builds himself differently from all the others but with the same objective.[183] It can be, therefore, said that humanism prompted a process of profound modification of the conception of man, which only developed fully in the following centuries.

The literary genre devoted to the topic of dignity ended with the Enlightenment (mid-seventeenth to eighteenth centuries) when the tension between the religious nature of man and the humanity within man was replaced by an emphasis on man's role within society,[184] in his individuality.[185] The works

177 See Gentile, *supra* n 175, 92.

178 As Heller affirms, 'it was no longer simply a case of the secularization of one problem or another, as had occasionally happened before in Christian philosophy. *Now Christianity itself was secularized. Christianity itself became a secular philosophical problem as soon as theology was transformed into philosophy*' (emphasis of the Author), Heller, *supra* n 172, 108ff.

179 Y Arieli, 'On the necessary and Sufficient Conditions for the Emergence of the Doctrine of the Dignity of Man and His Rights' in Kretzmer and Klein, *supra* n 9, 1, 9.

180 H de Groot (Grotius), *De Jure Bellis ac Pacis (On the Law of War and Peace)*, 1625, transl. AC K Campbell (Batoche Books 2001), Book II, chap. 19.

181 See J Finnis, *Aquinas: Moral, Political, and Legal Theory* (Oxford University Press 1998), 176–180, 280.

182 See Pascal, *Pensées*, n. 210, 162.

183 See Kristeller, *supra* n 171, 26ff.

184 Arieli, *supra* n 179, 7.

185 Englard, *supra* n 25, 1917.

of two influential figures are illustrative of this time. John Locke (1632–1704) discussed the concept of a person's identity seen as an ethical self. He examined the role of man's rationality in his individuality[186] and called for equality in the protection of life and in the exercise of political power.[187] Man's individuality is forged by his rational capacity, his consciousness, his pursuit of happiness, memory and responsibility before the divinity.

The transition from the Renaissance perception of man's dignity to a new notion of dignity connected to a normative dimension of rights and duties is even more emphasized by another important Enlightenment figure, Samuel von Pufendorf (1632–94).[188] In his view, equality and liberty derive from dignity,[189] which belongs to all rational human beings.[190]

Still with an aristocratic vision of man's status, in his *De iure naturae et gentium* (1672), Pufendorf describes man's 'supreme' dignity as embodying his privileged role in the world.[191] Stoic philosophy influences the text, with input from Platonic doctrine on the immortality of the soul.[192] Subsequently, however, Pufendorf develops the idea of the equality of men, basing it upon man's rational nature.[193] This reflection shows an important ontological change from a more traditional concept of dignity, with connected duties towards a divinity, to a notion founding basic human rights within man's community.[194]

It appears, however, that dignity is not yet conceived of as a value worthy of normative protection. Moreover, the ancient views on man's failures were by no means eradicated. Late in the Renaissance and during the Enlightenment, a number of important philosophers, such as Montaigne (1533–1592), Hobbes (1599–1679), Pascal (1623–1662), and Hume (1711–1776), were sceptical and pessimistic about the recognition of a particular dignity only to some individuals.[195] Only with Immanuel Kant (1724–1804), however, did the transition toward man's right within the society find firm ground, with human rationality and freedom placed at the core of the debate. The following

186 J Locke, *An Essay concerning Human Understanding* (Baffet 1690), Book II, Chapter 27.
187 J Locke, *Two Treatises of Government* (Awnsham Churchill 1690), Book II, Chapter 2.
188 Englard, *supra* n 25, 1917.
189 Starck, *supra* n 79, 181.
190 S Pufendorf, *De Iure Naturae et Gentium Libri Octo* (1706), transl. CH & WA Oldfather (Clarendon Press 1995), Book II, Chapters 1, 35.
191 *Ibid.*, Chapters 1, 5.
192 Cancik, *supra* n 9, 31.
193 Pufendorf, *supra* n 190, Book II, Chapters 2, 1.
194 Englard, *supra* n 25, 1918.
195 On Montaigne, see P Magnard, 'La dignité de l'homme de Raymond de Sebond à Montaigne' in *Actes du Colloque tenu à la Sorbonne, November 1992* (Champion 1995), 161, 166–172; Englard, *supra* n 25, 1918.

sections introduce the Kantian and post-Kantian reflections on human dignity.

2.3.2.1 Kantian Dignity

The concept of human dignity largely entered into political theories only with Immanuel Kant's philosophy. The Kantian view of human dignity has, on one reading, a structural similarity to the Catholic view, with an important distinction. Where the Catholic claims that our rational nature has absolute, unconditional and incommensurable value as a result of man being the image and likeness of God, whose own rational nature is the source of all existing value, Kant argues that our rational nature has absolute, unconditional and incommensurable value because *we* are the source of the existing value. In his view, dignity means the intrinsic value of the independent individual.

It is, therefore, relevant to analyse how Kant's writings develop this new understanding of dignity. Looking more analytically at his writings, *Würde*, which means 'dignity' in German, is a word etymologically linked to *Wert*, meaning 'worth' or 'value'.

In the *Groundwork to the Metaphysics of Morals* (1785), the most widely known and influential of Kant's writings, he refers to the term *Würde* 16 times. The concept is therefore considered as having a central place in his thought.[196] It introduces a distinction between two types of value:[197] fungible values (substitutable) and those possessing an 'inner value' or that have, as he subsequently writes, 'an unconditional, incomparable value'.[198] When Kant writes that 'autonomy is therefore the ground of the dignity of human nature',[199] the autonomy he is referring to is an unconditional and incomparable value of human nature.

Similarly, in Aquinas' notion of dignity, whatever has dignity has an 'unconditional, incomparable' value intrinsic to it, as the greatness that something has 'on account of itself'. However, for Aquinas, dignity is a value in itself and of different kinds, potentially at least, at all levels of God's creation. For Kant, dignity is a 'kind of value' and restricted to human beings, since someone has 'morality, and humanity itself insofar as it is capable of morality'.[200] A person acts ethically when he is moved by a rational force that commands on his will. Only human beings are able to act morally and

196 Most significantly, it is used four times in Ak. 4: 434–435.

197 Rosen, *supra* n 47, 21.

198 Ak. 4:436.

199 Ak. 4:436.

200 Rosen, *supra* n 47, 22–23.

feeling the force of moral claims. If for Pico della Mirandola, Bacon and Pascal the main question was the type of dignity human beings possess, Kant has introduced a conception of dignity in its full sense as both *human* and egalitarian, which all human beings have, without deriving it from God.

Opening a secular reading of man's dignity, Kant reflects on dignity of man by building constructional relations with other principles or concepts. First, he asserts that the moral nature of man derives from the fact that God has created him *free*, but 'we can know that moral nature independently of any belief that we have in God'.[201] Free will is the right of every person as such (*angeborn*), where her humanity lies.[202] Second, Kant also emphasizes the role of *autonomy*, the basis of dignity of the rational human being that only follows its own rules. Autonomy, as freedom of will, is the supreme principle of morality and it is only through morality, seen as autonomy, that a rational human being is a purpose in itself.[203] From this concept, Kant derives the following statement of the categorical imperative: 'Act in such a way that you treat humanity, both in your person and in the person of each other individual, always at the same time as an end, never as a mere means.'[204] Therefore, the idea of dignity is linked to Kant's specific concept of morality[205] and Kant's notion of dignity represents a *moral postulate* rather than a social value. It means that using another man as a mere instrument violates the agent's moral duty, and the non-recognition of someone else's dignity constitutes a vice (*laster*).[206]

Third, Kant also creates a link between dignity and *respect*, writing: 'and the word respect alone provides a becoming expression for the estimate of it that a rational being must give'.[207] In this way, he relates dignity to its original meaning as *status*, which is, however, attributed to the lawgiving function of morality, an inalienable aspect of all human beings. I would also consider this reflection on the role of respect as part of the relational character of dignity.

Fourth, this reflection supports a further consideration. Kant discusses the concepts of humility and self-respect, in sections 11 and 12 of the 'Doctrine of Virtue', in the *Metaphysics of Morals* (1797). Humility, he writes, derives from looking inward and comparing ourselves and our actions with moral

201 *Ibid.*

202 A Ripstein, *Force and Freedom: Kant's Legal and Political Philosophy* (Harvard University Press 2009), 9–13.

203 *Ibid.*, 77.

204 *Ibid.*, 67; for an analysis of Kant's idea of humanity as an *end in itself*, see TE Hill, Jr., *Dignity and Practical Reason in Kant's Moral Theory* (Cornell University Press 1992), 38–57.

205 Hill, *supra* n 204, 38–57.

206 I Kant, *The Doctrine of Virtue*, Part II of 'The Metaphysics of Morals', 1797, Chapter 1, para 2, 41.

207 Ak. 4:436.

requests.[208] Thus, dignity is something that we have because of the 'humanity in our person', and self-respect, the form of pride in oneself, is a matter of honour, which is different from arrogance. No person should transform himself in an instrument for the fulfilment of someone else's free will.[209] Therefore, once again, Kant promulgates the idea of the inherent dignity of morality, with a strong egalitarian view of *honour*, as something that is owed to everyone.

Lastly, the term 'dignity' is used in the *Groundwork* in association with the word *sublimity* (*Erhabenheit*).[210] Here Kant associates 'sublimity and dignity' as qualities 'in the person who fulfills all his duties'. The outcome is that the concept of dignity is seen as an intrinsic quality, a feature of those who respect the moral law's demands.

Thus, from Kant's perspective, human beings have dignity because the moral law, intrinsically and unconditionally valuable, is embodied only in them and they all share it equally. The concept of the moral personality's intrinsic worth was shown to be most influential in the constitutional context of the twentieth century, even if with a meaning transcending the strict Kantian conception. Outside the religious view, Kant opens the door to a view of dignity that is exclusively human and inherently connected to equality.

2.3.2.2 Post-Kantian Dignity

During the nineteenth century, other philosophers used and reviewed the Kantian concept of dignity to support social reforms. Schiller, in *On Grace and Dignity* (*Über Anmut und Würde*, 1793), discusses grace and dignity to reconcile Kant's philosophy with the pagan ideal of the integration of mind and body, advanced by Goethe. Dignity is seen as an aesthetic quality and is 'tranquillity in suffering'.[211] For Schiller, grace and dignity are elements of action. He states that the graceful person is someone who acts rightly with no internal struggle, in harmony with moral duties. When an inner conflict arises and the individual shows moral strength, the natural feature of such action of self-control, in Schiller's words, is dignity: 'Just as grace is the expression of a beautiful soul, so dignity is the expression of a sublime disposition,' recalling Kant's phrase about the 'dignity and sublimity' of the person who complies with all his duties.

In one of the footnotes to the 2nd edition of *Religion within the Limits of Reason Alone* (1794), Kant argues against Schiller's moral 'grace', by saying: 'I

208 Ak. 6:436.
209 See Ripstein, *supra* n 202, 36–37.
210 Ak. 4:439–440.
211 See Rosen, *supra* n 47, 55.

am unable to associate grace with the concept of duty, by reason of duty's very dignity. For the concept of duty includes unconditional necessitation, to which gracefulness stands in direct contradiction.'[212] However, Kant's view of the moral law, a characteristic of 'unconditional, in-comparable' value, which is 'raised above' any inclination from the senses, is an expression of the sublime within human beings, and this is in line with Schiller's idea that human beings are dignified when their acts overcome their impulses.

When Kant and Schiller were writing, the system of social status in Europe was responding to the impact of the French Revolution. Aristocracy privileges (*dignités*) had been revoked and the concept of equality asserted in their place.[213] The French Revolution was a strongly egalitarian political approach to the status concept of dignity. At the same time, Kant and Schiller advanced an egalitarian view of dignity of their own accord. For Kant, the idea of dignity as an intrinsic value was to be identified with a character that only human beings share, while Schiller moralized the idea of dignified action into something achievable by everyone in light of the constant human conflict between duty and inclination.

Notwithstanding this enthusiasm for the use of dignity in the political discourse, critics came from both the left and the right. In 1837, Arthur Schopenhauer, in his critique of Kant, stated that 'this expression "Human Dignity", once it was uttered by Kant, became the shibboleth of all perplexed and empty-headed moralists'.[214] Human dignity was thus defined as a content-less concept.[215] A radical denial of any religious basis for human dignity is also evident in Karl Marx's writings. In 1847, he strongly criticized another German socialist, Karl Heinzen, and argued that his uses of dignity were 'empty phrases' applied only to '[taking] refuge from history in morality'.[216] In 1872, Friedrich Nietzsche wrote one of the most vehement critical reviews of the time about this notion of dignity in his essay 'The Greek State'.[217] Nietzsche affirmed that the notion of dignity of labour is a way of trying to make more

212 Ak. 6:23.

213 Rosen, *supra* n 47, 61–62.

214 A Schopenhauer, *The Basis of Morality*, Part II, Critique of Kant's Basis of Ethics, trans. and intro. AB Bullock (Dover Publications 2005).

215 Rosen, *supra* n 47, 41.

216 K Marx, *Moralising Criticism and Critical Morality, a Contribution to German Cultural History Contra Karl Heinzen*, Deutsche-Brüsseler-Zeitung Nos 86, 87, 90, 92 and 94, 28 and 31 October, 11, 18 and 25 November 1847. See also Starck, *supra* n 79, 185.

217 It was one of the *Five Prefaces to Five Unwritten Books*, a gift for Cosima Wagner's birthday in 1872 (the year of the publication of *The Birth of Tragedy*), F Nietzsche, *The Greek State, Five Prefaces to Five Unwritten Books*, transl. MW Grenke, MK Davis, L van Boxel (St. Augustine's Press 2005).

attractive, in the form of a mere consolation, what is in reality a necessity for those who have to exercise it. Thus, labour and human existence gain a value that they do not naturally possess or deserve. In this view, slavery finds justification in that it is necessary to the life of the free aristocrat – the only person with an intrinsic value. Nietzsche writes just after the Franco-Prussian War and contrasts the modern State with the ancient Greek warrior-state, where its military structure of organization led to a division of people into military castes, which was the basis for the edifice of a 'martial society'. He explains that the one of the features of such a system is the absolute subordination of those in lower levels to higher classes – which constitutes a hierarchy not inimical to dignity.[218]

At the same time, other developments in the secularization of the notion of dignity had occurred under the influence of socialist and anarchist thinkers, such as Pierre-Joseph Proudhon (1809–65), who conceived dignity as a natural human sense and merged this view into the concept of justice – and, most importantly, detached from religion.[219]

2.3.2.3 A 'Non-relational' Dignity

From the seventeenth century onward, the concept of human dignity is cleaned from the religious nature proper of humanist approaches and centred instead on human reason. In the Enlightenment, the dignity of the human being is placed at the centre of philosophical reflections. With Samuel Pufendorf, one of the leading exponents of modern natural law, we witness not only the accomplishment of the secularization process of the concept of dignity, but also, above all, the use of this concept as a foundation of specific legal duties. The idea of human dignity as a legal category is outlined as imposing certain obligations of behaviour: the duty to cause benefit to others; the duty to recognize equal rights; the prohibition on considering oneself superior to others and on insulting them.[220] A final relevant consequence is the rejection of the Aristotelian assumption that there were men born to be slaves, a view held by the German philosopher in opposition to the principle of natural equality.[221] The work of Samuel Pufendorf has the merit of introducing a centuries-old concept of human dignity, which is then fully developed

[218] See Rosen, *supra* n 47, 45–46.

[219] See PJ Proudhon, *De La Justice dans La Revolution et dans l'eglise* (Garnier frères 1858), 299–300, 313.

[220] See Pufendorf, *supra* n 190, III, II, IV–VII.

[221] *Ibid.*, III, II, VIII.

by Kant, and placing dignity at the centre of the reflection of modern modern natural law.[222]

With Immanuel Kant's reflection on human dignity, we move more squarely to 'the central existential claim of modernity – man's autonomy, his capacity to be lord of his fate and the shaper of his future'.[223] The conception of dignity usually associated with Kant is human dignity as autonomy and man's capability to freely decide.

Although the principle of human dignity does not find, with Kant, a translation from the moral plane to the juridical one, starting from Kant, the concept of dignity abandons the ancient meaning in order to assume the fully fledged new one of 'human dignity' or 'equal dignity'. This new presentation is conveyed with the use of the term 'dignity' in the singular, which identifies a quality *intrinsic* to the human being and implies the negation of a hierarchical order. Dignity is a characteristic that belongs indistinctly and in an equal manner to all human beings. This concept of dignity is expressed by the syntagma '*non-relational dignity*', since it does not have nor need a characteristic to define itself, except that of belonging to the human race.[224] Such qualification, possessed equally by each person, renders human dignity an *intangible*, *invulnerable* and *inaccessible* concept.[225] Thus, the Kantian human dignity is described as an absolute concept and universal, capable of being the moral foundation of human rights.[226]

It is with political philosophy and the growth of republicanism that the concept gains a popular flavour.[227] During the nineteenth century, the concept of dignity started to be used for a variety of other social and political movements advocating specific types of social reform.[228] In Europe and in Latin America, human dignity came to be aligned with the abolition of slavery and the idea of the 'dignity of labour' was used to enclose some of the egalitarian aims of these social movements, as we shall see in Chapter 3.[229]

222 See MA Cattaneo, *Giusnaturalismo e dignità umana* (Edizioni Scientifiche Italiane 2006), 17.

223 Arieli, *supra* n 179, 12.

224 Spiegelberg, *supra* n 72, 191–192 and 195.

225 A Kolnai, *Dignity* [1976] 51 *Philosophy* 197, 253.

226 MA Cattaneo, *Dignità umana e pena nella filosofia di Kant* (Giuffrè 1981), 54.

227 T Paine, *Rights of Man* (1791); W Wordsworth, *The Prelude* (1805), Book Thirteenth, lines 76–88; C Renouvier, *Manuel Républicain de l'homme et du citoyen* (1848); PG Carozza, 'From Conquest to Constitutions: Retrieving a Latin American Tradition of the Idea of Human Rights' [2003] 25 *HRQ*, 281, 301.

228 McCrudden, *supra* n 74, 658.

229 Simón Bolivar, *Message to the Congress of Bolivia* (Lima, 25 May 1826), quoted in Carozza, *supra* n 228, 301; Decree of 27 April 1848, Preamble; A Flanders, *Management and Unions*

The threat from socialism, particularly with the development of communism by Marx and fear of class war and totalitarianism, encouraged the use of dignity in the new Catholic social doctrine developed at the end of the nineteenth century.[230] It mostly emphasized the importance of solidarity in society, giving a more communitarian colour to the concept, though still interpreted as a gift from God.

2.4 THE TURN TO HUMAN DIGNITY

The two conceptions just described, that is, *sovereign* and *human* dignity, the latter in its religious and philosophical connotations, could be summed into a semantic structure, by which 'dignity' unifies (or, as it were, aspires to unite) related but distinct features, namely rank or status and inherent worth. The twofold structure of dignity conceptions, or circles, seems to persist throughout its long and difficult history in international law, as we shall see throughout the following chapters.

It can be said that the relevance of the difference between a secularized conception of human dignity and a vision religiously connoted of human dignity lies in this: while the latter identifies the trait that equalizes human beings as the result of God's attribution to all men of a position of superiority (over other beings), the former conception identifies the same trait in the common characteristic of each personality – notwithstanding the attribution – or not – by God ('*etsi daremus non esse deum*').[231] The gradual emergence of the meaning of dignity as a concept that does not discriminate between men, but unifies them, regardless of any status, is certainly intertwined with the *Wirkungsgeschichte* of some ideas of Kantian moral philosophy. Nonetheless, the emergence of the concept remains, above all, the development of a central theme in Christian theology.[232]

One could add that a further relevant distinction is also between dignity as a 'dowry' and dignity 'as a performance'.[233] In the first sense, dignity is an innate quality which everyone has from birth as belonging to the human race

(Faber 1970), p. 239; J Eckert, ' Legal Roots of Human Dignity in German Law' in Kretzmer and Klein, *supra* n 9, 41, 47.

230 Pope Leo XIII, *Rerum Novarum* (1891). See also Curran, *supra* n 132; Pope Pius XI, *Quadragesimo Anno* (1931); Pope John XXIII, *Pacem in Terris* (1963); *Gaudium et Spes*, Vatican Council II (1965); Pope Paul VI, *Populorum Progressio* (1967); Pope John Paul II, *Centesimus Annus* (1991); see also J Maritain, *Man and the State* (University of Colorado Press 1951).

231 See also on the history of secularization, JC Monod, *La querelle de la secularisation, de Hegel à Blumenberg* (Librarie Philosophique J. Vrin 2002), 313.

232 This is synthesized from Paul in a verse from the *Letter to the Galatians* (3, 28).

233 See H Hofmann, 'La promessa della dignità umana. La dignità dell'uomo nella cultura giuridica tedesca' [1999] 76 *Rivista Internazionale di Filosofia del Diritto* 4, 625.

and it cannot be increased or decreased. In the second meaning, dignity is not a given, but a result to be achieved – the product of human actions. The Christian vision clearly expresses the idea that dignity is an intrinsic quality in every man; however, dignity remains a dynamic and hierarchical conception, linked to the experience of original sin and to the conquest of salvation.

A review of the roots of the two circles of dignity may leave a reader overwhelmed by the amount of intertwined reflections and interpretations. The different concept of sovereign dignity has today still important manifestation, as it is still adopted to refer to the status of sovereign States.[234] This conception of dignity will not be object of direct analysis. Rather, it will be dignity that inheres to personhood. This book will specifically shed a light on human dignity as an *attribution of the human being*. As described, dignity took a radical twist in the last two centuries, turning into a quintessentially personal feature of all people and a marker of equality. The emergence during the twentieth century of dignity as a right of individuals, and the rejection of prior practices of colonization and discrimination against racialized and ethnic groups, imposed constraints on sovereignty and on its scope. The rise of *human* dignity (inter alia) has, however, simultaneously also influenced the latitude of application of expressions of sovereign dignity. Sovereign and human dignity ultimately constitute rival but interlocking circles of dignity, as detailed in Chapter 1. The research, therefore, also flags the uses of sovereign dignity claims, as well as the purposes for which they are raised. More fundamentally, it explores the conceptual battlefront opened by the concept of human dignity, when the very assertion of human dignity to protect the individual conflicts with the powers of the State.

[234] J Resnick and J Chi-hye Suk, 'Adding Insult to Injury: Questioning the Role of Dignity in Conceptions of Sovereignty' [2003] 55 *SLR* 1921.

3

Three Constitutive Stages

3.1 INTRODUCTION

The main conceptions of thinking related to human dignity described in Chapter 2 found expression and slowly permeated the fabric of international law. This chapter now traces the legal concept of human dignity to its root causes and shows how distinct and theoretical conceptions of the past have influenced debates at the origins of international law, often blending with each other. It thus describes the historical process that for the first time shaped the various manifestations of human dignity in international law by way of its different instruments. It reveals that, at first, human dignity, as an attribution of every human being, entered into international law as a Christian dignity, which slowly secularized to become of universal application and, at a later stage, actionable. In this process, the scope of the circle of human dignity has extended to covering all humans, considered first in their individual dimension and later also in their collective one, and found itself in constant opposition with the first, more classical conception of sovereign dignity.

This historical progress is the outcome of three consecutive but overlapping constitutive stages of human dignity, all spanning from the nineteenth century until today. Each of them shows a different chronological consolidation of dignity that distinguishes itself from the others and is associated to a specific language, framework and instrument.

In particular, the emergence of international humanitarian law (IHL) represents the body of law in which the first constitutive stage of human dignity takes shape. It begins in the first half of the nineteenth century, showing dignity's first entry point with the adoption and entry into force of the Hague Law.[1] The consolidation of this stage was only completed with the

[1] Convention (IV) Respecting the Laws and Customs of War on Land and Regulations, The Hague, 18 October 1907 (Hague Convention IV 1907).

adoption of the Four Geneva Conventions in 1949,[2] into which the Two Additional Protocols were integrated in 1977.[3] During this first constitutive stage, human dignity enters into the laws of war mainly in its Christian sense.

However, human dignity consolidates as the foundation of the International Bill of Rights only in the 1960s. Its first manifestations in international human rights law (IHRL) were in the 1920s (first entry point) and later in 1945 (second entry point). In 1948, with the adoption of the Universal Declaration of Human Rights (UDHR),[4] human dignity is finally crystallized and completely consolidated in 1966. In the UDHR, human dignity is fully recognized as a secularized and inherent attribution of all individuals, rooted in the Enlightenment – despite still visible traces of a Christian legacy. In the subsequent years, the scope of human dignity is slowly expanded in other human rights instruments to cover not only the individual sphere but also the collective one. The two 1966 Covenants, the International Covenant on Civil and Political Rights (ICCPR)[5] and the International Covenant on Economic, Social and Cultural Rights (ICESCR),[6] ultimately succeed in fully capturing unexpressed currents and a universal-collective nature of dignity.

The evolution of international criminal law (ICL) embodies the third and last constitutive stage of human dignity, which turned into an actionable concept. Its first manifestations coincide with the adoption and entry into force of the Hague Law (1899 and 1907, first entry point) and the 1919 Treaty of Versailles (Article 227, second entry point). In 1945, with the Nuremberg Charter, human dignity first crystallizes in ICL. The legal and institutional criminal framework of the 1990s, and in particular, the adoption of the Statute

[2] ICRC, Geneva Convention for the Amelioration of the Condition of the Wounded and Sick in Armed Forces in the Field (First Geneva Convention), 12 August 1949, 75 UNTS 31; Geneva Convention for the Amelioration of the Condition of Wounded, Sick and Shipwrecked Members of Armed Forces at Sea (Second Geneva Convention), 12 August 1949, 75 UNTS 85; ICRC, Geneva Convention Relative to the Treatment of Prisoners of War (Third Geneva Convention), 12 August 1949, 75 UNTS 135; Geneva Convention Relative to the Protection of Civilian Persons in Time of War (Fourth Geneva Convention), 12 August 1949, 75 UNTS 287.

[3] ICRC, Protocol Additional to the Geneva Conventions of 12 August 1949, and relating to the Protection of Victims of International Armed Conflicts (Additional Protocol I or AP I), 8 June 1977, 1125 UNTS 3; ICRC, Protocol Additional to the Geneva Conventions of 12 August 1949, and relating to the Protection of Victims of Non-International Armed Conflicts (Additional Protocol II or AP II), 8 June 1977, 1125 UNTS 609.

[4] UNGA, Universal Declaration of Human Rights, 10 December 1948, 217 A (III).

[5] UNGA, International Covenant on Civil and Political Rights, 16 December 1966, UNTS 999, 171.

[6] UNGA, International Covenant on Economic, Social and Cultural Rights, 16 December 1966, UNTS 993, 3.

of the International Criminal Court (ICC Statute),[7] provides a final consolidation ground for human dignity in the history of ICL.

The historical timeline of human dignity, presented in Figure 3.1, shows (and introduces) these three stages. Each constitutive stage will be discussed in turn.

It should be noted now, however, that establishing these three distinct stages does not exclude each one from developing, clarifying and expanding in time through further 'legal peaks'. My aim is, more specifically, to shed light on the first entry points and consolidation of human dignity in the legal framework corresponding to each stage. For this reason, and on this basis, this research adopts a partition not based on branches per se, but it instead follows these three historical stages, which represent an analytical category developed as an outcome of visualizing embossed historical features. In this chapter, I will thus carefully explain the process of consolidation of human dignity in each historical stage and how its first expressions took shape, providing also an explanation of the context, to help facilitate the assessment of future developments, declines or growth.

In the next three chapters, instead, the study will examine the three distinct legal frameworks of human dignity in which human dignity manifested itself and that also represent three interlinked (but different) historical passages: (i) IHL (Chapter 4), (ii) IHRL (Chapter 5) and (iii) ICL (Chapter 6). Each chapter will draw from the conclusions presented in this chapter and examine the specific legal instruments adopted to manifest dignity, clarifying their terminological formulations, meaning and uses, at the regional and international level, as well as their specific functions. By displaying the synoptic legal evolution of human dignity, it may be possible to shed a clear light on the manner in which it has been perceived and the aspirations associated with its recognition or constitution. Even if the historical analysis overall reveals components of continuity behind this process, certain phases, instead, will open the stage to fundamental departures and distinct developments.

3.2 FIRST CONSTITUTIVE STAGE: CHRISTIAN DIGNITY AS A BENCHMARK FOR CIVILIZATION

3.2.1 *Overview*

The concept of human dignity had its first legal expression in the laws of war, a set of rules based on chivalry, religion and humanity, designed to protect

[7] UNGA, Rome Statute of the International Criminal Court (ICC), 17 July 1998.

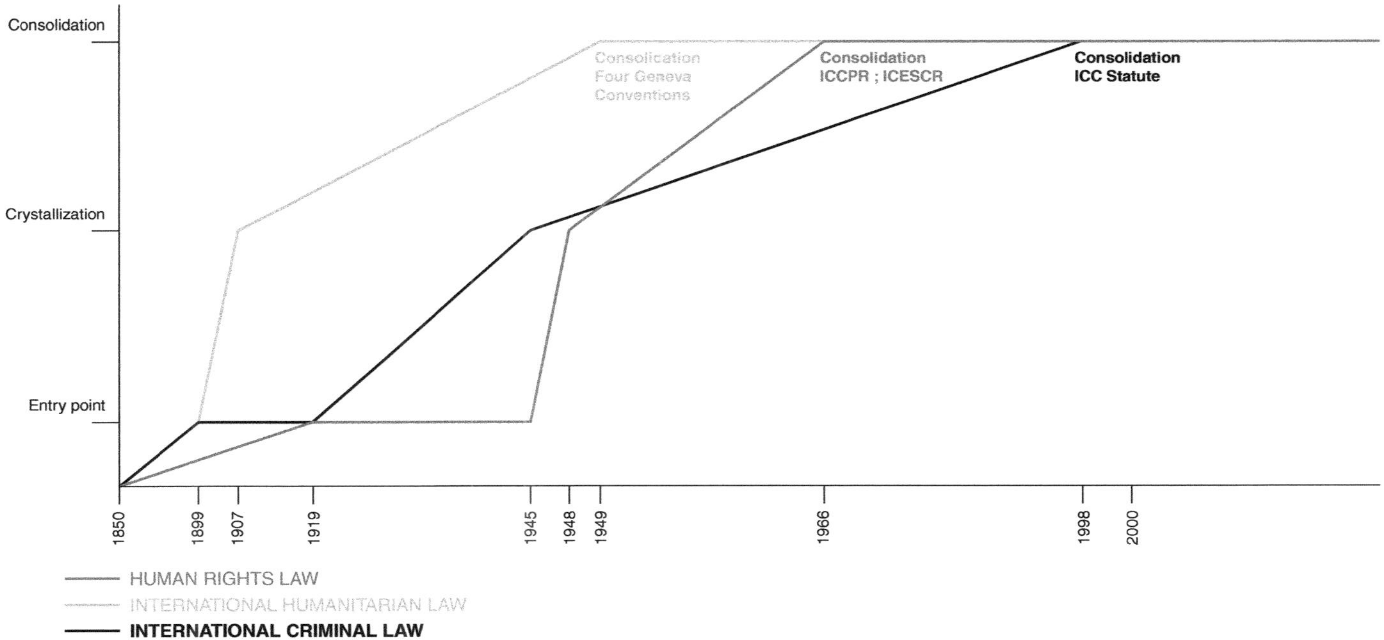

FIGURE 3.1 Three constitutive stages of human dignity

non-combatants and combatants.[8] Since ancient times, humanitarian considerations have pushed for the imposition of limitations on the conduct and means of warfare. This was the beginning of what became known as *ius in bello*. In particular, from the time of the Old Testament to the Chivalric period and to modern times, the concept of human dignity found its place in the laws of war in its Christian sense.

The sixteenth century was the age of religious wars in Europe, as well as of European colonial conquests.[9] However, in this century, the concept of human dignity started to appear in international legal debate,[10] with the Spanish School discussions on whether converting Indians to Christianity in Latin America was justified. On this matter, the Dominican Francisco de Vitoria (d. 1546), in his *De Indis*, argued that Indians were entitled to their lands and insisted that those who could not bear arms, such as women and children, including non-Christians, were to be considered as 'innocents' and had to remain immune from any attacks. He affirmed that all men share the same nature and are next of kin, offering an argument in favour of the equal dignity and inviolable rights of the people of the New World.[11] His arguments remained influential as a line of natural law thinking in the Catholic Church and in the subsequent human rights discourse.[12] Yet, notwithstanding Vitoria's reprimands, the expropriations and depredations went on. Dutch trades in the East Indies led to further considerations by Hugo Grotius (1583–1645). Grotius's opera *On the Law of War and Peace* was a catalyst for rules during armed conflict, introducing the principle that the law imposes limits on the destructive power of weapons during warfare. He argued that 'the power of the

8 See T Meron, *Henry's Wars and Shakespeare's Laws: Perspectives on the Law of War in the Later Middle Ages* (Oxford University Press 1993); T Meron, *Bloody Constraint: War and Chivalry in Shakespeare* (Oxford University Press 1998); T Meron, *The Humanization of International Law* (Martinus Nijhoff 2006), 2.

9 DJ Bederman, *The Spirit of International Law* (University of Georgia Press 2002), 121.

10 See JA Frowein, 'Human Dignity in International Law' in D Kretzmer and E Klein (eds), *The Concept of Human Dignity in Human Rights Discourse* (Brill 2002), 121; see also W Preiser, 'History of the Law of Nations: Ancient Times to 1648' in R Bernhardt (ed.), *Encyclopedia of Public International Law* (North Holland 1995), 740–741, 722; K Partsch, 'Individuals in International Law' in R Bernhardt (ed.), *Encyclopedia of Public International Law*, vol. 2 (North Holland 1995), 957–958.

11 F de Victoria, *De Indis Recenter Inventis et de Jure Belli Hispanorum*, in Barbaros Relectiones, para 3, n 3 (1539), reprinted in W Schätzel (Hrsg.) (ed.), 2 *Die Klassiker des Völkerrechts* (Mohr Siebeck GmbH & Co. KG 1952), 96–97; see JB Scott, *The Spanish Conception of International Law and Sanctions* (Clarendon Press 1934), 3–5.

12 See RJ Araujo, 'Foundations of Human Rights: The Work of Francisco de Vitoria' in MJ Schuck and J Crowley-Buck (eds), *Democracy, Culture, Catholicism: Voices from Four Continents* (Fordham University Press 2015), 280–297.

sword must be *restrained* from inflicting promiscuous death'[13] and connected moderation to humanity, stating that 'all actions no way conducive to obtain a contested right, or to bring the war to a termination, but calculated merely to display the strength of either side are totally repugnant to the duties of a Christian and to the *principles of humanity*'.[14] Though much indebted to Aquinas and Vitoria, Grotius secularized the Christian ethic of war by developing natural law theory as the universal basis for a new international legal order. Soon after his death, and in the aftermath of an appalling time of religious warfare ending in the Peace of Westphalia (1648), Europe gave public recognition to the sovereignty of the emerging European monarchs, and new Enlightenment doctrines slowly helped to forge the rules of IHL.[15]

Accordingly, various significant events began injecting humanitarian considerations into the regulations of warfare. First, by the end of the eighteenth century, enemy commanders concluded agreements for mutual respect of the wounded and sick.[16] Moreover, thanks to the commitment of Henri Dunant (1828–1910), Francis Lieber (1800–1872) and Fyodor Fyodorovich de Martens (1845–1908), whose action was strongly influenced by their Christian faith, the concept of human dignity was inserted in the rules on war to lay the foundations of modern IHL.

In parallel, it is also in this time that the 1815 Declaration Relative to the Universal Abolition of the Slave Trade[17] (the 1815 Declaration) was adopted, the first international instrument to condemn slavery.[18] It declared that the trade of slaves 'was considered by just and enlightened men throughout time to be *repugnant to the principles of humanity and universal morals*'.[19] During the final decades of the eighteenth century, Britain and the American colonies, which were about to become the United States, were the stage for a vocal movement that sought the abolition of slavery. It was driven by economic reasons and by sensitivities about human dignity flowing from the

13 H de Groot (Grotius), *De Jure Bellis ac Pacis (On the Law of War and Peace)*, 1625, ACK Campbell (trans.) (Batoche Books 2001), 286 (emphasis added).

14 *Ibid.*, 324 (emphasis added).

15 E de Vattel, *The Law of Nations* (T. & J. W. Johnson, Law Booksellers 1844), section 137; JJ Rousseau, *The Social Contract*, 1762, GDH Cole (trans.) (Dutton 1950), 8.

16 See the Treaty of Amity and Commerce, 10 September 1785, Kingdom of Prussia and the United States. See also G Butler and S Maccoby, *The Development of International Law* (Longmans Green 1928), 134; see also H Coursier, *The International Red Cross* (ICRC 1961), 10.

17 Declaration Relative to the Universal Abolition of the Slave Trade, 8 February 1815, Consolidated Treaty Series, vol. 63, No. 473. Final Act of the Congress of Vienna, ACT, No. XV.

18 See R Sawyer, *Slavery in the Twentieth Century* (Routledge & Kegan Paul 1986), 1–8; see also K Bales and PT Robbins, 'No One Shall be Held in Slavery or Servitude: A Critical Analysis of International Slavery Agreements' [2001] 2 *HRR* 18.

19 Emphasis added.

Enlightenment, and manifested mostly in radical, puritan Protestant circles and civil societies.[20] The British Anti-Slavery Society had started campaigning in 1787 to abolish slavery and succeeded in prohibiting the slave trade in the British Empire later in 1807. After the French Revolution, an 1848 decree of the French Republic abolished slavery as 'an affront to human dignity'.[21] The trade was also prohibited in the 1841 Quintuple Treaty[22] and the General Act of the Berlin Conference of 1885.[23] A large number of agreements, both multilateral and bilateral, dating from the early nineteenth century contain provisions prohibiting slavery in both war and peace.[24]

This section first presents the system of the laws of war at the end of the nineteenth century in order to explain the initial movement towards the recognition of humanitarian considerations in the regulation of warfare, at the detriment of state's freedom (Section 3.2.2). Starting with the beginning of the twentieth century, it identifies the first constitutive stage of human dignity in the adoption and entry into force of the Hague Law (Martens Clause, 1899 and 1907), which crystallizes human dignity in the system of IHL in its Christian expression. The section subsequently clarifies how and when human dignity fully consolidated in humanitarian law (Section 3.2.3). The consolidation of this phase only occurs in 1949, with the adoption of the four Geneva Conventions, which enhanced the protection of human dignity in its provisions, marking the beginning of a 'humanitarian age'.[25] The chronology

20 J Allain (ed.), *The Legal Understanding of Slavery: From the Historical to the Contemporary* (Oxford University Press 2012); JS Martinez, *The Slave Trade and the Origins of International Human Rights Law* (Oxford University Press 2012); DB Davis, *The Problem of Slavery in the Age of Revolution 1770–1823* (Oxford University Press 1999); T Hugh, *The Slave Trade: The Story of the Atlantic Slave Trade, 1440–1870* (Simon & Schuster 1997).

21 Decree of 27 April 1848, Preamble.

22 Treaty for the Suppression of the African Slave Trade, 20 December 1841, signed by Austria, Great Britain, France (which did not ratify it), Prussia and Russia for the Suppression of the African Slave Trade, 73 CTS 32 [Quintuple Treaty].

23 AM Trebilock, 'Slavery' in R Bernhardt (ed.), *Encyclopaedia of Public International Law* (North Holland 1985), vol. 8, 481–482; WG Grewe (ed.), *Fontes Historiae Iuris Gentium 1815–1945. Sources Relating to the History of the Law of Nations* (De Gruyter 1988), 306–307, 376, 379.

24 The signatories to the Brussels Conference Act of 1890 'declared that they were equally animated by the firm intention of putting an end to the traffic in African slaves'. The Brussels Conference Act was supplemented and revised by the Treaty of Saint-Germain, signed at Saint-Germain-en-Laye by the Allied Powers of the First World War on 10 September 1919, see Convention revising the General Act of Berlin, 26 February 1885, and of the General Act and the Declaration of Brussels, 2 July 1890, signed at Saint-Germain-en-Laye, 10 September 1919 (1922) LNTSer 19, 8 LNTS 27. The signatories undertook to 'endeavour to secure the complete suppression of slavery in all its forms and of the slave trade by land and sea' (Art. 11).

25 R Kolb, 'The Main Epochs of Modern International Humanitarian Law since 1864 and Their Related Dominant Legal Constructions' in KM Larsen, CG Cooper and G Nystuen (eds),

of this first constitutive stage, which will be followed in this section, is summarized in Figure 3.2.

3.2.2 A *Christian Dignity: From Dunant to the 'Laws of Humanity'*

After the Battle of Solferino in June 1859,[26] Henry Dunant, a Swiss businessman who witnessed the suffering of thousands of wounded men in the conflict who were left to die for lack of medical attention, planned medical relief in the battlefield and recorded his memories in a book titled *Un Souvenir de Solférino* (1862).[27] In the book he suggested the establishment of a voluntary relief agency to aid the war wounded and proposed an international legal instrument on the humane treatment of those sick and injured by war.[28] Moved by his Christian understanding,[29] he created the ICRC in 1863. Dunant's proposed treaty became reality on 22 August 1864 with the adoption of the First Geneva Convention for the Amelioration of the Condition of the Wounded of Armies in the Field, which marked the start of the development of the *Geneva Law*.[30] The first president of the ICRC, Gustave Moynier, affirmed that, in his view, the moral roots of the new laws of war were 'direct fruit of Christianity'.[31] He denied any influence of the secular doctrine propagated by the French Revolution. When presenting the laws of war in the history of philosophies, he asserted the relation between the two traditions, seeing the laws of war as a result of the new idea of progress.[32]

Searching for a 'Principle of Humanity' in International Humanitarian Law (Cambridge University Press 2013), 45.

26 See H McCoubrey, *International Humanitarian Law: The Regulation of Armed Conflicts* (Dartmouth 1990), 10–11.

27 H Dunant, *Un Souvenir de Solférino* (Jules-Guillaume Fick 1862), A *Memory of Solferino* (English version, ICRC 1986).

28 H Dunant's proposals were well received and, after the publication of his booklet, Gustave Moynier, President of the Geneva Public Welfare Society, set up a committee of five – all Swiss members, including Dunant – to understand the possibilities for enforcing proposal C (the commission was the forerunner of the ICRC).

29 M Huber, *The Good Samaritan: Reflections on the Gospel and Work in the Red Cross* (Gollancz 1945), 32 – original in German (Schulthess 1944), 10; Dunant, *supra* n 27, 116; KJ Partsch, 'The Western Concept' in UNESCO, *International Dimensions of Humanitarian Law*, Henry-Dunant Institute (UNESCO, Martinus Nijhoff 1988), 61.

30 Source of the 'Geneva Law' include: Convention for the Amelioration of the Condition of the Wounded in Armies in the Field, Geneva 22 August 1864; see *supra* n 2 and 3.

31 G Moynier, *Essai sur les caracteres generaux des lois de la guerre* (Eggiman, C&Cie 1895), 120.

32 *Ibid.*, 95 ff. As the third president of the ICRC, Huber stated that the ethics of the ICRC directly incorporated the idea of humanity and practical humanism and were neutral toward any religious doctrine, see M Huber, *The Red Cross: Principles and Problems* (ICRC 1941), and *Glaube und Kirche in Vermischte Schriften*, Band II (Atlantis Verlag 1948).

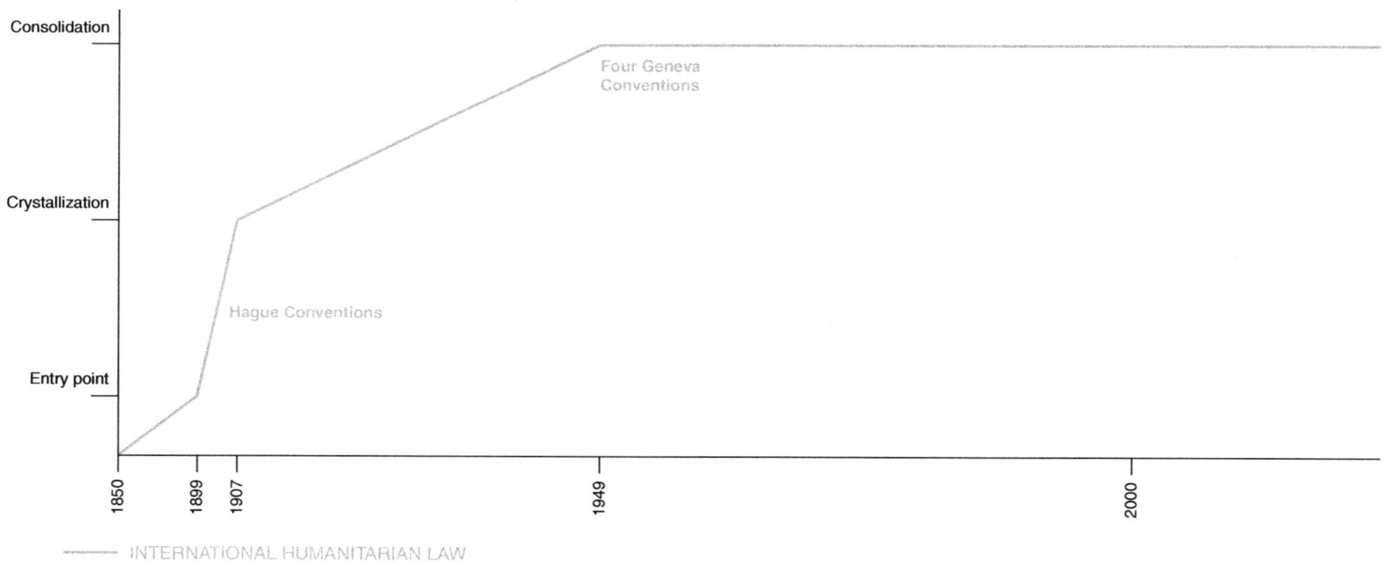

FIGURE 3.2 First constitutive stage

The desire to reduce suffering in war and to protect prisoners in the hands of the enemy, the wounded or sick, as well as civilians, started a humanitarian movement, which developed in the current humanitarian law.[33] This new trend was favoured by three influential persons of the nineteenth century:[34] not only the Genovese merchant Henry Dunant, but also the jurists Francis Lieber and Fyodor Fyodorovich de Martens. In 1863, by order of President Lincoln, Francis Lieber used the customary law of land warfare to draft and adopt written military instructions, which were issued as 'Army Order N.100' (*Instructions for the Government of Armies of the US in the Field*, or the Lieber Code).[35] It consisted of 157 articles and was promulgated as law with binding effect for the conduct in the field of the Union Army of the United States during the American Civil War. In 1913, Root enthusiastically described the Code as 'an instinctive selection of the best and most humane practice' in time of war.[36] Despite the Code 'balancing humanitarian concerns with military necessity did not always further the dictates of humanity',[37] it was grounded on 'broad humanitarian principles' and was an expression of an 'overall humanitarian spirit'.[38] There are various provisions where humanitarian considerations indeed regulate the conduct of hostilities, but the reference made in the Code to a more general 'principle of humanity' is relevant.[39]

A few years later, a form of a 'principle of humanity' was invoked for a specific purpose in the 1868 St Petersburg Declaration.[40] The Declaration was adopted to impose a ban on a particular type of ammunition, 'rifle shells', which were small projectiles that exploded or caught fire on impact, causing more harm than the ordinary bullets used at the time. However, it gained a relevance beyond this narrow scope, namely for its codification of the general principle prohibiting the infliction of unnecessary suffering.[41] The Preamble of the Declaration reads as follows:

33 According to Kolb, this stage runs from 1864 until 1899, see Kolb, *supra* n 25, 23.

34 GIAD Draper, 'The Development of International Humanitarian Law' in UNESCO, *supra* n 29, 70.

35 Instructions for the Government of Armies of the United States in the Field, 24 April 1863.

36 E Root, 'Francis Lieber' [1913] 7 *AJIL* 456.

37 T Meron, 'Francis Lieber's Code and Principles of Humanity' [1998] 36 *ColumJTransnatlL* 269, 271.

38 *Ibid.*, 274; see also JF Witt, 'Two Conceptions of Suffering in War' in A Sarat (ed.), *Knowing the Suffering of Others: Legal Perspectives on Pain and Its Meanings* (University of Alabama Press 2014), 129; see D Luban, 'Human Rights Thinking and the Laws of War' in JD Ohlin (ed.), *Theoretical Boundaries of Armed Conflict and Human Rights* (Cambridge University Press 2016), 50.

39 Lieber Code, Articles 4 and 75.

40 Declaration Renouncing the Use, in Time of War, of Explosive Projectiles under 400 Grammes Weight, made in St Petersburg, 29 November/11 December 1868.

41 See e.g. Y Dinstein, *The Conduct of Hostilities under the Law of International Armed Conflict* (Cambridge University Press 2004), 57; C Greenwood, 'Historical Development and Legal

> [T]he progress of civilization should have the effect of alleviating as much as possible the calamities of war; the only legitimate objective which states should endeavour to accomplish during war is to weaken the military forces of the enemy; for this purpose it is sufficient to disable the greatest possible number of men; this object would be exceeded by the employment of arms which uselessly aggravate the sufferings of disabled men, or render their death inevitable; the employment of such arms would, therefore, be contrary to the *laws of humanity*.[42]

Although the reference to 'the laws of humanity' did not achieve any independent legal impact, it built in the law of a new general standard, which also supported the more specific principle of unnecessary suffering. The Declaration was the precursor of what is now known as the 'Hague Law' on the means and methods of warfare, which had its genesis in a conference convened in Brussels by Tsar Alexander II in 1874. On that occasion, Professor Lieber's *Instructions* was adopted as a preparatory text, but the conference did not ratify the text.[43] The Brussels conference, however, was the basis for l'Institut de Droit International's 1880 *Oxford Manual of the Laws of War on Land*.[44] The latter and the Lieber Code, although not legally binding, were highly influential on the Hague Regulations. During the second part of the nineteenth century, the law of war was mostly formed by soft law instruments, such as the Lieber Code or the Oxford Manual, and by national legal instruments.[45] It was essentially a part of military law, focusing on the means and methods of warfare and on the care of wounded, sick or shipwrecked military persons. As a result, the law had to be further developed to protect civilians and to expand the protection for prisoners of war (PoWs). For this reason, under a Christian influence towards mitigating the cruelties of war,[46] the initiatives of the tsars of Imperial Russia, Alexander II and later Nicolas II, led to an important change in this direction.

Basis' in D Fleck and M Bothe (eds), *The Handbook of International Humanitarian Law* (2nd ed, Oxford University Press 2008), 23.

42 Emphasis added.

43 Project of an International Declaration Concerning the Laws and Customs of War, Brussels, 27 August 1874 [hereinafter 'Brussels Project']; see D Schindler and J Toman, *The Laws of Armed Conflicts* (4th ed, Martinus Nijhoff 2004), 25.

44 The *Laws of War on Land*, Manual published by the Institute of International Law (Oxford Manual), Adopted by the Institute of International Law at Oxford, 9 September 1880.

45 G Balladore–Pallieri, *La Guerra* (Cedam 1935), 116. This approach can still be viewed in the 1899 Hague Convention II (on land warfare), Article 1.

46 See C Tocornal, *Nociones de Derecho Internacional* (Impr. litog. y encuadernación Barcelona 1902).

In particular, the proposals advanced during the 1874 conference in Brussels were used by the first Hague Conference, held in 1899 and convened by Tsar Nicolas II. The first Hague Conference concluded three main treaties and three additional declarations.[47] The second Hague Conference, in 1907, resulted in conventions little advanced from the 1899 Convention.[48] As it can be seen in the commentaries to the Conventions, in 1906/1907, in convoking a second Peace Conference, 'the Imperial Government had in view the necessity of giving fresh development to the humanitarian principles which formed the basis of the work of the great international meeting of 1899' and was pleased by 'how deep and widespread' was 'the wish to-day to give effect to ideas having as their *object the welfare of humanity*'.[49] During the 1899 and 1907 Conferences, the collected Powers 'not only ... learnt to understand one another and to draw closer together, but ... succeeded in the course of this

47 (I) Convention for the Pacific Settlement of International Disputes; (II) Convention with respect to the Laws and Customs of War on Land and its Annex: Regulations concerning the Laws and Customs of War on Land; (III) Convention for the Adaptation to Maritime Warfare of the Principles of the Geneva Convention of 22 August 1864; Declarations (i) concerning the Prohibition of the Discharge of Projectiles and Explosives from Balloons or by Other New Analogous Methods; (ii) concerning the Prohibition of the Use of Projectiles with the Sole Object to Spread Asphyxiating Poisonous Gases; (iii) concerning the Prohibition of the Use of Bullets which can Easily Expand or Change their Form inside the Human Body such as Bullets with a Hard Covering which does not Completely Cover the Core, or containing Indentations. The Hague Peace Conference of 1899, in its Final Act, expressed the importance of holding a special conference for the revision of the Geneva Convention of 1864. In 1906 this conference was organized and adopted the new Convention, which replaced the 1864 Convention in the relations between the States parties.

48 The 1907 Hague Conference concluded thirteen treaties, of which twelve were ratified and entered into force, and one declaration: (I) Convention for the Pacific Settlement of International Disputes; (II) Convention respecting the Limitation of the Employment of Force for Recovery of Contract Debts; (III) Convention relative to the Opening of Hostilities; (IV) Convention respecting the Laws and Customs of War on Land; (V) Convention relative to the Rights and Duties of Neutral Powers and Persons in case of War on Land; (VI) Convention relative to the Legal Position of Enemy Merchant Ships at the Start of Hostilities; (VII) Convention relative to the Conversion of Merchant Ships into War-ships; (VIII) Convention relative to the Laying of Automatic Submarine Contact Mines; (IX) Convention concerning Bombardment by Naval Forces in Time of War; (X) Convention for the Adaptation to Maritime Warfare of the Principles of the Geneva Convention (of 6 July 1906); (XI) Convention relative to Certain Restrictions with regard to the Exercise of the Right of Capture in Naval War; (XII) Convention relative to the Establishment of an International Prize Court; (XIII) Convention concerning the Rights and Duties of Neutral Powers in Naval War; (XIV) Declaration Prohibiting the Discharge of Projectiles and Explosives from Balloons.

49 M. Le Secrétaire d'Etat, in A Pearce Higgins, *The Hague Peace Conferences and Other International Conferences Concerning the Laws and Usages of War Texts of Conventions with Commentaries* (Cambridge University Press 1909), 53 (emphasis added).

long collaboration in evolving a *very lofty conception* of the common welfare of humanity'.[50]

Throughout this codification process, the Russian jurist Fyodor Fyodorovich de Martens had a prominent role in the unfolding of humanitarian law and was the author of what became known as the Martens Clause.[51] It marked an important achievement for the time. The clause was included in the preambles of the Hague Convention of 1899 (para. 9) and the 1907 Hague Convention (para. 8) and 'crystallized and summarized the nineteenth century development of the humanitarian law of war'.[52] The clause and the preambles read:

> Until a more complete code of the laws of war has been issued, the High Contracting Parties deem it expedient to declare that, in cases not included in the Regulations adopted by them, *the inhabitants and the belligerents remain under the protection and the rule of the principles of the law of nations, as they result from the usages established among civilized peoples, from the laws of humanity, and the dictates of the public conscience.*[53]

This extract well expresses the essence of the ideas that motivated the drafters of the codification of the laws of war and reflects 'with precision of language, the ideas of the positive jurists and of the essential nexus between military requirements, the dictates of humanity, the standards of civilization and the

50 *Ibid.*, 67 (emphasis added).

51 Martens used several names over his lifetime: Fedor Fedorovitsch, Frédéric, and Friedrich. See VV Poustogarov, *Au Service de la Paix: Frédéric de Martens et les Conférences Internationales de la Paix de 1899 et 1907* (University of Geneva 1999), 15; on the Martens clause, see ibid., 174–176; see also L Mälksoo, 'F.F. Martens and His Time: When Russia Was an Integral Part of the European Tradition of International Law' [2014] 25(3) *EJIL* 811–829.

52 Draper, *supra* n 34, 72.

53 Emphasis added. The 1907 English version was somewhat different: 'inhabitants' replaced 'populations', the older term 'law of nations' was substituted for 'international law,' and 'requirements' gave way to 'dictates.'; MN Hayashi, 'The Martens Clause and Military Necessity' in HM Hensel (ed.), *The Legitimate Use of Military Force, The Just War Tradition and the Customary Law of Armed Conflict* (Routledge 2008), 135 ff.; A Cassese, 'The Martens Clause: Half a Loaf or Simply Pie in the Sky?' (2000) 11 *EJIL* 187; VV Poustogarov, 'The Martens Clause in International Law' [1999] 1 *JHIL* 125–135; AR Ticehurst, 'The Martens Clause and the Laws of Armed Conflict' in N Sanajaoba (ed.), *A Manual of International Humanitarian Laws* (Regency 2004), 312 (see already in [1997] 37 IRRC 125); T Meron, 'On Custom and the Antecedents of the Martens Clause in Medieval and Renaissance Ordinances of War' in U Beyerlin (ed.), *Essays in Honour of R. Bernhardt* (Springer 1995), 173 ff.; S Miyazaki, 'The Martens Clause and International Humanitarian Law' in C Swinarski (ed.), *Essays on International Humanitarian Law and Red Cross Principles in Honour of Jean Pictet* (Martinus Nijhoff 1984), 433 ff.; see H Strebel, 'Martens Clause' R Bernhardt (ed.), *Encyclopaedia of Public International Law*, vol 3 (North Holland 1982), 326–7.

value of codification of international law'.[54] Of relevance is the declaration of Baron Marschall von Bieberstein, who, speaking at the 1907 Hague Conference about submarine mines, said 'Military operations are not governed solely by stipulations of international law' but also by '[c]onscience, good sense, and the sense of duty imposed by *the principles of humanity*' and by '*the unwritten law of humanity and civilization*'.[55]

The Martens Clause did not arise out of a philosophical or religious vacuum. It was the culmination of the religious and Christian beliefs of Dunant, Lieber and de Martens in the second half of the nineteenth century. For this reason, the year 1899 and the adoption of the preambles of the Hague Convention of 1899 and the 1907 Hague Convention are the first legal peak and crystallization of human dignity in international law. The need to regulate armed conflicts and guarantee protection for civilians sets the stage for the first entry point and crystallization of human dignity in an international legal sphere. The 1907 Hague Convention was a 'Western Europe exercise', and the concept of laws of humanity reflected 'the evolution of Western European Christian values as they emerged from the natural law doctrine of these Christian States',[56] the pre-Christian Greco-Roman doctrine of the fifth century BCE and the doctrine of Islamic civilizations.[57]

The development of the laws of war in Europe occurred in the nineteenth century, thanks to the circulation of ideas of progress, civilization and philanthropism.[58] In this context, it was commonly believed that the social phenomenon of 'war' would be overcome by limitations placed through humanitarian progress.[59] The laws of war were no longer, as noted by Kolb, questions of natural law, opposed to positive law of nations,[60] or of personal morals – which is, in Vattel's terms, the personal conscience before God.[61]

54 Draper, *supra* n 34, 73.

55 See Commission on the Responsibility of the Authors of the War and on Enforcement of Penalties, Report Presented to the Preliminary Peace Conference, 29 March 1919, reprinted in [1920] 14(1) *AJIL*, 95–154, footnote 65 (emphasis added).

56 MC Bassiouni, *Crimes against Humanity: Historical Evolution and Contemporary Application* (Cambridge University Press 2011), xxviii.

57 *Ibid*.

58 On the idea of civilization in the nineteenth century, see WG Grewe, *The Epochs of International Law* (De Gruyter 2000), 445 ff., with further references.

59 See Kolb, *supra* n 25, 34. On the progress of limitations on war, see J Guelle, *La guerre continentale et les personnes* (Librairie Militaire De J. Domaine 1881), 99 (in the context of reprisals); JS Risley, *The Law of War* (Innes 1897), 73. It was later still noted in Balladore-Pallieri, *supra* n 45, 113 ff.

60 This distinction has a prominent place in Grotius, *supra* n 13, Book III. See P Haggenmacher, *Grotius et la doctrine de la guerre juste* (Graduate Institute Publications 1983), 568 ff.

61 See, e.g., *Le droit des gens*, (1758) Book III, ch. VIII, 137.

They had to be rules established by the positive law of nations. This faith in progress had some corollaries,[62] one of which was that the laws of war applied only to 'civilized' states – not to colonial territories or in the 'barbarian' and 'savage' world.[63] The standard of civilization 'is not just a historical curiosity, but forms an important thread in the social, legal, and institutional fabric of contemporary international society'.[64] The laws of armed conflict were perceived as a specific Christian and occidental practice, benefiting only a small and closed group of States. The 1872 *Maria Luz* Affair is a well-known example of this conception. Japan, a 'non-Christian countr[y] of the East', in the words of de Martens, in the defence of human principles, refused to return Chinese indentured labourers, victims of irregular recruitment and inhumane treatment, who escaped from a Peruvian ship. Japan was seen as a 'civilized state' when the arbiter, Tsar Alexander II, with the assistance of his adviser de Martens, refused Peru's claim to extra territorial rights.[65] Whereas it is inferred that the concept of human dignity first entered the laws of war as part of the Christian value of humanity, because of the Christian belief of the founders of this legal framework, in a century of declared faith to a religion of progress and civilization, however, this implied a discriminatory approach and the application of the principle *ab origine*. It meant that in colonial territories or in the 'barbarian' and 'savage' world, there was no place for the laws of humanity, international law, and its core principles, among which State sovereignty could have been extended to countries with partial political recognition, that is, not fully considered participants to the 'family of nations',[66] only after 'completely

[62] J Lorimer, *The Institutes of the Law of Nations*, vol. I, (William Blackwood and Sons 1883), 101; see Kolb, *supra* n 25, 35.

[63] See J Guelle, *Precis Des Lois de La Guerre Sur Terre*, vol. I, (Pedone Lauriel 1884), 5–6.

[64] GW Gong, *The Standard of 'Civilization' in International Society* (Clarendon Press 1984), 93. For an analysis, see L Obregón Tarazona, 'The Civilized and the Uncivilized' in B Fassbender and A Peters (eds), *The Oxford Handbook of the History of International Law* (Oxford University Press 2012), 918–940; M Koskenniemi, *The Gentle Civilizer of Nations: The Rise and Fall of International Law 1870–1960* (Cambridge University Press 2002).

[65] See Foreign Department, Tokyo, Japan, *Case of the Peruvian Barque Maria Luz*, with Appendix (Yokohama: n.p., 1872); a copy is included in FO 84/1442: 220–6; see AM Stuyt, *Survey of International Arbitrations 1794–1938*, n. 68, n. 104 (Springer 1939); FF Martens, *Traité de droit international*, trans. Albert Leo, vol. 2 (Librairie Marescq ainé 1883–1887), 339f; D Howland, *International Law and Japanese Sovereignty* (Palgrave McMillan 2016), 37; 'The Maria Luz Incident: Personal Rights and International Justice for Chinese Coolies and Japanese Prostitutes' in SL Burns and BJ Brooks (eds), *Gender and Law in the Japanese Imperium* (University of Hawaii Press 2013), 21–47.

[66] PCW Chan, 'China's approaches to International Law since the Opium War' [2014] 27(4) *LJIL* 859–892, 868.

recasting all non-Western political entities into the mould of modern European states'.[67]

3.2.3 A 'Humanitarian' Age

Even if the edifice of the laws of war opened the doors to the first considerations of human dignity in international law, its limits became visible during the First World War. At this time, the relationship between respect for human dignity, humanitarian standards and the laws of war appeared inadequate for three reasons: first, the Geneva Sick and Wounded Convention of 1906 did not seem appropriate for the types and number of casualties in war; second, the rules on the treatment of PoWs were inadequate, given that during the course of the war, belligerents concluded agreements, such as the Berne Agreements of 1917 and 1918, to overcome gaps in the Hague Regulations;[68] third, poisonous gas was used for the first time in warfare by Germany, causing unnecessary suffering and breaching Article 23(e) of the Hague Regulations of 1907, shocking public opinion and signalling the beginning of chemical warfare.

Although the prevailing opinion was that a revision of the laws of war would threaten the confidence in the League of Nations and the new methods of preventing war, the three aforementioned issues soon found a legal answer. A diplomatic conference called by the Swiss Government concluded in 1929 the Convention for the Amelioration of the Condition of the Wounded and Sick in Armies in the Field, replacing the Conventions of 1864 and 1906, and the Third Geneva Convention, relative to the treatment of prisoners of war, which did not supersede the Hague Convention (IV) of 1907. Under the auspices of the League of Nations and with the support of the ICRC, two rudimentary Protocols on the prohibition of the use of poisonous gases (Geneva Protocol of 1925, No. 13) and on submarine warfare (London Protocol of 1936, No. 87) were adopted. Further attempts to regulate new problems in the interwar period, especially the protection of neutrals and non-combatants at sea in warfare[69] and air warfare,[70] were instead

[67] E Jouannet, 'Universalism and Imperialism: The True–False Paradox of International Law?'[2007] 18 *EJIL* 379, at 382. See G. Le Moli, "'Parity with all nations': The 'coolie' trade and the quest for recognition by China and Japan" [2021] 34 LJIL, forthcoming.

[68] J Pictet, et al., *The Geneva Conventions of 12 August 1949: Commentary*, vol. III, Third Geneva Convention relative to the treatment of prisoners of war (ICRC 1960), 5 (Pictet et al., *Commentary*, III).

[69] Treaty of Washington of 1922; LFL Oppenheim, *International Law. A Treatise*, vol. II, Disputes, War and Neutrality', H Lauterpacht (ed.) (7th ed., Longman 1952), 490 [Oppenheim, *International Law*]; Schindler and Toman, *supra* n 43, 877–879.

[70] Hague Draft Air Warfare Rules of 1923, which attempted to limit lawful bombardment to specific military objectives, Article 24 (2); see Oppenheim, *supra* n 69, 518–523; Schindler and Toman, *supra* n 43, 207–217.

abortive. Nevertheless, these efforts can be seen as part of an important endeavour to expand the laws of war.[71]

When the Second World War broke out, the law of armed conflicts could, however, not fully cope with the horrors of the war, which superseded those of the First World War. It exposed legal weaknesses, and the tide of inhumanity attained a level more appalling and outrageous than the world had ever had the misery to witness. This phase, out of necessity, pushed the law towards a new era. After the recoil from the inhumanity exposed in the war crimes trials at Nuremberg, Tokyo and in national jurisdictions, the 1948 Genocide Convention[72] was the first international humanitarian instrument adopted after the war. It signalled the beginning of a new historical phase centred on the concept of humanitarian protection of victims of war, with limits on the freedom of States.

The second substantial response came with the adoption of the Four Geneva Conventions.[73] At the core of the Conventions lay the need to consolidate, clarify and enhance the protection of human dignity in times of war: the laws of war became *international humanitarian law*.[74] To guarantee protection of all victims of (modern) war, it was necessary to abandon both the old concept of model provisions present in municipal legislation and the minimum-codification system adopted by the Hague Conferences. The adoption of the Geneva Conventions in 1949 represented the start of a 'humanitarian age',[75] materializing the first consolidation of human dignity in international law.[76]

[71] See Article 52, Additional Protocol I.

[72] Convention on the Prevention and Punishment of the Crime of Genocide, 9 December 1948, 78 UNTS 277 (Genocide Convention).

[73] See *supra* n 2.

[74] Kolb, *supra* n 25, 45.

[75] *Ibid.*

[76] On the Geneva Conventions of 1949, see JAC Gutteridge, 'The Geneva Conventions of 1949' [1949] 26 *BYIL* 294; F Siordet, 'La Conférence diplomatique de Genève' [1949] 31 *RICR* 475, 554; J Pictet, 'La Croix–Rouge et les Conventions de Genève' [1950] 76 *RCADI* 1; S Tschirkovitch, 'Les nouvelles Conventions internationales de Genève relatives à la protection des victimes de la guerre du 12 août 1949' [1950] 54 *RGDIP* 97, at 525; P De La Pradelle, *La Conférence diplomatique et les nouvelles Conventions de Genève du 12 août 1949* (Les éditions internationals 1951); GIAD Draper, *The Red Cross Conventions* (Stevens & Sons 1958); GIAD Draper, 'The Geneva Conventions of 1949' [1965] 114 *RCADI* 59; A Maresca, *La protezione internazionale dei combattenti e dei civili: Le Convenzioni di Ginevra del 12 agosto 1949* (Giuffrè 1965); T Meron, 'The Geneva Conventions as customary law' [1987] 81 *AJIL* 348; A Clapham, P Gaeta, and M Sassòli, *The 1949 Geneva Conventions. A Commentary* (Oxford University Press 2015). See also the commentaries to the Four Geneva Conventions edited by the ICRC in the 1950s: Pictet et al., *Commentary*, I; J Pictet et al., *The Geneva Conventions of*

To examine the meaning and construction of human dignity in the Geneva Conventions of 1949, their *travaux préparatoires* not only provide a deeper contextual texture and colour to the provisions ultimately agreed by States Parties, but also demonstrate that the principle of human dignity was perceived throughout the drafting process as a fundamental core of IHL and at the heart of the ICRC activity.[77] As noted in 1946, during the first debates, by the Belgian delegate Frick-Cramer, there was a strong need to reaffirm the protection of the dignity of human personality.[78] It was considered as the core of the right of the enemy to be treated with dignity[79] and the right of civilians to protection.[80] It was thus suggested that 'the new Convention should comprise a General Part, guaranteeing in all circumstances the essential rights of the individual, as well as *the respect of the human dignity of all persons* who, for any reason whatever, are in the hands of the enemy or of a Power whose authority they do not recognize'.[81] For this reason, it was believed that the ICRC embodied *'the principles of the worth and dignity of*

12 August 1949: Commentary, Vol. II, Geneva Convention for the Amelioration of the Condition of Wounded, Sick and Shipwrecked Members of Armed Forces at Sea (ICRC 1960) [Pictet et al., *Commentary*, II]; Pictet et al., *Commentary*, III; J Pictet et al., *The Geneva Conventions of 12 August 1949: Commentary*, Vol. IV, Geneva Convention relative to the Protection of Civilian Persons in Time of War (ICRC 1958) [Pictet et al., *Commentary*, IV]. For the Additional Protocols of 1977, see essentially Y Sandoz, C Swinarski and B Zimmermann (eds), *Commentary on the Additional Protocols of 8 June 1977 to the Geneva Conventions of 12 August 1949* (ICRC 1987).

77 To conduct this research, the analysis has been based on the 101 folders of the *travaux préparatoires* of the Four Geneva Conventions and Two Additional Protocols, ICRC library database, available online at https://library.icrc.org/library/Direct.aspx?searchfield=856u&searchterm=https://library.icrc.org/library/docs/CDDH%25 (accessed 30 May 2019).

78 Preliminary Conference of National Red Cross Societies for the Study of Conventions and Various Problems Relating to the Red Cross (Geneva, July 26 – August 3, 1946) [Preliminary Conference 1946]: Minutes: Vol. III: sessions of Commission II (Saturday July 27 to Thursday 1 August 1946): convention relating to the treatment of prisoners of war and convention relating to civilians, sessions I to III from Saturday 27 July 1946 to Monday 29 July 1946, 10, Madame Frick – Cramer, ICRC member, 10; *ibid.*, see also sessions VII to X from Wednesday, 31 July 1946 to Thursday, 1 August 1946, 203, A. Prisoners of War Convention, a) General questions, Introduction; see also Preliminary Conference of National Red Cross Societies for the Study of Conventions and Various Problems Relating to the Red Cross (Geneva, 26 July to 3 August 1946): Minutes: Vol. VII: plenary meeting of Saturday August 3, 1946: examination of the report of Commission II, closure, plenary meeting of Saturday 3 August 1946, 3–4.

79 Preliminary Conference 1946: Minutes: Vol. VII: plenary meeting of Saturday 3 August 1946: examination of the report of Commission II, closure, plenary meeting of Saturday 3 August 1946, 3–4.

80 Preliminary Conference 1946: documentation provided by the ICRC, Vol. IV: Specific Problems of the Red Cross, 25–26, 26.

81 Summary report on the work of the Preliminary Conference 1946, I.– Convention Relative to the Treatment of Prisoners of War, (A) General Questions, 1. Introduction, 12. This was also reaffirmed in 1947, see Commission of government experts for the study of Conventions for the

man'[82] and, according to Max Huber, it was 'not *primarily concerned* with the interests of any State, but *with the human individual, his physical safety and personal dignity, without regard to nationality or any affinity whatever*'.[83] The need to guarantee human dignity had to prevail over the interests of sovereign dignity.

Similarly, in 1947, it was discussed that 'the revised Convention should embody a Preamble confirming the fundamental rights of man and *ensuring respect of the dignity of the human person*'.[84] In particular, it was affirmed the importance of providing a protection to the dignity of *women*, who 'have the right to be treated with unconditional respect to their honour, decency *and dignity*, in all circumstances whatsoever'.[85] After 1947, the drafting process advanced with increasing reflections on the fundamental principle of human dignity.[86] In 1949, the ICRC submitted a proposal which set forth the main principle underlying all the humanitarian Conventions and could appear in the Preambles of all four Draft Conventions. Accordingly, if not for disagreement over minor changes to it, the Geneva Conventions would have included the following text in their Preambles:

protection of war victims (Geneva, 14 to 26 April 1947): preliminary documents submitted by the ICRC [Preliminary Documents Commission 1947], Vol. II: Geneva Convention of 27 July 1929, relative to the treatment of prisoners of war, Classification of Treaty Stipulations, 227; in 1948, see Summary of the proceedings of the sub-commissions of the Legal Commission [of the] XVII International Conference of the Red Cross, Stockholm, August 1948.

82 See *supra* n 80, Vol. IV, VIII, The Role of the International Committee and its financial resources, 25 (emphasis added).

83 Conference of Governmental Experts for the Study of Conventions Protecting Victims of War (Geneva, 14–26 April 1947) [Conference Governmental Experts 1947]: program, committee reports, document No. 3, Opening address by Max Huber, 9, para 8 (emphasis added).

84 Proceedings of the Meeting for the study of Treaty Stipulations relative to the spiritual and intellectual needs of prisoners of war and civilian internees (Geneva, 3 and 4 March 1947), Convention relative to Prisoners of War, Art. 2 and 4, 27 (emphasis added).

85 Emphasis added. See also Conference Governmental Experts 1947, Chapter III, Protection of Women, 47; Report on the work of the Conference of Governmental Experts for the Study of Conventions Protecting Victims of War (Geneva, 14–26 April 1947), Report of the Third Committee, 301, 317, in section 4, 317; Joint Commission responsible for examining the texts of the draft Conventions to be submitted to the XVIIth International Conference of the Red Cross (Geneva, 15-16 September 1947): minutes of meetings 3 and 4, 4th Meeting, September 16 at 3 p.m., 128. This concern was also raised a few months earlier by M.M. Maier, see Conference Governmental Experts 1947: IV: minutes of Commission III: condition and protection of civilians in time of war, sessions VII to X from 17 April 1947 to 23 April 1947, M. Maier (rapporteur).

86 XVIIth International Conference of the Red Cross, Stockholm, August 1948: documents B.III, Resolution, 1, 2 (ICRC).

> *Respect for the personality and dignity of human beings constitutes a universal principle* which is binding even in the absence of any contractual undertaking.
>
> Such a principle demands that, in time of war, all those not actively engaged in the hostilities and all those placed hors de combat by reason of sickness, wounds, capture, or any other circumstance, shall be given due respect and have protection from the effects of war, and that those among them who are in suffering shall be succoured and tended without distinction of race, nationality, religious belief, political opinion or any other quality.
>
> The High Contracting Parties solemnly *affirm their intention to adhere to this principle*. They will ensure its application, by the terms of the present Convention, to the wounded and sick of armed forces in the field, and pledge themselves to respect, and at all times to ensure respect for, the said Convention.[87]

Thus, it was considered that 'respect for the person and the dignity of human beings *constitutes a universal principle* which is binding even without a contract'.[88] Human dignity was seen as the source of '*guarantees*'[89] and as part of the '*principes généraux du droit des gens*'.[90] Interestingly, the Irish delegate, Mr Cashman, referred to the Christian roots of the principle of human dignity, in support of the proposal by the Holy See that the Preamble had to expressly recognize the dignity and rights of man derived from God. In his words, '*the essential dignity of man, which is the basis on which this Convention rests, derives from his divine origin and destiny*'.[91] Mr Clattenburg (USA) expressed similar support.[92] Mr Nassif, delegate for

87 Emphasis added. Revised and new Draft Conventions for the protection of war victims: remarks and proposals submitted by the ICRC: document for the consideration of governments invited by the Swiss Federal Council to attend the Diplomatic Conference at Geneva (21 April 1949), 8. See also, in the same document: (i) 26, Revision of the Tenth Hague Convention of October 18, 1907, for the Adaptation to Maritime Warfare of the Principles of the Geneva a Convention of 1906, Preamble; (ii) 36, Revision of the Convention signed at Geneva on July 27, 1929, Relative to the Treatment of Prisoners of War, Preamble.

88 Diplomatic Conference of Geneva (21 April to 12 August 1949: Geneva) [Diplomatic Conference 1949], stenograms of Commission I, volume II, 24th meeting of May 31, 1949 at 10 a.m., 13 (see also 5); see also stenograms of Commission II, volume II, 19th meeting of June 14, 1949 at 3.15 pm, M. Vilhelm (ICRC), 55; see also stenograms of Commission I, volume III, 35th meeting of July 1, 1949 at 10 a.m., 42, 48.

89 Diplomatic Conference 1949, stenograms of Commission I, Volume III, 30th meeting of 21 June 1949 at 10 a.m., President, 2 (emphasis added).

90 Diplomatic Conference 1949, stenograms of Commission II, Volume I, 9th meeting of 5 May 1949 at 3.15 p.m., Baistrocchi (Italy), 29.

91 Diplomatic Conference 1949, stenograms of Commission III, Volume II, 23rd meeting of 25 May 1949 at 3 p.m., W. M. Cashman (Ireland), 55 (emphasis added).

92 Diplomatic Conference 1949, stenograms of Commission III, Volume II, 24th meeting of 27 May 1949 at 3 p.m., Mr. Clattenburg (U.S.A.), 9.

Lebanon, noted the importance of the UDHR and of including in the text of the Conventions an express reference to the principle of human dignity, a higher standard.[93] Delegates frequently also emphasized the need to guarantee the protection of women's dignity.[94]

There was a common urgency to adopt international conventions capable of providing a system of protection for human dignity in times of conflict.[95] It is therefore quite logical that, throughout the *travaux préparatoires*, delegates condemned acts 'contrary'[96] to human dignity, which could 'diminish'[97] or 'affect'[98] its full expression. We see, throughout the debates just reported, a *humanitarian shift* of the law, from a State-centric system to a set of provisions through which individuals – be they military or civilian – could enjoy a certain level of protection. Overall, the strength of this shift favoured a reconnection of the laws of war with the dictum of the Martens Clause and with the convictions of its drafters. IHL of this time is therefore coloured with 'humanitarianism'[99] and fully consolidates human dignity in its frame.

93 *Ibid.*, Mr. Nassif (Lebanon), 15.

94 Diplomatic Conference 1949, stenograms of Commission III, volume I, 10th meeting of 6 May 1949 at 3 p.m., delegate M. Maresca (Italy), 8; see also Draft of the 4 Geneva Conventions of 1949 and proposals and comments from Governments, Document no. 4: Draft Convention for the Protection of Civilian Persons in Time of War, Article 27, 15.

95 See also Mgr. Comte (Holy See), Diplomatic Conference 1949, stenograms of Commission II, volume II, 20th meeting of 16 June 1949 at 10am, 3; Mr Bammatte, the delegate from Afghanistan, Diplomatic Conference 1949, stenograms of Commission I, volume III, 35th meeting of 1 July 1949 at 10am, 33 (see also 29–30).

96 See Conference Governmental Experts 1947, program, committee reports, see (i) Report on the work of Commission III, 7, Part III, civilian population of a territory occupied by belligerent, Article 25; (ii) Documents presented by France, 5, Title II, Protection of civilians who are in the territory occupied by a belligerant, Article 21.

97 See Conference Governmental Experts 1947, Vol. III, volumes 1 and 2: minutes of Commission II: revision of the 1929 Convention relative to the treatment of prisoners of war, sessions I to V from 14 April 1947 to 16 April 1947, in session April 16, 1947 from 2 p.m. 50 to 5 p.m. 05, Col. R. Devyver (Belgium), 111.

98 *Ibid.*, sessions IX to X from 18 April 1947 to 19 April 1947, Brig. Gen. BM Bryan (U.S.A.), 256.

99 On these evolutions, see R Kolb, 'Aspects historiques de la relation entre le droit international humanitaire et les droits de l'homme' [1999] 37 *CYIL* 57; R Kolb, 'Human Rights and Humanitarian Law' [2008] 37 *CYIL* 57–97; See also L Doswald–Beck and S Vité, 'International Humanitarian Law and Human Rights Law' [1993] 293 *IRRC* 94; HP Gasser, 'International Humanitarian Law and Human Rights Law in Non–International Armed Conflict: Joint Venture or Mutual Exclusion?' [2002] 45 *GYIL* 149; R Provost, *International Human Rights and Humanitarian Law* (Cambridge University Press 2002); FF Martin, SJ Schnably, R Wilson, J. Simon and M Tushnet, *International Human Rights and Humanitarian Law: Treaties, Cases and Analysis* (Cambridge University Press 2006); R Arnold and N Quénivet (eds), *International Humanitarian Law and Human Rights Law: Towards a New Merger in International Law* (Martinus Nijhoff 2008).

However, a growing discrepancy between the revised Geneva Conventions and the Hague Conventions of 1899 and 1907, which had remained unchanged, was evident. It was only in the mid-1960s that various factors played a role in promoting further legal endeavours towards a closer respect for humanitarian rules and respect for human dignity.[100] Contemporary developments in IHRL provided support to changes in the laws of war. The International Conference on Human Rights in Teheran, convened by the United Nations (UN) and the UN General Assembly (GA) in 1968, adopted resolutions under the title 'Respect for human rights in armed conflicts', linking the development of the law of war with the international protection of human rights. This close affinity had an important impact on the edifice of humanitarian law, in particular with the adoption of the two Protocols, adopted in 1977, in addition to the Geneva Conventions of 1949. In 1980, the two Additional Protocols were supplemented by the UN Convention on prohibitions or restrictions on the use of certain conventional weapons.[101] With the end of the Cold War, IHL became increasingly 'humanized', less State-centred and more 'humankind-centred'.[102]

3.3 SECOND CONSTITUTIVE STAGE: THE SECULARIZATION OF HUMAN DIGNITY AS A NORM

3.3.1 *Overview*

The Great War in Europe led to a breakdown of many of the codified rules of war and an unprecedented catastrophe for the destruction it caused.[103] The laws of war developed during the first constitutive stage became a victim of the evolution of a system where sovereignty prevailed over the Martens Clause.[104] At a time when only State sovereignty and independence mattered in international relations, regardless of the dictates of the Martens Clause and

100 Draper, *supra* n 34, 82.

101 Convention on Prohibitions or Restrictions on the Use of Certain Conventional Weapons Which May be Deemed to be Excessively Injurious or to Have Indiscriminate Effects (and Protocols) (as Amended on 21 December 2001), 10 October 1980, 1342 UNTS 137. In 1976, the UN GA had already adopted a Convention on the prohibition of military or any hostile use of environmental modification techniques, Convention on the Prohibition of Military or any Hostile Use of Environmental Modification Techniques, 10 December 1976, A/Res./31/72.

102 According to Kolb, this stage runs from 1993 until today, see *supra* n 25.

103 A Becker, *Les cicatrices rouges, 14–18: France et Belgique occupées* (Fayard 2010).

104 See Kolb, *supra* n 25, 40–45.

considerations of humanity,[105] the law of the interwar period was also affected.[106] The dominant principle was State freedom.[107]

Moreover, during the First World War, the general anti-colonialist conscience became particularly active in demonstrating that the preservation and protection of peace and peoples' right to development were increasingly incompatible with the maintenance of colonial regimes.[108] On 8 January 1918, when addressing the US Congress, President Wilson presented his Fourteen Points, principles for peace, outlining his proposals for an end to war peace settlement that would 'vindicate the principles of peace and justice in the life of the world', not merely produce 'a new balance of power'.[109] Wilson's Fourteen Points became the foundation for the Versailles peace treaty in 1919, establishing the League of Nations.

Starting from 1919, we can trace a second constitutive stage of human dignity. From a religious conception, human dignity here evolves and emerges from this stage as a secular and individual conception, as a foundational principle of the international human rights legal system and as a human right of all human beings. This evolution runs from 1919 until 1966 and can be divided into three phases. In the aftermath of the First World War, the League of Nations and intellectual debates placed the individual at the centre of the international agenda. Human dignity here began its integration in a secularization process. Only by the 1940s, and mostly after the Second World War, human dignity was fully recognized as a fundamental attribution of the human person in the preambles of founding instruments of two international organizations, the UN,[110] here still in its religious sense, and the UN Educational, Scientific and Cultural Organization (UNESCO).[111] Whereas

105 See B Simma, 'From Bilateralism to Community Interest' [1994] 250 *RCADI*, 229.

106 Article 5(1) of the Covenant of the League of Nations, 28 April 1919, which establishes unanimity as the general voting modality (the rule of liberum veto was meant to guarantee States' equality).

107 Some authors affirmed that the law of armed conflict was based on a simple 'de facto freedom' to engage in specific acts of violence, see Balladore-Pallieri, *supra* n 45, 163–4.

108 Q Wright, *Mandates under the League of Nations* (UCP 1930); HD Hall, *Mandates Dependencies and Trusteeship* (Carnegie Endowment for International Peace 1948); CL Upthegrove, *Empire by Mandate* (Bookman Associates 1954); A Anghie, 'Colonialism and the Birth of International Institutions: Sovereignty, Economy, and the Mandate System of the League of Nations' [2001] 34 *NYUJIL&P* 513 ff.

109 A month later, on 11 February 1918, in a speech before Congress, President Wilson generally defined the Four Principles of any final peace settlement. President Wilson's Four Principles, 11 February 1918. See also A Millot, *Les Mandats internationaux*, (Émile Larose, Libraire-Editeur 1924), 36. See 'Remarks about Giuseppe Mazzini' and 'Further Remarks in Genoa' by Woodrow Wilson, in *The World Court*, Vol. 5, International Peace Forum, 1919, 28.

110 Charter of the United Nations, 24 October 1945, 1 UNTS XVI (UN Charter).

111 UNESCO Constitution, 16 November 1945, 3 Bevans 1311.

they established the duty to respect human dignity, further steps of a legislative character were still necessary to fully recognize and protect human dignity as an attribution of all human beings. The crystallization of human dignity in this second constitutive stage occurs when human dignity finds for the first time a clear expression as a fundamental principle, as an individual right and a source of other individual rights in the UDHR. Human dignity as secular and universal concept, in its individual dimension, fully consolidates in the human rights framework of the 1960s, and, more specifically, with the adoption of the Two Covenants. The consolidation corresponds to the expansion of the scope of universality to include also the collective dimensions of human dignity. The chronology of this second constitutive stage, followed in this section, is summarized in Figure 3.3.

Whereas, from the perspective of human dignity, the 1960s represent the decade of its consolidation in international human rights law, one may say otherwise for the history of human rights law. From such a distinct perspective, the scholarly literature has primarily focused on the 1940s[112] as well as on the 1970s.[113] The history of the 1960s has also been addressed by a few authors,[114] some also focusing on the link between human rights and

112 See, for instance, PG Lauren, 'First Principles of Racial Equality: History and the Politics and Diplomacy of Human Rights Provisions in the UN Charter' [1983] 5(1) *HRQ* 1–26; PG Lauren, *The Evolution of International Human Rights: Visions Seen* (University of Pennsylvania Press 1998); J Morsink, *The Universal Declaration of Human Rights: Origins, Drafting and Intent* (University of Pennsylvania Press 1999); G Alfredsson and A Eide, *The Universal Declaration of Human Rights. A Common Standard of Achievement* (Martinus Nijhoff 1999); MA Glendon, *A World Made New. Eleanor Roosevelt and the International Human Rights: Visions Seen* (Random House 2002).

113 R Afshari, 'On Historiography of Human Rights Reflections on Paul Gordon Lauren's the Evolution of the International Human Rights: Visions Seen' [2007] 29(1) *HRQ Human Rights Quarterly* 1–67; SL Hoffmann, Introduction: Genealogies of Human Rights' in SL Hoffmann (ed.), *Human Rights in the 20th Century* (Cambridge University Press 2011), 1–26; P Alston, 'Does the Past Matter? On the Origins of Human Rights' [2013] 126(7) *HLR* 2043–2081; S Moyn, *The Last Utopia: Human Rights in History* (Harvard University Press 2010); A Iriye, P Goedde and WI Hitchcock (eds), *The Human Rights Revolution* (Oxford University Press 2012); B Keys, *Reclaiming American Virtue, The Human Rights Revolution of the 1970s* (Cambridge University Press 2014).

114 R Burke, *Decolonization and the Evolution of International Human Rights* (University of Pennsylvania Press 2010); DJ Whelan, *Indivisible Human Rights. A History* (University of Pennsylvania Press 2010); SLB Jensen, *The Making of International Human Rights: The 1960s, Decolonization, and the Reconstruction of Global Values* (Cambridge University Press 2016); J Eckel, *Die Ambivalenz des Guten. Menschenrechte in der internationalen Politik seit den 1940ern* (Vandenhoeck & Ruprecht 2014).

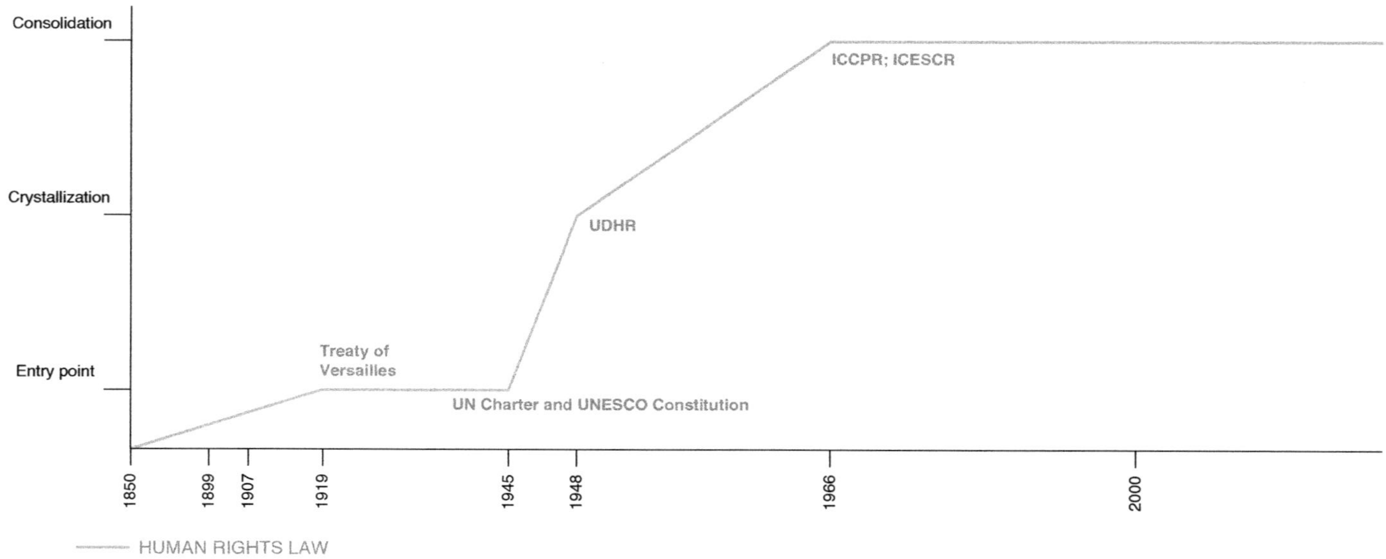

FIGURE 3.3 *Second constitutive stage*

decolonization.[115] From the point of view of human dignity, the 1960s negotiations of binding human rights treaties were fundamental to its consolidation. Moreover, if it is true that until the early 1960s the UDHR carried little weight in international politics, at the domestic level it was a significant source of inspiration for the drafting of constitutions in emerging States.[116] The story seen from the perspective of dignity begets a specific historical context, with a peculiar set of subjects, causalities, factors and trajectories. This approach also links these three periods (1940s, 1960s and 1970s) in a new way. From 1948, it took 18 years to complete the text of the Two Covenants. Between 1948 and 1966, human dignity sometimes made an appearance, while other times it acted as a 'shadow' human dignity or silently. It evolved through various steps of diplomatic negotiations and political debates, and in 1966 its universal nature was reshaped by the larger historical processes, thereby acquiring a collective guise. This evolution will be discussed next.

3.3.2 *The Transformation of Human Dignity in the Inter-war Period*

Distancing itself from the previous faith in civilization as a concept placed at the service of State sovereignty, the Preamble of the first draft of the Covenant of the League of Nations, written by Colonel House, Wilson's chief adviser, and carefully edited by the president, read: '*International civilisation proved a failure because there has not been a fabric of law* to which nations have yielded with the same obedience and deference as individuals submit to intra national laws.'[117] In 1933, House's 1919 Preamble was still cited as evidence that

[115] Rejecting the idea that human rights were central to the anti-colonial struggles, see Moyn, *supra* n 113, 84–119; S Moyn, 'Imperialism, Self-Determination, and the Rise of Human Rights' in A Iriye, P Goedde and WI Hitchcock (eds), *The Human Rights Revolution* (Oxford University Press 2012), 158–178; J Eckel, 'Human Rights and Decolonization: New Perspectives and Open Questions' [2010] 1 *Humanity:IJHR*, Fall, 111–135. Dissimilarly, Fabian Klose has emphasized the history of human rights and anti-colonial movements in the 1950s, see F Klose, *Human Rights in the Shadow of Colonial Violence. The Wars of Independence in Kenya and Algeria* (University of Pennsylvania Press 2013); see also B Simpson, 'Self-Determination, Human Rights and the End of Empire in the 1970s' [2013] 4(2) *Humanity: IJHR* 239–260.

[116] On the application of the Declaration in African countries, see E Schwelb, *Human Rights and the International Community. The Roots and Growth of the Universal Declaration of Human Rights, 1948–1963* (Quadrangle Books 1964), 51; see also CO Parkinson, *Bills of Rights and Decolonization. The Emergence of Domestic Human Rights Instruments in Britain's Overseas Territories* (Oxford University Press 2008).

[117] League of Nations Covenant (First Draft), in RS Baker, *Woodrow Wilson and the World Settlement* (Doubleday, Page 1922), 82 (emphasis added).

even if 'there is no mention of religion or the Church in the Preamble' of the Covenant of the League of Nations (the Covenant),[118] a quasi-religious 'moral consciousness' was one of its central inspirations.[119] The League of Nations was a realization of ideas already advanced by Vitoria and Grotius on a joint community of purpose, inspiring the coexistence of nations in a framework of law. As I will now examine in more detail, the concept of human dignity entered into the law through various legal elaborations and institutions established, or favoured, by the League of Nations and by the personal commitment of scholars, diplomats and humanitarian workers. During the interwar period, human dignity first permeated the law in a religious sense and slowly evolved into a secular and individual attribution. This transformation and transition can be traced throughout three distinct developments: the adoption of mandates systems and of minority treaties; the institutional answer to the refugee question; and, lastly, in the adoption of the ILO Constitution.

The League of Nations elaborated a so-called Mandate System to govern non-self-governing entities and to supervise powers performing colonial and post-colonial administration in such territories.[120] The system, developed and eventually established by the Covenant, was a compromise to meet a political dilemma. In order to, inter alia, prevent destabilization of the territories that were liberated from German and Ottoman colonial authority but considered to be not yet capable of self-government, the victorious powers established a type of condominium over most of these former colonies. Article 22(1) of the Covenant of the League of Nations referred to 'the principle that the well-being and development of such peoples form *a sacred trust of civilisation*'. On this basis, one view considered the mandate system as an '*oeuvre de civilization*',[121] dedicated to the promotion of the well-being and development of the peoples concerned and fortified by safeguards for the protection of their rights.[122] The other view, instead, regarded it as a mere instrument of imperial power,[123] perpetrating the

[118] Covenant of the League of Nations, 28 April 1919.

[119] See N Bentwich, *The Religious Foundations of Internationalism* (Allen & Unwin 1933), 246.

[120] In his publication '*The League of Nations. A Practical Suggestion*', the South-African General JC Smuts made its first proposal of this system, which became known as the 'Smuts Plan', reprinted in: DH Miller, *The Drafting of the Covenant*, vol. 2 (G.P. Putnam's Sons 1928), 23ff.

[121] Président du Conseil italien, M. Vittorio-Emanuele Orlando (intervention du 28 janvier 1919 à la Conférence de la paix à Paris), in *La prassi italiana di diritto internazionale. Terza serie* (1919–1925) (vol. IV, Rome, 1995), 2317.

[122] *South West Africa Cases*, Second Phase, [1966] ICJ Reports 1966, 6 [*South West Africa Cases*, Second Phase] Diss. Opinion Judge Tanaka, 268; *Legal Consequences for States of the Continued Presence of South Africa in Namibia*, ICJ Advisory Opinion, (1971) ICJ Reports 1971, 16, Separate Opinion Judge De Castro, 202.

[123] F Ermacora, 'Mandates' in R Wolfrum (ed.), *United Nations: Law, Policies and Practice* (Springer 1995), 871 ff. (871).

practice of foreign rule over the former colonies based upon an assessment of capability and civilization according to the leading States' perspectives.[124] These two interpretations of the same system most precisely reflect the compromise-like character of the system. The second view seems to find support in the terminology adopted, which once again recalls the nineteenth-century typical distinction between 'civilized' and 'uncivilized' societies. Despite its careful wording, the idea behind the establishment of different types of mandate was clearly based upon allegations that some peoples were not civilized enough to be able to govern themselves on a short-term or even medium-term basis.[125] This idea only changed when, after the creation of the UN and the establishment of the principle of self-determination, what was formerly called a 'sacred trust' was equated with speedy development of structures for self-government.[126]

At the Paris Peace Conference of 1919, France, Great Britain and the United States were behind not only territorial and economic changes in Eastern Europe but also history's first minority treaties.[127] The protection of religious and minority rights was an object of international consideration following the Peace of Westphalia.[128] In 1919, the Supreme Council established the Committee on New States and for the Protection of Minorities. All the new successor States were compelled to sign minority rights treaties as a precondition of diplomatic recognition. To preserve international peace, and 'to a lesser extent, to protect the legitimate interests of members of national minorities',[129] the Peace Conference insisted that the defeated or newly reconfigured States accept a set of obligations drafted to protect

124 TM Franck, *The Power of Legitimacy among Nations* (Oxford University Press 1990), 160.

125 N Matz, 'Civilization and the Mandate System under the League of Nations', [2005] 9(1) UNYB 47, 71.

126 Franck, *supra* n 124, 160.

127 See C Fink, 'The Minorities Question at the Paris Peace Conference' in MF Boemeke, GD Feldman and E Gläser (eds), *The Treaty of Versailles: A Reassessment After 75 Years* (Cambridge University Press 1998), 249–76 and P Thornberry, *International Law and Minorities* (Clarendon Press 1993). On the central question of the rights of minority groups, see C Fink, *Defending the Rights of Others: The Great Powers, The Jews, and International Minority Protection, 1878–1938* (Cambridge University Press 2004); for a synthesis of this history of international relations, see Z Steiner, *The Lights that Failed: European International History, 1919–1933* (Oxford University Press 2005).

128 C Fink, 'Minority Rights as an International Question' [2000] 9(3) *ContempEurHist* 385, 385. See Treaty between Great Britain, Germany, Austria, France, Italy, Russia, and Turkey for the Settlement of Affairs in the East, Berlin, 13 July 1878, 153 CTS 171 (Treaty of Berlin), Arts 5, 27, 35, 44 at 176 (Bulgaria), 182 (Montenegro), 184 (Serbia), 187 (Romania).

129 D Wippman, 'The Evolution and Implementation of Minority Rights' [1997] 66 *FLR* 597, 600.

the interests of minorities' members.[130] The resulting Minorities Treaties included provisions mandating non-discrimination and equal treatment under the law, and protections designed to ensure factual equality for individuals of minority groups. This was to be accomplished through provisions mandating positive steps to enable minorities to maintain the cultural, linguistic, religious and other differences that distinguished them from the rest of the State's population. Thus, with some exceptions, the Minorities Treaties did not formally establish collective rights; instead, they offered protections to members of minorities as *individuals*.[131] Nonetheless, special measures designed to enhance the ability of minorities to enjoy group-specific interests, including language, religion and culture, had the practical effect of advancing the interests of minorities as *collectivities*.[132] Even within its modest scope, the League's system was, however, undoubtedly deficient.[133] The minorities and their defenders pleaded for more publicity, direct access to the League and a permanent minorities commission.[134] The organization tried to balance three irreconcilable interests, those of the minority states, of the minorities and, lastly, those of the international community, and the first invariably prevailed. As George Scelle aptly put it, the system for protecting minority groups was a 'kind of transition law',[135] considered as a 'transition between the old practice of intervention and the inter-State procedure of guaranteeing freedoms' and 'a transition between forced allegiance to the State and the right of people to exercise self-determination'.[136] Although the problems were still enormous and the public and the minorities expected the League to act energetically on their behalf, the League of Nations' protection regime set some elements of individual and collective rights and

[130] A Walworth, *Wilson and His Peacemakers* (Norton 1986), 468–484; A Sharp, 'Britain and the Protection of Minorities at the Paris Peace Conference, 1919' in AC Hepburn (ed.), *Minorities and History* (Edward Arnold 1978), 170–188.

[131] F Capotorti, 'Study of the Rights of Persons Belonging to Ethnic, Religious and Linguistic Minorities, Sub-Commission on Prevention of Discrimination and Protection of Minorities', U.N. ESCOR, 30th Sess., EJCN.41Sub. 2/3841 REV. 1 (1979), para 101. See, e.g., Advisory Opinion, *Minority Schools in Albania*, 1935 P.C.I.J. (ser. A/B) No. 62, at 17; Fink, *supra* n 128, 389.

[132] Minorites were at times recognized the *right of petition*, see Capotorti, *supra* n 131, para 100.

[133] N Lerner, 'The Evolution of Minority Rights in International Law' in C Brölmann, R Lefeber and M Zieck (eds), *Peoples and Minorities in International Law* (Martinus Nijhoff 1993), 82–86.

[134] See, The League and the Minorities Treaties, *Bulletin of International News*, Vol. 5, No. 18 (16 March 1929), 3–10 (Royal Institute of International Affairs), 439–440.

[135] For example, in his *Précis de droit des gens* (Sirey 1932), 252.

[136] *Ibid.*

dignity of peoples recognized as having a distinct identity for their racial and religious peculiarities, traditions and national characteristics.

In addition, in 1921, the League of Nations established the High Commission for Russian Refugees, which started to work on both the humanitarian and legal levels of the refugee question.[137] For four long years, from 1914 to 1918, the war had left many displaced populations, forced to flee their lands on both the Western and Eastern fronts.[138] From 1918 to 1922, the numbers of refugees kept increasing in Europe,[139] because of the war or religious persecution.[140] In this time, Western countries focused on themselves in response to the crises in a process that created, in the words of Gérard Noiriel, 'a tyranny of the national',[141] setting institutional and ideological frontiers between nationals and others. Many countries adopted the practice of collectively stripping people of their citizenship on the basis of their class, race, ethnicity, political allegiances or religion.[142] In the early 1920s, around three million people were recognized as 'stateless'.[143] This figure became an emblem of the modern human condition, with humankind in the grip of States,[144] and a new focus for legal scholars who examined the concept of national sovereignty.[145]

137 C Gousseff, *L'exil Russe. La Fabrique de réfugié apatride 1920–1928* (CNRS Editions 2011), 218.

138 See on the topic, P Gatrell, *A Whole Empire Walking: Refugees in Russia during World War I* (Indiana University Press 1999); VG Liulevicius, *War Land on the Eastern Front: Culture, National Identity, and German Occupation in World War I* (Cambridge University Press 2000); N Baron and P Gatrell, (eds), *Homelands: War, Population, and Statehood in Eastern Europe and Russia, 1918–1924* (Anthem Press 2004); P Nivet, *La France occupée, 1914–1918* (Armand Colin 2011).

139 See on the topic, A Zolberg, 'The Formation of New States as a Refugee-Generating Process' [1983] 467 (1) AAPSS 24–38; M Marrus, *The Unwanted: European Refugees in the Twentieth Century* (Oxford University Press 1985), 51–121; CM Skran, *Refugees in Inter-War Europe: The Emergence of a Regime* (Clarendon Press 1995), 13–61.

140 DA Harvey, 'Lost Children or Enemy Aliens? Classifying the Population of Alsace After the First World War' [1999] 34 *JCH* 537–554; T Zahra 'The Minority Problem: National Classification in the French and Czechoslovak Borderlands' [2008] 17 *CEH* 137–165.

141 G Noiriel, *La tyrannie du national: le droit d'asile en Europe (1793–1993)* (Calmann-Lévy 1991).

142 E Audinet, 'Le retrait des naturalisations accordées aux anciens sujets de puissances en guerre avec la France' [1915] 42 *JDI* 129–140; P Weil, *Qu'est-ce qu'un Français? Histoire de la nationalité française depuis la Révolution* (Grasset 2002), 118, transl. by Catherine Porter as *How to Be French: Nationality in the Making Since 1789* (Duke University Press 2008), 108; see also J Schefgel, *L'Apatridie des réfugiés russes* (Éditions Godde 1934).

143 D Kévonian, *Réfugiés et diplomatie humanitaire* (Publications de la Sorbonne, 2004), 230.

144 For example, see the novel by B Traven, *Das Totenschiff* [The Death Ship] (Büchergilde Gutenberg 1926).

145 Many legal academics studied the issue of refugees' rights in this period. See, for instance, N Vindry, *L'Apatridie (absence de nationalité)* (Vadon 1925); V Sukiennicki, *Essai sur la*

In June 1921, the Norwegian Fridtjof Nansen was appointed the League of Nations' High Commissioner for Russian Refugees. The document that carries his name, the Nansen Certificate, created in 1922, also commonly called the Nansen Passport, made it possible for stateless people to move and settle abroad.[146] For the first time, refugees without protection from their country of origin were considered under the patronage of the League of Nations and the High Commission for Refugees.[147] In 1930, the League of Nations established the Nansen International Office for Refugees, a semi-autonomous body under the League's authority, which secured the agreement of 14 countries[148] to the Refugee Convention of 1933. In October 1933, the League established a High Commission for Refugees Coming from Germany, which was dissolved in 1938 when the League of Nations opened the Office of the High Commissioner for Refugees. During this time, when the concept of political refugees was increasingly remembered,[149] the 'individual' started to be factored into discussions related to refugees.[150] This evolution of refugees' legal status took place, for Égidio Réale, through a recognition of the League of Nations' 'moral protection'.[151] This protection would replace the protection by sovereign States, which, by then, had already been called into question.

Moreover, as the flow of people from agriculture to industry accelerated, the twentieth-century world also witnessed a change in the character of work. Workers organized and demanded dialogue, opportunity, decent incomes and dignity. In 1919, the Treaty of Versailles referred to another important institutional and legal milestone to be developed.[152] The ILO's first constitution was prepared by the Commission on International Labour Legislation to the

souveraineté des États en droit international moderne (Pédone 1926); A Colanéri, *La condition des 'Sans-patrie': Étude critique de l'Heimatlosen* (Librairie générale de droit et de jurisprudence 1932); Scelle, *supra* n 135; M Vichniac, 'Le statut international des apatrides' [1933] 43 *RCADI* 119–245.

146 It was not until Article 2, Convention Relating to the Status of Refugees, 28 July 1951, UNTS vol. 189, 137 (Refugee Convention), that the right of return would be recognized as an integral part of the Nansen Passport.

147 The Nansen Passport was, however, restricted in its use, see B Cabanes, *The Great War and the Origins of Humanitarianism, 1918–1924* (Cambridge University Press 2014), 180.

148 RJ Beck, 'Britain and the 1933 Refugee Convention: National or State Sovereignty?' [1999] 11 (4) *IJRL* 597–624.

149 See, for instance, the 'Political Refugee Certificate', which allowed for the holder to obtain a residency visa, see D Kévonian, 'Question des réfugiés, droits de l'homme: éléments d'une convergence pendant l'entre-deux-guerres' [2003] 72 *Matériaux pour l'histoire de notre temps* 40–49.

150 Skran, *supra* n 139, 113–116, 194–223; see also Cabanes, *supra* n 147, 187.

151 É Réale, *Le régime des passeports et la Société des Nations* (Rousseau 1930).

152 Treaty of Versailles, Articles 387 to 427.

Peace Conference in 1919.[153] Albert Thomas was appointed as the ILO's first director and was known to be one of the most influential figures of the labour reform movement that followed the Great War.[154] The ILO was a child of the war; it embodied the aspirations born out of the war years and people's faith in the importance of social dialogue[155] and was built on the belief that peace and justice could go hand in hand.[156] Thus, this was the first attempt to construct a universal organization to address the social and economic problems facing the early twentieth-century world. The starting point of all human activity was *man* himself'.[157] Man, that is to say, his activities and the conditions of his intellectual and moral development. 'The worker must emancipate himself in order to become fully a man', explained Albert Thomas.[158] Moreover, the ILO's Constitution laid out the rationale for the organization and established standards founded on a belief in universal justice.[159] An even greater ambition was behind its quest for social justice. In the minds of its founders, the development of social rights and the promotion of peace were inseparable.[160] To reach this purpose it was important to recognize and guarantee a truly humane system of work, respectful of all individuals' rights.[161] Lastly, this combat for social justice

153 Constitution of the International Labour Organization (ILO), 1 April 1919, entry into force 28 June 1919 (ILO Constitution).

154 JJ Becker, 'Albert Thomas d'un siècle à l'autre. Bilan de l'expérience de guerre' [2008] 2 *Les Cahiers de l'Irice* 2, 9–15; E Phelan, *Albert Thomas et la création du B.I.T.* (Grasset 1936).

155 A Thomas, 'Le Bureau International du Travail,' *Speech*, November 5, 1920 (ABIT, CAT/2/20/10); see also A Thomas, *Speech*, October 27, 1926 (ABIT, CAT/2/26/8)(Cambridge); see also A Thomas, 'Organisation Internationale du Travail: origine, développement, avenir' [1921] 1 *RIT* 1, 5–22, cited by I Lespinet-Moret and V Viet, 'Introduction' in *L'Organisation Internationale du Travail: origine-développement-avenir* (Presses universitaires de Rennes 2011), 13.

156 G Rodgers, et al., *The ILO and the Quest for Social Justice, 1919–2009* (ILO 2009), 7.

157 E Hiitonen, *La compétence de l'Organisation Internationale du Travail* (Rousseau & Cie 1929), 193 (emphasis added).

158 BW Schaper, *Albert Thomas: trente ans de réformisme social* (Van Gorcum 1959), 308. The primary mission of the ILO is to 'establish everywhere a truly humane system of work [. . .], to ensure [. . .] better, and as far as possible, equal conditions for all the workers of the world', see A Thomas, *L'Organisation Internationale du Travail et la première année de son activité* (ILO 1921), 5.

159 In 1944, the Declaration of Philadelphia reasserted the principles and goals of the ILO and was incorporated in the ILO Constitution, see International Labour Conference, 26th session, The Declaration of Philadelphia, 1944. One of the key principles of the Declaration is that lasting peace cannot be achieved unless it is based on social justice, grounded in freedom, dignity, economic security and equal opportunity. See JM Bonvin, *L'Organisation Internationale du Travail: essai sur une agence productrice de normes* (Presses universitaires de France 1998).

160 A Thomas, *Speech on Disarmament*, 21 November 1921 (ABIT, CAT/2/21/5) (Geneva).

161 A Thomas, 'Justice sociale et paix universelle. Réflexions sur un texte' [1924] 6 *La Revue de Paris* 241–261.

and peace reveals the progressive emergence of a base of shared values. As an historical novelty, the universality of specific social values was recognized by many countries and made official in the 'general principles' of the 'Labour Charter' of the Treaty of Versailles (Article 427) of 1919. This process ran in parallel with the League of Nations' efforts to eliminate slavery and slavery-related practices following the First World War.[162] According to Article 22 of the League of Nations Covenant, 'the Mandatory must be responsible for the administration of the territory under conditions which will guarantee … the prohibition of abuses such as the slave trade'. A Temporary Slavery Commission was appointed by the Council of the League of Nations in June 1924 and on 25 September 1926 it adopted the Slavery Convention that provided the first definition of slavery.[163] Only after the Second World War, the UN continued working toward the elimination of slavery.[164]

These intellectual, institutional and legal developments shaped the transition of human dignity from a purely religious to a secular and individual conception and right. It was indeed in the aftermath of the First World War that a new type of narrative emerged. A 'crisis of sovereignty' was at work in the milieu of internationalists, including, among many, Alejandro Álvarez, André Mandelstam, Nicolas Politis, René Cassin and Georges Scelle. Scelle, for instance, appealed to his colleagues 'to reject the idea of sovereignty deliberately and definitively, for it is false and it is harmful'.[165] For all these jurists, the individual and human rights had to have priority in international law. In the post-war world, for President Wilson, the new world order had to move in parallel with a reconstruction of international law on the basis of new standards.[166] All these intellectual strands desired to see an established international protection for populations that had been victims of attacks or who were otherwise vulnerable in wartime or peacetime. These strands ultimately converged during the Second World War.[167]

162 ME Burton, *The Assembly of the League of Nations* (Howard Fertig 1974).

163 Convention to Suppress the Slave Trade and Slavery, 25 September 1926, 60 LNTS 253, entered into force on 9 March 1927.

164 The Convention for the Suppression of the Traffic in Persons and of the Exploitation of the Prostitution of Others, 2 December 1949, A/RES/317; Supplementary Convention on the Abolition of Slavery, the Slave Trade and Institutions and Practices Similar to Slavery of 1956, United Nations Treaty Series, vol. 226, 3, entered into force on 30 April 1957.

165 G Scelle, 'Une ère juridique nouvelle', *La paix par le droit* (July–August 1919), 297–298.

166 AS Link, *The Papers of Woodrow Wilson*, vol. 58 (Princeton University Press 1966–1994), 598–600.

167 J Maritain, *The Person and the Common Good*, trans. JJ Fitzgerald (UNDP 1947), 13; for a reconstruction, see S Moyn, 'Personalism, Community and the Origins of Human Rights', in Hoffmann, *supra* n 113, 85–106.

3.3.3 *The Human Dignity of the Individual*

3.3.3.1 Dignity as an Individual Entitlement

Only by the 1940s, and mostly after the Second World War, did a global consensus emerge on considering human rights and democracy essential foundations for the post-war order and human dignity as a universal foundational principle, as a right and source of other rights. This time period can thus be considered as the beginning of a further constitutive phase of dignity, a time in which there was an increasing acknowledgment that human dignity represented an individual and inherent right.

In this time, together with the intellectual and political strands discussed in the previous section, other factors played an influential role. There had been a significant Catholic Church conversion to personalism[168] when in the mid-1930s Pius XI committed the Church to anti-totalitarianism.[169] Pope Leo XIII had already played a key catalysing role in universalizing the concept of the dignity of labour. His influential papal encyclical *Rerum Novarum*, or the Rights and Duties of Capital and Labor (1891), had entered directly into the nineteenth-century political conversation about the antagonism between classes, condemning exploitation and tying dignity to personhood.[170] In 1937, Eugenio Pacelli, soon to become Pius XII, wrote about 'a vast and dangerous conspiracy' threatening 'the inviolability of the human person that, in his sovereign wisdom and infinite goodness, the Creator has honored with an incomparable dignity'.[171] Further, Pacelli cited the critical line from Pius XI's *Mit brennender Sorge* to make clear that this inviolable dignity gave rise to a set of rights. Moreover, a central political novelty was the rise of Christian Democracy, a conservative political movement that prevailed in Western

168 For a variety of contemporary commentaries on the novel surge of the human person after 1936 in statements by Pius XI and XII, see *The Foundations of International Order* (proceedings of the Catholic Congress on International Peace, The Hague, 1938); L Watt, *Pope Pius XII on World Order* (Catholic Social Guild 1940), chapter 5, 'The Dignity of the Human Person'.

169 See, on the topic, S Moyn, 'Jacques Maritain: le origini dei Diritti umani e il pensiero politico cristiano' in L Bonanate and R Papini (eds), *Dialogo interculturale e diritti umani: la Dichiarazione Universale dei Diritti Umani, Genesi, evoluzione, e problemi odierni* (1948–2008) (Il Mulino 2008), 97–124; P de la Chapelle, *La Déclaration universelle des droits de l'homme et le catholicisme*, pref. René Cassin (LGDJ 1967).

170 In this sense, already Proudhon, in his *System of Economical Contradictions, or the Philosophy of Misery* (1846) (John Wilson & Son 1888), condemned the conditions of some work – modern, industrial, poorly paid work, which not only lacked dignity, but they deprived their *practitioners* of dignity.

171 Lettre de S. Em. Le Cardinal Pacelli, 1937, in Semaines sociales de France, *La Personne humaine en péril* (Clermont-Ferrand 1937), 5–8.

Europe, in which uses of the language of 'human dignity' hugely increased, as demonstrated in the history of post-war domestic constitutions. After Ireland's Constitution, dignity appeared once again in the 1946 conservative Catholic Bavaria's Constitution, then, subsequently, in the 1948 Christian Democratic Italy. The Italian Constitution referred to human dignity in three instances, as expressions of dignity, as a foundational principle and as a parameter for the implementation of human rights.[172] In 1949, the West German Constitution stated: 'Human dignity is inviolable'.[173]

Individual rights also attracted increasing interest among scholars.[174] Moreover, at the international level, on 1 January 1942, representatives of 26 Allied nations along with the countries of the tripartite pact – Germany, Italy and Japan – signed a UN Declaration, subscribing to the purposes set in the Atlantic Charter.[175] The UN Declaration, although it was only a mere declaration of political principles, represented the first international document mentioning human rights,[176] building on the language first used in the Atlantic Charter.[177] By 1 March 1945, 21 further States had acceded to this declaration. This group would then become the core of the 51 original member states of the UN.[178] The creation of a new international organization was formally agreed by Churchill, Roosevelt and Joseph Stalin at the Tehran Conference (1943) and further progress toward the establishment of the UN was made at the Dumbarton Oaks Conference (1944) and the Yalta Conference (1945).

As it will be discussed in this section, during this historical phase, the dignity of the human person found a first preliminary recognition in the preambles of constitutive documents of two international organizations, the UN, here still in its religious sense, and UNESCO (Section 3.3.3.2). The UN human rights

[172] Article 3, 27 and 41; see P Becchi, *Il Principio Dignità Umana* (Morcelliana 2009). On human dignity as an attribute of the *person* and, in this sense, as a possible supreme value of the legal system, see G Azzoni, 'Dignità umana tra autonomia e solidarietà', lecture in the course 'Umanesimo cristiano – costruire il bene comune oggi' (Almo Collegio Borromeo, 30 agosto – 4 settembre 2010).

[173] West German Constitution, approved in Bonn on 8 May 1949 and entered into force on 23 May 1949 (Basic Law).

[174] See above section 3.3.2.; see also HG Wells, *The Times*, 23 October 1939; DC Smith, *H.G. Wells: Desperately Mortal: A Biography* (Yale University Press 1986), 46; H Lauterpacht, *An International Bill of the Rights of Man* (Cambridge University Press 1945); A Clapham, *Human Rights a Very Short Introduction* (2nd ed., Oxford University Press 2014), 24–29.

[175] Declaration by United Nations, done 1 January 1942, entered into force 1 January 1942, 204 LNTS 381 [Atlantic Charter].

[176] M Bennouna, *Atlantic Charter* (1941), [2007] *MPEPIL*.

[177] E Borgwardt 'When You State a Moral Principle, You Are Stuck with It: The 1941 Atlantic Charter as a Human Rights Instrument' [2006] 46 *VJIL* 501, 526.

[178] Smith, *supra* n 174, 32.

movement inaugurated by the UN Charter[179] was a direct consequence of the barbarities of the Second World War[180] and rooted not so much in philosophical doctrines, but most likely in Catholic usage and in a shared instinctive understanding of the unhuman acts perpetrated,[181] in order to avoid 'a return to inhuman ideologies and practices'.[182] Further legislative efforts were, however, still needed. In the words of Professor Jessup, the expansion of the duty to '*respect for human dignity*' imposed by the Charter and its translation into specific rules required 'further steps of a legislative character'.[183] The crystallization of human dignity in this second constitutive stage can indeed be set at the time of the adoption of the 1948 UDHR. Here human dignity finds for the first time a clear expression as a fundamental principle, as an individual right and a source of other individual rights (Section 3.3.3.3). All these instruments influenced the framework of human rights protection. In particular, the 1950 European Convention on Human Rights ('ECHR')[184] and the 1951 Refugee Convention represent two cases of recognition of a 'shadow' human dignity (Section 3.3.3.4). Despite its absence in their text, human dignity indeed permeated and highly influenced their preparatory works. Whereas the mid-1950s appeared to be a transitional phase in the human rights project, human dignity maintained its central role, at times expressly or other times by shadow-acting, and slowly expanded its scope until reaching its final consolidation in the 1960s.

3.3.3.2 Human Dignity at the Heart of International Organization

After the war, it was felt that all nations had to work to create the spirit of peace, 'one of the guarantees (and maybe the surest) of peace itself',[185] in order to

179 G Kaeckenbeeck, 'La Charte de San-Francisco dans ses rapports avec le droit international' [1948] 70 *RCADI* 260.

180 See Y Arieli, 'On the Necessary and Sufficient Conditions for the Emergence of the Doctrine of the Dignity of Man and His Rights', in Kretzmer and Klein, *supra* n 10, 1; C Tomuschat, *Human Rights: Between Idealism and Realism* (3rd ed., Oxford University Press 2014), 22–23; T Buergenthal, 'The Evolving International Human Rights System' [2006] 100(4) *AJIL* 783–807, 786.

181 See JP Humphrey, 'International Protection of Human Rights' [1948] 255 *The Annals of the American Academy of Political and Social Science* 15–21, 21. See also Frowein, *supra* n 10, 122–123.

182 R Andorno, 'The Paradoxical Notion of Human Dignity' [2001] 5(2) *Rivista Internazionale di Filosofia del Diritto* 156.

183 P Jessup, A *Modern Law of Nations* (Macmillan 1948), 91 (emphasis added); see also Dissenting Opinion of Judge Tanaka in the *South West Africa Cases*, Second Phase.

184 European Convention for the Protection of Human Rights and Fundamental Freedoms, as Amended by Protocols No. 11 and 14, Rome, 4 November 1950.

185 L Blum, ECO/Conf.F, 41, quoted in HH Krill de Capello, 'The Creation of the United Nations Educational, Scientific, and Cultural Organization' [1970] 24(1) *IO* 1, 20–21.

elaborate the principles of intellectual and moral reconstruction of a deeply shaken world. The UN Charter was signed on 26 June 1945 in San Francisco and came into force on 24 October 1945. Hersch Lauterpacht affirmed, as early as in 1948, that the UN Charter could be described as a 'landmark in the recognition of the status of the individual and his protection by international society'.[186] Another major concern after the war was educational reconstruction. On 16 November 1945, the UNESCO Constitution came into force. Both instruments recognize the human dignity of the individual. It is interesting, however, to compare the rationales behind the references to human dignity included in the preambles of these two constitutive instruments:[187] in the case of the UN Charter, it was inserted almost by accident, and the wording used in the text still reflected a concept religiously rooted, while in the case of the UNESCO Constitution, it was made clear in the preparatory works that human dignity was explicitly detached from competing theologies or doctrines and enshrined as a democratic and guiding principle and right of all individuals.

In particular, as regards the UN Charter, its drafters succeeded in including only a few references to human dignity in the Preamble as well as in Article 1 (3). According to Smuts' first draft of the Preamble, the UN was established, inter alia, 'to re-establish the faith of men and women in fundamental human rights [and] in the sacredness, essential worth and integrity of the human personality'.[188] A slightly rephrased version stated 'to re-establish faith in fundamental human rights, in the sanctity and ultimate value of human personality, in the equal rights of men and women and of nations large and small'.[189] Some members regarded the Smuts text as inelegant and excessively long. The general challenge for Gildersleeve, Smuts and others at the conference, as Moyn noted, was 'to prettify the great power settlement of the

186 H Lauterpacht, 'Human Rights, the Charter of the United Nations, and the International Bill of the Rights of Man, – Preliminary Report, E/CN.4/89, International Law Association Conference (43rd ed., 1948), 9.

187 J Huxley, *UNESCO: Its Purpose and Its Philosophy* (Preparatory Commission of UNESCO 1946), 7.

188 Draft Preamble to the Charter of the United Nations Proposed by the Union of South Africa, 26 April 1945, UNCIO, vol. 3, 474–475.

189 See the Preamble to the Charter of the United Nations Submitted by the South African Delegation in Revision of Draft of April 26, 1945, May 3, 1945, idem, 476–477; see RD Russell, *A History of the United Nations Charter: The Role of the United States 1940–1945* (Brookings 1958), 911–915. See also Library of Congress and UN Information Organizations, Documents of the UN Conference on International Organization [UNCIO Documents] (UNCIO, 1945), vol. 6, 277. For the Smuts text, see *supra* n 188, 476–477.

Dumbarton Oaks agreement a year before, and the insertion of dignity and even "human rights" were part of this endeavour'.[190]

It seems that 'dignity' was included almost by accident in the original text of the UN Charter. The American delegate Virginia Gildersleeve credited herself in her memoirs, *Many a Good Crusade* (1954), for having proposed on her own authority a revision in which the first two clauses of the passage just quoted are replaced with the phrase 'to reaffirm faith in the dignity and value of every human being'.[191] Thus, in Gildersleeve's version, 'dignity' took the place of 'sanctity'; the rest stayed mostly the same. However, according to the UN official transcripts, during committee (I/1/A), it appears that the New Zealand delegation made the proposal first, by suggesting the Preamble include the determination of the peoples of the UN 'to assert the dignity of man, so grievously outraged'. Whereas this expression was not adopted, it was agreed to follow and merely edit Smuts' draft. Gildersleeve's version may have been advanced on 3 May 1945.[192]

The drafting committee accepted the proposal, and the passage survives nearly verbatim in the final version of the Preamble. The revision did not trigger any further discussion at the time. As Virginia Gildersleeve was the dean of Barnard College and a doctor in English and comparative literature at Columbia University (New York), it was most likely thought that she had enough talent to present a politically harmless text that was rhetorically inspiring.[193] Aside from the alteration of 'value' to 'worth' and Smuts' change of 'human being' to 'human person', not many changes were made to this part of the Preamble after these edits. There is no indication that there was any consideration of the substitution of 'dignity' for 'sanctity' or, for that matter, of the meaning or more general significance of the idea of dignity for human rights. The rapporteur described the major motives of the revisions of the Smuts text as avoidance of redundancy with the main body of the Charter and an achievement of a 'harmony in ideas and words' that would 'awaken the imagination of the common man'.[194]

190 S Moyn, 'Why Is Dignity in the Charter of the United Nations?', *Humanity Journal (online blog)*, 14 June 2014, http://humanityjournal.org/blog/why–is–dignity–in–the–charter–of–the–united–nations–2/.

191 VC Gildersleeve, *Many a Good Crusade: Memoirs of Virginia Gildersleeve* (Macmillan 1954), 346.

192 This appears from the notes wrote on a side of Smuts' text in Doc. 2 (English), G/14 (d) (1), 3 May 1945, cited in Moyn, *supra* n 190.

193 P Van Kemseke, '"We the peoples […]" The Interaction of Power, Ideas and Ideology in the United Nations Charter' in J de Maeyer and V Viaene (eds), *World Views and Worldly Wisdom · Visions et expériences du monde: Religion, Ideology and Politics, 1750–2000* (Liverpool University Press 2016), 369.

194 UNCIO Documents, vol. 6, 366, 358; see also C McCrudden, 'Human Dignity and Judicial Interpretation of Human Rights' [2008] 19(4) *EJIL* 655, 675–676.

Beitz noted that '[t]he employment of the term "human dignity" is evidence that this term had a positive valence in the vernacular of the moment, but the off-handedness of the decision to place it early in the preamble and the absence of any consideration of its significance argue against inferring any shared, articulate purpose'.[195] However, as persuasive as Beitz's argument is, the preparatory works of the draft, as well as the legal and political context of the time, support a different reasoning related to the exclusive use of human dignity – expression of a religious grounding of the concept. First, an interesting change in Smuts' draft was the replacement of the word 're-establish' with 'reaffirm'. The reason for this change was that, according to the relevant subcommittee, 'that faith [in the dignity and value of every human being] ha[d] never faded', and that it was this faith in human dignity and rights 'which moved men and women in all lands to accept the sacrifices by which victory [was] achieved'.[196] However, 'that faith needed reaffirmation in our Charter especially after it ha[d] been trampled upon by Nazism and Fascism in Europe as well as in other instances elsewhere'.[197] With one minor change, the subcommittee's formulation was adopted by the Committee and then the Commission. The reference to the dignity and value of the 'human being' was changed into that of the 'human person' at the request of Smuts.[198] During the Thirteenth Meeting of Committee I/1, the Committee adopted the revised text. The Commission also adopted the same text and during the Eleventh Meeting of Steering Committee, on 23 June 1945, where one last change was made, the word 'value' was deleted.[199] Second, Moyn correctly affirms that Beitz's argument does not do well in explaining the near-exclusive use of human dignity in Western European constitutions in the moment just after the Second World War, coinciding and overlapping rather precisely with the time and place that conservative Christian Democracy ascended to rule. Last, as a confirmation of the influence of Christianity, Christians celebrated the language adopted in the UN Charter as grounded in Christian roots. Carlos Romulo, Philippines delegate to the UN and crucial American ally, noted in

[195] CR Beitz, 'Human Dignity in the Theory of Human Rights: Nothing But a Phrase?' [2009] 41 (3) *PhilosPublicAff* 259–290, 266.

[196] Report of Rapporteur, Subcommittee I/1/A, Section 3, to Committee I/1, 5 June 1945, UNCIO, vol. 6, 359. See also Report of Rapporteur of Committee 1 to Commission I, UNCIO, vol. 6, 392.

[197] *Ibid.*

[198] See Report of Rapporteur of Committee 1 to Commission I, UNCIO, vol. 6, 461, and the Thirteenth Meeting of Committee I/1, 5 June 1945, idem, 366.

[199] See First Session of Commission I, 14 June 1945, 20. See further the Summary Report of Forty-First Meeting, 25 June 1945, UNCIO, vol. 17, 380 and the Summary Report of Eleventh Meeting of Steering Committee, 23 June 1945, UNCIO, vol. 5, 307.

1949: 'We discern in the Charter's avowal of ... the dignity of the human person, the Christian belief in a brotherhood of men equally precious in the eyes of God, each deserving of His Justice and worthy of His love.' And that '[i]t was by restoring the basis of natural law to the national and international future, with all the moral implications that went along with it, that dignity found its stride'.[200]

According to Moyn, Beitz is, however, correct when noting that dignity is not 'earmarked' in any particular sense, since no debates around interpretation of the term took place in UN circles at any point in time.[201] Thus, it can be said, in agreement with Moyn,[202] that the language seems most traceable to Catholic usage. A Christian vision of dignity played a catalysing role in universalizing the concept of the dignity. The affirmation in the Preamble of the UN Charter was strengthened in Article 1 of the Charter, which recites the purposes of the UN, which involve respect for human rights, and the dignity and worth of the human person.[203] Therefore, human dignity, as enshrined in the UN Charter, resulted to be considered 'as the cardinal unit of value in the global society of the future'.[204]

Similarly, the Preamble of the UNESCO Constitution defined the aims of the new organization. The American poet, diplomat and Librarian of Congress Archibald MacLeish penned the lines that open the Preamble – 'Since wars begin in the minds of men, it is in the minds of men that the defences of peace must be constructed' – in line with the aim expressed during the conference by M. Léon Blum. The Preamble then continues by stressing the dangers of ignorance and noting that the Second World War denied certain basic principles – 'the *democratic principles of the dignity*, equality and mutual respect of men' – and replaced them with 'the doctrine of the inequality of men and races'.[205] Based on these premises, it adds that 'the wide diffusion of culture, and the education of humanity for justice and liberty and peace, are *indispensable to the dignity of man* and constitute a sacred duty which all the nations must fulfil in a spirit of mutual assistance and concern'. Human dignity was thus a fundamental democratic principle violated by war and a guiding principle for the diffusion of culture.

200 CP Romulo, 'On Natural Law and International Law' [1949] 35(8) *VaLRev* 1052, 1053.
201 See Moyn, *supra* n 190.
202 S Moyn, *Human Rights and the Uses of History* (Verso 2014), 53.
203 See, in this sense, *Legality of the Threat or Use of Nuclear Weapons*, Advisory Opinion, (1996) I.C.J. Reports 1996, Dissenting Opinion of Judge Weeramantry, 434.
204 *Ibid.*, Dissenting Opinion of Judge Weeramantry, 442.
205 Emphasis added.

Julian Huxley, who played a leading part in the creation of UNESCO and was elected as its Director-General in 1946,[206] expressly clarified in a pamphlet published in 1946 that the drafters of the UNESCO Constitution chose not to embrace any particular doctrines of the world, 'partly because it is contrary to its charter and essence to be sectarian, partly for the very practical reason that any such attempt would immediately incur the active hostility of large and influential groups, and the non-cooperation or even withdrawal of a number of nations'.[207]

The two references to human dignity in the Constitution are the expression of two different approaches. First, the drafters decided not to base the organization exclusively on any special philosophy, whether existentialism, rationalism or an economic-determinist theory. By focussing on democracy and the principles of human dignity, equality and mutual respect, the Constitution's drafters refused to adopt the view that the State had to be placed in a higher or more important position than the individual or to consider any class theory of society. This is the reason why the Preamble refuses racialism and any belief in superior or inferior 'races', nations or ethnic groups.

Second, the Preamble confirms that its core must be rooted '[i]n some form of humanism'.[208] As Huxley explained, it must be interpreted as a 'scientific' and 'evolutionary' humanism, which first seeks 'to bring in all the peoples of the world, and ... [treat] all peoples and all individuals within each people as equals in terms of *human dignity*, mutual respect, and educational opportunity'.[209] It is a scientific humanism, since science provides the material foundation for human culture, based on a monistic, unitary philosophic approach. It is 'evolutionary' as opposed to an ideal humanism as it provides 'the link between natural science and human history ... [and] it not only shows us the origin and biological roots of our human values, but gives us some basis and external standards for them among the apparently neutral mass of natural phenomena'.[210]

At the founding meeting of UNESCO in London on 16 November 1945, Cassin addressed the delegates with a statement revealing the path about to start: the Soviet Union had to be taken on board and considerations of a moral order had to be considered in order to protect and ensure peace against States'

206 'General Conference, First Session', UNESCO House, Paris, from 20 November to 10 December 1946. UNESCO/C/30 [1 C/Resolutions] Item 14, 73: UNESCO, 1947.

207 J Huxley, *UNESCO: Its Purpose and Its Philosophy* (Preparatory Commission of UNESCO 1946), 7.

208 *Ibid.*

209 *Ibid.* (emphasis added).

210 *Ibid.*

abuses.[211] Sovereignty itself caused the failures of the League of Nations in the 1930s, and it was clear that State powers had to be refrained through an international moral, and possibly legal, order. That 'required action not only in the educational sphere, though that dimension was critical to Cassin, but in the realm of international law'.[212] If UNESCO was one lane of this path, another was the creation of the Commission on Human Rights (HRC) within the orbit of the Economic and Social Council of the UN, per Article 68 of the UN Charter. Laugier prepared a document for the Economic and Social Council of the UN (ECOSOC) that precisely listed the rights that the States signatories of the UN Charter had agreed to defend, and he asked John Humphrey to head the secretariat of the new commission.[213] Here lies the link between UNESCO and the development of human rights work in the late 1940s.

3.3.3.3 Crossing the Rubicon: The Two 1948 Declarations

At the San Francisco Conference, the proposal to include a declaration of human rights was left aside because of time constraints and because it was felt that the organization, once formed, would be best placed to implement the suggestion of promoting 'respect for human rights and fundamental freedoms'.[214] The UN organs took early action to consider the necessary steps to implement the obligation to respect human rights. One of the first results was the UDHR, drafted by the HRC, chaired by Eleanor Roosevelt,[215] and proclaimed by the UN GA in Paris on 10 December 1948. A few months earlier, however, on 2 May 1948, in Bogotà, the Ninth International Conference of American States had

211 Conference for the establishment of the UNESCO, Institute of Civil Engineers, London, 1–16 November 1945, ECO/CONF./29, 91–92.

212 J Winter and A Prost, *René Cassin and Human Rights from the Great War to the Universal Declaration* (Cambridge University Press 2013), 234.

213 See AJ Hobbins (ed.), *On the Edge of Greatness: The Diaries of John Humphrey, First Director of the United Nations Division of Human Rights, 1948–49*, vol. 1 (McGill University Press 1994).

214 The Dumbarton Oaks Proposals for a General International Organizations contained in Chapter IX (Arrangements for International Economic and Social Cooperation) Section A (Purpose and Relationships) which established that the Organization had to 'promote respect for human rights and fundamental freedoms'; see J Robinson, *Human Rights and Fundamental Freedoms* (Institute of Jewish Affairs 1946), xix (Introduction).

215 For a detailed account of the drafting history and the debates, see Morsink, *supra* n 112; R Normand and S Zaidi, *Human Rights at the UN: The Political History of Universal Justice* (Indiana University Press 2008), 177–182; see also N Robinson, *The Universal Declaration of Human Rights* (Institute of Jewish Affairs 1958), 25–30.

already finalized the American Declaration on the Rights and Duties of Man ('Bogotà Declaration'),[216] the first international human rights instrument of a general nature. During the Conference, delegates confirmed their careful consideration of the draft of the Universal Declaration[217] and the working group on rights of man also took the UN draft as one of its basic working documents.[218] Importantly, both projects enshrine and recognize the human dignity of the individual and, despite a few similarities, they also present points of departures.

During the drafting works on the Preamble of the Bogotà Declaration, it was stated that the first paragraph of the Preamble was taken from the UN project, 'hardly changing it'.[219] Both the preparatory work and the final wording of the Declaration considered human dignity as the source of human rights on the basis of the 'recognition of the moral value of the individual human being'.[220] It was argued during the drafting process that '[t]he Declaration of Rights and Duties is inspired by the concept that the human being has dignity and inherent value'.[221] At the time, Latin American thinking was at a sort of juncture of different world approaches on human rights: the Western Anglo-Saxon liberal individualist vision of the world, and the more communitarian one.[222] The Latin American approach did recognize not only the importance of civil and political rights – a central concern for the Western bloc – but also the function of social property and solidarity toward the most vulnerable, which was the

216 Out of six working commissions, the Sixth was subdivided into three sub-commissions. In principle, Subcommittee A would analyse the issue of the international rights and duties of man, the Sixth Committee was devoted to the analysis of the Draft Declaration ('PDADDH'). In addition to the work of the Sixth Commission and the Subcommittee A, it is relevant for the purposes of the Declaration the work that was carried out by the Working Group on Human Rights. The report of the work can be read in the Novena Conferencia Internacional Americana, Actas y Documentos (Ministerio de Relaciones Exteriores de Colombia, Bogotá, 1953) ['NCV']; see P Álvaro, *Los trabajos preparatorios de la Declaración Americana de los Derechos y Deberes del Hombre y el origen remoto de la Corte Interamericana* (Instituto de Investigaciones Jurídicas UNAM, 2017).

217 For instance, see statement by the Cuban delegate in NCV, 544 and 562.

218 NCV, 475.

219 NCV, 513; see also NCV, 477.

220 See Comité Jurídico Interamericano, Informe anexo al Anteproyecto de Declaración de los derechos y deberes internacionales del hombre, Rio de Janeiro, 31 December 1945 ['AD'], 15.

221 See AD, 32.

222 MA Glendon, 'The Forgotten Crucible: The Latin American Influence on the Universal Human Rights Idea' [2003] 16 *HHRJ* 32–34.

core belief of the Soviet bloc.[223] Catholic social doctrine influenced this Latin American intermediate position.[224]

During the discussions, the Cuban delegate openly affirmed that 'the rights of the individual ... are based on natural law'.[225] By comparing the Preamble of the American Declaration on the Rights and Duties of Man with that of the UDHR, it is quite evident that one of the main differences is that the former Declaration, though equally affirming that human beings are endowed with reason and consciousness, adds that such attributes are endowed 'by nature'. The drafters also engaged in other philosophical discussions on typical characteristics associated with human nature. They argued that '[t]he man is, undoubtedly, by his nature, a social being'. They conceived the State as a 'cooperative community'[226] and considered that the State 'exists for the man, not the man for the State'.[227] These provisions also demonstrate that the Inter-American Juridical Committee considered that there are rights that must be exercised 'for the general good of the community and the conservation of public order and security'[228] and broad autonomy is not compatible with duties required by the Declaration.[229] In 1945, the drafters were aware of the universal importance of the Declaration and clearly recognized that it 'may serve as a precedent for the universal declaration, thus facilitating greater encouragement to respect of 'human rights and fundamental freedoms', in accordance with the provisions of the Charter'.[230] The work carried out in this region was taken into account by the UN HRC as a basis for the preparation of the UDHR.[231]

In the words of Morsink, 'the Holocaust shocked the moral consciousness of all civilized peoples into an increased awareness of the inherent dignity of every human being',[232] and the Universal Declaration can be seen as an act of protest, a revolutionary document, or 'a trumpet call of

223 *Ibid.*, 33–36; Paolo Carozza refers to some rules in which the Latin American influence permeated not only the drafting of the Universal Declaration of Human Rights, but also, several years earlier, the Charter of the United Nations, see Carozza, *From Conquest to Constitutions*, 286–287, 289–311.

224 Glendon, *supra* n 222, 30–31.

225 See NCV, 544.

226 AD, 14.

227 AD, 35 and 40.

228 AD, 25, also, on the principle of reciprocity of rights and duties (see also NCV, 477); on the right to vote and correlative obligation, AD, 40.

229 AP Díaz, '*La Génesis de la Declaración Americana de los Derechos y Deberes del Hombre y la Relevancia Actual de sus Trabajos Preparatorios*' [2016] XLVII *Revista de Derecho de la Pontificia Universidad Católica de Valparaíso* 361–395, 386–387.

230 AD, 54.

231 Glendon, *supra* n 222, 30–31.

232 For the first quote, see Morsink, *supra* n 112, 59–60.

victory after battle'.[233] On 27 January 1947, the first formal meeting of the HRC was held. As Henri Laugier, who on that occasion acted as the UN Assistant Secretary-General in charge of social affairs, aptly put it:

> The mission of the HRC consists of continuing in peacetime the struggle of the people begun in wartime repelling every attack against the rights and *dignity of man*, and in drafting, according to the principles of the Charter of the UN, an international declaration of human rights which can be strong enough to overcome all obstacles.[234]

The Declaration was intended as 'a general statement of principles in simple, brief, and unambiguous language'[235] and was considered an authoritative interpretation of the references to human rights in the UN Charter.[236] The sense of urgency played a major role.[237] Through the UDHR, the human dignity of the individual is crystallized in IHRL as a secularized and universal concept, rooted in the Enlightenment – despite still visible traces of a Christian legacy. The final text of the UDHR has five references to human dignity (two in the Preamble; Article 1; and Articles 22 and 23) and provides a unifying thread to the approach and vision of human rights recognition. The first three expressions well demonstrate the rationales followed by the drafters in the decision to enshrine human dignity in the text of the Declaration. They will now be examined in turn.

First, the Preamble of the Declaration affirms the reasons behind the importance of proclaiming the rights enshrined in its text. Two of them include an explicit reference to human dignity.

The first reason for proclaiming the Declaration is that:

> recognition of the inherent dignity and of the equal and inalienable rights of all members of the human family is the foundation of freedom, justice and peace in the world.
>
> (Preamble, para 1)

This recital reflects three central considerations, all being part of the so-called founding function of human dignity.[238] First, by stating that human dignity

233 See *ibid*., 38.

234 Emphasis added. See Winter and Prost, *supra* n 212, 243; On Laugier, see C Morelle and P Jakob, *Henri Laugier. Un esprit sans frontières* (Bruylant 1997), 249; and JL Crémieux-Brilhac and JF Picard (eds), *Henri Laugier en son siecle* (CHRS Editions 1995).

235 A/C.3/SR/165, 21.

236 For an account on the debates on the point during the preparatory work, see Robinson, *supra* n 215, 36–37. See also LB Sohn, 'The Improvement of the UN Machinery on Human Rights' [1979] 23(2) *International Studies Quarterly* 188.

237 Winter and Prost, *supra* n 212, 247.

238 K Dicke, 'The Founding Function of Human Dignity in the Universal Declaration of Human Rights', in Kretzmer and Klein, *supra* n 10, 114.

has to go through a process of recognition, which is associated with a 'faith' in the second reference of the Preamble, it implies that such pre-existence creates a corresponding obligation. The act of recognition, therefore, is not human dignity itself,[239] which pre-exists, but implies an obligation to recognize it. Second, this obligation is necessary since such recognition is at the basis of freedom, justice and peace. Last, 'all members of the human family' own an inherent dignity, which is therefore 'an expression of the unity of mankind'.[240] Dicke therefore concludes that it can be inferred that human dignity is a fundamental principle 'in light of which each and every policy and law-making to secure freedom, to implement justice and to maintain peace must be seen'.[241]

The first recital itself was not introduced into the text of the Declaration until quite late in the drafting process. Officers of the Committee on the Preamble – Eleanor Roosevelt, Chang, Rene Cassin and Charles Malik – were (to various degrees) in agreement with the inherence view of human rights. During the debates, the drafters agreed that a standard should be established, 'with a view to elevating the concept of man's dignity',[242] to affirm 'one common human nature and the fundamental unity of the human race'.[243] In particular, Charles Malik argued that '[t]he deepest danger of the age' is posed by a collectivism that demands 'the extinction of the human person as such in his own individuality and ultimate inviolability'.[244] His view found support in Mrs Roosevelt, who noted, 'individual must have rights that are guarded,'[245] and in René Cassin, who recognized the predominant importance of an individual's freedom of conscience, since it is a right that 'gives man *his value and dignity*'.[246] Their first proposal to the Third Session in May and June of 1948 was never seriously questioned by the Third Committee, which adopted this recital unanimously.

In the text of the preamble, it is thus possible to trace similarities with the language adopted in declarations of the eighteenth century, mostly in the first

239 *Ibid.*
240 *Ibid.*
241 *Ibid.*, 115, who refers to German Enlightenment as a background source. In particular, see J Fries, *Philosophische Rechtslehre und Kritik aller positive Gesetzgebung* (Jena 1803).
242 PC Chang, HRC, First Session, Summary Records, E/CN.4/SR.7, 4.
243 R Cassin, ibid.
244 *The More Important Speeches and Interventions of Charles Malik*, Verbatim Records of the First Session of the Human Rights Commission (Papers of Charles Habib 'Malik, Library of Congress, Manuscript Division), 35–37; Human Rights Commission, First Session, Summary Records, E/CN.4/SR.9, 3.
245 *Ibid.*, 38–39.
246 *Ibid.*, 42–43 (emphasis added).

parts of the document. The first recital of the 1948 Preamble mentions 'inherent dignity' and 'equal and inalienable rights', both of which reflect Enlightenment views present in the Virginia Declaration of Rights of 1776, in the American Declaration of Independence and in the French Declaration of 1789, which qualified rights as 'natural, imprescriptible, and inalienable'. Also, Rene Cassin[247] and other delegates,[248] in various instances, confirmed these roots and that human beings were endowed with them simply by virtue of their own humanity. As Morsink notes, natural rights philosophies of the eighteenth century believed they had found a sound basis for a morality that was both universal and secular.[249] Considering the clear Enlightenment echoes of the words 'inherent' and 'inalienable', these words did not lead to much controversy in the debate on the Preamble. The words 'inherent', 'inalienable' in the first recital, and 'born', in Article 1, build the so-called *inherence view* of human rights. This is the view that human rights belong to people as people. Human beings have these moral rights because of their humanity and their membership in the human family, not because of any external force or agency. Human beings have inherent dignity, being born with 'equal and inalienable' rights, as recognized in Article 1 of the Declaration. This means that dignity has not been assigned but simply assessed as pre-existing and provided with protection. Therefore, since no organ has given dignity or moral rights to individuals, it cannot take it away – which is what the word 'inalienable' means.[250]

The second reference to human dignity comes straight from the first paragraph of the UN Charter:

247 Verbatim Record of the Hundred and Eightieth Meeting of the GA, A/PV. 180, 9 December 1948.

248 See Ninety-Eighth Meeting of the Third Committee, A/C.3/SR.98, 9 October 1948 (Peng-chun Chang, 114); Hundred and Twenty-Seventh Meeting of the Third Committee, 9 November 1948, A/C.3/SR.127 (Peng-chun Chang, 397). Anze Matienzo, the delegate from Bolivia, argued that the right to a nationality was 'an inalienable human right' and he later referred to all of the rights in the Declaration as being 'inherent', see Hundred and Twenty-Third Meeting of the Third Committee, 5 November 1948, A/C.3/SR.123 (Anze Matienzo 35 and 111). Similarly, the Egyptian delegation (A/C.3/264); the representative from Uruguay (Verbatim Record of the Hundred and Eighty-First Meeting of the GA, 10 December 1948, A/PV.181, Enrique Armand Ugon, 887); the Yugoslavian delegate (Memorandum by the Division of Human Rights, E/CN.4/31, Yugoslav proposal, 35). The Indian delegation presented its version of an international bill, which started by affirming 'Recognizing the fact that the United Nations has been established for the specific purpose of enthroning the natural rights of man' (E/CN.4/11, Draft of a Resolution for the GA Submitted by the Representative of India, 31 January 1947, 1).

249 Morsink, *supra* n 112, 282.

250 *Ibid.*, 293.

> Whereas the peoples of the United Nations have in the Charter reaffirmed their faith in fundamental human rights, in the dignity and worth of the human person and in the equal rights of men and women and have determined to promote social progress and better standards of life in larger freedom
>
> (Preamble, para 5)

In this second reference to human dignity, the wording 'reaffirmed their faith' notes the pre-existing nature of dignity. It does not, however, mention earlier episodes of such affirmation but simply implies that the fundamental character of human rights and of dignity is well known by the reader. The Declaration refers implicitly to past political experiences, particularly the atrocities of National Socialist practices.[251] This consideration could imply that 'faith' in dignity calls for the establishment of democratic states under the rule of law.[252] Lastly, this second recital of dignity shows that the concept carries a moral or personal value ('worth') and is a feature of every 'human person', a concept deriving from the Christian persona.[253]

The most innovative reference to dignity is instead in Article 1, which, introducing the subsequent list of rights, provides that:

> [a]ll human beings are born free and equal in dignity and rights. They are endowed with reason and conscience and should act towards one another in a spirit of brotherhood.

Article 1, together with Article 3, is a general foundational declaration of principles. It was agreed by the members of the Third Committee that a provision that epitomizes the contents of the Declaration would carry greater weight as a first Article of the Declaration, rather than as part of the Preamble. The roots of the language adopted by the drafters are therefore interesting and worth consideration.

First, the expression '*are born free*', as a substitution for 'are by nature free', is of central importance. Justino Jimenez de Arechaga, the Uruguayan delegate, voted to delete 'by nature' from the draft, noting that '*rights were derived from the nature of man and not from the acts of States*'.[254]

In spite of the obvious metaphysical implications of the expression 'by nature', its insertion was first suggested during the Third Committee in the autumn of 1948, when it was deleted in a trade-off to avoid references to God.

251 J Morsink, 'World War Two and the Universal Declaration' [1993] 15 *Human Rights Quarterly* 357–405.

252 Dicke, *supra* n 238, 116.

253 A Trendelenburg, 'Zur Geschichte des Wortes Person' [1908] 13 *Kant-Studien XIII* 1–17.

254 A/C.3/SR.96, 101 (emphasis added).

Two suggested amendments sought to introduce a reference to God in the Declaration,[255] which led to long discussions, but neither of the amendments was voted upon.[256] The first sentence contains an affirmation of the inherence of human rights. It supports the position of the drafters who considered a connection between human nature and individual's rights. In line with the Enlightenment roots of the Preamble, the first sentence of Article 1 is a virtual rewrite of the first Article of the 1789 French Declaration, which states that all 'men are born, and always continue, free and equal in respect of their rights'. Given these connections, it is no surprise that this sentence was a joint French and Philippine proposal.[257] Most drafters used the word 'born' in a dual capacity, a physical birth that is accompanied by a moral birth into the human family of rights and duties.[258]

Second, Article 1 declares that all human beings are not only born free and equal, but adds that they are born '*in dignity and rights*'. Therefore, it follows that individuals cannot be held in slavery or servitude (Article 4);[259] each of them is 'a person before the law' (Article 6); individuals have a remedy in cases of violation of the rights (Article 8); and they are entitled to a status in the community (Articles 15, 16, 17, 21 and 28). Mr Cassin emphasized this, saying that the 'two initial articles stated general principles, within the framework of which individual rights were defined. There was a regular progression from individual rights to social rights.'[260] According to Robinson, Article 1 also has a practical application, and it recognizes a *right* to dignity. In fact, it not only establishes equality in dignity and rights but also affirms the inherent right of all human beings to 'dignity' itself.[261] Consequently, Article 1 militates against events in which individuals are treated inhumanely and their dignity is

255 See proposals by the Brazilian delegation, A/C.3/243; Dutch delegation, A/C.3/219.

256 See Morsink, *supra* n 112, 285–290.

257 The word 'born' was questioned in the Third Committee, where both the Lebanese and Chinese delegations suggested its deletion (A/C.3/235 and 326). Since both of these delegations accepted the inherence view of human rights, these amendments did not mean that the Declaration 'to be philosophically totally open', as Morsink notes, see *supra* n 112, 291. After a lively debate, the word 'born' was kept in with a sizable majority of 20 votes to 12, with 5 abstentions.

258 For a clear report of the debate on the topic, see Morsink, *supra* n 112, 291–292.

259 The Economic and Social Council based its Resolution 475(XV) in 'Slavery' on the principle of 'dignity and worth of the human person' proclaimed in the UN Charter and the UDHR.

260 Between the two groups, first were physical protection's rights; second, individual's relations with others and things, such as property; third, public freedoms; and fourth, guarantee of social security. See A/C.3/SR 173, 4. Differently, Chang described the logical structure of the Declaration as the expression of the three main ideas of the 18th century: 'Article 1 expressed the idea of fraternity, Article 2 that of equality, and Article 3 that of liberty', A7C.3/SR 103, 5–6.

261 Robinson, *supra* n 215, 103–104.

violated.[262] On this basis, it has also been argued that two genealogies of human rights meet in Article 1 of the UDHR: first, 'the fight for universal recognition and equal protection of the dignity of each and every human being'; and, second, 'the struggle for inalienable fundamental rights as a way to protect citizens against abuse of power, in particular by their own sovereign (the state)'.[263] Article 1 includes the two principles that underlie differentiated genealogies, one of a substantive and the other of a procedural nature: universal human dignity and fundamental rights.[264] As regards human dignity in particular, it is seen as the *core value* sustaining human rights to which three basic values, liberty, equality and solidarity ('brotherhood'), relate and against which the exercise of any human right must be tested.[265]

The reference to 'human family' in the first Recital of the Preamble is linked with this Recital to the 'spirit of brotherhood' in Article 1, and both formulations were intended to reverse the order of the rallying cry of the French Revolution, placing fraternity first rather than last. Dicke argues that even if the expression 'freedom equality and brotherhood' appears to be an inheritance from the French Revolution, the term 'reason' is accompanied by 'conscience', thus referring to a moral reasoning at the basis of equality among human beings. In the words of Cassin, the term '*reason*' added 'the particular spark that distinguishes [people] from animals and at the same time obligates them to more grandeur and to more duties than any other beings on earth'.[266] The UDHR is, thus, closer to a Rousseaunian and Kantian vision of dignity than to that of the physiocratic school.[267] Morsink concluded, in relation to the long debates about references to nature and God:

> It is clear from this segment of drafting history that the Universal Declaration is a *secular document by intent*. This outright secularism is a more honest stance than the ambiguous trickledown theory of the classical period. And for that very reason certain fundamentalist or evangelical groups are uncomfortable with or even antagonistic toward the document.[268]

262 See Resolution 445C (XIV) (1952) on Deprivation of Women of Certain Essential Rights and Resolution 547 H (XVIII) (1954) on Customs, Ancient Laws and Practices Affecting the Human Dignity of Women.

263 B de Gaay Fortman, 'Equal Dignity in International Human Rights' in M Düwell, J Braarvig, R Brownsword and D Mieth, (eds), *The Cambridge Handbook of Human Dignity: Interdisciplinary Perspectives* (Cambridge University Press 2014), 355–356.

264 *Ibid.*

265 *Ibid.*, 356.

266 SR.13/, 4. See Chang, SR.8/, 2. On the debate on the expression '*reason and conscience*', see Morsink, *supra* n 112, 296.

267 *Ibid.*

268 Morsink, *supra* n 112, 289 (emphasis added).

This feature was later confirmed by Cassin, called the 'father' of the UDHR.[269] He noted that 'the secularism of the Declaration is in direct relation to its universality'[270] and the success of the Declaration derived directly from its secular nature.[271] On 9–10 December 1948, the Universal Declaration was opened to a vote. Cassin concluded by reporting that the 'firm support of France' for the Declaration, which, 100 years after the Revolution of 1848 and the abolition of slavery on all French territory, constituted a global step in the long struggle for the rights of man' and which represented 'the most vigorous, the most essential *protest of humanity* against the atrocities and the oppression which millions of human beings suffered through the centuries and in particular during and after the two world wars'.[272]

For this reason, the UDHR, together with the human rights idea in general, is embedded securely in the ambiance of the war's aftermath, as part of the moral reconstruction of Europe perceived to be essential to stave off future conflicts and atrocities.[273] In the Declaration, human dignity becomes a 'formal, transcendental norm to legitimize human rights claims'[274] and shows that human rights contain 'at their heart unconditional inviolability'.[275] Cassin strongly felt that a moral manifesto, a statement of principles on human rights, and thus a non-legally binding covenant, gaining the support of those who had won against the Nazi regimes, was the most he could achieve. The main drive was to avoid the reoccurrence of horrors committed in the past and guarantee, through a moral manifesto, a limit to the omnipotence of States' sovereignty over their citizens and an international recognition of human dignity as a right of every human being. The UDHR carries a legal shift from the individual to the *person*[276] and represents a central instrument on the path toward the universalization and secularization of human dignity, a process that will be completed only in the third consolidation phase – as we will see below in Section 3.4.

269 M Agi, *René Cassin* (Perrin 1998).

270 R Cassin, 'Quelques souvenirs sur la Déclaration Universelle de 1948' [1968] 1 *Revue de droit contemporain, Bruxelles, Association Internationale des Juristes Démocratiques* 21–22 (my translation).

271 See R Cassin, 'Historique de la Déclaration Universelle de 1948', in René Cassin, *La Pensée et l'action*, 116.

272 382AP/128, dossier 3, 'Discours de René Cassin, Délégué de la France à l'Assemblée Générale des Nations Unies à Paris', 9 December 1948 (emphasis added).

273 Moyn, *supra* n 167, 121.

274 Dicke, *supra* n 238, 118.

275 *Ibid.*, 119.

276 See M Mazower, 'The Strange Triumph of Human Rights, 1930–1950' [2004] 47(2) *Historical Journal*, 379–398; see also Winter and Prost, *supra* n 212, 239.

3.3.3.4 'Shadow' Human Dignity

Whereas the UN Charter represented a milestone in the new international normative edifice built in this second constitutive stage and it firmly showed that human dignity is one of its foundational principles, the UDHR finally proclaimed, with a new language, the 'inherent dignity of all members of the human family'[277] and of 'the human person'[278] – with a focus that is sometimes centred around the transcendent dimension of humanity (the human family), and at other times around its immanent dimension (the human person). The dignity as an attribution of the person is, however, never questioned. The influence of these two instruments resonated in subsequent treaties part of the wider framework of human rights protection. In particular, the 1950 ECHR and the 1951 Refugee Convention constitute two relevant illustrations of cases enshrining a 'shadow' human dignity. Even if human dignity is not expressly included in their texts, it moved, permeated and highly influenced their preparatory works. A review of the drafting debates of both treaties shows how human dignity was considered part and parcel of the two instruments and why only practical reasons led to the absence from the final documents.

The ECHR was adopted in 1950 by the Parliamentary Assembly.[279] Notwithstanding the surprising absence of a clear reference to human dignity in the text of the Convention, the minutes reported in the *travaux préparatoires* of various meetings of the Assembly of the Council well demonstrate that human dignity was on the minds of many delegates, even though it was differently perceived. In particular, at the first session of the Council's Consultative Assembly, a member of the Greek delegation, Mr Antonopoulos, considered human dignity as a foundation of the European common heritage,[280] while the Italian delegate, Mr Cingolani, referred to human dignity by framing it, instead, within the doctrines of the Catholic faith.[281] The Danish delegate, Mr Kraft, noted that Europe had a '*common spiritual basis* in its views on man, his *dignity* and his rights'.[282] The Belgian representative, Mr de la Vallée-Poussin, referred to human dignity as the essential expression of

[277] Preamble, UDHR.

[278] *Ibid.*

[279] See, WA Schabas, *The European Convention on Human Rights: A Commentary* (Oxford University Press 2015), vii.

[280] Council of Europe, Collected Edition of the '*Travaux Préparatoires*' of the ECHR, Vol. 1, Preparatory Commission of the Council of Europe, Committee of Ministers, Consultative Assembly, 11 May–8 September 1949, First Session of the Consultative Assembly, Strasbourg, Eight Sitting, 19 August 1949 (Martinus Nijhoff, 1975), 56 [Preparatory Commission August 1949].

[281] *Ibid.*, 60–64.

[282] *Ibid.* (emphasis added).

European civilization as opposed to others forms of social life.[283] Moreover, Sir David Maxwell-Fyfe, the delegate for Great Britain, also referred to human dignity. In his view, the central purpose of the Council's Assembly and of the Convention was: 'to delimit the conditions in which alone the *dignity* of the human spirit will stand free, firm and unassailed'.[284] M Yetkin, delegate for Turkey, argued that 'if we wish to safeguard the values upon which *human dignity* depends, we must coordinate on thoughts and actions'.[285] For this reason, in the words of the Irish representative, Mr Norton, 'We have to make human rights and *human dignity realistic and tangible, a something which can be felt, something which can be enjoyed, something from which one can benefit.*'[286] Human dignity was indeed considered part and parcel of a European traditional heritage that the Convention aimed to protect. Human dignity was seen as an essential democratic principle connected to the concept of liberty, against the servitude of man under Nazi and communist regimes, as the delegates Teitgen[287] and Jaquet from France,[288] Fayat (Belgium)[289] and Nally (United Kingdom)[290] argued.

The absence of the term 'dignity' in the Convention is surprising, the more so if one takes into account that the Treaty reflects, in many ways, the UDHR and most of the rights are analogous to some of those recognized in the Declaration. In Jean-Paul Costa's view, it may simply mean that 'the Convention is a more practical, pragmatic, and mechanism-oriented text than that of the Declaration: it created a commission and a court'.[291] Conciseness may have been a reason.[292] Perhaps the diversity of opinions on the exact meaning or its religious roots was also a reason why the term was not included in the text. Admittedly, the Treaty was conceived to be fully functional, leaving no scope for possible difficulties of interpretation. The spiritual and moral sphere, to which human dignity was perceived as belonging, was perhaps seen as distinct from the more technical solution to be found for the purpose of 'the safeguarding and further realisation of human rights and fundamental freedoms'. The goal of the Committee was to find 'the means

283 *Ibid.*, 102 (emphasis added).
284 *Ibid.*, 124 (emphasis added).
285 *Ibid.*, 126 (emphasis added).
286 *Ibid.*, 130 (emphasis added).
287 *Ibid.*, 40.
288 *Ibid.*, 134–138.
289 *Ibid.*, 86.
290 *Ibid.*, 144–150.
291 JP Costa, 'Human Dignity in the Jurisprudence of the European Court of Human Rights' in C McCrudden, (ed.), *Understanding Human Dignity* (Oxford University Press 2013), 394.
292 Schabas, *supra* n 207, 66.

for arriving at an effectual organisation of peace, which is the supreme aim of our Union',[293] and not rely on vague concepts.[294] Sir David Maxwell-Fyfe summarized the position by importantly referring to the implications for State sovereignty

> [W]e *cannot let the matter rest at a declaration of moral principles and pious aspirations* . . . Like all treaties, the proposed Convention would involve some *voluntary surrender of sovereignty*: namely the sovereign right to suppress liberty and democratic institutions.[295]

Therefore, it is not difficult to understand that an express reference to values of humanity or to human dignity in the final text of the Convention might have been seen as superfluous or, in any event, beyond (and misleading from) the more concrete purpose of the Assembly and of the Convention itself. By examining the Convention's drafting history, however, it appears that references to 'human dignity' reduced, or almost disappeared, at a precise moment. It seems that the term fell between two procedural moments. More specifically, the deliberations of the Assembly, in which European delegates expressed their views by also referring to human dignity – such as those mentioned above – were summed up and largely presented on 5 September 1949 in a report to the Assembly by the rapporteur Pierre Henri-Teitgen on behalf of the Commission on Legal and Administrative Questions.[296] On that occasion, in his opening remarks, on the preliminary question on whether such a collective guarantee of essential freedoms and fundamental rights was useful, the Rapporteur stated that:

> the Committee replied in the affirmative, considering that this guarantee would demonstrate clearly the common desire of the Member States to build a European Union in accordance with the *principles of natural law, of humanism and of democracy*; it would contribute to the development of solidarity and would fulfil the longing for security among their peoples.[297]

293 Persico (Italy), Council of Europe, Preparatory Commission August 1949, *supra* n 280, 112. See also M Schmal (Netherlands), Council of Europe, Collected Edition of the 'Travaux Préparatoires' of the ECHR, Vol. 2, Consultative Assembly, Second Session of the Committee of Ministers, Standing Committee of the Assembly, 10 August–18 November 1949; First Session of the Consultative Assembly, Eighteenth Sitting, 8 September 1949 (Martinus Nijhoff 1975), 22–24 (emphasis added).

294 M Schmal (Netherlands), *supra* n 293, 22–24, 24.

295 *Ibid.*, 114, 122 (emphasis added).

296 *Ibid.*, 32 (emphasis added).

297 Report presented by Mr P.H. Teitgen, 5 September 1949, Doc. A 290, I TP 192–213, at 192; Report [of the Committee on Legal and Administrative Questions], 5 September 1949, Doc. AS (1) 77, I TP 216–39, at 216.

Thus, Teitgen merely summed up references to human dignity made during the Committee's debates by using the broader formulation '*principles of natural law, of humanism and of democracy*'.[298] A few references to human dignity made sporadic reappearances later in the debates. The view Teitgen expressed was shared by other delegates, who subsequently recollected, in a few instances, the importance of protecting the '*fundamental dignity of the human family*',[299] the '*dignity of man*',[300] and the need 'to give the personal opportunity to the individual to establish the *dignity of the individual human spirit* and to prevent injustice'.[301]

It can be concluded from the *travaux préparatoires* that, despite its textual absence, human dignity inevitably was seen as an inherent part and universal foundational value of the future Convention, in line with the UDHR. This peculiar aspect did not prevent the Convention's bodies from invoking the concept. In particular, the ECtHR declared that '[t]he very essence of the Convention is respect for human dignity and human freedom'[302] and that secularism is 'consistent with the values underpinning the Convention'.[303] Not only has the Court maintained neutrality in relation to any particular religion, but it has also proclaimed 'visions of human dignity and values that, while certainly compatible with those of established religions, are not essentially spiritual'.[304] Chapter 5 will further explore the manifestations of human dignity in the jurisprudence of the ECtHR

As much as the ECHR, the essence of the Refugee Convention is also the protection of human dignity, adopted just one year later, in 1951. It was modelled on the 1933 Refugee Convention,[305] which was the 'first binding

298 He had already used the expression 'value of our humanism' during the first session of the Consultative Assembly on 19 August, 1949, Teitgen (France), Council of Europe, Preparatory Commission August 1949, *supra* n 280, 40.

299 Mr Sweetman (Ireland), *ibid.*, 90.

300 M. Teitgen (France), *ibid.*, 174.

301 Sir David Maxwell-Fyfe (United Kingdom), *ibid.*, 200.

302 *Svinarenko and Slyadnev* v. *Russia* [GC], nos 32541/08 and 43441/08, 17 July 2014, para 118 and 138; *Pretty* v. *the United Kingdom*, no. 2346/02, ECHR 2002–III, para 65. See also B Maurer, *Le principe de respect de la dignité humaine et la Convention Europeéene des Droits de l'Homme* (La Documentation Française 1999).

303 *Leyla Şahin* v. *Turkey* [GC], no. 44774/98, ECHR 2005–XI, para 114.

304 See Schabas, *supra* n 207, 413. In particular, this universal outreach of the Convention and its connection with the UDHR can be seen in Recital 4 of its Preamble. The phrase repeats Recital 1 of the UDHR Preamble.

305 Convention Relating to the International Status of Refugees, 28 October 1933, League of Nations, Treaty Series Vol. CLIX No. 3663, In 1928, for instance, negotiations had been convened, but 'the majority of participating States proved unwilling to contract formal obligations on behalf of these refugees', Beck, *supra* n 148, 604; JC Hathaway, 'The Evolution of Refugee Status in International Law: 1920–1950' [1984] 33 *ICLQ* 348, 357.

multilateral instrument to afford refugees legal protection' and to 'articulate the principle that refugees should not be returned involuntarily to their country of origin'.[306] The Convention had formalized a clear understanding of the principle of non-refoulement.[307] However, the Convention had important limits: it applied only to groups of refugees who already had League of Nations protection; only sixteen States became parties to it, and various States set strict reservations.[308] This discourse changed radically after the Second World War. Western States 'considered it necessary to put human considerations above political ones'.[309] The final steps were to set up an organization capable of advancing these goals and reflect this new sensibility – the International Refugee Organization (IRO) in 1947, and the UN High Commissioner for Refugees (UNHCR) in 1950 – as well as to entrench this understanding in international law. The Constitution of the IRO had started this process, and the establishment of UNHCR in 1950 and the adoption of the Refugee Convention in 1951 solidified the normative understandings that had emerged twenty years earlier.[310] The Preamble to the Convention declares that it represents an integral part of the wider framework of human rights protection,[311] placing at its core the principle of humanity.[312] Although the

306 Beck, *supra* n 148, 603.

307 In 1932, for instance, the 13th Assembly urged 'Governments not to proceed to the expulsion of a refugee unless he has obtained permission to enter an adjoining country.' As a report of 1933 noted, 'in spite of the earnest resolution adopted by the last Assembly . . . this unfortunate practice [expulsion of refugees] has increased in certain European countries during the past year', see League of Nations, Nansen International Office for Refugees, A.19.1933 Report of the Governing Body, 1, 5.

308 See Beck, *supra* n 148, 621.

309 LW Holborn, *The International Refugee Organization: A Specialized Agency of the United Nations: Its History and Work, 1946–1952* (Oxford University Press 1956), 32.

310 After the adoption of the 1951 Convention, refugee concerns began to arise around the world and the UN Refugee Convention was opened for accession on 31st January 1967, Protocol Relating to the Status of Refugees, 31 January 1967, UNTS vol. 606, 267. See V Chetail, *International Migration Law* (Oxford University Press 2019), chapter 3.

311 A Zimmermann, J Dörschner and F Machts (eds), *The 1951 Convention Relating to the Status of Refugees and Its 1967 Protocol* (Oxford University Press 2011), 346; JC Hathaway, *The Law of Refugee Status* (Cambridge University Press 2014), 110; P Kourula, *Broadening The Edges: Refugee Definition And International Protection Revisited* (Martinus Nijhoff 1997), 92; among court decisions, see *Canada (Attorney-General)* v. *Ward* [1993] 2 SCR 689 (Canada), 733 (La Forest J); *Horvath* v. *Secretary of State for the Home Department* [2001] 1 AC 489 [2000] UKHL 37 (UK) (Bingham LJ); *Refugee Status Appeals Authority (New Zealand)*, Refugee Appeal No. 74665/03 [2005] NZAR 60, para 58 ff.; *Minister or Immigration and Multicultural Affairs* v. *Khawar* [2002] HCA 14 (2002) 210 CLR 1, para 19 (Gleeson CJ); *Abebe* v. *Ashcroft*, 379 F.3d 755 (US), 760.

312 D Cantor and JF Dorieux, *Refuge from Inhumanity? War Refugees and International Humanitarian Law* (Martinus Nijhoff 2014), 9.

Convention does not refer to human dignity in its text, its *travaux préparatoires* show that compatibility and consistency of human dignity were viewed as benchmarks or standards for the assessment of the concept of persecution ex Article 1A(2) and of the level of protection and treatment of refugees' human rights.[313]

3.3.4 *The Expansion of Human Dignity: Individual and Collective Expression*

3.3.4.1 Two Competing Views: An Initial Synthesis

The 1940s can be considered a starting point for contemporary human rights history as well as the preparatory decade of an international consolidation of human dignity that only arrives in the 1960s. As described in Section 3.3.3, the 1940s generated a milestone document that has shaped the entire field, namely the UDHR. Over time, this document has aroused considerable interest and mixed, or even contrasting, opinions: some authors regard it as 'a monumental achievement'[314] while others as a 'funeral wreath laid on the grave of wartime hopes'.[315] The history of the human rights project in the 1940s has been differently framed and defined, considered as '[a] New Deal for the World', '[a] World Made New'[316] and, conversely, 'Death by Birth' or, simply, a 'stillborn' work.[317] These conflicting views call for an accurate political and legal analysis of this period, which may also be able to demonstrate the central role of the 1960s in this history.

On 9 December 1948, the day before the adoption of the UDHR Rights, Eleanor Roosevelt predicted that the Declaration would turn into 'the Magna Carta of all mankind'.[318] At the same time, elsewhere, and, more particularly, in Guadeloupe, French West Indies, the rhetoric was less grandiose (or generous). In 1946, the third West Indian Conference of the Caribbean Commission decided that the Caribbean Commission should consider drafting a regional 'Bill of Human Rights and Obligations'.[319] The third session of

313 A/Conf.2/34–36 (France); see also The Refugee Convention, 1951, *The Travaux Préparatoires analysed with a Commentary by Dr Paul Weis* (UNHCR 1990), 76 (France) and 204 (Denmark).

314 DJ Whelan, *supra* n 114, 60.

315 Moyn, *supra* n 113, 2.

316 See, respectively, E Borgwardt, *A New Deal for the World: America's Vision for Human Rights* (Harvard University Press 2005); Glendon, *supra* n 112.

317 See, respectively, Moyn, *supra* n 113, 44–83 and S Moyn, 'Human Rights in History' *The Nation*, August 11, 2010.

318 Mrs Roosevelt (SA), UNGA, 3rd Session, 180th meeting, 9 December 1948, 362.

319 See Recommendation 8 from 'Report by Secretary General on the Action taken by the metropolitan and territorial Governments on the Recommendations of the previous session

the West Indian Conference opened at Guadeloupe, on 1 December 1948, and closed on 14 December, after reviewing policy to be followed by the Caribbean Commission for the next two years.

The 1948 human rights debate proved to be a quite controversial item. The colonial powers in the Caribbean, namely the United Kingdom, France and the Netherlands, considered the issue with some concern.[320] During the session of the West Indian Conference of the Caribbean Commission, the Trinidadian delegate suggested a regional adaptation of the UDHR,[321] while the Puerto Rican delegate called a Committee to be set up to 'submit concrete proposals for practical implementation' of the UDHR 'in the life of the Caribbean people' and urged the Caribbean Commission to avoid waiting for actions from 'the United Nations or the Metropolitan Governments'.[322] The delegation submitted a resolution demanding implementation of the UDHR.

Time again plays an interesting role, considering that this statement was made only three days before the vote on 10 December which led to the universal adoption of the UDHR. Although the Puerto Rican Resolution was passed and later reached the Drafting Committee, at this second stage, however, the specific recommendation on human rights did not advance.[323] It is, therefore, not difficult to see that the debates in Guadeloupe ended with no real effect, while, by contrast, in Paris the adoption of the UDHR was celebrated as a great achievement. The parallel occurrence of these two events in December 1948, one in Paris and the other in Guadeloupe, the colonial territory, shows how the history of human rights can be 'a history of the simultaneous coexistence of proclamation and denial'.[324] Elements of this

of the West Indies conference and on the work of the Commission since the previous session, U.S. National Archives, RG/59/150/70/28/6 – Box 40. File: Report by the Secretary General on Progress of West Indies Conference. The Commission had been originally created in 1942 for its strategic location during the Second World War.

320 U.S. National Archives, RG/ 59/ 150/ 70/ 28/ 6 – Box 40: U.S. Department of State, 'Draft Declaration of Human Rights (Item 5); Background Information for use of the United States Commissioners on the Caribbean Commission', 22 November 1948, 12. See also JC Parker, *Brother's Keeper: The United States, Race, and Empire in the British Caribbean, 1937–1962* (Oxford University Press 2008), 70 (also 52–55); RC Alomar, *Revisiting the Transatlantic Triangle: The Constitutional Decolonization of the Eastern Caribbean* (Kingston 2009), 18–24.

321 U.S. National Archives, RG 59/ 150/ 70/ UD 07D 68 – Box 39 (Caribbean Commission series): Mr. Gomes (Trinidad), 3rd West Indian Conference, Daily Journal no. 6, December 7, 1948.

322 *Ibid*: Mr. Ramos Antonini (Puerto Rico), 3rd West Indian Conference, Daily Journal no. 6, December 7, 1948.

323 *Ibid.* 3rd West Indian Conference, Recommendations of the Conference, 28 January 1949.

324 Jensen, *supra* n 114, 20.

equation are not only human rights, but also sovereignty, as well as universality and relativism. In particular, when on 9 December 1948 René Cassin declared before the UN GA that '[t]he chief novelty of the Declaration was its universality',[325] it was clear to many that its claim to universality was still dubious.[326]

The coexistence of proclamation and denial, with gaps between ideals and reality,[327] provides the contextual foundation to ground a discussion on the entrance of human dignity in the debates and international legal provisions of the following two decades. In particular, this time is also characterized by important legal developments that ultimately led to the expansion of the circle of human dignity from its individual dimensions to include its collective dimension, in order to explicitly guarantee the dignity of collective subject, such as peoples or groups. In particular, this evolution can be seen in the process behind the adoption of three specific instruments related to distinct phenomena: the 1948 Genocide Convention; the 1955 Declaration on Promotion of World Peace and Cooperation;[328] and the 1965 International Convention on the Elimination of All Forms of Racial Discrimination (ICERD).[329]

The first is represented by the adoption, on 9 December 1948, of the Convention on the Prevention and Punishment of the Crime of Genocide, through which the States parties confirmed 'that genocide, whether committed in time of peace or in time of war, is a crime under international law' and undertook 'to prevent and to punish'.[330] In 1941, 'a crime without a name' was the expression that Winston Churchill used to refer to the atrocities committed by the Nazi regime.[331] The legal term 'genocide' is relatively new. Between the two world wars, Raphael Lemkin coined this concise term based on a neologism with Ancient Greek and Latin roots: the Greek *genos*, meaning race,[332] and *caedere*, meaning to kill in Latin.[333] He defined genocide as '[A]

325 Mr. Cassin (France), UNGA, 3rd Session, 180th meeting, December 9, 1948, 866.

326 H Lauterpacht, 'The Universal Declaration of Human Rights' [1948] 25 *BYIL* 354–381, 358, 372–373; see also Jensen, *supra* n 114, 36.

327 Jensen, *supra* n 114, 21.

328 Final Communiqué of the Asian-African Conference, Bandung, 24 April 1955, 9.

329 International Convention on the Elimination of All Forms of Racial Discrimination, 21 December 1965, UNTS vol. 660, p. 195.

330 Article 1, Genocide Convention.

331 R Lemkin, 'Genocide' [1946] 15(2) *American Scholar* 227.

332 HG Liddell and R Scott, *A Greek-English Lexicon* (Clarendon Press 1996), 344; WF Arndt and FW Gingrich, *A Greek-English Lexicon of the New Testament and Other Early Christian Literature* (University of Chicago Press 1957), 155; P Chantraine, *Dictionnaire étymologique de la langue grecque* (Editions Klincksieck 1968), 222.

333 During the drafting works, some argued the term was an unclear combination of Latin and Greek and the term 'generocide', with pure Latin origin, would have been more appropriate, see A/PV.123, Henriquez Urena (Dominican Republic).

co-ordinated plan of different actions aiming at the destruction of essential foundations of the life of national groups, with the aim of annihilating the groups themselves'.[334] One of the objectives of such plan would be the 'destruction of the personal security, liberty, health, *dignity* and even the lives of the individuals belonging to such groups'.[335] The Genocide Convention came into force in January 1951. Like the ECHR and the Refugee Convention, it also enshrined a 'shadow' human dignity. Even though the final document does not include explicit references to human dignity, it figured at the core of the debate in the drafting process[336] and was regarded as the protected object of the crime of genocide.[337] All the delegates recognized that genocide was an international offence against human dignity.[338] As put by Hartley Shawcross, the United Kingdom representative, 'it was necessary [...] that *international law should limit the omnipotence of certain States over their citizens* and in certain cases protect them against their own Government'.[339] Mr De La Tournelle, the French representative, stated that France was determined to advance 'the greatest efforts to speed up the progress of international law in a sphere which touches so nearly on the destinies and *dignity* of human society'.[340] Thus, recognizing the human dignity of individual and collective subjects meant also protecting the dignity of human society and civilization.[341]

By the mid-1950s there appeared to be a stalemate on the UN human rights project[342] or, at least, a transitional phase.[343] At the same time, the project found different platforms of discussion and of evolution outside the UN doors.

334 R Lemkin, *Axis Rule in Occupied Europe* (Carnegie Endowment for International Peace, Division of International Law 1944), 79.

335 *Ibid.*

336 Mr Chagla, the Indian delegate, A/C.6/84, 25 November 1946, 22nd Meeting, Sixth Committee on the Legal Questions; E/SR.218, General Statements on Draft Convention on the Crime of Genocide, 218th Meeting of ECOSOC, Palais de Nations, Geneva, 26 August 1948, in H Abtahi and P Webb, *The Genocide Convention: The Travaux Préparatoires* (Martinus Nijhoff 2008), 1234.

337 Mr Riad Bey, the Saudi Arabian delegate, A/C.6/91, 28 November 1946, 23rd Meeting, Sixth Committee on the Legal Questions (emphasis added).

338 A/C.6/177, 30 October 1947, Sixth Committee on the Legal Questions, Draft Convention on the Crime of Genocide, Resolution of the National Assembly of Panama; Mr Riad Bey, the Saudi Arabian delegate, A/C.6/91, 28 November 1946, 23rd Meeting, Sixth Committee on the Legal Questions

339 A/C.6/84, 25 November 1946, 22nd Meeting, Sixth Committee on the Legal Questions (emphasis added).

340 A/PV.123, 21 November 1947, GA Hall, Flushing Meadow, New York, in Abtahi and Webb, *supra* n 336, 450 (emphasis added).

341 A/C.6/177, 30 October 1947, Sixth Committee on the Legal Questions, Draft Convention on the Crime of Genocide, Resolution of the National Assembly of Panama (emphasis added).

342 Jensen, *supra* n 114, 41.

343 Burke, *supra* n 114, 15.

In April 1955, the Bandung Conference 'marked out many of the basic contours that came to define key human rights battles, such as that on self-determination'.[344] It was a landmark event in the emergence of the non-aligned movement and the birth of the Third World.[345] A 10-point Declaration on Promotion of World Peace and Cooperation (the Declaration), integrating the principles of the UN Charter, was adopted unanimously in the same year[346] and included, as the first two principles, 'respect for fundamental human rights and for the purposes and principles of the charter of the United Nations' and '[r]espect for the sovereignty and territorial integrity of all nations'. The fourth principle declared a commitment to abstain 'from intervention or interference in the internal affairs of another country'. During the drafting works, debates on human rights and universal dignity[347] ran alongside considerations related to safeguards of sovereign forms of dignity, expressed through principles of respect for State sovereignty and non-interference.[348] Importantly, however, Prince Wan of Thailand argued that Western and Eastern religions have all a common basis for rights, since 'all teach the same lesson – the dignity and worth of man, faith in fundamental human rights, and respect for fundamental freedom for all without distinction as to creed, color or race'.[349] Dignity was seen as a common and universal bond among cultures and universal rights and the UDHR as a valid normative standard for all. Moreover, several delegates associated the pursuit of human rights with the pursuit of self-determination.[350] The Bandung delegates ultimately recognized the UDHR

344 *Ibid.*, 13; see also R Burke, 'The Compelling Dialogue of Freedom, Human Rights at the Bandung Conference' [2006] 28(4) *HRQ* 947–965.

345 G McTurnan Kahin, *The Asian-African Conference* (Cornell University Press 1956), 1.

346 Final Communiqué of the Asian-African Conference, Bandung, 24 April 1955, 9.

347 Ali Sastroamidjojo, Conference Introductory Address, as reproduced in F Hassan, Collected Documents of the Asian-African Conference, 18–24 April 1955 (Centre for the Study of Asian-African and Developing Countries), 18–19, https://digitalarchive.wilsoncenter.org/collection/16/bandung-conference-1955. Of the twenty-five delegates who took the floor on the same day, eleven invoked human rights, see Royal Highness, Foreign Minister Sardar Mohammed Naim of Afghanistan, Prime Minister Zhou Enlai of communist China, and the delegates of Egypt, Iran, Japan, Jordan, Lebanon, Thailand, Turkey, South Vietnam and Yemen, see Asian-African Conference, Speeches and Communiqués, passim; Charles Malik, 'Talk Given by Dr. Charles Malik at Luncheon,' Canberra: Department of External Affairs, Australia, 28 April 1955, 2, National Archives of Australia, A1838/278, 3002/1 Pr 5, File No. 156/3/3.

348 Opening Address of China, as reproduced in Hassan, *supra* n 347, 39; see also Opening Address of Lebanon, as reproduced in Hassan, *supra* n 347, 77 (emphasis added).

349 Opening Address of Thailand, in Hassan, *supra* n 347, 109.

350 Opening Address of Afghani Foreign Minister, Sardar Mohammed Naim, as reproduced in Hassan, *supra* n 347, 27; Opening Address of Iran, Mr Abdoh, as reproduced in *ibid.*, 59.

as 'a common standard of achievement for all peoples and all nations'.[351] The Bandung Conference was a 'historic'[352] event and, in the words of Carlos Romulo, the Philippines delegate, its outcome 'fully supported' the UDHR,[353] because of the universality of 'ideals of freedom'.[354]

Moreover, when the issue of racial discrimination strongly remerged in the late 1950s,[355] the foundational role of human dignity was openly proclaimed in both the Article 1 of the 1960 Convention against Discrimination in Education[356] and in the Preamble and Article 1 of the 1963 Declaration on the Elimination of All Forms of Racial Discrimination.[357] At the time, the prevalence of cases of racial discrimination, in particular the policy of apartheid in South Africa, was a great spur to international reaction.[358] The latter declaration included three references to human dignity in its Preamble in connection with the recognition of UN international instruments, namely the UN Charter (para 1) and the UDHR (para 2). Moreover, before turning to the core of the agreed text, it 'solemnly' declared 'the necessity of speedily eliminating racial discrimination throughout the world, in all its forms and manifestations, and of securing understanding of and respect for the *dignity of the human person*' (my emphasis). In Article 1, the Declaration condemned discrimination between human beings on the ground of race, colour or ethnic origin as '*an offence to human dignity*', which is seen 'as a denial of the

351 Final Communiqué of the Asian-African Conference, 24 April 1955, at 80, Article C–1. Malik advanced a proposal to recognize the 1948 UDHR in the final declaration. This proposal was supported by Ceylon, Iran, Iraq, Japan, Pakistan, Thailand, Turkey and South Vietnam. It was instead opposed by communist China, India, Indonesia and North Vietnam, with Zhou Enlai the opposition leader, see GH Jansen, *Afro-Asia and Non-Alignment* (Faber 1966), 198.

352 C Malik, 'A.B.C Sunday Radio Program Transcript. Guest of Honour Charles Malik,' Australian Broadcasting Corporation, 5 May 1955, 1, National Archives of Australia, A1838/278, 3002/1 Pr 5.

353 CP Romulo, *The Meaning of Bandung* (North Carolina University Press 1956), 14. It cannot be disregarded the strong opposition of the communist China's delegate Zhou, who, however, consented to the inclusion of a mere acknowledgement, see *ibid.*, 14.

354 Emphasis added. See Romulo, *The Meaning of Bandung*, 36; similarly, see Djalal Abdoh, 'The Bandung Conference. An Appreciation', Tehran: British Foreign Office, Tehran Embassy, 3 May 1955, 1–2, National Archives UK, Kew, FO 371/116984, 1071/55/55, D2231/336, 1.

355 See MS McDougal, HD Lasswell and LC Chen, 'The Right to Religious Freedom and World Public Order: The Emerging Norm of Nondiscrimination' [1975] 74 *MichLR* 865.

356 UNESCO, Convention Against Discrimination in Education, 14 December 1960 ('CADE'), Article 1.

357 UN Declaration on the Elimination of All Forms of Racial Discrimination, 20 November 1963, A/RES/1904.

358 See E Schwelb, 'The International Convention on the Elimination of All Forms of Racial Discrimination' [1966] 15 *ICLQ* 996; N Lerner, *The UN Convention on the Elimination of All Forms of Racial Discrimination* (2nd ed., Sijthoff & Noordhoff International 1980).

principles of the Charter of the United Nations, as a violation of the human rights and fundamental freedoms proclaimed in the UDHR, as an obstacle to friendly and peaceful relations among nations and as a fact capable of disturbing peace and security among peoples'. The adoption of the Declaration was saluted as an historic event. 'The twentieth of November 1963 will be, to our mind, as historic as 10 December 1948', declared the Egyptian delegate.[359] During the 1965 GA Session, devoted to the drafting of the ICERD, delegates recognized the need to 'assume a legal responsibility to the international community',[360] and the representative from Jordan stated that '*[t]he meaning of sovereignty had changed*', as it 'had lost its absolute character'.[361] The Convention was 'designed to safeguard human dignity'[362] and proclaim human dignity as a foundational principle of the Convention, in continuity with (and confirmation of) the UN Charter, the UDHR and the 1963 Declaration, by including three references in its Preamble.[363] All these instrument captured the need to include provisions protecting individuals and groups of the population from acts of racial discrimination regarded as '*incompatible with human dignity*'.[364]

All these legal developments realized an initial synthesis of the individual-collective dimensions of human dignity and played a significant role only a few months later, when the two 1966 Covenants were completed and adopted. They indeed sowed the seeds for the consolidation of human dignity in the human rights framework. As it will be discussed next, the two Covenants realized a higher synthesis compared to the 1948 UDHR and succeeded in capturing unexpressed currents and a universal-collective nature of dignity.

3.3.4.2 The Two Human Rights Covenants: Two Paradigms of Human Dignity

On 7 December 1966, after lengthy negotiations, the Third Committee voted and unanimously adopted two Covenants, the ICCPR and the ICESCR. This was followed by another unanimous vote in the GA on 16 December.[365] The

359 Mr Ghorbal (United Arab Republic/Egypt), UNGA, 18th Session, 1261th meeting, November 20, 1963, 15.

360 Miss Hart (New Zealand), UNGA, Third Committee, 20th session, 1347th meeting, November 18, 1965, 340.

361 Mr Sharaf (Jordan), UNGA, Third Committee, 20th session, 1347th meeting, November 18, 1965, 337 (emphasis added).

362 *Ibid.*

363 See Preamble, ICERD, recital 1, 2 and 5.

364 Article 1, CADE (emphasis added).

365 On Monday, December 19, 1966, the two Covenants opened for signature. On the first day, they were signed by Jamaica, the Philippines, Costa Rica, Honduras and Israel. Cyprus

delegate from Cyprus assessed the significance of this achievement most poignantly: '[t]he *moral obligations for respect of human rights will become a legal duty*'.[366] A reference to human dignity was introduced in the Preamble and in substantive Articles of both the ICESCR and the ICCPR, recognizing specific human rights, namely the right to education[367] and treatment of persons deprived of their liberty.[368]

In particular, for the purpose of this study, it is interesting to note that in the Preambles of the ICESCR and the ICCPR (and with identical wording), human dignity is proclaimed twice as a founding principle of the international human rights project started in 1945. The *travaux préparatoires* show the reason why the Commission on Human Rights, which adopted two provisional texts of separate covenants for each set of rights in its eighth session in 1952, had agreed on the text of the Preambles of both Covenants as they appear today.[369]

First, the opening lines declare:

> Considering that, in accordance with the principles proclaimed in the Charter of the United Nations, recognition of the *inherent dignity* and of the equal and inalienable rights of all members of the human family is the foundation of freedom, justice and peace in the world.[370]

As the Commission on Human Rights clarified,

> [t]he first paragraph of each preamble is a *statement of the general principle that 'recognition of the inherent dignity* and of the equal and inalienable rights of all members of the human family is the foundation of freedom, justice and

signed the Covenant on Civil and Political Rights on this day, while Colombia signed both on December 21.

366 Mr Rossides (Cyprus), UNGA, 21st session, 1495th meeting, December 16, 1966, 16 (emphasis added).

367 Article 13 of the ICESCR.

368 Article 10 of the ICCPR.

369 For the *Preamble of the Draft Covenant on Economic, Social and Cultural Rights*, see E/CN.4/L.54, 54/Rev.1–3, paras 167, 171; E/CN.4/SR.308; 333; E/CN.4/666/Add.15; E/2256, paras 161–162; Preamble of the *Draft Covenant on Civil and Political Rights*, see Preamble of the draft covenant prepared at the sixth session, E/1992, annex I ; E/CN.4/528, para 66; E/CN.4/528/ Add.1, para 39; E/CN.4/L.148, 208; E/CN.4/666/Add.15; E/CN.4/SR.331, 333; E/CN.4/668/Add.18, Add.18/Corr.1 (French only); E/2256, paras 286–289; see also Report of the Commission on Human Rights (Ninth Session), Draft International Covenants on Human Rights, ECOSOC document E/2447, E/CN.4/689, 6 June 1953, Annex I, 39 (for the Preamble of the Draft Covenant on Economic, Social and Cultural Rights); 41 (for the Preamble of the Draft Covenant on Civil and Political Rights).

370 Preamble, ICCPR; Preamble, ICESCR, emphasis added.

> peace in the world'. This clause was taken from the first paragraph of the preamble of the Universal Declaration.[371]

The wording of the second part of the preambular provision is inevitably a direct tribute to (and manifestation of continuity with) the UDHR. However, the paragraph includes the phrase 'in accordance with the principles proclaimed in the Charter of the United Nations', whereas the Declaration does not.[372] During the debates on the Preambles, the expression 'principles of the Charter' was considered too indefinite by one delegate. It was argued that it can be interpreted broadly as to include the entire Charter, or narrowly so as to only refer to the principles set forth in Article 2 of the Charter, leaving out the 'purposes' in Article 1 – among which was the achievement of 'international cooperation … in promoting and encouraging respect for human rights and for fundamental freedoms for all without distinction as to race, sex, language or religion'.[373] After a number of drafting changes, which included the approval of an amendment advanced by Australia and Sweden[374] related to the individuals' duty of cooperation,[375] the text was adopted unanimously.[376]

However, both Covenants introduce a legal novelty into the international human rights project started in 1945. They declare, in the second paragraph of the Preamble:

> Recognizing that *these rights derive from the inherent dignity* of the human person.[377]

The *travaux préparatoires* of the Preamble to the draft covenant on civil and political rights clarify that, during the 333rd meeting, after the Commission had adopted its text, all the delegates decided unanimously to insert this

371 E/CN.4/SR.308, 12 (Belgium), emphasis added. See also A/2929, Chapter III, para 3. During the *6th Session* (1950) of the Commission on Human Rights, many proposals were advanced, which were not voted upon but were referred to the Working group, namely: E/CN.4/365 (USA); E/CN.4/365 (France); E/CN.4/376/ (Chile); E/CN.4/377 (Australia); E/CN.4/377/ Rev.1 (Australia). The proposal E/CN.4/491 (Working Groups composed by France, Australia, Chile, Lebanon, United Kingdom, USA and Yugoslavia) was adopted, see E/ CN.4/SR.193, para 50; see documents E/1681 and E/1992, preamble, para 1. See also MJ Bossuyt, *Guide to the 'Travaux Préparatoires' of the International Covenant on Civil and Political Rights* (Kluwer Academic 1987), 4–5.

372 E/CN.4/SR.137, para 34 (Australia), para 38–39 (Chile).

373 A/2929, Chapter III, para 5.

374 E/CN.4/L.171.

375 E/CN.4/SR.308, 13.

376 E/CN.4/SR.308, 14; see also E/CN.4/666/Add.15; E/2256, para 161 (25).

377 Emphasis added.

paragraph between the second and third paragraphs of the text of the Preamble.[378] Its content was debated throughout the 5th session (1949), 6th session (1950) and 8th session of the Commission. In particular, during the 6th session (1950), it was suggested that the recognition that the rights set forth in the covenants 'are inalienable and derive from the inherent dignity of the human person' be integrated into the text of the Preamble.[379] One proposal read as follows:

> [T]he States parties hereto declare that they recognize the rights and freedoms set forth in part II hereof as being among the inalienable human rights and fundamental freedoms *flowing from the inherent dignity of the human person*.[380]

There was indeed general acceptance of the idea that the rights recognized set forth in the covenants derived from the *inherent dignity* of the human person. Thus, through these two references in their Preambles, the two Covenants specified and consolidated the international legal status of human dignity within the human rights framework by affirming that human dignity is a mother-right from which other rights derive. This important manifestation of human dignity will be discussed in more detail in Chapter 5.

Importantly, in both Covenants, Article 1 recognizes the right of all peoples to self-determination. Such recognition has impacted the development of the juridical concept of dignity, understood in its universal sense. It was during the closing phases of drafting the Universal Declaration in 1948 that self-determination and, more precisely, the *right* to self-determination became the source of intense and open controversy. During the drafting, efforts to include it in the final text were eventually rejected by the preponderant Western group,[381] which declined to insert self-determination as a human right in the text of the Declaration.[382] In the early 1950s, however, two strands were visible in both the Human Rights Commission (HRC) and the GA's Third (Social, Humanitarian, and Cultural) and Fourth (Special Political and

378 E/CN.4/SR.333; see also E/CN.4/666/Add.15 (which included the expression 'in accordance with' instead of 'in conformity' and was adopted unanimously E/CN.4/SR.333, 8), see E/2256, para 162 (25), see also E/2247 and A/2929, preamble para 1; see Bossuyt, *supra* n 371, 6–7.

379 E/CN.4/SR.138, para 10–11 (Lebanon); E/CN.4/SR. 331, 9 and 11 (Lebanon); E/CN.4/SR. 333, 5 and 7 (Australia), 6 (Greece) and (Lebanon).

380 E/CN.4/379 (Lebanon), Commission of Human Rights, 6th session (1950) (emphasis added). The proposal was not voted upon but was referred to the Working Group.

381 JP Humphrey, *Human Rights and the United Nations: A Great Adventure* (Transnational 1984), 66.

382 Moyn, *supra* n 113, 84–119.

Decolonization) Committees. These strands can be traced in the records of the discussions related to the drafting of the two Covenants. In fact, already by 1950, during the first consideration by the HRC on whether to include an Article on self-determination, a preliminary question divided the members, namely, whether 'self-determination' was a political principle or a legal right.[383]

The first school of thought argued that 'self-determination' was a political principle, not a human right or an individual right.[384] It was a 'nebulous term',[385] which meant 'different things to different persons': from the right to 'local autonomy', to 'self-government', to 'secession or association' or to 'independent and sovereign statehood'. Also, the concepts of 'people' or 'nation' were considered 'extremely vague'[386] as no 'scientific definitions of such terms existed'.[387] In particular, the members of this school of thought opposed the inclusion of an Article on self-determination in the two Covenants for various reasons: its inclusion would have limited the number of ratifications;[388] the UN Charter made no reference to 'right' of self-determination, but only to a principle 'with a strong moral force', too 'complex to be translated into legal terms in an instrument which was to be legally enforced';[389] the UDHR, which 'was intended to cover all human rights', curiously contained no Article on self-determination;[390] self-determination was not an individual

383 Commission on Human Rights, 7th Session (1951), A/2929, Chapter IV, para 2.

384 E/CN.4/SR.253, 7 (United Kingdom); E/CN.4/SR.255, 5 (Australia); see A/2929, Chapter 4, para 3.

385 E/CN/.4/SR.243, 11 (Belgium); E/CN.4/SR.259, 5 (Sweden); E/CN.4/SR.260, 5 (United Kingdom); see A/2929, Chapter 4, para 3.

386 E/CN.4/SR.252, 7 (Belgium); E/CN.4/SR.259, 5 (Sweden); E/CN.4/SR.260, 5 (United Kingdom); see A/2929, Chapter 4, para 3.

387 *Ibid.*; see A/2929, Chapter 4, para 3.

388 A/C.3/SR.579, para 3 (Norway); A/C.3/SR.642, para 3 (China), para 21 (United Kingdom), para 22 (Netherlands); A/C.3/SR.643, para 17 (Belgium), para 39 (Israel); A/C.3/SR.644, para 4 (Denmark), para 31 (Venezuela); A/C.3/SR.646, para 11 and para 20 (Union. Sov. Soc. Rep.); A/C.3/SR.647, para 27 (Australia); A/C.3/SR.650, para 4 (Brazil), para 8 (Denmark), para 12 (EG); A/C.3/SR.651, para 5 (India); A/C.3/SR.654, para 13 (New Zealand), para 20 (Afghanistan); A/C.3/SR.677, para 8 (Norway); see A/3077, para 29.

389 A/C.3/SR.311, para 21–23 (France); A/C.3/SR.367, para 8 (New Zealand); A/C.3/SR.371, para 29 (France); A/C.3/SR.399, para 26 (France); A/C.3/SR.400, para 19–20 (Australia), para 29 (New Zealand), para 31 (Turkey); para 36 (Czechoslovakia); A/C.3/SR.401, para 27 and paras 31–32 (United Kingdom); A/C.3/SR.572, para 6 (Syrian Arab Republic); A/C.3/SR.641, para 27 (Saudi Arabia); A/C.3/SR.642, para 11–12 (United Kingdom); A/C.3/SR.647, para 19 (Australia); A/C.3/SR.652, para 20–22 (United Kingdom); A/C.3/SR.677, para 8 (Netherlands); see A/3077, para 31.

390 A/C.3/SR.210, para 7 (Mexico); para 24 (Union. Sov. Soc. Rep.); A/C.3/SR.363, para 27 (France); A/C.3/SR.366, para 28 (Lybian Arab Republic); A/C.3/SR.566, para 30 (France); A/C.3/SR.642, para 13 (United Kingdom), A/C.3/SR.644, para 12 (Afghanistan); A/C.3/

right but 'a collective right, and, therefore, inappropriate for inclusion in a covenant which was attempting to lay down the rights of individuals'.[391]

In the same year, a different school of thought maintained that self-determination was a right as well as a principle – the most fundamental of all human rights.[392] It was argued that it was 'a collective right appertaining to all peoples and all nations',[393] a 'prerequisite of the enjoyment of all the rights and freedoms'.[394] It was also added that the principle of self-determination of peoples in accordance with Articles 1 and 55 of the UN Charter has the same essence as the right to self-government or independence, ex Articles 73b and 76b, 'were not different in essence'[395]and it would be 'absurd' to recognize the latter and not the former as a right.[396] Thus, 'the right to self-determination was a universal right; it was a right of all peoples and all nations'.[397] A third line of argument suggested dealing with the issue in a separate declaration or a separate covenant[398] or, to avoid possible legal uncertainty, as subject of a clause in the Preamble of each Covenant.[399] Those who wanted to include a specific Article on self-determination in the draft Covenants supported their claim through different arguments. First, in their view, the right to self-determination was 'essential for the enjoyment of all other rights' and it had to 'appear in the forefront of the covenants'. 'In many cases, individual rights could not be exercised because peoples did not enjoy the right of self-determination.'[400] Moreover, Resolution 5454 (VI) of the GA included an

SR.647, para 20 (Australia); A/C.3/SR.648, para 16 (Saudi Arabia); A/C.3/SR.652, para 18 (United Kingdom); See also A/3077, para 33.

391 A/C.3/SR.309, para 62 (France); A/C.3/SR.310, para 30 (Brazil); A/C.3/SR.312, para 5 (Nicaragua); A/C.3/SR.398, para 40 (Netherlands); A/C.3/SR.399, para 28 (France); A/C.3/SR.400, para 15 (Canada); para 30 (Turkey), para 39 (Czechoslovakia), para 55 (Union. Sov. Soc. Rep.); A/C.3/SR.562, para 13 (United Kingdom); A/C.3/SR.567, para 3 (Netherlands); A/C.3/SR.568, para 27 (Israel); A/C.3/SR.570, para 5 (Canada), para 17 (China); A/C.3/SR.571, para 59 (New Zealand); see also A/3077, para 34.

392 E/CN.4/SR.254, 8 (Lebanon); A/2929, Chapter IV, para 4.

393 E/CN.4/SR.255, 6 (Poland); E/CN.4/SR.256, 7 (Yugoslavia); A/2929, Chapter 4, para 4.

394 E/CN.4/SR.253, 3 (China); A/2929, Chapter IV, para 4.

395 E/CN.4/SR.253, 8 (United Kingdom); E/CN.4/SR.254, 10 (Lebanon).

396 *Ibid.*; see also A/2929, Chapter IV, para 7.

397 *Ibid.*; see also A/2929, Chapter IV, para 7.

398 E/CN.4/SR.255, 5 (Australia), 7 (F); A/2929, Chapter IV, para 5.

399 E/CN.4/SR.255, 7 (France); see also Third Committee, 6th Session (1951), A/C.3/SR.402, para 14 (France); 9th Session (1954) A/C.3/SR.580, paras 2–6 (Brazil), paras 18–26 (Saudi Arabia), para 29 (Bolivia), paras 31–32 (Uruguay); A/2929, Chapter IV, para 5.

400 A/C.3/SR.309, para 52–53 (Afghanistan), para 60 (Union. Sov. Soc. Rep.); A/C.3/SR.310, para 14–15 (India), para 33 (Poland), para 44 (Iraq); A/C.3/SR.311, para 4 (Syrian Arab Republic), para 10 (Byelorussian S.S.R.); A/C.3/SR.358, para 27 (Afghanistan); A/C.3/SR.359, para 8 (Union. Sov. Soc. Rep.); para 21 (Byelorussian S.S.R.); A/C.3/SR.362, para 64 (Chile), para 66 (Syrian Arab Republic); A/C.3/SR.365, para 28 (Egypt), para 32 (Uruguay); A/C.3/SR.366,

Article on the right self-determination[401] and in Articles 1 and 55 of the UN Charter, member States had already 'undertaken to respect the right to self-determination',[402] for 'furthering universal peace'.[403] Last, 'if self-determination constituted a collective right, it nevertheless affected each individual'[404] and to be deprived of the right to self-determination entailed the loss of human rights.[405]

para 18 (Indonesia); A/C.3/SR.367, para 19 (Ukrainian S.S.R.), para 43 (SA); A/C.3/SR.368, A/C.3/SR.367, para 19 (Ukrainian S.S.R.), para 43 (Saudi Arabia); A/C.3/SR.368, para 15 (Byelorussian S.S.R.); A/C.3/SR.397, para 4 (Syrian Arab Republic); A/C.3/SR.399, para 23 (Byelorussian S.S.R.), para 45 (Ethiopia), para 50 (Iran); A/C.3/SR.401, para 4 (Byelorussian S.S.R.), para 15 (Pakistan), para 35 (Uruguay), para 45 (Indonesia); A/C.3/SR.566, para 10 (Burundi), para 35 (Saudi Arabia); A/C.3/SR.569, para 24 (India); A/C.3/SR.572, para 50 (Liberia); A/C.3/SR.573, para 3 (Indonesia); A/C.3/SR. 641, para 7 (Ukrainian S.S.R.); A/C.3/SR.644, para 20 (Byelorussian S.S.R.), para 25 (Indonesia) A/C.3/SR.645, para 8 (Chile), para 12 (Czechoslovakia), para 29 (Iran); A/C.3/SR.646, para 12 (Union. Sov. Soc. Rep.); A/C.3/SR.647, para 1 (Greece), para 38 (Yugoslavia); see also A/3077, para 35.

401 A/C.3/SR.565, para 27 (Union. Sov. Soc. Rep.); A/C.3/SR.572, para 29 (Greece); A/C.3/SR.641, para 6 (USSR); A/C.3/SR.643, para 34 (Poland); A/C.3/SR.644, para 13 (Afghanistan); A/C.3/SR.645, para 16 (Czechoslovakia); A/C.3/SR.646, para 39 (Philippines); A/C.3/SR.652, para 6 (Afghanistan); see also A/3077, para 36.

402 A/C.3/SR.310, para 18 (Afghanistan); A/C.3/SR.364, para 18 (USA); A/C.3/SR.367, para 44 (Saudi Arabia); A/C.3/SR.398, para 36–37 (Saudi Arabia); A/C.3/SR.399, para 24 (Byelorussian S.S.R.); A/C.3/SR.400, para 9 (Lybian Arab Republic), para 38 (Czechoslovakia); A/C.3/SR.401, para 3 (Byelorussian S.S.R.); A/C.3/SR.570, para 27–28 (Bolivia); A/C.3/SR.645, para 25 (El Salvador); A/C.3/SR.647, para 3 (United Kingdom); A/C.3/SR.649, para 22 (Costa Rica); A/C.3/SR.650, para 14 (Ecuador); see also A/3077, para 37.

403 A/C.3/SR.310, para 6 (Mexico), para 12 (Uruguay), para 47 (Ukrainian S.S.R.); A/C.3/SR.311, para 4 (Syrian Arab Republic), para 9 (Byelorussian S.S.R.); A/C.3/SR.363, para 31 (Peru'); A/C.3/SR.364, para 19 (USA); A/C.3/SR.365, para 12 (Yugoslavia); A/C.3/SR.366, para 46 (Cuba), para 52 (Ecuador), para 58 (Czechoslovakia); A/C.3/SR.370, para 11 (Union Sov. Soc. Rep.); A/C.3/SR.397, para 8–9 (Syrian Arab Republic); para 12 (Mexico); A/C.3/SR.399, para 3 (India), para 52 and para 54 (Iran); A/C.3/SR.400, para 42 (Dominican Republic); A/C.3/SR.565, para 24 (Union. Sov. Soc. Rep.); A/C.3/SR.570, para 40 (Mexico); 575, para 9 (Ukrainian S.S.R.); A/C.3/SR.641, para 28 (Saudi Arabia); A/C.3/SR.645, para 15 (Czechoslovakia); A/C.3/SR.646, para 22 (Union. Sov. Soc. Rep.); A/C.3/SR.650, para 25 (Panama); A/3077, para 38.

404 A/C.3/SR.310, para 35 (Poland); A/C.3/SR.311, para 12 (Byelorussian S.S.R.), para 33 (Mexico), para 48 (Saudi Arabia), A/C.3/SR.365, para 12 (Yugoslavia), A/C.3/SR.568, para 47–49 (Yugoslavia); A/C.3/SR.571, para 17 (Poland); A/C.3/SR.572, para 4–5 (Syrian Arab Republic), para 30 (United Kingdom); A/C.3/SR.575, para 21 (El Salvador); A/C.3/SR.646, para 4 (Pakistan); A/C.3/SR.647, para 39 (Yugoslavia); A/C.3/SR.651, para 34 (Egypt), para 39 (Israel), A/C.3/SR.654, para 27 (Denmark), para 32 (Bolivia); see also /A/3077, para 40.

405 A/C.3/SR.311, para 5 (Syrian Arab Republic); A/C.3/SR.367, para 43 (Saudi Arabia); A/C.3/SR.397, para 30 (Saudi Arabia); A/C.3/SR.400,para 2–5 (Syrian Arab Republic), para 8 (Libyan Arab Republic); A/C.3/SR.402, para 4 (Mexico); A/C.3/SR.565, para 23 (Union. Sov. Soc. Rep.); A/C.3/SR.571, para 4 (Egypt); A/C.3/SR.642, para 5 (China), para 27 (Netherlands); A/C.3/SR.644, para 21 (Byelorussian S.S.R.), para 28–29 (RI); A/C.3/SR.645,

In 1966, the concept of self-determination was recognized as a fundamental and universal human right[406] and a pre-condition for the existence of other individual human rights, with the inclusion in the ICESCR and in the ICCPR of the identically worded Articles 1. The *travaux préparatoires* make clear that the word 'peoples' meant 'peoples in all countries and territories, whether independent, trust or non-self-governing':[407] it had to be understood in 'its most general sense and no definition was necessary'.[408] Moreover, the definition of the right to self-determination, provided in Article 1(1),[409] was regarded as a 'very comprehensive conception', meaning that 'every people should be free to establish its own political institutions, to develop its own economic resources and to direct its own social and cultural evolution, without the interference of other people or nations'.[410] Self-determination had to be recognized as a collective human right,[411] and the '[a]chievement of self-determination' had to 'mark renewed efforts to guarantee human rights and the *dignity* of the individual'.[412] From the perspective of human dignity,

para 22 (El Salvador); A/C.3/SR.646, para 21 (Union Sov. Soc. Rep.); A/C.3/SR.647, para 8–9 (GR); A/C.3/SR.651, para 35 (Egypt); see also A/3077, para 40.

406 Commission on Human Rights, 8th Session (1952), E/CN.4/SR.254, 5 (Union Sov. Soc. Rep.); see also A/2929, Chapter 4, para 8.

407 E/CN.4/SR.253, 4 (Greece).

408 E/CN.4/SR.256, 7 (Yugoslavia); 9 (Belgium); E/CN.4/SR.257, 9 (Lebanon). Suggestions were made to the effect that 'peoples' should apply to [E/CN.4/SR.256, 5 (India); E/CN.4/SR.257, 6 (USA), 'large compact national groups', to 'ethnic religious or lingustic minorities', to 'racial units inhabiting well defined territories [E/CN.4/SR.256, 7 (Yugoslavia)]. The 'right to minorities was a separate problem of great complexity', see A/2929, Chapter IV, para 9 (Commission on Human Rights, 8th Session, 1952).

409 Commission on Human Rights, 8th Session (1952), E/2556, Article 1, para 1 (see also documents E/2447 and A/2929, Article 1, para 1. The Article was adopted by 12 votes to none, with 1 abstention (E/CN.4/SR.259, 7); Third Committee, 10th Session, 1955, see A/3077, para 74, which 'adopted Paragraph 1 as a whole' by 'a roll-call vote [G.A. N.10 of 31 to 9, with 18 abstentions' (A/C.3/SR.676, para 21)].

410 Commission on Human Rights, 8th Session (1952), A/2929, Chapter IV, para 12; see also Third Committee, 10th Session (1955): A/C.3/SR. 643, para 36 (Poland).

411 See also I Brownlie, 'The Rights of Peoples in Modern International Law' in J Crawford (ed.), *Rights of Peoples* (Clarendon Press 1992), 1, 5; see also the *Kitok case*, Report of the Human Rights Committee, A/43/40, 221, 228; 96 ILR, 637, 645; the *Lubicon Lake Band case*, A/45/40, vol. II, 1, 27; 96 ILR, 667, 702; *EP* v. *Colombia*, A/45/40, vol. II, 184, 187; and *RL* v. *Canada*, A/47/40, 358, 365; 96 ILR, 706. However, in *Mahuika et al.* v. *New Zealand*, the Committee took the view that the provisions of article 1 may be relevant in the interpretation of other rights protected by the Covenant, in particular Article 27 on the rights of persons belonging to minorities, A/56/40, vol. II, annex X, A. See also *Diergaardt et al.* v. *Namibia*, A/55/40, vol. II, annex IX, sect. M, para 10.3.

412 US Mission to the UN, *Press Release*, USUN–114(75), 10 October 1975, 3; see also Telegram 4928 from U.S. Mission United Nations to State, October 10, 1975, State Department FOIA Electronic Reading Room, Central Foreign Policy Files, 1973–1976.

the Two Covenants indeed consolidated human dignity as a universal concept, in its individual and collective dimension.

Thus, more specifically, the ICCPR and the ICESCR consolidate different trends, more or less liberal, that had not found complete manifestation in the Universal Declaration. Starting from 1945, in the transition from religious human dignity to a more universal one, there are two main streams of *universal* human dignity that manifest themselves, one more individual and the other more collective. In particular, the attempt of UDHR drafters in 1948 to create a less religious and more universal ecumenical instrument managed to capture different currents of dignity, but leaving unexpressed those that later converged into the movement for the recognition of the concept of self-determination – a very diverse current in itself.

The two Covenants realize a higher synthesis compared to the 1948 Covenant. Unlike the Universal Declaration, the two instruments succeed in capturing unexpressed currents and a universal-collective nature of dignity. This is perhaps a peculiarity of the two Covenants. The two treaties, indeed, collect these two different paradigms of dignity: on the one hand, human dignity as an attribution of the individual, to be found crystallized in the UDHR; while on the other, an expression of dignity in its collective nature. In particular, self-determination appears as a legal paradigm of a whole series of previous concerns – partly similar and partly different from those that had found expression elsewhere. The fact that the only common Articles of the two Covenants are Article 1, on the right to self-determination, together with the prohibition of discrimination on the basis 'race, colour, sex, language, religion, political or other opinion, national or social origin, property, birth [or other status]',[413] confirms the evolution and crystallization of this broader and more universal reflection.

This does not imply that the earlier recognition in 1948 of the physical protection of the group as such, for instance, through the prohibition of genocide (by the Genocide Convention), did not take into account the collective nature of dignity or that this feature was not relevant when the regime of protection of minorities started to materialize in the 1920s. In a periodization focused on dignity and human rights, it is, however, interesting to note the evolution of the qualification of universality in relation to human dignity as such. In fact, if in itself the 'universal' nature of dignity can possess various and infinite shades, by considering its legal manifestations, human dignity appears expressed in its two dimensions: the individual (more liberal, more 'Wilsonian', more political, less economic, less social), and the

413 Article 2, ICESCR; 26 ICCPR (see also its Article 24).

collective one, which is also manifested through collective rights.[414] The Covenants confirmed and consolidated the process of collectivization of human dignity in international law, against the circle of sovereign dignity – a process started back in 1919 and crystallized in 1948. Although it may seem natural to consider that the first manifestation of human dignity appeared in the UDHR, looking at it more closely, in reality we note that the Declaration did not give expression to a strand of dignity that did not fit in its predominantly individualistic connotation, Catholic or Western. It is not enough that dignity presents itself as universal, because its dimensional connotations qualify its true scope. Therefore, it is not only the difference between (and the passage from) Catholic dignity and universal human dignity that is important, but rather, as explained, the shades within the conception (and qualification) of 'universal'. These specific shades of dignity are also expressions of different historical trends. The consolidation of this bi-dimensional nature of universal human dignity blossomed only with the 1966 Covenants, which, for this reason, can be seen as the apical instruments for the expression of human dignity in the human rights sphere.

3.4 THIRD CONSTITUTIVE STAGE: THE CRIMINALIZATION OF ASSAULTS TO HUMAN DIGNITY

3.4.1 *An Actionable Human Dignity*

A further constitutive stage of human dignity can be followed throughout the nineteenth century and the twentieth century. ICL, or similar versions of it, has a long history,[415] with the chivalric system in the medieval era as the first precursor.[416] The international criminal system has historically evolved and consolidated around two main pillars, namely (i) the development of an international definition of crimes and (ii) the inception and consolidation of

414 See D Sanders, 'Collective Rights' [1991] 13 *HRQ*368; M Shaw, *International Law* (8th ed., Cambridge University Press 2018), 220–231.

415 See TLH McCormack, 'From Sun Tzu to the Sixth Committee, The Evolution of an International Criminal Law Regime' in TLH McCormack and GJ Simpson (eds), *The Law of War Crimes, National and International Approaches* (Kluwer Law International 1997), 31; MC Bassiouni, 'From Versailles to Rwanda in Seventy-Five Years, The Need to Establish an International Criminal Court' [1997] 10 *HHRLJ* 11.

416 See, MH Keen, *The Laws of War in the Late Middle Ages* (University of Toronto Press 1965); Meron, *supra* n 8; G Schwarzenberger, *International Law as Applied by International Courts and Tribunals* (Stevens & Sons 1968), vol. II, chapter 39; R Cryer, *Prosecuting International Crimes: Selectivity in the International Criminal Law Regime* (Cambridge University Press 2005), Chapter 1.

principles and procedures governing the international investigation and prosecution of these crimes. These two pillars and foundations are the starting point for the historical search for human dignity in ICL. In particular, because of this dual foundation, which arose and evolved at different paces, human dignity makes its entrance in ICL in two ways and at two different speeds. In this process, it is slowly vested with an actionable nature.

The first constitutive element, the concept of international crime, emerges for the first time in 1899 with the Hague Conventions, then slightly develops with the Treaty of Versailles in 1919. In 1943, Kelsen observed that, at the time of writing, international law was certainly well equipped with the definition of the crimes, but had no system of international criminal responsibility.[417] He noted:

> Since the demand to punish the war criminals aims at individual responsibility of the persons who by their own conduct have performed the crimes, it seems impossible to satisfy this demand on the basis of general international law.[418]

In 1943 the problem was considered of 'impossible solution'.[419] It was only in 1945 that the Nuremberg Charter established a first recognition of the criteria of international criminal responsibility (and its prosecution). The second component of the international criminal system will, however, only consolidate in the 1990s, with the establishment of the ICC. Here, the definition of international crime, already set in 1945, finds a final confirmation and internationalization. This legal and institutional development consolidates a system of protection of human dignity, transforming it into an actionable concept.

The two components of ICL just described, the definition of an international crime and the concept of individual criminal responsibility, are inherently connected (and moved) by two distinct considerations, namely *humanitas* and *utilitas*. As Kelsen correctly said, those committing piracy (or slave trading) have long been regarded as guilty of crimes against international society (*crimina iuris gentium*) for which there is direct responsibility.[420] It is

417 H Kelsen, 'Collective and Individual Responsibility in International Law with Particular Regard to the Punishment of War Criminals' [1943] 31 *CalifLRev* 530; see also V Pratt and JE Viñuales, 'Rétroactivité et non-rétroactivité en droit international: essai de clarification conceptuelle à partir de l'éxpérience du Procès de Nuremberg' [2013] 59 *Annuaire français de droit international* 327–358.

418 Kelsen, *supra* n 417, 534.

419 *Ibid.*, 534.

420 See Article 9, Universality—Piracy, [1935] 29 AJIL, *Supplement: Research in International Law*, 563-572; see JC Bluntschli, *Le Droit International Codifie* (Lardy's transl., Guillaumin 1895), Art. 346; P Fauchille, *Traité de Droit International Public* (Librarie Arthur Rousseau

a long-established principle of the world community[421] that all States may have jurisdiction and can therefore both arrest and punish pirates, as long as pirates are apprehended on the high seas[422] or in the territory of the State concerned. The principle is one of *universality*, which will be examined in more detail in Chapter 6. Here, this principle is just a starting point to reflect on its *origins*.[423] The more specific reason is that we can trace a further continuing line with the rival relation between the two circles of dignity, at the inception of the international criminal system. The principle of universal jurisdiction has its first origin in the concept of *utilitas* and only subsequently did its *humanitarian* connotation evolve, leading to an expansion of the meaning and application of the principle.

On the basis of the above considerations, the following section will first clarify the distinction between the concept of *utilitas* and of *humanitas*. Subsequently, it presents the consolidation process of human dignity in ICL by first focusing on the crystallization of human dignity, in a period spanning from the end of 1800 to 1945. This time corresponds to the first recognition and adoption of a complete set and definition of international crimes (first phase) which enshrine human dignity as a protected good. Subsequently, it examines its development and final consolidation in 1998, with the establishment of an international and permanent system of prosecution with the entry into force of the ICC Statute (second phase). The chronology of this third constitutive stage, which will be followed in this section, is summarized in Figure 3.4. Chapter 6 will instead examine in detail the manifestations of human dignity in this legal framework.

3.4.2 Utilitas *versus* Humanitas

The distinction between a universal jurisdiction that could be called 'utilitarian' and another one of 'humanitarian' source seems an essential stage in the

1922), sec. 483; D Field, *Outlines of an International Code* (2nd ed. 1876), Art. 650; P Fiore, *International Law Codified* (Borchard's transl., Baker Voorhis 1918), Art. 299; WE Hall, *International Law* (8th ed., Oxford University Press 1924), sec. 81. See also *Draft Convention on Piracy, Research in International Law* [1932], 739, 751–754, 757–765, 852.

421 See *In re Piracy Jure Gentium* [1934] AC 586; 7 AD, 213; see also DH Johnson, 'Piracy in Modern International Law' [1957] 43 *Transactions of the Grotius Society* 63; GE White, 'The Marshall Court and International Law: The Piracy Cases' [1989] 83 *AJIL* 727. See also the Separate Opinion of Judge Guillaume in *Congo* v. *Belgium*, ICJ Reports, 2002, 3, 37–38; 128 ILR, 60, 92–94; and *R* v. *Jones* [2006] UKHL 16; 132 ILR, 668.

422 Article 105 of the Law of the Sea Convention, GA Res. 48/263, 1833 UNTS 396, 10 December 1982 (reproducing Article 19 of the Geneva Convention on the High Seas, 1958).

423 Perhaps the more detailed account can be found in H Donnedieu De Vabres, 'Le système de la répression universelle. Ses origines historiques – Ses formes contemporaines' [1922] *Revue de droit international privé* (devenue Revue critique de droit international privé), 547.

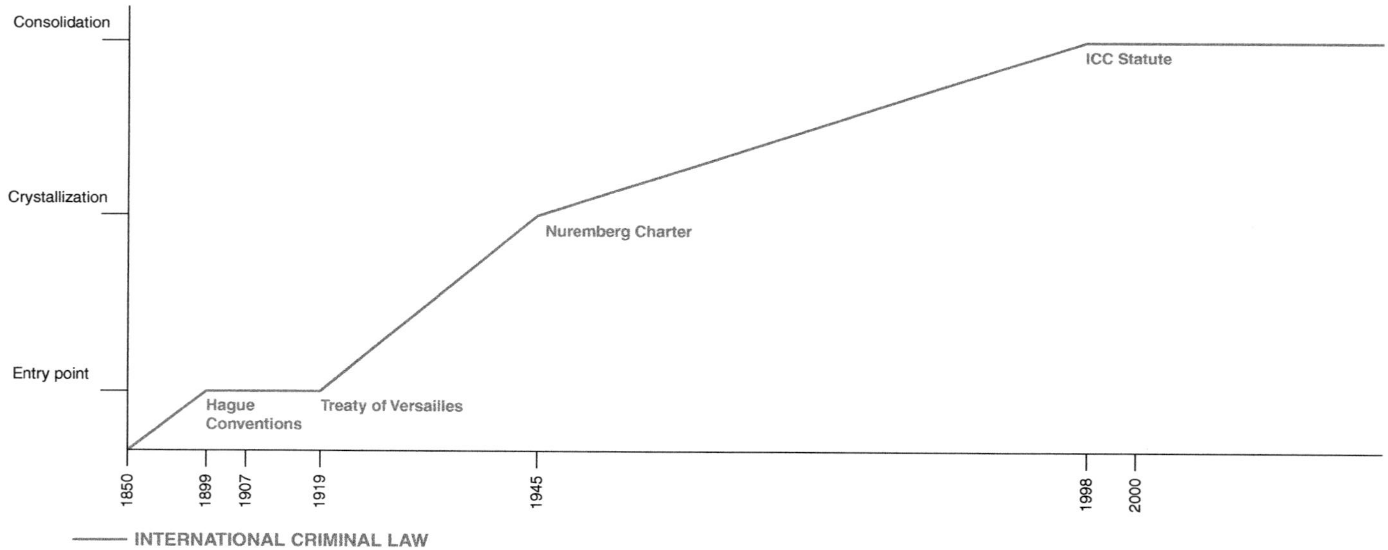

FIGURE 3.4 *Third constitutive stage*

exploration of the meaning of the current idea of universal jurisdiction and of the evolution of human dignity in ICL. Many legal scholars since the nineteenth century have advocated the theory of universal jurisdiction without necessarily clarifying the philosophical foundation of that theory or its legal elements. Instead, much like the early universalists, they argue that certain international crimes imply that all States, irrespective of any existing national legislation, and even contrary to national legislation, have the power to prosecute, irrespective of any territorial connection to the crime or any connection to the nationality of the perpetrator or the victim. Perhaps the most articulate expression of the question was made in 1924 by Donnedieu de Vabres[424] when he observed, 'Universal jurisdiction is not based on the dogmatic, philosophical conception of a human fraternity, but on the indisputable reality of a community of interests'.[425] However, a few pages later, he noted, 'it is not possible to build exclusively on utilitarian basis the rational and final solution of conflicts of criminal jurisdiction'.[426] These remarks by one of the greatest specialists of universal jurisdiction serve as a reference for structuring the exploration of the sources of this institution. Universal jurisdiction only gained positive law through its reformulation in strictly utilitarian terms. However, this formulation has never been enough to exhaust the reality of universal jurisdiction. Nowadays, this last statement is almost self-evident, so much of the humanitarian ideology developed following the horrors of the Second World War, but it was less obvious at the time when Donnedieu de Vabres wrote, when ideas such as human solidarity and human dignity were still growing at a slow pace in the international legal dimension. In this vein, it is first necessary to expose the utilitarian theorizations of universal jurisdiction before examining the humanitarian aspect of this institution.

The different interpretations of universal jurisdiction that can be described as utilitarian are, as a general rule, still dependent on Bartole de Sassoferrato's conception of the *forum of deprehensionis*.[427] Universal jurisdiction is envisaged as a means of dealing with the possible impact on the State of the forum

[424] H Donnedieu De Vabres, *Les Principles Modernes Du Droit Penal International* (Sirey 1928), 135–136; see also A Rubin, *The Law of Piracy* (2nd ed., 1998).

[425] Donnedieu De Vabres, *supra* n 423, 535, original 'La compétence universelle ne repose pas sur la conception dogmatique, philosophique d'une fraternité humaine, mais sur la réalité incontestable d'une communauté d'intérêts' (my translation).

[426] *Ibid.*, 563, '... that it is not possible to raise on an exclusively utilitarian basis the rational and definitive solution of conflicts of criminal jurisdiction' (my translation).

[427] Dig. 47.2 – De furtis ; Dig. 13.1, De condictione furtiva; see C Guenoux, *Histoire du droit romain au Moyen Âge* (Charles Hingray 1839); G Le Bras, C Lefebvre and J Rambaud, *L'âge classique (1140–1378), Sources et théorie du droit* (Sirey 1965); Donnedieu De Vabres, *supra* n 424, 136ff

of the commission of certain crimes abroad. In particular, the presence of the unpunished criminal on the territory of a State would undermine the rule of law and civil peace because of the scandal of impunity.[428] The legitimacy of the jurisdiction is thus derived, in the final analysis, from the principle of the place of commission.[429] Among authors for whom universal jurisdiction was mainly for utilitarian reasons, we could include the French penalist Maurice Travers, for whom the idea of a universal repression based on the existence of a moral and legal solidarity between the States neglects the evidence that, since the sovereignty of the State is limited, it can not act on behalf of all humanity.[430]

The humanitarian source of universal competence must be sought in the thoughts of authors such as Covarrubias[431] and Grotius.[432] They identified a category of individual crimes damaging the interests of the international community as a whole, whose authors were seen as enemies of humankind (*communis hostis omnium* or *hostis humani generis*).[433] At the end of the nineteenth and at the beginning of the twentieth century, however, this interpretation of the foundation of the institution had only a limited scope. Reflecting the belief of his time, Donnedieu de Vabres spoke of two kinds of internationalism, one 'idealist' and the other 'realist', adding that:

> the former is more attractive to philosophers and philanthropists (while) the latter fits better with the practical concerns of statesmen. It also penetrates more easily into positive law.[434]

A number of scholars have affirmed the need for a universal repression of certain crimes on the basis of the existence of a human solidarity, human

428 See JLE Ortolan, *Eléments de droit pénal* (4ème édition, 1875), vol. 1, 381; Donnedieu De Vabres, *supra* n 423, 536; A Mercier, 'Le conflit des lois pénales en matière de compétence' [1931] 87(1) *Annuaire de l'Institut de droit international* 134.

429 Donnedieu De Vabres, *supra* n 423, 538–539.

430 M Travers, *Le droit pénal international et sa mise en œuvre en temps de paix et en temps de guerre*, vol. I (Sirey 1920–1922), 75–76.

431 D Covarrubias y Leyva, *Opera omnia* (1762).

432 P Haggenmacher, 'Grotius et le droit international – Le texte et la légende' in A Dufour, et al. (eds), *Grotius et l'ordre juridique international* (travaux du colloque Hugo Grotius, Genève 10–11 November 1983) (Payot 1985), 118.
Grotius, *supra* n 13, Book I, chap. I.

433 For a long period, piracy juris gentium was included among international crimes.

434 Donnedieu De Vabres, *supra* n 423, 557, original 'law [L]e premier séduit davantage les philosophes et les philanthropes (alors que) le second s'accorde mieux avec les préoccupations pratiques des hommes d'Etat. Aussi pénètre-t-il plus aisément dans le droit positif' (my translation).

dignity and/or a natural right, such as the Italian criminal lawyer Francesco Carrara[435] or the Brazilian Silvestre Pinheiro-Ferreira.[436]

The ideologies underlying both forms of the institution are distinct. At the origin of the concept of *judex deprehensionis*, there was the idea of an administrative distribution, which has subsequently become 'inter-State', of the competences. In the case of universal *humanitarian* jurisdiction, such a distribution plays no role as long as it is the gravity of the crime, and gravity alone, that puts the judge in a position to adjudicate the crime. It is understandable then that these two methods lead to different outcomes. In other words, from a theoretical point of view, the court of a State could be competent to know of a certain crime because of its particular gravity without being so on the basis of the principle of the *forum deprehensionis* and vice versa.

Both sources have, however, been confused or, more precisely, brought together by legal practice in a composite entity. There is an essential difference between the idea of utilitarian universal jurisdiction and that of universal humanitarian jurisdiction. Certainly, the principle of universal jurisdiction has its first origin in the concept of *utilitas* and only later was it expanded by way of a *humanitarian* source. The *nature* of the crime lies at the core of the distinction between the two sources. For the purpose of my study, this distinction enables me to reduce the scope of my analysis only to those crimes that trigger a humanitarian jurisdiction and are against human dignity and against humanity. This focus will be maintained also in the analysis of the manifestations of human dignity presented in Chapter 6.

3.4.3 *From The Hague to Nuremberg: The Rise of Individual Criminal Responsibility*

In the second half of the nineteenth century, efforts intensified at international level for the codification of the laws of war.[437] In the aftermath of the experiences of the American Civil War and the Franco-Prussian War of 1870, the question of the individual responsibility for violations of these norms arose clearly to the attention of the international community.

No indication of actual effort can, however, be derived from the first instruments concluded in the middle of the century, namely the 1856 Paris

435 F Carrara, *Programme du cours de droit criminel* (trad. P. Baret) (Paris 1876), par. 1057, in Donnedieu De Vabres, *supra* n 423, 544 (emphasis added).

436 S Pinheiro-Ferreira, *Droit des gens*, t. II, art. 3 para. 12, 31; *Cours de droit public*, t. II, 32 ss et 179 ss, cited in *ibid.*

437 See G Balladore Pallieri, *Diritto bellico* (Cedam 1955); E David, *Principes de droit des conflits armés* (Bruylant 1999). See also Section 3.2.

Declaration Respecting Maritime Law, the First Geneva Convention for the Amelioration of the Condition of the Wounded in Armies in the Field of 1864 and the St Petersburg Declaration of 1868.[438] In fact, the government delegates who drew up the Geneva Convention of 1864 had expressly removed from the draft Convention a provision, formulated in very limited terms, on the question of the penal repression of the crimes committed by individuals.[439]

The solution referred to in the 1906 Geneva Convention for the Amelioration of the Condition of the Wounded and Sick in Armies in the Field is instead quite significant. According to its Article 28, the Contracting States undertook to take

> the necessary measures to repress, in time of war, individual acts of robbery and ill treatment of the sick and wounded of the armies, as well as to punish, as usurpations of military insignia, the wrongful use of the flag and brassard of the Red Cross by military persons or private individuals not protected by the present convention.[440]

The rule, however, said nothing about whether a State could only punish members of its own armed forces or those of enemy States; it is therefore not possible to consider the accepted jurisdiction criteria.[441]

The question also remains rather ambiguous in the light of the so-called Hague law and, in particular, the Hague Regulations annexed to the Fourth Hague Convention of 1907, concerning the laws and customs of land war. They recognize, but only in a very general and limited way, the punishment of the perpetrators of certain violations.[442] The time did not seem ripe for States to show an interest in exercising the faculty to repress behaviours not connected in any way to their own social sphere, which is what the principle of universality calls for. The experience of the First World War, which will be now discussed, does not seem to deny this conclusion.

438 See also the project for the Declaration of Bruxelles, S Glaser, *Droit international pénal conventionnel*, vol. I (Bruylant 1970), 75 s.

439 See J Pictet et al. (ed.), *The Geneva Conventions of 12 August 1949: Commentary, Vol. I*, Convention for the Amelioration of the Condition of the Wounded and Sick in Armies in the Field (ICRC 1952), 396 [Pictet et al., *Commentary*, I].

440 1906 Geneva Convention for the Amelioration of the Condition of the Wounded and Sick in Armies in the Field, 6 July 1906, Article 28.

441 See Pictet et al., *Commentary*, I, 398 s.; Y Sandoz, 'Penal Aspects of International Humanitarian Law' in MC Bassiouni, (ed.), *International Criminal Law*, vol. I (Transnational Publishers Dobbs Ferry 1986), 213.

442 See Articles 41 and 56.

After the end of the First World War, the Allies set up a commission of 15 members to investigate the responsibility for the start of the war and violations of the laws of war and assess what type of tribunal would be appropriate for trials.[443] In March 1919, the Commission to the Preliminary Peace Conference established the liability of the central powers for starting the war[444] and that *violations of the laws of war and humanity* had been committed.[445] The Commission recommended that high officials, including the Kaiser, be tried for ordering such crimes and on the basis of command responsibility.[446]

The work carried out within the Commission is undoubtedly of great importance with respect to the question that interests us, namely the identification of a further entry point of human dignity in international law and the related limits to the repressive power of States with regard to *crimina juris gentium*. In particular, it also represents a stage in the process of affirmation in the practice of governments of new indictments attributable to the category of *crimina juris gentium*, that is, crimes against peace and those against humanity.

The report presented to the Supreme Council on 29 March 1919 established a fundamental distinction between two categories of crime: the acts that led to the conflict and those in violation of the laws and customs of war. On this last category there was a general consensus and a fairly detailed but not exhaustive list of the criminal cases was compiled.[447] The delegations welcomed the principle of individual responsibility of the authors of violations of war law without difficulty: 'Whoever has been guilty of offenses against the laws and customs of humanity, is liable to criminal prosecution.'[448] The possibility of an amnesty for the guilty parties was excluded, correlatively, foreseeing the respective States as having a precise obligation to deliver the guilty parties in order to allow for judgment against them.[449] This was an innovative principle compared to the previous practice of tacit amnesties.

The Commission subsequently suggested the establishment of an Allied 'High Tribunal', with members from all of the Allied countries, to try violations of the laws and customs of war and the laws of humanity.[450] This was

443 Report of the Commission to the Preliminary Peace Conference [1920] 14 *AJIL* 95.
444 *Ibid.*, 107.
445 *Ibid.*, 114–115.
446 *Ibid.*, 116–117, 121. See also T Meron, 'Reflections on the Prosecution of War Crimes by International Tribunals' [2006] 100 *AJIL* 551.
447 *Ibid.*, 114–115.
448 *Ibid.*, 115–117.
449 *Ibid.*, 123.
450 *Ibid.*, 122.

criticized by the Commission's US and Japanese members. The US members said that they knew 'of no international statute or convention making violation of the laws and customs of war – not to speak of the *laws or principles of humanity* – an international crime'.[451] The Japanese representatives questioned 'whether international law recognizes a penal law applicable to those who are guilty'.[452] The majority, however, clearly considered there to be a body of ICL, albeit one that did not include aggression as a crime.[453] Accordingly, the 1919 Treaty of Versailles included, in Article 227, that '[t]he Allied and Associated Powers publicly arraign William II of Hohenzollern, formerly German Emperor, for a *supreme offence against international morality* and the sanctity of treaties'.[454] The disputed crimes were expressed with a formula of compromise, vague and indeterminate – 'supreme offense against international morality' and 'the sacred authority of the treaties' – which had provoked criticism from many parties regarding respect for the principle *nullum crimen, nulla poena, sine praevia lege*.[455] But it is clear that the Commission's debate on the responsibilities of the authors of the war was a fundamental step in the process that led, in 1945, to the elaboration of the category of crimes against peace.[456] This provision was not implemented as the Netherlands refused to hand the Kaiser over to the Allies because of the political nature of the offence.[457] In addition, the Treaty of Versailles, in Articles 228 and 229, also provided for prosecutions of German nationals for war crimes before Allied courts, including mixed commissions where the victims came from more than one State. These provisions, however, never materialized into practice. Some prosecutions, but far fewer than the Allies wanted, were undertaken by Germany itself in Leipzig between 1921 and 1923. The proceedings were biased toward the defendants, leading to questionable acquittals and lenient sentences.[458] Even if some of these cases later formed important precedents in ICL,[459] we cannot consider that a system

451 *Ibid.*, 144–146.
452 *Ibid.*, 152.
453 *Ibid.*, 118.
454 *Ibid.*, 122. This provision was contested by the Italian Prime Minister Vittorio Emanuele Orlando, see *La prassi italiana di diritto internazionale* (terza serie (1919–1925)), a cura di Marchisio, Ferrajolo, Javicoli, Marcelli, (Roma, 1995) vol. IV, 2348ff.
455 Ibid. 2351ff.
456 See E Schwelb, 'Crimes against Humanity' [1946] *BYIL*, 182ff.
457 See MC Bassiouni, 'World War I, The War to End All Wars and the Birth of a Handicapped International Criminal Justice System' [2002] 30 *DJIL&P* 244, 269–273; WA Schabas, *The Trial of the Kaiser* (Oxford University Press 2018).
458 C Kress, 'Versailles-Nuremberg-the Hague: Germany and International Criminal Law' [2006] 40 *IL* 15, 16–20.
459 *The Dover Castle* (1922) 16 AJIL 704; *The Llandovery Castle* (1922) 16 AJIL 708. See Kress, *supra* n 458, 16–18.

of international criminal justice was active at the time. Significant developments followed the experience of the Second World War and the Conventions stipulated immediately afterwards on the subject.

In August 1945, six months after Yalta, the Allies issued a Charter establishing the Nuremberg International Military Tribunal to try the 'major war criminals of the European Axis',[460] setting forth guidelines known as the Nuremberg Principles. By sanctioning prosecutions for atrocities committed in wartime, the Nuremberg Principles was 'a determination to *punish the most violent sorts of assaults on human dignity*'.[461] The Nuremberg Charter defined three categories of crimes: crimes against peace, war crimes, and the category of crimes referred to as 'crimes against humanity'. More specifically, the concept of 'crime against humanity' was defined in Article 6(c).

The notion of crimes against humanity had already appeared on the legal scene on 24 May 1915, following the massacre of the Armenians, in the Joint Declaration by France, Great Britain and Russia regarding the Armenians.[462] In the original proposal, however, Russian Foreign Minister Sazanov had suggested 'crimes against Christianity and civilisation'.[463] Taking issue with the term 'Christianity', fearing the reaction from the Muslim population, the French Minister Delcassé advanced the suggestion to replace the word with 'humanity'.[464] The proposal was accepted by the other delegations. At the time, however, the term seems to have been adopted a little by chance,[465] considering the subsequent legal developments. Various other attempts to act at the diplomatic level on behalf of humanity did not succeed. In 1919, the Commission on the Responsibilities of the Authors of War and on Enforcement of Penalties, in addition to considering German responsibility for the war, sought to charge Turkish officials and other individuals for 'crimes

460 Article 1, Charter of the International Military Tribunal – Annex to the Agreement for the prosecution and punishment of the major war criminals of the European Axis [Nuremberg Charter] 8 August 1945.

461 See Glendon, *supra* n 112, 14 (emphasis added).

462 France, Great Britain and Russia Joint Declaration, 24 May 1915; see Jean-François Roulot, *Le crime contre l'humanité* (L'Harmattan 2002), 75; see also A Clapham, *Human Rights a Very Short Introduction* (2nd ed., Oxford University Press 2014), 34.

463 Russian Dispatch of 11 May 1915, in A Beylerian, *Le Grandes Puissances, l'Empire Ottoman et les Arméniens dans les archives françaises (1915–1918) Recueil de documents* (Paris, 1983), 23 (doc. n. 29).

464 *Ibid.*, 23.

465 A Cassese, *Cassese's International Criminal Law* (3rd ed., Oxford University Press 2013), 84–85.

against the laws of humanity'[466] based on the so-called Martens Clause contained in the Preamble of the 1907 Hague Convention (IV).[467] Moreover, the 1920 Treaty of Sèvres (1920), between the Allies and Turkey, punished the 'acts in violation of the laws and customs of war'[468] and 'criminal acts'[469] allegedly committed by Turkish government, but did not expressly refer to 'humanity'. The Treaty was never ratified and was replaced on 24 July 1923 by the Treaty of Lausanne, which not only removed the clause, but also granted immunities to those responsible for such crimes.[470] Political considerations prevailed over moral ones.[471]

If the connection between humanity and crime was established, the expression 'crime against humanity' was only included in the Nuremberg Charter at the very end of the Conference,[472] after the drafter had already defined the crime. This category of crimes came to incorporate 'all actions running contrary to those basic values that are, or should be, considered inherent in any human being'.[473] The Charter demonstrated that, in the words of British Chief Prosecutor Sir Hartley Shawcross, 'the omnipotence of the State' was limited and 'the individual human being, the ultimate unit of all law, is not disentitled to the protection of mankind when the State tramples upon his rights in a manner which outrages the conscience of mankind'.[474] The term 'crime against humanity' was regarded as more suitable to catch the attention of the general, public conscience.[475] The concept of 'humanity' carries a strong symbolic meaning. It was for the images that it conveys, rather than for strictly legal reasons, that it was originally incorporated in the law. This term evokes much more than what it may literally describe:[476] it is 'a thought

466 'Report presented to the Preliminary Peace Conference by the Commission on the Responsibilities of the Authors of War and on the Enforcement of Penalties' (Carnegie Endowment for International Peace, Division of International Law, 1919), 25–26. The action was paralyzed by the Memorandum of Reservations submitted by the US delegates.

467 Hague Convention IV 1907, preamble, 2779–2780.

468 Treaty of Sèvres, 10 August 1920, Article 226.

469 *Ibid.*, Article 227.

470 G Bass, *Stay the Hand of Vengeance: The Politics of War Crimes Tribunals* (Princeton University Press 2001); Bassiouni, *supra* n 457, 244–291.

471 Bassiouni, *supra* n 56, xxix–xxx.

472 Ibid., 47.

473 A Cassese, *supra* n 465, 87.

474 Sir H Shawcross, *Speeches of the Chief Prosecutors at the Close of the Case against the Individual Defendants* (HM Stationery Office, Cmd 6964, 1946), 63.

475 H Meyrowitz, *La Repression par les tribunaux allemands des crimes contre l'humanité et l'appartenance à une organisation criminelle en application de la loi n° 10 du Conseil de Contrôle allié* (LGDP 1961), 47.

476 M Massé, 'Après Nuremberg et Eichmann, entre Barbie et Touvier: les crimes contre l'humanité', Actes, droit et humanité, *Les cahiers d'action juridique*, (1989), n 67–68, 33.

of what we might be, that is, an awareness of what we might also not be'.[477] This consideration explains why the word 'humanity' has never been otherwise defined, and only by the enumeration of behaviours described as crimes against humanity.[478] The concept of humanity serves as a prism to describe the constituent elements of the offense.[479] It appears in itself ambivalent – considering the immanent and transcendent nature of its entity. The individual victim of such a crime is perceived not only as a member of humanity, and thus a victim of that specific crime, but also as its depositary,[480] which allows them to be distinguished from the 'ordinary' victim. The criminal act inevitably takes the individual out of humanity: the perpetrator confiscates the inherent humanity of the victim.[481] It also undermines, at the same time, the entire human race, which is the main or direct victim of the crime. The Nazi regime had materialized repeated attacks on human dignity that would be considered as crimes against both human dignity and the human race.[482] The word 'humanity' made it possible to take into account all of these parameters, that is, to include a human dimension, condemning attacks on an individual's dignity and on humankind. Thus, in the expression 'crime against humanity', the concept of humanity is adopted in all its semantic meaning: it refers to humankind in its entirety, in 'its individual and collective manifestations'.[483]

Providing a definition of crimes against humanity was the Nuremberg Charter's most relevant and advanced contribution to international law,[484]

477 J Allard, 'L'humanité, un concept juridique sans précédent?' in T Berns (ed.), *Le droit saisi par le collectif* (Bruylant 2004), 206, original 'une pensée de ce que nous pourrions être, c'est-à-dire une conscience de ce que nous pourrions également ne pas être' (my translation).

478 M Delmas-Marty, *Vers un droit commun de l'humanité* (Les éditions Textuel 1996), 85. During the Commission's work on the Draft Code of Crimes against the Peace and Security of Mankind, it was proposed to introduce a definition of the term 'humanity', but this idea was not taken up by the Commission, see CDI, 'Summary records of meetings of the 41st session, 2098th meeting, 9 May 1989', CIDA 1989, vol. I, 20, para 18 (statement by Mr. Sepulveda Gutiérrez).

479 These features will be examined in more detail in Chapter 6 of this study; see also C Le Bris, *L'humanité saisie par le Droit International Public* (LGDJ 2012), Chapter 1.

480 RJ Dupuy, *L'humanité dans l'imaginaire des nations, conférences, essais et leçons du Collège de France* (Julliard 1991), 203: 'Il y a crime contre l'humanité parce que la victime est dépositaire de celle-ci en même temps qu'elle en est membre'.

481 See R Roussillon, 'Crime contre l'humanité "psychique"' in M Colin (ed.), *Le crime contre l'humanité* (Erès 1996), 111f.

482 Le Bris, *supra* n 479, 241–242.

483 T Doudou, 'Quatrième rapport sur le projet de code des crimes contre la paix et la sécurité de l'humanité', [1986] ACDI vol. II (1st part), 57, para 15.

484 As previously considered, the concept of crimes against humanity can be traced back to the France, Great Britain and Russia Joint Declaration, 24 May 1915.

although it kept the law of war imprint by confining the crimes to crimes 'before or during the war'. Inspired by this instrument, on 19 January 1946, the Declaration of Supreme Command of the Allied Forces Far East established the Tokyo International Military Tribunal[485] to try the 'major war criminals in the Far East'[486] and Law No. 10 promulgated by the Control Council in Germany[487] included the notion of 'crime against humanity', which did not include the nexus requirement and was adopted to establish a uniform legal basis for the prosecution of war criminals in occupation courts in Germany.[488] Even though it is undeniable that the Nuremberg Tribunal, composed of four principal judges (from the US, UK, USSR and France) and four alternates, was the first international criminal tribunal, it was only meant as a finite (in time) measure. It was specifically designed to bring Nazi war criminals to justice, and carried out 13 trials between 1945 and 1949. The provisions of the Nuremberg Charter, however, marked the first crystallization of human dignity in its third constitutive stage and triggered a chain of developments in ICL, particularly since the GA in 1946 affirmed the Charter's principles.[489]

3.4.4 *Back to The Hague: The Institutionalization of International Prosecution*

The massive violations of IHL and IHRL rights in the former Yugoslavia, and subsequently, the Rwanda massacres of 1994, led to the establishment of two ad hoc criminal tribunals, the International Criminal Tribunal for the former Yugoslavia (ICTY)[490] and the International Criminal Tribunal for Rwanda (ICTR),[491] by virtue of the authority of the UN Security Council (SC) to adopt decisions binding upon all member States ex Chapter VII of the UN Charter.

485 Charter of the International Military Tribunal for the Far East, 19 January 1946.

486 Article 1, *ibid.*

487 Law of 20 December 1945, published in *Journal officiel du Conseil de contrôle en Allemagne*, n° 3, Berlin, 31 January 1946, 50f.

488 Allied Control Council Law No. 10 Punishment of Persons Guilty of War Crimes, Crimes Against Peace and Against Humanity, 20 December 1945, Official Gazette of the Control Council for Germany, No. 3, Berlin, 31 January 1946. 1 Friedman 908, Article II.

489 UNGA Resolution 95(I) of 11 December 1946, Affirmation of the Principles of International Law recognized by the Charter of the Nuremberg Tribunal. See also the International Law Commission's Report on Principles of the Nuremberg Tribunal, Yearbook of the ILC, 1950, vol. II, 195, and the Convention on the Non-Applicability of Statutory Limitations to War Crimes and Crimes against Humanity, 1968.

490 Statute of the International Tribunal for the Prosecution of Persons Responsible for Serious Violations of International Humanitarian Law Committed in the Territory of the Former Yugoslavia since 1991, Annex to Security Council S/RES/827, 25 May 1993 [ICTY Statute].

491 Statute of the International Tribunal for Rwanda, Annex to S/RES/955, 8 November 1994 [ICTR Statute].

Importantly, both tribunals included a definition of international crimes under their jurisdiction. Articles 2 to 5 of the ICTY Statute include the crimes with regard to which the Tribunal can exercise jurisdiction, namely grave breaches of the Geneva Conventions of 1949, violation of the laws or customs of war, genocide and crimes against humanity. The Statute of the ICTR largely resembles that of the ICTY – it was referred to as the 'adjustment of the ICTY Statute to the circumstances in Rwanda'.[492] Articles 2 to 4 of the Statute stipulated the crimes over which the Tribunal had jurisdiction. Article 2 dealt with genocide; Article 3 with crimes against humanity; and Article 4 dealt with violations of Article 3 common to the Geneva Conventions and of Additional Protocol II. Another important feature of these tribunals was that both had concurrent jurisdiction with national courts.[493] The origins and case law of the ad hoc Tribunals are an essential component in the constitutive history of human dignity in ICL, as we shall see in Chapter 6. Although both tribunals had a limited scope and timespan, they were a fundamental step on the path toward the equipment by the international criminal system of an international criminal court.

On 15 December 1997, the GA organized a State Conference for the establishment of the ICC in Rome.[494] It started on 15 June 1998 and was concluded on 17 July 1998 with the adoption of the ICC Statute,[495] which entered into force on 1 July 2002, ex Article 126. The creation of a permanent criminal court was a landmark moment in the path toward prevention and repression of international crimes. The adoption of the Statute of the ICC is not only a fundamental historical event in the international cooperation for the purpose of exercising punitive activity in the matter of *crimina juris gentium*, but also consolidates the protection of the legal good human dignity by providing both a definition of such crimes as well as a permanent structure to prosecute them. This was the outcome of a long evolution that started at the end of the nineteenth century.

The ICC distinguishes itself from previous courts and tribunals and mechanisms of criminal justice for four main reasons. In primis, unlike the two international criminal tribunals (for the former Yugoslavia and for Rwanda),

492 Report ICTR, 1995, 491.

493 Article 9, ICTY Statute; Article 8, ICTR Statute.

494 UNGA Resolution 52/160, 15 December 1997.

495 See Triffterer, O, (ed.), *Commentary on the Rome Statute of the International Criminal Court* (2nd ed., Hart 2008); C Stahn (ed.), *The Law and Practice of the International Criminal Court* (Oxford University Press 2015); WA Schabas, *The International Criminal Court: a commentary on the Rome Statute, Oxford Commentaries on International Law* (2nd ed., Oxford University Press 2016).

the ICC is the product not of a binding SC resolution, but of an international treaty. This was essentially because States, while prepared to agree on the establishment of geographically limited (the former Yugoslavia) and temporally constrained (in Rwanda's case) tribunals by SC action, were not willing to be so bound by the establishment of a permanent international criminal court with much more extensive jurisdiction without express consent. Second, the ICC is an institutional prosecutorial mechanism whose jurisdiction is inherently different from its predecessors, such as the Nuremberg Tribunal, the ICTY or the ICTR. A third key feature of the ICC is that it is based on the principle of complementarity, which is a functional principle aimed at granting jurisdiction to a subsidiary body (in this case, the ICC) when the main body (a national court) fails to exercise its jurisdiction: when the latter fails to act, the former, in the presence of certain circumstances, can represent a possible venue to avoid impunity.[496] Lastly, the Statute provides that the jurisdiction of the ICC is limited to the 'most serious crimes of concern to the international community as a whole', being genocide, crimes against humanity, war crimes and aggression. Thus, the ICC Statute, as we shall see in more detail in Chapter 6, intends to provide penal protection against the violations of the most basic human rights protecting the dignity of the persons in their individuality and in their social and collective dimension. The Statute therefore protects also the collective legal interests of international peace and security, as well as more concrete legal interests of individuals, such as life, bodily integrity, liberty and personal autonomy.

These four distinctive features of the ICC are the reason why human dignity consolidates as a protected interest in ICL, becoming an actionable concept. The agreement of the States parties on the full institutionalization of the system of prosecution at the international level of international crimes through the creation of an international criminal court, not geographically nor temporally limited, finalize the third constitutive stage of the criminal protection of human dignity. This last phase is the outcome of the previous entry points and developments that occurred since the nineteenth century.

[496] Article 17 ICC Statute. See C Stahn and MM El Zeidy, *The International Criminal Court and Complementarity* (University of Colorado Press 2014); A Cassese, *supra* n 465, 351; JT Holmes, 'Complementarity: National Courts versus the ICC' in A Cassese, P Gaeta and JRWD Jones (eds), *The Rome Statute of the International Criminal Court: A Commentary* (Oxford University Press 2002), Chapter 18.1, 672.

4

Human Dignity in International Humanitarian Law

4.1 INTRODUCTION

In the words of Jean Pictet, international humanitarian law (IHL) finds 'its inspiration in humane ideals', and 'focuses on the protection of the individual in time of war'.[1] Such definition, bridging a legal and a moral notion, reflects the nature of a legal discipline based on instilling moral, or specifically, humanitarian, considerations in international law when war casts a sinister shadow over human life. Since the 1863 Lieber Code onwards, upholding human dignity has been one of the main goals of the modern quest to regulate hostilities.

In Chapter Three, the study concluded that the concept of human dignity first entered the laws of war through the Christian value of humanity, because of the Christian belief of its founders, and was at the basis of a foundational guiding principle. The entry date and first crystallization of human dignity in international law and, more specifically, in IHL occurred with the adoption of the Martens Clause. In 1949, instead, the adoption of the Four Geneva Conventions defined the true consolidation of human dignity in the laws of war.[2] It is said that their entry into force marked the

[1] J Pictet, 'International Humanitarian Law: Definition' in UNESCO, *International Dimensions of Humanitarian Law*, Henry–Dunant Institute (UNESCO, Martinus Nijhoff 1988), xix.

[2] On the Geneva Conventions of 1949, see JAC Gutteridge, 'The Geneva Conventions of 1949' [1949] 26 *BYIL* 294; F Siordet, 'La Conférence diplomatique de Genève' [1949] 31 *RICR* 475, 554; J Pictet, 'La Croix–Rouge et les Conventions de Genève' [1950] 76 *RCADI* 1; S Tschirkovitch, 'Les nouvelles Conventions internationales de Genève relatives à la protection des victimes de la guerre du 12 août 1949' [1950] 54 *RGDIP* 97, at 525; P De La Pradelle, *La Conférence diplomatique et les nouvelles Conventions de Genève du 12 août 1949* (Les éditions internationals 1951); GIAD Draper, *The Red Cross Conventions* (Stevens & Sons 1958); GIAD Draper, 'The Geneva Conventions of 1949' [1965] 114 *RCADI* 59; A Maresca, *La protezione internazionale dei combattenti e dei civili: Le Convenzioni di Ginevra del 12 agosto 1949* (Giuffrè 1965); T Meron, 'The Geneva Conventions as Customary Law' [1987] 81 *AJIL*

beginning of a 'humanitarian age',[3] transforming the law of armed conflict into a 'humanitarian law'. The protection of the individual became the pivotal core of the entire system. There was no longer room for a system of rules merely (or even essentially) considered as 'military law'. As the Commentary to the GC IV (article 2) notes, 'the Conventions have been drawn up first and foremost to protect individuals, and not to serve State interests'.[4]

Building on the conclusions drawn on the main consolidated features of the first constitutive stage of human dignity, this chapter moves into the examination of the legal manifestations of dignity in IHL. The laws of armed conflict deploy four main manifestations of human dignity: first, human dignity acts as a foundational *principle* and structural element of IHL; second, human dignity injects considerations of humanity in the law and represents the basis of an *inviolable right*, from which other rights derive; third, it is an obligation-creating principle, directly deriving from its legal substance and from its concretizations; and lastly, human dignity acts a protected good of specific international *crimes*. This assessment inspires the structure of this section. The following sections will explain in detail how three main instruments, that is, *principle* (Section 4.2), *right* (Section 4.3) and *obligation* (Section 4.4), characterize and manifest human dignity in the laws of armed conflict framework, outlining the various linguistic articulations of human dignity for each of them and their interrelation. Differently, the manifestations of human dignity as a *crime* will be presented and examined in Chapter Six. In line with the argumentative narrative of this study, the chapter will conclude

348; A Clapham, P Gaeta and M Sassòli, *The 1949 Geneva Conventions. A Commentary* (Oxford University Press 2015). See also the commentaries to the Four Geneva Conventions edited by the ICRC in the 1950s: J Pictet et al., *The Geneva Conventions of 12 August 1949: Commentary*, Vol. I, Convention for the Amelioration of the Condition of the Wounded and Sick in Armies in the Field (ICRC 1952); J Pictet et al., *The Geneva Conventions of 12 August 1949: Commentary*, Vol. II, Geneva Convention for the Amelioration of the Condition of Wounded, Sick and Shipwrecked Members of Armed Forces at Sea (ICRC 1960); J Pictet et al., *The Geneva Conventions of 12 August 1949: Commentary*, Vol. III, Third Geneva Convention Relative to the Treatment of Prisoners of War (ICRC 1960); J Pictet et al., *The Geneva Conventions of 12 August 1949: Commentary*, Vol. IV, Geneva Convention Relative to the Protection of Civilian Persons in Time of War (ICRC 1958). For the Additional Protocols of 1977, see essentially Y Sandoz, C Swinarski and B Zimmermann (eds), *Commentary on the Additional Protocols of 8 June 1977 to the Geneva Conventions of 12 August 1949* (ICRC 1987).

3 R Kolb, 'The Main Epochs of Modern International Humanitarian Law since 1864 and Their Related Dominant Legal Constructions' in KM Larsen, CG Cooper and G Nystuen (eds), *Searching for a 'Principle of Humanity' in International Humanitarian* Law (Cambridge University Press 2012), 45.

4 Pictet et al., *Commentary*, IV, *supra* n 2, Art. 2(1).

with an analysis of the tension between the two circles of dignity, sovereign and human, within the framework of humanitarian law (Section 4.5).

4.2 HUMAN DIGNITY AS A PRINCIPLE

Respect for human dignity, in the words of Jean Pictet, is a 'principle of human law' and 'military necessity and the maintenance of public order must always be compatible with respect for the human person'.[5] This section examines two 'cardinal principles contained in the texts constituting the fabric of humanitarian law',[6] which constitute a direct manifestation of human dignity: the principle of humanity and the principle of distinction. Whereas the principle of humanity animates the spirit and content of IHL, the principle of distinction guarantees the protection of certain categories of persons in times of conflict on the basis of humanitarian considerations. They are both 'deontological' principles, which define what is a morally mandatory conduct and from which deontological constraints derive.[7] A focus on these two principles is thus based on strict evaluation of the inherent role of human dignity in their formation and development. On the contrary, the principles of military necessity and proportionality, which also lie at the foundations of much of IHL, are rather 'consequentialist', as they determine legality according to an assessment of the consequences of an act.[8] They therefore suggest if an action is right or wrong depending on the outcome of such assessment, which includes evaluations related to sovereign dignity. The principles of humanity and of distinction instead determine legality according to a clear set of rules based on human dignity. The interrelation between human dignity and the principles of military necessity and proportionality, as expression of sovereign dignity, will be discussed in Section 4.5.

5 J Pictet, *Development and Principles of International Humanitarian Law*, Henry–Dunant Institute (Martinus Nijhoff 1985), 61. See also I Brownlie, *Principles of Public International Law* (5th ed., Clarendon Press 1998), 27; H Sultan, 'La conception islamique du Droit international humanitaire dans les conflits armés' [1978] 34 *Revue egyptienne de Droit international* 1, 4, 7–9.

6 *Legality of the Threat or Use of Nuclear Weapons*, Advisory Opinion, (1996) ICJ Reports 1996, p. 226, para 78.

7 Deontology is a theory whose name derives from the Greek word *deon*, meaning duty. Actions that obey these rules are ethical, while actions that do not, are not. This ethical theory is most closely associated with German philosopher Immanuel Kant.

8 The paradigm case of consequentialism is utilitarianism, whose classic proponents were Jeremy Bentham (1789), John Stuart Mill (1861) and Henry Sidgwick (1907).

4.2.1 *The Principle of Humanity*

The principle of humanity overarches the whole body of IHL[9] and provides the law with a 'unique identity'.[10] As the International Criminal Tribunal for the former Yugoslavia (ICTY) aptly put it in the notable early case *Prosecutor* v. *Furundžija*:

> The essence of the whole corpus of international humanitarian law as well as human rights law lies in the protection of the human dignity of every person. . . . The general *principle of respect for human dignity* is . . . the very *raison d'être* of international humanitarian law and human rights law; indeed in modern times it has become of such paramount importance as to permeate the whole body of international law.[11]

The principle is commonly understood as meaning that the protection of human beings in times of conflict is warranted by the inherent dignity of the human person. In particular, this section will examine three core aspects of the principle of humanity: first, the historical role of the Martens Clause in recognizing 'the laws of humanity', or 'principles of humanity', as a substantive principle of IHL and as the 'most general norm of the Laws of War';[12] second, the meaning of the concept 'humanity' and its relation with 'human dignity'; and, lastly, the operational functions of the principle under IHL from a conceptual and practical perspective. The principle also constitutes the core source of cardinal manifestations of human dignity, namely of specific rights and obligations. The content and implications of such rights and obligations will be examined below in Sections 4.3 and 4.4, respectively.

4.2.1.1 The Martens Clause and 'Principles of Humanity'

The Martens Clause, introduced in Chapter Three (Section 3.2.2), needs now to be singled out for its central relevance in the present debate. This section will first clarify its legal basis and subsequently its purpose and meaning.

The Martens Clause was originally crafted to provide residual humanitarian norms in order to guarantee the protection of the population of occupied

9 See R Liivoja, 'Technical Change and the Evolution of the Law of War' [2015] 97(900) *IRRC* 1157, 1165–1166.

10 BB Jia, 'Principle of International Humanitarian Law' in JE Viñuales (ed.), *The UN Friendly Declaration at* 50 (Cambridge University Press 2020), 272.

11 *Prosecutor* v. *Furundžija*, IT–95–17/1–T, 10 December 1998, ICTY, para 183.

12 G Balladore-Pallieri, *La Guerra* (CEDAM 1935), 139.

territories.[13] In this context, it seems clear that the purpose of the Clause is disclosed by the Preamble to the Hague Convention, which clarifies that cases not provided for in the Convention 'should [not] for want of a written provision be left to the arbitrary judgment of the military commanders'. Taking this a step further, the Nuremberg Tribunal interpreted the Martens Clause as follows:

> The Preamble is much more than a pious declaration. It is a general clause, making the usages established among civilized nations, the laws of humanity and the dictates of public conscience into the legal yardstick to be applied if and when the specific provisions of the Convention and the Regulations annexed to it do not cover specific cases occurring in warfare, or concomitant to warfare.[14]

Subsequently, the Clause appeared in common provisions of the Geneva Conventions and in the 1977 Additional Protocols. It is present in the denunciation clauses of the Geneva Conventions (Common Article 63/62/142/158) for a different, but parallel, objective. If a State Party denounces the Conventions, it will remain bound by the principles of international law, as a result of the usages established among civilized peoples, the laws of humanity and the dictates of public conscience. Therefore, the Clause becomes a fundamental guarantee that international customary law will still apply to States no longer bound by the Geneva Conventions as treaty law.[15] In addition, Common Article 3 of the Conventions also sets forth the fundamental principle that persons taking no active part in the hostilities shall in all circumstances be 'treated humanely'. The implication of this provision and obligation will be examined in Section 4.4.1.

The Additional Protocols introduced instead a 'modernized' version of the Clause. Additional Protocol I moved the Clause from the Preamble of the Hague Conventions to the text of Protocol I, in its Article 1(2), to clarify the gradual development of written humanitarian law as well as to demonstrate that a common law had to be respected.[16] The ICRC Commentary to Article 1(2) AP I stated that there were two reasons why it was considered useful to include this Clause in the Protocol. First,

[13] FW Holls, *The Peace Conference at The Hague* (Macmillan 1900), 135–138; Ministère des Affaires Etrangères, La Haye, *Conférence Internationale de la Paix 1899*, Troisième partie, Deuxième Commission, at 111–116 (1899).

[14] *In re Krupp and others*, 15 Ann. Dig. 620, 622 (U.S. Mil. Trib. 1948).

[15] G Abi-Saab, 'The Specificities of Humanitarian Law' in C Swinarski (ed.), *Studies and Essays on International Humanitarian Law and Red Cross Principles in Honour of Jean Pictet* (Martinus Nijhoff 1984), 265, 275.

[16] Diplomatic Conference on the Reaffirmation and Development of International Law Applicable in Armed Conflicts, Official Records, Doc. CDDH/I/SR.3, para 11 (1978).

> it is not possible for any codification to be complete at any given moment; thus the Martens Clause prevents the assumption that anything which is not explicitly prohibited by the relevant treaties is therefore permitted. Secondly, it should be seen as a dynamic factor proclaiming the applicability of the principles mentioned regardless of subsequent developments of types of situation or technology.[17]

Additional Protocol II to the Geneva Conventions confirms in its Preamble that 'in cases not covered by the law in force, the human person remains under the protection of the principles of humanity and the dictates of the public conscience'.[18] The ICRC Commentary to the formulation of the Martens Clause in the Preamble in AP II states that since 'they reflect public conscience, the principles of humanity actually constitute a universal reference point and apply independently of the Protocol'.[19] There are other important examples of restatements of the Martens Clause in later treaties[20] as well as cited or otherwise referred to in several national military manuals.[21]

The Clause's main purpose – pursuant to the wise premonition of the Russian jurist and diplomat Fyodor Fyodorovich de Martens – is to extend juridically the protection to civilians and combatants in all situations, even though not contemplated by the treaty norms. To this end, it invokes 'the principles of international law' derived from 'established custom', as well as 'the principles of humanity' and the 'dictates of public conscience'. In particular, respect for the intrinsic worth of the human person is, in practice, the foundation of the higher interests of the international community which give rise to *jus cogens*.[22] The International Court of Justice has maintained in several instances that States' sovereign powers are limited in times of peace

17 Sandoz et al., *supra* n 2, 55.

18 Protocol Additional to the Geneva Conventions of 12 August 1949, and Relating to the Protection of Victims of Non-International Armed Conflicts, 1125 UNTS 609, 8 June 1977 (entered into force 7 December 1978) [Additional Protocol II or AP II], Preamble, para 4, which does not include references both to custom and to international law.

19 Sandoz et al., *supra* n 2, para 4434.

20 See Final Act of the International Conference on Human Rights, Res. XXIII, para 2, at 18, UN Sales No. E.68.XIV.2 (1968).

21 For the US Manuals, see US Department of the Army, *The Law of Land Warfare*, para 6 (Field Manual No. 27–10, 1956); US Department of the Air Force, *International Law – The Conduct of Armed Conflict and Air Operations*, 1–7(b) (AFP No. 110–31, 1976); UK Manual, see UK War Office, *The Law of War on Land*, being part III of the Manual of Military Law, paras 2, 3, 5 (1958) ; see also United Kingdom Ministry of Defence, *The Manual of the Law of Armed Conflict* (2004); for the German manual, see Federal Ministry of Defense, *Humanitarian Law in Armed conflicts – Manual*, para 129 (ZDv 15/2, 1992).

22 See for instance, ICTY, *Prosecutor* v. *Martić*, Review of the Indictment Pursuant to Rule 61, No. IT–95–11– R61, 13 March 1996, paras 12–13; ICTY, *Prosecutor* v. *Furundžija*, *supra* n 11; ICTY, *Prosecutor* v. *Aleksovski*, IT–95–14/ 1–T, Trial Judgement, 25 June 1999, paras 47– 57.

and war by 'elementary considerations of humanity',[23] by 'principles of morality'[24] or the 'laws of humanity'.[25] In the words of Judge Weeramantry, all law depends on 'the fundamental principle of the dignity and worth of the human person'.[26] Moreover, 'dictates of public conscience' can be instead considered from two perspectives: first, they may refer to the influential role of public opinion, capable of shaping the conduct of the parties to a conflict and promoting the development of IHL, including customary law;[27] second, they can reflect *opinio juris* since public opinion may help form the opinion of governments.[28] As Meron aptly notes, it is, however, necessary 'to mold public opinion through the infusion of moderating and humanitarian views to make it worthy of public conscience'.[29]

The 'principles of humanity' and the 'dictates of public conscience' have been limiting factors on the freedom of States to do what is not expressly prohibited by the law.[30] As will be described below, the influence of the Martens Clause on the battlefield goes hand in hand with the application of other central principles of IHL, including the principles of distinction and proportionality and the prohibitions of indiscriminate attacks and unnecessary suffering. It is undeniable that the principle of humanity has influenced the

See also *Prosecutor* v. *Kallon and Kamara*, Decision on Challenge to Jurisdiction: Lomé Accord Amnesty, SCSL–04– 15–PT–060–I, 13 March 2004, para 71; *Armed Activities on the Territory of the Congo* (New Application: 2002) (*Democratic Republic of the Congo* v. *Rwanda*) (2006) ICJ Reports 2006, para 64.

23 *Corfu Channel case* (*UK* v. *Albania*), Merits (1949) ICJ Reports 1949, 22; *Military and Paramilitary Activities in and against Nicaragua* (*Nicaragua* v. *United States of America*), Judgment, ICJ Reports 1986, p. 14, para 218; *Legality of the Threat or Use of Nuclear Weapons*, *supra* n 6, paras 79, 95.

24 *Reservations to the Convention on the Prevention and Punishment of the Crime of Genocide*, ICJ, Advisory Opinion (1951) ICJ Reports 1951, p. 15, 23 and see also 108; see also *Armed Activities on the Territory of the Congo*, *supra* n 22.

25 *Nicaragua Case*, *supra* n 23, para 218.

26 *Ibid.*, Dis. Op. Weeramantry, 433; see also Dis. Op. Schwebel, 318–319. *Legal Consequences of the Construction of a Wall in the Occupied Palestinian Territory*, Advisory Opinion (2004) ICJ Reports 2004, p. 136, para 157 (referring to the resultant obligations as 'of an erga omnes character').

27 See T Meron, *War Crimes Law Comes of Age* (Oxford University Press 1998), 304–309.

28 UN GAOR, 6th Comm., 28th Sess., 1452d mtg., at 306, para 46, UN Doc. A/C.6/SR.1452 (1973). See also Reglamento para el servicio de campaña, Art. 826 (1882), reprinted in Estado Mayor del Ejército, Manual de derecho de guerra 329–30 (M–O–23–1, 1986); UK Manual, *supra* n 21, para 619; see also Australian Defence Force, Law of Armed Conflict Training, para 7 (DI(G) OPS, 1994).

29 T Meron, *The Humanization of International Law* (Martinus Nijhoff 2006), 25.

30 See L Doswald-Beck, 'International Humanitarian Law and the Advisory Opinion of the International Court of Justice on the Legality of the Threat or Use of Nuclear Weapons' [1997] 316 *IRRC* 35, 49.

development of IHL and that some humanitarian restraints can be considered as its offspring.[31] The rhetorical and ethical code words of the Martens Clause were a pull toward normativity and attained a central role in the progressive humanization of IHL.[32]

4.2.1.2 'Humanity' and 'Human Dignity'

In the words of Jean Pictet, humanity refers to 'something understood but not actually expressed',[33] which indicates that the ordinary meaning may facilitate the investigation. According to the *Oxford English Dictionary*, 'humanity' may describe on one hand, 'the human race; mankind; human beings collectively', but also, 'the character or quality of being humane', a 'behaviour or disposition towards others such as befits a human being'.[34] If one side reflects humanity as a collective group ('humankind'), the second represents a form of yardstick to evaluate a certain conduct, the moral notion close to altruism and philanthropy. 'Humanity' has two sets of meanings. The first refers to the human race, or to those attributes that make us, as human beings, distinctive. The second refers to a virtue, meaning acting with humanity. On this premise, Coupland makes a distinction between humanity–humankind and humanity–sentiment.[35] Interestingly, both of these concepts are expressed with the same term in English, as is the case in French (*la humanité*) and Spanish (*la humanidad*), whereas in German they manifest themselves through different terms *Menschlichkeit* and *Menschheit*, respectively.[36]

Traditionally, scholars seem to have preferred to refer to the notion of humanity–humankind,[37] while humanitarians approach humanity as benevolence and altruism. Humanitarianism is, in fact, 'simply this attitude of humanity laid down as a social doctrine and extended to mankind as

31 US Manuals, *supra* n 21.

32 Meron, *supra* n 29, 29.

33 Pictet et al., *Commentary*, IV, *supra* n 2, 15.

34 *Oxford English Dictionary* (Clarendon Press 1989); see R Coupland, 'Humanity: What Is It and How Does It Influence International Law?' [2001] 844 *IRRC* 969–990.

35 Coupland, *supra* n 34, 972.

36 See E Wartel, 'Humanitarians and Their Moral Stance in War: The Underlying Values' [2009] 91 *IRRC* 779–802; the dilemma seems to have been clarified when the original wording of the Martens Clause, described below, referring to 'laws of humanity', was modified into 'the principles of humanity'.

37 G Robertson, *Crimes against Humanity: The Struggle for Global Justice* (Penguin Books 2000), 239; T Meron, 'The Martens Clause, Principles of Humanity and Dictates of Public Conscience' [2000] 94 *AJIL* 78–89; A Cassese, 'The Martens Clause: Half a Loaf or Simply Pie in the Sky?' [2000] 11 *EJIL* 187.

a whole'.[38] The latter approach, indeed, is at the heart of the foundation of the ICRC. After witnessing the horrific sufferings of thousand of wounded and dying men moaning for surcease during the Battle of Solferino in that Italian War of Unification in 1859, the Swiss merchant Henry Dunant wrote his book A *Memory of Solferino*.[39] Moved by feelings of human empathy, and motivated by his Christian understanding, he created the institution four years later. The ICRC is the guardian of the Geneva Conventions, and its mandate includes monitoring the application of IHL.[40] Humanity itself remains the 'ideal [of the institution], the reason for its existence and its object'.[41] In 1985, the 20th International Conference of the Red Cross (Vienna) formulated seven Fundamental Principles of the Red Cross. These principles are instrumental to the actualization of humanity, the first principle, from which, according to Pictet, 'all other principles hang'.[42] It was here stated:

> Humanity – The Red Cross, born of a desire to bring assistance without discrimination to the wounded on the battlefield, endeavours – in its international and national capacity – to prevent and alleviate human suffering wherever it may be found. Its purpose is to protect life and health and to ensure respect for the human being. It promotes mutual understanding, friendship, co-operation and lasting peace amongst all peoples.[43]

The history of the formation of the ICRC and of humanity as its *raison d'être* are closely connected to the original endeavours in the codification of IHL, as described. In 1983, Pictet recognized that IHL was linked to 'the formidable struggle which has been carried on from the very beginning of human society between those who wish to preserve, unite and liberate mankind and those who seek to dominate, destroy or enslave it'.[44] Thus, the crystallization stage of human dignity in the framework of

38 J Pictet, *Red Cross Principles* (ICRC 1956), 14–31.

39 H Dunant, A *Memory of Solferino* (English version, ICRC 1986).

40 Statutes of the International Red Cross and Red Crescent Movement (adopted by the 25th International Conference of the Red Cross at Geneva in 1986, amended in 1995 and 2006), Art. 5.

41 Pictet, *supra* n 38, 12; The founders of the organization described their aim as preventing and alleviating human suffering, protecting life and health, ensuring respect for the human being and promoting mutual understanding, friendship, co-operation and lasting peace amongst all peoples; A Durand, *The International Committee of the Red Cross* (ICRC 1981), 54.

42 Pictet, *supra* n 38, 14.

43 Durand, *supra* n 41, 54.

44 Pictet, *supra* n 5, 5. See also F Maurice, 'Humanitarian Ambition' [1992] 289 *IRRC* 371.

IHL was rendered possible because States showed to be committed to guarantee the protection of fundamental values as well as the application of elementary considerations of humanity.[45]

The general legal principle of human dignity subsumes the two concepts of humanity-humankind and humanity-sentiment, effectively representing the interests of the international community. Both approaches are indeed grounded on the moral concept of human dignity applicable to every single human individual. It has a particular normative force, implying certain basic human rights and duties which delineate its content.[46] The connection between humanity and human dignity is thus fairly intuitive since each human being, as part of humankind, has an inherent value (their dignity). The protection of human beings in times of conflict is warranted by the inherent dignity of the human person and any conduct assaulting this essence in times of war, this humanness, is then an action against humanity. The broader concept of 'humanity' as a normative standard heavily relies on human dignity.[47] Therefore, human dignity allows the concept of humanity to inform the content of universal IHL instruments as well as to guide conduct in warfare.

4.2.1.3 Principle of Humanity and Its Functions

The principle of humanity has two main functions, which should be viewed as distinct but also possibly overlapping:[48] an *architectural* or *axiological* function and an *auxiliary* function. Through the latter, the principle is then used to clarify ambiguities when primary sources of law are absent (*suppletive* function) or unclear or inadequate (*interstitial* or *conciliatory* function), as it will be described below.

First, the principle of human dignity has an *architectural* function, in the sense that, as described, it has influenced the creation of the IHL

45 See, for instance, B Simma, 'From Bilateralism to Community Interest' [1994] 250 *RCADI* 217–384; AA Cançado Trindade, 'International Law for Humankind: Towards a New Jus Gentium' [2005] 317 *RCADI* 1–717.

46 AH Robertson, 'Humanitarian Law and Human Rights' in C Swinarski (ed.), *Studies and Essays on International Humanitarian Law and Red Cross Principles in Honour of Jean Pictet* (Martinus Nijhoff 1984), 793, 795.

47 See R Urueña, 'Deciding What is Humane: Towards a Critical Reading of Humanity as a Normative Standard in International Law' in B van Beers, L Corrias and WG Werner (eds), *Humanity across International Law and Biolaw* (Cambridge University Press 2014), 188.

48 See also Cassese, *supra* n 37, 189–192.

system as we know it today and may favour future changes. It serves an *axiological function* since it is the *raison d'etre* and 'common link'[49] for rules within the international legal order,[50] being a social value around which there is broad acceptance that it must be protected.[51] As seen above, human dignity has been recognized not only as the foundation of human rights law and humanitarian law, but of the entire international legal order, as a broader thread running through it.[52]

This function can be closely linked to two strands of uses of the principle of human dignity and, in particular, of the Martens Clause. The first identifies human dignity with the whole of morality,[53] according to which acting against morality is, as such, acting against human dignity or, more precisely, against the agent's own human dignity.[54] Thus, it has been held that the Martens Clause allows for certain moral imperatives to enter into the law.[55] Moreover, the Clause has also an impact on the assessment of the international customary law status of norms or principles in IHL, in the sense that it 'loosens' the

49 A Verdross, 'Les principes généraux du droit applicables aux rapports internationaux' [1938] 45 *RGDIP* 52 (English translation).

50 See, on this aspect, C Tomuschat and JM Thouvenin (eds), *The Fundamental Rules of the International Legal Order: Jus cogens and Obligations Erga omnes* (Martinus Nijhoff 2006).

51 D Feldman, 'Human Dignity as a Legal Value: Part I' [1999] *PL* 682–702; L Lafrance, 'International Humanitarian Law and Cultural Relativism' in M Sassòli, A Bouvier and A Quintin (eds), *How Does Law Protect in War?*, vol. 1 (ICRC 2011), 98 (noting the broad acceptability of notions of dignity); J Donnelly, 'Human Rights and Human Dignity: An Analytic Critique of Non-Western Conceptions of Human Rights' [1982] 76(2) *AmPolSciRev* 303–316.

52 ICTY, *Prosecutor* v. *Furundžija*, *supra* n 11, para 183; *Reservations to the Convention on the Prevention and Punishment of the Crime of Genocide*, *supra* n 24.

53 See *supra* n 24.

54 P Asaro, 'On Banning Autonomous Weapon Systems: Human Rights, Automation, and the Dehumanisation of Lethal Decision-Making' [2013] 94 *IRRC* 886, 708.

55 TJ Lawrence, *The Principles of International Law* (4th ed., London: McMillan 1911), 395. See also P-M Dupuy, 'Les "considérations élémentaires d'humanité" dans la jurisprudence de la Cour internationale de justice' in R-J Dupuy and L-A Sicilianos (eds), *Mélanges en l'honneur de Nicolas Valticos. Droit et justice* (Paris: Pédone 1999), 117, 127; C Tomuschat, 'International Law: Ensuring the Survival of Mankind on the Eve of a New Century: General Course on Public International Law' [1999] 281 *RCADI* 9, 356; R Ticehurst, 'The Martens Clause and the Laws of Armed Conflict' [1997] 317 *IRRC* 125, 134; and VV Pustogarov, 'Fyodor Fyodorovich Martens (1845–1909) – A Humanist of Modern Times' [1996] 312 *IRRC* 322, 132. Of contrary view, see A Shibata, 'The Court's Decision in Silentium on Sources' in K Bannelier, T Christakis and S Heathcote (eds), *The ICJ and the Evolution of International Law* (Routledge 2012), 207.

conditions prescribed for State practice, while at the same time 'elevates' opinio juris to a higher rank.[56]

Second, the principle of human dignity operates also at the level of interpretation of international principles and norms, serving an *auxiliary* function. This argument can be viewed from two perspectives. One understanding is that it rules out the *a contrario* argument that when a matter is not covered by the Hague Regulations or by later documents in which it is reiterated, belligerents can act freely. Already being part of the international humanitarian legal order, the principle of human dignity becomes essential for situations in which IHL is not applicable. Before the Second World War, the Martens Clause had provided support and justification for the criminalization of inhumane conducts when not explicitly done so by the law.[57] This can be considered a *suppletive* function, which in turn helps in any decision-making process in the absence of an IHL norm.

The other understanding is that the principle of human dignity serves as a general interpretative guideline, in the sense that whenever there are unclear norms or doubts about their interpretation, it demands to consider requirements of humanity in interpreting international rules, reorganizing the order of priorities. The principle of humanity expresses the spirit behind the rules of IHL and serves the purpose of circumscribing the discretionary power of belligerents in case of loose international provisions.[58] In the words of Benvenisti, '[t]he human dignity principle informs the interpretation of the law on the conduct of hostilities and provides a *built-in* mechanism for improving armies' treatment of enemy civilians'.[59] This can be called an *interstitial* or *conciliatory* function.[60] The Martens Clause should also be

56 Cassese, *supra* n 37, 214; ICTY, *Prosecutor* v. *Kupreškić*, IT-95-16-T, 14 January 2000, para 527; Meron, *supra* n 37, 87–88; G Distefano and E Henry, 'Final Provisions, including the Martens Clause', in Clapham, Gaeta and Sassòli, *supra* n 2, 184–185.

57 For torture, see 'Trial of Kriminalassisstent Karl-Heinz Hermann Klinge' in United Nations War Crimes Commission (UNWCC) (ed.), *Law Reports of Trials of War Criminals*, vol. III (London: HMSO 1947–1949), 12; arbitrary trials, 'Trial of Hans Paul Helmuth Latza and Two Others' in UNWCC (ed.), *ibid.*, vol. XIV, 58; human medical experiments, 'Trial of Erhard Milch' in UNWCC (ed.), *ibid.*, 51; or the killing of hostages, 'Trial of Hans Albin Rauter' in UNWCC (ed.), *ibid.*, vol. XIV, 119.

58 ICTY, *Prosecutor v. Kupreškić*, *supra* n 57, paras 525–528.

59 E Benvenisti, 'Human Dignity in Combat: The Duty to Spare Enemy Civilians' [2006] 39 *ILR* 81 (emphasis added).

60 V Lowe, 'The Politics of Law-Making: Are the Method and Character of Norm Creation Changing?' in M Byers (ed.), *The Role of Law in International Politics* (Oxford University Press 2000), 216.

interpreted today as reflecting the adaptability of the principle of humanity to the 'changing conditions, inclusive of changes in the means and methods of warfare and the outlook and tolerance levels of the international community'.[61]

4.2.2 *The Principle of Distinction*

The principle of distinction is an undisputed cornerstone of IHL and part of *jus cogens*.[62] It demands that a clear distinction be drawn between armed forces and civilians, or between combatants and non-combatants and between objects that may and may not be legitimately attacked.[63] In other words, 'in a situation of armed conflict, every person is either a legitimate military target (military objective) or a protected person - *tertium non datur*'.[64] The cardinal importance of this principle was confirmed in the *Legality of the Threat or Use of Nuclear Weapons* of the ICJ, in which the Court held that the principle of distinction between combatants and non-combatants, together with other basic principles of humanitarian law, constitutes one of the 'intransgressible principles of international customary law'.[65] The principle is fundamental to the respect of the human person and can be derived directly from a general principle of law, namely 'elementary considerations of humanity'. It originated in the preamble of the St Petersburg Declaration, which stated that 'the only legitimate object which states should endeavour to accomplish during war is to weaken the military forces of the enemy'. By emphasizing military forces as the object of attacks, the content of the principle 'overlaps' with the principle of military necessity, which is 'also concerned with the circumstances and purpose of military operations'.[66] The current version of the principle is enshrined in Article 48 of AP I, which describes the fundamental rule of distinction as follows:

> In order to ensure respect for and protection of the civilian population and civilian objects, the Parties to the conflict shall at all times distinguish

61 *Legality of the Threat or Use of Nuclear Weapons*, *supra* n 6, 406 (Shahabuddeen, J, dissenting).

62 ILC, Report on State Responsibility, YILC, 2001, vol. II, Part Two, Draft Art. 40, Commentary, 112.

63 JM Henckaerts and L Doswald –Beck, *Customary International Humanitarian Law*, vol. 1 Rules (ICRC and Cambridge University Press 2005), rules 1 and 7.

64 N Melzer, 'The Principle of Distinction between Civilians and Combatants' in A Clapham and P Gaeta (eds), *Oxford Handbook of International Law in Armed Conflict* (Oxford University Press 2014), 296–297.

65 *Legality of the Threat or Use of Nuclear Weapons*, *supra* n 6, para 78. See also ICRC Customary Law Study, Commentary Rule 1 at 3ff.

66 Jia, *supra* n 10, 260.

> between the civilian population and combatants and between civilian objects and military objectives and accordingly shall direct their operations only against military objectives.

The principle of distinction is made operational through two fundamental provisions prohibiting attacks on civilians and civilian objects (in Articles 51(2) and 52(1) AP I, respectively). Article 52(1) AP I defines civilians objects as 'all objects which are not military objectives'. Military objectives are defined, in Article 52(2) AP I, as 'those objects which by their nature, location, purpose or use make an effective contribution to military action and whose total or partial destruction, capture or neutralization, in the circumstances ruling at the time, offers a definite military advantage'.[67] Thus, '[a]ttacks shall be limited strictly to military objectives', as added by Article 52(2) AP I. Article 50(1) also adds that 'in case of doubt whether a person is a civilian, that person shall be considered to be a civilian'. The condition of taking direct part in hostilities may, however, excuse the attackers from breaching the principle.[68]

The customary rule of distinction is also applicable in situation of non-international armed conflicts (NIACs).[69] During the conduct of hostilities, in both international armed conflicts (IACs) and NIACs, for the purposes of the principle of distinction, IHL protects the same categories of persons, namely civilians, medical and religious personnel and persons *hors de combat*.[70] Persons not entitled to immunity thus include: State armed forces, dissident armed forces and other organized armed groups, such as belligerent parties, civilians directly participating in hostilities and medical, religious and civil defence personnel or persons *hors de combat* who commit hostile acts, thus losing their protected status.

The principle, which derives from the need to prioritize considerations of humanity, constitutes the source of one cardinal obligation of IHL, namely the prohibition of indiscriminate attacks, regulated by Article 51(4) AP I. As a consequence, as the ICJ stated, that 'States must never make civilians the

[67] See also A Jachec-Neale, *The Concept of Military Objective in International Law and Targeting Practice* (Routledge 2015), chapters 2–5.

[68] See ICRC, *Interpretative Guidance on the Notion of Direct Participation in Hostilities* (ICRC 2009), 49.

[69] Customary law Study, vol. 1, Rule 1.

[70] In IACS, see Art. 51 AP I (civilians); Art. 24 GC I (medical and religious personnel on land), 36 GC II (on ships) and Customary Law Study, vol. I, Rules 25 (medical) and 27 (religious); Art 12 AP I (medical units); Art. 67(1) AP I (civil defence personnel); see Art. 41(1) and (2) AP I and Customary law Study, vol. 1, Rule 47 and Art. 23(c) of the 1907 Hague Regulations (persons hors de combat). In NIACs, see Arts 13, 9(1) AP II; Customary Law Study, vol. 1, Rules 25 (medical) and 27 (religious); Art. 7(1) AP II and Customary Law Study, vol. 1, Rule 47 (hors de combat).

object of attack and must consequently never use weapons that are incapable of distinguishing between civilian and military targets.'[71] This obligation will be further explored below in Section 4.4.2.1. The principle of distinction can thus define the juridical nature of military actions. An attack is thus *prima facie* illegal if it is conducted in disregard of the principle, unless mitigating circumstances recognized under IHL apply. The principle has nevertheless not always proved simple to apply in practice.[72]

The principle of proportionality follows the principle of distinction in application. The principle prohibits an attack that may be expected to cause incidental loss of civilian life, injury to civilians, damage to civilian objects, or a combination thereof, which would be excessive in relation to the concrete and direct military advantage anticipated.[73] Proportionality should thus be found between the losses and the advantage: when assessing the legality of a prospective attack against a lawful target, it must be examined whether the expected collateral (or ancillary) damage to civilians comes within the limits of proportionality. Therefore, 'even a legitimate target may not be attacked if the collateral civilian casualties would be disproportionate to the specific military gain from the attack'.[74] The same can be said for damages to civilian property. The principle of proportionality thus provides 'a further restriction' by disallowing attacks against lawful targets owing to the envisaged disproportionate injury or damage to civilians or civilian objects.[75]

4.3 HUMAN DIGNITY AS A RIGHT

4.3.1 *Individual Rights and Human Dignity*

As introduced in Chapter One, one of the central reasons why rights and obligations are approached in this study as two separate legal instruments and manifestations of dignity lies in their different normative natures: if obligations fall within the category of *prescriptive* instruments, human rights provisions can be considered as *permissive* norms. Several norms of the four Geneva

71 *Legality of the Threat or Use of Nuclear Weapons*, *supra* n 6, para 78.

72 F Kalshoven, 'Prohibitions or Restrictions on the Use of Methods and Means of Warfare' in I Dekker and H Post (eds), *The Gulf War of 1980–1988* (Martinus Nijhoff 1992), 97, 102–106. See also ICTY, *Prosecutor* v. *Stanislav Galić*, IT-98-29-A, Judgment, 30 November 2006, para 136; ICTY, *Prosecutor* v. *Tihomir Blaškić*, IT-95-14-A, Appeal Judgment, 29 July 2004, paras 114–115.

73 See Art. 51(5)(b) and 57(2)(b) AP I; Y Dinstein, 'The Principle of Proportionality' in Larsen, Cooper and Nystuen, *supra* n 3, 75.

74 *Legality of the Threat or Use of Nuclear Weapons*, *supra* n 6, 587.

75 E Rauch, 'Conduct of Combat and Risks Run by the Civilian Population' [1982] 21 *RDMDG* 66, 67.

Conventions, their two APs, and parallel customary international law confer protection on individuals. At the time of the early Geneva Conventions, it was not clear and settled whether such provisions were able to directly create rights for individuals. Whereas some maintain that it is only States that have rights and obligations under the rules of IHL, which in this view only set standards for the treatment of individuals,[76] there is a case to be made for the rules directly endowing individuals with rights and obligations. This is notably the position taken in the Commentary to the Geneva Conventions,[77] as well as by jurisprudence of national courts[78] and by certain authors[79] who view the move away from reciprocity as a condition of the application of IHL rules as intrinsically linked to the existence of individual rights.

The 1929 Geneva Prisoners of War Convention made, for the first time, references to rights of individuals in several provisions.[80] The 1949 Conventions 'conferred [rights] on protected persons'[81] through various cardinal provisions. Some of the norms in the existing treaties expressly mention 'rights', 'claims', 'entitlements', 'liberty' and 'guarantees' of the individual.[82]

In order to avoid the texts of the 1949 Conventions being left to 'modifications dictated by chance, events or under the pressure of wartime circumstances',[83] Common Article 6/6/6/7 expressly states:

> No special agreement shall adversely affect the situation of the wounded and sick, of members of the medical personnel or of chaplains, as defined by the present Convention, *nor restrict the rights which it confers upon them.*[84]

76 See R Provost, *International Human Rights and Humanitarian Law* (Cambridge University Press 2002), 27–34; K Parlett, *The Individual in the International Legal System* (Cambridge University Press 2011), 176–228.

77 Pictet et al., *Commentary*, IV, *supra* n 2, Art. 8, 77.

78 See for instance, BVerfGE 112, 2004, 1 et seq., para 38; A Peters, *Beyond Human Rights: The Legal Status of the Individual in International Law* (Cambridge University Press 2016), 232.

79 D Jinks, 'The Applicability of the Geneva Conventions to the *Global War on Terror*' [2005] 46 *VJIL* 168; Peters, *supra* n 79, 195.

80 Arts. 42, 62 and 64.

81 Pictet et al., *Commentary*, I, *supra* n 2, 82.

82 *Annex to Hague Convention IV* (1907), see Art. 3, Art. 12, Art. 13, Art. 18, Art. 23(1)(h), Art. 32 and Art. 46(1). The Annex consists of the regulations respecting the laws and customs of war on land; *GC III*, see Art. 6(1), Art. 7, Art. 14(1), Art. 50(2), Art. 54(2), Art. 78(1) and (2), Art. 84(2), Art. 96(4), Art. 105(1), Art. 106, Art. 113(1), Art. 129(4) and Art. 130; *GC IV*, see Art. 5(3), Art. 7(1), Art. 8, Art. 27(1), Art. 35 (1) and (2), Art. 38, Art. 40(4), Art. 43(1), Art. 48, Art. 52(1), Art. 72(1), Art. 73, Art. 75(1), Art. 76(3), (6) and (7), Art. 78(2), Art. 80, Art. 101(1) and (2), Art. 146(4) and Art. 147; *AP I*, see, referring to 'rights', Art. 11(5), Art. 32, Art. 44(2), (5) and (6), Art. 79(2) and Art. 85(4)(e); Art. 45 ('claim') and Art. 56(3) ('entitlement'); *AP II*, see Art. 4(1), Art. 5(1)(e), Art. 6(2) (a) and (e) and Art. 6(3).

83 Pictet et al., *Commentary*, IV, *supra* n 2, 71.

84 Emphasis added.

It was explained by the ICRC that the choice of the term *'confers upon them'*, instead of 'stipulates on their behalf', as was suggested at the Conference,[85]

> had doubtless been influenced by the concomitant trend of doctrine, which also led to the universal proclamation of Human Rights, to define in concrete terms a concept which was implicit in the earlier Conventions. But it had at the same time complied with the unanimous recommendation of the Red Cross Societies, meeting in conference in Geneva in 1946, to confer upon the rights recognized by the Conventions 'a personal and intangible character allowing' the beneficiaries 'to claim them irrespective of the attitude adopted by their home country'.[86]

Pictet attributes the deliberate focus on individual rights to the influence of the recognition of international human rights.[87] The emphasis on personal rights is a consequence of the recognition that people are better protected through the conferral of individual rights than by a mere stipulation of objective duties of protection.[88] For example, according to Article 30, protected persons can appeal to Protecting Powers and the ICRC, providing a means of ensuring that individual rights under the Conventions are respected.[89]

A further indicator of the intention to establish individual rights in these texts is the two types of non-disposal clauses. *In primis*, each of the four Geneva Conventions contains a *non-renunciation clause* (Article 7/7/7/8):

> [Protected persons] may in no circumstances renounce in part or in entirety *the rights secured to them* by the present Convention, and by the special agreements referred to in the foregoing Article, if such there be.

85 *Final Record of the Diplomatic Conference of Geneva of 1949* (New York: William S. Hein 2004), Vol. II, Sec. B, 76 (Special Committee, Joint Committee, 23rd meeting). The Conference considered that the expression 'on their behalf' would have implied only 'an "indirect" benefit deriving from the attitude prescribed to the States'. For this reason, the Diplomatic Conference chose the formulation previously proposed by the ICRC ('confers upon them'), Pictet et al., *Commentary*, I, *supra* n 2, 82– 83.

86 Pictet et al., *Commentary*, I, *supra* n 2, 83, citing the Report on the Work of the Preliminary Conference of National Red Cross Societies for the Study of the Conventions and of Various Problems relative to the Red Cross (Geneva, 26 July–3 August 1946), Geneva, 1947, 71.

87 Pictet et al., *Commentary*, I, *supra* n 2, 83, stating the formulation was influenced by 'the concomitant trends of doctrine, which also led to the universal proclamation of Human Rights'.

88 Peters, *supra* n 79, 199.

89 ICRC, Commentary on the First Geneva Convention: Convention (I) for the Amelioration of the Condition of the Wounded and Sick in Armed Forces in the Field, 2nd edition, 2016, or (in brief) as ICRC, Commentary on the First Geneva Convention, 2016, 'Article 7: Non–Renunciation of Rights', 2016, para 1001; Pictet et al., *Commentary*, IV, *supra* n 2, 78–79.

According to Article 11 of AP I, no scientific experiments may be conducted or organs removed, or similar acts performed even with the consent of the person concerned.

The non-renunciation clauses show that the Conventions directly confer rights on the individual, regardless of whether national laws of States Parties have enacted them.[90] The non-renunciation clauses are intended to move the guarantees closer to human rights. The reference to the prohibitions of deviations by way of agreements between States imply, on the one hand, that specific guarantees are provided by States; on the other, they also withdraw other guarantees from the power of the States. Therefore, because the States are not the obligees of the owed duties of protection, then individuals must be the obligees.[91] Remarkably, Pictet noted that the non-renunciation clause in Convention (IV) relative to the Protection of Civilian Persons is 'of the greatest assistance to all protected persons. It allows them to claim the protection of the Convention, not as a privilege, but as a right.'[92] The non-disposability of such protective norms can therefore be seen as showing the importance of protected rights and of human dignity.

Thus, in principle, 'individual rights have an *emancipatory potential* that is best suited to the moral status of the individual and also is able to provide argumentative support for efforts to improve their practical enforceability'.[93] Human dignity act as the foundation and object of personal rights conferred by various provisions of IHL. It therefore manifests itself as *mother-right* and/or in its *derivative-rights*. In Jean Pictet's words, '[t]he initiators of the 1864 and following Conventions wished to *safeguard the dignity of the human person*, in the profound conviction that imprescriptible and inviolable rights were attached to it even when hostilities were at their height'.[94] Thus, human dignity in IHL also acts as a *source* of rights. It lies at the basis of *all rights* and must be respected and protected, creating corresponding positive and negative obligations. When dignity functions as a *mother-right*,

90 On the contrary, Parlett, in contrast, assumes that the wording of the non-renunciation clause leaves open the possibility that rights are to be conferred only by national law (*supra* n 77, 184); on the contrary, as Anne Peters notes, that reading is not compatible with the official German translation, in Peters, *supra* n 79, 232; see also Pictet et al., *Commentary*, I, *supra* n 2, 82 refers to 'secure' as the 'still stronger term' than 'confer'. See also Advisory Opinion concerning Jurisdiction of the Courts of Danzig, (1928), P. C. I. J., Ser. B. No. 15, at 17–18 (Advisory Opinion of 3 March 1928); R Higgins, 'Conceptual Thinking about the Individual' [1978] 4(1) *BJIS* 1–19; T Meron, 'Human Rights in Internal Strife' [1984] 78(4) *AJIL* 33–40.

91 Peters, *supra* n 79, 199–232. See RJ Wilhelm, 'Le caractère des droits accordés à l'individu dans les Conventions de Genève' [1950] 32 *RICR* 561–590, 587.

92 Pictet et al., *Commentary*, IV, *supra* n 2, 79. Similarly, see Pictet et al., *Commentary*, I, *supra* n 2, 84 on GC I on wounded and sick persons.

93 Peters, *supra* n 79, 200 (emphasis in the text).

94 Pictet et al., *Commentary*, I, *supra* n 2, 82, also 81 (emphasis added).

the *unique* aim that characterizes each right is distinct from the *general* aim of that specific right, which is represented by the realization of the foundational value and principle of human dignity.[95] Within each human right, both its general and unique aims are eventually combined by the ultimate realization of the foundational value of human dignity.

4.3.2 *Human Dignity as a Mother-Right*

Considering the strong influence of HRL on the humanization process of IHL, Rosen, providing a clarification of the specific content of human dignity in this sphere, interestingly argues that there is a difference between the use of dignity in the Geneva Convention and in the UDHR (as well as in the German *Grundgesetz*), which made dignity (presumably) foundational to basic rights.[96] In the Geneva Convention, in its Common Article 3, there is a clear contrast between clauses 1(a) and 1(c) – between dignity and other human rights. If clause 1(a) outlaws violence to life and person (murder, cruel treatment and torture), clause 1(c) prohibits violations of dignity, expressed as humiliating and degrading treatment. He argues that what is at stake in the Geneva Convention is dignity as 'a requirement that people (in this case, prisoners of war) should be treated respectfully – that they have a right to be treated "with dignity"'.[97] Thus, the Geneva Conventions show a sense of dignity close to 'a right to dignified treatment' as opposed to the one adopted in the UDHR (or the *Grundgesetz*), where dignity appears as a foundation of human rights.

Whereas this consideration also emerges from the analysis of the *travaux préparatoires*,[98] it should not limit the reading of the manifestations of human dignity in IHL. A holistic and comprehensive reading which takes into account the role and manifestations of human dignity in human rights law and in IHL shows that human dignity acts as a principle and as a mother-right but is also source of different rights and obligations. It is therefore manifested by way of various instruments.

In times of IACs, humanitarian law provides for 15 categories of protected persons – four related to combatants and eleven concerning civilians.[99] In

95 A Clapham, 'Non-State Actors' in D Moeckli, S Shah and S Sivakumaran (eds), *International Human Rights Law* (2nd ed., Oxford University Press 2014), 533.

96 M Rosen, *Dignity: Its History and Meaning* (Harvard University Press 2012), 58–60.

97 *Ibid.*, 60.

98 See Chapter 3 for details (3.2.3).

99 These are: (i) *The wounded and sick in armed forces in the field.* Such persons are protected by the GC I (in particular, Arts. 12–18) and by AP I (in particular, Arts. 8–20); (ii) *The wounded, sick, and shipwrecked members of armed forces at sea.* Such persons are protected by the entire GC II (in particular, Arts. 12–21) and by AP I (in particular, Arts. 8–20); (iii) *Medical and religious*

times of NIACs, humanitarian law defines five categories of protected persons and specific guarantees and related obligations.[100] In particular, the relationship between human dignity as a mother-right and derivative rights can be examined in light of an analysis focused on categories of persons whose rights are recognized by certain IHL provisions. A few illustrations can support this reading.

First, the *wounded, sick and shipwrecked* have the right to be respected,[101] protected[102] and treated humanely and cared for (to the fullest extent practicable and with the least possible delay) by the party in whose power they are, without any adverse distinction.[103]

Moreover, the Third Geneva Convention gives a detailed description of the rights granted to *prisoners of war*, and the correlative obligations incumbent upon the belligerents: (i) *right to be treated humanely:* prisoners of war shall be protected against acts of violence, intimidation, insults and public curiosity[104] and have rights to quarters, food, clothing, hygiene, medical attention and inspections,[105]

personnel attached to armed forces. Such persons are protected by the GCs I and II (GCI Arts. 24, 25; GCII Arts. 36, 37); (iv) *Prisoners of war.* Such persons are protected by the GC III (in particular, Arts. 4, 12–16) and by AP I (Arts. 43–47); (v) *Wounded and sick civilians*. Such persons are protected by the GC IV (in particular, Arts. 3, 16–23) and by AP I (Arts. 10–16). Pregnant women, maternity cases, newborn infants and infirm persons are included in the humanitarian law definition of 'wounded and sick' (AP I Art. 8); (vi) *Medical and religious civilian personnel.* This category is defined, and such persons are protected, by the GC IV (Art. 20) and by AP I (Art. 15); (vii) *Parliamentarians*. Such persons are protected by the Hague Convention IV (1907) on the laws and customs of war; (viii) *Personnel of civil defense organizations*. Such persons are protected by AP I (Arts. 61–68); (ix) *Relief personnel*. Such persons are protected by AP I (Art. 71); (x) *The civilian population and civilian persons*. Such persons are mainly protected by the GC IV and by AP I (Arts. 48–67); (xi) *Persons detained, interned, or otherwise deprived of liberty* (GC IV Arts. 41, 42 and 79–135; AP I Art. 75); (xii) *The population of an occupied territory* (GC IV Arts. 47–78; AP I Arts. 63, 69); (xiii) *Women*. Women are protected by Additional Protocol I (in particular, Art. 76, GC IV Art. 14). Women prisoners of war, internees and detainees also benefit from specific protection under the GCs III and IV; (xiv) *Children*. Children are protected by Additional Protocol I (in particular, Arts. 77, 78). Children prisoners of war, internees and detainees also benefit from specific protection under the GCs III and IV; (xv) *Foreigners, refugees, and stateless persons* (GC IV Arts. 35–46; AP I Art. 73).

100 They are the following: (i) everyone who does not or no longer participates in the hostilities must benefit from the minimum guarantees (GCI–IV Common Art. 3; AP II Art. 4); (ii) the civilian population and objects indispensable to their survival (AP II Arts. 13, 14); (iii) persons deprived of their liberty for reasons related to the armed conflict (AP II Art. 5); (iv) wounded and sick (GC IV Art. 3; AP II Arts. 7, 8); (v) Medical and religious personnel (AP II Art. 9).

101 See GCs I and II, Arts 12.

102 See GCI, Art. 15(1); CIHL Rule 111.

103 See GCs I and II, Arts 12(2) and (3); AP I, Art. 10(2); GCs, common Art. 3(2); AP II, Art. 7(2); CIHL Rule 110.

104 GC III, Arts. 13(1)–(2).

105 *Ibid.*, Arts. 25–31.

property,[106] or representation;[107] (ii) *right to equal treatment*: prisoners of war shall be treated without any discrimination on the basis of race, nationality, religion, opinions and similar criteria;[108] (iii) *security rights*: prisoners of war shall be evacuated from combat and danger zone;[109] (iv) *labour rights*: prisoners of war could be utilized by the Detaining Power for work, respecting their age, sex, rank, physical aptitude;[110] (v) *procedural rights*: the Detaining Power can prosecute the prisoner of war according to it own laws, regulations and orders in force and judicial proceedings against the prisoners of war shall be carried out in accordance with the fair trial canons;[111] (vi) *right to repatriation*: seriously wounded or sick prisoners of war shall be sent back to their country regardless of number or rank. The rest of the prisoners of war shall be released and repatriated after the cessation of active hostilities.[112]

According to the Fourth Geneva Convention, the rights of protected *civilian persons* are absolute and inalienable. As a consequence, parties of armed conflicts cannot conclude special agreements that will 'adversely affect the situation of protected persons';[113] protected persons cannot renounce their rights;[114] and, lastly, protected persons of occupied or annexed territories cannot be deprived of the rights established in the Geneva Convention.[115] In the words of Pictet, Article 27 'proclaims the principle of respect for the human person and the inviolable character of the basic rights of men and women', and is the 'basis on which the Convention rests, the central point in relation to which all its other provisions must be considered'.[116] In particular, the basic rights granted and conferred to civilian persons are the following: (i) *right to be treated humanely*: protected persons are 'entitled, in all circumstances, to respect for their persons, their honour, their family rights, their religious convictions and practices, and their manners and customs', and they shall be protected against acts of violence, intimidation, insults and public curiosity;[117] (ii) *right to equal treatment*: protection should be provided without any discrimination on the basis of race, religion, opinions and with no prejudice to the provisions relating to their state of health,

106 *Ibid.*, Arts. 58–68.
107 *Ibid.*, Arts. 79–81.
108 *Ibid.*, Art. 16.
109 *Ibid.*, Art. 19.
110 *Ibid.*, Arts. 49–57.
111 *Ibid.*, Arts. 82–108.
112 *Ibid.*, Arts. 109–119. See also Meron, *supra* n 29, 45.
113 GC IV, Art. 7.
114 *Ibid.*, Art. 8.
115 *Ibid.*, Art. 47.
116 Pictet et al., *Commentary*, IV, *supra* n 2, 200–201.
117 GC IV, Art. 27.

age and sex;[118] (iii) *security rights*: protected persons cannot be used as a human shield and corporal punishment, torture, murder, collective penalties and experiments are forbidden, together with hostage-taking and pillage.[119] The Geneva Conventions also expressly grant special protection to *women* in all circumstances. Wounded and sick women (members of the army, prisoners of war) shall be treated taking into consideration their sex.[120] During captivity, they should be housed in separate dormitories from the men, have separate facilities,[121] and be supervised by women.[122] In particular, Article 27(2) of the 1949 Geneva Convention IV provides that '[w]omen shall be especially protected against any attack on their honour'.[123]

In NIACs, humane treatment is granted by the Common Article 3 of the Geneva Conventions. The implication of this provision will be seen in more detail in Section 4.4.1, and in Chapter Six. AP II complements Article 3 of the Geneva Conventions and grants protected persons the rights to 'respect for their person, honour and convictions and religious practices"[124] and prohibits the forced movements of civilians.[125] The study on the rules of customary IHL published by the ICRC in 2005 (Customary IHL Study) clarifies the rights of specific categories of protected persons that are applicable in IACs and NIACs.[126]

Human dignity manifests itself in IHL not only by way of rights but also by way of a further legal instrument. In particular, the principle of human dignity acts as an obligation-creating principle as much as the *mother-right* human dignity and its derivative rights. Obligations deriving directly from their legal substance are examined in the following section.

4.4 HUMAN DIGNITY AS AN OBLIGATION

The rules enshrined in the laws of war are binding not only upon States but also upon every protected individual.[127] As Jean Pictet writes,

118 *Ibid.*
119 *Ibid.*, Art. 29.
120 GC I and II, Art. 12; GC III, Art. 14.
121 GC III, Arts. 25, 29; GC IV, Art. 76.
122 GC III, Arts. 97, 108; GC IV, Art. 76.
123 GC IV, Art. 27.
124 Additional Protocol II, Art. 4.
125 Additional Protocol, Art. 17.
126 Henckaerts and Doswald–Beck, *supra* n 64, in relation to medical personnel, Rule 25 and Rule 26; to religious personnel, Rule 27: journalists, Rule 34; to persons hors de combat, Rule 47; to women, Rule 134; to children, Rule 135; to elderly, disabled and infirm, Rule 138.
127 LFL Oppenheim, *International Law. A Treatise*, vol. II, 'Disputes, War and Neutrality', H Lauterpacht (ed.) (7th ed., Longman 1952), 341.

> *Rights entail obligations*. With reference to the individual, . . . the rules of the Conventions, or certain of them, can also be considered as obligations directly incumbent on the persons protected. It is an indisputable fact that certain obligations, such as the respect due to the wounded and sick under Article 16, are also laid upon persons who can claim protection under the Convention.[128]

Individuals have indeed 'an active role to play as bearers of individual rights and obligations under international humanitarian law'.[129] In particular, this section will detail a twofold typology of legal obligations and constraints to the free exercise of power in armed conflict. The first set of constraints is related to the protective regime granted to categories of persons under IHL and, the second, relates to rules on means and methods of warfare.

4.4.1 *Constraints Related to the Protective Regime*

After the horrors of the Second World War, the requirement of humane treatment was placed at the very heart of the laws of armed conflict. As noted in the 1958 Pictet Commentary, '[t]he obligation to grant protected persons humane treatment is in truth the "leitmotiv" of the four Geneva Conventions'.[130] Each of the four 1949 Geneva Conventions and their 1977 APs applies to a specific category of person (with the Protocols applying more generally to 'victims'). They define the rights and protections that must be respected and which each category is entitled to receive, as discussed in Section 4.3.2.

Humane treatment encompasses all aspects of a person's existence[131] and requires that the individual concerned is granted a 'minimum treatment' so as to have an acceptable life with dignity.[132] The scope of humane treatment is very broad and, in general terms, 'acts or omission which cause mental or physical suffering represent attacks on bodily or mental integrity or on human

128 Pictet et al., *Commentary*, IV, *supra* n 2, 79 (italics mine).

129 D Fleck, 'The Role of Individuals in International Humanitarian Law and Challenges for States in its Development' in MN Schmitt and LC Green (eds.), *The Law of Armed Conflicts: Into the Next Millenium* (US Naval War College 1998), 119–139, 136; see Peters, *supra* n 79, 220–230. See also, L Zegveld, *Accountability of Armed Opposition Groups in International Law* (Cambridge University Press 2002), 10–12; S Sivakumaran, 'Binding Armed Opposition Groups' [2006] 55 *ICLQ* 369–394.

130 Pictet et al., *Commentary*, IV, *supra* n 2, 204.

131 J Pictet, 'The Fundamental Principles of the Red Cross: Commentary' (Henry Dunant Institute 1979), I, (Principle of Humanity), at 137.

132 *Ibid.*

dignity clearly fall short of the standard'.[133] Thus, the essential criterion is that of the preservation of human dignity. To understand what humane treatment comprises is 'a matter of common sense and good faith', in the words of Pictet, and a detailed definition might be a straitjacket limiting the reach of the protection.[134]

The notion of humane treatment has been enshrined in the set of minimum humanitarian standards to be respected in both NIACs and IACs, as stipulated in Common Article 3 and its corresponding customary international law rule. The specific meaning of the principle was not further detailed, the focus being instead on the absolute prohibitions listed in Common Article 3, that result from the principle of humane treatment itself, including violence to life and person, mutilation, cruel treatment, and torture; the taking of hostages; or outrages upon personal dignity, in particular humiliating and degrading treatment. This approach shows that instead of defining humane treatment, the States Parties chose to define the prohibited acts that are incompatible with humane treatment and thus, the obligations arising from the protection of the principle of humanity. As the Trial Chamber aptly put it in *Aleksovski* (1999), 'the purpose of Common Article 3 [of the Geneva Conventions] is to uphold and protect the inherent human dignity of the individual'.[135] The ICTY Appeals Chamber confirmed the role of human dignity as a general legal principle in its 2000 judgment in the same case, stating generally that where 'outrages upon personal dignity' are defined as a criminal offence, 'it was the broader concept of human dignity that was emphasized' as 'the important value protected by the offence' at issue.[136]

Such protection in fact defines the content of the obligations constraining the exercise of powers in conflict. Beyond the minimum protection ex Common Article 3, each of the Geneva Conventions entails its own regime on that matter.[137] The provisions vary slightly from category to category, but

133 *Ibid.* See also ICTY, *Kordić & Čerkez*, IT-95-14/2, Appeals Chamber, 17 December 2004, para 39.

134 J Pictet, 'The Medical Profession and International Humanitarian Law' [1985] 25 *IRRC* 247, 194. The delegations to the Diplomatic Conference looked for some flexibility in adopting the wording of the provision, see Pictet et al., *Commentary*, I, *supra* n 2, 3, 53–54. For an opposite view, see DA Elder, 'The Historical Background of Common Article 3 of the Geneva Convention of 1949' (1979) 37 *Case Western Reserve JIL* 37, 61.

135 ICTY, *Prosecutor* v. *Aleksovski*, *supra* n 22, paras 47–57.

136 ICTY, *Prosecutor* v. *Aleksovski*, IT–95–14/ 1–A, Appeals Chamber Judgement, 24 June 2000, para 25.

137 The requirement features in all four Conventions: Art. 12 GC I; Art. 12 GC II; Arts. 13, 20, 46 GC III; Arts. 27, 37, 127 GC IV.

two obligations constitute the foundation of the protective regime established by the GCs, AP I and AP II as well as customary IHL: the obligation to 'respect' and 'protect' protected persons. The obligation to 'respect' alludes to sparing the protected persons and not attacking them. The obligation 'to protect' means that parties to the conflict must take all the precautions and measures in their power to prevent the proscribed acts and, thus, ensure that the rights of a protected person are safeguarded. Importantly, each of the Geneva Conventions also includes a broad prohibition of discrimination against persons protected by that specific Convention.[138]

By way of illustration, I will here examine the main obligations arising from the protection of the principle of humanity and deriving from rights recognized to three specific categories: the wounded, sick and shipwrecked, prisoners of war and civilian population and of individual civilians.

As regards the *wounded, sick and shipwrecked*, to whichever party they belong, shall be respected and protected in all circumstances,[139] and any attempts on their lives are prohibited. They shall be treated humanely and cared for without distinction.[140] The obligation to respect and protect is applicable 'in all circumstances', a formulation which epitomizes that, in case of non-compliance, military necessity cannot be a ground precluding wrongfulness.[141] Obligations to the wounded and sick laid out in GC III show the scope of the obligation to treat humanely the wounded and sick who are in enemy hands. They must be provided, inter alia, with sufficient food and water,[142] clothing[143] and with accommodation that guarantees sufficient standards of health and hygiene.[144] They must freely exercise their religious practices[145] and be protected from insults and public curiosity.[146] As such, humane treatment covers 'all aspects of a man's existence'.[147] The protection of the wounded and sick has been also further developed through the elaboration of AP II, which developed the content of Common Article 3. The obligations to provide protection and to ensure medical care made explicit in AP

138 See G Rona and RJ McGuire, 'The Principle of Non-Discrimination' in Clapham, Gaeta and Sassòli, *supra* n 2, 191–205.

139 Art. 12(1), 35(1) GC I; Art. 12(1) GC II; Art. 3(1) n2, GC III; Art. 16 GC IV; Art. 10(1) AP I; Art. 7(1) AP II.

140 Art. 12(2) GC I; Art, 12(2) GC II; Art. 10(2) AP I; Art. 7(2), AP II.

141 F Kalshoven and L Zegveld, *Constraints on the Waging of War: An Introduction to International Humanitarian Law* (4th ed., ICRC 2011), 37, 84.

142 Art. 26 GC III; Art. 89 GC IV.

143 Art. 27 GC III; Art. 90 GC IV.

144 Arts. 22 and 29 GC III; Art. 85 GC IV.

145 Art. 34 GC III; Arts. 86 and 93 GC IV.

146 Art. 13(2) GC III; Art. 27(4) GC IV.

147 Pictet et al., *Commentary*, I, *supra* n 2, Art. 12, at 137.

II[148] constitute 'an authoritative interpretation of the general requirement laid down in Common Article 3, deriving from the duty to collect and care for, as well as the requirement of humane treatment'.[149] As noted by Mehring, the principle of human dignity surely entails that a physician treat their patient with humanity, yet it does not specify much regarding such treatment. However, in this respect, Articles 11 AP I and 5(2)(e) AP II and 16 AP I and 10 AP II provide much more clarity. Thus, although human dignity is integral in the legal regime related to medical care, it does not give further guidance on medical issues.[150]

Second, *prisoners of war* must be treated humanely[151] and equally.[152] The obligation also applies 'at all times', meaning that a detaining power cannot justify inhuman treatment by reference to the circumstances of the hostilities or other reasons related to the conflict, such as its perceived duration.[153] In particular, the obligation requires that the detaining power does not commit inhuman acts, such as acts or omission causing death or seriously endangering the health of the prisoners, also by way of not providing adequate space, food or drinking water.[154] It also implies that the detaining power prevents such acts by another party [155] and protects prisoners from harm and acts of violence and intimidation, insults and public curiosity.[156]

Moreover, with regard to the protection of the category of *civilian population* and of *individual civilians*, the duty to protect, respect and treat them humanely is part of customary international law.[157] Article 27 GC IV

148 See Art. 7(1) and (2) AP II.

149 G Giacca, 'The Obligations to Respect, Protect, Collect and Care for Wounded, Sick and Shipwrecked' in Clapham, Gaeta and Sassòli, *supra* n 2, 799.

150 S Mehring, *First Do No Harm: Medical Ethics in International Humanitarian Law* (Brill 2015), 332.

151 Common Art. 3 GCs; Art. 13–14 GC III; Art. 75 AP I; Art. 4 AP II; Art. 10 ICCPR. The obligation of humane treatment 'imposes a minimum standard, namely a duty to respect prisoners' inherent human dignity and inviolable quality as human beings', see ICRC, *Commentary on the Third Geneva Convention* (Cambridge University Press 2021), para 1570. For an analysis of Article 13 and of the nature and implications of this obligation, see *ibid.*, paras 1562–1650.

152 Art. 16 GC III; Art. 26 ICCPR. However, on positive discrimination, see Art. 22(3) GC III; Art. 14(2) GC III.

153 S Krähenmann, 'Protection of Prisoners in Armed Conflict' in D Fleck (ed.), *Handbook of International Humanitarian Law* (Oxford University Press 2013), 373. The expression 'at all times' has also been interpreted as underlining that the principle of military necessity cannot be invoked as a justification for not fulfilling the obligation of humane treatment, see ICRC Commentary, GC III, 2021, *supra* n 152, para 1580.

154 Art. 26 GC III, Art. 27 GC III and Arts. 29–31 GC III. See SN Rodley, *Treatment of Prisoners* (Oxford University Press 2009), 377–426.

155 Art. 13(2) GC III.

156 *Ibid.* See ICRC Commentary, GC III, 2021, *supra* n 152, paras 1610–1632.

157 Henckaerts and Doswald-Beck, *supra* n 64, Rules 87–105.

proclaims the basic principle of protection for human beings and the right to humane treatment. In particular, parties to a conflict shall direct operations only against military objectives[158] and civilians shall be respected and protected,[159] and not be objects of attacks.[160]

If detained, they must be treated humanely.[161] Moreover, they must also be able to receive all necessary relief.[162] Any attack on the honour of women or form of indecent assault is prohibited,[163] and children shall be the object of special respect and protection.[164] Civilians should not be used as a shield to render areas immune from military operations.[165] This prohibition follows directly from the rule that civilians shall not be involved in hostilities. They also benefit from the fundamental guarantees protected by the conventions.[166] Accordingly, the obligation to treat humanely all persons once they are in the power of the adverse party must be respected in all circumstances. Those who find themselves in the hands of a party to a conflict or an occupying power of which they are not nationals benefit from the status of protected persons.[167]

AP I has relaxed the strict definition of the categories of protected persons and consolidated the provisions ensuring a minimal level of protection. It also establishes the fundamental guarantees that remain applicable to all victims of a situation of conflict who do not benefit from a specific, preferential regime or categorization.[168]

4.4.2 *Constraints on the Means and Methods of Warfare*

The second set of constraints deriving from human dignity applicable in times of conflict relates to rules on means and methods of warfare. In particular, they are closely related to two fundamental principles: (i) means and methods of warfare are not unlimited[169] and weapons should not be used in a manner that will indiscriminately affect both combatants and non-combatants (principle of

158 Art. 48, AP I.
159 Art. 27(1), GC IV; Art. 46(1), Hague Regulations.
160 Art. 51(2) AP I; Art. 13(2) AP II.
161 Art. 27, 76, 79–134 GC IV; Arts. 11, 75, AP I; Art. 5 AP II.
162 Art. 23, 38 GC IV; Art. 70 AP I.
163 Art. 27(2) GC IV; Art. 76(1) AP I.
164 Art. 24 GC IV; Art. 77(1) AP I.
165 Art. 28 GC IV; Art. 51(7) AP I.
166 GC I–IV Common Art. 3; Art. 75, AP I.
167 Art. 4, GC IV.
168 Art. 75, AP I.
169 Art. 35 (1), Additional Protocol I, para 1; Art. 22 of both the 1899 Hague Convention II and the Hague Convention IV (1907).

distinction);[170] (ii) weapons should not inflict either superfluous injury or unnecessary suffering (principle of humanity).[171] As the Trial Chamber of the ICTY clarified in the *Martić case*, these principles 'emanate from elementary considerations of humanity, which constitute the foundation of the entire body of IHL applicable to all armed conflicts', and are all incorporated in the Martens Clause.[172]

In light of the protection of human dignity, this section will examine the content of the obligations arising from the above principles in the context of the current legal regime and, lastly, focus on the main challenges posed today by new technologies and, more specifically, by autonomous weapons.

4.4.2.1 Prohibition of Indiscriminate Attacks

The right of the parties to an armed conflict to choose means and method of warfare is not unlimited.[173] The prohibition against unlimited warfare constitutes the basis of any regulation of the methods and means of warfare. It derives from the principle of humanity, from the 'dictates of public conscience' and also from the assumption of the final rejection of 'total war'.[174] Importantly, this obligation requires striking a balance between conflicting concerns of humanity and military necessity.[175]

The principle of distinction, clarified in Section 4.2.2, defines the content of a central obligation prohibiting indiscriminate attacks. Article 51(4) (a) of AP I prohibits attacks that are not directed at a specific military objective. This represents a self-evident consequence of the principle of distinction. The same provision subsequently defines indiscriminate attacks as: '(b) those which employ a method or means of combat which cannot be directed at a specific military objective; or (c) those which employ a method or means of combat the effects of which cannot be limited as required by this Protocol'; and

170 Art. 51(4) Additional Protocol I; S Haines, 'The Developing Law of Weapons: Humanity, Distinction, and Precautions in Attack' in Clapham and Gaeta, *supra* n 65, 282–289.

171 Art. 35 (2) Additional Protocol I, para 2.

172 *Prosecutor* v. *Martić*, *supra* n 22, para 13. See also W Kälin, Special Rapporteur on the Situation of Human Rights in Kuwait under Iraqi Occupation, Report E/CN.4/1992/26, para 36.

173 Art. 35 (1), Additional Protocol I, para 1; Art. 22 of both the 1899 Hague Convention II and the Hague Convention IV (1907).

174 ICRC, *Commentary on the Additional Protocols of 8 June 1977 to the Geneva Conventions of 12 August 1949* (ICRC and Martinus Nijhoff 1987), Additional Protocol I (and Annex I), Part III, 382, para 1367.

175 Y Dinstein, *The Conduct of Hostilities under the Law of Armed Conflict* (2nd ed., Cambridge University Press 2010), 4–8; see also J Gardam, *Necessity, Proportionality, and the Use of Force by States* (Cambridge University Press 2004).

consequently, in each such case, means and methods are of a nature to strike military objectives and civilians or civilian objects without distinction. This provision only addresses indiscriminate attacks, and not weapons that are themselves indiscriminate. It is inevitably dependent on the existence of weapons to fulfil the requirements of distinction in the context of an attack. One of the criteria for labelling a weapon to be inherently indiscriminate is that it cannot be used in a manner consistent with the principle of distinction and 'is likely to … randomly hit combatants and civilians to a significant degree'.[176]

Therefore, the weapon's discriminatory capacity is ordinarily related to particular targets and is not something that is likely to be an inherent feature of any weapon. Bacterial weapons or poisons in water supplies, for instance, would not be capable themselves of discriminating between combatants and non-combatants. Even weapons that are not inherently indiscriminate can be used to strike without distinction. Such use is, of course, proscribed. We are in the 'realm between designed use and inappropriate use'.[177] In its Advisory Opinion on the *Legality of the Threat or Use of Nuclear Weapons*, the ICJ confirmed that weapons the use of which violates the fundamental principles of humanitarian law are illegal.[178] In the ICRC's view, the total prohibition of certain weapons, from exploding bullets to chemical and bacterial weapons, 'was not based on an objective analysis of the suffering caused by the weapons concerned; such means of warfare were simply deemed abhorrent or inhuman'.[179] As Haines notes, 'virtually any weapon can be used indiscriminately' since 'we are in the realm of the difference between means and methods, between designed use and inappropriate use'.[180]

The quite broad definition of what constitutes an 'indiscriminate attack', ex Article 51(4) AP I, is supplemented in Paragraph 5 by two illustrations. In particular, they concern: (a) the case of an attack by bombardment which combines a series of distinct military objective located in an area; and (b) 'an attack which may be expected to cause incidental loss of civilian life, injury to civilians, damage to civilian objects, or a combination thereof, which would be excessive in relation to the concrete and direct military advantage anticipated'. The latter establishes that all damaging effects of military operations

176 Doswald-Beck, *supra* n 30, 41.

177 Haines, *supra* n 171, 283.

178 *Legality of the Threat or Use of Nuclear Weapons*, *supra* n 6, paras 78–79.

179 Report of the ICRC for the Review Conference of the 1980 United Nations Convention on Prohibitions or Restrictions on the Use of Certain Conventional Weapons Which May Be Deemed to Be Excessively Injurious or to Have Indiscriminate Effects, February 1994, at 132.

180 Haines, *supra* n 171, 283.

shall be measured on the proportionality yardstick. Collateral damage can only be justified if losses are commensurate to the military advantage. The principle of proportionality thus requires a subjective assessment and a careful balancing.[181]

4.4.2.2 Prohibition of Unnecessary Suffering

The prohibition of superflous injury or unnecessary suffering applies to the use of weapons, projectiles and material and to methods of warfare that can cause physical or moral additional suffering for no military gain.[182] The Preamble of the 1868 Saint Petersburg Declaration mentioned the principle for the first time, by clarifying that 'the employment of arms which uselessly aggravate the sufferings of disabled men, or render their death inevitable' [...] 'would [...] be contrary to the laws of humanity'. As a general prohibition of arms or material, of 'a nature to cause superfluous injury' (in the Hague Regulation of 1899) or 'calculated to cause unnecessary suffering' (in the Hague Regulation of 1907), it was included in Article 23 (e) of the Hague Regulations.[183] They both specify the features of the obligation arising from the principle of humanity.[184] It remains, however, unclear what constitutes an unnecessary suffering, what is a superfluous injury and what is the specific threshold that should not be crossed.[185]

Two different tests could be adopted to characterize a weapon as causing unnecessary suffering.[186] The first is linked to *military necessity*. The latter requires a comparative assessment as to how much suffering various weapons may cause and whether other means could still result in the same outcome with less harm.[187] The prohibition of causing 'unnecessary suffering' would prohibit or limit the use of weapons capable of causing suffering unnecessary to the accomplishment of legitimate military objectives.[188] A traditional

181 S Oeter, 'Methods and Means of Combat' in Fleck, *supra* n 154, 196–198.

182 Art. 35 (2) Additional Protocol I, para 2. See also C Greenwood, 'Historical Development and Legal Basis' in D Fleck and M Bothe (eds), *Handbook of International Humanitarian Law* (Oxford University Press 2008), 19–20.

183 See also Art. 35(2) of AP I and the Preamble, CCW, para 3.

184 Haines, *supra* n 171, 284.

185 The questions are discussed by F Kalshoven, 'Les principes juridiques qui sous-tendent la Convention sur les armes classiques' (1990) 72 *IRRC* 556–567, at 563–566; E David, *Principes de droit des conflits armés* (Bruyland 2002), 316–25.

186 Meron, *supra* n 29, 70–73.

187 W Solf, in M Bothe, KJ Partsch and W Solf, *New Rules for Victims of Armed Conflict* (Martinus Nijhoff 1982), 196.

188 See US Air Force Pamphlet 110–131, 19 November 1976, para 6.

reading of the prohibition would thus imply the prohibition of causing a physical or emotional impairment which cannot be justified by military necessity[189] and, in the words of the ICJ, 'a harm greater than that unavoidable to achieve legitimate military objectives'.[190] This type of assessment is, however, mostly subjective and, in practice, legality is considered in light of the weapon's intended purpose.[191] It is unclear whether 'the disablement of the greatest possible number of enemy combatants' is the only criteria by which to evaluate military advantage or if other military requirements may play a role.[192] A more objective assessment would require a comparison with existing weapons in use on the battlefield.[193]

A second test relies on the *effects of weapons*, a test that stems from the wording of the Saint Petersburg Declaration. Cassese has noted that '[w]eapons are to be deemed unlawful when they are such as to produce death whenever and in whatever manner they hit the enemy' and, thus, 'it is not in keeping with international law if it always results in killing all persons who in some way happen to be struck by it'.[194] At the 1899 Hague Conference, members regarded weapons causing 'incurable wounds' as unlawful,[195] taking into account different factors.[196] This view was integrated in the German Military Manual,[197] but more generally, it has not prevailed.[198] The ICRC's superfluous injury and unnecessary suffering (SIrUS) project studied and assessed the health effects

189 N Sitaropolous, 'Weapons and Superfluous Injury or Unnecessary Suffering in International Humanitarian Law: Human Pain in Time of War and the Limits of Law' (2001) 54 *Revue Hellénique de Droit International* 71–108, 91.

190 *Legality of the Threat or Use of Nuclear Weapons*, *supra* n 6, at 257, para 78.

191 Doswald-Beck, *supra* n 30, 45.

192 The position is expressed in the US representative's formulation of the proportionality test at the Lucerne Conference (1974): Statement of the Chief of the International Affairs Division (W Solf), at the Lucerne Conference, [1974] Digest of United States Practice in International Law 708–709, at 709 (Arthur W Rovine ed. 1973 and 1974).

193 See Memorandum of Law on Sniper Use of Open-Tip Ammunition (1990), in US Practice Report (ICRC Study), Annex 3 14, at 3.

194 A Cassese, 'Weapons Causing Unnecessary Suffering: Are they Prohibited?' [1975] 58 *Rivista di Diritto Internazionale* 12, 18.

195 *Ibid.*, 17.

196 Such as the risks of death, medical effects, as well as the laws of humanity, see ICRC, Report on the Work of the Conference of Government Experts on the use of Certain Conventional Weapons, para 6–12 (1974), 10; P Robblee, 'The Legitimacy of Modern Conventional Weaponry' [1976] 71 *MLR* 95–148; Art. 23(b) of the Regulations annexed to the 1899 Hague II and the Hague Convention IV (1907).

197 See German Military Manual, *supra* n 21, para 407. See also H Meyrovitz, 'The Principle of Superfluous Injury or Unnecessary Suffering' [1994] 299 *IRRC* 98, 118.

198 It has been argued that perhaps the regulation of the use of weapons was seen as a question of technology, instead of in light of the effects of them on humans, see RM Coupland, *The SirUS Project* (ICRC 1997), 14.

of weapons, such as disease, permanent disability, and inevitable or virtually inevitable death, to be considered when the legality of new weapons was examined, in particular when determining whether the purpose of the weapon 'could reasonably be achieved by other lawful means that do not have such effect'.[199]

The more typical approach is to balance military necessity with unnecessary suffering. Thus, it can be argued that the assessment of a possible superfluity of an injury or the level of need to inflict suffering can only matter for (informed) subjective judgement, which should be influenced by humanitarian considerations. Thus, 'attempts to achieve total objectivity in relation to them would be intellectually flawed'.[200] The use of specific weapons may also change because of the humanizing effect of public opinion[201] or limited military effectiveness.[202] Despite problems in the evaluation of superfluous injury and unnecessary suffering, 'the principle arising from the desire to eradicate them is vitally important and it is an essential permanent customary backdrop to weapons law'.[203]

4.4.2.3 Autonomous Weapons

Recent years have witnessed a dramatic increase in the adoption of robotic systems by military forces, in particular different unmanned systems used in the air, on land and on – or under – the sea.[204] New studies in robotics and computing combined with military operational demands are influencing the development and adoption of novel robotic systems with more degrees of autonomy.[205] Unmanned systems are increasingly crafted and used to deliver weapons, thereby becoming weapon systems.[206] Three main categories of control and automation can be defined: (1) remote-controlled or tele-operated systems, which are under the direct control of a remote operator; (2) automated systems (also defined as semi-autonomous), which can act independently of

199 See R Coupland and P Herby, 'Review of the Legality of Weapons: A New Approach, the SIrUS Project' [1999] 835 *IRRC* 583–592; See J McClelland, 'The Review of Weapons in accordance with Art. 36 of Additional Protocol 1' [2003] 850 *IRRC* 397–415, 399–400.

200 Haines, *supra* n 171, 286.

201 L Doswald–Beck, 'Implementation of International Humanitarian Law in Future Wars' [1998] 71 *US Naval War College* 39, 46–47.

202 M Aubert, 'The International Committee of the Red Cross and the Problem of Excessively Injurious or Indiscriminate Weapons' [1990] 279 *IRRC* 477–497, at 477–478.

203 *Ibid.*

204 See, for instance, PW Singer, *Wired for War* (Penguin 2009).

205 See US Department of Defense, Defense Science Board, Task Force Report: The Role of Autonomy in DoD Systems (19 July 2012), 78.

206 US Department of Defense, *Unmanned Systems Integrated Roadmap 2013*, FY2013-2038 (2013), 73.

external control but only according to a predefined set of programmed rules; and (3) autonomous systems, which can operate with no external control, defining their own acts but within the limitations set up in their programming and software.[207] Autonomy in machines can be understood as 'the capacity of a robot, following activation, to operate without any external control in some or all areas of its operation for extended periods of time'.[208]

There is no agreed definition of an AWS,[209] although various definitions proposed by different countries and organizations share similar themes.[210] It is, however, clear that these weapon systems can independently select and attack targets, with or without human oversight. The distinction between autonomous and automated is only based on the degree of 'freedom' with which the weapon system can select and attack different targets. Weapon systems that select and attack targets only under remote control by a human operator are usually excluded from AWS. This would exclude, in principle, armed unmanned air systems (i.e. drones) since targeting and firing would be remotely controlled by humans. If drones are instead developed with the capability to select and/or attack targets (with or without human supervision), they would be considered de facto semi-autonomous or AWS.[211] For the purposes of this section, the term 'autonomous weapon systems' refers to weapon systems for which critical functions (i.e. acquiring, tracking, selecting and attacking targets) are autonomous. Thus, autonomous weapons would enable the release of force from unmanned systems that are not directly or remotely controlled by humans. Instead, once a human has activated an AWS, on-board computers will take the decision, independent from direct human control, selecting the target and releasing force.[212] Therefore, as Heyns noted, the development of autonomous weapons will enable humans to be

207 ICRC, 'Autonomous Weapon Systems: Technical, Military, Legal and Humanitarian Aspects', Expert meeting, Geneva, Switzerland, 26–28 March 2014 (ICRC 2014), 62.

208 *Ibid.*

209 See C Heyns, 'Autonomous Weapons in Armed Conflict and the Right to a Dignified Life: An African Perspective' [2017] 33(1) *SAJHR* 46–71, 47, footnote 3.

210 See, for instance, US Department of Defense, Autonomy in Weapon Systems, Directive 3000.09 (21 November 2012); C Heyns, Report of the Special Rapporteur on extrajudicial, summary or arbitrary executions, UN General Assembly, A/HRC/23/47 (9 April 2013), para 38 [Report of the Special Rapporteur on extrajudicial, summary or arbitrary executions 2013]; B Docherty, 'Losing Humanity: The Case against Killer Robots' (Human Rights Watch 2012); ICRC, International Humanitarian Law and the challenges of contemporary armed conflicts, Official working document of the 31st International Conference of the Red Cross and Red Crescent (28 November – 1 December 2011), 39; ICRC, 'Autonomous Weapons: States Must Address Major Humanitarian, Ethical Challenges' (ICRC 2013).

211 ICRC, *IHL 2011*, *supra* n 211, 39–40.

212 See M Schmitt, 'Autonomous Weapon Systems and International Humanitarian Law: A Reply to the Critics' [2013] 1 *HNSJF* 3–7.

physically absent from the point of release of force, as happens with armed drones, and also to be 'psychologically' absent, to the point that they do not take the on-the-spot decision to direct and open fire.[213] The actual release of force takes place elsewhere and some time after the system was activated. It is, therefore, said that unmanned systems are pushing a process of depersonalization in the use of force and the development and acquisition of weaponized unmanned systems are likely to expand globally in the coming years.[214] Notwithstanding the fact that such force can be directed against objects, the concern of this section is confined to the role of human dignity and its violations.

My analysis will now, therefore, focus on barriers to autonomy and on the role of human dignity in the debate.

The growing levels of autonomy of robotic systems are favoured by a series of drivers[215] and benefits to the users, such as stronger capability over a broader area, higher performance and speed in taking the decision, longer persistence in the battlefield and in the enemy's territory, reduced military personnel and reduced risks for them.[216] There are, however, barriers to autonomy: (i) *unpredictability*: since autonomous systems are adaptable, within the boundaries of their software and programmes, they are necessarily unpredictable, and it is only possible to test possible situations they might be faced with[217] – and testing itself may raise safety issues;[218] (ii) *unreliability*: added to the problem of unpredictability is the issue of reliability, since failures may derive from errors, malfunctions, software failures, breakdown in human–machine interaction or cyberattacks, among many other things;[219] (iii) *vulnerability*: autonomous systems present risks associated with malfunctions, accidents and vulnerabilities in their use.[220] These barriers have led further research to focus on autonomous unmanned systems that can make decisions and react to circumstances without

213 Heyns, *supra* n 210, 47.

214 ICRC, *supra* n 208, 60.

215 US Department of Defense, *supra* n 207, 3.

216 *Ibid.*, vi; UK Ministry of Defence, Development, Concepts and Doctrine Centre, *The UK Approach to Unmanned Aircraft Systems*, Joint Doctrine Note 2/11 (30 March 2011), 5–10. See also V Boulanin and M Verbruggen, Mapping the Development of Autonomy in Weapon Systems (SIPRI 2017).

217 US Air Force, Report on Technology Horizons: A Vision for Air Force Science & Technology During 2010–2030: Volume 1 (15 May 2010), 105.

218 US Department of Defense, *supra* n 206, 64.

219 US Department of Defense, Autonomy in Weapon Systems, Directive 3000.09 (21 November 2012); JL Chameau, W Ballhaus and H Lin (eds), *Emerging and Readily Available Technologies and National Security – A Framework for Addressing Ethical, Legal, and Societal Issues*, National Research Council, US National Academies (The National Academies Press 2014), 3–2.

220 US Department of Defense, *supra* n 206, 7–8.

human intervention,[221] involving studies in information, communications technology and artificial intelligence, the cognitive and behavioural sciences.[222] However, it is not clear whether such technological developments would be sophisticated enough to enable autonomous functioning in highly complex decision-making, such as the process of selecting and attacking targets with weapon systems. At the moment, when unmanned systems are adopted to carry weapons, the decision to fire at a specific target is still taken by a person (and not by the machine).[223] However, many of the functions allowing that person to take those decisions are automated and delegated to sensors and computer-based systems.[224] Therefore, in theory, it would not take much to enable an unmanned system to use fire without human intervention, but it would require a technological leap in capability while also raising important legal and ethical questions,[225] as will be discussed in the following paragraphs.

Both civilians and combatants can be threatened by attacks from AWS.[226] The threat to human dignity of AWS used in times of conflict lies in the risk they pose to the dignity and rights of both civilians and combatants.[227] In order to clarify the role of human dignity, it should be investigated whether AWS can be considered *inherently* contrary to human dignity, by presenting the relevant IHL principles and rules at stake and providing an overview of the status of the current debate on the topic.

First, it should be noted that it is well accepted that new technologies of warfare must abide by existing international law, in particular rules and principles of IHL, such as distinction, proportionality and precautions in attack. Achieving such capacity would appear to present significant challenges. In particular, it is important to carry out rigorous legal reviews of new technologies of warfare to ensure that they may be used lawfully, as required by Article 36 of AP I to the Geneva Conventions of 1949.[228] The

221 US Department of Defense, *supra* n 207, 68.

222 *Ibid.*, 13.

223 *Ibid.*, 24. See also Boulanin and Verbruggen, supra n 217, 57–83.

224 UK Ministry of Defence, *supra* n 217, 2–3.

225 *Ibid.*, 5–4. See, recently, V Boulanin, N Davison, N Goussac and MP Carlsson, *Limits on Autonomy in Weapon Systems* (ICRC and SIPRI 2020); J Galliott, D MacIntosh and JD Ohlin, *Lethal Autonomous Weapons: Re-Examining the Law and Ethics of Robotic Warfare* (Oxford University Press 2020).

226 See in this sense, D Birnbacher, 'Autonomous Weapons Systems and Human Dignity' in N Bhuta, S Beck, R Geiss, HY Liu and C Kress (eds), *Autonomous Weapons Systems: Law, Ethics, Policy* (Cambridge University Press 2016), 113; E Lieblich and E Benvenisti, 'The Obligation to Exercise Discretion in Warfare: Why Autonomous Weapons Systems are Unlawful' in *ibid.*, 245–283.

227 Heyns, *supra* n 210, 49.

228 See Schmitt, *supra* n 213.

aim of Article 36 is to prevent the use of, and set restrictions on, recourse to weapons that would violate international law in some or all circumstances, by determining their lawfulness before they are developed, acquired or otherwise included in a State's arsenal.[229] The acceptability of AWS should also be assessed according to the principles of humanity and the dictates of public conscience. This refers to the Martens Clause, formulated in Article 1(2) of AP I and in the Preamble (4) of AP II. In its Advisory Opinion on the Legality of the Threat or Use of Nuclear Weapons, the ICJ affirmed that the Martens Clause had 'proved to be an effective means of addressing rapid evolution of military technology'.[230] A weapon that is not covered by existing rules of IHL would be deemed to be contrary to the Martens Clause if it cannot *per se* act in line with the principles of humanity or the dictates of public conscience.[231]

This issue has triggered different views. Waxman and Anderson have noted the importance of developing internal norms and practices for the design of AWS and clarifying principles at the basis of the AWS's assessment.[232] However, Schmitt has argued that 'as with most other weapon systems, their lawfulness as such, as well as the lawfulness of their use, must be judged on a *case-by-case* basis'.[233] In Sassòli's view, it is important to consider that 'politically, there is a risk that once the technology has been developed at great expense, vested interests will make it nearly impossible to conclude that the result is unlawful. The solution may be to accompany the development process with *constant reviews*.'[234]

Together with the barriers to autonomy explained above (unpredictability, unreliability, vulnerability), concerns have been raised that AWS would not be able to choose a 'higher purpose' and to act like 'human beings in the same situation'[235] when taking decisions.[236] It has been noted that, because AWS cannot be emotive, it is doubtful whether the delegation to

[229] See, for more details, ICRC, *ICRC's Guide to the Legal Review of New Weapons, Means and Methods of Warfare* (ICRC 2006), 4.

[230] *Legality of the Threat or Use of Nuclear Weapons*, *supra* n 6, para 78.

[231] ICRC, *supra* n 230, 7.

[232] M Waxman and K Anderson, *Law and Ethics for Autonomous Weapon Systems: Why a Ban Won't Work and How the Laws of War Can* (Jean Perkins Task Force on National Security and Law 2013), 13; see also UK Ministry of Defence, *supra* n 217, para 503.

[233] Schmitt, *supra* n 213, 8 (emphasis added).

[234] M Sassòli, 'Autonomous Weapons and International Humanitarian Law: Advantages, Open Technical Questions and Legal Issues to be Clarified' [2014] 90 *US Naval War College, International Law Studies* 308–340.

[235] Heyns, *supra* n 210, 51.

[236] See UK Ministry of Defence, *supra* n 217, paras 520–521; D Saxon, 'Introduction' in D Saxon (ed.), *International Humanitarian Law and the Changing Technology of War* (Martinus Nijhoff 2013), 7.

machines of life and death choices is morally acceptable. Waxman and Anderson have stated that 'this is a difficult argument to engage, since it stops with a moral principle that one either accepts or not', but also that 'it raises a further question as to what constitutes the tipping point into impermissible autonomy, given that the automation of weapons functions is likely to occur in incremental steps'.[237] It could be, however, concluded that when 'the decision to take life or to subject people to other grave consequences is at stake, the decision making power should be exercised by humans'.[238] This is implied by IHL, the rules of which assume conduct by human soldiers or commanders, rather than machines.[239]

This leads to the central concern, that is, whether AWS can be considered *inherently* contrary to human dignity. Heyns reflected on whether it would be '*inherently* wrong to let autonomous machines decide who and when to kill. . . . The question here is whether the deployment of LARs [lethal autonomous robots] against . . . enemy fighters, is in principle acceptable, because it entails non-human entities making the determination to use force.'[240] There are three main reasons put forward to demonstrate that AWS are intrinsically incompatible with human dignity, starting from the consideration that, as machines, AWS:[241] (i) cannot comprehend the value of human life, so they 'could undermine the principle of dignity, which implies that everyone has a worth deserving of respect. As inanimate machines, fully autonomous weapons could truly comprehend neither the value of individual life nor the significance of its loss. Allowing them to make determinations to take life away would thus conflict with the principle of dignity';[242] (ii) cannot take responsibility, since 'when viewed from the perspective of engineering and design ethics, intentionally designing systems that lack responsible and accountable

237 Waxman and Anderson, *supra* n 233, 7.

238 Report of the Special Rapporteur on extrajudicial, summary or arbitrary executions 2013, para 89. See also Asaro, *supra* n 55, 700. On the role of the human operator in 'framing the environment' in which AWS operate, see J Thurnher, 'Examining Autonomous Weapon Systems from a Law of Armed Conflict Perspective' in H Nasu and R McLaughlin (eds), *New Technologies and the Law of Armed Conflict* (TMC Asser Press 2014), 223–224.

239 See Hague Convention II with Respect to the Laws and Customs of War on Land and its annex: Regulations concerning the Laws and Customs of War on Land, adopted on 29 July 1899, entered into force on 4 September 1900; the Hague Convention IV (1907); Additional Protocol I, Art. 1(2).

240 C Heyns, Report of the Special Rapporteur on extrajudicial, summary or arbitrary executions, A/HRC/23/47, 9 April 2013, para 92 (emphasis added).

241 On the opposite, see Birnbacher, *supra* n 227, who notes that 'What is contrary to human dignity is not these weapons themselves but, rather, the uses to which they might be put' (118) and warns to 'beware of idealizations of human warfare' (121).

242 Human Rights Watch, *Shaking the Foundations – The Human Rights Implications of Killer Robots* (HRW 2014), 3.

agents is in and of itself unethical, irresponsible, and immoral';[243] and (iii) unlike human actors, cannot act mercifully or compassionately, since '[t]he most offensive part is probably not the fact of being killed by a machine, but rather the deprivation of hope for some kind of mercy or reprieve that this technology brings. Since there is no deliberative process, there is no possibility of a higher appeal, no prospect of human empathy.'[244] Recently there has been discussion of a 'human-on-the-loop' model of weapon systems, entailing human supervision of one or more systems that have autonomous functions in the decision cycle to carry out lethal force.[245]

In light of the above reflections, it can be affirmed that, in the absence of rules of IHL explicitly prohibiting or restricting AWS, when the 'law runs out', the principle of human dignity plays an influential role when examining the importance of (or appeal of) both developing and using AWS, becoming a standard for the acceptability of AWS. Human dignity constitutes an inherent limit and constraint to the use of this type of weapons. This consideration has three corollaries: first, a weapon that is not covered by current rules of IHL would be deemed inherently contrary to the Martens Clause if it can *per se* operate against the principles of humanity or the dictates of public conscience; second, the potential impact of AWS on human dignity demands the development of internal norms and practices for the design of AWS systems and the conduct of an assessment on a cases-by-case level, with constant reviews, as regards their compliance with IHL rules; third, once the weapon is adopted in a mission, the principle of human dignity would also act as moral guideline, opening the question on whether rules would allow delegating life-and-death decisions to machines on the battlefield. On this last remark, IHRL would also be able to provide a moral and an accountability framework.[246]

4.5 HUMAN DIGNITY VERSUS SOVEREIGN DIGNITY

The developments in the laws of armed conflict show a move from a State-centred to a human-centric approach. As clarified by the ICTY in the *Kupreskić* case, 'the so-called "humanisation" of international legal obligations' refers 'to the general erosion of the role of reciprocity in the application of humanitarian law over the last century'.[247] In particular, the 'underpinning

243 Asaro, *supra* n 55, 695.
244 C Heyns, 'Challenge of Autonomous Weapons Systems to Legal Regulation', working paper, Conference EUI Autonomous weapons systems: Law, Ethics, Policy, 24–25 April 2014, 13.
245 Asaro, *supra* n 55, 694–695.
246 ICRC, *supra* n 230, 9.
247 ICTY, *Prosecutor* v. *Kupreškić*, *supra* n 57, para 518.

of this shift was that it became clear to States that norms of international humanitarian law were not intended to protect State interests; they were primarily designed to benefit individuals qua human beings'.[248] This shift, or move from a sovereign dignity paradigm to a human dignity paradigm, is evidenced by the legal path that led to the incorporation of considerations of humanity in the law and by recent practice and implementation.

As seen in Chapter Three, the humanization process can be dated back to the adoption of the Geneva Conventions of 1929 and 1949.[249] In particular, the term 'dignity' appears most prominently in Common Article 3 to the 1949 Conventions, which prohibits, inter alia, 'outrages upon personal dignity, in particular humiliating and degrading treatment',[250] conducts that 'are and shall remain prohibited at any time and in any place whatsoever'. By prohibiting various kinds of mistreatment of captives, Common Article 3 of the 1949 Conventions is 'clearly a mini-human rights treaty within the broader protections of the Conventions'.[251] The Geneva Conventions of 1949 are to be regarded 'as the most advanced effort made to introduce some humane regulation to wartime situations' and respond 'to the quest of modern man to secure as far as possible the overriding aim of human dignity'.[252] It is here that human dignity consolidates in its first constitutive stage. Furthermore, as discussed, both Additional Protocols extended such protection. This process was also favoured by various developments accelerated in the 1990s, such as the rebirth of international criminal law, at the core of which lies 'the vindication of human dignity, not (or not only) the reduction of aggregate suffering',[253] or the increased attention to human rights concerns (due process of law, torture, inhuman treatment, arbitrary arrest/detention, non-refoulement, non-discrimination, etc.).

In particular, to understand how the principle of human dignity and humanitarian considerations are gaining in importance today, taking ground from sovereign dignity, their role shall be examined in comparison with considerations of military necessity. It is said that IHL is grounded on the balance between military necessity and humanitarian considerations.[254] The principle of military necessity permits a party engaged in the conflict to use

248 *Ibid.*

249 See, on the reasons, Kolb, *supra* n 3, 45–52.

250 GC III, Art. 3.

251 D Luban, 'Human Rights Thinking and the Laws of War' in J Ohlin (ed.), *Theoretical Boundaries of Armed Conflicts and Human Rights* (Cambridge University Press 2016), 20.

252 Kolb, *supra* n 3, 55.

253 Luban, *supra* n 252, 21.

254 See Y Dinstein, *The Conduct of Hostilities under the Law of International Armed Conflict* (3rd ed., Cambridge University Press 2016), 8–9; I Detter, *The Law of War* (Cambridge University Press 2010), 395–396.

a certain degree of force, allowed under IHL, in order to achieve the legitimate purpose of the conflict, which is to partially or completely weaken the military forces of the enemy with the minimum expenditure of life and resources.[255] However, necessity can never justify actions prohibited by IHL and civilians, and the civilian population as such should never be object of attack.[256] The relation between human dignity and military necessity will be assessed in two contexts, namely the norm-creation process and in the interpretation and application of specific norms.

As regards the first issue, humanitarian considerations have acquired a relatively stronger impact compared to considerations of military necessity in the norm-creation process. The background example can be found in the adoption of two international conventions: the Mine Ban Convention in 1997,[257] the first instance in which humanitarian considerations prevailed in the negotiation of treaties prohibiting the use of specific weapons, compared to military considerations,[258] and the Cluster Munitions Convention in 2008.[259] The significance of both treaties was that they went far beyond a prohibition of use of these weapons; they also drew a framework for stockpile destruction, clearing of contaminated areas and assisting victims.[260] Even if at the time the Mine Ban Convention was being negotiated it was believed that anti-personnel mines could create significant military advantages, humanitarian considerations prevailed, and their use was nevertheless prohibited (similarly for cluster munitions).

The principle of human dignity is also increasingly influential in the application of already existing rules, to the point of having an independent legal impact. IHL includes various provisions that leave actors with a considerable discretion.[261] In particular, the principle of proportionality establishes a connection between interests equally entitled to legal protection: on one side, the need of combatants to perform military action and,

255 See St Petersburg Declaration, Preamble. See also ICTY, *Prosecutor* v. *Galic*, IT-98-29.T, Trial Judgement, paras 44 and 76.

256 E Cannizzaro, 'Proportionality in the Law of Armed Conflict' in Clapham and Gaeta, *supra* n 65, 335–336.

257 1997 Convention on the Prohibition of the Use, Stockpiling, Production and Transfer of Anti–Personnel Mines and on Their Destruction [Mine Ban Treaty], adopted 18 September 1997, 2056 UNTS 211, entered into force 1 March 1999.

258 T Meron, 'The Humanization of Humanitarian Law' [2000] 94 *AJIL* 239.

259 Convention on Cluster Munitions, 30 May 2008, Treaty Series, vol. 2688, p. 39.

260 KM Larsen, CG Cooper and G Nystuen, 'Introduction by the Editors: Is There a "Principle of Humanity" in International Humanitarian Law?' in Larsen, Cooper and Nystuen, *supra* n 3, 9.

261 See ICTY, *Prosecutor* v. *Kupreškić*, *supra* n 57, paras 525–526.

on the other, the need of non-combatants to remain unaffected by the pursuit of hostilities; second, the duty to balance military gains expected with prospective collateral damage is also 'subjectively symmetrical' since it is equally on both sides, regardless of any inquiry upon the legality of their ultimate purpose.[262] The proportionality rule is 'simply one feature of the broader principle of distinction, and that principle should be understood as a recognition of the human dignity of non-combatants'.[263] If the principle of distinction can be interpreted as an effort to minimize unnecessary suffering in war,[264] the principle of proportionality shows, at a minimum, that human dignity has an autonomous legal impact. More specifically, the principle of proportionality in fact intends to protect civilians from collateral damage even when they are not the direct target of attack.

Put in practice, the *UK Manual of the Law of Armed Conflict* suggests the same consideration:[265] first, it states that humanity 'forbids the infliction of suffering, injury or destruction not actually necessary for the accomplishment of legitimate military purposes'; and second, that

> [t]he principle of humanity is based on the notion that once a military purpose has been achieved, the further infliction of suffering is unnecessary. Thus, if an enemy combatant has been put out of action by being wounded or captured, there is no military purpose to be achieved by continuing to attack him [...] civilians and civilian objects make no contribution to military action.

Quoting the definition included in the *UK Manual of the Law of Armed Conflict*, the ICRC's 'Interpretive Guidance on the Notion of Direct Participation in Hostilities under International Humanitarian Law' affirms that the 'principle of humanity' is '[c]omplementing and implicit in the principle of military necessity', and that '[i]n conjunction, the principles of military necessity and of humanity reduce the sum total of permissible military action from that which IHL does not expressly prohibit to that which is actually necessary for the accomplishment of a legitimate military purpose in the prevailing circumstances'.[266]

262 *Ibid.*

263 Luban, *supra* n 252, 9.

264 In this sense, Luban supports his argument that the 'concern to alleviate the calamities of war rather than respect for human dignity' seems the more plausible origin of the principle of distinction by recalling the preamble to the 1868 St Petersburg Declaration, see *ibid.*, 10.

265 See UK Ministry of Defence, *The Manual of the Law of Armed Conflict* (Oxford University Press 2005), 23.

266 Interpretive Guidance on the Notion of Direct Participation in Hostilities under International Humanitarian Law, adopted by the Assembly of the ICRC on 26 February 2009, 1042. For an analysis, see A Clapham, *War* (Oxford University Press 2021), 313-316.

Examining this issue through a practical example, Larsen notes that 'military operations in multilateral enforcement operations are subjected to stronger demands to be guided by humanitarian considerations than other military operations are, especially when these multilateral operations are not involving the survival of the states whose forces are involved, but rather in support of peace in another state'.[267] This reflection is also supported by a useful example. The United Nations-authorized peace operations and the UN Secretary-General's Bulletin on observance by UN forces of IHL clearly set a prohibition against the use of incendiary weapons in peace operations,[268] whereas IHL only contains rules that restrict the use of such weapons.[269] It may well be thought that such refrain from the use of otherwise lawful weapons most likely derives from the application of the principle of human dignity and, thus, from humanitarian considerations.[270] Dahl and Cooper conclude on this point that '[i]t may also be speculated on whether humanitarian considerations will always weigh relatively more than military necessity, thereby restricting the military acts more than the laws require, as long as this military necessity is not dictated by one's own country's struggle for survival'.[271]

Therefore, the independent legal impact of the principle of human dignity is the outcome of its uses and functions. First, the principle of human dignity increasingly shows its *architectural* function, in cases in which humanitarian concerns are incorporated into the rules of IHL. Second, it serves as an element of interpretation and as a moral test that ensures that the applicability of the law is not too far from the expectations of the general public.[272] Third, the role of such a principle is most relevant in those cases where the rules of IHL are inadequate or non-existent, playing an *interstitial* or *suppletive* function, in particular in the case of NIACs. In these cases, there are arguably two possible approaches: either further development of IHL through treaty or custom, or broadening the application of IHRL. It has been suggested that the principle of human dignity could actually represent a constructive *middle road* between supporters and opponents of a stronger impact of

267 Larsen et al., *supra* n 261, 10–11.

268 UN doc. ST/SGB/1999/13, para 6.2.

269 Protocol on Prohibitions or Restrictions on the Use of Incendiary Weapons (Protocol III to the Convention on Certain Conventional Weapons), 10 October 1980, and the ICRC Customary Law Study, rules 84 and 85.

270 Larsen lists various incentives in this direction, see Larsen et al., *supra* n 261, 11.

271 AW Dahl and CG Cooper, 'Implementation in Practice: 60 Years of Dissemination and Other Implementation Efforts from a Norwegian Perspective' in Larsen, Cooper and Nystuen, *supra* n 3, 343.

272 KM Larsen and CG Cooper, 'Conclusions: Is There a "Principle of Humanity" in International Humanitarian Law?' in Larsen, Cooper and Nystuen, *supra* n 3, 356.

IHRL on the conduct of hostilities. It has been argued that the principle would decrease tendencies to call for the applicability of IHRL in contexts that would be better assessed in light of IHL.[273] Thus, 'it could further support a more coherent relation between IHL and HRL, since it would function as a "humanitarian exception" entirely within the framework of IHL and thereby reduce the need to turn to external rules, such as HRL, which may or may not fit in the particular context'.[274]

273 See KM Larsen, 'A "Principle of Humanity" or a "Principle of Human–Rightism"?' in Larsen, Cooper and Nystuen, *supra* n 3, 141; AM Gross, 'Human Proportions: Are Human Rights the Emperor's New Clothes of the International Law of Occupation?' [2007] 18 *EJIL* 1, who argues 'that the merging of IHRL into IHL, rather than expanding human protection may serve to undermine it as well as to legitimize violations of people living under occupation' (4–5).

274 Larsen, *supra* n 274, 142.

5

Human Dignity in Human Rights Law

5.1 INTRODUCTION

The decolonization process, described as the largest transfer of sovereign power in history,[1] caused a 'tectonic shift', from South to North and East to West, when the issue of human rights emerged and evolved rapidly.[2] It led to reforms in international relations and to new legal and institutional approaches to the 'universal' nature of human rights. More specifically, the universal character of human dignity, which made its first appearance in the UN Charter, in the UNESCO Constitution and in the UDHR, in connection with an individual paradigm, expanded to reach a new collective and broader paradigm. The nexus between decolonization and human rights refined the discourse and the legal manifestations of human dignity. In particular, late 1962 was a time when various developments happened. The human rights project that had been faltering since 1945 was pushed in a new legal direction and trajectory by two major developments that occurred at the United

[1] J Herbst, 'Let Them Fail: State Failure in Theory and Practice' in R Rotberg (ed.), *When States Fail: Causes and Consequences* (Princeton University Press 2004), 312; see J Sheehan, *Where Have All the Soldiers Gone? The Transformation of Modern Europe* (Houghton Mifflin 2008), 166.

[2] See S Pedersen, 'The Meaning of the Mandates System: An Argument' [2006] 32 *Geschichte und Gesellschaft* 560–582; S Pedersen, *The Guardians. The League of Nations and the Crisis of Empire* (Oxford University Press 2015), 13; F Cooper, *Colonialism in Question: Theory, Knowledge, History* (University of California Press 2005), 231; F Cooper, *Citizenship between Empire and Nation. Remaking France and French Africa, 1945–1960* (Princeton University Press 2014); AG Hopkins, 'Rethinking Decolonization' [2008] 200(1) *Past and Present* 241–247; C Reus-Smit, *Individual Rights and the Making of the International System* (Cambridge University Press 2013), 161.

Nations. The first development was related to a new legal dynamic flavoured by concerns around race and religion. Four UN GA debates, which started in 1962 and ended in 1966, secured a human rights breakthrough on international law and demonstrated how those two issues, race and religion, transcended the sacred notion of sovereignty that for years was firmly secured by UN member states. On this foundation, the Convention on Elimination of All Forms of Racial Discrimination, adopted in 1965, paved the way for the legal recognition of a universal and collective paradigm of human dignity and for the recognition of the right to self-determination in the 1966 Covenants. The second development was that human rights became an essential component of international norm-making endeavours. In 1962, the UN started the process of elaboration of 'the principles of international law concerning friendly relations and cooperation among states based on the UN Charter', which lasted from 1962 to 1970[3] and led to the adoption of Resolution 2625 in 1970, and, a few years later, to the 1975 Helsinki Final Act, which acknowledged the universal significance of human rights.

Between 1948 and 1966, human dignity sometimes made an appearance, while at other times it was silent. It evolved through various steps of diplomatic negotiations and political debates, and in 1966 its universal nature was reshaped by the larger historical processes, thereby acquiring a collective guise. Building on the conclusions drawn in Chapter 3 on the main consolidated features of the second constitutive stage of human dignity, this chapter moves into the examination of the legal manifestations of dignity in the human rights legal framework. Here, it is possible to trace three main levels of relationships between human dignity and human rights and, thus, three main instruments that are typically adopted to manifest them: first, human dignity as a foundation of human rights, which is formulated as a *principle* and is the most common and predominant legal form; second, dignity as the foundation and object of rights and which therefore manifests itself as *mother-right* and/or in its *derivative-rights*; and, last, human dignity as the basis of specific *obligations*. This assessment grounds the structure of this chapter. The following paragraphs explain in detail how these three main instruments (i.e. *principle*, *right* and *obligation*) characterize and manifest human dignity in international human

[3] UNGA resolutions 1815 (XVII) of 18 December 1962; 1966 (XVIII) of 16 December 1963; 2103 (XX) of 20 December 1965; 2181 (XXI) of 12 December 1966; 2327 (XXII) of 18 December 1967; 2463 (XXIII) of 20 December 1968 and 2533 (XXIV) of 8 December 1969.

rights law (IHRL), taking into account the regional and international dimensions, from both the normative and the judicial perspectives, outlining the various linguistic articulations of human dignity for each of them. Indeed, while examining traces and patterns of human dignity in international law, in order to assess the framework language of human dignity, I have considered terminological variations and variety of different legal formulations able to convey and carry the same meaning. This approach allows the identification of underlying trends in the manifestations of human dignity.

This chapter begins by examining human dignity as foundational principle (Section 5.2), as a right (Section 5.3) and as an obligation (Section 5.4). Subsequently, in line with the argumentative narrative of this study, the chapter concludes by showing how the circle of human dignity, by way of its manifestations in human rights law, is placing limits to the full operation of sovereign dignity (Section 5.5).

5.2 HUMAN DIGNITY AS A FOUNDATIONAL PRINCIPLE

The 1948 Preamble of the UDHR declares that the recognition of 'the inherent dignity and of the equal and inalienable rights of all members of the human family is the *foundation* of freedom, justice and peace in the world'.[4] As discussed in Chapter 3, this recital reflects the so-called founding function of human dignity,[5] explicitly conceived as a universal foundational principle of all rights or, more generally, of a world order. As a foundational principle, human dignity featured in constitutional documents, and in regional as well as in international provisions. As human dignity became a central feature of human rights discourse after the Second World War, many newly independent States began including chapters on human rights, which included references to human dignity, in their constitutions. Today, dignity acts as a central feature of constitutional architectures, as a constitutional value and as a constitutional right.[6] This section presents the evolution of the recognition of the foundational principle of human dignity at the regional

[4] Emphasis added.

[5] K Dicke, 'The Founding Function of Human Dignity in the Universal Declaration of Human Rights' in D Kretzmer and E Klein (eds), *The Concept of Human Dignity in Human Rights Discourse* (Brill 2002) 114.

[6] For an analysis, see A Barak, *Human Dignity: The Constitutional Value and the Constitutional Right* (Cambridge University Press 2015).

level and international level. Due account will be given to the linguistic nuances of this principle, to pay tribute to the long history of consolidation of human dignity in international law and to provide a clearer picture of the ingredients that are part of the foundational principle of human dignity today.

In particular, all human rights instruments deploy human dignity as a foundational principle with essentially three features: (i) first, it is a structural element and necessary foundational inclusion of the international legal system; (ii) second, it possesses a legal substance, which is to protect human dignity of all, in its individual and collective dimension, and to inject considerations of humanity concretized through a series of legal norms in different areas of international law; (iii) third, it is an obligation-creating principle, directly deriving from its legal substance and from its concretizations. More specifically, these three features are normally substantiated by three legal expressions. Human dignity is (i) the first value at the *foundation* of the world order; (ii) qualified as *inherent* to all human persons and the basis of an *inviolable right*; (iii) and a non-balanceable basis for all rights which *derive* from it, provide it with a concrete and contextually specific form, and correspond to positive and negative *obligations*. Thus, the fundamental value and principle of human dignity serve also as a normative foundation of two separate manifestations of human dignity (as a right and as obligation).

This section examines the instrument principle at the regional and international level, by first considering its various formulations and also by presenting what conducts are considered incompatible with its core meaning. This approach allows the easy tracing and identification of trends in the expressions, use and functions of the principle as well as its relation and interplay with other manifestations of human dignity.

5.2.1 *Regional Dimension*

5.2.1.1 Formulations and Terminology

Human dignity is referred to as a foundational principle in various regional human rights laws and, more specifically, in African,[7] Latin American,[8] and

7 Preamble, Protocol to the ACHPR on the Rights of Women in Africa, 11 July 2003 [Maputo Protocol].

8 Preamble, American Declaration of the Rights and Duties of Man, Organization of American States (OAS), 2 May 1948 [American Declaration of the Rights and Duties of Man]; Preamble, Maputo Protocol.

European instruments.[9] The 'belief' in dignity is also a driving attitude and standpoint in the 'Arab nation'[10] and represents the foundation of 'equality' in Asia[11] as well as in the Arab world.[12] In the African Union, dignity is mainly listed among the 'essential objectives' that African States shall aim to realize[13] and 'core values' on which human rights are founded.[14]

By looking at the formulations of human dignity in the regional context, three prisms can be identified: one related to the terminological formulations of the principle; one associated to its attribution; and a last one on the relations with other principles.

First, one can notice that the foundational nature of human dignity is expressed as a 'principle of dignity'[15] and as 'universal value of dignity'.[16]

9 Preamble, Charter of Fundamental Rights of the European Union, European Union: Council of the European Union, 2007/C 303/01, 14 December 2007, C 303/1 [EU Charter of Fundamental Rights]. In *bioethics*: Convention for the Protection of Human Rights and Dignity of the Human Being with regard to the Application of Biology and Medicine: Convention on Human Rights and Biomedicine, Oviedo, ETS 164, 4 April 1997 [Oviedo Convention on Human Rights and Biomedicine], Preamble and Art. 1; Additional Protocol to the Convention on Human Rights and Biomedicine concerning Transplantation of Organs and Tissues of Human Origin, ETS 186, 24 January 2002 [AP on Transplantation of Organs and Tissues of Human Origin], Preamble and Art. 1; Additional Protocol to the Convention on Human Rights and Biomedicine, concerning Biomedical Research, Strasbourg, ETS 195, 25 January 2005 [AP on Biomedical Research], Preamble, Art. 1, Art. 9(2); Additional Protocol to the Convention on Human Rights and Biomedicine, concerning Genetic Testing for Health Purposes, ETS 203, 27 November 2008 [AP on Genetic Testing for Health Purposes], Preamble and Art. 1; Guidelines, Recommendation Rec(2006)4 of the Committee of Ministers to member states on research on biological materials of human origin and its Explanatory Memorandum, 15 March 2006 [Rec(2006)4], Preamble, and para 14; (Guidelines), Recommendation CM/Rec(2016)6 of the Committee of Ministers to member States on research on biological materials of human origin, 11 May 2016 [CM/Rec (2016)6], Preamble and Art. 1.

10 Preamble, 1994, Arab Charter on Human Rights, 15 September 1994; version of 2004, in force 15 March 2008 [Arab Charter].

11 Principle 1, Association of Southeast Asian Nations (ASEAN) Human Rights Declaration [ASEAN 2009], principle 1.

12 Art. 3, Arab Charter, 1994; Art. 1 (a), Art. 6 (a), Cairo Declaration of Human Rights in Islam (OIC, 1990). Art. 1: (a); Art. 6: (a).

13 Preamble, African [Banjul] Charter on Human and Peoples' Rights, adopted 27 June 1981, OAU Doc. CAB/ LEG/ 67/ 3 rev. 5, 21 ILM 58 (1982) [African Charter].

14 Preamble (5), (Mauritius) Declaration and Plan of Action (OAU Grand Bay 12–16 April 1999) CONF/HRA/ Dec 1; see also Preamble, African Union, Maputo Protocol.

15 Preamble, *ibid.*

16 Preamble, 2000, EU Charter of Fundamental Rights.

Here dignity is expressed in three forms: 'human dignity',[17] 'inherent dignity'[18] or, more simply, as 'dignity'.[19]

Moreover, human dignity is associated to either individual or collective subjects. In the former case, it is attributed to the individual, denoted as 'man',[20] 'human person',[21] 'human being'[22] or 'individual'.[23] In this type of attribution, documents may also refer to the specific dignity of the 'child'[24] or of the 'woman'.[25] In its collective dimension, dignity is also attributed to a group of people, variously called 'all human beings',[26] 'all

17 Preamble, American Declaration of the Rights and Duties of Man; Preamble, 2000, EU Charter of Fundamental Rights; Preamble, Arab Charter; Art. 3, Arab Charter, 1994; Art.1 (a), Art.6 (a), Cairo Declaration of Human Rights in Islam; Preamble, Oviedo Convention on Human Rights and Biomedicine; Preamble, AP on Biomedical Research; Preamble, AP on Transplantation of Organs and Tissues of Human Origin; Preamble, AP on Genetic Testing for Health Purposes; Preamble, Art.1 (Guidelines), CM/Rec(2016)6.

18 Art. 5, (2), American Convention on Human Rights, San José, Costa Rica, 22 November 1969 [ACHR]; Preamble, OAS(OAS), Inter-American Convention on the Elimination of All Forms of Discrimination against Persons with Disabilities, 7 June 1999, AG/RES. 1608 (XXIX–O/99) [Inter-American Convention on the Elimination of All Forms of Discrimination against Persons with Disabilities]; Preamble, Inter-American Convention to Prevent and Punish Torture, OAS TS No. 67, 9 December 1985 [Inter-American Convention to Prevent and Punish Torture]; Preamble, 2002, Protocol No. 13 to the Convention for the Protection of Human Rights and Fundamental Freedoms concerning the abolition of the death penalty in all circumstances, 3 May 2002 [Protocol No. 13 to the Convention for the Protection of Human Rights and Fundamental Freedoms]; Preamble, African Charter on the Rights and Welfare of the Child, 1 July 1990; Art. 20, Arab Charter, 1994.

19 Preamble, African Charter; Preamble, African Charter on the Rights and Welfare of the Child, 1990; Preamble, 2003, Maputo Protocol; Art. 33, (3), Arab Charter, 1994; Art. 8, (g), Inter-American Convention on the Prevention, Punishment, and Eradication of Violence against Women, 9 June 1994 [Inter-American Convention on Violence against Women]; Art. 16, (1–2), Convention on Action against Trafficking in Human Beings, ETS 197, 16 May 2005 [Convention on Action against Trafficking in Human Beings]; Principle 1, ASEAN 2009.

20 Preamble, Inter-American Convention to Prevent and Punish Torture.

21 Art. 5, (2), ACHR; Art. 20 Arab Charter, 1994; Preamble, Inter-American Convention on the Elimination of All Forms of Discrimination against Persons with Disabilities; Art. 16, (1–2), Convention on Action against Trafficking in Human Beings.

22 Preamble, Oviedo Convention on Human Rights and Biomedicine.

23 *Ibid.*, preamble; AP on Transplantation of Organs and Tissues of Human Origin, preamble; Preamble, AP on Biomedical Research, preamble; AP on Genetic Testing for Health Purposes, preamble; Rec(2006)4, preamble; CM/Rec(2016)6, preamble.

24 Preamble, African Charter on the Rights and Welfare of the Child, 1990.

25 Art. 6 (a), Cairo Declaration of Human Rights in Islam.

26 Preamble, 2002, Protocol No. 13 to the Convention for the Protection of Human Rights and Fundamental Freedoms; Art. 1, I. Oviedo Convention on Human Rights and Biomedicine; Additional Protocol to the Convention for the Protection of Human Rights and Dignity of the Human Being with regard to the Application of Biology and Medicine, on the Prohibition of Cloning Human Beings, ETS 168, 12 January 1998, Preamble [AP on the Prohibition of Cloning Human Beings]; Preamble, AP on Transplantation of Organs and Tissues of Human Origin; Preamble, Art. 1, AP on Biomedical Research; Preamble, Art. 1, AP on Genetic Testing for

persons',[27] 'all men'[28] and 'peoples'.[29] More specific legal provisions also refer to the dignity of specific vulnerable peoples, such as 'women',[30] 'men and women',[31] or, more generally, 'of everyone'.[32]

Lastly, the principle of dignity appears also coupled with other principles, namely equality,[33] freedom,[34] 'democracy',[35] 'peace'[36] and 'justice'.[37] To illustrate the core role and functioning of the principle in the regional human rights systems, also in its relation with other rights and principles, it is helpful to refer to two relevant examples from regional practice. First, the European Committee of Social Rights has emphasized that '*human dignity is the fundamental value and indeed the core of positive European human rights law* – whether under the European Social Charter or under the European Convention of Human Rights'.[38] Thus, it has been affirmed that human dignity 'is behind almost every Convention right and the Court should take it into account when interpreting Convention provisions'.[39] Moreover, when interpreting and applying the American Convention, the Inter-American

Health Purposes; Preamble and para 14 (guidelines) Rec(2006)4; Preamble, Art. 1 (Guidelines), CM/Rec(2016)6.

27 Principle 1, ASEAN 2009.

28 Art. 1 (a), Cairo Declaration of Human Rights in Islam.

29 Preamble, African Charter.

30 Art. 8 (g), Inter-American Convention on Violence against Women.

31 Art. 3, Arab Charter.

32 Art. 1, Oviedo Convention on Human Rights and Biomedicine; Art. 1, AP on Transplantation of Organs and Tissues of Human Origin.

33 Preamble, Inter-American Convention on the Elimination of All Forms of Discrimination against Persons with Disabilities; Preamble, African Charter; Preamble, 2003, Maputo Protocol; Preamble, EU Charter of Fundamental Rights; Preamble, Arab Charter, version 2004 (not in 1994 version); Principle 1, ASEAN 2009 (General Principles); Art. 3, Arab Charter, 1994; Art. 1 (a), Art. 6 (a), Cairo Declaration of Human Rights in Islam.

34 Preamble, Inter-American Convention on the Elimination of All Forms of Discrimination against Persons with Disabilities; Preamble, African Charter; Preamble, EU Charter of Fundamental Rights; Preamble, 2002, Protocol No. 13 to the Convention for the Protection of Human Rights and Fundamental Freedoms; Preamble and Art. 33(3), Arab Charter, 1994; Preamble, Inter-American Convention to Prevent and Punish Torture.

35 Preamble, 2003, Maputo Protocol; Preamble, EU Charter of Fundamental Rights.

36 Preamble, 2003, Maputo Protocol; Preamble, Arab Charter, 1994.

37 Preamble, African Charter; Preamble, 2003, Maputo Protocol; Preamble, EU Charter of Fundamental Rights; Preamble, Arab Charter, 1994 and 2004 version.

38 Digest of the case law of the European Committee of Social Rights, 2008, pp. 81–89. See also *Lopes De Sousa Fernandes* v. *Portugal*, [GC], No. 56080/13, 19 December 2017, Partly Concurring, Partly Dissenting Opinion of Judge Pinto De Albuquerque, para 24.

39 *Simeonovi* v. *Bulgaria*, [GC], No. 21980/04, 12 May 2017, Partly Dissenting Opinion of Judge Serghides, para 48, p. 72; see also *Svinarenko and Slyadnev* v. *Russia*, No. 32541/08 and 4431/08, 17 July 2014, para 138.

Court has consistently invoked the general principles of law,[40] among which those endowed with a truly fundamental character constituting the *substratum* of the legal system itself.[41] In the domain of IHRL, it clarified that 'the *principle of the dignity of the human being* and that of the *inalienability of his inherent rights* belong to this category of fundamental principles'.[42] As aptly put by Judge Sergio García Ramírez, '*the object and purpose of the American Convention on Human Rights are to uphold human dignity* and recognize the demands that the protection and fulfillment of the human person pose, to articulate attendant obligations, and to provide juridical instruments that preserve that human dignity and meet those demands'.[43]

5.2.1.2 Incompatibility with the Principle of Human Dignity

Regional instruments describe conducts that are deemed against human dignity as acts 'contrary to'[44] or that can 'affect'[45] or 'endanger'[46] dignity. These are also considered 'offence(s) to'[47] or 'against'[48] human (or 'inherent')[49] dignity. By way

40 See IACtHR: *Five Pensioners* v. *Peru*, Judgment of 28 February 2003, para 156; *Cantos* v. *Argentina*, Judgment of 7 September 2001, para 37; *Baena Ricardo et al.* v. *Panama*, Judgment of 2 February 2001, para 98; *Neira Alegría* v. *Peru*, Preliminary Objections, Judgment of 11 December 1991, para 29; *Velásquez Rodríguez* v. *Honduras*, Judgment of 29 July 1988, para 184; and *cf.* also Advisory Opinion No. 17 on *The Juridical Status and Human Rights of the Child*, 28 August 2002, paras 66 and 87; Advisory Opinion No. 16 on *The Right to Information on Consular Assistance in the Framework of the Guarantees of the Due Process of Law*, 1 October 1999, paras 58, 113 and 128; Advisory Opinion No. 14 on *International Responsibility for the Promulgation and Enforcement of Laws in Violation of the ACHR*, 9 December 1994, para 35.

41 AA Cançado Trindade, *Tratado de Direito Internacional dos Direitos Humanos*, III (SA Fabris ed. 2003), 524–525.

42 *Plan de Sánchez Massacre* v. *Guatemala*, IACtHR, Judgment of 29 April 2004, (Merits), Separate Opinion of Judge AA Cançado-Trindade, para 16, p. 5; see also *Advisory Opinion No. 18, on Juridical Condition and Rights of the Undocumented Migrants* 17 September 2003, IACtHR, para 157.

43 *Mayagna (Sumo) Awas Tingni Community* v. *Nicaragua*, IACtHR, Judgment of 31 August 2001, Concurring Opinion of Judge Sergio García Ramírez, para 2 and 4 (emphasis added).

44 AP on the Prohibition of Cloning Human Beings, Preamble; Preamble, AP on Biomedical Research.

45 Art. 6, ACHR; Preamble, 1990, African Charter on the Rights and Welfare of the Child.

46 Preamble, Oviedo Convention on Human Rights and Biomedicine; Preamble, AP on Transplantation of Organs and Tissues of Human Origin.

47 Preamble, Convention on Action against Trafficking in Human Beings.

48 Preamble, Inter-American Convention to Prevent and Punish Torture; Preamble, Inter-American Convention on Violence against Women.

49 Preamble, Inter-American Convention on Forced Disappearance of Persons, OAS, 9 June 1994.

of illustration, in the context of biomedicine, the 'instrumentalisation of human beings through the deliberate creation of genetically identical human beings' is declared '*contrary* to human dignity' and 'a misuse of biology and medicine'.[50] Similarly, 'the misuse of organ and tissue transplantation' may lead to 'acts endangering human life, well-being or dignity'.[51] Moreover, the Preamble of the 1994 Inter-American Convention on the Prevention, Punishment and Eradication of Violence against women states that violence against women is an offence against their human dignity.

The jurisprudence of the regional courts provides a clarification of what, in specific cases, has been considered an offence or a violation of the principle of human dignity.

As regards the ECHR, the Court has referred to conducts incompatible with the principle of human dignity in the assessment of the following infringements: discrimination on account of gender,[52] ethnicity[53] or race;[54] ill-treatment or degrading treatment in detention, where conditions should be 'compatible with respect for human dignity';[55] severe

50 Preamble, AP on the Prohibition of Cloning Human Beings.

51 Preamble, AP on Transplantation of Organs and Tissues of Human Origin.

52 S.A.S. v. *France*, [GC], No. 43835/11, Judgment, 1 July 2014, para 120.

53 See ECtHR: *Perinçek* v. *Switzerland*, No. 27510/08, 15 October 2015, para 155 and 280; on the upsetting effect of statement, see *Orban and Others* v. *France*, No. 20985/05, 15 January 2009, para 52; *PETA Deutschland* v. *Germany*, No. 43481/09, 8 November 2012, paras 17–18. See also Concurring Opinion of Judge Zupančič, Joined by Judge Spielmann, para 8, p. 17; *Vona* v. *Hungary*, No. 35943/10, 9 July 2013, 9 December 2013, para 61; *D.H. and Others* v. *The Czech Republic*, [GC], No. 57325/00, 13 November 2007, para 178; *Soulas and Others* v. *France*, No. 15948/03, 10 July 2008, paras 43–44; and *Féret* v. *Belgium*, No. 15615/07, 16 July 2009, paras 69–71; *Nachova and Others* v. *Bulgaria*, [GC], No. 43577/98 and 43579/98, 2005–VII, para 145; and *Timishev* v. *Russia*, [GC], No. 55762/00 and 55974/00, ECtHR 2005–XII, para 56. See also, often quoted by the ECtHR, Report of the Special Rapporteur on freedom of religion or belief, Mr Heiner Bielefeldt, 22 December 2011 A/HRC/19/60, para 61.

54 See *East African Asians* v. *the United Kingdom*, No. 4403/70–4419/70, 4422/70, 4423/70, 4434/70, 4443/70, 4476/70–4478/70, 4486/70, 4501/70 and 4526/70–4530/70 (joined), 14 December 1970, Decisions and Reports (DR), p. 62; *Abdu* v. *Bulgaria*, No. 26827/08, 11 March 2014, para 38; see *Ananyev and Others* v. *Russia*, No. 42525/07 and 60800/08, 10 January 2012, paras 139–142; regarding transport conditions, see also, mutatis mutandis, *Khudoyorov* v. *Russia*, No. 6847/02, ECHR 2005–X, para 116ff.

55 ECtHR: *M.S.S.* v. *Belgium and Greece*, [GC], No. 30696/09, 21 January 2011, para 263; *Kudła* v. *Poland*, [GC], No. 30210/96, 26 October 2000, para 94; *Yaroslav Belousov* v. *Russia*, No. 2653/13, 4 October 2016, para 92; *Khudoyorov* v. *Russia*, *supra* n 54, para 103; *McGlinchey and Others* v. *United Kingdom*, No. 50390/99, 29 April 2003, para 46; *Alimov* v. *Turkey*, No. 14344/13, 6 September 2016, para 71; *Kalashnikov* v. *Russia*, No. 47095/99, 15 July 2002, para 95; *Popov* v. *Russia*, No. 26853/04, 13 July 2006, para 208; *Bouyid* v. *Belgium*, [GC], No. 23380/09, 28 September 2015, paras 87–90, 103; *Van der Ven* v. *The Netherlands*, No. 50901/99, 4 February 2003, para 50; also *Lorse and Others* v. *The Netherlands*, No. 52750/99, 4 February 2003, para 74; *Frerot* v. *France*, No. 70204/01, 12 June 2007, paras 37–39, 48;

physical and verbal bullying or violence;[56] physical exercise during military service that exacerbates a health condition;[57] limitation on the freedom of choice, with regard to end-of-life decision-making;[58] bans on home births,[59] gestational surrogacy[60] or on the use of cryopreserved embryos for stem cell research,[61] and on freedom of expression;[62] forced labour, mostly related to child protection;[63] severe mental suffering caused to relatives of a victim or a disappeared person;[64] in cases of extradition or expulsion of migrants,[65] and in relation to degrading treatment and inhuman conditions migrants can be subjected to in detention centres for asylum seekers.[66]

Valašinas v. *Lithuania*, No. 44558/98, 24 July 2001, para 117; *Wiktorko* v. *Poland*, No. 14612/02, 31 March 2009, para 53–54; *Iwanczuk* v. *Poland*, No. 25196/94, 15 November 2001, para 59; *Svinarenko and Slyadnev* v. *Russia*, *supra* n 39, paras 138–139; *Głowacki* v. *Poland*, No. 1608/08, 20 October 2012, paras 81, 90.

56 *Dordević* v. *Croatia*, No. 41526/10, ECtHR, 24 July 2012, para 152.

57 *Chember* v. *Russia*, No. 7188/03, ECtHR, 3 July 2008, para 50.

58 *Lambert and Others* v. *France*, [GC], No. 46043/14, Judgment, 5 June 2015, para 142; *Pretty* v. *The United Kingdom*, No. 2346/02, 29 July 2002, para 65; *Mcdonald* v. *The United Kingdom*, No.4241/12, Judgment, Court (Fourth Section), 20 May 2014, para 47.

59 *Dubská and Krejzová* v. *The Czech Republic*, [GC], No. 28859/11 and 28473/12, 15 November 2016, Dissenting Opinion of Judges Sajó, Karakaş, Nicolaou, Laffranque and Keller, 56–57, para 29.

60 *Paradiso and Campanelli* v. *Italy*, [GC], No. 25358/12, 24 January 2017, Joint Concurring Opinion of Judges De Gaetano, Pinto De Albuquerque, Wojtyczek And Dedov, para 7, p. 59; see also Concurring Opinion of Judge Dedov, 62–64. Respect for family life, through the existence of a biological link, was a decisive criterion in the previous surrogacy cases against France, namely *Mennesson* v. *France*, No. 65192/11, ECtHR, Judgment [Extracts], 26 June 2014 and *Labassee* v. *France*, No. 65941/11, 26 June 2014, which were decided in favour of the applicants.

61 See *Parrillo* v. *Italy case*, [GC], No. 46470/11, ECtHR, 27 August 2015, para 174; *Ibid.*, *Concurring Opinion of Judge Pinto De Albuquerque*, 43 at 70–71; Joint Partly Dissenting Opinion of Judges Casadevall, Ziemele, Power-Forde, De Gaetano and Yudkivska, 78, para 6. The Court has maintained in *VO* v. *France*, No. 53924/00, 8 July 2004, paras 28, 35and 84; see however also *ibid.*, Dissenting Opinion of Judge Mularoni, joined by Judge Strážnická, p. 38.

62 *Vereinigung Bildender Künstler* v. *Austria*, No. 68354/01, Judgment, First Section, 25 January 2007, Final 25 April 2007; see also *Vona* v. *Hungary*, *supra* n 53, Concurring Opinion of Judge Pinto De Albuquerque, pp. 34–35.

63 *Siliadin* v. *France*, No. 73316/01, ECtHR 26 October 2005, para 142; *Rantsev* v. *Cyprus and Russia*, No. 25965/04, ECHR 10 May 2010, para 282.

64 *Bitiyeva and X* v. *Russia*, Nos. 57953/00 and 37392/03, ECtHR, 21 June 2007, paras 105, 152.

65 *Khlaifia and others* v. *Italy*, [GC], No. 16483/12, 15 December 2016, paras 158, 160(c), 169, 175 and 184; *Ibid.*, Concurring Opinion of Judge Raimondi, para 4, p. 94; *ibid.*, Partly Dissenting Opinion of Judge Serghides, para 52, p. 119 (emphasis added).

66 *S.D.* v. *Greece*, No. 53541/07, 11 June 2009, para 47; *Tabesh* v. *Greece*, No. 8256/07, 26 November 2009, para 36; on severe conditions of detention which 'undermined the very

The jurisprudence of the IACtHR has also referred to the principle of human dignity as a driving principle to define conducts as incompatible with its object and purpose. This approach concerns cases of inhuman treatment in detention centres[67] as well as instances of violence against women[68] or violations of children's rights.[69] Importantly, in the latter case, the Court has indeed reiterated on various occasions that 'the *regulating principle regarding children's rights is based on the very dignity of the human being*'.[70]

Lastly, the African Commission on Human and Peoples Rights has also considered various conducts as contrary to the principle of human dignity. In particular, it regarded the denial of legal status,[71] when States force individuals 'to live as stateless persons under degrading conditions', depriving them of their family and 'depriving their families of the men's support',[72] to be 'a *violation of the dignity of a human being*'. Similarly, 'incompatible with *the principle*[s] *of human dignity*' is dispossessing indigenous peoples from their ancestral land.[73] The Commission also assessed as contrary to the principle of human dignity execution of a death sentence by hanging,[74] the denial of

essence of human dignity' of an unaccompanied minor, see *Rahimi* v. *Greece*, No. 8687/08, ECtHR, 5 April 2011, paras 86, 110 (see also 60).

A.A. v. *Greece*, No. 12186/08, 22 July 2010, paras 57–65.

67 *López Álvarez* v. *Honduras*, Judgment of 1 February 2006, Series C No. 141, paras 105–106; *García Asto and Ramírez Rojas* v. *Peru*, Judgment of 25 November 2005, Series C No. 137, para 221; and *Raxcacó Reyes* v. *Guatemala*, Judgment of 15 September 2005, Series C No. 133, para 95; *Miguel Castro-Castro Prison* v. *Peru*, Judgment of 25 November 2006, paras 315, 321; *Gómez-Paquiyauri Brothers* v. *Peru*, Judgment of 8 July 2004, para 109; *Loayza Tamayo* v. *Peru*, Judgment of 17 September 1997, Series C No. 33, para 57.

68 Preamble, Inter-American Convention on Violence against Women; *Fernández Ortega et al.* v. *Mexico*, Judgment of 30 August 2010, para 118; *Rosendo Cantú et al.* v. *Mexico*, Judgment of 31 August 2010, para 108.

69 Advisory Opinion No. 17, *supra* n 40, para 56; *Gómez-Paquiyauri Brothers* v. *Peru*, *supra* n 67, para 163; *Ituango Massacres* v. *Colombia*, Judgment of 1 July 2006, para 244.

70 *Atala Riffo and Daughters* v. *Chile*, Judgment of 24 February 2012, para 108; *Gómez-Paquiyauri Brothers* v. *Peru*, *supra* n 67, Concurring Opinion of Ad Hoc Judge Francisco Eguiguren Praeli, p. 4; *The Río Negro Massacres* v. *Guatemala*, Judgment of 4 September 2012 (Preliminary objection, merits, reparations and costs), para 142.

71 *John K. Modise* v. *Botswana*, ACommHPR, Comm. 97/93_14AR, 6 November 2000, para 92; *Amnesty International* v. *Zambia*, ACommHPR, Comm. 212/98, 5 May 1999, para 58.

72 *Amnesty International* v. *Zambia*, *supra* n 71, para 58.

73 *Centre for Minority Rights Development and Minority Rights Group International on behalf of Endorois Welfare Council* v. *Kenya*, ACommHPR, Comm. 276/2003, 25 November 2009, para 216.

74 *Ibid.*, para 169 (emphasis added).

medical attention in detention,[75] hate speech or discriminatory behaviours,[76] and enforced disappearance.[77]

All these cases well illustrate the operation and extent of the principle of human dignity in the jurisprudence of regional bodies and its role in the protection of specific human rights. The relation between human dignity and the instrument right will be discussed in detail in Section 5.3.

5.2.2 *International Dimension*

5.2.2.1 Formulations and Terminology

Human dignity appears for the first time as a central value and structural element in two landmark international documents of the 1940s, namely the UN Charter and the UDHR. Drafters of subsequent human rights instruments have modelled the wording of their preambular or substantive articles on them, to manifest continuity not only with the approach adopted but also with the history behind them. The dignity of the individual is today considered as 'the fundamental guiding principle of international human rights law'.[78] There is an established 'core human rights principle[s] of human dignity'.[79]

For this reason, human rights instruments not only equally 'reaffirm', in the words of the UN Charter, 'faith ... in the dignity'[80] of the human person, but also acknowledge human dignity as the foundation of four different concepts.

75 See *Huri – Laws* v. *Nigeria*, ACommHPR, Comm. 25/98, 6 November 2000, para 41.

76 See *Zimbabwe Lawyers for Human Rights and the Institute for Human Rights and Development in Africa* v. *Zimbabwe*, ACommHPR, Comm. 293/04, 22 May 2008, para 51 (emphasis added); *Eyob B. Asemie* v. *the Kingdom of Lesotho*, ACommHPR, Comm. 435/12, 13 February 2015, para 56; *Darfur Relief and Documentation Centre* v. *Sudan*, ACommHPR, Comm. 310/05, 25 November 2009, para 67; *Luke Munyandu Tembani and Benjamin John Freeth* v. *Angola and Thirteen Others*, ACommHPR, Comm. 409/12, 30 April 2014, para 92; *Zimbabwe Lawyers for Human Rights & Associated Newspapers of Zimbabwe* v. *Republic of Zimbabwe*, ACommHPR, Comm. 284/03, 3 April 2009, para 91; *Purohit and Moore* v. *Gambia (The)*, ACommHPR, Comm. 241/01, 29 May 2003, para 58.

77 *J.E Zitha & P.J.L.Zitha* v. *Mozambique*, ACommHPR, Comm. 361/08, 1 April 2011, para 81 (emphasis added).

78 CESCR, GC 13, The right to education (Art. 13 of the Covenant), E/C.12/1999/10, 8 December 1999, para 41. See also CRC, GC 8, The right of the child to protection from corporal punishment and other cruel or degrading forms of punishment (arts. 19, 28, para 2 and 37, inter alia), CRC/C/GC/8, 2 March 2007, para 16.

79 CERD, GR 35, Combating racist hate speech, CERD/C/GC/35, 26 September 2013, para 10.

80 Preamble, Charter of the UN, 24 October 1945, 1 UNTS XVI [UN Charter]; Preamble, para 5, Art. 1, Universal Declaration of Human Rights, GA Resolution 217(III), adopted 10 December 1948 [UDHR]; Preamble, UN GA, Vienna Declaration and Programme of Action, 12 July 1993, A/CONF.157/23 [Vienna Declaration and Programme of Action]; Preamble, para 1, UN GA, Convention on the Elimination of All Forms of Discrimination

Human dignity, *in primis*, 'is the foundation of freedom, justice and peace in the world', as declared for the first time by the Universal Declaration.[81] Moreover, all human beings enjoy 'equality in dignity',[82] in line with Article 1 of the UDHR, which recognizes that 'all human beings are born free and equal in dignity and rights',[83] and have the right to pursue their 'spiritual

against Women, 18 December 1979, UNTS, vol. 1249, p. 13 [CEDAW]; Preamble, GA resolution 46/91, UN Principles for Older Persons, 16 December 1991 [UN Principles for Older Persons]; Preamble, GA resolution 2856 (XXVI), Declaration on the Rights of Mentally Retarded Persons of 20 December 1971 [Declaration on the Rights of Mentally Retarded Persons]; Preamble, GA resolution 3447 (XXX), Declaration on the Rights of Disabled Persons, of 9 December 1975 [Declaration on the Rights of Disabled Persons]; Preamble, GA resolution 48/96, Standard Rules on the Equalization of Opportunities for Persons with Disabilities, A/RES/48/96, 4 March 1994, [Standard Rules on the Equalization of Opportunities for Persons with Disabilities]; Preamble, Declaration on the Rights of Persons Belonging to National or Ethnic, Religious and Linguistic Minorities, GA resolution 47/135 of 18 December 1992 [Declaration on the Rights of Persons Belonging to National or Ethnic, Religious and Linguistic Minorities]; Preamble, UN Declaration on the Granting of Independence to Colonial Countries and Peoples, GA resolution 1514 (XV) of 14 December 1960.

81 Preamble, para 1, UDHR; Preamble, UN GA, International Covenant on Economic, Social and Cultural Rights, 16 December 1966, UNTS, vol. 993, p. 3 [ICESCR]; Preamble, UN GA, International Covenant on Civil and Political Rights, 16 December 1966, UNTS, vol. 999, p. 171 [ICCPR]; Preamble, UN GA, Convention on the Rights of the Child, 20 November 1989, UNTS, vol. 1577, p. 3 [CRC]; Preamble, (a), UN GA, Convention on the Rights of Persons with Disabilities, 13 December 2006, A/RES/61/106, Annex I [CRPD]; Preamble, Convention against Torture and Other Cruel, Inhuman or Degrading Treatment or Punishment, adopted and opened for signature, ratification and accession by GA resolution 39/46 of 10 December 1984, entry into force 26 June 1987 [CAT] in which dignity is not openly expressed, however see Preamble, paras 1–2; GA resolution 47/133, Declaration on the Protection of All Persons from Enforced Disappearance, of 18 December 1992 [Declaration on the Protection of All Persons from Enforced Disappearance], Preamble, para 1. *UN GCs*, see: Preamble, Forty-ninth session (1996), CERD, GR XXII on article 5 of the Convention on refugees and displaced persons; GC 8, *supra* n 78, para 17; Preamble, Sixty-fifth session (2005), CERD, GR 30 (XXX) on discrimination against non-citizens; Preamble, GR 34, CERD/C/GC/34, 3 October 2011; Eleventh session (1994), GC 5: Persons with disabilities, CESCR, para 5.

82 The formulation 'all human beings are born free and equal in dignity' can be found in the following documents: UDHR, Art. 1; Preamble, para 2, Art. 1, 1963, 1904 (XVIII) UN Declaration on the Elimination of All Forms of Racial Discrimination, A/RES/18/1904, 20 November 1963 [UN Declaration on the Elimination of All Forms of Racial Discrimination]; Preamble, para 2 and 3 UN GA, International Convention on the Elimination of All Forms of Racial Discrimination, 21 December 1965, UNTS, vol. 660, p. 195 [ICERD]; Declaration on Race and Racial Prejudice, adopted and proclaimed by the General Conference of the UN Educational, Scientific and Cultural Organization at its twentieth session, on 27 November 1978, Arts 1, 4, 5, 6 (para 1), 7, 9 (para 1, 2, 3, 4), 10, refer to the '*principle of equality in dignity*' [Declaration on Race and Racial Prejudice]; Arts. 10, 11, 12, 28, Universal Declaration on Bioethics and Human Rights, 19 October 2005, Art. 10 [Universal Declaration on Bioethics and Human Rights].

83 GR XXII, *supra* n 81; Fifty-first session (1997), GR 23 (XXIII) on the rights of indigenous peoples, CERD, para 4; Sixty-first session (2002), GR 29 on Art. 1, paragraph 1, of the Convention (Descent), CERD, para 8; GR 30, *supra* n 81, preamble; GR 34, *supra* n 81;

development' in condition of dignity.[84] For this reason, 'social progress and development' are founded on respect for dignity.[85] Thus, there is an overall recognition that human dignity grounds the concepts and principles of 'freedom, justice and peace', of 'equality', of 'spiritual development' and of 'social progress and development'.

Even when an international instrument is silent on this principle, human dignity still remains of 'central importance' for personal autonomy[86] and as a foundational objective. For instance, GC No. 13 (Twenty-first session, 1999) on the right to education (Article 13 of the Covenant) clearly states that '[t]he Committee notes that, although it is absent from article 26(2) of the Declaration, the drafters of ICESCR [International Covenant on Economic, Social and Cultural Rights] expressly included the dignity of the human personality as one of the *mandatory objectives* to which all education is to be directed'.[87] It is generally agreed that respecting human dignity is 'a fundamental and universally applicable rule', as recognized by GC No. 21: Article 10 (Humane treatment of persons deprived of their liberty).[88]

However, when human dignity is expressly mentioned, it appears, as it does at the regional level, under different formulations, which can be seen through

GC 5, *supra* n 81, para 5; GC 20, Non-discrimination in economic, social and cultural rights (art. 2, para 2, of the International Covenant on Economic, Social and Cultural Rights), E/C.12/GC/20, 2 July 2009, footnote 10, which recalls para 6 of the Durban Review Conference; GC 22 (2016) on the right to sexual and reproductive health, E/C.12/GC/22, 2 May 2016, see Report of the International Conference on Population and Development, Cairo 5–13 September 1994 (E.95.XIII.18), chap. I, resolution 1, annex. Principle 1; GC 10 (2007), Children's rights in juvenile justice, CRC/C/GC/10, 25 April 2007, para 13; Sixteenth session (1997), CEDAW, GR 23: Political and public life, para 1; GR 32 (2014) on the gender-related dimensions of refugee status, asylum, nationality and statelessness of women, CEDAW/C/GC/32, 14 November 2014, para 24 (l); GR 36 (2017) on the right of girls and women to education, CEDAW/C/GC/36, 27 November 2017, para 57; GR 29, *supra* n 83, para 1(a); GR 32 (2009), The meaning and scope of special measures in the International Convention on the Elimination of All Forms Racial Discrimination, CERD/C/GC/32, 24 September 2009, paras 6, 20; GR 35, *supra* n 79, para 10; GC 16 (2005), The equal right of men and women to the enjoyment of all economic, social and cultural rights, E/C.12/2005/4, 11 August 2005, para 1.

84 Preamble, C122 Employment Policy Convention, ILO 1964 [C122 Employment Policy Convention]; in an equal wording, see Preamble, Discrimination (Employment and Occupation) Convention, ILO 1958 (No. 111) [C111 Discrimination (Employment and Occupation)]; Preamble, Indigenous and Tribal Populations Convention, ILO 1957 (No. 107) [C107 Indigenous and Tribal Populations Convention].

85 See Art. 2, Declaration on Social Progress and Development, Proclaimed by GA resolution 2542 (XXIV) of 11 December 1969 [Declaration on Social Progress and Development]; GCs: GC 13 (1999), *supra* n 78, para 4.

86 GC 36 (2018) on Art. 6 of the ICCPR, CCPR/C/GC/36, para 9.

87 GC 13 (1999), *supra* n 78, para 18.

88 HRC, GC 21: Art. 10 (Humane treatment of persons deprived of their liberty), HRI/GEN/1/Rev.9 (Vol. I), 13 March 1993, para 4.

three lenses: a linguistic one; one associated with its attribution; and one on the relationship with other principles.

As regards its various formulations, although they all convey 'the message of the inherent dignity of all human beings',[89] the following expressions are often used: 'the democratic principle of the dignity of men';[90] 'basic principle of the dignity inherent in all human beings';[91] 'fundamental principle associated with human dignity';[92] 'principle of respect for human dignity';[93] 'principle

89 GR 29, *supra* n 83, para 8; GR 34, *supra* n 81, para 61.

90 Constitution of the UNESCO, 16 November 1945, 3 Bevans 1311, preamble, para 3 [UNESCO Constitution]; Preamble, para 1, 1978, Declaration on Race and Racial Prejudice; Preamble, UNESCO, Universal Declaration on the Human Genome and Human Rights, 11 November 1997 [Universal Declaration on the Human Genome and Human Rights].

91 Preamble, UN GA, Declaration on the Elimination of All Forms of Intolerance and of Discrimination Based on Religion or Belief, 25 November 1981, A/RES/36/55 [Declaration on the Elimination of All Forms of Intolerance and of Discrimination Based on Religion or Belief].

92 Preamble, Universal Declaration on the Eradication of Hunger and Malnutrition, 16 November 1974, GA resolution 3348 (XXIX) of 17 December 1974.

93 Preamble, para 3, CEDAW and GC 9, Art. 10 (Humane treatment of persons deprived of their liberty) [GC 9 has been replaced by GC 21, *supra* n 88], 30 July 1982, CCPR, para 4. Similarly, at the basis of the right to be treated with dignity, see *UN GCs*: GC 9 (2006), The rights of children with disabilities, 27 February 2007, CRC/C/GC/9, para 43; GC 15 (1986), The position of aliens under the Covenant, 30 September 1986, CCPR, para 7; GC 6 (2005), Treatment of unaccompanied and separated children outside their country of origin, CRC/GC/2005/6, 1 September 2005, para 31(1); GC 8, *supra* n 78, para 19; GC 10, *supra* n 83, paras 13, 40, 89; GC 16 (1988), Art. 17 Right to privacy, CCPR, 28 September 1988, para 8; GC 20 (1992), Art. 7 (Prohibition of torture, or other cruel, inhuman or degrading treatment or punishment), 30 September 1992, para 2; GC 21, *supra* n 88, paras 1, 3, 4; GC 28 (2000) Art. 3, The equality of rights between men and women (Replaces GC 4), CCPR/C/21/Rev.1/Add.10, 29 March 2000, para 15; GC 29 (2001) states of emergency (Art. 4), CCPR/C/21/Rev.1/Add.11, 31 August 2001, para 13(a); CEDAW, GR 19: Violence against women, 1992, para 14, 24(b); GR 23, *supra* n 83, para 1; CEDAW, GR 24: Art. 12 of the Convention (women and health), 1999, paras 22, 25; GR 27 on older women and protection of their human rights, 16 December 2010, CEDAW/C/GC/27, para 10; Joint GR 31 of the CEDAW/GC 18 of the UN CRC on harmful practices, 14 November 2014, CEDAW/C/GC/31–CRC/C/GC/18, para 14; GR 32 (2014), *supra* n 83, para 24(l); GR 36, *supra* n 83, paras 57, 69; CERD, GR 13 (XIII) on the training of law enforcement, officials in the protection of human rights, 1993, para 2; GR 29, *supra* n 83, para 1 (a); CERD, GR 31 on the prevention of racial discrimination in the administration and functioning of the criminal justice system, 2005, para 19; GC 2 on the rights of migrant workers in an irregular situation and members of their families, CMW/C/GC/2, 28 August 2013, paras 36, 44; GC 5, *supra* n 81, para 34; GC 21, Right of everyone to take part in cultural life (art. 15, para 1 (a), of the ICESCR), E/C.12/GC/21, 21 December 2009, para 40; GC 1 (2001), Art. 29 (1), The Aims Of Education, CRC/GC/2001/1, para 8; GC 4 (2003), Adolescent Health and Development in the context of the CRC, CRC/GC/2003/4, 1 July 2003, para 69; GC 7 (2005) Implementing child rights in early childhood, CRC/C/GC/7/Rev.1, 20 September 2006, paras 14, 28, 29, (a) and (d); GC 8, *supra* n 78, paras 2, 5, 7, 16, 17, 21, 29; GC 14 (2013) on the right of the child to have his or her best interests taken as a primary consideration (art. 3, para 1), CRC/C/GC/14, para 2; GC 20 (2016) on the

with regard to dignity of all human beings';[94] 'principle of human dignity';[95] and, last, the 'spirit of dignity'.[96] Human dignity, in all of these manifestations, still represents one of the 'fundamental principles of international law [. . .], [e]xpressing the will and the aspirations of all peoples to eradicate war from the life of mankind'.[97]

From a purely linguistic perspective, it is interesting to notice that these legal documents make reference to the following terms, which show which concept of human dignity has entered into international law: 'human dignity',[98] 'inherent dignity'[99] and 'dignity and worth

implementation of the rights of the child during adolescence, 6 December 2016, CRC/C/GC/20, para 4.

94 Preamble, UN GA, Declaration on the Elimination of Violence against Women, 20 December 1993, A/RES/48/104 [Declaration on the Elimination of Violence against Women].

95 Declaration on the Elimination of Violence against Women, preamble; International Convention on the Protection of the Rights of All Migrant Workers and Members of Their Families, GA resolution 45/158, 18 December 1990 [ICPMW], Art. 70; I. Values and Principle, 2, UN GA, UN Millennium Declaration, GA resolution, A/RES/55/2, 18 September 2000 [UN Millennium Declaration]; Preamble, Declaration on the Rights of Mentally Retarded Persons; Preamble, Declaration on the Rights of Disabled Persons; Preamble, Standard Rules on the Equalization of Opportunities for Persons with Disabilities; Preamble, para 1, UN Declaration on the Elimination of All Forms of Racial Discrimination; Preamble, para 1, ICERD; GR 32 (2009), *supra* n 83, para 6; GC 19, The right to social security (art. 9), E/C.12/GC/19, 4 February 2008, CESCR, para 22.

96 CRC, Preamble para 3.

97 Preamble, GA resolution 39/11, Declaration on the Right of Peoples to Peace of 12 November 1984 [Declaration on the Right of Peoples to Peace].

98 Preamble, para 3, CEDAW; UN Millennium Declaration, Values and Principle, 2; Preamble, UN GA, Second Optional Protocol to the ICCPR, Aiming at the Abolition of the Death Penalty, 15 December 1989, A/RES/44/128; Art. 31, GA resolution 45/113, UN Rules for the Protection of Juveniles Deprived of their Liberty, 14 December 1990; Art. 2, GA resolution 34/169, Code of Conduct for Law Enforcement Officials, 17 December 1979; Declaration on the Use of Scientific and Technological Progress in the Interests of Peace and for the Benefit of Mankind, GA resolution 3384 (XXX), 10 November 1975, Preamble, para 2, Principle 8 [Declaration on the Use of Scientific and Technological Progress]; Preamble, Arts. 10, 15, 21, 24, Universal Declaration on the Human Genome and Human Rights; Art. 4, UNESCO, Universal Declaration on Cultural Diversity, 2 November 2001; Art. 1, UN Declaration on the Elimination of All Forms of Racial Discrimination; Preamble, Declaration on Race and Racial Prejudice; UNESCO International Declaration on Human Genetic Data, 22 July 2003, Preamble, Arts. 1(a), 26; Universal Declaration on Bioethics and Human Rights, Arts. 2, 3, 11, 12, 28; Art. 70, ICPMW.

99 Preamble, para 1, UDHR; Preamble, ICESCR; Preamble and Art. 10, ICCPR; Preamble, para 1 and Art. 37, CRC; Preamble, GA resolution 46/119, Principles for the protection of persons with mental illness and the improvement of mental health care, 17 December 1991; Preamble, (a) and (h), Art. 3 (a), CRPD; GA resolution 45/111, Basic Principles for the Treatment of Prisoners, 14 December 1990, at 1; Principle 1, GA resolution 43/173, Body of Principles for the Protection of All Persons under Any Form of Detention or Imprisonment, 9 December 1988;

[inherent in] of the human person'.[100] Each of the terms has a distinct historical and philosophical background, based on beliefs or mere stylistic choices of the individuals involved in the drafting processes, as discussed in Chapter 3. Notably, the wording adopted in the UN Charter and in the UDHR has been maintained as legal models in many subsequent legal documents.

Moreover, dignity is attributed to either individuals or to collective entities. In relation to the former, terms such as 'man',[101] 'human person'[102] and 'individual'[103] are used. When the legal document refers to a specific subject, it is possible to find a more specific reference, such as in the case of the dignity of

GA resolution 45/113, *supra* n 98; Preamble, CAT; GA resolution 45/110, UN Standard Minimum Rules for Non-custodial Measures (The Tokyo Rules), 14 December 1990, Art. 6.2; Universal Declaration on the Human Genome and Human Rights, Preamble, para 2, Art. 1; Preamble, Declaration on the Protection of All Persons from Enforced Disappearance; Preamble, para 1, ICERD; Preamble, Declaration on the Elimination of All Forms of Intolerance and of Discrimination Based on Religion or Belief; Art. 17, ICPMW.

100 Preamble, UN Charter; Preamble, para 5, UDHR; Preamble, Vienna Declaration and Programme of Action; Preamble, para 1, CEDAW; Preamble, para 2, CRC; Preamble, UN Principles for Older Persons; Preamble, Declaration on the Rights of Mentally Retarded Persons; Declaration on the Rights of Disabled Persons, Preamble; Standard Rules on the Equalization of Opportunities for Persons with Disabilities, Preamble; Preamble, (a) and (h), CRPD; Guidelines for Action on Children in the Criminal Justice System Recommended by Economic and Social Council resolution 1997/30 of 21 July 1997, Art. 11 (a) [Guidelines for Action on Children]; Declaration on Social Progress and Development, Preamble, Art. 2; Preamble, Supplementary Convention on the Abolition of Slavery, the Slave Trade, and Institutions and Practices Similar to Slavery, Economic and Social Council resolution 608 (XXI), 7 September 1956, entry into force 30 April 1957 [Supplementary Convention on the Abolition of Slavery]; Preamble, Declaration on the Rights of Persons Belonging to National or Ethnic, Religious and Linguistic Minorities.

101 Preamble, para 4, UNESCO Constitution; Preamble, UNESCO Universal Declaration on Cultural Diversity, 2 November 2001 [UNESCO Universal Declaration on Cultural Diversity]; Art. 1, UNESCO Convention against Discrimination in Education, 14 December 1960.

102 Preamble, UN Charter; Preamble, para 5, UDHR; Art. 10, ICCPR; Preamble, Vienna Declaration and Programme of Action; Art. 37, CRC; Preamble, UN Principles for Older Persons; Preamble, Declaration on the Rights of Mentally Retarded Persons; Preamble, Declaration on the Rights of Disabled Persons; Preamble, GA resolution 46/119, *supra* n 99; Preamble, Standard Rules on the Equalization of Opportunities for Persons with Disabilities; Preamble, (h), CRPD; GA resolution 43/173, *supra* n 99, Principle 1; Preamble, para 2, CAT; Declaration on Social Progress and Development, Preamble and Art. 2; Declaration on the Use of Scientific and Technological Progress, Preamble and Art. 8; Preamble, Supplementary Convention on the Abolition of Slavery, Preamble; Preamble, operative principle 1, UN Declaration on the Elimination of All Forms of Racial Discrimination; ICERD, Preamble, para 3; International Declaration on Human Genetic Data, Preamble; ICPMW, Art. 17; Declaration on the Rights of Persons Belonging to National or Ethnic, Religious and Linguistic Minorities, Preamble.

103 International Declaration on Human Genetic Data, Preamble.

the 'juvenile'.[104] However, it is more common to find various expressions of dignity of collective groups. Provisions refer to the dignity of 'all members of the human family',[105] 'of all human beings',[106] 'of persons',[107] 'of groups'[108] or 'of all peoples',[109] 'of human beings',[110] 'of men'[111] and 'of individuals'.[112] At times these collective groups are specified, for example, with reference to the dignity 'of juveniles as human beings',[113] 'of child victims'[114] and 'of victims'.[115] More broadly, norms also protect the dignity 'of mankind',[116] of 'humankind'[117] and 'of humanity'.[118] Inevitably, this collective attribution paints a clearer picture of the universal scope and ultimate purpose of this principle.

Lastly, a third lens enables us to notice that the principle of human dignity qualifies or is also associated with other principles. It can be found in connection with the concepts of 'autonomy',[119] 'peace'[120] and

104 Art. 66, GA resolution 45/113, *supra* n 98.

105 Preamble, para 1, UDHR; Preamble, ICESCR; Preamble, ICCPR; Preamble, CRC; Preamble, (a) CRPD; Preamble, para 2, Universal Declaration on the Human Genome and Human Rights; Preamble, C111 Discrimination (Employment and Occupation).

106 Art. 1, UDHR; Preamble, Declaration on the Elimination of Violence against Women; Preamble, C122 Employment Policy Convention; Preamble, paras 1, 2, 1963, UN Declaration on the Elimination of All Forms of Racial Discrimination; Preamble, paras 1, 2, ICERD; Arts. 1, 4, 5, Declaration on Race and Racial Prejudice; Art. 9, para 1, Declaration on Race and Racial Prejudice; Preamble, Declaration on the Elimination of All Forms of Intolerance and of Discrimination Based on Religion or Belief.

107 Art. 3, CRPD; Art. 2, GA resolution 34/169, *supra* n 98; Art. 69, GA resolution S–26/2, Declaration of Commitment on HIV/AIDS, 27 June 2001.

108 Art. 9, para 2, 3, Declaration on Race and Racial Prejudice.

109 Art. 9, para 1, Declaration on Race and Racial Prejudice.

110 Art. 60 (1), Standard Minimum Rules for the Treatment of Prisoners, Economic and Social Council by its resolutions 663 C (XXIV) of 31 July 1957 and 2076 (LXII) of 13 May 1977, (Part II); GA resolution 45/111, *supra* n 99, 1; GA resolution 45/110, *supra* n 99, Art. 6.2.

111 Preamble, para 3, UNESCO Constitution; Preamble, para 1, Universal Declaration on the Human Genome and Human Rights; Preamble, para 1, Art. 10, Declaration on Race and Racial Prejudice.

112 Art. 10, Universal Declaration on the Human Genome and Human Rights; Art. 6 (all individuals and all groups), 7 (individuals), Declaration on Race and Racial Prejudice; Art. 9, para 2, Declaration on Race and Racial Prejudice.

113 Art. 66, f, GA resolution 45/113, *supra* n 98.

114 Art. 45, Guidelines for Action on Children.

115 Principle 4, A/RES/40/34, Declaration of Basic Principles of Justice for Victims of Crime and Abuse of Power, 29 November 1985.

116 Preamble, para 1, Universal Declaration on the Human Genome and Human Rights.

117 Preamble, Universal Declaration on Bioethics and Human Rights.

118 Art. 1, Universal Declaration on the Human Genome and Human Rights.

119 GC 36, *supra* n 86, para 9.

120 Preamble, para 1, UDHR; Preamble, ICESCR; Preamble, ICCPR; Preamble, CRC; Preamble, Declaration on the Rights of Mentally Retarded Persons; Preamble, Declaration on the Rights of Disabled Persons; Preamble, CRPD; Preamble, CAT; Preamble, Declaration on the Right of Peoples to Peace; Declaration on the Protection of All Persons from Enforced Disappearance;

'justice'.[121] The most common pairs of human dignity are equality[122] and freedom.[123]

Preamble, UNESCO Universal Declaration on Cultural Diversity; Preamble, para 2, Art. 1, UN Declaration on the Elimination of All Forms of Racial Discrimination; Preamble, para 1, 1978, Declaration on Race and Racial Prejudice; Art. 4, Declaration on Race and Racial Prejudice; Preamble, Declaration on the Rights of Mentally Retarded Persons; Preamble, Declaration on the Rights of Disabled Persons; Preamble, Standard Rules on the Equalization of Opportunities for Persons with Disabilities; Preamble, Universal Declaration on the Human Genome and Human Rights; Preamble, para 1, 1978, Declaration on Race and Racial Prejudice; Preamble, para 4, UNESCO Constitution; Preamble, para 3, CRC. Among *UN GCs*: GC 8 (2006), The right of the child to protection from corporal punishment and other cruel or degrading forms of punishment (Arts. 19, 28, para 2 and 37, inter alia), CRC/C/GC/8, 2 March 2007, para 17.

121 Preamble, para 1, UDHR; Preamble, ICESCR; Preamble, ICCPR; Preamble, CRC; Declaration on Social Progress and Development, Art. 2; Preamble, Declaration on the Rights of Mentally Retarded Persons; Preamble, Declaration on the Rights of Disabled Persons; Preamble, Standard Rules on the Equalization of Opportunities for Persons with Disabilities; Preamble, CRPD; Preamble, CAT; Declaration on the Protection of All Persons from Enforced Disappearance; Preamble, UNESCO Universal Declaration on Cultural Diversity; Preamble, para 1, 1978, Declaration on Race and Racial Prejudice; Art. 10, Universal Declaration on Bioethics and Human Rights; Arts. 8 (a) and 45, Guidelines for Action on Children; Principle 4, A/RES/40/34, Declaration of Basic Principles of Justice for Victims of Crime and Abuse of Power, 29 November 1985; International Declaration on Human Genetic Data, Preamble, Art. 1(a); Preamble, Declaration on the Rights of Mentally Retarded Persons; Preamble, Declaration on the Rights of Disabled Persons; Preamble, Standard Rules on the Equalization of Opportunities for Persons with Disabilities; Arts. 31, 66, 66 (f), GA resolution 45/113, *supra* n 98; Preamble, Universal Declaration on the Human Genome and Human Rights; Preamble, para 1, 1978, Declaration on Race and Racial Prejudice; Preamble, para 4, UNESCO Constitution; Art. 10, Universal Declaration on Bioethics and Human Rights.

122 Preamble, para 1, 1978, Declaration on Race and Racial Prejudice; Arts. 1, 4, 5, 6 (para 1), 7, 9 (para 1, 2, 3, 4), 10, Declaration on Race and Racial Prejudice; Preamble, Declaration on the Elimination of All Forms of Intolerance and of Discrimination Based on Religion or Belief; Art. 10, Universal Declaration on Bioethics and Human Rights; Preamble, para 3, CEDAW; Preamble, Declaration on the Elimination of Violence against Women; International Declaration on Human Genetic Data, Preamble, Art. 1(a), 26; UN Millennium Declaration, Values and Principle, 2; Preamble, Declaration on the Elimination of Violence against Women; Preamble, Universal Declaration on the Human Genome and Human Rights; Preamble, para 1, UN Declaration on the Elimination of All Forms of Racial Discrimination; Preamble, para 1, ICERD; Preamble, para 1, 1978, Declaration on Race and Racial Prejudice; Preamble, Declaration on the Elimination of All Forms of Intolerance and of Discrimination Based on Religion or Belief; Preamble, paras 3, 4, UNESCO Constitution; Preamble, para 3, CRC. Among *UN GCs*: Preamble, Forty-ninth session (1996), GR XXII on Art. 5 of the Convention on refugees and displaced persons, CERD; GR 23 (XXIII) *supra* n 83; GR 29, *supra* n 83, para 8; GR 30, *supra* n 81; GR 34, *supra* n 81; GC 5, *supra* n 81, para 5; GC 20 (2009), *supra* n 83, footnote 10, which recalls para 6 of the Durban Review Conference; GC 22, *supra* n 83; see Report of the International Conference on Population and Development, *supra* n 83, chap. I, resolution 1, annex. Principle 1; GC 10, *supra* n 83, para 13; GR 23, *supra* n 83, para 1; GR 32 (2014), *supra* n 83, para 24(1); GR 36, *supra* n 83, para 57; GR 29, *supra* n 83, para 1(a); GR 32 (2009), *supra* n 83, paras 6, 20; GR 35, *supra* n 79, para 10; GC 16 (2005), *supra* n 83, para 1.

123 Preamble, para 1, UDHR; Preamble, ICESCR; Preamble, ICCPR; Preamble, CRC; Preamble, Declaration on the Rights of Mentally Retarded Persons; Preamble, Declaration on the Rights of Disabled Persons; Preamble, Standard Rules on the Equalization of

5.2.2.2 Incompatibility with the Principle of Human Dignity

Recognizing the principle of human dignity and its foundational function also implies condemning those acts that run against its inner value. We can trace a rich variety of formulations used to convey that dignity is the main international standard against which the compatibility of a certain conduct shall be measured. In particular, the practice of UN Treaty Bodies as well as of the Hague Court provides us with relevant grounds for consideration.

UN Treaty Bodies' GCs adopt different formulations to describe infringements of human dignity, as we shall see by way of illustration.

First, '*violations*' of 'human dignity'[124] or of 'the principle of respect for human dignity'[125] are considered acts '*incompatible* with the dignity and worth of the human person'.[126] Moreover, documents also deplore '*attacks on*',[127]

Opportunities for Persons with Disabilities; Preamble, CRPD; Preamble, CAT; Preamble, Declaration on the Right of Peoples to Peace; 41/128, Declaration on the Right to Development, A/RES/41/128, 4 December 1986; Declaration on the Protection of All Persons from Enforced Disappearance; Preamble, C122 Employment Policy Convention; Preamble, C111 Discrimination (Employment and Occupation); Preamble, para 2, Art. 1, UN Declaration on the Elimination of All Forms of Racial Discrimination; Preamble, paras 2, 3, ICERD; Preamble, para 1, Declaration on Race and Racial Prejudice; Art. 6 (para 1) Declaration on Race and Racial Prejudice; Preamble, Declaration on the Elimination of All Forms of Intolerance and of Discrimination Based on Religion or Belief; Preamble, Arts. 11, 12, 28, Universal Declaration on Bioethics and Human Rights; Art. 37, CRC; UN Principles for Older Persons, Section 'Care'; GA resolution 46/119, *supra* n 99, Principle 1; Art. 3, CRPD; Declaration on the Use of Scientific and Technological Progress, Preamble; Preamble, Arts. 1, 10, 15, Universal Declaration on the Human Genome and Human Rights; Art. 4, UNESCO Universal Declaration on Cultural Diversity; International Declaration on Human Genetic Data, Preamble, Arts. 1(a), 26; Preamble, Arts. 2, 3, Universal Declaration on Bioethics and Human Rights; Preamble, Declaration on the Rights of Mentally Retarded Persons; Preamble, Declaration on the Rights of Disabled Persons; Preamble, Standard Rules on the Equalization of Opportunities for Persons with Disabilities; Preamble, para 1, UN Declaration on the Elimination of All Forms of Racial Discrimination; Preamble, para 1, ICERD; Preamble, para 1, 1978, Declaration on Race and Racial Prejudice; Preamble, Declaration on the Elimination of All Forms of Intolerance and of Discrimination Based on Religion or Belief; Preamble, paras 3, 4, UNESCO Constitution; Preamble, para 3, CRC. Among *UN GCs*: GC 18 on the Right to Work, Art. 6 of the ICESCR, E/C.12/GC/18, 6 February 2006, para 4.

124 Vienna Declaration and Programme of Action, Part I, 25; Preamble (h), CRPD; GC 28 (2000), *supra* n 93, para 24; GR 33 on women's access to justice, CEDAW/C/GC/33, 3 August 2015, para 18.

125 Preamble, CEDAW.

126 Vienna Declaration and Programme of Action, Part I, 15 (para 2); Art. 1, UNESCO, Convention against Discrimination in Education, 14 December 1960, Arts. 1, 1(d); Preamble, Supplementary Convention on the Abolition of Slavery.

127 Preamble, UN GA, Declaration on the Protection of Women and Children in Emergency and Armed Conflict, 14 December 1974, A/RES/3318(XXIX).

'*offence to*',[128] acts '*prejudicial to*'[129] or '*infringement of*'[130] human dignity. In addition, harmful acts are described as '*contrary to*'[131] or able to '*affect*'[132] or to represent 'an *affront* to'[133] human dignity.

Beyond the different linguistic nuances, all of these acts are internationally condemned simply because they are harmful practices, a '*denial of dignity*',[134] carrying 'a *negative impact*' on dignity and moral integrity.[135] In particular, the Committee has deplored incompatibility with this principle in various contexts, namely the protection of refugees;[136] the prohibition of torture and ill-treatment,[137] since '[t]he humane treatment and the respect for the dignity of all persons deprived of their liberty is a *basic standard of universal application*';[138] and with respect to Article 16 of the ICCPR, on the right of everyone to 'recognition everywhere as

128 Art. 2, GA resolution 3452 (XXX), Declaration on the Protection of All Persons from Being Subjected to Torture and Other Cruel, Inhuman or Degrading Treatment or Punishment, 9 December 1975; GA resolution 34/169, *supra* n 98, Art. 5, Commentary, (a); Art. 1, Declaration on the Protection of All Persons from Enforced Disappearance; Preamble, Declaration on Race and Racial Prejudice; Art. 1, UN Declaration on the Elimination of All Forms of Racial Discrimination; GC 1 (2001), *supra* n 93, para 10.

129 GC 11 (2009), Indigenous children and their rights under the Convention, CRC/C/GC/11, 12 February 2009, para 22 (emphasis added).

130 Art. 19, International Convention for the Protection of All Persons from Enforced Disappearance, 20 December 2006, GA resolution 61/177 (12 January 2007); Universal Declaration on the Human Genome and Human Rights, Art. 6; International Declaration on Human Genetic Data, Art. 7(a).

131 Arts. 11, 24, Universal Declaration on the Human Genome and Human Rights; International Declaration on Human Genetic Data, Art. 27; Joint GR 31 CEDAW/GC 18 UN CRC, *supra* n 93, para 25; GC 17 (2005), The right of everyone to benefit from the protection of the moral and material interests resulting from any scientific, literary or artistic production of which he or she is the author (Art. 15, paragraph 1 (c), of the Covenant), E/C.12/GC/17, 12 January 2006, para 35.

132 Art. 11, Declaration on the Right and Responsibility of Individuals, Groups and Organs of Society to Promote and Protect Universally Recognized Human Rights and Fundamental Freedoms, GA resolution 53/144 (9 December 1998); GR 34 (2016) on the rights of rural women, CEDAW/C/GC/34, 7 March 2016, para 23.

133 Art. 3, Declaration on the Elimination of All Forms of Intolerance and of Discrimination Based on Religion or Belief.

134 Joint GR 31 CEDAW/GC 18 UN CRC, *supra* n 93, para 16 (emphasis added).

135 *Ibid.*, para 15.

136 *Abdilafir Abubakar Ali and Mayul Ali Mohamad* v. *Denmark* (CCPR/C/116/D/2409/2014), Annex III, Individual opinion of Committee members Anja Seibert-Fohr joined by Yuji Iwasawa (dissenting), para 1 (emphasis added).

137 See GC 20 (1992), *supra* n 93, para 2; A.H.G. *and* M.R. v. *Canada* (CCPR/C/113/D/2091/2011), 5 June 2015, para 10.4.

138 GC 9 (1982), *supra* n 93, para 1; GC 13 (1999), *supra* n 78, para 41; A.H.G. *and* M. R. v. *Canada*, *supra* n 137, Individual opinion of Committee member Anja Seibert-Fohr (concurring), in Appendix 1, see para 2.

a person before the law';[139] racial hatred;[140] 'reproductive cloning of human beings', 'germ-line interventions',[141] and misuse of scientific and technical progress;[142] and polygamy.[143] Thus, the UN treaty bodies' approach shows that dignity is a 'core value',[144] the realization and reparation of which, in case of damage, is the 'ultimate objective' and first 'priority'.[145]

The Hague Court, in its 'judicial' activity, has engaged in interpreting and applying human rights,[146] with consideration of their historical development.[147] While the Court's opportunities to deal with human rights have heavily relied on the nature of the disputes brought to The Hague, these opportunities unfolded 'in tandem with the widening and thickening of international human rights'.[148] In particular, the Court has recognized 'elementary considerations of humanity'[149] as the basis of peremptory *jus cogens*

139 *Mevlida Ičić* v. *Bosnia and Herzegovina* (CCPR/C/113/D/2028/2011), 20 August 2015, para 4 (emphasis added); *Nura Hamulić and Halima Hodžić* v. *Bosnia and Herzegovina* (CCPR/C/113/D/2022/2011), 20 August 2015, Separate opinion of Committee members Olivier de Frouville, Mauro Politi, Victor Manuel Rodríguez-Rescia and Fabián Omar Salvioli (partly dissenting), para 3. See also, Similarly, *Chhedulal Tharu and others* v. *Nepal* (CCPR/C/114/D/2038/2011), 21 October 2015, Individual opinion of Committee member Olivier de Frouville (concurring), Appendix I, para 3.

140 *Mohamed Rabbae, A.B.S and N.A.* v. *The Netherlands* (CCPR/C/117/D/2124/2011), 29 March 2017, Annex I, Individual opinion of Committee member Dheerujlall Seetulsingh, para 1 and Opinion partiellement concordante, partiellement dissidente de Olivier de Frouville, footnotes (q), p. 35 and footnote (t), pp. 35–36; see X v. *Sri Lanka* (CCPR/C/120/D/2256/2013), 22 August 2017, para 7.6.

141 Arts. 11, 24, Universal Declaration on the Human Genome and Human Rights.

142 GC 17 (2005), *supra* n 131, para 35.

143 Joint GR 31 CEDAW/GC 18 UN CRC, *supra* n 93, para 25.

144 GC 1 (2001), *supra* n 93, para 1.

145 GC 3 (2012), Implementation of Art. 14 by States parties, CAT/C/GC/3, 13 December 2012, para 4; GC 13 (1999), *supra* n 78, para 18; GR 35 on gender-based violence against women, updating GR 19, CEDAW/C/GC/35, 26 July 2017, para 33(b).

146 With regard to human rights, see B Simma, 'Human Rights before the International Court of Justice: Community Interest Coming to Life?' in C Tams and J Sloan (eds), *The Development of International Law by the ICJ* (Oxford University Press 2013), Chapter 13, 301–325.

147 See G Zyberi, *The Humanitarian Face of the International Court of Justice* (Intersentia 2008); see also R Higgins, 'The International Court of Justice and Human Rights' in R Higgins (ed.), *Themes and Theories: Selected Essays, Speeches, and Writings in International Law*, vol. 1 (Oxford University Press 2009), 639; S Sivakumaran, 'The International Court of Justice and Human Rights' in S Joseph and A McBeth (eds), *Research Handbook on International Human Rights Law* (Edward Elgar 2010), 299.

148 Simma, *supra* n 146, 303.

149 *Corfu Channel case* (*UK* v. *Albania*), Merits, (1949) ICJ Reports 1949, 4, 22 (emphasis added); *Legality of the Threat or Use of Nuclear Weapons*, Advisory Opinion, ICJ Reports 1996, p. 226257, para 79; *Military and Paramilitary Activities in and against Nicaragua* (*Nicaragua* v. *United States of America*), Judgment, ICJ Reports 1986, p. 14, para 218; *Legal Consequences*

norms.[150] The principle of elementary considerations of humanity referred to by the ICJ is 'a step forward . . . in the development of law',[151] having considerably broadened the scope of the human rights law and of human dignity's application. Of particular relevance for the argumentative narrative line of this study is the reflection of the notion of State sovereignty made by Judge Alvarez in his Separate Opinion in the *Corfu Channel Case*. He recognized the limits to the traditional concept and noted:

> [State sovereignty] has evolved, and we must now adopt a conception of it which will be in harmony with the new conditions of social life [. . .] Today, owing to social interdependence and to the predominance of the general interest, the States are bound by many rules which have not been ordered by their will. The sovereignty of States has now become an institution, an international social function of a psychological character, which has to be exercised in accordance with the new international law.[152]

The 'new international law', whose finality, among others, is to *restore human dignity*,[153] has placed the dignity of human beings at the centre of many rules and set 'limitations on the classical international law based on the principle of State sovereignty'.[154] Human dignity has thus gained a territory and place in international law to the detriment of the predominant position previously held by sovereign dignity. This dynamic is further explored in Section 5.5.

5.3 HUMAN DIGNITY AS A RIGHT

In this section, my analysis focuses on the express manifestations of human dignity through the instrument 'right' in human rights law. As detailed in Chapter 1, this instrument characterizes human dignity in two main ways: first, it expresses dignity as a right or as a mother-right through a *permissive* formulation included in a primary norm which protects it; and, second, it identifies individuals as right-holders and connects to their right specific obligations

of the Construction of a Wall in the Occupied Palestinian Territory (Advisory Opinion), ICJ Reports 2004, 136, para 157.

150 *Armed Activities on the Territory of the Congo* (New Application: 2002) (*Congo* v. *Rwanda*), ICJ Reports 2006, 3, para 64. See also Chapter 4 (4.2.1.1.).

151 M Lachs, 'Some Reflections on the Contribution of the International Court of Justice to the Development of International Law' [1983] 10 *SyracuseJIntlL&Com* 1, 241.

152 *Corfu Channel Case, supra* n 149, Individual Opinion Judge Alvarez.

153 *East Timor* (*Portugal* v. *Australia*), ICJ Reports 90 1995, 102, para 29, Judge ad hoc Skubiszewski, in his Dissenting Opinion, 238, paras 44–45 (emphasis added).

154 SRS Bedi, *The Development of Human Rights Law by the Judges of the International Court of Justice* (Hart 2007), 321.

binding one or more duty-bearers. In particular, the relationship between human dignity and the instrument 'human right' can be seen more closely from three perspectives.

The first perspective considers the relationship between *value* and right. In line with a purposive interpretation, the content of a right is determined by its underlying purpose. More specifically, the purpose of the right to human dignity is to realize the foundational value of human dignity and each person's inviolable humanity. The second and third levels, instead, view the relationship of dignity and right from two configurations that human dignity assumes. Human dignity appears not only as a value principle but also as the *object* and *source* of rights. First, human dignity is qualified as *inherent* to all human persons, considered in their individuality and in their sociality. It can therefore be an *inviolable and fundamental right* in itself. Moreover, human dignity can be the *source* of other rights. It lies at the basis of *all rights* and must be respected and protected, thus creating corresponding positive and negative obligations.

This twofold formulation of human dignity as an *inviolable and fundamental right* and as mother-right of *all rights* will be the conceptual structure traced in the analysis of two dimensions, regional and international. Each dimension will be analysed, identifying how human dignity relates to the instrument, how it is formulated and, lastly, its relationship with other rights.

5.3.1 *Right to Dignity*

Human dignity constitutes the essence of an *inviolable and fundamental right*, whose content reflects the value that it embodies.[155] This section examines the right to dignity from the regional (Section 5.3.1.1) and international (Section 5.3.1.2) perspectives. Therein, three prisms are identified: one related to the formulation of the right; one associated to its attribution; and a last one on the relations with other rights. Moreover, the practice of regional courts and international bodies provides a clarification of what, in specific cases, has been considered an offence or a violation of the right.

5.3.1.1 Regional Dimension

Regional instruments indistinctively adopt the following expressions to refer to the right to dignity: 'the right to have the inherent dignity of the

[155] See, however, C O'Mahony, 'There Is No Such Thing as a Right to Dignity' [2012] 10 *IJCL* 551.

persons [respected]',[156] 'the right to the respect of the dignity inherent in a human being'[157] and 'right to dignity'.[158] In particular, by way of illustration, it is worth referring to the Preamble of the Nice Charter, which, in its opening, declares: 'Conscious of its spiritual and moral heritage, the Union is founded on the *indivisible, universal values of human dignity*, freedom, equality and solidarity.'[159] In view of this statement, its Article 1 subsequently clarifies that 'Human dignity is inviolable. It must be respected and protected.' A comparison of the two phrases shows that that the qualification 'inviolable' refers to a right, while the adjective 'indivisible' to the universal value.[160] The adjective 'inviolable' has been used only to characterize the content of dignity, but it does not recur in sections of the Charter related to other rights. In the title of the European Union Charter, all rights are defined as 'fundamental' and, thus, inevitably, from this point of view, nobody could prevail over another.[161] However, the unique statement included in Article 1 is a quite strong confirmation that the manifestation of human dignity in the Charter of Nice appears as a fundamental right enjoying a primary status, almost more fundamental than others.[162]

Moreover, the express formulations of the right to dignity are mainly associated with an individual paradigm, namely the dignity of a 'person',[163] of 'man'[164] or of the 'human being'.[165] In its plural paradigm, it is expressly attributed to 'all human beings',[166] and to specific vulnerable groups, such as persons with disabilities,[167]

156 Inter-American Convention on Violence against Women, Art. 4(e).

157 African Charter, Art. 5.

158 EU Charter of Fundamental Rights, Chapter I, Dignity, Art. 1; European Social Charter, Art. 26, Part I.

159 Emphasis added.

160 The expression 'inviolable' is also associated to 'rights' by the 1948 UDHR in its preamble.

161 P Grossi, 'Dignità umana e libertà nella Carta dei diritti fondamentali dell'Unione europea' in M Siclari (ed.), *Contributi allo studio della Carta dei diritti fondamentali dell'Unione europea* (Giappichelli 2003), 44.

162 9 October 2001 in Case C–377/98 *Netherlands* v. *European Parliament and Council* [2001] ECR I–7079, at grounds 70–77; see also, Explanations Relating to the Charter of Fundamental Rights, 14 December 2007, Official Journal of the European Union, C 303/17, (2007/C 303/02).

163 Inter-American Convention on Violence against Women, Art. 4.

164 Inter-American Convention to Prevent and Punish Torture, Preamble.

165 African Charter, Art. 5.

166 Preamble, Protocol No. 13 to the Convention for the Protection of Human Rights and Fundamental Freedoms.

167 Guidelines on the conditions of arrest, police custody and pre-trial detention in Africa, ACommHPR, 2017, 33(a)(ii) on persons with disabilities.

women[168] and 'refugees, asylum seekers and internally displaced persons'.[169]

Lastly, the right to dignity is described as a constitutive and primary right to be considered while interpreting other human rights, namely the right to life,[170] the right to work,[171] right to privacy[172] and the prohibition of torture.[173] The relation between these rights and the right to dignity is further explored in Section 5.3.2.

These legal bases have grounded regional courts' decisions assessing violations of the right to dignity. In the European system, the majority of references to the right to human dignity appear in judgments of the ECtHR related to cases of inhuman treatment in detention.[174] The IACtHR has instead referred to the right to dignity in decisions related to violations of the right to privacy[175] and of the right to humane treatment in detention.[176] The African Commission and the African

168 Organization of American States, Inter-American Convention on the Prevention, Punishment and Eradication of Violence against Women ('Convention of Belem do Para'), 9 June 1994, Art. 4(e); Maputo Protocol, Art. 3 (1); GC 2 on Art. 14.1 (a), (b), (c) and (f) and Art. 14. 2 (a) and (c) of the Maputo Protocol; GCs on Art. 14 (1) (d) and (e) of the Maputo Protocol, para 11; Guidelines on the conditions of arrest, police custody and pre-trial detention in Africa, *supra* n 167, para 32(b), (v) on women.

169 Kigali Declaration, ACommHPR, 8 May 2003, para 11.

170 EU Charter of Fundamental Rights, Art. 25; See also 2002, Protocol No. 13 to the Convention for the Protection of Human Rights and Fundamental Freedoms, Preamble; GC 3 on the ACHPR: The Right to Life (Art. 4), ACommHPR held from 4 to 18 November 2015, Introduction, para 3.

171 Art. 26, European Social Charter (ESC) and Revised Social Charter, ETS 163, 3 May 1996, Art. 26 [European Social Charter].

172 Art. 11, ACHR.

173 Art. 5, African Charter on Human and Peoples Rights. This right is also recalled in Guidelines for the Policing of Assemblies by Law Enforcement Officials in Africa, ACommHPR, 2017, para 1.2.1; GC 4 on the ACHPR: The Right to Redress for Victims of Torture and Other Cruel, Inhuman or Degrading Punishment or Treatment (Art. 5), ACommHPR, 2017, paras 3, 8, 10, 18, 44, 61, 70; Principles and Guidelines on Human and Peoples' Rights while Countering Terrorism in Africa, ACommHPR, 2015, part 3 Liberty, Arrest, and Detention, Part 3, para D, (i).

174 *Khamtokhu and Aksenchik* v. *Russia*, [GC], Nos. 60367/08 and 961/11, Judgment, 24 January 2017, Concurring Opinion of Judge Turković, p. 42, para 11. See also *Vinter and Others* v. *The United Kingdom*, [GC], Nos. 66069/09, 130/10 and 3896/10, para 113; see also *Dubská and Krejzová* v. *The Czech Republic, supra* n 59, para 56; *Khlaifia and Others* v. *Italy, supra* n 65, paras 160, 169; *Vasyukov* v. *Russia*, Nos. 2974/05, 5 April 2011, para 59.

175 *Kimel* v. *Argentina*, Judgment of 2 May 2008, paras 55–56 and *Ibid.*, Concurring Opinion of Judge Diego García-Sayán, para 14, p. 4; *Ricardo Canese* v. *Paraguay*, Merits, Reparations and Costs, 31 August 2004, Series C No. 111, para 101; *Manuel Cepeda Vargas* v. *Colombia*, Judgment of 26 May 2010, para 174 and p. 87; *Fernández Ortega et al.* v. *Mexico, supra* n 68, para 177, p. 92; *Rosendo Cantú et al.* v. *Mexico, supra* n 68, para 121.

176 *Bulacio*, Judgment of 18 September 2003, Series C No. 100, para 126; *García-Asto and Ramírez-Rojas, supra* n 67, para 221; *Bámaca Velásquez case*, Judgment of 25 November 2000, Series C No. 70, para 150 (emphasis added); *Cantoral Benavides case*,

Court, instead, have also frequently referred to the 'the right to respect of the dignity inherent in a human being' on the basis of Article 5 of the African Charter, which recognizes the right to dignity.[177] In particular, the Commission has also on many occasions referred to the strict relationship between the right to respect human dignity and right to life. In *Sudan Human Rights Organisation & Centre on Housing Rights and Evictions (COHRE)* v. *Sudan*, the African Commission clarified the meaning of the right to life and its relationship with the right to dignity, stating that: 'The term "life" itself has been given a relatively broad interpretation by courts internationally, *to include the right to dignity* and the right to livelihood.'[178] Moreover, the Commission has elaborated the link between the right to respect human dignity and the right to be treated with humanity.[179] In *Purohit and Moore* v. *Gambia*, a case on conditions of detention of mentally ill persons, the Commission detailed the content of this right, saying:

> Human dignity *is an inherent basic right* to which all human beings, regardless of their mental capabilities or disabilities as the case may be, are entitled to without discrimination. It is therefore an inherent right which every human being is obliged to respect by all means possible and on the other hand it confers a duty on every human being to respect this right.[180]

According to the Commission, this right should be 'zealously guarded and forcefully protected by all States party to the African Charter in accordance

Judgment of 18 August 2000, Series C No. 69, paras 82–89; and *Fairén Garbi and Solís Corrales case*, Judgment of 15 March 1989. Series C No. 6, para 149; *Loayza Tamayo* v. *Peru*, *supra* n 67, para 57 (emphasis added), and *J.* v. *Peru*, Preliminary objection, merits, reparations and costs, Judgment of 27 November 2013, Series C No. 275, para 363; *Rodríguez Vera et al.* (The Disappeared from the Palace of Justice) v. *Colombia*, Judgment of 14 November 2014, para 419.

177 African Commission: see *John K. Modise* v. *Botswana*, *supra* n 71, para 92; *Amnesty International* v. *Zambia*, *supra* n 71, para 58; with reference to unremunerated work, see *Malawi Africa Association et al.* v. *Mauritania*, ACommHPR, Comm. 54/91–61/91–96/93–98/93–164/97_196/97–210/98, 11 May 2000, para 135; with reference to poor conditions of detention, see *Media Rights Agenda* v. *Nigeria*, ACommHPR, Comm. 224/98, 6 November 2000, para 72; with regard to enforced disappearance, see *J.E Zitha & P.J.L. Zitha* v. *Mozambique*, *supra* n 77, para 81. For the African Court's case law, see *In the Matter of Peter Joseph Chacha* v. *The United Republic of Tanzania*, No. 003/2012, ACtHPR, Ruling on Admissibility, 28 March 2014, paras 64, 67.

178 *Sudan Human Rights Organisation & COHRE* v. *Sudan*, ACommHPR, Comm. 279/03–296/05, 27 May 2009, para 146 (emphasis added); see also *Malawi Africa Association, et al* v. *Mauritania*, *supra* n 177, para 135.

179 See *supra* n 76.

180 *Purohit and Moore* v. *Gambia (The)*, *supra* n 76, para 57 (emphasis added); see also *Egyptian Initiative for Personal Rights and INTERIGHTS* v. *Egypt*, ACommHPR, Comm. 323/06, 12 October 2013, para 190; see also *Sudan Human Rights Organisation & COHRE* v. *Sudan*, *supra* n 178, paras 158, 163 and 164.

with the well established principle that all human beings are born free and equal in dignity and rights'.[181]

The aformentioned jurisprudence not only clarifies the meaning of the right to dignity but is also indicative of its operativity in relation with other human rights in the practice of regional bodies.

5.3.1.2 International Dimension

Multilateral treaties, declarations, proclamations, and agreements promulgated in the late 1940s (and thereafter) promoted the centrality of human dignity as 'it became necessary to defend, not merely some rights, some truths, or some moral principles, but the very existence of human rights, truth, and of morality'.[182] As we saw in detail in Chapter 3, the UN Charter affirms in its Preamble that 'the peoples of the United Nations' have 'faith in fundamental human rights' that include 'the dignity and worth of the human person'. The UN Charter, and later the UDHR, set an internal 'tuning key' to which the right to dignity and all the other human rights would have to be harmonized.[183]

This is also probably the reason why the contours of the right to dignity remain somewhat undefined. There are very few provisions expressly referring to dignity as a *right* in international legal documents. When present, this right is expressed with different but almost similar linguistic formulations, namely '(inherent) right to respect for human dignity'[184] and 'right to dignity',[185] the latter of which is also interchangeably referred to as 'right to human dignity'.[186]

181 *Purohit and Moore* v. *Gambia (The)*, *supra* n 76, para 61, referring to Art. 1 of the UDHR (emphasis added).

182 KJ Hasson, 'Religious Liberty and Human Dignity: A Tale of Two Declarations' [2003] 27 *HarvJL&PP* 81, 82.

183 See MA Glendon, 'Reflections on the UDHR' [1998] 82 *First Things* 23, 24.

184 See Art. 3, Declaration on the Rights of Disabled Persons; Art. 2 (a), Universal Declaration on the Human Genome and Human Rights. See also GC 11 (2009), *supra* n 129, para 7, (c), 13; GC 13, The right of the child to freedom from all forms of violence, 18 April 2011, CRC/C/GC/13, para 13.

185 UN GA, UN Declaration on the Rights of Indigenous Peoples, 2 October 2007, A/RES/61/295 [UN Declaration on the Rights of Indigenous Peoples], Art. 15, (1); see also GC 13 (2011), *supra* n 184, para 11 (d); GC 20 (2016), *supra* n 93, para 75; GC 11 (2009), *supra* n 129, para 17.

186 See GC 14 (2000), The right to the highest attainable standard of health (Art. 12 of the ICESCR), E/C.12/2000/4 11 August 2000, para 3; GC 15 (2002), The right to water (arts. 11 and 12 of the ICESCR), E/C.12/2002/11 20 January 2003, CESCR, para 1; GC 11 (2009), *supra* n 129, para 17; GC 13 (2011), *supra* n 184, para 17; GC 20 (2016), *supra* n 93, para 75.

It is interesting to notice that these manifestations are associated to the 'man'[187] or to 'the human person',[188] but are predominantly linked to a collective paradigm, such as 'all members of the human family'[189] and, in specific provisions, to 'disabled persons',[190] 'indigenous people',[191] 'children',[192] 'adolescents'[193] or 'older persons'.[194]

Although undefined, the contours of this right are not shapeless. This right has been mostly formulated by way of interpretation by the UN Treaty Bodies' practice. In particular, here the right to dignity is defined by three main features.

First, the right to human dignity is expressed as an 'imperative' and primary right, which imposes on States the obligations to respect, protect and ensure this right. For example, with regard to children's rights, two GCs of the CRC are of particular relevance. First, the GC No. 10 (2007) on children's rights in juvenile justice states:

> This *inherent right to dignity and worth*, to which the preamble of CRC makes explicit reference, has to be respected and protected throughout the entire process of dealing with the child, from the first contact with law enforcement agencies and all the way to the implementation of all measures for dealing with the child.[195]

Moreover, GC No. 13 (2011) recognized the importance of securing the right to dignity[196] and 'promoting children's fundamental rights to respect for their human dignity'.[197] As described, the prevention 'of all forms of violence, is essential for promoting the full set of child rights in the Convention'.[198] As a consequence, the absolute right to dignity implies

187 UNESCO Constitution, Preamble, para 4.
188 ICCPR, Art. 10; CRPD, Art. 16 (4).
189 GA resolution 47/133, Declaration on the Protection of All Persons from Enforced Disappearance; Preamble, Universal Declaration on the Human Genome and Human Rights, Preamble and Art. 1. For a similar wording, see also Preamble, ICESCR; Preamble, ICCPR. They all refer to UDHR, Preamble, para 1.
190 Art. 3, Declaration on the Rights of Disabled Persons, Art. 3; Art. 24 (1), (a), CRPD
191 UN Declaration on the Rights of Indigenous Peoples, Arts. 15(1), 43; Proposed American Declaration on the Rights of Indigenous Peoples, IACommHR, OEA/Ser/L/V/.II.95 Doc.6 (1997), Art. XXIV.
192 GC 13 (2011), *supra* n 184, para 11 (d), 13.
193 GC 20 (2016), *supra* n 93, para 75.
194 UN Principles for Older Persons, principle 17, 'Dignity'.
195 GC 10, *supra* n 83, para 13.
196 GC 13 (2011), *supra* n 184, para 11(d), 13.
197 *Ibid.*, para 13.
198 *Ibid.*, para 17.

that there are no exceptions permitted. This aspect represents its second constitutive feature.[199]

The right to dignity is also associated to a 'sense of uniqueness'[200] and it is an *integral component* of other rights, the realization of which is described as strictly related and dependent upon dignity's realization. In this sense, the GC No. 14 (2000) of the CESCR on the right to the highest attainable standard of health affirms that

> The right to health is closely related to and dependent upon the realization of other human rights, as contained in the International Bill of Rights, including the rights to food, housing, work, education, human dignity . . . These and other rights and freedoms address integral components of the right to health.[201]

Moreover, in a significant number of cases, the Human Rights Committee has repeatedly found, with respect to many substantiated claims, that poor conditions of detention violate a person's '*right to be treated with humanity and with respect for the inherent dignity of the human person*'.[202] The Committee has therefore concluded that these inhumane conditions are contrary to Article 7

199 *Ibid.*

200 GC 20 (2016), *supra* n 93, para 75.

201 GC 14 (2000), *supra* n 186, para 3; see also GC 15 (2002), *supra* n 186, para 1.

202 *Egor Bobrov* v. *Belarus* (CCPR/C/122/D/2181/2012), 12 November 2018, para 8.2 (emphasis added); *Yuba Kumari Katwal* v. *Nepal* (CCPR/C/113/D/2000/2010), 5 May 2015, para 3.6; *Zafar Abdullayev* v. *Turkmenistan* (CCPR/C/113/D/2218/2012), 19 May 2015, para 7.3; *Mahmud Hudaybergenov* v. *Turkmenistan* (CCPR/C/115/D/2221/2012), 22 December 2015, para 7.3; *Dzhakishev Mukhtar* v. *Kazakhstan* (CCPR/C/115/D/2304/2013), 9 December 2015, para 7.3; *Sunnet Japparow* v. *Turkmenistan* (CCPR/C/115/D/2223/2012), 17 December 2015, para 7.3; *A.S.* v. *Nepal* (CCPR/C/115/D/2077/2011), 4 January 2016, para 8.4; *Shadurdy Uchetov* v. *Turkmenistan* (CCPR/C/117/D/2226/2012), 26 September 2016, para 7.4; *Dovran Bahramovich Matyakubov* v. *Turkmenistan* (CCPR/C/117/D/2224/2012), 26 September 2016, para 7.3; *Matkarim Aminov* v. *Turkmenistan* (CCPR/C/117/D/2220/2012), 27 September 2016, para 9.3; *Kayum Ortikov* v. *Uzbekistan* (CCPR/C/118/D/2317/2013), 27 January 2017, para 10.4; *Abdelkader Boudjemai* v. *Algeria* (CCPR/C/121/D/2283/2013), 1 December 2017, para 8.2; *Zhaslan Suleimenov* v. *Kazakhstan* (CCPR/C/119/D/2146/2012), 12 May 2017, para 8.7; *Evans* v. *Trinidad and Tobago* (CCPR/C/77/D/908/2000), 5 May 2003, para 6.4; *Mwamba* v. *Zambia* (CCPR/C/98/D/1520/2006), 10 March 2010, para 6.4; *Bozbey* v. *Turkmenistan* (CCPR/C/100/D/1530/2006), 27 October 2010, para 7.3; *Bennet* v. *Jamaica* (CCPR/C/65/D/590/1994), 25 March 1999, paras 10.7–10.8; *Simpson* v. *Jamaica* (CCPR/C/73/D/695/1996), 31 October 2001, para 7.2; *Shaw* v. *Jamaica* (CCPR/C/62/D/704/1996), 2 April 1998, para 7.1; *McLeod* v. *Jamaica* (CCPR/C/59/D/734/1997), 31 March 1998, para 6.4; *Mezine* v. *Algeria* (CCPR/C/106/D/1779/2008), 25 October 2012, para 8.8; *Gorji-Dinka* v. *Cameroon* (CCPR/C/83/D/1134/2002), 17 March 2005, para 5.2; *Djebrouni* v. *Algeria* (CCPR/C/103/D/1781/2008), 31 October 2011, para 8.2; *Zarzi* v. *Algeria* (/C/101/D/1780/2008), 22 March 2011, para 7.8; *Guezout and Rakik* v. *Algeria* (CCPR/C/105/D/1753/2008), 19 July 2012, para 8.8; *Berzig* v. *Algeria* (CCPR/C/103/D/1781/2008), 31 October 2011, para 8.8; *Ammari* v. *Algeria* (CCPR/

and Article 10(1) of the ICCPR, which deals specifically with the situation of persons deprived of their liberty, and encompasses for such persons the criteria generally expressed in Article 7.[203] Thus, the practice of UN Treaty Bodies frames human dignity as an absolute and imperative right, whose realization is a necessary and integral component of other human rights.

5.3.2 *Dignity as a Mother-Right*

Human dignity is the basis of an inviolable right and a source of all rights that derive from it. Oscar Schachter considers that to state that all human rights and fundamental freedoms derive from the inherent dignity of the human person should be read in a *philosophical* sense rather than an historical one.[204] It clearly implies that rights are not derived from the State or any other external authority. In his view, this affirmation carries two corollaries: the first, that 'basic rights are not given by authority and therefore *may not be taken away*; the second [...] that they are rights of the person, *every person*'.[205] A further implication of recognizing human dignity as a 'source' of human rights is that '[d]rawing upon the conception of human dignity and the intrinsic worth of every person, we can *extend and strengthen* human rights by formulating new rights or construing existing rights to apply to new situations'.[206] Thus, in light of their mother-source, namely human dignity, human rights acquire an inherent nature and belong to all people. For this reason, they are not limited in number and can expand in light of contextual and practical needs.

As a mother-right, human dignity lies at the basis of all rights and must be respected and protected, creating corresponding positive and negative obligations. Each human right is thus eventually combined by the ultimate realization of the foundational value of human dignity. To better understand the relationship between human dignity as a mother-right and human rights,

C/112/D/2098/2011), 30 October 2014, para 8.2; *Rouba Alhaj Ali* v. *Morocco* (CAT/C/58/D/682/2015), 13 September 2016, para 7.3; *Rafik Belamrania* v. *Algeria* (CCPR/C/118/D/2157/2012), 17 March 2017, para 6.4; *Malika El Boathi* v. *Algeria* (CCPR/C/119/D/2259/2013), 17 March 2017, para 7.2; *Lounis Khelifati* v. *Algeria* (CCPR/C/120/D/2267/2013), 21 September 2017, para 6.3. See also GC 21 (1992) on humane treatment of persons deprived of their liberty, paras 3–4.

203 See also *Ahmadou Sadio Diallo* (*Republic of Guinea* v. *Democratic Republic of the Congo*), Merits, Judgment, ICJ Reports 2010 (II), 692, para 165, sub-para (2) (3) of the operative part. See also the Separate Opinion of Judge Cançado Trindade, paras 222–242.

204 O Schachter, 'Human Dignity as a Normative Concept' [1983] 77 *AJIL* 848, 853.

205 *Ibid.*

206 *Ibid.* (emphasis added).

examples of this connection will be first examined at the regional level and subsequently at the international level.

5.3.2.1 Regional Dimension

At the regional level, human dignity as a mother-right generally has two main features, which are reflected also at the international level: it is a *source* and *foundation* of rights, which derive and 'flow' from it; and, as an integral component of human rights, it *qualifies* their content. These features can be traced in both regional legal instruments and in the jurisprudence of regional bodies.

As regards the European human rights legal framework, in the words of Judges Spielmann and Jebens, 'the concept of dignity *prevails* throughout the European Convention on Human Rights, even if it is not expressly mentioned in the text of the Convention'.[207] The ECtHR has indeed made it clear on various occasions that '[t]he *very essence* of the Convention is respect for human dignity and human freedom'.[208] In particular, '[d]ignity is a *quality inherent* to the human being that does not depend on age, the crime committed or – still less – gender, in democratic societies'.[209] Thus, as noted by Judge Dedov, '[t]o respect persons as ends, to view them as having basic human dignity, seems to be inextricably bound up with viewing persons as possessors of rights'.[210] Human dignity has a central role in the European system and is regarded as a foundational right to be considered while interpreting other rights. As clearly declared by Judge Serghides: 'Human dignity is behind almost every Convention right.'[211]

Moreover, human dignity may also be used as a qualification of other rights. In this sense, for instance, the EU Charter of Fundamental Rights refers to the

207 *Vereinigung Bildender Künstler* v. *Austria, supra* n 62, Joint Dissenting Opinion, Judges Spielmann and Jebens, paras 7–8.

208 *Pretty* v. *The United Kingdom, supra* n 58, para 65; and *Christine Goodwin* v. *The United Kingdom*, [GC], No. 28957/95, ECtHR 2002–VI, para 90. See also *Valašinas* v. *Lithuania, supra* n 55, para 102.

209 *Khamtokhu and Aksenchik* v. *Russia, supra* n 174, Dissenting Opinion of Judge Pinto de Albuquerque, p. 77, para 47.

210 *Naït-Liman* v. *Switzerland*, [GC], No. 51357/07, Judgment, Dissenting Opinion of Judge Dedov, 15 March 2018, p. 77, referring to N Bowie and R Simon, The Individual and the Political Order, 1977).

211 *Simeonovi* v. *Bulgaria, supra* n 39; see also *Regner* v. *The Czech Republic*, [GC], No. 35289/11, 19 September 2017, para 24.

right 'to lead a life of dignity'[212] and the 'right to work with dignity'.[213] A significant number of cases refer to dignity violations in cases about the right to human treatment in detention,[214] the 'right to hope',[215] the right to a fair trial,[216] the right to personal or professional reputation and honour[217] or the right to health care.[218]

Also, Inter-American human rights instruments and jurisprudence of the IACtHR follow the same approach. First, human dignity acts as a source and foundation of rights. As aptly put by Judge Cançado Trindade, '[i]n the domain of international human rights law, the *principle of the dignity of the human being* and that of the *inalienability of his inherent rights* belong to this category of fundamental principles'.[219] In particular, human dignity is a primary principle and right by virtue of which 'all individuals must be respected (both their honour and their beliefs), based on the mere fact of belonging to the human race, irrespective of any other circumstance'.[220] Thus, human dignity acts is a mother-right and source of rights in different contexts and in relation to a variety of human rights. For instance, civil and political rights and social and economic rights are declared to 'constitute an *indivisible whole based* on the recognition of the dignity of the human person'.[221] Moreover, human dignity is the foundation and source of the right not to be discriminated against based on disability, which '*flow* from the inherent dignity and equality of each person'.[222]

212 EU Charter of Fundamental Rights, Art. 25; see also Protocol No. 13 to the Convention for the Protection of Human Rights and Fundamental Freedoms, Preamble.

213 EU Charter of Fundamental Rights, Art. 31.

214 See *Muršić* v. *Croatia*, [GC], No. 7334/13, 20 October 2016, paras 96–101; see also *supra* n 174.

215 See *Vinter and Others* v. *The United* Kingdom, *supra* n 174, paras 107–113; see on the point, *Rooman* v. *Belgium*, [GC], No. 18052/11, Judgment, 31 January 2019, Partly Dissenting Opinion of Judge Nussberger, para 9, p. 82.

216 E Brems and L Lavrysen, 'Procedural Justice in Human Rights Adjudication: The European Court of Human Rights' [2013] 35 *HRQ* 35, 184–188; *Regner* v. *The Czech Republic*, *supra* n 211, Partly Dissenting Opinion of Judge Serghides, paras 24, 31.

217 *Medžlis Islamske Zajednice Brčko and Others* v. *Bosnia And Herzegovina*, No. 17224/11, 27 June 2017, para 106.

218 *Lopes De Sousa Fernandes* v. *Portugal*, *supra* n 38, Partly Concurring, Partly Dissenting Opinion of Judge Pinto De Albuquerque, para 71 (emphasis added). He refers in footnote to the Maastricht Guidelines on Violations of Economic, Social and Cultural Rights, Maastricht, 1997, paras 6 and 8.

219 *Plan de Sánchez Massacre* v. *Guatemala*, *supra* n 42, Separate Opinion of Judge AA Cançado-Trindade, para 16, p. 5 (emphasis added); see also Advisory Opinion No. 18, *supra* n 42, para 157.

220 *Plan de Sánchez Massacre* v. *Guatemala*, *supra* n 42, Separate Opinion of Judge AA Cançado-Trindade, para 17, p. 5.

221 See Preamble, Additional Protocol to the ACHR in the Area of Economic, Social and Cultural Rights, OAS TS No. 69, 17 November 1988; Preamble, AP on Genetic Testing for Health Purposes.

222 *Ibid.*, Preamble.

Human dignity also qualifies the content of human rights, such as the right to be treated humanely in detention.[223] In particular, the IACtHR has referred to the inherent relationship between human dignity and the right to life,[224] while examining the scope of protection[225] or the legal status of the embryo,[226] and between human dignity and right to truth, which is '*fundamental to the inherent dignity of the human person*'.[227]

Similarly, on the basis of Article 5 of the African Charter, human dignity is mostly understood in the following forms: as a source and foundation of rights, such as the right to social security, the right to food and the right to water,[228] and thus a reference for the realization of human rights;[229] as a qualification and integral component of other human rights, namely when there are references to the right to be treated *with dignity*[230] or the right to life *in dignity*.[231] On these bases, the case law of the African Commission has also referred to human dignity as a source and component of the right to life,[232] the right to food[233] and the right to be treated with humanity.[234]

223 Art. 2, ACHR; Preamble, Inter-American Convention to Prevent and Punish Torture.

224 *Rosendo Cantú et al.* v. *Mexico*, *supra* n 68, para 119; *Atala Riffo and Daughters* v. *Chile*, *supra* n 70, para 162.

225 *Artavia Murillo et al. ('In Vitro Fertilization')* v. *Costa Rica*, Judgment of 28 November 2012, para 143 (emphasis added); see also *Gelman* v. *Uruguay*, Merits and reparations, Judgment of 24 February 2011, Series C No. 221, para 97; similarly, see ECtHR, *Evans* v. *United Kingdom*, No. 6339/05, Judgment of 10 April 2007, paras 71 and 72; *Dickson* v. *United Kingdom*, No. 44362/04, Judgment of 4 December 2007, para 66; *S.H. and others* v. *Austria*, No. 57813/00, Judgment of 3 November 2011, para 82; *P. and S.* v. *Poland*, No. 57375/08, Judgment of 30 October 2012, para 96.

226 *Artavia Murillo et al.* v. *Costa Rica*, *supra* n 225, paras 247 and 248.

227 See OHCHR, Study on the right to the truth, E/CN.4/2006/91, 9 January 2006, paras 57 and 59, recalled in *Rodríguez Vera et al.* v. *Colombia*, Judgment of 14 November 2014, Concurring Opinion of Judge Eduardo Ferrer Mac-Gregor Poisot, para 17.

228 Principles and Guidelines on the Implementation of Economic, Social and Cultural Rights in the ACHPR, ACommHPR, 10 to 24 November 2010, para 81 (right to social security); 84 (right to food); 87 (right to water).

229 *Ibid.*, Preamble, para 24.

230 *Ibid.*, para 59 (ee) and para 71(q); Maputo Protocol, Arts. 22(b), 23(b), 24(b); Guidelines on the conditions of arrest, police custody and pre-trial detention in Africa, *supra* n 167, paras 24, 25 (d), 32(b), (i); Principles and Guidelines on Human and Peoples' Rights while Countering Terrorism in Africa, *supra* n 173.

231 *Ibid.*, para 78; GC 3 on the ACHPR, *supra* n 170, Introduction, paras 3, 6, 11, 36, 43; Principles and Guidelines on Human and Peoples' Rights while Countering Terrorism in Africa, *supra* n 173, para E, Part 3 Liberty, Arrest, And Detention; Ouagadougou Declaration and Plan of Action on Accelerating Prisons and Penal Reforms in Africa, 6–20 November 2003, para 2.

232 *Sudan Human Rights Organisation & COHRE* v. *Sudan*, *supra* n 178, para 146 (emphasis added).

233 *Social and Economic Rights Action Center (SERAC) and Center for Economic and Social Rights (CESR)* v. *Nigeria*, ACommHPR, Comm. 155/96, 27 October 2001, para 65.

234 See *supra* n 76.

Arab and Asian human rights documents, in a different way, instead make reference to human dignity as mother-right in two forms: to qualify specific human rights, namely the right to life (or to a dignified existence),[235] the right to social security[236] or the right to education;[237] and to recognize and affirm the principle of equality between men and women.[238]

5.3.2.2 International Dimension

International human rights norms traditionally present human dignity as a mother-right with two characteristics: as a *source* of rights and as a *qualification* of rights. In the first sense, human rights provisions declare that 'rights *derive* from the inherent dignity [and worth] of the human person'.[239] Dignity also equips human rights with a virtuous shape when it is instead adopted to qualify a specific right, such as the 'right to live with dignity',[240] the 'right to be treated with dignity',[241] the 'right to pursue spiritual development in conditions of dignity',[242] the 'right to representation with dignity'[243] and the 'right to return in dignity'.[244] In this sense, human dignity ultimately is a foundational right necessary for the development of the personality[245] and individuals' self-perception of dignity ('sense of dignity') should drive the enhancement and realization of other human rights, such as the right to education.[246] Thus, such human rights are 'indispensable' for dignity.[247]

These considerations can be further combined and supported with reflections on the relationship of dignity-rights given by UN Treaty Bodies in their GCs to UN human rights treaties. Various GCs refer explicitly to dignity as

235 Preamble, Arab Charter, 2004.
236 Art. 30(1), ASEAN 2009.
237 *Ibid.*, Art. 31(3).
238 Arts. 1(a) and 6(a), Cairo Declaration of Human Rights in Islam.
239 ICESCR, Preamble; ICCPR, Preamble; Vienna Declaration and Programme of Action, Preamble; CAT, Preamble, para 2.
240 Declaration on Social Progress and Development, part I principles, Art. 1; 'Dignity', UN Principles for Older Persons, principle 17.
241 Art. 10, ICCPR; see also Basic Principles for the Treatment of Prisoners, *supra* n 99, principle 1.
242 C122 Employment Policy Convention, Preamble; Discrimination (Employment and Occupation) Convention, 1958 (No. 111), Preamble.
243 Proposed American Declaration on the Rights of Indigenous Peoples, *supra* n 191, Art. XVI (3).
244 UN Millennium Declaration, para 26, Section VI.
245 UDHR, Art. 22.
246 ICESCR, Art. 13 (1); CRPD, Art. 24 (1) (a), (a).
247 UDHR, Art. 22; UNESCO Constitution, preamble, para 4.

a source of rights,[248] clarifying four important characteristics and functions of human dignity, some of them already developed by other regional bodies.

First, human dignity is composed [of] and expressed in its amplitude by human rights, which therefore form an *inseparable* part of it and are of necessary importance in guaranteeing dignity. This feature has been expressed, for instance, with regard to the right to work[249] and the right to social security.[250]

Second, human dignity, as a source of rights, *expands* the scope of protection of derivative-rights, such as the right to housing,[251] right to water,[252] the right to health,[253] the right to access to adequate sanitation,[254] the right to food,[255] and cultural rights, which are 'essential for the maintenance of human dignity'.[256]

Moreover, human dignity acts as a *distinctive criteria*, enabling human rights to be distinguished from other entitlements.[257] The CESCR has noted that the right of everyone to benefit from the protection of the moral and material interests resulting from any scientific, literary or artistic production of which they are the author:

> is a human right which *derives* from the inherent dignity and worth of all persons. This fact *distinguishes* article 15, paragraph 1(c), and other human rights from most legal entitlements recognized in intellectual property systems.[258]

Here, human dignity functions as *distinctive criteria* among different entitlements, in this case, those guaranteed in intellectual property systems. Thanks to human dignity, human rights possess a different nature that makes them

[248] GC 4 (1991), The right to adequate housing (art. 11 (1) of the ICESCR), CESCR, paras 7, 9; GC 17 (2005), *supra* n 131, para 1; GC 18, *supra* n 123, paras 1, 4; GC 19, *supra* n 95, paras 1, 41; GC 1 (2001), *supra* n 93, para 2.

[249] GC 18, *supra* n 123, para 1, 4; GC 16 (2005), *supra* n 83, para 1.

[250] GC 19, *supra* n 95, paras 1, 22, 41 (emphasis added); see also GC 24 (2017) on State obligations under the ICESCR in the context of business activities, E/C.12/GC/24, 10 August 2017, footnote 16; see also Constitutional Court of South Africa, *Daniels* v. *Scribante and others*, case CCT 50/16, Judgment of 11 May 2017, paras 37–39 (leading judgment by J Madlanga).

[251] GC 4 (1991), *supra* n 248, para 7 (emphasis added).

[252] GC 15 (2002), *supra* n 186, paras 1 and 11.

[253] GC 14 (2000), *supra* n 186, para 3.

[254] GC 15 (2002), *supra* n 186, para 29.

[255] GC 12 (1999), The right to adequate food (art. 11), E/C.12/1999/5, 12 May 1999, CESCR, para 4.

[256] GC 21 (2009), *supra* n 93, para 1.

[257] GC 17 (2005), *supra* n 131, para 1 (emphasis added).

[258] *Ibid.*

distinguishable from other legal instruments, namely entitlements deriving from a distinct regime.

Lastly, human dignity is a *qualification* of specific rights, namely the 'right to life (or live) with dignity',[259] 'right to die with dignity',[260] 'right to age with dignity'[261] and 'right to be treated with dignity'.[262] In this sense, the jurisprudence of the UN Treaty Bodies also reports human dignity as a qualification of the following human rights: the 'right to social security'[263] – for its 'central importance in guaranteeing human dignity';[264] the 'right to life';[265] the 'right to access good, product and services'[266] of persons with disabilities; the 'right to housing';[267] the right to have personal honour, dignity and reputation respected, in light of Article 17 of the ICCPR.[268]

259 See GC 36, *supra* n 86, paras 3, 26, 62; CEDAW, GR 21: Equality in marriage and family relations, 1994, para 28; CEDAW, GR 24, *supra* n 93, para 22; CEDAW, GR 25: Art. 4 (1) of the CEDAW (temporary special measures), 2004, para 19; GR 33, *supra* n 124 ('empowerment' instead of right), para 15; CERD, GR 21: on the right to self-determination, 1996, para 5; GC 4 (1991), *supra* n 248, paras 7, 8 (e); GC 6 (1995), The economic, social and cultural rights of older persons, CESCR, para 5; GC 12 (1999), *supra* n 255, para 4; GC 13 (1999), *supra* n 78, footnote 4; GC 14 (2000), *supra* n 186, para 1 and footnote 13; GC 15 (2002), *supra* n 186, Introduction; GC 18, *supra* n 123, paras 1, 31(a); GC 9 (2006), *supra* n 93, para 41; GC 21 (2017) on children in street situations, CRC/C/GC/21, 21 June 2017, paras 29, 50.

260 See GC 36, *supra* n 86, para 9; GC 14 (2000), *supra* n 186, para 25.

261 See CEDAW, GR 27, *supra* n 93, para 9.

262 See GC 9 (2006), *supra* n 93, para 43; GC 9 (replaced by GC 21), *supra* n 93, para 1; GC 15 (1986), *supra* n 93, para 7; GC 10, *supra* n 83, paras 13, 40, 89; GC 16 (1988), *supra* n 93, para 8; GC 20 (1992), *supra* n 93, para 2; GC 21, *supra* n 88, paras 1, 3, 4; GC 28, *supra* n 93, para 15; GC 29 (2001), *supra* n 93, para 13(a); GR 19, *supra* n 93, paras 14, 24(b); GR 23, *supra* n 83, para 1; GR 24, *supra* n 93, paras 22, 25; GR 27, *supra* n 93, para 10; Joint GR 31 CEDAW/GC 18 UN CRC, *supra* n 93, para 14; GR 32 (2014), *supra* n 83, para 24(l); GR 36, *supra* n 83, paras 57, 69; GR 13 (1993), *supra* n 93, para 2; GR 29, *supra* n 83, para 1(a); GR 31 (2005), *supra* n 93, para 19; GC 2 (2013), *supra* n 93, paras 36, 44; GC 5, *supra* n 81, para 34; GC 21 (2009), *supra* n 93, para 40; GC 1 (2001), *supra* n 93, para 8; GC 4 (2003), *supra* n 93, para 69; GC 6 (2005), *supra* n 93, para 31(i); GC 7 (2005), *supra* n 93, paras 14, 28, 29, (a) and (d); GC 8, *supra* n 78, paras 2, 5, 7, 16, 17, 19, 21, 29; GC 14 (2013), *supra* n 93, para 2; GC 20 (2016), *supra* n 93, para 4.

263 *Marcia Cecilia Trujillo Calero* v. *Ecuador* (E/C.12/63/D/10/2015), CESCR, 14 November 2018, para 11.1.

264 GC 19 (2008) on the right to Social Security, paras 1–3.

265 *Marcia Cecilia Trujillo Calero* v. *Ecuador*, *supra* n 263, para 22.

266 *Simon Bacher* v. *Austria* (CRPD/C/19/D/26/2014), 6 April 2018, para 9.6.

267 *Mohamed Ben Djazia and Naouel Bellili* v. *Spain* (E/C.12/61/D/5/2015), CESCR, 21 July 2017, para 15.3; see also GC 4 (1991), *supra* n 248, paras 7, 8 (c), 13. See Special Rapporteur on adequate housing as a component of the right to an adequate standard of living, and on the right to non-discrimination in this context, and her report, A/HRC/31/54, paras 28–38.

268 *Khidirnazar Allakulov* v. *Uzbekistan* (CCPR/C/120/D/2430/2014), 22 August 2017, para 7.6; X v. *Sri Lanka*, *supra* n 140, para 7.6; X v. *United Republic of Tanzania* (CRPD/C/18/D/22/2014), CRPD, 5 October 2017, para 8.7; GC 16 (1988), *supra* n 93, para 11.

Thus, each reference to human dignity directs the human rights content by specifying what they imply and how they shall be respected and exercised. It is, perhaps, a call for closer attention to the inherent nature of both dignity and rights.

5.4 HUMAN DIGNITY AS AN OBLIGATION

As also introduced in the first chapter, the principle of human dignity acts as an obligation-creating principle. Positive and negative obligations derive directly from its legal substance and from its concretizations.

In a more nuanced conceptualization of negative and positive obligations, the universal system of human rights developed the tripartite typology of obligations to respect, protect, and fulfil,[269] which was originally associated to economic, social and cultural rights, and later developed to apply to all human rights.[270] The obligation to *respect* is a negative obligation, which requires States to not interfere with or curtail the enjoyment of human rights.[271] The obligation to *protect* is, instead, a positive obligation, demanding that States protect individuals and groups against abuses by others. Lastly, the obligation to *fulfil* also has a positive nature, requiring States to take an active role in facilitating the enjoyment of rights.[272] There are, however, variations of these typologies, with the initial framework being refined by additional layers, such as the obligation to promote and the obligation to facilitate,[273] around which there is no agreement on their scope and on their levels.[274]

Arguably, these flaws reflect the lack of clarity surrounding the typologies, which proved to be difficult to apply in practice.[275]

However, these typologies have the merit of showing the linkages between the various obligations, which also demonstrate that not all obligations fit in one category. More specifically, the obligations related to and manifesting

[269] See A Eide, 'Economic Social and Cultural Rights as Human Rights' in A Eide, C. Krause and A. Rosas (eds), *Economic Social and Cultural Rights. A Textbook* (Martinus Nijhoff 2001), 23ff.

[270] H Steiner, P Alston and R Goodman, *International Human Rights in Context* (3rd ed., Oxford University Press 2008), 180–185.

[271] M Nowak, *UN Covenant on Civil and Political Rights: CCPR Commentary* (2nd ed., Engel 2005), xxi.

[272] V Waisman, 'Human Trafficking: State Obligations to Protect Victims' Rights, the Current Framework and a New Due Diligence Standard' [2010] 33 *HICLR* 385, 406.

[273] See Steiner et al., *supra* n 270, 184.

[274] For an overview of the typologies proposed in legal scholarship, MM Sepulveda, *Nature of Obligation under the International Covenant of Economic Social and Cultural Rights* (Intersentia 2003), 157–172; P Mazzeschi, 'Responsabilité de l'Etat pour violation des obligations positives relatives aux droits de l'homme' [2008] 333 *RCADI* 243–249.

[275] Mazzeschi, *supra* n 274, 240–249.

human dignity, both in regional and international legal frameworks and in the case law of regional and international bodies, are mainly three: the obligation to respect, the obligation to protect, and the obligation to ensure, promote and foster ('fulfil') human dignity. This section thus analyses, in turn, these set of obligations, showing common patterns in their formulation and connections between them and with other manifestations of human dignity.

5.4.1 *Obligation to Respect Human Dignity*

The '*obligation to respect*' human dignity defines the duty to refrain and abstain from interfering with or curtailing the enjoyment of the dignity of persons.[276] In particular, this obligation is framed at the regional and international level in four main ways: (i) in simple form; (ii) as a derivative expression of the principle of respect for human dignity or the right to be treated with dignity; (iii) as a standard of implementation; (iv) as the ultimate objective of a different obligation.

First, it can be expressed with a formulation that, rather explicitly, refers directly to the duty to respect. For instance, Article 3 of the Universal Declaration on Bioethics and Human Rights declares that '[h]uman dignity, human rights and fundamental freedoms are to be fully respected'.[277] The ECtHR has reiterated on many occasions that 'the *very essence* of the Convention is respect for human dignity'.[278] Similarly, in the Inter-American legal system, human rights provisions expressly refer to the obligation to enhance respect for dignity.[279]

Second, the obligation to respect also arises from the adoption of two different manifestations of human dignity, namely *the principle of respect for human dignity* or the *right to be treated with dignity*. In this case, these instruments are used as a direct source of the obligation. In the first case, by way of example, GC No. 19 (2008) (on the right to social security (Article 9)) of the CESCR affirms that 'States parties must also pay *full respect to the principle of human dignity*

276 See Nowak, *supra* n 271, 37–41; M Scheinin, 'Economic and Social Rights as Legal Rights' in Eide et al., *supra* n 269, 32ff.

277 Art. 3, Universal Declaration on Bioethics and Human Rights; see also Art. 2, GA resolution 34/169, *supra* n 98; see also, in this form, Declaration on the Use of Scientific and Technological Progress, Preamble (2); Preamble, International Declaration on Human Genetic Data; GC 13 (2011), *supra* n 184, para 59; GC 21 (2017), *supra* n 259, para 32.

278 See *supra* 208; see also, on treatment during hospitalization, *Fernandes De Oliveira* v. *Portugal*, [GC], No. 78103/14, Judgment, 31 January 2019, para 112 (see also 69, 75); see also, on conditions of detention, *Khlaifia and Others* v. *Italy*, *supra* n 65, para 160, 169; on the respect for the dignity of persons in custody, see *Rooman* v. *Belgium*, *supra* n 215, para 143.

279 Art. 8, (g) 1994, Inter-American Convention on Violence against Women.

contained in the preamble of the Covenant'.[280] The HRC has also noted that Article 16 of the ICCPR, 'undoubtedly one of the most direct expressions of the principle of respect for the dignity of the human person in international human rights law',[281] 'requires the State party to show concern for the fate of every person and to treat everyone in a manner that *respects the inherent dignity of the human person*'.[282] Moreover, according to the ECtHR, states parties to the ECHR are under the 'obligation to guarantee' that the conditions of detention are 'compatible with the *principle of respect for their human dignity*, having regard to the absolute terms of Article 3 of the Convention'.[283]

By way of illustration of the second case, on the linkages between the obligation to respect and the right to be treated with dignity, the Convention on the Rights of the Child, for instance, affirms that '[e]very child deprived of liberty *shall be treated with humanity and respect for the inherent dignity of the human person*'.[284] Moreover, in 2014, the International Law Commission (ILC) adopted a set of 'Draft articles on the expulsion of aliens'. This text was submitted to the United Nations GA, which took note of it.[285] Of interest is Article 13, entitled '[o]bligation to respect the human dignity and human rights of aliens subject to expulsion', which expressly declares that '[a]ll aliens subject to expulsion *shall be treated with humanity and with respect for the inherent dignity* of the human person at all stages of the expulsion process' (para 1). Moreover, with regard to the prohibition of inhuman or degrading treatment, the ECtHR has reiterated in various instances that it is 'a value of civilisation closely bound up with respect for human dignity, part of the very essence of the Convention'.[286] Thus, a person detained should be under conditions that are compatible with respect for human dignity.[287]

280 GC 19, *supra* n 95, para 22.
281 *Mevlida Iĉić* v. *Bosnia and Herzegovina*, *supra* n 139, para 4 (emphasis added).
282 *Lounis Khelifati* v. *Algeria*, *supra* n 202, para 6.3 (emphasis added).
283 *Khlaifia and Others* v. *Italy*, *supra* n 65, Concurring Opinion of Judge Raimondi, para 4, p. 94.
284 Art. 37, (c), CRC (emphasis added); see also Art. 17, Universal Declaration on Bioethics and Human Rights; see also Art. 10, ICCPR; see also GA resolution 45/111, *supra* n 99, Principle 1; see also Art. 17, ICPMW; GC 9 (replaced by GC 21), *supra* n 93, para 1; GC 15 (1986), *supra* n 93, para 7; GC 20 (1992), *supra* n 93, para 2; GC 28, *supra* n 93, para 15; GC 29 (2001), *supra* n 93, para 13(a); GR 19, *supra* n 93, paras 14, 24; GR 24, *supra* n 93, paras 22 and 25; Joint GR 31 CEDAW/GC 18 UN CRC, *supra* n 93, para 14; GR 32 (2014), *supra* n 83, para 24 (l); GR 36, *supra* n 83, paras 57 and 69; GR 13 (1993), *supra* n 93, para 2; GR 29, *supra* n 83, para 1(a); GR 31 (2005) *supra* n 93, para 19; GC 2 (2013), *supra* n 93, paras 36, 44; GC 4 (2003), *supra* n 93, para 69; GC 7 (2005), *supra* n 93, para 29 (d); GC 8, *supra* n 78, paras 2, 5.
285 Resolution A/RES/69/119 10 December 2014.
286 See *Bouyid* v. *Belgium*, *supra* n 55, paras 81 and 89–90 (emphasis added).
287 See, for instance, *Muršić* v. *Croatia*, *supra* n 214, paras 47, 55 (obligation to respect), 56, 58, 98, 99, 100.

Thirdly, the obligation to respect dignity can also be the *standard of implementation* of a more specific obligation. This is normally the case when a provision indicates that a specific obligation should be performed 'with due respect'[288] or 'with due regard for'[289] human dignity. In this case, the protected good or obligation defined by the norm is different from human dignity, but the obligation to respect human dignity appears as a possible standard (or limit) for its implementation. The object of the provision may thus potentially cause conflict with the obligation to respect human dignity and constitute a harmful conduct to its inherent content. For this reason, the provision expressly refers to the need to maintain respect for human dignity, which acts as standard of application. For instance, the Protocol against the Smuggling of Migrants by Land, Sea and Air, supplementing the UN Convention against Transnational Organized Crime, states that '[e]ach State Party involved with the return of a person who has been the object of conduct set forth in article 6 of this Protocol shall take all appropriate measures to carry out the return in an orderly manner and with *due regard for the* safety and *dignity* of the person'.[290]

Lastly, the obligation to respect human dignity can also be formulated as the *ultimate objective* of a distinct and more specific obligation. This formulation occurs when a provision describes the protected good or obligation and human dignity is defined as complementary to its protection. This is normally the case when a provision indicates that a specific obligation should be performed 'in order to' respect human dignity. For instance, Article 15 of the Universal Declaration on the Human Genome and Human Rights reads 'States should take appropriate steps to provide the framework for the free exercise of Research on the human genome with due regard for the principles set out in this Declaration, *in order to safeguard respect for* human rights, fundamental freedoms *and human dignity*'.[291]

[288] Preamble, Universal Declaration on Bioethics and Human Rights.

[289] Art. 12, (a), Universal Declaration on the Human Genome and Human Rights; Art. 26, International Declaration on Human Genetic Data. Similarly, Rule 60 (1), Standard Minimum Rules for the Treatment of Prisoners, *supra* n 110.

[290] Art. 18 (5), Protocol against the Smuggling of Migrants by Land, Sea and Air, supplementing the UN Convention against Transnational Organized Crime; see also Art. 8 ('Removal'), Directive 2008/115/EC of the European Parliament and of the Council, 16 December 2008.

[291] Emphasis added.

5.4.2 *Obligation to Protect Human Dignity*

The '*obligation to protect*' human dignity,[292] recognized at the regional and international level, encompasses the duty to prevent third parties from interfering, protecting persons from mistreatment or abuse. The jurisprudence of the HRC as well as of regional bodies constitutes an important source of interpretation of this type of obligation. In particular, it finds expression in two main ways: (i) in a simple form; and (ii) as a derivative expression of the principle of respect for human dignity or the right to be treated with dignity.

In its first expression, it can be found in the practice of the HRC, which has affirmed the obligation to protect dignity in relation to Article 7, 10[293] and Article 17 of the ICCPR, on the right to have recognized reputation, honour and dignity.[294] This obligation is also normally combined with the obligation to respect and fulfil dignity.[295] The ECtHR has also affirmed that, as recognized by regional instruments,[296] the 'obligation to protect' human dignity requires the State to adopt or strengthen preventive measures.[297]

In its second expression, illustrations can be found in the jurisprudence of the IACtHR and of the African Commission. Pursuant to Article 5 of the Inter-American Convention, the Inter-American Court has clarified in various instances that the right to live in a situation of imprisonment 'compatible with the personal dignity'[298] implies the obligation for the State to protect a person's dignity.[299] Moreover, the African Commission, has reiterated this

292 Similarly, it also used the verb 'safeguard', see GC 21 (2017), *supra* n 259, para 27; see also *Blokhin* v. *Russia*, [GC], No. 47152/06, 23 March 2016, para 146.

293 *John-Jacques Lumbala Tshidika* v. *Democratic Republic of the Congo* (CCPR/C/115/D/2214/2012), 24 December 2015, para 6.5.

294 *Khidirnazar Allakulov* v. *Uzbekistan*, *supra* n 268, para 7.6; GC 16 (1988), *supra* n 93, para 11.

295 See, for instance, Guidelines on the Role of Prosecutors, 8th UN Congress on the Prevention of Crime and the Treatment of Offenders, 27 August to 7 September 1990, Art. 12; Art. 2, GA resolution 34/169, *supra* n 98.

296 Or 'obligation to safeguard dignity', see Preamble, Oviedo Convention on Human Rights and Biomedicine; Preamble, AP on Transplantation of Organs and Tissues of Human Origin; Preamble, AP on Genetic Testing for Health Purposes; Rec(2006)4, preamble and para 14 of Guidelines; CM/Rec(2016)6, preamble, art. 1 (Guidelines); Preamble, AP on Biomedical Research; Art. 6, (d), Convention on Action against Trafficking in Human Beings.

297 See, for instance, *Khlaifia and Others* v. *Italy*, *supra* n 65, paras 41 and 46; *Muršić* v. *Croatia*, *supra* n 214, paras 47, 55, 98, 99, 100; *Garib* v. *The Netherlands*, [GC], No. 43494/09, 6 November 2017, Dissenting Opinion of Judge Kūris, para 6, p. 79.

298 *López Álvarez*, *supra* n 67, paras 105–106; *García Asto and Ramírez Rojas*, *supra* n 67, para 221; *Raxcacó Reyes* v. *Guatemala*, *supra* n 67, para 95; *Miguel Castro-Castro Prison* v. *Peru*, *supra* n 67, paras 315, 321.

299 See *García Asto and Ramírez Rojas*, *supra* n 67, para 221; *Raxcacó Reyes* v. *Guatemala*, *supra* n 67, para 95; *Fermín Ramírez* v. *Guatemala*, Judgment of 20 June 2005, Series C No. 126, para 118; *Miguel Castro-Castro Prison* v. *Peru*, *supra* n 67, para 315; with regard to children's

obligation in cases related to conditions in detention and the right to be treated with dignity[300] and with regard to the right to food, described as 'inseparably linked to the dignity of human beings'.[301] This relationship, according to the African Commission, implies a positive obligation for the State 'to protect and improve existing food sources and to ensure access to adequate food for all citizens', coupled with the negative obligation 'not destroy or contaminate food sources'.[302]

5.4.3 *Obligation to Ensure, Promote and Foster Human Dignity*

States are under a duty to take all necessary measures to realize dignity, which may include taking appropriate legislative, administrative, budgetary, judicial and other actions toward the full realization of human dignity.[303] In particular, human rights documents refer to the following obligations: (i) obligation to *ensure* (the respect of) human dignity; (ii) obligation to *promote* respect for human dignity; (iii) obligation to *foster* (respect for) dignity.

The obligation to *ensure* dignity[304] is framed in three main forms. First, it can be expressed with a formulation that, in a rather simple and explicit form, refers directly to the duty to ensure the respect of dignity. For instance, the 2019 Global Compact for Safe, Orderly and Regular Migration declares that States shall foster institutional contacts (between consular authorities and relevant officials from countries of origin and destination), as well as provide adequate consular assistance to returning migrants, 'to ensure predictability, safety and dignity in return and readmission'.[305] Also, in Europe, regional human rights instruments refer to the obligation to ensure (full respect for)

rights, see *Atala Riffo and Daughters* v. *Chile*, *supra* n 70, para 108; *Gómez-Paquiyauri Brothers* v. *Peru*, *supra* n 67, Concurring Opinion of Ad Hoc Judge Francisco Eguiguren Praeli, p. 4; *The Río Negro Massacres* v. *Guatemala*, *supra* n 70, para 142 and Advisory Opinion No. 17, *supra* n 40, para 164.

300 *Purohit and Moore* v. *Gambia (The)*, *supra* n 76, para 61.

301 *SERAC and CESR* v. *Nigeria*, *supra* n 233, para 65.

302 *Ibid.*

303 See MC Craven, *The International Covenant on Economic Social and Cultural Rights. A Perspective on its Development* (Clarendon Press 1995), 107–114; Steiner et al., *supra* n 270, 182–184.

304 See Vienna Declaration and Programme of Action, principle 11, para 3, part I; Art. 23, CRC; Art. 24, CRPD; Global Compact for Safe, Orderly and Regular Migration, GA, 19 December 2018, A/RES/73/195, 11 January 2019, para 37(d), under Objective 21; Art. 20, (c) 1990, African Charter on the Rights and Welfare of the Child; Art. 40 (1), Arab Charter, 2004.

305 Global Compact, *supra* n 304, para 37(d), under Objective 21. See also International Declaration on Human Genetic Data, Art. 1; Vienna Declaration and Programme of Action, principle 11, para 3, part I; GC 2 (2013), *supra* n 93, para 44.

dignity, often in the legal frameworks on biomedicine and on the protection of asylum seekers.[306] The ECtHR has also held that 'a positive obligation exists upon States to ensure respect for human dignity'.[307]

Moreover, like the obligation to respect human dignity, the obligation to ensure dignity can also act as a *standard of implementation*. This formulation is mostly adopted in cases where human dignity acts as a qualifying force of specific rights, such as the right to live with dignity[308] or with regard to humane treatment in detention.[309] Lastly, the obligation to ensure dignity can also be formulated as the *ultimate objective* of a distinct and more specific obligation.[310] For instance, GC No. 21 (2017) on children in street situations, reads that '[s]tates should also put in place procedural and practical funeral arrangements *to ensure dignity* and respect for children who die on the streets'.[311]

The obligation to *promote* dignity, instead, is normally expressed in combination with the obligation to respect and protect human dignity.[312] Thus, like the obligation to respect and ensure human dignity, also the obligation to promote dignity can act as the *standard of implementation* of a distinct obligation.[313] By way of example, GC No. 7 (2005) on implementing child rights in early childhood, urges '[s]tates parties to incorporate the particular situation of young children into all legislation, policies and interventions to promote physical and psychological recovery and social reintegration *within an environment that promotes dignity* and self-respect'.[314]

306 Preamble, Oviedo Convention on Human Rights and Biomedicine; Council Directive 2004/83/EC, of 29 April 2004, para (10); see Regulation (Eu) No 604/2013 of the European Parliament and of the Council of 26 June 2013, art. 24; Directive 2011/95/EU of the European Parliament and of the Council of 13 December 2011, para (16).

307 See *Dordević* v. *Croatia*, *supra* n 56, para 152.

308 GC 9 (2006), *supra* n 93, para 11; *Dordević* v. *Croatia*, *supra* n 56, para 152; *L.* v. *Lithuania*, No. 27527/03, ECtHR 2007–IV, 11 September 2007, para 56; mutatis mutandis, *Pretty* v. *United Kingdom*, *supra* n 58, para 65.

309 *Mozer* v. *The Republic of Moldova and Russia*, [GC], No. 11138/10, 23 February 2016, para 178; *Muršić* v. *Croatia supra* n 214, para 100, see also Joint Partly Dissenting Opinion of Judges Sajó, López Guerra and Wojtyczek, para 7, p. 67.

310 See Art. 24, CRPD; International Declaration on Human Genetic Data, Art. 7 (a); GC 36, *supra* n 86, para 62 (emphasis added); see also GR 25, *supra* n 259, para 19; GC 8 (2006), *supra* n 120, paras 19, 27; GC 21 (2017), *supra* n 259, para 32.

311 GC 21 (2017), *supra* n 259, para 32.

312 Art. 2 Universal Declaration on Bioethics and Human Rights; see also Preamble, (y), Art. 1, CRPD, Preamble (y); Art. 1; see also GC 14 (2013), *supra* n 93, para 5; GC 21 (2017), *supra* n 259, para 28.

313 Art. 40(1), CRC (emphasis added); see also Principle 11, (a), Guidelines for Action on Children; GC 7 (2005), *supra* n 93, para 37.

314 GC 7 (2005), *supra* n 93, para 37.

Similarly, the obligation to *foster* dignity is normally expressed in a direct form[315] and together with other obligations. Thus, like the obligation to respect, ensure and promote human dignity, also the obligation to foster dignity is adopted as a *standard of implementation* of a different obligation. For instance, GC No. 4 (2003) on adolescent health and development in the context of the CRC, makes clear that adolescents 'have the right to physical and psychological recovery and social reintegration *in an environment that fosters* health, self-respect and *dignity*'.[316] This formulation implies that the right to physical and psychological recovery and social reintegration should be implemented with due regard to the obligation to foster human dignity. The obligation to foster dignity can also at times be expressed as the *ultimate objective* of specific conducts.[317]

5.5 HUMAN DIGNITY VERSUS SOVEREIGN DIGNITY

Mapping human dignity through its manifestations in human rights law allows one to trace how far the circle of human dignity has gone to conquer the space originally covered by the first circle, namely sovereign dignity. Like in international humanitarian law (IHL), human dignity manifests itself in IHRL as a deontological principle, defining what is a morally mandatory conduct and triggering deontological constraints. Human dignity in IHRL is not based on a 'consequentialist logic' but rather allows a clearly distinction between right or wrong according to a set of rules based on its core content. This 'deontological' character is transferred in all the other instruments, such as rights and obligations, that manifest (and derive from) human dignity. Each right protects the individual from intrusions, by the State or otherwise, which constitute an assault and attack to the essence of dignity. Such rights thus are granted a special protection.

For this inherent character, the principle of human dignity, the mother-right dignity, its derivative rights and obligations can act as limits to the full operation of sovereign dignity. This can be seen in the operativity of human dignity in two examples: in the case of derogations to human rights law (Section 5.5.1); and, second, with regard to the so-called 'unilateral coercive

[315] See, for instance, Art. 8, (a), CRPD; Art. 1, (a) Cairo Declaration of Human Rights in Islam, which uses the verb 'enhance'.

[316] GC 4 (2003), *supra* n 93, para 37 (emphasis added); see also GC 8 (2006), *supra* n 120, para 37; GC 3 (2012), *supra* n 145, para 36; Art. 39, CRC; see also Art. 16, CRPD.

[317] Art. 2(3), C107 Indigenous and Tribal Populations Convention; GC 36, *supra* n 86, para 50; GC 3 (2012), *supra* n 145, para 4 (see also 12, 16).

measures' (UCMs) (Section 5.5.2). These are two vantage points from which a much wider reflection on human dignity in international law can be conducted and helpful to the understanding of the transformation international law has undergone, particularly since the end of the Second World War.

5.5.1 *Derogations and Human Dignity*

In times of serious public emergency, the framework of IHRL presents some flexibility and a margin of adjustment to face challenging national events by allowing states to derogate from certain human rights provisions without violating their obligations under the human rights treaties.[318] However, State powers are not without limits. Beyond the requirement of notification,[319] IHRL sets specific conditions under which a derogation to human rights can be justified.

First, states cannot derogate to non-derogable rights. The list of non-derogable rights differs from one international instrument to another. The ECHR[320] includes the right to life,[321] prohibition of torture and ill-treatments,[322] prohibition of slavery,[323] and no punishment without law.[324] Interestingly, the Arab Charter also expands the list to the right to liberty and security,[325] to the freedom to leave one's country[326] and to the right to seek political asylum.[327] The HRC has clarified that certain rights are defined as

[318] ICCPR, art. 4; ACHR, art. 27; ECHR, art. 15. The ACommHPR does not contain a derogation clause. See *Media Rights Agenda and Constitutional Rights Project* v. *Nigeria*, ACommHPR, Comm. Nos. 105/93, 128/94, 130/94, 152/96, 31 October 1998, paras 67–70. See also HRC, GC 29: Derogations during a State of Emergency, CCPR/C/21/Rev.1/Add.11, 31 August 2001.

[319] Art. 4(1) ICCPR also asks for an official recognition of the emergency. See also GC 29, *supra* n 318, para 2. See also *Zambrano Vélez et al.* v. *Ecuador*, Judgment, IACtHR, 4 July 2007, para 70.

[320] Additional protocols to the ECHR include clauses excluding derogation to the abolition of death penalty (see Protocols 6 and 13), the principle *ne bis in idem* (see Protocol 7). See C Schreuer, 'Derogation of Human Rights in Situations of Public Emergency: The Experience of the European Convention on Human Rights' [1982] 9 *YJIL* 113,129.

[321] Art. 2 ECHR; Art. 6 ICCPR; Art. 4 ACHR; Art. 5 Arab Charter.

[322] Art. 3 ECHR; Art. 7 ICCPR; Art. 5 ACHR; Art. 8; see also Art. 9 Arab Charter.

[323] Art. 4 ECHR (slavery and forced labor); Art. 8 ICCPR (slavery, servitude, but not including forced labor); Art. 6 ACHR (slavery and forced labor); Art. 10 Arab Charter (slavery and forced labor).

[324] Art. 7 ECHR; Art. 15 ICCPR; Art. 9 ACHR; Art. 15 Arab Charter.

[325] Art. 14 Arab Charter.

[326] Art. 27 Arab Charter.

[327] Art. 28 Arab Charter.

non-derogable on the basis of four reasons:[328] (i) since 'their suspension is irrelevant to the legitimate control of the state of national emergency'; (ii) because 'derogation may indeed be impossible' for certain rights like freedom of conscience; (iii) 'because without them there would be no rule of law'; and (iv) because of their status as peremptory norms, which according to the Vienna Convention on the Laws of Treaties excludes any derogation.[329] The Committee has also clarified that there are other rights that, in the Committee's opinion, cannot be made subject to lawful derogation under Article 4. Some illustrative examples, among others, include that 'All persons deprived of their liberty shall be treated with humanity and with respect for the inherent dignity of the human person.'[330] In the words of the Committee

> [A]lthough this right, prescribed in article 10 of the Covenant, is not separately mentioned in the list of non-derogable rights in article 4, paragraph 2, the Committee believes that here the Covenant expresses a norm of general international law not subject to derogation. This is supported by the reference to the *inherent dignity* of the human person in the preamble to the Covenant and by the close connection between articles 7 and 10.[331]

Thus, the recognition and protection of human dignity in the ICCPR, according to the HRC, is not only a reason to support the non-derogability of some rights but also an inherent reason to expand the list of non-derogable rights included in the ICCPR. The HRC reiterated this view also in its statement on derogations from the ICCPR in connection with the COVID-19 pandemic,[332] where it insisted on the States' duty 'to treat all persons, including persons deprived of their liberty, *with humanity and respect for their human dignity*'.[333]

Second, the ECHR also states that derogating measures must be 'strictly required by the exigencies of the situation' and 'not inconsistent with its other obligations under international law' and that measures cannot discriminate between national and non-nationals.[334] Thus, strict necessity requires evidence of a link between the situation and the measures as

[328] GC 23, Issues Relating to Reservations Made upon Ratification or Accession to the Covenant or the Optional Protocols thereto, or in Relation to Declarations under Article 41 of the Covenant, CCPR/C/21/Rev.1.Add.6, 11 November 1994, para 10.

[329] Vienna Convention on the Laws of Treaties, 23 May 1969, UNTS vol. 1155, p. 331, Art. 53.

[330] GC 29, *supra* n 318, para 13.

[331] *Ibid.*, para 13 (a).

[332] HRC, Statement on derogations from the Covenant in connection with the COVID-19 pandemic, CCPR/C/128/2, 24 April 2020.

[333] *Ibid.*, para 2(e) (emphasis added).

[334] *A and others* v. *The United Kingdom*, [GC], No. 3455/05, 19 February 2009, para 190; see also ICCPR, Art. 4(1). See also IACtHR, Advisory Opinion No. 18, *supra* n 42, para 101.

well as that no other measures could have been adopted to face the emergency. The HRC has stated, in its GC No. 29 on Article 4 of the ICCPR, that the principle of proportionality is indeed 'common to derogation and limitation powers'.[335] In this assessment, it is clear how human dignity and derivative rights play a role in directly constraining sovereign dignity. Protected non-derogable rights, of particular importance to secure the dignity of individuals and to guarantee their survival in situations of emergency,[336] restrict the authority of the State and its powers of derogation and interference.

5.5.2 *Unilateral Coercive Measures and Human Dignity*[337]

The terms 'reprisal', 'retorsion', 'countermeasure', 'sanction' and 'UCM', among several others, differ in their scope and implications, sometimes in important ways, but they also share a deeper dimension, that is, the self-assessed and horizontal nature of the response to an event or action from another entity. This turns the question of 'horizontal responses' – to use a neutral term – into much more than the analysis of a specific concept; more accurately, the question unveils the inner structure of the international legal order and the transformation and shift it has gone through.

International law, as law in general, is a language, and the selection of specific terms depends on what a proposition is intended to convey, not to convey or to leave ambiguous. Thus, whereas the term 'retorsion' is unambiguously used to convey action which is inimical but lawful, the terms 'reprisal' or, at present, 'countermeasure' convey action which is normally unlawful except for the reason that it is justified as a response to prior unlawful conduct. The use of these terms does not say much about their unilateral or collective nature. The term 'sanction' instead conveys the idea that it is a reaction to illegality adopted in a concerted (collective) manner, typically acting within or prompted by an international organization, although unilateral sanctions are also possible. The term UCM emphasises both the 'unilateral' and the 'coercive' nature of the measure, but both features remain

335 GC 29, *supra* n 318, para 4.

336 See J Fitzpatrick, *Human Rights in Crisis* (University of Pennsylvania Press 1994), 64; A. Müller, 'Limitations to and Derogations from Economic, Social and Cultural Rights' [2009] 9 *HRLR* 557–601, 562.

337 This section draws upon G Le Moli and JE Viñuales, 'Today as Yesterday? Unilateral Coercive Measures and Human Dignity' [2019] 18(2) *Chinese JIL* 437–447.

ambiguous.[338] 'Unilateral' is not understood as action by a single State but, rather, as action which has not been required or authorized by an international organization which has the power to do so. 'Coercive' is intended to be more than merely inimical but not necessarily unlawful. Such is the – rather wide – scope ascribed to the very terminology of UCMs.

In such a context, asking whether UCMs are lawful or unlawful is self-defeating, because the very expression has been coined to cover action that is unlawful and unjustified, unlawful but justified, *and* lawful but inimical. In other words, it is an artificially created dilemma, the answer to which must begin with a reformulation of the problem. But the deeper question of how far the exercise of 'private justice'[339] can be recognized in international law remains essential. The question of UCMs shows the degree of transformation of international law from a horizontal to a mixed 'horizontal-vertical' legal order. This transformation is manifested by the values (such as the main one, human dignity) from which limits to private justice (that only convey that private justice is legally recognized to some extent) increasingly arise and the legal mechanisms through which they find expression. When considered together, these values and mechanisms instil a significant degree of verticality in the international legal order.

The two major strands of the contemporary debate on private justice concern economic coercion[340] and 'third-party' or 'collective' or, still, 'general interest' countermeasures.[341] In the first case, the debate unfolds mostly at the level of the primary norm (is the exercise of economic coercion a breach of a primary norm of conduct, particularly a norm of general international law?). The debate relating to the second strand unfolds instead at the level of secondary norms (can a State other than the 'injured State' adopt countermeasures against a State which has breached international law?). The

338 Research-based progress report of the Human Rights Council Advisory Committee containing recommendations on mechanisms to assess the negative impact of unilateral coercive measures on the enjoyment of human rights and to promote accountability, A/HRC/28/74, 10 February 2015, paras 7–13.

339 D Alland, *Justice privée et ordre juridique international. Etude théorique des contre-mesures en droit international public* (Pedone 1994).

340 See e.g. A Hofer, 'The Developed/Developing Divide on Unilateral Coercive Measures: Legitimate Enforcement or Illegitimate Intervention?' [2017] 16 *Chinese JIL* 175. See generally D Bowett, 'Economic Coercion and Reprisals by State' [1972] 13 *VJIL* 1; L Boisson de Chazournes, *Les contre-mesures dans les relations économiques internationales* (Pedone/IUHEI 1992).

341 See M Akehurst, 'Reprisals by Third States' [1970] 44 *BYIL* 1; LA Sicilianos, *Les réactions décentralisées à l'illicite, des contre-mesures à la légitime défense* (LGDJ 1990); D Alland, 'Countermeasures of General Interest' [2002] 13 *EJIL* 1221; M Davidowicz, *Third-Party Countermeasures in International Law* (Cambridge University Press 2017).

distinction between the level of primary and secondary norms is useful to frame the, sometimes confusing, terms of the more specific debate over UCMs and human rights.

As noted earlier, UCMs is an expression coined to encompass three main hypotheses: (i) action which is unlawful (under a primary norm) and unjustified (under secondary norms); (ii) action which is unlawful (under a primary norm) but justified (under secondary norms); and (iii) action which is inimical but lawful (under the applicable primary norms). Analytically, any attempt to consider UCMs unlawful must therefore turn hypotheses (ii) and (iii) into hypothesis (i). To turn (ii) into (i), the analysis will unfold under the conditions for justification of otherwise unlawful action, particularly the conditions for the adoption of a valid countermeasure. This applies to countermeasures by both the 'injured State' (whose action will be assessed in the light of the conditions for valid countermeasures) and third States (here the ILC Articles are of limited help, but the question of third States' 'entitlement' to adopt countermeasures remains one governed by secondary norms). To turn (iii) into (i), the analysis will begin instead at the level of the primary norm before moving to the level of secondary norms. Is the UCM in question a breach of a primary norm of conduct? The answer can be sought in the primary norms arising from a treaty, but a general assessment will need to pay particular attention to primary norms arising from general international law and hence applicable to all. Only in the case a primary norm is breached will the analysis move to the level of secondary norms, and it will be similar to that conducted for hypothesis (ii).

Importantly, in theory, this analytical cartography is applicable irrespective of whether the analysis of lawfulness (breach of a primary norm) or justification (under secondary norms) is conducted by one of the States involved (the self-assessment of a private justice situation) or by a third party *ex post facto*. In practice, however, who conducts the assessment makes a world of difference. The recognition of private justice or, to continue with the neutral terminology used earlier, of 'horizontal responses' assumes that States themselves are recognized as possessing the power to assess the legality of the action of another State, irrespective of any involvement of a third party (e.g. an adjudicator). Limits to UCMs arise more and more from fundamental values recognized at the international level. In particular, the value of human dignity has found expression in international law through different legal instruments, understood here as ways of formulating a norm (principles, obligations, rights, crimes). These instruments, most widely relied upon in specific areas of law, have introduced important limits to private justice in general and to certain forms of UCMs specifically, making them unlawful and widening the forums before which they can be characterized as such.

The manifestations of 'human dignity' in international law have taken many forms, including primary norms of conduct (as discussed – human rights and their correlative obligations for States), the violation of which can be reviewed by a dense network of courts and committees, as well as secondary norms, such as the rules formulated in Article 50(1)(b) and (c) of the ILC Articles, which transform certain primary norms of human rights and humanitarian law into secondary norms placing conditions for the validity of countermeasures.

Such legal manifestations of human dignity have turned a range of actions/omissions falling under the hypotheses (ii) and (iii) described above into hypothesis (i). As discussed in this chapter, IHRL expresses the centrality of human dignity, which is recognized as a foundational principle of the international legal order a as well as a primary 'mother' human right, which are a both sources of obligations. The recognition of human dignity has also translated considerations of humanity into a series of legal norms, both 'primary' and 'secondary', also in other areas of international law, as IHL, as discussed in Chapter 4, and international criminal law, as Chapter 6 will examine. As seen, these instruments that express human dignity can transform measures from lawful into unlawful, under the applicable primary norms, placing important limitations on the lawfulness of 'horizontal responses' or UCMs.

Because human dignity is distinct from the traditional interests of States, that is, the interests a State can dispose of transactionally, and because the legal expressions of human dignity in international law, both through certain instruments (principles, obligations, human rights and international crimes) and through certain institutions (adjudicatory and quasi-adjudicatory bodies), exclude or significantly limit the horizontal or transactional dimension of classical international law, their implications are far-reaching. They cannot be merely seen as traditional limitations to unilateral action (e.g. the principle of non-intervention, the prohibition of the use of force, encroachments on the territorial integrity of a State, etc.). A State can authorize another State to intervene in its internal affairs, but it does not have the legal power to permit other States to encroach on the manifestations of human dignity of the peoples and individuals under its jurisdiction.

Some of dignity's legal manifestations are 'primary norms' that specifically aim to protect human dignity by banning or restricting certain conduct. Thus, conduct under hypothesis (iii) in violation of such primary norms is no longer merely inimical; it is unlawful. Importantly, these primary norms are to a significant extent taken up and made to perform also the function of 'secondary norms' limiting the possibility of justification, thus making the bulk of situations which are unlawful under (iii) also unjustified, hence moving from (iii) and (ii) directly to (i) in a single blow. Indeed, Article 50(1) of the ILC Articles clearly states that 'countermeasures shall not affect [...] (a) obligations for the protection of fundamental human rights; (b) obligations of a humanitarian character prohibiting reprisals'.[342] This understanding of the limitations on countermeasures has deep historical roots. In a resolution dating back to 1934, the *Institut de droit international* declared that a State must 'abstain from any harsh measure which would be contrary to the laws of humanity or the demands of the public conscience'.[343] The same logic underpins more recent illustrations of such limitations. Due to the collateral effects on civilian populations, economic sanctions 'should always take full account' of the provisions of the ICESCR.[344] The safeguards of IHL have been established primarily to protect civilians in times of war, but 'there is no reason why those safeguards should not apply to economic sanctions imposed in the course of or outside an armed conflict'.[345] Importantly, Article 50(1)(d) of the ILC Articles reaffirms, in line with Article 26, that the circumstances precluding wrongfulness described in chapter V of Part One do not affect the wrongfulness of any act of a State not in accordance with an obligation set by a peremptory norm of international law.

Therefore, the legal manifestations of the fundamental value of human dignity are able to touch upon both primary and secondary norms rendering an action unlawful (under a primary norm) and unjustified (under secondary norms), and thereby moving from (iii) to (i) in a single stroke.

Two conclusions can be drawn from the analysis above. First, the subset of actions/omissions that are in violation of certain legal manifestations of human dignity (e.g. certain principles, obligations, human rights, international crimes) can thus be analysed under this more granular analytical cartography. At this analytical level, there is a significant difference between norms governing 'horizontal' or transactional relations among States and

342 Draft articles on Responsibility of States for Internationally Wrongful Acts, with commentaries 2001, See Portuguese Colonies case (*Naulilaa incident*), II RIAA 1011 (1928), 1026.

343 Annuaire de l'Institut de Droit International, vol. 38 (1934), 710.

344 E/C.12/1997/8, para 1.

345 Report of the Special Rapporteur on the negative impact of unilateral coercive measures on the enjoyment of human rights, A/HRC/39/54, 10–28 September 2018, 9, which, for instance, makes references to the reimposition of a comprehensive trade embargo on the Islamic Republic of Iran in May 2018 by the USA; HP Gasser, 'Collective Economic Sanctions and International Humanitarian Law. An Enforcement Measure under the UN Charter and the Right of Civilians to Immunity: An Unavoidable Clash of Policy Goals?' [1996] 56 *ZaöRV* 871–880.

norms expressing human dignity: whereas in the first case, a two-step analysis is normally – but not always[346] – required (i.e. the conduct is unlawful under a given primary norm and it is not justified under secondary norms), moving from (iii) to (ii) and then to (i), in the second case the very primary norms that make a conduct unlawful are subsequently made to play at the level of secondary norms to make it also unjustified, thus moving from (iii) to (i) in one stroke. This is not the case for every legal manifestation of human dignity in international law but of a substantial part of them (Article 50(1)(b), (c) and (d) of the ILC Articles).

Second, the nature of human dignity as a value and its legal and institutional expression add a strong component of verticality in the assessment of UCMs. This has important implications both at the theoretical and practical levels. At the theoretical level, the exercise of 'private justice' is deprived of one of its fundamental corollaries, that is, the possibility of 'transacting' justice. Human dignity cannot be given away by either the State who takes the initial action or by the State that adopts a horizontal response. Cooperation remains, of course, possible but only to protect human dignity, with no lawfully recognized concession on this front (as an example, one can think of the forced population exchanges of classical international law, which were recognized despite their encroachment on human dignity).

Thus, perhaps the main manifestation of the horizontal structure of classical international law, namely enforcement through reprisals, is now placed under a new 'vertical' light stemming from the legal expressions of human dignity. At the practical level, a constitutive aspect of reprisals (and of private justice in general), that is, the self-assessment of the lawfulness of the situation to which the horizontal action responds, is also significantly limited, because it is increasingly brought under the remit of a dense network of courts and committees with power to legally assess the situation. Over the last century and a half, the effects of human dignity are felt virtually everywhere, even in the strongholds of the old horizontal logic, such as reprisals or countermeasures.

346 The main example is the prohibition of the use of force, which operates both as a primary norm and as a limitation to the validity of countermeasures.

6

Human Dignity in International Criminal Law

6.1 INTRODUCTION

The path of human dignity in international criminal law (ICL) has been marked by two main phases, through which it slowly turned into an actionable concept. As discussed in Chapter 3, immediately after the Second World War, the protection of dignity crystallized in the Nuremberg Principles. In the mid-1990s, after the creation of the ad hoc tribunals, the International Criminal Tribunal for the former Yugoslavia (ICTY) and International Criminal Tribunal for Rwanda (ICTR),[1] the highest point of the consolidation of human dignity in ICL was reached with the adoption of the Statute of the International Criminal Court (ICC) and the subsequent establishment of the Court.[2] The ICC began its work as the first *permanent forum* of international criminal justice in 2003.[3]

1 Statute of the International Tribunal for the Prosecution of Persons Responsible for Serious Violations of International Humanitarian Law Committed in the Territory of the Former Yugoslavia since 1991, Annex to Security Council S/RES/827, 25 May 1993 [ICTY Statute] and Statute of the International Tribunal for Rwanda, Annex to S/RES/955, 8 November 1994 [ICTR Statute].

2 Rome Statute of the International Criminal Court (last amended 2010), 17 July 1998 (ICC Statute).

3 See RS Lee (ed.), *The International Criminal Court. The Making of the Rome Statute* (Kluwer Law International 1999); M Politi and G Nesi (eds), *The Rome Statute of the International Criminal Court* (Routledge 2001); A Cassese, P Gaeta and JRWD Jones (eds), *The Rome Statute of the International Criminal Court: A Commentary* (Oxford University Press 2002); D McGoldrick, P Rowe and E Donnelly, *The Permanent International Criminal Court* (Hart 2004); C Kreß, 'The International Criminal Court as a Turning Point in the History of International Criminal Justice' in A Cassese (ed.), *The Oxford Companion to International Criminal Justice* (Oxford University Press 2009), 143; O Triffterer and K Ambos, *The Rome Statute of the International Criminal Court A Commentary* (3rd ed., Beck/Hart 2016); WA Schabas, *The International Criminal Court A Commentary on the Rome Statute* (Oxford University Press 2016); C Stahn, *The Law and Practice of the International Criminal Court* (Oxford University Press 2015).

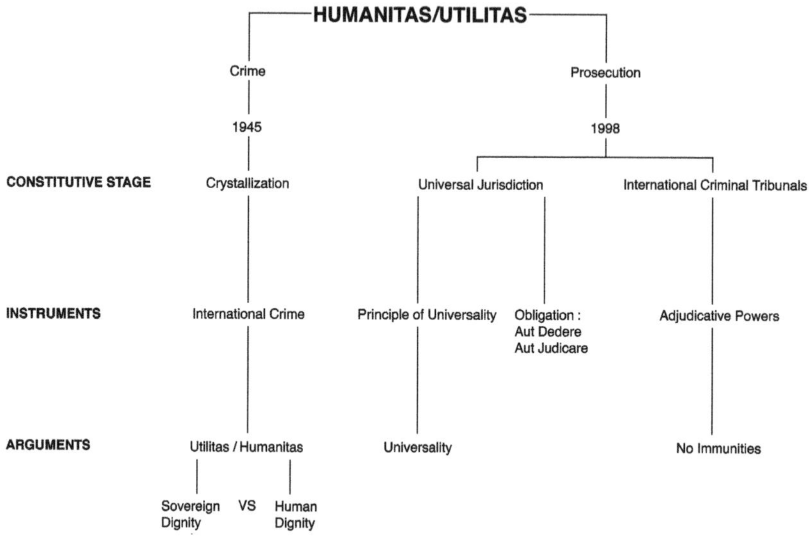

FIGURE 6.1 *Human dignity and international criminal law*

The ICC Statute represents the first comprehensive codification of international crimes and of the principles of the international criminal system. In particular, human dignity arose and evolved at different paces, following the development of these two constitutive pillars. Figure 6.1 summarizes this structural evolution.

The distinction between crimes and prosecution, and therein, between domestic and international enforcement, constitute the foundational architecture of this chapter, where I examine the main manifestations and instruments through which human dignity is expressed in ICL. The dual structure (crimes and prosecution) shares a common root, namely the protection of *humanitas*. The ICC Statute represents the legal foundation and starting point of the analysis. In particular, in Section 6.2, the instrument *crime* is examined, by analysing three main crimes, the crime of genocide, crimes against humanity and war crimes. The selection is dictated by the role given to human dignity as protected good, both in their definition as international crimes and in the related practice. Section 6.3, instead, looks into the relationship between *humanitas* and international prosecution. Reasons of *humanitas* change the nature of the prosecution normally assigned to ordinary crimes. The prosecution is internationalized on two levels: at the national level, through the principle of universal jurisdiction and the obligation *aut dedere aut judicare*; at the international level, through the establishment of a system organized at the international level to prosecute *hostes humani generis* and bring justice to victims of international crimes. The adoption of a permanent court consolidates a system of protection of human dignity. As will be seen in this chapter, human dignity is thus able to shape not only the definition of the core international crimes but also the nature of their prosecutorial system, acquiring, in turn, an actionable nature. In this process, which is still ongoing, as it is discussed in Section 6.4, the circle of human dignity exercises a normative power capable of slowly and partially displacing the circle of sovereign dignity.

6.2 INTERNATIONAL CRIMES

6.2.1 *Genocide*

The prohibition of genocide is a peremptory norm of international law (*jus cogens*) and an *erga omnes* obligation of States.[4] Despite the adoption of the Genocide Convention in 1948,[5] the history of the prosecution of this crime

4 ICJ, *Reservations to the Convention on the Prevention and Punishment of the Crime of Genocide, International Court of Justice, Advisory Opinion* (1951) ICJ Reports 1951, p. 23; *Case Concerning the Application of the Convention on the Prevention and Punishment of the Crime of Genocide* (*Bosnia and Herzegovina* v. *Yugoslavia*) (1996) ICJ Reports 1996, 595, para 31; *Application of the Convention on the Prevention and Punishment of the Crime of Genocide* (*Bosnia and Herzegovina* v. *Serbia and Montenegro*) (2007) ICJ Reports 2007, para 161 [*Genocide Case*]; *Prosecutor* v. *Akayesu*, ICTR-96-4-T, 2 September 1998, para 495 [*Akayesu*]; *Prosecutor* v. *Blagojević and Jokić*, IT-02-60-T, 17 January 2005, ICTY, para 639 [*Prosecutor* v. *Blagojević and Jokić*] with further references in note 2053; see G Mettraux, *International Crimes and the ad Hoc Tribunals* (Oxford University Press 2005), 199. On *jus cogens* and obligation *erga omnes* concerning international crimes, see MC Bassiouni, *Introduction to International Criminal Law* (Martinus Nijhoff 2013), 155, 236–246. On the customary international law aspect, see M Salter and M Eastwood, 'Establishing the Foundations' in P Behrens and R Henham (eds), *Elements of Genocide* (Routledge 2013), 26 ff; E Wilmshurst, 'Genocide' in R Cryer, H Friman, D Robinson and E Wilmshurst (eds), *An Introduction to International Criminal Law and Procedure* (3rd ed., Cambridge University Press 2014), chapter 10, 205.

5 Convention on the Prevention and Punishment of the Crime of Genocide, 9 December 1948, 78 UNTS 277 [Genocide Convention]. For an analysis see (Chapter 3 Section 3.3.4.1). Moreover, on the history of the adoption of the Genocide Convention, see PN Drost, *The Crime of State, vol. II: Genocide* (AW Sythoff 1959), 1ff; J Dülffer, 'The United Nations and the Origins of the Genocide Convention 1946–1948' in CJM Safferling and E Conze (eds), *The Genocide Convention Sixty Years after its Adoption* (Asser Press 2010), 55; JL Kunz, 'The United Nations Convention on Genocide' [1949] 43 *AJIL* 738; P Akhavan, *Reducing Genocide to Law* (Cambridge University Press 2012); M Lippman, 'The Drafting and Development of the 1948 Convention on Genocide and the Politics of International Law' in HG van der Wilt et al. (eds), *The Genocide Convention: The Legacy of 60 Years* (Martinus Nijhoff 2012), 15; N Robinson, *The Genocide Convention. A Commentary* (World Jewish Congress 1960) 17 ff.; WA Schabas, *Genocide in International Law, The Crime of Crimes* (2nd ed., Cambridge University Press 2009), 17 ff, 59 ff; Y Shany, 'The Road to the Genocide Convention and Beyond' in P Gaeta (ed.), *The UN Genocide Convention. A Commentary* (Oxford University Press 2009), 3; Y Ternon, *L'État criminel, les Génocides au XX siècle* (Seuil 1995), 17 ff, 39 ff.

shows that it would nearly take 50 years before international criminal tribunals, the ICTY and ICTR, were created to deal specifically with it, though with temporal and territorial limitations.[6] In 1998, the establishment of the ICC meant a stable international institution now existed for the prosecution of the crime of genocide.[7] Article II of the Genocide Convention defined the crime, reflecting the *ius cogens* norm.[8] During the drafting process of the ICC Statute, delegates maintained the same definition as the one adopted in the Genocide Convention.[9] Thus, Article 6 of the ICC Statute mirrors Article II of the Genocide Convention and is the basis of the following analysis.

The historical path of the international recognition of this crime was discussed in relation to the consolidation of human dignity in Chapter 3. For the purpose of this study, although acknowledging the many issues (and vast literature) related to the crime of genocide,[10] the discussion will be limited to the analysis of the protected interest and legal good of human dignity.

6 A review of ICTY's jurisprudence on the crime of genocide can be found in S Malmström, 'Genocide Case Law at the ICTY' in R Bellelli (ed.), *International Criminal Justice* (Routledge 2010), 267. On the ICTR, see RS Lee, 'The Rwanda Tribunal' [1996] 9 *LJIL* 37; V Morris and M Scharf, *The International Criminal Tribunal for Rwanda* (Transnational 1998); DDN Nsereko, 'Genocidal Conflict in Rwanda and the ICTR' [2001] 48 *NILR* 31. On the Tribunals' jurisprudence, see GW Mugwanya, *The Crime of Genocide in International Law* (Cameron May 2007); G Verdirame, 'The Genocide Convention in the Jurisprudence of the ad hoc Tribunals' [2000] 49 *ICLQ* 578; WA Schabas, 'Genocide Trials and Gacaca Courts' [2005] 3 *JICJ* 879.

7 For an overview of national prosecutions of genocide, see H Kreicker, 'National Prosecution of Genocide from a Comparative Perspective' [2005] 5 *ICLR* 313; WJ van der Wolf and D de Ruiter (eds), *Genocide on Trial* (Wolf Legal 2011), 11 ff.

8 Chapter 3 presented the debates about the notion of genocide during the negotiation process, see Section 3.3.4.1. See *Armed Activities on the Territory of the Congo* (New Application: 2002) (*Democratic Republic of the Congo* v. *Rwanda*) (2006) ICJ Reports 2006, p. 3, para 64; *Genocide Case*, para 161; *Prosecutor* v. *Jelisic*, IT-95-10-T, 14 December 1999, ICTY, para 60 [*Jelisić*]; *Prosecutor* v. *Krstić*, IT-98-33-T, 2 August 2001, ICTY, para 541 [*Krstić*]; *Akayesu*, para 495; *Prosecutor* v. *Karadžić*, IT-95-5/18, Trial Chamber, 24 March 2016, para 539. *Jorgić* v. *Germany*, no. 74613/01, ECHR 2007–III, para 68; Report by the UN Secretary-General of 3 May 1993 on the ICTY Statute, S/25704 (1993), para 35; A Cassese, *International Criminal Law* (3rd ed., Oxford University Press 2013), 113. The wording of the crime in the Genocide Convention was adopted verbatim into Article 4(2) ICTY Statute and Article 2(2) of the ICTR Statute.

9 See WA Schabas, 'Article 6' in Triffterer and Ambos, *supra* n 3, Art. 6, para 1, at 128.

10 See, *supra* n 5. See also M Odello and P Łubiński (eds), *The Concept of Genocide in International Criminal Law* (Routledge 2020); R Amir, *Twentieth Century Forcible Child Transfers: Probing the Boundaries of the Genocide Convention* (Lexington 2019); C Tams, L Berster and B Schiffbauer, *Convention on the Prevention and Punishment of the Crime of Genocide: A Commentary* (Nomos 2014); A Szpak, 'National, Ethnic, Racial, and Religious Groups Protected against Genocide in the Jurisprudence of the ad hoc International Criminal Tribunals' [2012] 23 *EJIL* 155; E Novic, *The Concept of Cultural Genocide* (Oxford University Press 2016); D Bloxham and AD Moses (eds), *The Oxford Handbook of Genocide Studies* (Oxford University Press 2010); L May, *Genocide: A Normative Account* (Cambridge

First, genocide protects a *collective* legal interest, that is, the existence of certain groups and their right to contribute to their social dimension.[11] In Resolution 96(1) of 1946, the General Assembly defined genocide as 'denial of the right of existence of entire human groups in the same way as homicide is the denial of the right to live for individual human beings'.[12] The physical and social right of the group to exist is therefore the primary protected interest in the norm's protective scope.[13] Victims of a genocidal attack are subjected to serious violations of their human dignity: the victim of the crime suffers not only because of their membership in a specific group but also because they are depersonalized and objectivized. Therefore, the human dignity of the individual victim is protected together with the primary protected right, namely the existence of the group.[14] By requiring that the perpetrator intends the destruction of the group as such, the definition makes it very clear that the victim of genocide is chosen on account of her or his membership of a protected group.[15] From this perspective, the target or (intended) victim of the crime of genocide is the group itself and not (only) the individual.[16] The crime of genocide pertains to the destruction of a race, tribe, nation, or other group with a particular positive identity, not to the destruction of various people lacking a distinct identity.[17]

In addition to collective group interests, it cannot be denied that the fundamental rights of the individual parts of the group are also harmed by genocidal acts.[18] They are usually the targets of attack. However, any injury or danger to individual rights falls under Article 6 of the ICC Statute if the individual is specifically attacked because of her membership in the group. Only the presence of the *dolus specialis* renders a violation of individual rights

University Press 2010); DL Nersessian, *Genocide and Political Groups* (Oxford University Press 2010); C Kreß, 'The Crime of Genocide under International Law' [2006] 6 *ICLR* 461.

11 R Lemkin, *Axis Rule in Occupied Europe* (Carnegie Endowment for International Peace 1944), 91.

12 A/RES/1/96 (1946), which also says: '[S]uch denial of the right of existence . . . results in great losses to humanity in the form of cultural and other contributions represented by these human groups'.

13 See E Fronza, 'Genocide in the Rome Statute' in F Lattanzi and WA Schabas (eds), *Essays on the Rome Statute of the International Criminal Court*, vol. I (Il Sirente 1999), 105, 118 ff; A Zahar and G Sluiter, *International Criminal Law* (Oxford University Press 2008), 179. See *Krstić*, paras 574 ff, 580.

14 See Fronza, *supra* n 13, 119; Kreß, *supra* n 10, 465; A Planzer, *Le crime de genocide* (St. Gallen 1956), 79 ff.

15 Lemkin, *supra* n 11, 79.

16 *Akayesu*, para 521; *Jelisić*, para 79; cf. also, *Prosecutor* v. *Kayishema and Ruzindana*, ICTR-95-1-T, 21 May 1999, ICTR, para 97; *Prosecutor* v. *Ndindabahizi*, ICTR-2001- 71-I, 15 July 2004, ICTR, para 454 (15 July 2004); *Prosecutor* v. *Stakić*, IT-97-24-T, 31 July 2003, paras 520–521 [*Stakić*]; *Krstić*, para 561; *Prosecutor* v. *Sikirica*, IT-95-8-T, Judgment on Defence Motions to Acquit, 3 September 2001, para 89; see also Commentary on the ILC's 1996 Draft Code (Art. 17, para 7).

17 *Stakić*, Appeal Judgement, paras 21–24.

18 See Fronza, *supra* n 13, 119; Planzer, *supra* n 14, 79–80.

an actual crime of genocide.[19] The *mens rea* required for genocide is a specific intent to destroy, in whole or in part, a national, ethnic, racial or religious group, as such.[20] The term 'destroy' is limited to the physical or biological destruction of the group.[21]

In Chapter 3, I maintained that, unlike the Universal Declaration of Human Rights (UDHR), the two Covenants of 1966 succeeded in capturing a universal collective nature of dignity. The two treaties collect these two different dimensions of dignity. The recognition, in the 1948 Genocide Convention, of the physical protection of the group as such by the prohibition on genocide is part of the consolidation process of dignity in its collective nature of dignity, as clarified in Section 3.3.4.2. In a periodization focused on dignity and human rights, the qualification of universality in relation to human dignity, in both its individual and collective nature, found its full consolidation in human rights law in the 1960s.

6.2.2 *Crimes against Humanity*

As seen in Chapter 3, human dignity's first entrance in ICL occurred when the definition of crimes against humanity was first explicitly formulated as a category of crimes in Article 6(c) of the Nuremberg Charter.[22] The International Law Commission's (ILC) draft of Crimes against the Peace and Security of Mankind played an important part in the negotiations on the ICC Statute.[23] During the negotiations in Rome, there was agreement that crimes against humanity should be included in the list of core crimes. In spite of this broad consensus, formulating crimes against humanity was a difficult task. Ultimately, however, a precise definition was developed in

[19] See *Jelisić*, para 66; *Akayesu*, para 522.

[20] See *Prosecutor* v. *Mladić*, IT-09-92, Trial Chamber, 22 November 2017, para 3435.

[21] *Krstić*, Appeal Judgment, para 25.

[22] See Chapter 3 (3.4.3). Charter of the IMT, Nuremberg, 8 August 1945, Art. 6(c). See MC Bassiouni, *Crimes against Humanity* (Cambridge University Press 2011), 111 ff; RS Clark, 'Crimes against Humanity at Nuremberg' in G Ginsburgs and VN Kudriavtsev (eds), *The Nuremberg Trial and International Law* (Kluwer Academic 1990), 177; E Schwelb, 'Crimes against Humanity' [1946] 23 *BYIL* 178.

[23] See 1996 Draft Code, Art. 18. See RS Clark, 'History of Efforts to Codify Crimes Against Humanity, From the Charter of Nuremberg to the Statute of Rome' in LN Sadat (ed.), *Forging a Convention for Crimes against Humanity* (Cambridge University Press 2011), 15 ff; M McAuliffe de Guzman, 'Crimes against Humanity' in WA Schabas and N Bernaz (eds), *Routledge Handbook of International Criminal Law* (Routledge 2011), 121, 124.

Article 7, building on earlier definitions, as well as on the jurisprudence of the ICTY.[24]

The material elements of crimes against humanity require the commission of one of the individual acts precisely described in Article 7(1). Moreover, Article 7(1) provides, in its chapeaux, the context element for these violations, requiring that the crime must be 'committed as part of a widespread or systematic attack directed against any civilian population with knowledge of the attack'. Thus, within the context pictured by Article 7(1), the individual acts gain a different level of criminality. The rationale of the 'internationalization' of certain crimes is to protect fundamental human rights and underlying '*human dignity*'[25] against serious systematic and widespread human rights violations caused, supported or tolerated by States or certain non-state organizations. The mental element requires intent and knowledge (Article 30, ICC Statute) regarding the material elements of the crime, including the contextual element. The literature focusing on crimes against humanity is vast.[26] For the purpose of this research, the analysis will focus on the protected interest and legal good of human dignity, providing examples of criminal conducts inherently connected to its protection.

The core legal good protected by the crime against humanity is, *in primis*, the dignity of the person, in its individual and social dimension. Crimes against humanity target fundamental recognized human rights, such as the right to life, health or dignity itself. However, from a broader perspective, they call into question *humanity* as such,[27] in the sense of a 'minimum standard of

24 On the negotiations on Art. 7 of the ICC Statute, see D Robinson, 'Defining Crimes against Humanity at the Rome Conference' [1999] 93 *AJIL* 43; D Robinson, 'Crimes against Humanity, Reflections on State Sovereignty, Legal Precision and the Dictates of the Public Conscience' in Lattanzi and Schabas, *supra* n 13, 139. See also RS Clark, 'Crimes against Humanity and the Rome Statute of the International Criminal Court' in Politi and Nesi, *supra* n 3, 75; P Hwang, 'Defining Crimes against Humanity in the Rome Statute of the International Criminal Court' [1998] 22 *FILJ* 457; M McAuliffe deGuzman, 'The Road from Rome, The Developing Law of Crimes against Humanity' [2000] 22 *HRQ* 335; LN Sadat, 'Crimes against Humanity in the Modern Age' [2013] 107 *AJIL* 334, 355 ff.

25 *Prosecutor* v. *Kupreškić*, IT-95-16-T, 14 January 2000, para 547 ('[crimes against humanity] are intended to safeguard basic human values by banning atrocities *directed against human dignity*', emphasis added) [*Kupreškić*].

26 Bassiouni, *supra* n 22; A Cassese, 'Crimes against Humanity' in Cassese, Gaeta and Jones, *supra* n 3, 353; Clark, *supra* n 23, 8; G Werle and B Burghardt, 'Do Crimes against Humanity Require the Participation of a State or a "State-Like" Organization?' [2012] 10 *JICJ* 1151.

27 For a discussion of the interpretation of humanity as a legal concept, see G Radbruch, 'Zur Diskussion über das Verbrechen gegen die Menschlichkeit' [1947] *Süddeutsche Juristenzeitung* 131 ff; see also Cassese, *supra* n 26, 360. On the interests protected by crimes against humanity from the perspective of Kant's theory of law, see K Gierhake, *Begründung des Völkerstrafrechts auf der Grundlage der Kantischen Rechtslehre* (Duncker & Humblot 2005), 271 ff.

the rules of human coexistence'.[28] Therefore, crimes against humanity are also a threat to peace in a broader sense, including the security of humankind. The crime affects not only the individual victim but also the international community as a whole.[29]

By way of illustration, in the *Erdemović* case decided by ICTY, Judges McDonald and Vohrah, in their separate opinion, stated:

> [R]ules proscribing crimes against humanity address the perpetrator's conduct not only towards the immediate victim but also towards the whole of humankind. . . . It is therefore the concept of humanity as victim which essentially characterises crimes against humanity . . . Because of their heinousness and magnitude they constitute an *egregious attack on human dignity*, on the very notion of humaneness. They consequently affect, or should affect, each and every member of mankind, whatever his or her nationality, ethnic group and location. . . . This aspect of crimes against humanity as injuring a broader interest than that of the immediate victim . . . is shown by the intrinsic elements of the offence.[30]

Despite different approaches, the relationship between human dignity and criminal acts against humanity has also been identified by legal scholars. By way of illustration, Antonio Cassese considered crimes against humanity as 'particularly odious offences in that they constitute a serious attack on human dignity or a grave humiliation or degradation of one or more persons'.[31] Mireille Delmas-Marty considers the criminalization of crimes against humanity as protecting the dignity of the individual and that of humanity.[32] In David Luban's words, crimes against humanity are 'politics gone horribly wrong',[33] 'politics gone cancerous'.[34] They are a double assault on *individuality* – considered as the individual and political 'quality of being human', 'humanness' – and on *groups* – meaning a 'set of individuals' or 'humankind'.[35] As aptly put by Paul Martens, 'as soon as the essence of man is touched, the whole humanity appears as a victim'.[36]

28 HH Jescheck, 'Gegenstand und neueste Entwicklung des internationalen Strafrechts' in FC Schroeder and H Zipf (eds), *Festschrift für Reinhart Maurach zum 70 geburtstag* (Muller 1972), 579, 590 (from German).

29 See also Cryer et al., *supra* n 4, 230.

30 *Prosecutor* v. *Erdemović*, IT-96-22, 7 October 1997, ICTY, separate opinion of Judges McDonald and Vohrah, para 21 [*Erdemović*] (emphasis added).

31 Cassese, *supra* n 8, 90.

32 M Delmas-Marty, *Trois défis pour un droit mondial* (Seuil 1998), 192.

33 *Ibid.*, 108.

34 *Ibid.*, 116.

35 *Ibid.*, 86 ff. R Vernon, 'What is Crime against Humanity?' [2002] 10 *JPP* 231–249, 237–238.

36 P Martens, 'L'humanité comme sujet de droit' in T Berns (ed.), *Le droit saisi par le collectif* (Bruylant 2004), 222; see also C Le Bris, *L'humanité saisie par le Droit International Public* (LGDJ 2012).

In 2014, the ILC started working on a project of a comprehensive convention on crimes against humanity, with the aim to develop a draft treaty on the prevention and punishment of crimes against humanity.[37] In August 2019, the Report of the ILC on the work of the seventy-first session (Chapter IV) presented the draft text of 15 articles and a draft annex, which includes, among other provisions, a definition of crimes against humanity (Article 2). The latter resembles the text of Article 7 of the ICC Statute and specifies the state's obligation to refrain from committing and to prevent crimes against humanity (Articles 3 and 4). Importantly, the first preambular paragraph clarifies that 'over the course of history, millions of people have been victimized by acts that deeply shock the conscience of humanity' and 'because of their gravity, constitute egregious attacks on humankind itself'.[38] The fourth preambular paragraph also recalls that the prohibition of crimes against humanity is a peremptory norm of general international law (*jus cogens*). The Commission decided, in conformity with Article 23 of its Statute, to recommend the draft articles to the General Assembly. In particular, the ILC recommended the elaboration of a convention by the General Assembly or by an international conference of plenipotentiaries on the basis of the draft articles.

The practice of international tribunals provides clarifications on how individual acts that may amount to crimes against humanity have been regarded as attacks on human dignity. This will be discussed next. The purpose is not to present an exhaustive list of cases but rather to give illustrations of how human dignity, as a protected interest, manifests itself in relation to this specific crime.

6.2.2.1 Murder

The Rome Statute lists the crime of murder in Article 7(1)(a), and it requires that the perpetrator kills[39] one or more persons in a given context. The jurisprudence of the ad hoc tribunals does not make a distinction between 'murder', as a crime against humanity, and 'wilful killing', as a war crime. The difference is the distinct context elements.[40] In the case *Kupreškić TC*, the

37 ILC 66th Sess., 3227th mtg. at 3, A/CN.4/SR.3227 (18 July 2014).

38 Draft articles on Prevention and Punishment of Crimes Against Humanity, with commentaries, ILC 71st mtg, A/74/10, 4, (2).

39 The respective footnote 7 provides: 'For the purposes of this definition the term "killed" is interchangeable with the term "caused death." This footnote applies to all elements which use either of these concepts.'

40 The Trial Chamber in *Prosecutor* v. *Delalić et al.*, IT-96-21-T, Judgment, 16 November 1998, paras 421 ff., concluding that there is no qualitative difference between 'wilful killing' and

ICTY considered that the two offences are not in a relationship of 'reciprocal speciality'.[41] In assessing the nature of the legal values protected by the norm that criminalizes each conduct, the Chamber considered that the two offences (murder and wilful killing) constitute part of the common general legal framework of the Statute. They have the same general aims and protect the same values in that they are drafted to ensure *respect for human dignity*, no matter what their specific purposes and values are.[42] Therefore, a distinctive interpretation of the respective conducts of killing would be 'inconsequential'.[43] The crime of taking of life is the underlying act of all main crimes,[44] as 'killing (of) members of the group' (i.e. genocide),[45] 'murder' (i.e. crimes against humanity),[46] or 'wilful killing', 'violence to life' (i.e. war crimes).[47]

6.2.2.2 Imprisonment or Other Severe Deprivation of Physical Liberty

Article 7(1)(e) of the ICC Statute covers the crime of 'imprisonment or other severe deprivation of physical liberty in violation of fundamental rules of international law'. Two decisions have considered this criminal conduct: *Kordić and Čerkez* and *Krnojelac*.[48]

In *Kordić and Čerkez*, the Trial Chamber found that the contextual element is the only criterion that differentiates the crime against humanity of

'murder' (para 433), including regarding the mens rea required (para 439) [*Delalić*]. In the same vein *Prosecutor* v. *Blaškić*, IT-95-14-T, 3 March 2000, para 181 [*Blaškić*]; *Prosecutor* v. *Kordić and Čerkez*, IT-95-14/ 2-T, 26 February 2001, paras 229, 236 [*Kordić and Čerkez*]; *Prosecutor* v. *Tolimir*, IT-05-88/2-T, 12 December 2012, ICTY, para 714; *Prosecutor* v. *Stanišić and Župljanin*, IT-08-91-T, 27 March 2013, ICTY, Vol. I, para 42 [*Stanišić and Župljanin*]. See also the Separate and Dissenting Opinion of Judge Cassese, in *Erdemović*, footnote 8.

41 *Kupreškić*, para 701.

42 *Ibid.*, para 702 (emphasis added).

43 *Ibid.*, para 703. See also on this issue, O Swaak-Goldman, 'Crimes against Humanity' in K McDonald and O Swaak-Goldman (eds), *Substantive and Procedural Aspects of International Criminal Law*, vol. 2 (Brill Nijhoff 2000), 164 ff.

44 With the exception of the special case of the crime of aggression.

45 Article 2(a) Genocide Convention; Article 4 of the ICTY Statute; Article 2 of the ICTR Statute; Article 5 of the ICC Statute; and section 4(a) of Regulation 15/2000.

46 Article 6(c) IMT, Article 5(c) of the Tokyo Charter, Article II(1)(c) of CCL 10, Principle VI(c) of the ILC's Nuremberg Principles (YbILC, ii, (1950), 374), Article 2(11) Draft Code, YbILC, ii, (1954), 151 and Article 18(a) of the 1996 Draft Code (YbILC, ii/2, 15); Article 5(a) of the ICTY Statute, Article 3(a) of the ICTR Statute and Article 7(1)(a) of the ICC Statute.

47 Article 2(a) of the ICTY Statute, Article 4(a) of the ICTR Statute; Article 8(1)(a)(i) and (c)(i) of the ICC Statute; and section 5, 6.1.(a)(i) of UNTAET Regulation 2000/15.

48 However, deprivation of liberty has been regarded as a persecutory act in, for instance, *Prosecutor* v. *Simić*, IT-95-9, 17 October 2003, ICTY, paras 59–66; *Prosecutor* v. *Gotovina*, IT-06-90-T, 15 April 2011, ICTY, paras 1848 ff [*Gotovina*].

imprisonment or other severe deprivation of liberty from unlawful confinement as a grave breach of the Geneva Conventions.[49] The Trial Chamber held that the imprisonment of civilians is unlawful where: civilians have been detained in the absence of reasonable grounds that the security of the detaining power makes it absolutely necessary; the procedural safeguards required by Article 43 of the Geneva Convention IV are not complied with in respect of detained civilians; it occurs as part of a widespread or systematic attack directed against a civilian population.[50]

In the *Krnojelac* case, the Trial Chamber moved beyond *Kordić*, holding that imprisonment as a crime against humanity can exist even if the requirements of unlawful confinement are not met.[51] A case of arbitrary physical deprivation of liberty may constitute imprisonment if the other conditions of the crime are satisfied. Arbitrariness is assessed on the basis of the rules of due process.[52] In times of armed conflict, Articles 42(1), 43(1) (Geneva Convention, GC, IV)[53] and Article 5 (Additional Protocol, AP, II) apply,[54] while in peacetime, Article 9(1) and Article 14 of the International Covenant on Civil and Political Rights (ICCPR) applies.[55]

Article 7(1)(e) ICC Statute considers both 'imprisonment' and 'deprivation of liberty'. The latter must be 'severe' – in light of the wording that it is 'other' than imprisonment – while imprisonment is in itself already qualified as severe. Conditions of detentions play an important role in the assessment of the level of severity and should be 'compatible with respect for human dignity',[56] as also discussed in Chapter 5. Persons deprived of their liberty 'shall be treated with humanity and with respect for the inherent dignity of the human person'.[57] It is considered that the 'severity' threshold would be met

49 *Kordić and Čerkez*, para 301.

50 *Ibid.*, para 303.

51 *Prosecutor* v. *Krnojelac*, IT-97-25-T, 15 March 2002, para 111 [*Krnojelac*].

52 *Ibid.*, paras 112, 113.

53 ICRC, Geneva Convention Relative to the Protection of Civilian Persons in Time of War (Geneva Convention IV), 12 August 1949, 75 UNTS 287.

54 ICRC, Protocol Additional to the Geneva Conventions of 12 August 1949, and relating to the Protection of Victims of Non-International Armed Conflicts (Additional Protocol II, APII), 8 June 1977, 1125 UNTS 609.

55 International Covenant on Civil and Political Rights, 16 December 1966, 999 UNTS 171. See *Kordić and Čerkez*, para 303.

56 See, for instance, ECtHR: M.S.S. v. *Belgium and Greece*, [GC], No. 30696/09, 21 January 2011, para 263; *Kudła* v. *Poland*, [GC], No. 30210/96, 26 October 2000, para 94; *Yaroslav Belousov* v. *Russia*, No. 2653/13, 4 October 2016, para 92; *Bouyid* v. *Belgium*, [GC], No. 23380/09, 28 September 2015, paras 87–90, 103.

57 Article 10, ICCPR.

also in case of a short period of detention under inhumane conditions, with insufficient food, hygiene, and space, accompanied by inhumane treatment.[58]

6.2.2.3 Sexual Violence

Sexual violence has been described as the 'forgotten' crime in international law,[59] especially considering its absence in the trials after the Second World War.[60] The protected good of this crime[61] is, *in primis*, physical and mental integrity[62] as well as dignity and personal (sexual) autonomy;[63] as part of international crimes, the prosecution of sexual violence offences may also contribute to the maintenance of international peace and security.[64] Second, as to the method of criminalization, sexual violence may be criminalized explicitly or implicitly. A classic implicit criminalization is the classification of a sexual offence as an offence against the honour or dignity of the victim. International humanitarian law (IHL) focuses on the attack on the woman's honour.[65] In domestic law, in a similar way,

58 See K Ambos, *Treatise on International Criminal Law*, vol. II, The Crimes and Sentencing (Oxford University Press 2014), 89.

59 See C Chinkin, 'Gender-related Violence' in Cassese, *supra* n 3, 76; KD Askin, 'Women' in KD Askin and DM Koenig (eds), *Women and International Human Rights Law* (Transnational 2001), 64. In a similar vein, see N Hayes, 'Definition of Rape' in S Darcy and J Powderly (eds), *Judicial Creativity at the International Criminal Tribunals* (Oxford University Press 2010), 129.

60 See A Cole, 'International Criminal Law and Sexual Violence: An Overview' in C McGlynn and V Munro (eds), *Rethinking Rape Law* (Routledge 2010), 48–50, 58–59, on the Nuremberg and Tokyo trials.

61 See K Ambos, *Treatise on International Criminal Law*, vol. I, Foundations and General Part (Oxford University Press 2013), 60 ff.

62 See also W Schomburg and I Peterson, 'Genuine Consent to Sexual Violence Under International Criminal Law' [2007] 101 *AJIL* 121–140, 126.

63 For instance, the English Sexual Offences Act 2003, Chapter 43, 20 November 2003, protects various interests, punishing non-consensual sexual activity. Therefore, sexual crimes on adults include the element of lack of consent of the victim (see Sexual Offences Act 2003, Part 1, 1–4). In the German Criminal Code ('German StGB'), instead, sexual offences are defined 'Offences against sexual self-determination', see Chapter 13, German Criminal Code, 13 November 1998, Federal Law Gazette (Bundesgesetzblatt) I, p. 3322.

64 See UN SC Res. 1820, 19 June 2008, para 1; UN SC Res. 1880, 30 September 2009, para 1 and UN SC Res. 1960, 16 December 2010 all stating that 'sexual violence may impede the restoration of international peace and security'. In conflict situations, references to sexual violence can be previously found in UN SC Res. 820, 17 April 1993, para 6; UN SC Res. 1325, 31 October 2000, paras 10–11.

65 See, for example, Article 27 GC IV and Article 75(2) (b) AP I. See also CK Hall and K Ambos, 'Article 7' in Triffterer and Ambos, *supra* n 3, paras 53–54, at 206–207; M Cottier and J Grignon, 'Article 8' in Triffterer and Ambos, *supra* n 3, paras 731–733, at 500–501; see also KD Askin, 'Crimes against Women' in BS Brown (ed.), *Research Handbook on International Criminal Law* (Cheltenham et al., Elgar 2011), 86 ff.

sexual violence is often considered as an offence against sexual integrity or autonomy,[66] while the specific act is defined as an offence against dignity.[67] The link with honour and dignity also clarifies the reason why, during the drafting of the Rome Statute, sexual offences were still considered under the war crime of outrages upon personal dignity. The Preparatory Committee later drafted a distinct category for sexual offences. The ICC Statute, unlike the constitutive statutes of the ICTY and the ICTR,[68] includes criminalization of sexual violence both as crimes against humanity (Article 7(1)(g)) and as war crimes (Article 8(2)(b)(xxii) and (e)(vi)) and has been widely praised for that.[69] Moreover, one may also implicitly see behind the criminalization of sexual offences other crimes against humanity (as well as war crimes), in particular those referring to offences against physical integrity or the right to reproduction. These criminal offences are identical in nature but differ only in the context element.

In particular, Article 7(1)(g) of the ICC Statute covers rape, sexual slavery, enforced prostitution, forced pregnancy, enforced sterilization and any other form of sexual violence of comparable gravity.[70] The perpetrator must commit an act of a sexual nature against one or more persons or cause such person or persons to engage in an act of a sexual nature by using force, threat of force or by coercion, according to the Elements of Crimes.[71] The conduct must be comparable in gravity to the offences included in Article 7(1)(g) of the Rome Statute. The Elements of Crimes are the outcome of the judgment of the ICTR in the *Akayesu* case.[72] Here, the Tribunal decided a case related to an order to strip a female student and force her to perform physical exercise naked before many people.[73]

66 See *supra* n 63.

67 Rape once was regarded as an offence against property or against the honour of the women's owner. The criminalization of sexual violence is now closely connected to the current recognition of gender rights, see Dube, *Rape Laws in India* (Butterworths 2008), 1–2, 11–15 and 161 ff. See, for example, the Indian Penal Code, 6 October 1860, Section 375, Chapter 12 'Offences against Women'. See also, in Uruguay, Article 272 of the Código Penal, 'good customs and family order'.

68 For the legal position in these Statutes, see Chinkin, *supra* n 59, 76 ff.

69 *Ibid.*, 77; on gender issues during the negotiations of the ICC Statute, see B Bedont and K Hall-Martinez, 'Ending Impunity for Gender Crimes under the International Criminal Court' [1999] 6 *BJWA* 66 ff.

70 See KD Askin, 'Crimes Within the Jurisdiction of the International Criminal Court' [1999] 10 *CLF* 33, 45.

71 See Elements of Crimes for Art. 7(1)(g)-6 of the ICC Statute. In the decision *Prosecutor* v. *Muthaura et al.*, ICC-01/09-02/11, 23 January 2012, ICC (PTC), paras 265–266.

72 *Akayesu*, para 598.

73 *Ibid.*, para 688.

Similarly, sexual acts on dead bodies were also regarded by the ICTR as 'a form of sexual violence of comparable severity'.[74]

Importantly, the Trial Chamber in *Furundžija* case affirmed that:

> international criminal rules punish not only rape but also any serious sexual assault falling short of actual penetration. It would seem that the prohibition embraces all serious abuses of a sexual nature inflicted upon the physical and moral integrity of a person by means of coercion, threat of force or intimidation in a way that is degrading and humiliating for the *victim's dignity*.[75]

When searching for an international definition of the crime of rape, the ICTR found different views among domestic jurisdictions regarding the question of whether oral penetration could amount in itself to the crime of rape.[76] Later, looking into the general principles of ICL and international law, it focused on the 'general principle of respect for human dignity', declaring that:

> The general principle of respect for human dignity is the basic underpinning and indeed the very *raison d'être* of international humanitarian law and human rights law; indeed in modern times it has become of such paramount importance as to permeate the whole body of international law.[77]

By assessing that human dignity is meant to 'shield people' from humiliation and degradation, the ICTR held that a definition of rape that also included oral penetration is 'consonant' with human dignity. In the words of the Tribunal, the fundamental principle of protecting human dignity 'favours broadening the definition of rape'.[78] The Tribunal later overrode any concerns about possible clashes with the principle of legality (*nullum crimen sine lege*),[79] though not without leading to controversy.[80]

74 See Hall and Ambos, *supra* n 65, 53. See also the *Prosecutor* v. *Niyitegeka*, ICTR-96-14-A, 9 July 2004, ICTR, para 465; *Prosecutor* v. *Kajelijeli*, ICTR-98- 44A-A, 1 December 2003, ICTR, para 936. See also G Werle and F Jessberger, *Principles of International Criminal Law* (3rd ed., Oxford University Press 2014), 372.

75 *Prosecutor* v. *Furundžija*, IT-95-17/1-T, 10 December 1998, ICTY, para 186 (emphasis added) [*Furundžija*]. See *Prosecutor* v. *Aleksovski*, IT-95-14/1-T, 25 June 1999, ICTY, para 54 [*Aleksovski*].

76 *Furundžija*, para 182.

77 *Ibid.*, paras 182–183.

78 *Ibid.*, para 184.

79 *Ibid.*

80 I Bantekas, 'Reflections on Some Sources and Methods of International Criminal and Humanitarian Law' [2006] 6 *ICLR* 121, 127.

6.2.2.4 Persecution

Article 7(1)(h) of the ICC Statute covers the crime against humanity of persecution. A good illustration of this crime can be found in the 'Media Trial' case decided by the ICTR. Here, the Tribunal clarified that hate speech targeting a population based on ethnicity, or on any discriminatory reason, amounts to persecution. The Trial Chamber stated that hate speech is 'a discriminatory form of aggression that *destroys the dignity* of those in the group under attack' and found in the specific case that hate speech on discriminatory grounds reached the level of gravity necessary for persecution.[81] The Appeals Chamber subsequently reasoned that hate speech violates the *right to respect for the dignity of the members* of the targeted group as human beings and the group's right to security.[82] The Appeals Chamber also clarified that it is 'the cumulative effect of all the underlying acts of the crime of persecution which must reach a level of gravity equivalent to that for other crimes against humanity' and it is 'the context in which these underlying acts take place' that is important to consider in the assessment of their gravity.[83]

6.2.2.5 Other Inhuman Acts

'Other inhumane acts' is the residual category of the acts that are crimes against humanity.[84] The statutes of the ad hoc tribunals refer to 'other inhumane acts' (Article 5(i) ICTY and Article 3(i) ICTR statutes), and the jurisprudence has on several occasions noted its uncertain scope, especially in light of the principle of legality.[85] The ICC Statute defines these acts more

81 *Prosecutor* v. *Nahimana et al.*, ICTR-99-52, 3 December 2003, ICTR, paras 1070 ff (emphasis added). See also WA Schabas, *The UN International Criminal Tribunals. The Former Yugoslavia, Rwanda and Sierra Leone* (Cambridge University Press 2006), 217. For a more restrictive approach, see also *Mugesera* v. *Canada* (Minister of Citizenship and Immigration), Supreme Court of Canada, decision of 28 June 2005, 2005 SCC 40, [2005] 2 Supreme Court Reports 100, paras 146 ff; J Rikhof, 'Hate Speech and ICL: The Mugesera Decision by the Supreme Court of Canada' [2005] 3 *JICJ* 1121–1133.

82 See *Prosecutor* v. *Nahimana et al.*, ICTR-99-52-A, 28 November 2007, ICTR, para 986. In this regard, in *Prosecutor* v. *Kvočka et al.*, IT-98-30/1-A, 28 February 2005, paras 323–325, violations of human dignity, such as harassment, humiliation and psychological abuse, if sufficiently serious constitute acts of persecution.

83 *Ibid.*, para 987.

84 On the importance of this norm, see J Pictet et al., *Commentary on the Geneva Conventions of 12 August 1949, I* (ICRC 1952), 54; *Kupreškić*, para 563.

85 See *Kupreškić*, para 563. See also *Prosecutor* v. *Blagojević and Jokić*, para 625; *Stakić*, para 719; *Prosecutor* v. *Kordić and Čerkez*, IT-95-14/2-A, para 117; but see also *Stakić*, IT-97-24-A, para 315 and *Prosecutor* v. *Muvunyi*, ICTR-2000-55A-T, 12 September 2006, para 527 [*Muvunyi*] with references to the *Stakić* decision in Appeal, footnote omitted.

clearly.[86] Article 7(1)(k) ICC Statute says that other inhumane acts are 'acts of a similar character intentionally causing great suffering, or serious injury to body or to mental or physical health'. Therefore, the perpetrator must cause 'great suffering, or serious injury to body or to mental or physical health' of the victims and the act must be 'of a character similar to any other act' referred to in Article 7(1) ICC Statute.[87]

Whether (basic) human rights violations fall into the category of 'other inhumane acts' seems difficult. Article 7(1)(k) ICC Statute requires in fact 'great suffering' and 'serious injury'. In this sense, in fact, the case law of the ad hoc tribunals, in its assessment of the 'inhumane' qualification of an act,[88] has also developed two restrictive criteria, applied in a few cases,[89] namely '(i) the occurrence of an act or omission of similar seriousness to the other enumerated acts under the Article; (ii) the act or omission caused serious mental or physical suffering or injury or constituted a *serious attack of human dignity*'.[90]

6.2.3 *War Crimes*

After the Second World War, Article 6(b) of the Nuremberg Charter – the basis for the Nuremberg trials – granted jurisdiction to the International Military Tribunal (IMT) over 'violations of the laws and customs of war' and, on this basis, it was able to prosecute those responsible for war crimes. At Nuremberg, the Tribunal noted that many of the prohibitions in the Hague Convention existed long before its adoption and that their prosecution as crimes had been 'punishable as offenses against the laws of war' since 1907.[91]

86 *Prosecutor* v. *Katanga and Chui*, Closing Statements, 23 May 2012, Trial Chamber II, ICC-01/04-01/07-T, ICC, para 450.

87 See Element 1 and 2 of the Elements of Crimes.

88 *Kordić and Čerkez*, IT-95-14/2-A, 17 December 2004, para 117; *Muvunyi*, para 527.

89 See only *Prosecutor* v. *Stakić*, IT-97-24-A, 22 March 2006, para 317 (forcible transfer of civilians); *Prosecutor* v. *Kamuhanda*, ICTR-95-54a-T, 22 January 2004, para 710 (sexual violence) [*Kamuhanda*].

90 *Prosecutor* v. *Vasiljević*, IT-98-32-T, 29 November 2002, para 234 (emphasis added) [*Vasiljević*]; confirmed by *Vasiljević*, IT-98-32-A, para 165. Similar *Galić*, IT-98-29-T, para 152; *Prosecutor* v. *Blagojević and Jokić*, para 626–629; *Kordić and Čerkez*, IT-95-14/2-A, para 117; *Prosecutor* v. *Lukić and Lukić*, IT-98-32/1-T, 20 July 2009, para 960 [*Lukić*]; *Kamuhanda*, para 718; *Prosecutor* v. *Bagosora et al.*, ICTR-98-41-T, 18 December 2008, para 2218; *Krstić*, para 532 (dicta); *Prosecutor* v. *Brđanin*, IT-99-36-T, 1 September 2004, para 544 (forcible transfer punishable as other inhumane acts) [*Brđanin*]; *Prosecutor* v. *Kvočka*, IT-98-30/1-T, 2 November 2001, ICTY, para 208 (dicta), (citing *Kupreškić*) [*Kvočka*]; *Kupreškić*, para 566 (dicta). In the latter, the Trial Chamber set a threshold for assessing the existence of an inhumane act ex article 5 of the ICTY Statute, establishing that they 'must be carried out in a systematic manner and on a large-scale'.

91 *France et al.* v. *Göring et al.* (1946) 22 IMT 411, 463.

After the Nuremberg Charter, there was a long-time gap before the creation of the ICTY and of the ICTR, which gave a new international structure to the prosecution of war crimes.[92] However, the outreach of these tribunals was limited temporally and geographically.

Today, the reference provision for war crimes is Article 8(1) of the ICC Statute, which is much more than a codification of earlier practice – mainly in light of its comprehensive codification of war crimes committed in Non-International Armed Conflicts (NIACs). Since its entry into force, the ICC Statute has played a significant role in the enforcement of IHL.[93] The provisions regulating war crimes are structurally distinct from those regulating crimes against humanity and genocide. According to Article 8(1) of the ICC Statute, the ICC's jurisdiction covers war crimes 'in particular' when committed as part of a plan or policy or as part of a large-scale commission.[94] The expression 'in particular' makes clear that single or isolated war crimes are not completely excluded, giving a broad discretion to the Prosecutor and to the judges in their exercise of jurisdiction over such crimes.[95] Although 'war crimes' are recognized both in 'international armed conflicts' (IACs) and 'non-international armed conflict' (NIACs), they are still different. Article 8 of the ICC Statute divides IACs and NIACs into grave breaches of the GCs and other serious violations of the law and customs of war (para. 2(a), (b)), and serious violations of Common Article 3 GCs and other serious violations of the laws and customs of non-international conflict (para. 2(c), (e)). Moreover, unlike the statutes of the ICTY and ICTY,[96] Article 8 includes an exhaustive list of crimes[97] in line with the principle of legality.[98]

The protected interest and legal good guaranteed by the provision that criminalizes conducts contrary to IHL in armed conflict are both the

92 See K Roberts, 'The Contribution of the ICTY to the Grave Breaches Regime' [2009] 7 *JICJ* 743.

93 Similarly, see M Sassòli, 'Humanitarian Law and International Criminal Law' in Cassese, *supra* n 3, 111; see O Triffterer, 'The Preventive and the Repressive Function of the International Criminal Court' in Politi and Nesi, *supra* n 3, 137.

94 On the works of the Preparatory Committee, see H von Hebel and D Robinson, 'Crimes within the Jurisdiction of the Court' in Lee, *supra* n 3, 107.

95 See *Prosecutor* v. *Jean-Pierre Bemba Gombo*, ICC-01/05-01/08, Pre-Trial Chamber II, Decision Pursuant to Article 61(7)(a) and (b) of the Rome Statute on the Charges of the Prosecutor Against Jean-Pierre Bemba Gombo, 15 June 2009, para. 211 [*Bemba*].

96 With an opening formula 'such violations shall include, but not be limited to', see Article 3 ICTY Statute and Article 4 ICTR Statute.

97 See also L Condorelli, 'War Crimes' in Politi and Nesi, *supra* n 3, 107, 112.

98 Similarly, WA Schabas, 'Follow Up to Rome: Preparing for Entry into Force of the International Criminal Court Statute' [1999] 20 *HRLJ* 157, 163. See also Ambos, *supra* n 61, 88 ff.

collective legal interests of international peace and security,[99] and the more concrete legal rights and interests of individuals, such as life, bodily integrity, liberty, personal autonomy and, above all, human dignity.[100] The provisions on war crimes protect fundamental individual rights during armed conflict, as is particularly evident in the case of grave breaches provisions of the GCs. Protected persons are exposed to specific dangers in armed conflict, where personal dignity and basic rights may be at risk. Similarly, in case of crimes addressed by the law of the Hague Conventions, individual legal interests are guaranteed by the prohibition of certain means and methods of warfare that cause unnecessary suffering.[101] In addition, the objective of the law of war crimes is to ultimately limit the disruption of peace and security and to make it easier to restore peace and the community after the conflict ends.[102]

To clarify the role of human dignity in this context, this section offers next some illustrations of war crimes that define offences related to bodily integrity and human dignity. The aim is quite modest, as the goal is not to provide a systematic overview of each crime that falls under Article 8. However, the focus is on offences to human dignity that may resemble some of the crimes against humanity, notably torture, persecution and other inhumane acts, although translated into the contextual elements applicable to war crimes.

6.2.3.1 Torture, Cruel or Inhuman Treatment

Torture is a grave breach of the GCs and is punishable under Article 8(2)(a)(ii) of the Rome Statute. It is also a serious violation of Common Article 3 of the GCs, regulated by Article 8(2)(c)(i) of the ICC Statute. Its definition reflects that mentioned in the jurisprudence of the ICTY and the ICTR.[103] Unlike torture as a crime against humanity, the victim of the war crime of torture does not have to be 'in the custody or under the control of the accused',[104] although normally this is the context of the crime.

99 See the Preamble of the ICC Statute, para 3.

100 On the protected legal interests, see Ambos, *supra* n 58, 48–49, with further references; Werle and Jessberger, *supra* n 74, 333.

101 See generally, on the increased significance of individual rights in international humanitarian law, T Meron, 'The Humanization of Humanitarian Law' [2000] 94 *AJIL* 239.

102 See Pictet et al., *supra* n 84, 361; Werle and Jessberger, *supra* n 74, 407–408.

103 *Prosecutor* v. *Kunarac, Kovac and Vukovic*, IT-96-23 and IT-96-23/1, Trial Judgment, 22 February 2001, para 497 and Appeal, 12 June 2002, para 142 [*Kunarac*]. See also *Krnojelac*, para 179; *Furundžija*, para 162; *Prosecutor* v. *Musema*, ICTR-96-13-T, 27 January 2000, para 285 [*Musema*].

104 *Prosecutor* v. *Mbarushimana*, ICC-01/04-01/10, 16 December 2011, ICC [*Mbarushimana*], Dissenting opinion of Judge Sanji Mmasenono Monageng, paras 29–30.

The Elements of Crimes define 'torture' as the infliction of 'severe physical or mental pain or suffering upon one or more persons' for purposes such as 'obtaining information or a confession, punishment, intimidation or coercion or for any reason based on discrimination of any kind'.[105] The war crime of torture has been described as a crime of specific intent[106] since it demands the satisfaction of a 'specific purpose requirement'.[107]

'Inhuman treatment' is a grave breach of the GCs, punishable pursuant to Article 8(2)(a)(iii) of the ICC Statute, which applies to IACs. 'Cruel treatment' is a serious violation of the Geneva Conventions punishable ex Article 8(2)(c)(i) of the ICC Statute, which instead applies to NIACs. Both inhuman treatment and cruel treatment are defined in the Elements of Crimes: 'The perpetrator inflicted severe physical or mental pain or suffering upon one or more persons.'[108]

It should be remembered that the ICTY first defined inhuman treatment on the basis of the provisions of the Geneva Convention prohibiting inhuman acts.[109] The Tribunal described humanity as the basic pillar of the GCs[110] and affirmed that acts or omissions that cause serious mental or physical suffering[111] are a serious attack on bodily or psychological integrity, or otherwise contravene the principle of humanity are inhuman and not consistent

105 *Mbarushimana*, para 169; Elements of Crimes, War Crimes, art. 8(2)(a)(ii)-1, War crime of torture, paras 1–2; Elements of Crimes, War Crimes, art. 8(2)(c)(i)-4, War crime of torture, para 4.

106 *Bemba*, ICC-01/05-01/08-424, para 294.

107 *Mbarushimana*, Dissenting opinion of Judge Sanji Mmasenono Monageng, para 29; Bemba, paras 195, 293, 299–300.

108 Elements of Crimes, War Crimes, art. 8(2)(a)(ii)-2, War crime of inhuman treatment, para 1; Elements of Crimes, War Crimes, art. 8(2)(c)(i)-3, War crime of cruel treatment, para 1. Jurisprudence of the ad hoc tribunals support the opinion that the two crimes are identical: *Delalić*, para 443; *Kordić and Čerkez*, para 265.

109 See ICRC: Art. 12, Geneva Convention for the Amelioration of the Condition of Wounded, Sick and Shipwrecked Members of Armed Forces at Sea (Geneva Convention II), 12 August 1949, 75 UNTS 85, Art. 12; Arts 13, 20, 46, Geneva Convention Relative to the Treatment of Prisoners of War (Geneva Convention III), 12 August 1949, 75 UNTS 135; Geneva Convention IV, Arts 27, 32; Geneva Conventions I–IV, Art. 3; (ICRC), Protocol Additional to the Geneva Conventions of 12 August 1949, and relating to the Protection of Victims of International Armed Conflicts (Protocol I), 8 June 1977, 1125 UNTS 3 (Additional Protocol I, API I) Art. 75(1); AP II, Arts 4(1), 7(2).

110 *Prosecutor* v. *Mucić et al.*, IT-96-21, 16 November 1998, para 532 [*Mucić*]. See also S Vöneky, 'Implementation and Enforcement of International Humanitarian Law' in D Fleck and M Bothe (eds), *The Handbook of International Humanitarian Law* (3rd ed., Oxford University Press 2013), para 1412, who notes that '[t]he obligation of humane treatment is practically a guiding theme for the four Geneva Conventions'.

111 Similarly, see Elements of Crimes for Art. 8(2)(a)(ii)-2 of the ICC Statute, num. 1; Elements of Crimes for Art. 8(2)(c)(i)-3 of the ICC Statute, 1.

with the concept of humanity.[112] Inhuman treatment requires a violation of the basic principle of humane treatment, particularly respect for human dignity.[113] A perpetrator can also be guilty of inhuman treatment if they subjected the victim to inhuman conditions.[114] What conditions count as inhuman cannot, however, be defined in the abstract, but must be determined in light of the circumstances of the individual case.[115] The jurisprudence provides several examples, including injuries and mistreatment of detainees, and the use of persons as human shields.[116] 'Inhuman treatment', expressed in Common Article 3 of the GCs, is therefore considered as 'the umbrella under which the remainder of the listed "grave breaches" in the Conventions fall'.[117] Differently, 'cruel treatment' is described as an intentional act or omission 'which, judged objectively, is deliberate and not accidental, which causes serious mental or physical suffering or injury or constitutes a *serious attack on human dignity*'.[118] In the ICTR Statute, the definition of inhumane treatment includes a reference to corporal punishment, in line with Common Article 3 to the GCs.[119]

It is, however, doubtful that the ICTY case law on the distinction between torture, on the one hand, and inhuman and cruel treatment, on the other, can be considered applicable to the ICC Statute. As mentioned above, the Elements of Crimes define these crimes in an identical form, as they both require 'severe physical or mental pain or suffering'.[120] Unlike the approach adopted by the ICTY, it will also not be possible to consider every violation of

112 See *Lukić*, para 631; *Aleksovski*, paras 56 ff.; affirmed in *Prosecutor* v. *Naletilić and Martinović*, IT-98-34-T, 31 March 2003, para 246 [*Naletilić*]; *Prosecutor* v. *Haradinaj et al.*, IT-04-84bis-T, 29 November 2012, para 421; *Stanišić and Župljanin*, para 56. On inhuman treatment by causing serious mental suffering, see *Prosecutor* v. *Haradinaj et al.*, IT-04-84-A, 19 July 2010, para 95.

113 *Delalić*, para 442; *Kordić and Čerkez*, para 256.

114 *Mucić*, para 558.

115 See *Mucić*, para 544; *Blaškić*, para 155; *Martić*, IT-95-11, Trial Chamber, 12 June 2007, para 80; *Delić*, IT-04-83, 15 September 2008, para 51. On the factors to be considered when deciding individual cases, see *Gotovina Case*, para 1794.

116 *Kordić and Čerkez*, para 256; see also *Kvočka*, para 161 (concerning 'cruel treatment' as a violation of common article 3, where the same considerations apply).

117 *Blaškić*, paras 154–155.

118 *Kordić and Čerkez*, para 265 (emphasis added). See also *Blaškić*, para 186; *Jelisić*, paras 34, 41.

119 ICTR Statute, Art. 4(a).

120 See Elements of Crimes for Art. 8(2)(a)(ii)-2 of the ICC Statute, num. 1 (inhuman treatment); Elements of Crimes for Art. 8(2)(c)(i)-3 of the ICC Statute, num. 1 (cruel treatment); Elements of Crimes for Art. 8(2)(a)(ii)-1 of the ICC Statute, num. 1; and Elements of Crimes for Art. 8(2)(c)(i)-4 of the ICC Statute, num. 1 (torture). The ICC considered that holding civilians hostage for hours in a room filled with corpses was inhuman treatment: see *Prosecutor* v. *Katanga and Chui*, Decision on the Confirmation of Charges, 30 September 2008, Pre-Trial Chamber I, ICC-01/04-01/07, ICC, paras 361 ff [*Katanga*].

dignity as cruel or inhuman treatment. This also derives simply from the fact that attacks on dignity are regulated by Article 8(2)(b)(xxi) of the ICC Statute.[121]

The elements of the crime of cruel or inhuman treatment are, however, fulfilled if a violation of dignity causes severe physical or mental pain or suffering. For instance, charges of cruel treatment pursuant to Article 8(2)(c)(i) have been used in arrest warrants issued in the Situation referred to the ICC by the Government of Uganda, where the perpetration of acts such as restraining civilians, forcing them to carry plundered property,[122] while beating them,[123] under threat of death, and abduction was alleged.[124] The assault and/or injures to civilians and/or the act of forcing them to carry heavy loads of pillaged goods, causing pain and suffering or serious injury to body or mental or physical health, have also been considered as cruel treatments.[125] Moreover, in *Katanga et al.*, the Pre-Trial Chamber I considered that imprisoning citizens for many hours in a classroom filled with dead bodies[126] amounted to inhuman treatment under Article 8(2)(a)(ii). However, it ultimately discharged the two accused because the crimes could not be attributed to them.[127]

6.2.3.2 Outrages upon Personal Dignity

The ICC Statute also criminalizes 'committing outrages upon personal dignity, in particular humiliating and degrading treatment', in Articles 8(2)(b)(xxi) and 8(2)(c)(ii), which are identical for both IACs and NIACs.[128] The status of humiliating and degrading treatment as a war crime is recognized under customary international law.[129]

121 See R Arnold and S Wehrenberg, 'Article 8' in Triffterer and Ambos, *supra* n 3, paras 614–651, 469–476.

122 *Arrest Warrant for Kony* as Amended on 27 September 2005, Pre-Trial Chamber II, ICC-02/04-01/05, ICC, paras 17–19; *Arrest Warrant for Lukwiya*, 8 July 2005, Pre-Trial Chamber II, ICC-02/04, ICC, 9; *Arrest Warrant for Otti*, 8 July 2005, Pre-Trial Chamber II, ICC-02/04, ICC, 14.

123 *Ibid.*, 17; *Arrest Warrant for Otti*, *supra* n 122, 18.

124 *Ibid.*, 18–19; *Arrest Warrant for Otti*, *supra* n 122, 19; *Arrest Warrant for Ongwen*, 8 July 2005, Pre-Trial Chamber II, ICC-02/04, ICC, 10.

125 *Prosecutor* v. *Mudacumara*, ICC-01/04-01/12, Decision on the Prosecutor's Application under Article 58, 13 July 2011, ICC, paras 44–45 [*Mudacumara*].

126 *Katanga*, paras 361–364.

127 *Ibid.*, para 572.

128 See Arnold and Wehrenberg, *supra* n 121; A Zimmermann and R Geiß, 'Article 8' in Triffterer and Ambos, *supra* n 3, paras 900–901, at 553.

129 See *Kunarac*, IT-96-23-T, para 498; *Prosecutor* v. *Sesay et al.*, SCSL-04-15-T, 2 March 2009, Special Court for Sierra Leone (SCSL), para 174.

The definition is based on Common Article 3(1)(c) of the GCs. Article 75(2)(b) of AP I and Article 4(2)(e) of AP II also contain prohibitions on humiliating and degrading treatment.[130] The protection of human dignity is the central objective of Article 27(1) of Geneva Convention IV, which requires respect for one's person, honour, family rights, and religious convictions and practices. The right to respect for one's person is broadly considered and takes into account all rights that are inseparable from human existence, especially the right to physical, moral and intellectual integrity.[131] This crime can therefore be perpetrated in many ways.[132] In particular, the Elements of Crimes include two clarifications: 'The perpetrator humiliated, degraded or otherwise violated the dignity of one or more persons. The severity of the humiliation, degradation or other violation was of such degree as to be generally recognized as an outrage upon personal dignity.'[133] Moreover, the footnote to the first expression reads: 'For this crime, "persons" can include dead persons. It is understood that the victim need not personally be aware of the existence of the humiliation or degradation or other violation. This element takes into account relevant aspects of the cultural background of the victim.'[134]

With no consensus, the Preparatory Committee had advanced a proposal to include[135] 'as well as practices of apartheid and other inhuman and degrading practices involving outrages upon personal dignity based on racial

[130] Geneva Conventions I–IV, Art. 3(1)(c) contains a prohibition on 'outrages upon personal dignity, in particular humiliating and degrading treatment'. In addition to humiliating and degrading treatment, the wording in the Additional Protocols includes, as examples of prohibited acts, enforced prostitution and any form of indecent assault.

[131] See J Pictet et al., *Geneva Convention IV, Commentary* (ICRC 1958), 201.

[132] See Arnold and Wehrenberg, *supra* n 121, paras 622–641.

[133] Elements of Crimes, War Crimes, Art. 8(2)(b)(xxi), War crime of outrages upon personal dignity, paras 1–2; ibid., Art. 8(2)(c)(ii), War crime of outrages upon personal dignity, paras 1–2. See *Prosecutor* v. *Brima et al.*, SCSL-04-16-T, 20 June 2007, SCSL, para 716 and SCSL-2004-16-T, Decision on Defence Motions for Judgment of Acquittal Pursuant to Rule 98, 31 March 2006, SCSL, para 115.

[134] Elements of Crimes, War Crimes, art. 8(2)(b)(xxi), War crime of outrages upon personal dignity, para 1, fn. 49; Elements of Crimes, War Crimes, art. 8(2)(c)(ii), War crime of outrages upon personal dignity, para 1, fn. 57.

[135] References to apartheid appear in the following documents: UN Doc. A/CONF.183/C.1/SR.4, paras 44 (Syria), 48 (Lebanon), 63 (Libya), 65 (China), 66 (United Arab Emirates), 67 (Greece), 69 (Vietnam), 70 (Bahrain); UN Doc. A/CONF.183/C1/SR.5, paras 9 (Kuwait), 19 (Republic of Korea), 23 (Tunisia), 26 (Thailand), 33 (Egypt), 46 (Brazil), 48 (Algeria), 56 (Japan), 62 (Morocco), 69 (Cuba), 70 (Turkey), 72 (Iran), 83 (Senegal), 97 (South Africa). Opposing reference to apartheid: UN Doc. A/CONF.183/C.1/SR.4, paras 62 (Costa Rica), 75 (Sweden); UN Doc. A/ CONF.183/C1/SR.5, paras 7 (Belgium), 36 (Russia), 40 (United Kingdom), 58 (Switzerland), 60 (Macedonia), 66 (Italy), 92 (Chile).

discrimination'.[136] It can be noted here that, whereas the Bureau Proposal did not include modifications to the draft of the Preparatory Committee,[137] it added 'the crime of apartheid' to the notion of crimes against humanity.

As an example of the applicability of this crime, the Pre-Trial Chamber I of the ICC, while confirming a charge of outrages upon personal dignity, declared, referring to wording of the earlier judgment of the ICTY Trial Chamber in the *Furundžija Case*:

> The general principle of respect for human dignity is the basic underpinning and indeed the very raison d'être of international humanitarian law and human rights law ... This principle is intended to shield human beings from outrages upon their personal dignity, whether such outrages are carried out by unlawfully attacking the body or by humiliating and debasing the honour, the self-respect or the mental well-being of a person.[138]

In the *Aleksovski* decision, the ICTY emphasized that the overall purpose of Common Article 3(1) of the GCs is to protect dignity and ensure humane treatment.[139] The Tribunal considered that humiliating and degrading treatment is not only inhuman treatment that causes serious suffering, but it can also be the outcome of physical violence.[140] The severity, form and duration of the violence and the intensity and duration of the physical or mental suffering are the objective standards by which to assess the existence of this crime.[141] '[T]he humiliation of the victim must be so intense that any reasonable person would be outraged'[142] and such humiliation must be 'real and serious', but need not be 'lasting'.[143] It is a 'species of inhuman treatment that is deplorable, occasioning more serious suffering than most prohibited acts falling within the genus'.[144] In the *Musema* case, the ICTR defined humiliating or degrading

136 Preparatory Committee Draft Statute, pp. 20 (international armed conflict), 22 and 23 (non-international armed conflict). Each of the two categories of non-international armed conflict had an identical provision, and this redundancy was only removed in the Bureau Discussion Paper of 6 July 1998, A/CONF.183/C.1/SR.33, para 7.

137 Discussion Paper, Bureau, UN Doc. A/CONF.183/C.1/L.53; Bureau Proposal, UN Doc. A/CONF.183/C.1/L.59.

138 *Furundžija*, para 183, cited in *Katanga*, para 369, fn. 482.

139 *Aleksovski*, para 49.

140 *Ibid.*, paras 56 ff, in which the Court took the view that the crime had to be based on the perpetrator's contempt for the victim's dignity. The Trial Chamber found the circumstances in prison camps, characterized by physical violence and the use of prisoners as human shields and to dig trenches in dangerous areas, to be serious violations of personal dignity: see *Aleksovski*, paras 228 ff; affirmed by *Aleksovski*, IT-95-14/1-A, (AC), 24 March 2000, para 37.

141 *Ibid.*, paras 56–57.

142 *Kunarac*, IT-96-23-A and IT-96-23/1-A, para 162.

143 *Kunarac*, IT-96-23-T and IT-96-23/1-T, para 501.

144 *Aleksovski*, paras 54–56.

treatment as acts that undermine self-respect and '[l]ike outrages upon personal dignity, these offences may be regarded as a lesser forms of torture; moreover ones in which the motives required for torture would not be required, nor would it be required that the acts be committed under state authority'.[145]

In *Katanga et al.*, the Pre-Trial Chamber I considered that 'hanging naked from handcuffs or being forced to maintain a certain position for long periods of time' was a form of humiliating treatment of female prisoners, recalling the view of the UN Human Rights Council.[146] It also mentioned the jurisprudence of the ICTY and ICTR, when considering outrages upon personal dignity, such as forcing victims to dance naked on a table; compelling detainees to be human shields; threatening detainees with acts of physical, psychological or sexual abuse; compelling incest or, after killing their parents or tutors, leaving infants with no care.[147] The focus of violations of dignity is primarily on acts, omission, or words that do not necessarily involve long-term physical harm, but which nevertheless are serious offences deserving of punishment.[148] Moreover, in the preliminary examination in the Gaza Flotilla situation, the ICC Prosecutor stated that there was a reasonable basis to believe that Israel Defence Forces soldiers perpetrated humiliating and degrading treatment that was sufficiently serious to amount to an outrage upon the personal dignity of the *Mavi Marmara* passengers.[149] Among the various treatments, the Prosecutor listed being beaten, being denied access to toilet services, being blindfolded, being handcuffed for long times, being denied medical treatments, being given limited access to food and drink and facing physical and verbal violence.[150]

6.2.3.3 Causing Great Suffering

Article 8(2)(a)(iii) of the ICC Statute includes the grave breach of 'wilfully causing great suffering or serious injury to body or health'. 'Great suffering' is

145 *Musema*, para 285.
146 *Katanga*, para 370. The relevant cases are: *Isoriano de Bouton* v. *Uruguay* (37/1978), CCPR/C/12/D/37/1978; *Arzuaga Gilbao* v. *Uruguay* (147/1983), CCPR/C/26/D/147/1983.
147 *Ibid.*, para 371.
148 *Kvočka*, para 172. See also *Katanga*, paras 375–376; *Mudacumara*, paras 55–56.
149 Office of the Prosecutor, Situation on Registered Vessels of Comoros, Greece and Cambodia, 6 November 2014, para 90 (Situation on Registered Vessels of the Comoros, the Hellenic Republic of Greece and the Kingdom of Cambodia (ICC-01/13), Application for Review pursuant to Article 53(3)(a) of the Prosecutor's Decision of 6 November 2014 not to initiate an investigation in the Situation, 29 January 2015, Annex A).
150 *Ibid.*, para 90.

understood, as explained in the Elements of Crimes, as 'great physical or mental pain or suffering'.[151] There is no equivalent crime with respect to NIACs. The expression 'wilfully causing great suffering or serious injury to body or health' implies that it is formed by a single offence, the constitutive elements of which are set out as alternatives.[152] It includes conduct that does not fit in the notion of torture and, unlike torture, there is no need to establish a prohibited purpose.[153] According to the Commentary to Article 147 of the Fourth Geneva Convention, the criminal act may be inflicted for motives such as punishment, revenge, or out of sadism, and the length of time the victim is incapacitated is considered to assess the seriousness.[154]

Unlike the grave breach of inhuman treatment, there must be serious mental or physical injury, although it does not need to be permanent.[155] Acts that only relate to an individual's human dignity, and that may only cause temporary unhappiness or humiliation, are not sufficient to fall within the definition of this crime.[156] The crime includes mental as well as physical suffering, so that solitary confinement, for instance, can also be considered as an infliction of great suffering.[157] In the *Čelebići* case at the ICTY, the Prosecutor alleged that the inhumane conditions in the prison camp amounted to wilfully causing great suffering or serious injury to body or health, but the Trial Chamber held that such acts were more properly charged as inhuman treatment.[158]

6.2.3.4 Sexual Violence

In the context of IACs, Article 8(2)(b)(xxii) of the ICC Statute regulates crimes of rape, sexual slavery, forced prostitution, forced pregnancy, enforced sterilization and other forms of sexual violence that are grave breaches of the GCs. A similar provision for NIACs is present in Article 8(2)(e)(vi) of the Statute, which provides for the same method of commission as well as every other method of sexual violence that is a serious violation of Common Article 3 of the GCs.

151 Elements of Crimes, War Crimes, art. 8(2)(a)(iii), war crime of willfully causing great suffering, para 1.

152 *Blaškić*, para 156.

153 *Delalić*, para 442. Also: *Kordić and Čerkez*, para 245.

154 *Naletilić*, paras 339–343.

155 See K Dörmann, 'Article 8' in Triffterer and Ambos, *supra* n 3, paras 109, at 338.

156 *Kordić and Čerkez*, para 245; *Krstić*, para 513. See also *Akayesu*, para 502; *Prosecutor* v. *Kaing Guek Eay* (alias: Duch), 001/18-07-2007/ECCC/TC, 26 July 2010, para 454.

157 Vöneky, *supra* n 110, para 1412; *Krnojelac*, para 183.

158 *Delalić*, para 558.

Before the creation of the ICC, treaties did not expressly cover the crime of sexual violence, which was instead regarded as a 'mere' attack on personal honour or dignity. Article 27(2) of Geneva Convention IV, Articles 75(2) and 76(1) of AP I, and Article 4(2)(e) of AP II classified rape, enforced prostitution and 'any other form of indecent assault' as attacks on the victim's honour; they were not specifically considered as grave breaches of the GCs or their APs. The ICTR Statute adopted this reading and classified rape, enforced prostitution and other forms of sexual violence as outrages upon personal dignity,[159] as did the SCSL Statute.[160] If the ICTY Statute was silent regarding sexual violence as war crimes,[161] given the relevance of sexual violence as a method of warfare in the Bosnian conflict, the Tribunal therefore prosecuted sexual violence as a war crime on the basis of the grave breaches provisions of the GCs or other violations of the laws and customs of war.[162]

By including distinct provisions on crimes of sexual violence in the ICC Statute, it was ultimately expressly recognized that these crimes, in the context of organized violence, are international crimes.[163]

6.2.3.5 Slavery

Article 4(2)(d) of AP II prohibits 'slavery and slave trade in all their forms' and applies to '[a]ll persons who do not take a direct part or who have ceased to take part in hostilities, whether or not their liberty has been restricted'.[164] Although this protocol only applies to NIACs, slavery is also prohibited in IACs. The crime infringes upon the principle of humane treatment, which is recognized in Common Article 3 of the GCs, Article 13 of Geneva Convention III, Article 27 of Geneva Convention IV, and Article 4(1) of AP II.[165]

In 2002, because of the serious nature of this crime, the ICTY, in the *Krnojelac* judgment, considered that slavery committed in the context of an

159 See ICTR Statute, Art. 4(e).

160 See SCSL Statute, Art. 3(e).

161 However, the Tribunal can prosecute sexual violence as crimes against humanity: see ICTY Statute, Art. 5(g).

162 See e.g. *Furundžija*, para 172. See also *Mucić*, paras 476 ff; *Kvočka*, para 145; *Kunarac*, IT-96-23-A and IT-96-23/1-A, paras 150 ff; *Brđanin*, para 485 (rape as torture).

163 E La Haye, 'The Elements of War Crimes—Article 8(2)(b)(xxii)' in RS Lee (ed.), *The International Criminal Court, Elements of Crimes and Rules of Procedure and Evidence* (Transnational 2001), 184, 185 ff.

164 AP II, Art. 4(1). See SS Junod, in Y Sandoz, C Swinarski and B Zimmermann (eds.), *Commentary on the Additional Protocols* (ICRC 1987), para 4523.

165 See SS Junod, in Sandoz et al., *supra* n 164, para 4523.

armed conflict constituted a war crime.[166] The Tribunal also clarified the elements of the war crime, affirming that the elements are the same as the elements of the crime against humanity of enslavement.[167] Article 8(2) of the Rome Statute does not include slavery as a war crime as such. However, the conduct of enslavement as 'the exercise of any or all of the powers attaching to the right of ownership over a person'[168] could amount to the war crime of 'outrages upon personal dignity' under Article 8(2)(b)(xxi) and (c)(ii) of the ICC Statute.

6.3 PROSECUTION

6.3.1 *Universal Jurisdiction: Principle of Universality and* Aut dedere aut judicare

The principle of universal jurisdiction is traditionally described as 'a legal principle allowing or requiring a state to bring criminal proceedings in respect of certain crimes irrespective of the location of the crime and the nationality of the perpetrator or the victim'.[169] With a view only to adjudicative powers, universal jurisdiction is the ability of a national court of any State to bring to justice persons for crimes committed outside its territory which are not linked to the State by the nationality of the suspect or the victims or by harm to the State's own national interests. When a domestic court exercises jurisdiction over international crimes or ordinary crimes of international concern committed abroad, the court acts as an agent of the international community implementing international law.[170]

In Chapter 3, Section 3.4.2, I discussed the origins of the principle of universality. The distinction between a universal jurisdiction that could be called 'utilitarian' and a jurisdiction that is 'humanitarian' is an essential element of analysis in the exploration of the meaning of the current idea of universal jurisdiction. In particular, the principle of universal jurisdiction '*transcends* state sovereignty'.[171] Moreover, universal jurisdiction also displaces

166 See *Krnojelac*, paras 351–356.

167 *Ibid.*, para 356.

168 See ICC Statute, Art. 7(2)(c).

169 See KC Randall, 'Universal Jurisdiction under International Law' [1988] 66 *TLR* 785–788; International Law Association Committee on International Human Rights Law and Practice, 'Final Report on the Exercise of Universal Jurisdiction in Respect of Gross Human Rights Offences', 2000, 2.

170 See *Attorney General of Israel* v. *Eichmann*, 36 Int'l L. Rep. 277, 304 (Israel Sup. Ct. 1962).

171 See MC Bassiouni, 'Universal Jurisdiction for International Crimes' [2001] 42 *VJIL* 81, 96 (emphasis added).

the right of the accused to be tried by the 'natural judge', a foundational principle related to territorial jurisdiction.[172]

The *ratio* of a decision to trigger universal jurisdiction is based on three major points: '(i) no other state can exercise jurisdiction on the basis of the traditional doctrines; (ii) no other state has a direct interest; and (iii) there is an interest of the international community to enforce.'[173] But the rationale behind it is broader: '[I]t is based on the notion that certain crimes are so harmful to international interests that states are entitled – and even obliged – to bring proceedings against the perpetrator, regardless of the location of the crime and the nationality of the perpetrator or the victim.'[174] It was therefore accepted as a general principle that in certain circumstances sovereignty could be limited for such serious crimes. Hence, the State exercises universal jurisdiction as a surrogate for the international community with an *actio popularis* against individuals who are *hostes humani generis*.[175]

For this reason, it has been argued that the principle of universal jurisdiction is based on two theories:

> The first is the *universalist* position that stems from an idealistic *weltanschauung*. This idealistic universalist position recognizes certain core values and the existence of overriding international interests as being commonly shared and accepted by the international community and thus transcending the singularity of national interests. The second position is a *pragmatic policy-oriented* one that recognizes that occasionally certain commonly shared interests of the international community require an enforcement mechanism that transcends the interests of the singular sovereignty.[176]

These two theories have common features, namely: (a) the existence of fundamental and universal values; (b) the importance of extending the scope of enforcement mechanisms in order to prosecute possible serious violations; and (c) the deterrence and prevention effect that an expanded jurisdictional enforcement system will generate. Both positions ultimately provide all

172 See, e.g., Art. 13, ECHR; Art. 25, ACHR.

173 Bassiouni, *supra* n 171, 96.

174 M Robinson, 'Foreword' in S Macedo (ed.), *The Princeton Principles on Universal Jurisdiction* (Princeton University Press 2001), 16.

175 See R Boed, 'The Effect of a Domestic Amnesty on the Ability of Foreign States to Prosecute Alleged Perpetrators of Serious Human Rights Violations' [2000] 33 *CornellILJ* 297, 299–301; also M Ragazzi, *The Concept of International Obligations Erga Omnes* (Clarendon Press 1997); *Barcelona Traction, Light and Power Company Limited* (*Belgium* v. *Spain*), 2nd Phase, 5 February 1970, ICJ, para 32.

176 Bassiouni, *supra* n 171, 96 (emphasis added).

sovereign States, as well as international organs, with the power to individually or collectively implement and enhance international proscriptions.[177]

The *aut dedere aut judicare* (extradite or prosecute) obligation is inherently connected to the principle of universality. However, it requires a State to exercise jurisdiction (which would necessarily imply universal jurisdiction in some instances) over a person suspected of certain categories of crimes or to extradite the person to a State able and willing to do so or to surrender the person to the ICC with jurisdiction over the suspect and the crime.[178] Indeed, the 1952 International Committee of the Red Cross (ICRC) Commentary to Article 49 of the First Convention affirms that '[t]here is nothing in the paragraph to exclude the handing over of the accused to an international penal tribunal'.[179] This option was also expressly mentioned in the 1996 Draft Code of Crimes, adopted by the ILC.[180] In its Commentary on the 1996 Draft Code, the ILC also clarified that a State would satisfy its international obligations either by extraditing to another State the alleged offender, who is found in its territory, surrendering them to an international criminal court or prosecuting that person before its national courts.[181]

The ultimate purpose of this obligation is to ensure that those who are accused of certain international crimes are prosecuted consistently with international standards of criminal procedure by providing for prosecution by a court with competent jurisdiction. According to Bassiouni, violations of international crimes having a *jus cogens* character give rise to an obligation *erga omnes* on States to either extradite or prosecute any alleged offenders present on their territory, 'the consequence of which is that impunity cannot be granted'.[182] In essence, he argues that, because of the peremptory nature of *jus cogens*, a violation of such a norm gives rise to a corresponding obligation *erga omnes* on all States to, among other things, extradite or prosecute any

[177] These issues are discussed in MC Bassiouni and EM Wise, *Aut dedere Aut judicare: The Duty To Prosecute or Extradite in International Law* (Martinus Nijhoff 1995), 3–69.

[178] See generally M Henzelin, *Le Principe de l'Universalité en Droit Pénal International: Droit et Obligation pour les États de Poursuivre et Juger selon le Principe de l'Universalité* (Bruylant 2000); C Mitchell, *Aut Dedere, aut Judicare: The Extradite or Prosecute Clause in International Law* (Graduate Institute 2009); Bassiouni and Wise, *supra* n 177, 3–5; H Donnedieu de Vabres, *Introduction à l'étude du droit pénal international: essai d'histoire et de critique sur la compétence criminelle dans les rapports avec l'étranger* (Sirey 1922), 183.

[179] Pictet et al., *supra* n 84, 366.

[180] Draft Code of Crimes, Article 9, Obligation to extradite or prosecute.

[181] Yearbook of the ILC, 1996, vol. II, Part Two, p. 32. See also Art. 11, International Convention for the Protection of All Persons from Enforced Disappearance, 20 December 2006.

[182] See also MC Bassiouni, 'Searching for Peace and Achieving Justice: The Need for Accountability' [1996] 59 *LCP* 9–28, 17.

alleged offender on their territory.[183] Similarly, Goodwin-Gill affirms that '[i]nternational crimes, "by their very nature," produce an obligation *erga omnes* to extradite to another competent state, prosecute locally, or surrender the person concerned to the jurisdiction of a competent international tribunal; it is the *jus cogens/erga omnes* combination that makes prosecution (somewhere) unavoidable as a matter of duty'.[184]

In short, the obligation *aut dedere aut judicare* attempts to restore or protect fundamental rights through effective judicial remedies, ensure minimal decent treatment to restore dignity and judge and punish perpetrators.[185] Beyond the connection between the protection of human dignity, the *principle* of universality and the obligation *aut dedere aut judicare*, the following section explores the adjudicative power of criminal courts at the international level.

6.3.2 *Adjudicative Power*

Hannah Arendt, in her 1963 *Eichmann in Jerusalem*, considered that only a court that could genuinely claim to represent the entire humanity, the victim of the crimes committed by the accused, and would judge on the basis of a new understanding of the import of 'universal jurisdiction', would have been competent to prosecute Eichmann. In her view, the Jerusalem court should have declared itself incompetent and the 'Nazis and Nazi Collaborators Law' inapplicable. It should then have asked the UN to establish an international criminal court for this case, for 'the very monstrousness of the events is "minimized" before a tribunal which represents one nation only'.[186] Only such a scenario, in her opinion, would have guaranteed the development of the new legal category of 'humanity' and of the existing international legal order.

As seen in Chapter 3, the first special 'international' tribunal, composed by five judges of the victorious powers, was suggested in the Treaty of Versailles.[187] The Nuremberg and Tokyo tribunals were 'multinational tribunals', rather than

183 See also MC Bassiouni, 'International Crimes: Jus Cogens and Obligatio Erga Omnes' [1996] 59 *LCP* 63–74, 63; I Bantekas and S Nash, *International Criminal Law* (3rd ed., Cavendish 2007), 92.

184 GS Goodwin-Gill, 'Crime in International Law: Obligations Erga Omnes and the Duty to Prosecute' in GS Goodwin-Gill and S Talmon (eds), *The Reality of International Law: Essays in Honour of Ian Brownlie* (Clarendon Press 1999), 198–223, 220.

185 See P Capps, *Human Dignity and the Foundations of International Law* (Hart 2009), 211.

186 Hannah Arendt, *Eichmann in Jerusalem. A Report on the Banality of Evil* 267 (1992) (Orig. 1963), 270.

187 Treaty of Versailles (1919), 2 Bevans 235, art. 227.

'international tribunals in the strict sense'.[188] In the 1990s, the ICTY was the 'first truly international criminal tribunal'.[189] The Appeals Chamber of the ICTY in the *Tadić* case clearly explained that

> it would be a travesty of law and a betrayal of the universal need for justice, should the concept of State sovereignty be allowed to be raised successfully against human rights. Borders should not be considered as a shield against the reach of the law and as a protection for those who trample underfoot the most elementary rights of humanity.[190]

The Chamber also clarified that this 'is all the more so in view of the nature of the offences [. . .] which, if proven, do not affect the interests of one State alone but shock the conscience of mankind'.[191] Thus, for this reason, 'the principle of primacy of this International Tribunal over national courts must be affirmed',[192] and '[t]here can therefore be no objection to an international tribunal properly constituted trying these crimes on behalf of the international community'.[193]

Only a few years later, the Rome Statute was going to establish the new International Criminal Court, distinguishing it from previous other ad hoc tribunals. In 1998, reasons of *humanitas* drove States towards agreeing to set up an international system of prosecution that provides a permanent court with an adjudicative power, derived from the consent given by States. Article 1 of the ICC Statute opens by stating that '[a]n International Criminal Court is hereby established' and characterizes it as 'a permanent institution', reflecting the urgency expressed during the drafting debates.[194] In the historical path of

188 BVA Röling, 'The Law of War and the National Jurisdiction since 1945' [1960] 100 *RCADI* 356.

189 T Meron, 'War Crimes in Yugoslavia and the Development of International Law' [1994] 88 *AJIL* 78, 79.

190 *Tadić*, IT-94-1-AR72, Appeals Chamber, Decision on the Defence Motion for Interlocutory Appeal on Jurisdiction, 2 October 1995 [*Tadić AR72*], para 58.

191 It also notes that, already in 1950, the Supreme Military Tribunal of Italy stated in the case of General Wagener: 'These norms [concerning crimes against laws and customs of war], due to their highly ethical and moral content, have a universal character, not a territorial one. [. . .] They are, instead, crimes of lèse-humanité (*reati di lesa umanità*) and, as previously demonstrated, the norms prohibiting them have a universal character, not simply a territorial one,' see 13 March 1950, in *Rivista Penale* 753, 757 (Sup. Mil. Trib., Italy 1950; unofficial translation). See also Supreme Court of Israel in the *Eichmann*, *Israel* v. *Eichmann*, 36 International Law Reports 277, 291–293 (Isr. S. Ct. 1962).

192 *Tadić AR72*, para 59.

193 *Ibid.*, Decision at Trial, Decision on the Defence Motion on Jurisdiction, 10 August 1995, para 42.

194 A/CONF.183/SR.2, paras 19 (Norway), 57 (Venezuela); A/CONF.183/SR.3, para 57 (Romania); A/CONF.183/SR.7, para 21 (Mexico).

dignity consolidation in ICL, the ICC represents the first permanent institution with the 'power' to exercise jurisdiction over 'the most serious crimes of international concern' and, by way of comparison with the first pillar of the criminal system of prosecution of international crimes, it is a complementary system to national criminal jurisdictions.[195] Thus, Article 1 provides 'a synthetic presentation of the main characteristics of the International Criminal Court: its permanence, its complementarity and its scope limited to the crimes recognized by its Statute'.[196]

It can be concluded that human dignity defines not only the core international crimes but also the nature of their prosecutorial system. Crimes that are contrary to the protection of human dignity deserve to have a prosecution that supersedes national courts and can provide an international justice for horrors committed by *hostes humani generis* that shake the conscience of humankind, beyond concerns of State sovereignty.[197]

6.4 *HUMANITAS* AS THE FOUNDATION OF INTERNATIONAL CRIMINAL LAW

Human dignity entered and was consolidated in the legal frame of ICL by way of two processes, as described in Chapter 3. These two processes are closely connected to the formation of two main pillars of the international criminal system, namely the notion of international crime and the system of international prosecution, both at the national and at the international levels. This architecture shares a common basis, namely considerations of *humanitas*. In this process, human dignity not only acquired an actionable character but also slowly and partially displaced sovereign dignity. This transformation is visible in two illustrations.

195 On complementarity, see C Stahn and MM El Zeidy, *The International Criminal Court and Complementarity* (University of California Press 2014); S Nouwen, *Complementarity in the Line of Fire: The Catalysing Effect of the International Criminal Court in Uganda and Sudan* (Cambridge University Press 2013); JK Kleffner, *Complementarity in the Rome Statute and National Criminal Jurisdictions* (Oxford University Press 2008); F Gioia and M Politi, *The International Criminal Court and National Jurisdictions* (Routledge 2008); JT Holmes, 'Complementarity: National Courts versus the ICC' in Cassese, Gaeta and Jones, *supra* n 3, chapter 18.1, 672.

196 AA Mbaye and SS Shoamanesh, 'Article 1' in J Fernandez and X Pacreau (eds), *Statut de Rome de la Cour pénale internationale. Commentaire article par article*, 2 tomes (Pedone 2012), 311–325, 324 (my translation).

197 This is in line with Kelsen's view (see Chapter 3, section 3.4.1), and with Hannah Arendt's opinion expressed in her correspondence with Gershom Scholem, Letter of 24 July 1963, and in Hannah Arendt, *Eichmann In Jerusalem. A Report On the Banality of Evil* 267 (Penguin Classics 2006) (Orig. 1963), Epilogue.

First, as examined in Chapter 3, the dichotomy and tension between human dignity and sovereign dignity can be traced in the opposition between considerations of *utilitas* and *humanitas*, which guided both the definition and classification of international crimes, as well as the related prosecutorial apparatus. This distinction has first allowed me to reduce the scope of my analysis only to those crimes that trigger a humanitarian jurisdiction and are against human dignity and against humanity. The need for a universal repression of certain crimes on the basis of the existence of a human solidarity, human dignity and/or a natural right had been slowly advanced by scholars such as Francesco Carrara, Silvestre Pinheiro-Ferreira and Donnedieu de Vabres. This intellectual movement favoured a transformation in the sources of the principle of universal jurisdiction: whereas at first it was based solely on the concept of *utilitas*, it slowly expanded to reasons of *humanitas*. This development was predominantly favoured by an assessment of the nature of the crime. Only in 1945, the Nuremberg Charter established for the first time a definition of international crimes based on *humanitas* and a first recognition of the criteria of international criminal responsibility. This process was consolidated in the 1990s with the adoption of the Rome Statute and the establishment of a permanent international criminal court.

Moreover, human dignity pierces sovereign dignity and the State's screen by limiting the full operativity and functioning of the system of immunities. Immunity from jurisdiction enjoyed by the State and the Head of State has been traditionally grounded on the principle of State dignity.[198] In the words of Arthur Watts:

> Dignity, whether of States or their Heads, is an elusive notion, although it is still a convenient label. Some of the consequences formerly attributed to the need to respect the dignity of Heads of States now survive, if they survive at all, in the realms of protocol and State ceremonial . . . Some aspects of the respect due to the dignity of Heads of States still, however, survive as a matter of international law.[199]

The question of whether immunity from foreign criminal jurisdiction is subject to exceptions remains highly debated. The basic position, expressed by the ICJ in the *Arrest Warrant* case, is that customary international law

198 See *Certain Criminal Proceedings in France* (*Republic of the Congo* v. *France*) (Provisional Measures) [2003] ICJ Rep 102, Dissenting Opinion of Judge De Cara, pp. 122–123; *The Schooner Exchange* v. *McFaddon* (1812). See however, R Jennings and A Watts, *Oppenheim's International Law* (9th ed., Oxford University Press 1992), 341–342.

199 A Watts, 'The Legal Position in International Law of Heads of States, Head of Governments and Foreign Ministers' [1994] 247 *RCADI* 41.

provides no exceptions to this immunity.[200] The ICJ referred to two specific decisions, namely the decision of the House of Lords, of 24 March 1999, in the *Pinochet* case[201] and that of the French Court of Cassation, of 13 March 2001, in the *Gaddafi* case.[202] In the first case, the former Chilean head of State Augusto Pinochet invoked his immunity from foreign criminal jurisdiction *ratione materiae* against an extradition request made by Spain to the United Kingdom, in the context of criminal proceedings for the commission of the international crime of torture, within the meaning of the Convention against Torture. The reasoning of the various members of the House of Lords shows profound differences of opinion, but their majority converge in the conclusion that the adoption of the Convention against Torture had introduced a conventional exception to immunity from foreign criminal jurisdiction *ratione materiae*. As for the Gaddafi case, the French Court of Cassation upheld the Libyan head of State's immunity from criminal jurisdiction, considering that acts of terrorism were not subject to any conventional exception. Having examined the two cases, the ICJ found that they did not support a finding of any exception to immunity from foreign criminal jurisdiction under customary international law. Such exceptions must be provided for in an international treaty and are binding only on the States parties to it.

Moreover, the ILC's work on the issue of 'Immunity of State officials from foreign criminal jurisdiction' has been marked by profound disagreements, requiring the adoption of the draft article in question – draft article 7 – not by consensus but by a recorded vote, which is extremely rare.[203] The text of this draft article, entitled 'Crimes under international law in respect of which immunity ratione materiae shall not apply', reads as follows:

> Immunity *ratione materiae* from the exercise of foreign criminal jurisdiction shall not apply in respect of the following crimes under international law: (a) crime of genocide; (b) crimes against humanity; (c) war crimes; (d) crime of apartheid; (e) torture; (f) enforced disappearance.

200 *Arrest Warrant of 11 April 2000 (Democratic Republic of the Congo* v. *Belgium)*, Judgment, ICJ Reports 2002, p. 3, para 58.

201 *Regina* v. *Bow Street Metropolitan Stipendiary Magistrate and Others, ex parte Pinochet Ugarte (No. 3)* [2000] 1 AC 147.

202 *Gaddafi*, Court of Cassation, Criminal Chamber, public hearing of Tuesday, 13 March 2001, Appeal No: 00-87215.

203 Draft article 7 was adopted by 21 votes to 8, with 1 abstention. See Annual report of the ILC, A/72/10, 2017, chapter XI, chapter VII, para 74. Twenty members (most of whom voted against), submitted explanations of their vote. For the reasons for the reservations regarding the exceptions and limitations proposed, see para 93 of the Report.

During the vote, several members of the ILC, including its chairman, Mr Georg Nolte, and the former Special Rapporteur on immunity from foreign criminal jurisdiction, Mr Roman Kolodkin, recorded the reasons for their negative vote. These reasons are mainly due to the fact that the entire exercise conducted by the ILC on this issue is *de lege ferenda*.[204] The disagreement within the ILC could not be resolved on the merits because, as the commentary admits, it deliberately left open the question of whether certain crimes which demand official standing are committed in an official capacity or not.[205]

Various national courts have adhered to the doctrine according to which international crimes falling under mandatory law (*jus cogens*) constitute an exception to the immunity of a public official from foreign criminal jurisdiction. The Italian Court of Appeal in *Milde* considered the existence of a tension between sovereign immunity and respect for peremptory norms. It declared:

> Compliance with each person's inviolable rights is a fundamental principle of international law. It has the effect of reducing the scope of other traditional principles based on the sovereign equality of States, such as the customary norm granting every State immunity from the civil jurisdiction of foreign States. In fact, the jurisdictional immunity of foreign States is not absolute and cannot be invoked in proceedings relating to acts amounting to international crimes, i.e. acts *violating the universal values based on respect for human dignity which transcend, as such, the interests of a particular State community*.[206]

In a judgment rendered on 21 October 2008, following its decision in *Ferrini* v. *Germany* (2004),[207] the Court of Cassation upheld the jurisdiction of Italian courts over the sovereign immunity of Germany, grounding its decision on the

204 See, for instance, Chairman, ILC, Provisional summary record of the 3378th meeting, 20 July 2017, at 10 a.m., A/CN.4/SR.3378, 13.

205 The very definition of the term 'act performed in an official capacity' in draft article 2 (f), as 'any act done by a representative of a State in the exercise of State authority', was worded to avoid – without resolving – this difficulty, as the provisional commentary to this draft article notes: 'Using "authority" rather than "functions" avoids having to consider whether or not international crimes can arise out of the exercise of "state functions"'. See Annual report of ILC, A/71/10, 2016, chapter XI, Commentary to draft Article 2 (f), para 7.

206 *Germany* v. *Milde* (Max Josef), Appeal Judgment, Case No. 1072/2009, (2009) 92 *Riv Dir Int* 618, ILDC 1224 (IT 2009), 13 January 2009, Italy (emphasis added); Supreme Court of Cassation; 1st Criminal Section.

207 *Ferrini* v. *Germany*, Appeal Judgment, Case. No. 5044/04, ILDC 19 (IT 2004), 11 March 2004, Italy, Supreme Court of Cassation; see A Bianchi, 'Ferrini v Federal Republic of Germany' [2005] 99 *AJIL* 242; For scholarly comment see, A Gattini, 'War Crimes and State Immunity in the Ferrini Decision' [2005] 2 *JICJ* 224–242; P De Sena and F De Vittor, 'State Immunity

peremptory nature of the norms violated.[208] The Court of Cassation, in line with the decision of the Court of Appeal, connected *jus cogens* to 'respect for liberty and dignity as inherent values of every human person'.[209] It affirmed that human dignity is '*a fundamental principle due to its axiological content as a meta-value*'.[210] Since the recognition of State immunity may deprive the claimants of their rights, the decision of the Italian Court of Cassation clearly shows that in order to grant respect for fundamental rights of the victims, access to justice ought to be granted to them. The doctrine of *jus cogens* was used precisely because human dignity, the general principle of law at the core of peremptory norms, was perceived to determine and trigger overriding procedural and juridical effects.[211] Human dignity was adopted as a general principle of law underpinning *jus cogens* provisions and source of legal effects of peremptory norms. Although the ICJ later rejected the Italian courts' interpretation of the interaction between rules of *jus cogens* and the (procedural) rules of sovereign immunity,[212] in his Dissenting Opinion, Judge Cançado Trindade drew attention to the 'central principles at issue' in the case, and stated that they were '*the principle of humanity and the principle of human dignity*'.[213] In his words, 'State immunity cannot, in my view, be unduly placed above State responsibility for international crimes and its ineluctable complement, the responsible State's duty of reparation to the victims.'[214]

Consistent with this approach, in the *Nezzar* case,[215] the Court of Complaints of the Swiss Federal Criminal Court refused immunity to a former major general of the Algerian army and former minister of defence

and Human Rights: The Italian Supreme Court Decision on the Ferrini Case' [2005] 19 *EJIL* 89–112.

208 *Germany* v. *Milde*, Court of Cassation (First Criminal Section) (Italy), No. 1072/ 2009, ILDC 1224, reproduced in Iovane, States and Other Subjects of International Law, 330– 331 ('the real question to be decided is whether customary rules protecting fundamental values inherent to every human being should prevail over the rule on the jurisdictional immunity of foreign States').

209 Corte di Cassazione, Sez. I Penale, No. 1072 of 21 October 2008, registered 13 January 2009, Milde, in 92 Rivista di diritto internazionale (2009) 618ff, para 328. For comments, see A Ciampi, 'The Italian Court of Cassation Asserts Civil Jurisdiction over Germany in a Criminal Case Relating to the Second World War: The Civitella Case' [2009] 7 *JICJ* 597–615.

210 *Ibid.*, para 329 (emphasis added).

211 See *Jurisdictional Immunities of the State* (*Germany* v. *Italy*: Greece Intervening) Judgment of 3 February 2012, 113–115, paras 27–29.

212 *Ibid.*

213 *Ibid.*, Dis. Op. Cançado Trindade, p. 284, para 290, referring to para 57 of the Judgement.

214 *Ibid.*

215 Tribunal pénal fédéral, Cour des plaintes, A. c. *Ministère public de la Confédération, B. et C.* A, décision du 25 juillet 2012 (no de dossier : BB.2011.140).

because the acts for which the individual in question was being prosecuted (crimes of war and torture) would constitute international crimes of *jus cogens*.

Whether one follows the position maintained by a few national courts or that of draft Article 7 adopted by majority by the ILC after the recorded vote, the exceptions to immunity from foreign criminal jurisdiction appear to be recognized to certain international crimes of *jus cogens* status. Although the issue is not yet solved at the level of the ILC and still remains quite disputed, the decisions and the reasonings provided by national courts represent a valuable articulation of the principle of human dignity as the foundation of international law and underlying *jus cogens* norms.[216] Whereas this process is still ongoing, this constitutes an instance which allows one to seize human dignity in the making as it unfolds. Its normative power and circle are gradually acting *de lege ferenda* towards overriding or limiting the circle of sovereign dignity.

In conclusion, human dignity and *humanitas* shape not only the definition of core international crimes but also the nature and actual operativity of their prosecutorial system. In line with concerns expressed by both Kelsen and Arendt, at different historical moments, crimes that represent attacks on human dignity are recognized as deserving a prosecution that can provide an international justice beyond concerns of State sovereignty.

216 See T Weatherall, *Jus Cogens: International Law and Social Contract* (Cambridge University Press 2015), 66.

7

Bridging Narratives

Human Dignity and the Transformation of International Law

7.1 TWO CIRCLES OF DIGNITY

In this long journey, I relied on the distinction between the two circles of dignity to organize and structure the argumentative narrative of my research. This study has shown that dignity has been progressively and, in many ways, sequentially at the root of State sovereignty and of the efforts to defend – against that sovereignty – the dignity of human beings. From 'sovereignty' to 'human dignity', the concept of dignity underpins two competing circles and their claims. These concepts are both different and interlocked in a sequential and rival manner, which means the use of the concept to affirm the normative claim of one circle largely relies on the use of the concept by the other circle. Yet, at the same time, the two uses entertain a competing or rival relation in that one concept developed to limit the expansion of the other.

As regards the concept of sovereign dignity, it has three main features: it can attach to persons holding a specific position; it has a transient character, since the institutionalization of *dignitas* necessarily entails its detachment from the person holding the office and its conferral on the office itself; and it has an exclusionary character, as it draws a line between one group or circle and another. *Dignitas* is in fact defined in relation to certain qualities and carries with it a social distinction. Both the qualities conferring a special treatment and the treatment may change over time, but the exclusionary character of the concept remains. And it is this feature that, by its very definition, delimits a circle that leaves outside a wider circle of those not enjoying special treatment.

A challenge to exclusionary treatment can take two forms: either the circle is extended to include those left outside or the scope of the treatment is restricted. In both cases, the claim rests on the assertion of a competing form of dignity. The second conception and circle of dignity challenges in fact the distinction and the powers conferred by *dignitas*. It refers to a specific attribute of every human being for the simple reason that they are human and does not defer to any social degrees. Thus, dignity cannot be acquired or lost – it is not transient – and it attaches to every human being – thus not exclusionary within the circle of human beings, but excluding other entities, for example, legal persons. Its permanent and non-exclusionary features do not mean that this conception, with its many variations, is not 'rival'. This is important because, as mentioned earlier, the different circles of dignity are interlocked in a way that can be characterized as sequential (dependent on one another) and rival (competing). I maintained in this research a deliberate focus on dignity as an attribute of the human being. The rise of human dignity in the history of international law has, however, also influenced the latitude of application of the concept of sovereignty and expressions of 'institutional dignity'. For this reason, the conceptual battlefront opened by the concept of human dignity towards sovereign dignity was kept visible in the backstage of my analysis.

7.2 HUMAN DIGNITY AND THE ARCHITECTURE OF INTERNATIONAL LAW

What emerges from the conceptual examination of dignity and from the analysis of the three constitutive stages developed more specifically in Chapter 3 is that today we can still distinguish two circles of opposing dignities, sovereign and human; and that the second circle of human dignity developed at a later date and in opposition to the first. The classic and sovereign conception of dignity, and specifically that associated with the State, is traced in the past through, and remains today in, all manifestations of State sovereignty. For instance, this concept reappears when it is used today to support arguments associated with State immunities or with the principle of non-intervention in internal affairs. These are all corollaries of the principle of State sovereignty. Throughout the study, I have traced how sovereign dignity still manifests itself and relates with human dignity. The concept was subsequently, and by analogy, adopted at the religious level to affirm that humans are the holders of a dignity, given to them by God. In this way, human dignity in the Christian sense made its historical entrance associated to the human being, who had a *special status* being created in the image of God. This concept will be increasingly refined over time, becoming less theological and assuming a *limiting function* of the first conception of sovereign (and State) dignity.

The concept of human dignity assumes, in its entry into international law, a restraining role and, in a broader sense, a function of control over the first conception of sovereign dignity. Therefore, what is originally an analogy, once applied to human nature, developed into a limit to the first conception. In this process, human dignity touched upon the very architecture of international law. This study has identified that this process occurred at four different levels, by pointing out: (i) *when* it occurred, by identifying three constitutive stages of human dignity (Chapter 3); (ii) *where* it developed, and, more specifically, in three main areas of international law most directly influenced by human dignity (IHL, IHRL and ICL, see Chapters 3–6); (iii) *how* and, namely, with what instruments human dignity found expression (principle, right, crime and obligation, see Chapters 4–6); and, last, (iv) its *implications* (i.e. the argument). These lines of reasoning are brought together in this final chapter.

7.2.1 *Legal Consolidation*

I will here briefly retrace the main stages related to *when* and *where* dignity found expression *in* international law. In particular, I will refer to the most illustrative examples of the transformation of international law in the historical process leading to the recognition of human dignity, extracted from the previous chapters. Figure 7.1 sums up the three constitutive stages.

The Martens Clause, included in the preambles of the II Hague Convention of 1899 (para 9) and of the 1907 Hague Convention (para 8), 'crystallized and summarized the nineteenth-century development of the humanitarian law of war'.[1] It marks both the beginning and the crystallization of the first constitutive stage of human dignity in international law. The concept of *laws of humanity* reflected 'the evolution of Western European Christian values as they emerged from the natural law doctrine of these Christian States'[2] and the doctrine of Islamic civilizations.[3] The concept of human dignity entered for the first time in the laws of war through the Christian value of humanity, due to the Christian belief of its founders, and was posed at the basis of a foundational guiding principle. For the relevance and resonance of the Martens Clause in the IHL frame, we can easily set here the first *entry point* and *crystallization* of human dignity in international law and in IHL. By contrast, its *consolidation* in the IHL context will be reached

[1] GIAD Draper, 'International Dimensions of Humanitarian Law' in UNESCO, *International Dimensions of Humanitarian Law*, Henry-Dunant Institute (UNESCO, Martinus Nijhoff 1988), 72.

[2] MC Bassiouni, *Crimes against Humanity: Historical Evolution and Contemporary Application* (Cambridge University Press 2011), Introduction, xxviii.

[3] *Ibid.*

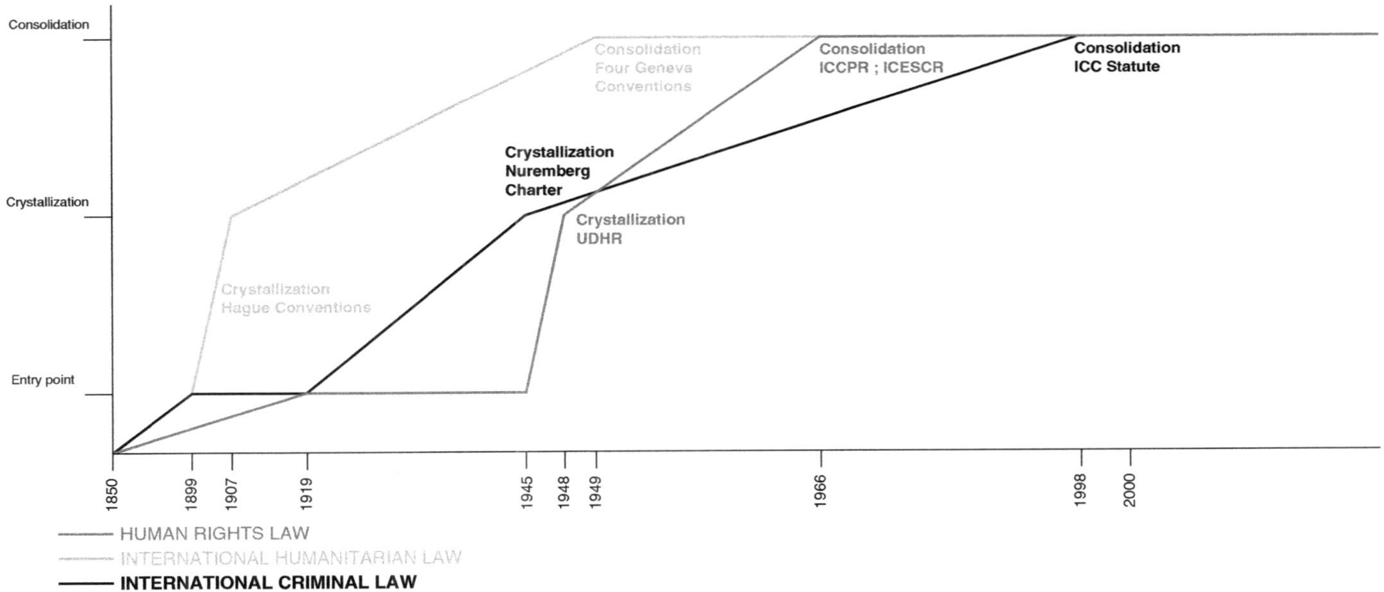

FIGURE 7.1 Three constitutive stages of human dignity

only later, in 1949, with the adoption of the Geneva Conventions, and with the adoption of the Additional Protocols of 1977.

Also in the nineteenth century, human dignity began to be associated with labour, although its formalization will occur only in the second constitutive stage of dignity. Pope Leo XIII played a key catalyst role in universalizing the concept of the dignity of labour. His influential papal encyclical *Rerum Novarum*, or the Rights and Duties of Capital and Labour (1891), enters directly into the nineteenth-century political conversation about the antagonism between classes. Through a Christian lens, workers' dignity as human beings was thus recognized.

The legal restraints on the conduct of hostilities which developed during the first constitutive stage were, however, a rather isolated inroad of human dignity into a system where State sovereignty and sovereign prerogatives remained at the foundations of international law.[4] In 1919, Wilsons' Fourteen Points became the basis for the Versailles Peace Treaty in 1919, establishing the League of Nations, which would guarantee the 'political independence and territorial integrity [of] great and small states alike'. Colonel House's 1919 preamble of the Covenant of the League of Nations, was still cited as evidence that even if 'there is no mention of religion or the Church in the Preamble' of the Covenant of the League of Nations,[5] a quasi-religious 'moral consciousness' was one of its central inspirations.[6] The League of Nations was a realization of ideas already advanced by Vitoria and Grotius on a joint community of purpose, inspiring the coexistence of nations in a framework of law.

From a religious conception, human dignity here evolves and emerges from this stage as a secular and individual conception, as a foundational principle of the international human rights legal system and as a human right of all human beings. This evolution runs from 1919 until 1966. Three phases, all constituting a second constitutive stage of human dignity, have been identified.

During the interwar period, human dignity first entered in the law in a religious sense and slowly evolved into a secular and individual attribution. This transformation has been followed throughout three distinct legal developments: the adoption of mandates systems and of minority treaties; the

4 See R Kolb, 'The Main Epochs of Modern International Humanitarian Law since 1864 and Their Related Dominant Legal Constructions' in KM Larsen, CG Cooper and G Nystuen (eds), *Searching for a 'Principle of Humanity' in International Humanitarian Law* (Cambridge University Press 2013), 40–45.

5 Covenant of the League of Nations, 28 April 1919.

6 See N Bentwich, *The Religious Foundations of Internationalism* (G. Allen & Unwin 1933), 246.

institutional answer to the refugee question; and, lastly, in the adoption of the ILO Constitution.

As narrated in Chapter 3, a 'crisis of sovereignty' was at work in the milieu of internationalists, including Georges Scelle, who appealed to his colleagues 'to reject the idea of sovereignty deliberately and definitively, for it is false and it is harmful'.[7] Meanwhile, there was a larger Catholic Church conversion to personalism,[8] when in the mid-1930s Pius XI committed the Church to anti-totalitarianism.[9] Thanks to Maritain above all, only the Christian vision placing rights in the framework of the common good afforded a persuasive theory.[10]

All the above events sowed the seeds of a new phase in the second constitutive stage of human dignity, when the dignity of the human person found a first preliminary recognition in the preambles of the UN Charter,[11] here still in its religious sense, and in the constitutive document of UNESCO.[12] The adoption of the 1948 UDHR represents the crystallization of human dignity, which finds for the first time a clear expression as a fundamental principle, as an individual right and a source of other individual rights. All these instruments influenced the human rights protection framework.

As examined in Section 3.3.3.2, the first line of the UN Charter reads that 'the peoples of the United Nations' are determined 'to reaffirm faith in fundamental human rights, in the dignity and worth of the human person, in the equal rights of men and women and of nations large and small'. This text constitutes a milestone in the new international normative edifice built in this second constitutive stage, and it firmly affirms that human dignity represents one of its foundational principles.

The UDHR, the first international human rights instrument, analysed in Section 3.3.3.3, constitutes instead a paradigmatic example of this specific historical time as well as the first legal pinnacle of dignity in the human rights

7 G Scelle, 'Une ère juridique nouvelle', *La paix par le droit* (July–August 1919), 297–298.

8 See *The Foundations of International Order* (proceedings of the Catholic Congress on International Peace 1938); L Watt, *Pope Pius XII on World Order* (Catholic Social Guild 1940), ch. 5.

9 See S Moyn, 'Jacques Maritain: le origini dei Diritti umani e il pensiero politico cristiano' in L Bonanate and R Papini (eds), *Dialogo interculturale e diritti umani: la Dichiarazione Universale dei Diritti Umani, Genesi, evoluzione, e problemi odierni (1948–2008)* (Il Mulino 2008), 97–124; P de la Chapelle, *La Déclaration universelle des droits de l'homme et le catholicisme* (LGDJ 1967).

10 S Moyn, 'Personalism, Community and the Origins of Human Rights' in SL Hoffmann (ed.), *Human Rights in the Twentieth Century* (Cambridge University Press 2011), 112.

11 Charter of the United Nations, 24 October 1945, 1 UNTS XVI.

12 UNESCO Constitution, 16 November 1945, 3 Bevans 1311.

frame. It refrains from giving a specific definition of human dignity or from directly associating it with a specific conception. The main drive is to avoid the reoccurrence of the horrors committed in the past and guarantee, through a moral manifesto, a limit to the omnipotence of States' sovereignty over their citizens and an international recognition of human dignity to every human being. In the Declaration, human dignity becomes a 'formal, transcendental norm to legitimize human rights claims'[13] and shows that human rights contain 'at their heart unconditional inviolability'.[14] The UDHR constitutes a central instrument for the path towards the universalization and secularization of dignity. It is a profoundly communitarian document and primarily constituted a shift afoot from the individual to the *person* – precisely a moral repudiation of dangerous individualism.[15] For this reason, the UDHR, together with the human rights idea in general, is embedded, rather than in Roman law and in Immanuel Kant's political conception, more securely in the ambiance of the war's aftermath, as part of the moral reconstruction of Europe perceived to be essential to stave off future conflicts and atrocities.[16]

The first proposals for a European Convention on Human Rights had been made a good six months before the completion of the UDHR, and the final version of the treaty text of the European Convention on Human Rights (ECHR) was signed by the member States of the Council of Europe on 4 November 1950,[17] less than two years after the UDHR's proclamation in December 1948. Importantly, the ECHR, like the 1951 Refugee Convention,[18] represents a case of 'shadow' human dignity: despite its absence in its text, human dignity highly influenced its preparatory works. Throughout the drafting process of the ECHR, the concept of human dignity made its appearance in various instances, even though, however, the term itself was not clearly defined and ended up not featuring in the final text of the Convention. From the analysis of the ECHR (see Section 3.3.3.4), it emerged that, even if the Convention is silent about human dignity, at the early stage of its drafting, the delegates have recognized it as the 'essential expression of European

13 K Dicke, 'The Founding Function of Human Dignity in the Universal Declaration of Human Rights' in D Kretzmer and E Klein (eds), *The Concept of Human Dignity in Human Rights Discourse* (Brill 2002), 118.

14 *Ibid.*, 119.

15 See M Mazower, 'The Strange Triumph of Human Rights, 1930–1950' [2004] 47(2) *HJ* 379–398.

16 Moyn, *supra* n 10, 121.

17 European Convention for the Protection of Human Rights and Fundamental Freedoms, as amended by Protocols No. 11 and 14, Rome, 4 November 1950.

18 Convention Relating to the Status of Refugees, 28 July 1951, UNTS vol. 189, 137.

civilisation',[19] as its common spiritual basis[20] and as the foundation of its common heritage[21]. For some members, human dignity was still a concept rooted in its Judeo-Christian conception,[22] while for the main part, it was a secular and universal concept, an essential democratic principle. As also the European Court emphasized, secularism was 'consistent with the values underpinning the Convention'.[23] Ultimately, even if the decision to exclude the term human dignity from the text of the Convention was probably taken to avoid '*a declaration of moral principles and pious aspirations*',[24] the ECHR represents an inspiration 'for the *triumph of human dignity*',[25] leading the world in the protection and further advancement of human rights, 'in accordance with the *principles of natural law, of humanism and of democracy*'.[26] In particular, during the European Convention's debates, it was felt important 'to give the personal opportunity to the individual to establish the *dignity of the individual human spirit* and to prevent injustice'.[27] To do so, states had to inevitably accept 'some *voluntary surrender of sovereignty*: namely the sovereign right to suppress liberty and democratic institutions'.[28]

A few years later, the Second Vatican Council, which started in 1952, led to a renewal of the Catholic teachings. On April 1963, Pope John XXIII issued the encyclical *Pacem in Terris*, which endorsed the UDHR, calling it 'an act of the

19 M Vallée–Poussin (Belgium), Council of Europe, Collected Edition of the '*Travaux Préparatoires*' of the ECHR, vol. 1, Preparatory Commission of the Council of Europe, Committee of Ministers, Consultative Assembly, 11 May–8 September 1949, First Session of the Consultative Assembly, Strasbourg, Eight Sitting, 19 August 1949 (Martinus Nijhoff 1975) [Preparatory Commission August 1949], 102.

20 M Kraft (Denmark), *ibid.*, 102.

21 M Antonopoulos (Greece), *ibid.*, 56.

22 See, for instance, M Maccas (Greece), *ibid.*, 106.

23 *Leyla Şahin* v. *Turkey*, [GC], No. 44774/98, ECHR 2005–XI, para 114.

24 Sir Maxwell-Fyfe (United Kingdom), Preparatory Commission August 1949, *supra* n 19, p. 114, p. 122 (emphasis added).

25 Council of Europe, Collected Edition of the '*Travaux Préparatoires*' of the ECHR, vol. 5, Legal Committee, Ad Hoc Joint Committee, Committee of Ministers, Consultative Assembly, 23 June–28 August 1950; Ninth Sitting of the Consultative Assembly, 16 August 1950 (Martinus Nijhoff, The Hague 1979), p. 278 (emphasis added).

26 Report presented by Mr PH Teitgen, 5 September 1949, Doc. A 290, I TP 192–213, at 192; Report [of the Committee on Legal and Administrative Questions], 5 September 1949, Doc. AS (1) 77, I TP 216–239, at 216.

27 Sir Maxwell-Fyfe (United Kingdom), Council of Europe, Collected Edition of the '*Travaux Préparatoires*' of the ECHR, vol. 2, Consultative Assembly, Second Session of the Committee of Ministers, Standing Committee of the Assembly, 10 August–18 November 1949; First Session of the Consultative Assembly, Eighteenth Sitting, 8 September 1949 (Martinus Nijhoff 1975), p. 200 (emphasis added).

28 Sir Maxwell-Fyfe (United Kingdom), Preparatory Commission August 1949, *supra* n 19, 114, 122 (emphasis added).

highest importance ... and an important step towards the juridical-political organization of all the peoples of the world'.[29] The document was a form of papal Bill of Rights[30] and the embodiment of a societal vision aiming at promoting rights and duties. The Second Vatican Council ended on 8 December 1965, approving the Declaration on Religious Liberty – *Dignitatis Humanae* – which was among the most important statements from the Council during its three years of deliberation. *Dignitatis Humanae*, as *Pacem in Terris*, constituted a major development in how the Catholic Church placed itself in the political world and on ecumenical issues.[31]

Also when the issue of racial discrimination re-emerged in the 1950s,[32] the foundational role of human dignity was this time openly proclaimed in both Article 1 of the 1960 Convention against Discrimination in Education[33] and in the Preamble and Article 1 of the 1963 Declaration on the Elimination of All Form of Discrimination. Importantly, this discourse about human dignity emerged in contraposition to considerations regarding State sovereignty. During the 1965 General Assembly Session, devoted to the drafting of a universal Convention on Elimination of All Forms of Racial Discrimination, delegates agreed to 'assume a legal responsibility to the international community'[34] and, in this respect, the representative from Jordan affirmed that '*[t]he meaning of sovereignty had changed*', as it 'had lost its absolute character'.[35] Once again, it was decided to proclaim human dignity as a foundational principle of the Convention, in continuity with (and confirmation of) the UN Charter, the UDHR and the 1963 Declaration, by including three references in its preamble.[36]

[29] See *Pacem in Terris*, para 143–244; see also JP Humphrey, *Human Rights and the United Nations: A Great Adventure* (Transnational 1984), 76.

[30] SLB Jensen, *The Making of International Human Rights: The 1960s, Decolonization, and the Reconstruction of Global Values* (Cambridge University Press 2016), 148.

[31] F Russell Hittinger, 'The Declaration on Religious Liberty, Dignitatis Humanae' in ML Lamb and M Levering (eds), *Vatican II: Renewal within Tradition* (Oxford University Press 2008), 375–376; see also A Francisco Carrillo de Albernoz, 'The Ecumenical and World Significance of the Vatican Declaration on Religious Liberty' [1966] 18(1) *Ecumenical Review* 65, emphasizing the important role of international authorities in matters of religious liberty (81).

[32] See MS McDougal, HD Lasswell and LC Chen, 'The Right to Religious Freedom and World Public Order: The Emerging Norm of Nondiscrimination' [1975] 74 *MichLR* 865.

[33] Convention against Discrimination in Education, 14 December 1960, 429 UNTS 93.

[34] Miss Hart (New Zealand), UN General Assembly, Third Committee, 20th session, 1347th meeting, 18 November 1965, p. 340.

[35] Mr Sharaf (Jordan), UN General Assembly, Third Committee, 20th session, 1347th meeting, 18 November 1965, p. 337 (emphasis added).

[36] See Recitals 1, 2 and 5 of the Preamble, International Convention on the Elimination of All Forms of Racial Discrimination, GA Res. 2106 (XX), 660 UNTS 195, 21 December 1965 (entered into force 4 January 1969).

This growing recognition of human dignity during this third phase of its second constitutive stage built the real momentum for its consolidation in international human rights law in 1966, with the adoption of the two Covenants. In both the preambles of the ICESCR and of the ICCPR, human dignity is proclaimed twice as a founding principle of the international human rights project started in 1945 and both declare, in the second paragraph of the preamble, that '*these rights derive from the inherent dignity* of the human person'.[37] From the perspective of human dignity, if Cassin paid tribute to its Christian legacy in 1963, the 1966 Covenants are instead the consolidation of human dignity as a universal concept. The two Covenants consolidate different trends, more or less liberal, that had not found complete manifestation in the Universal Declaration.

Starting from 1945, in the transition from religious human dignity to a more universal one, there are two main streams of *universal* human dignity that manifest themselves, one emphasizing the individual and the other of a more collective nature. The two Covenants realize a higher synthesis compared to the one that occurred in 1948. Unlike the Universal Declaration, the two instruments succeed in capturing unexpressed currents and a *universal-collective nature* of dignity. This is perhaps a peculiarity of the two Covenants. The two treaties, indeed, collect these two different dimensions of dignity: on the one hand, a more culturally situated formulation of dignity, to be found in the UDHR and ECHR; while on the other, an expression of dignity as a substratum of anticolonialism, of self-rule. In particular, self-determination appears as a legal paradigm of a whole series of previous concerns – partly similar and partly different from those that had found expression in instruments focusing on the individual.

The Covenants not only 'reaffirmed' this right and a consolidated customary rule, they also confirmed and consolidated the process of collectivization of human dignity in international law, against the circle of sovereign dignity – a process started back in 1919 and crystallized in 1948. Therefore, it is not only the difference between Catholic dignity and universal human dignity (and the transition from one to the other) that is important, but rather, as explained, the shades within the qualification of 'universal'. The consolidation of a bi-dimensional nature of universal human dignity, individual and collective, has its blossom with the 1966 Covenants, which, for this reason, can be seen as the apical instruments for the expression of human dignity in the human rights sphere.

37 Emphasis added.

Lastly, a third constitutive stage of human dignity has been traced throughout the nineteenth and the twentieth centuries. In particular, this process begins early but it consolidates late in time, compared to the two just examined, due to the peculiar character of ICL. The international criminal system has historically evolved and consolidated around two main pillars, namely the development of an international definition of crimes and the inception and consolidation of principles and procedures governing the international investigation and prosecution of these crimes. These two pillars constituted the basis for the historical search for human dignity in international criminal law. The first constitutive element, namely the concept of an international crime rooted in human dignity, emerged for the first time in 1899 with the Hague Conventions, then symbolically developed with the Treaty of Versailles in 1919 and consolidated in 1945 with the adoption of the Nuremberg Charter. The year 1945 is the first entry point and crystallization of human dignity in ICL, in line with the first definition of international crimes. The year 1945 also establishes a first recognition of the criteria of international criminal responsibility (and its prosecution) with the Nuremberg Charter. It is, however, a limited recognition because the Nuremberg Charter was a context-specific retrospective instrument. This second component of the international criminal system was only consolidated in the 1990s, with the establishment of other context-specific mechanisms, the ad hoc Tribunals for the former Yugoslavia and for Rwanda and, eventually, of the 1998 Rome Statute establishing a permanent, general and prospective International Criminal Court. Here, the definition of international crime, already mature in 1945, finds a final confirmation, clarification and internationalization. In particular, because of this dual foundation, which arose at different paces, human dignity makes its entrance in ICL in two ways and at two different speeds. In this process, it has been slowly vested with an actionable nature. The final consolidation of human dignity in its third constitutive stage is thus reached only in 1998. All these historical milestones are the expression of the narrative of the two circles, and all reveal how human dignity pushed sovereign dignity to place itself at the core of international law, transforming its original structure. This process, which is still ongoing, as discussed in Chapter 6, Section 6.4, thus shows how the circle of human dignity exercises a normative power capable of slowly and partially displacing the circle of sovereign dignity.

7.2.2 *Instruments*

In addition to *when* and *where* human dignity found expression in international law, this study also assessed *how* it did so by searching for its legal manifestations. In this respect, in order to develop this part of the study, three criteria have been researched within each selected legal framework, that is, IHL, IHRL and ICL, namely: (a) the specific language and terminological formulations adopted to express human dignity; (b) the features of the basic legal framework; and, lastly, (c) the specific legal instruments adopted to manifest dignity, their meaning as well as their specific functions. Four main legal instruments are used to express human dignity and conform its conceptual structure in international law, namely 'principle', 'human right', 'crime' and 'obligation'. The table of instruments, introduced in Chapter 1, is summarized in Figure 7.2.

The figure deliberately avoids referring to the areas of law examined as a result of the historical analysis. Its main purpose is not to show where human dignity has found expression but rather to summarize the types of instruments through which it has done so. I have therefore maintained the same conceptual cartography referred to in the first chapter of this study and combined the various legal manifestations. Since this theory was tested in various areas of law, the research led to the following results.

As detailed in Chapter 4, the laws of armed conflict deploy four main manifestations of human dignity: (i) human dignity acts as a foundational *principle* and

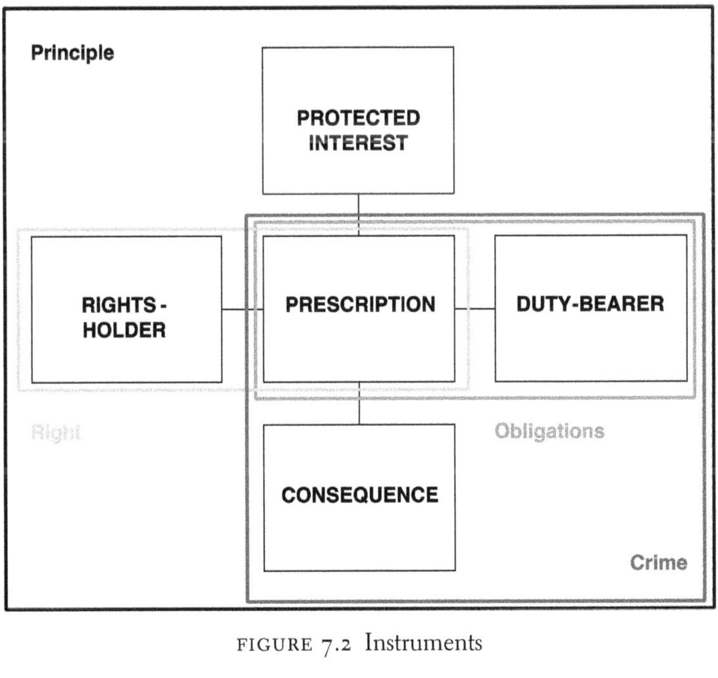

FIGURE 7.2 Instruments

structural element of IHL; (ii) human dignity injects considerations of humanity in the law and represents the basis of an *inviolable right*, from which other rights derive; (iii) it is an *obligation-creating* principle, directly deriving from its legal substance and from its concretizations (a first set of constraints is related the protective regime extended to categories of persons under IHL and, the second, relates to rules on means and methods of warfare); and (iv) human dignity is a protected good of specific international *crimes*. In particular, there are two cardinal principles which represent a direct manifestation of human dignity: the principle of humanity and the principle of distinction. Whereas the principle of humanity animates the spirit and content of IHL, the principle of distinction guarantees the protection of certain categories of persons in times of conflict on the basis of humanitarian considerations. The idea of humanity as a normative standard heavily relies on human dignity. The examination of instruments and judicial practice shows, in fact, that the common understanding today is that the protection of human beings is warranted by the inherent dignity of the human person.[38] Therefore, human dignity is a term of art that has served as a general principle of law since antiquity, which allows the concept of humanity to be captured for the agenda of either party in a given armed conflict and is thus capable today of informing the content of universal IHL instruments as well as guiding conduct in warfare. In particular, the 'principle of humanity' has been adopted with two main functions, which should be viewed as distinct but simultaneously overlapping uses:[39] an *architectural* or *axiological* function and an *auxiliary* function. Through the latter, the principle is used to clarify ambiguities when primary sources of law are absent (*suppletive* function) or unclear or inadequate (*interstitial* or *conciliatory* function). As concluded in Chapter 4, the 'principle of human dignity' should thus receive a wide understanding and be perceived as having more and more an independent legal impact. In cases in which humanitarian concerns are incorporated into the rules of international humanitarian law, the principle of human dignity shows its *architectural* function. In addition, it serves as an element of interpretation and as a moral test, which ensures that the applicability of the law is not too far from the expectations of the general public.[40] Above all, such a principle is most

38 See R Urueña, 'Deciding What is Humane: Towards a Critical Reading of Humanity as a Normative Standard in International Law' in B van Beers, L Corrias and WG Werner (eds), *Humanity across International Law and Biolaw* (Cambridge University Press 2014), 188.

39 See also A Cassese, 'The Martens Clause: Half a Loaf or Simply Pie in the Sky?' [2000] 11 *EJIL* 187, 189–192.

40 KM Larsen and CG Cooper, 'Conclusions: Is There a "Principle of Humanity" in International Humanitarian Law?' in KM Larsen, CG Cooper and G Nystuen (eds), *Searching for a 'Principle of Humanity' in International Humanitarian* Law (Cambridge University Press 2012), 356.

relevant in those cases where the rules of international humanitarian law are inadequate or non-existent, playing an *interstitial* or *suppletive* function, in particular in the case of non-international armed conflicts.

Secondly, there are instead three main levels of relations between *human dignity and human rights* and, thus, three main instruments that are typically adopted to manifest them: (i) human dignity as a foundation of human rights, which is formulated as a *principle* and as a result is the most common and predominant legal form; (ii) dignity as foundation and object of rights and which therefore manifests itself as both *mother-right* and/or in its *derivative rights*; and (iii) human dignity as the basis of specific *obligations*. More specifically, these three features are normally substantiated by three legal expressions. Human dignity is the first value at the *foundation* of the world order. It is characterized as *inherent* to all human persons and the basis of an *inviolable right*. It is further understood as a non-balanceable basis for all rights, which *derive* from it, provide it with a concrete and contextually specific form, and correspond to positive and negative obligations.

Thirdly, *human dignity is manifested in ICL* through the criterion or rationale relating to the protection of *humanitas* (by contrast to the mere *utilitas*). *Humanitas* in ICL in turn finds expression through three main instruments. First, the instrument of *crime*, namely the crime of genocide, crimes against humanity and war crimes. The selection was based on their recognition in the ICC Statute and on the role given to human dignity as a protected value in both the definition of the crimes and in the related case law. The relationship between *humanitas* and international prosecution determines the two other manifestations. Reasons of *humanitas*, in fact, change the nature of the prosecution normally assigned to ordinary crimes. The prosecution is internationalized by way of two instruments: at the national level, through the principle of universal jurisdiction and the obligation *aut dedere aut judicare*; at the international level, through the creation of a system which provides an international court with the adjudicative power to prosecute *hostes humani generis* and bring justice to victims of international crimes. The establishment of a permanent international criminal court constitutes the consolidation of this system of protection of human dignity, transforming it into an actionable concept. In ICL, human dignity is therefore able to shape not only the definition of the core international crimes but also of the nature of their prosecutorial system.

7.3 A SECULARIZED DIGNITY

As seen throughout this research, there are two broad strands in the conceptualization of human dignity: (i) a religious perspective, which looks at the concept as connected to the divine or to a metaphysical account; (ii) what could be called a set of 'secular' accounts that have enabled the development of human rights. The emergence and consolidation of human rights embodies not the triumph of one concept over the other but a more complex process of conceptual elaboration and generalization of a religious conception so as to make it more widely acceptable. The affirmation of human dignity in constitutional and international legal documents is indeed a product of a secular age. Yet the development of the underlying concept of what a human being is stems from religious thought[41] and, primarily, Christian thought.[42] It clearly arises from the historical record examined in this study that the latter acted as a driver of the legal elaboration of human rights in the aftermath of the Second World War and the process of adoption of the UDHR. There is a noticeable convergence[43] on the broad frame within which the process unfolded, one whereby an initially Christian conception of human dignity was progressively stripped of its idiosyncratic features as a condition for its generalization through international instruments.

Both the religious and the secularized conceptions of human dignity entail significant limitations, not only on the powers conferred by 'sovereign dignity', but, potentially, on its very recognition. After the Second World War, these limitations appeared as the most urgent task to be accomplished. The religious variant, whether in its Christian form or in its wider (and subsequent) cultural rooting, does not question the basis of authority of the State, but it entails limitations for the scope of the powers that States can claim over humans. The process of secularization stripped dignity out of its idiosyncratic origins in Christian thought. A secularized use of dignity became increasingly noticeable in legal language, alongside an ever-present dignity in its Christian meaning (e.g. in the field of bioethics). Therefore, by examining in a more detailed way the process by which secularization took place historically, it seems that a circular process took shape. As anticipated in the first chapter of this study, first, there was a detachment from the classical conception of dignity, through an extension by analogy of the concept to express an inherent and religious value of each human being, given by God. The concept of

41 A Barak, *Human Dignity: The Constitutional Value and the Constitutional Right* (Cambridge University Press 2015).

42 C Starck, 'The Religious and Philosophical Background of Human Dignity and its Place in Modern Constitutions' in D Kretzmer and E Klein (eds), *The Concept of Human Dignity in Human Rights Discourse* (Brill 2002), 180.

43 MA Glendon, *A World Made New. Eleanor Roosevelt and the Universal Declaration of Human Rights* (Random House 2001); S Moyn, *Christian Human Rights* (UPenn 2015); S Moyn, *The Last Utopia: Human Rights in History* (Harvard University Press 2010).

dignity was later re-secularized when viewed as an adequate term to express a universal purpose. This process can be interpreted as an 'inverse secularization': a universal and secular concept of dignity entered again and opposed itself to a form of sovereign dignity still used today in relation to State sovereignty. Even when dignity became 'secular', it did not lose sight of its religious origins. This level of analysis demonstrated that the concept of human dignity made its first appearance in legal history in a religious and later more secularized guise, as a reaction and limit to the classical conception of sovereign dignity and, thus, in opposition to the concept of State sovereignty.

Exploring the process through which dignity was turned against sovereignty and increasingly consolidated as the foundation of international law enables conclusions on the historical relevance of the theory of secularization. To explain human dignity, to seek its religious roots, to see its evolution and how it is manifested on a juridical level, ultimately allow us to demonstrate that the concept, originally rooted in religion, is today fully integrated into a secularized discourse, such as international law, not only at a superficial level but at a structural one. This is manifest in the emergence out of human dignity of a range of fundamental principles, obligations, rights and even crimes. Pulling all these threads highlights that international law has come to be reformulated and built on a religious concept, namely human dignity, in its secularized form. Thus, the permeation and eventual prevalence of human dignity in international law lends support to and can be rooted within the wider theory of secularization developed to describe other political and legal processes.

The concept of 'secularization'[44] – as expressed in the Löwith–Blumenberg controversies – is considered as (i) a division between the secular and the religious domains and the 'retreat of religion as the dominant sphere' of society, or (ii) the 'transfer' of religious meanings and values into secular form on the ideological and institutional levels.[45] The expressions 'secularization-retreat' and 'secularization-transfer' still exist in the present debate about the role of religion.[46] Interestingly, in this sense, Nathaniel Berman, in his work on the genealogy of modern internationalism and in his study on the relationship between religion and the international order, examines the role of religion in the 'imagination' of legal internationalists – without, however,

44 See JC Monod, *La querelle de la secularisation, de Hegel à Blumenberg* (Librarie Philosophique J. Vrin 2002).

45 *Ibid.*, from page 22, where Monod discusses the analysis of Hans Blumenberg, who most sharply made a distinction between the two senses of 'secularization'.

46 N Berman, '"The Sacred Conspiracy": Religion, Nationalism, and the Crisis of Internationalism' [2012] 25(1) *LJIL* 9–54, at 15.

digging into the historical 'effective results' of this process. He perceptively observes in this regard that:

> rejecting views which relegate religion to the margins, I maintain that religion has played a recurrent and highly fraught role in the internationalist imagination, with which it has maintained complex relations both of rivalry and of complicity.[47]

Berman criticizes the view of a pure process of secularization meant as a retreat of religion. He adopts instead a striking and creative use of the separation between a 'secularization-transfer' and a 'secularization-retreat' and engages with the mutual 'contamination' of the two. By way of illustration, in 1933, the preamble of first draft of the Covenant of the League of Nations was cited as evidence that, while 'there is no mention of religion or the Church in the Preamble' of the League Covenant, a quasi-religious '*moral consciousness*' was one of its key inspirations.[48] Norman Bentwich, first Attorney General of the British Mandate government in Palestine, made such an observation, emphasizing the connection between civilizational failure and the need to turn to religion as the foundation for a new beginning. In his view, this would have occurred only with an epochal shift in 'religion' itself. Berman, in line with Bentwich, argues against 'the conventional "supersessionist" account of the relationship between a definitively secularized international law and its medieval religious predecessors … in favour of … dialectical processes among secularization-retreat, re-entanglement through contagion, and secularization-transfer'.[49] In other words, the role played by religion 'cannot be limited to a … chapter of the genesis of international law, in which religion would be partly "relegated" … and would have otherwise played a "precursor" role with the theologian-lawyers such as Vitoria'.[50] According to Monod, this narrative:

> becomes illusionary when it suggests that, after, let's say, the sixteenth and seventeenth centuries, international law would have become a purely secular matter in which religion played only a marginal role. The colonial 'game' with the 'fanaticism' or the religious and moral 'backwardness' of the indigenous people, legitimating their need of a 'civilized' protection, is a convincing instance of this persistence.[51]

47 *Ibid.*, 14.

48 N Bentwich, *The Religious Foundations of Internationalism* (G. Allen & Unwin 1933), 246 (emphasis added).

49 Berman, *supra* n 46, 26.

50 JC Monod, 'What's New in Our Current "International Secularism"?' [2012] 25(1) *LJIL* 67–72, 68.

51 *Ibid.*, 68–69.

If the latter is but an illustration of the interlocked relation between religion and the crafting of international law, the present study has sought to unveil and, as much as possible, track in its more textured manifestations the process through which the legal and political structure of international law today has been transformed by the forces of secularization, embodied in the concept of human dignity. The secularized concept of human dignity, nowadays embraced by international law, carries along similar limits inherent in the original religious concept and, above all, the exclusionary character of dignity. The following section elaborates on this point to flesh out the *implications* of the current consolidation of human dignity in international law.

7.4 WIDENING THE CIRCLE: ANTHROPOCENTRISM AND THE DIGNITY OF NATURE[52]

Because of its extension to each and every individual, human dignity may appear as the ultimate horizon of dignity, with the ensuing suppression of dignity's exclusionary character. Indeed, if no one is left out of the human dignity circle, there is no excluded group to be integrated into it. However, on closer examination, human dignity draws a circle that excludes a range of other normative claims to dignity, including those of certain collective entities (such as 'peoples', 'communities' or even legal persons); other living things (such as flora and fauna); and even the full extent of what we call 'nature'. Expanding the circle of dignity to these other entities does not mean treating them on an equal footing with humans. But it does entail recognition of the dignity of such entities, which places limitations on the powers flowing from human dignity.

Much like the relationship between *dignitas* and human dignity, that between human dignity and this third circle of dignity is a rival one. Of the three examples of excluded entities, certain collective subjects, such as indigenous and tribal peoples or, more generally, 'peoples' as understood in international law, enjoy a range of specific human rights[53] and they are therefore not clearly excluded. For this reason, it is more accurate to leave them out from the discussion of the third circle. It must be noted, however, that the recognition of such collective rights is only partially grounded on 'human dignity', at least if the latter term is understood in its individual (rather than collective) and universal (rather than cultural) meaning. Yet, for other entities, the exclusionary character inherent to the concept of dignity, even of 'human' dignity, remains

[52] This section relies on G Le Moli, 'Three Circles of Dignity' [2019] 11(1) *JHRP* 258, 265–267.

[53] N Schrijver, *Sovereignty over Natural Resources: Balancing Rights and Duties* (Cambridge University Press 1997); J Crawford (ed.), *Rights of Peoples* (Clarendon Press 1992).

operative. The following discussion is not intended to fully spell out this argument, but only to note it as an important implication of the analysis of dignity conducted in this study. I first look at the work concerning religious dimensions and then move to the more recent work on environmental ethics.

The starting point is provided by the thesis of the historian Lynn White, Jr who, in an influential article published in the journal *Science* in 1967,[54] argued that Christianity was not only at the root of a conquering attitude of humankind over nature but also, for that very reason, it was at the root of what he called 'our ecologic crisis'. The relationship between the 'disenchantment of the world', enabled by Christianity's Weltanschauung, and the development of Western societies had been widely studied even before White's work.[55] But White linked it to the ecological crisis. His reasoning is essentially an exploration of the mentality of Latin Christianity in the Middle Ages as well as of the later connection between science and technology, which together have been the main drivers of both 'progress' and environmental degradation. This conjunction of science and technology was, according to White, enabled by the overall view in Latin Christianity of humans as masters of nature. He concluded from this analysis that:

> the fact that most people do not think of these attitudes as Christian is irrelevant. No new set of basic values has been accepted in our society to displace those of Christianity. Hence, we shall continue to have a worsening ecologic crisis until we reject the Christian axiom that nature has no reason for existence save to serve man.[56]

Similar views have resonated in different strands of philosophical and policy literature. But it is striking that perhaps the main extension of White's voice has been that of Pope Francis himself in the 2015 encyclical letter *Laudato Si'*.[57] White had noted at the end of his account that the main exception to the conquering message of Christianity was that of St Francis of Assisi, who he saw as professing a virtue of humility not only at the individual level, but also for humans as a species. The encyclical carries the title of St Francis' words in the Canticle of the Creatures, *Laudato Si', mi' Signore'* (Praise be to you, my Lord). The text of the encyclical is subtle and combines abundant references to the egalitarian doctrine of St Francis with an unequivocal assertion of the unique dignity of human beings. The possible tension is not ignored. Pope

54 L White, 'The Historic Roots of our Ecologic Crisis' [1967] 155(3767) *Science* 1203–1207.

55 M Weber, *Economy and Society: An Outline of Interpretive Sociology*, 1922, re-issued by G Roth and C Wittich (eds) (University of California Press 1978).

56 White, *supra* n 54, 1207.

57 Pope Francis, *Encyclical Letter Laudato Si'* (Vatican Press 2015).

Francis makes reference to the stance taken by some of his predecessors regarding the overexploitation of nature. Of particular note, he seems to echo – without making any express reference – the thought of White, who had proposed 'Francis as patron saint for ecologists'.[58] At paragraph 10 of the encyclical, Pope Francis mentions that St Francis 'is the patron saint of all who study and work in the area of ecology, and he is also much loved by non-Christians'. Then at paragraph 11, he notes that:

> If we approach nature and the environment without this openness to awe and wonder, if we no longer speak the language of fraternity and beauty in our relationship with the world, our attitude will be that of masters, consumers, ruthless exploiters, unable to set limits on their immediate needs. By contrast, if we feel intimately united with all that exists, then sobriety and care will well up spontaneously. The poverty and austerity of St Francis were no mere veneer of asceticism, but something much more radical: a refusal to turn reality into an object simply to be used and controlled.

The encyclical never crosses the line of equating humans and nature in terms of dignity. It does recognize the tension, albeit in veiled terms, and addresses it by redefining human dignity in terms that require harmony with nature. Thus, although it does not recognize an extension of the circle, it does accept the intrinsic value of nature and limits the powers associated with human dignity. The articulation between these two circles is thus comparable to that between *dignitas* and human dignity, although the dignity of nature is only brandished to limit the powers flowing from human dignity rather than to extend the circle.

Another parallel can be made with respect to the secularization of the debate, which has been reformulated in a terminology that makes a distinction between 'instrumental' and 'intrinsic' value. This distinction lies at the roots of global environmental governance and, more generally, of contemporary approaches to human rights and environmental protection. The field is vast, and one could make reference to a wide range of materials, from writings,[59] to political speeches,[60] to reports from expert

58 White, *supra* n 54, 1207.

59 R Routley, 'Is There a Need for a New, an Environmental Ethic?' [1973] 1 *Proceedings of the 15th World Congress of Philosophy* 205–210; R Routley and V Routley, 'Human Chauvinism and Environmental Ethics' in DS Mannison, MA McRobbie and R Routley (eds), *Environmental Philosophy* (Australian National University 1980), 96–189; H Rolston, 'Is There an Ecological Ethic?' [1975] 85(2) *Ethics* 93–109; H Rolston, *Environmental Ethics: Duties to and Values in the Natural World* (Tampere University Press 1988).

60 I Gandhi, 'Man and Environment', Statement by Indira Gandhi (Prime Minister of India) to the Plenary Session of the UN Conference on the Human Environment, Stockholm, 14 June 1972.

groups,[61] to policy and legal instruments.[62] Reviewing some of them, even briefly, may serve to illustrate how the circles of dignity are interlocked in a rival manner.

At the philosophical level, perhaps the main challenge to 'anthropocentrism' or human 'specism'[63] comes from 'deep ecology' as expounded in the writings of the Norwegian philosopher Arne Næss.[64] Næss initially distinguished between a 'shallow ecology movement' whose main feature was to be anthropocentric and, more specifically, to address pollution and resource depletion for the sake of 'the health and affluence of people in the developed countries'.[65] He contrasted this movement with a 'deep ecology', one based on the idea of 'biospheric egalitarianism'.[66] Interestingly, Næss spoke of an expanded version of the self which would be inherently connected to nature and hence inseparable from it. This is a subtle idea. It does not mean merely that humans are part of the biosphere, as one species among others, but that the very individuality of human beings is a construction that obscures their embeddedness in nature, the fact that the relationship with nature is a definitional feature. As Næss puts it, humans and other organisms are 'knots' in the biospherical net. This is a unequivocal extension of the circle of dignity from humans to other living things and nature, and it came under heavy criticism due to its unintuitive practical implications, which set the right of humans to live and blossom on the same footing with that of other creatures. Deep ecology was revised in the 1980s so as to become a 'platform' (rather than a doctrine) based on eight principles around which many religions and philosophical traditions were expected to converge.[67]

These principles embody the rivalry between the second and the third circles of dignity. They begin[68] with a statement of the intrinsic value of both human and non-human life (understood broadly to include non-living things, such as rivers and landscapes) as well as of its 'richness and diversity'. Then, a delicate balancing between two competing interests is attempted. Humans have 'no right to reduce

61 TEEB (The Economics of Ecosystems and Biodiversity), *Mainstreaming the Economics of Nature: A Synthesis of the Approach, Conclusions and Recommendations of TEEB* (TEEB 2010).

62 See Declaration of the UN Conference on the Human Environment (UN 1972), Principle 1; Rio Declaration on Environment and Development (UN 1992), Principle 1.

63 R Richards, *The Species Problem: A Philosophical Analysis* (Cambridge University Press 2010).

64 A Næss, 'The Shallow and the Deep, Long-Range Ecology Movement' [1973] 16(1) *Inquiry* 95–100; A Næss and G Sessions, 'The Basic Principles of Deep Ecology' (1984), www.deepecology.org/platform.htm; A Næss, *Ecology, Community, Lifestyle* (D Rothenberg, trans.) (Cambridge University Press 1989).

65 Næss, *The Shallow and the Deep*, *supra* n 64, 95.

66 *Ibid.*, 95–96.

67 Næss and Sessions, *supra* n 64.

68 Principles 1 and 2, *ibid.*, 3.

this richness and diversity except to satisfy vital needs'.[69] The term 'vital needs' is deliberately left open but it appears as the irreducible core of human dignity ensuring its overriding character. It represents, in other words, a redrawing of the second circle within the third circle of biospheric value.

Even in its revised and more ecumenical form, the expectations of the deep ecology platform remain far too ambitious when compared with the policy realities. In turning against sovereign dignity, human dignity has not only conquered much of the space of the first circle, it has also expanded to exclude the third one. At present, the recognition of the dignity of this third circle is nowhere near the expanse and importance of the second. That is perhaps the dilemma presented by human dignity. Due to the rival character of dignity as a concept, the assertion of human dignity against *dignitas*, or sovereign dignity, carries with it an encroachment on a third circle. The price of preserving human dignity and all the advancements that follow from it may well be, as suggested by White in his seminal essay, to remain entangled in the man–nature attitude deeply grounded in Christian dogma that is, still today, at the roots of our ecological crisis.

From 'sovereignty' to 'human dignity' to 'eco-centrism', the concept of dignity underlies the normative claims of all these three competing circles. More fundamentally, the concept of human dignity opens two conceptual battlefronts. These battlefronts are interdependent because the very assertion of human dignity to protect the individual against the powers of the State may also lay the foundations for an over-exploitation of nature. These are the implications of the concept of human dignity today. International law is therefore based on a secularized concept, that possesses the same exclusionary character that the original religious concept of human dignity – which puts all creation at the service of man. This process of secularization, in turn, finds expression in international law.

The implications of this process, examined in this chapter, lay the foundation of a possible fourth constitutive stage of human dignity. In this stage, dignity expands once again its universal scope beyond the individual and collective human nature and, thus, beyond the human circle. It once again silences its exclusionary character. This stage is, however, beyond the scope of this study. I have narrated the history of the '*protest of humanity*',[70] staging the conflict between human dignity and sovereign dignity. On a different script, the narrative of the history of the interlocked protest and revolt of nature, the third circle of dignity, may, however, find here its *incipit*.

69 Principle 3, *ibid.*, 3–4.

70 382AP/128, dossier 3, 'Discours de René Cassin, Délégué de la France à l'Assemblée Générale des Nations Unies à Paris', 9 December 1948.

Select Bibliography

BOOKS

Abbott, W and Gallagher, J (eds), *Documents of Vatican II* (America Press 1966)

Abtahi, H and Webb, P, *The Genocide Convention: The Travaux Préparatoires* (Martinus Nijhoff 2008)

Agi, M, *René Cassin* (Perrin 1998)

Akhavan, P, *Reducing Genocide to Law, Definition, Meaning, and the Ultimate Crime* (Cambridge University Press 2012)

Allain, J (ed.), *The Legal Understanding of Slavery: From the Historical to the Contemporary* (Oxford University Press 2012)

Alland, D, Chetail, V, de Frouville, O and Viñuales, JE (eds), *Unité et diversité du droit international/Unity and Diversity of International Law. Ecrits en l'honneur du Professeur Pierre-Marie Dupuy/Essays in Honour of Professor Pierre-Marie Dupuy* (Martinus Nijhoff 2014)

Ambos, K, *Treatise on International Criminal Law, vol. 1, Foundations and General Part* (Oxford University Press 2013)

Ambos, K, *Treatise on International Criminal Law, vol. 2, The Crimes and Sentencing* (Oxford University Press 2014)

Arnold, R and Quénivet, N (eds), *International Humanitarian Law and Human Rights Law: Towards a New Merger in International Law* (Martinus Nijhoff 2008)

Askin, KD and Koenig, DM, *Women and International Human Rights Law* (Transnational Publishers 2001)

Baker, HC, *The Image of Man. A Study of the Idea of Human Dignity in Classical Antiquity, the Middle Ages, and the Renaissance* (1947) (Harper 1961)

Baker, RS, *Woodrow Wilson and the World Settlement* (Doubleday, Page 1922)

Balladore-Pallieri, G, *La guerra* (Cedam 1935)

Bantekas, I and Nash, S, *International Criminal Law* (3rd ed, Routledge 2007)

Barak, A, *Human Dignity: The Constitutional Value and the Constitutional Right* (Cambridge University Press 2015)

Bariéty, J and Briand, A (eds), *La Société des Nations et l'Europe, 1919–1932* (Presses Universitaires de Strasbourg 2007)

Baron, N and Gatrell, P (eds), *Homelands: War, Population, and Statehood in Eastern Europe and Russia, 1918–1924* (Anthem Press 2004)

Bartelson, J, *A Genealogy of Sovereignty* (Cambridge University Press 1995)

Bassiouni, MC (ed.), *International Criminal Law*, vols 1–3 (2nd ed, Transnational Publishers 1999)

Bassiouni, MC (ed.), *International Criminal Law*, vols 1–3 (3rd ed, Martinus Nijhoff 2008)

Bassiouni, MC and Wise, EM, *Aut dedere Aut judicare: The Duty to Prosecute or Extradite in International Law* (Martinus Nijhoff 1995)

Bassiouni, MC, *Crimes against Humanity* (Cambridge University Press 2011)

Bassiouni, MC, *Crimes against Humanity in International Criminal Law* (2nd ed, Martinus Nijhoff 1999)

Bassiouni, MC, *Crimes against Humanity: Historical Evolution and Contemporary Application* (Cambridge University Press 2011)

Bayertz, K (ed.), *Sanctity of Life and Human Dignity* (Kluwer 1996)

Becker, A, *Les cicatrices rouges, 14–18: France et Belgique occupées* (Fayard 2010)

Bederman, DJ, *The Spirit of International Law* (University of Groningen Press 2002)

Behrens, P and Henham, R, *Elements of Genocide* (Routledge 2013)

Bellelli, R (ed.), *International Criminal Justice* (Routledge 2010)

Bentwich, N, *The Religious Foundations of Internationalism* (Allen & Unwin 1933)

Berman, HJ, *Law and Revolution* (Harvard University Press 1983)

Berman, N, '"The Sacred Conspiracy": Religion, Nationalism, and the Crisis of Internationalism' [2012] 25(1) *LJIL* 9–54

Bernhardt, R (ed.), *Encyclopaedia of Public International Law*, vol. 3 (North Holland Publishing 1982)

Bernhardt, R (ed.), *Encyclopaedia of Public International Law*, vol. 8 (North Holland Publishing 1985)

Bernhardt, R (ed.), *Encyclopaedia of Public International Law*, vol. 2 (North Holland Publishing 1995)

Berns, T (ed.), *Le droit saisi par le collectif* (Bruylant 2004)

Besson, S and Tasioulas, J (eds), *The Philosophy of International Law* (Oxford University Press 2010)

Betti, E, *La struttura dell'obbligazione romana e il problema della sua genesi* (Giuffrè 1985)

Bevilaqua, C, *Direito Público Internacional (A Synthese dos Princípios e a Contribuição do Brasil)* (Livr. Fr. Alves 1911)

Beyerlin, U (ed.), *Essays in Honour of R. Bernhardt* (Springer 1995)

Beyleveld, D and Brownsword, R, *Human Dignity in Bioethics and Biolaw* (Oxford University Press 2004)

Bhagavan, M, *India and the Quest for One World: The Peacemakers*, Transnational History Series (Palgrave Macmillan 2013)

Bhuta, N, Beck, S, Geiss, R, Liu, HY and Kress, C (eds), *Autonomous Weapons Systems: Law, Ethics, Policy* (Cambridge University Press 2016)

Bianchi, A, *International Law Theories. An Inquiry into Different Ways of Thinking* (Oxford University Press 2016)

Bodansky, D, Brunnée, J and Hey, E (eds), *The Oxford Handbook of International Environmental Law* (Oxford University Press 2007)

Bodin, J, *The Six Bookes of a Commonweale*, KD McRae (ed.) (Harvard University Press 1962)

Boemeke, MF, Feldman, GD and Gläser, E (eds), *The Treaty of Versailles: A Reassessment after 75 Years* (Cambridge University Press 1998)

Bonanate, L and Papini, R, *Dialogo interculturale e diritti umani: la Dichiarazione Universale dei Diritti Umani, Genesi, evoluzione, e problemi odierni (1948–2008)* (Il Mulino 2008)

Bonfante, P, *Corso di Diritto Romano, vol. 4: Le obbligazioni* (Giuffrè 1979)

Bonvin, JM, *L'Organisation Internationale du Travail: essai sur une agence productrice de normes* (Presses Universitaires de France 1998)

Borelli, G, *Ragion di stato e Leviatano* (Il Mulino 1993)

Borgwardt, E, *A New Deal for the World: America's Vision for Human Rights* (Harvard University Press 2005)

Bossuyt, MJ, *Guide to the 'Travaux Préparatoires' of the International Covenant on Civil and Political Rights* (Kluwer Academic Publishers 1987)

Brett, AS, *Liberty, Right and Nature: Individual Rights in Later Scholastic Thought* (Cambridge University Press 1997)

Brownlie, I, *Principles of Public International Law* (6th ed, Clarendon Press 2003)

Brunet, R, *La garantie internationale des droits de l'homme d'après la charte de San-Francisco* (Grasset 1947)

Burke, R, *Decolonization and the Evolution of International Human Rights* (University of Pennsylvania Press 2010)

Burns, JH and Goldie, M (eds), *The Cambridge History of Political Thought 1450–1700* (Cambridge University Press 1991)

Burns, SL and Brooks, BJ (eds), *Gender and Law in the Japanese Imperium* (University of Hawaii Press 2013)

Burton, ME, *The Assembly of the League of Nations* (Howard Fertig 1974)

Butler, G and Maccoby, S, *The Development of International Law* (Longmans Green 1928)

Cabanes, B, *The Great War and the Origins of Humanitarianism, 1918–1924* (Cambridge University Press 2014)

Cahn, E, *The Sense of Injustice* (New York University Press 1949)

Capps, P, *Human Dignity and the Foundations of International Law* (Hart Publishing 2009)

Cassese, A, *International Criminal Law* (3rd ed, Oxford University Press 2013)

Cassese, A, Gaeta, P and Jones, JRWD (eds), *The Rome Statute of the International Criminal Court: A Commentary* (Oxford University Press 2002)

Cassese, A et al. (ed.), *The Oxford Companion to International Criminal Justice* (Oxford University Press 2009)

Cassin, R, *La pensée et l'action* (Ed. F. Lalou 1972)

Cassirer, E, *Dall'Umanesimo all'Illuminismo* (La Nuova Italia 1995)

Cattaneo, MA, *Dignità umana e pena nella filosofia di Kant* (Giuffrè 1981)

Cattaneo, MA, *Giusnaturalismo e dignità umana* (Edizioni Scientifiche Italiane 2006)

Cheng, B, *General Principles of Law as Applied by International Courts and Tribunals* (Stevens 1953)

Chetail, V, *International Migration Law* (Oxford University Press 2019)

Clapham, A and P Gaeta (eds), *Oxford Handbook of International Law in Armed Conflict* (Oxford University Press 2014)

Clapham, A, Gaeta, P and Sassòli, M, *The 1949 Geneva Conventions. A Commentary* (Oxford University Press 2015)

Clapham, A, *Human Rights: A Very Short Introduction* (2nd ed., Oxford University Press 2014)
Clapham, A, *Human Rights Obligations of Non-state Actors* (Oxford University Press 2006)
Colanéri, A, *La condition des 'Sans-patrie': Étude critique de l'Heimatlosen* (Librairie générale de droit et de jurisprudence 1932)
Cooper, F, *Colonialism in Question: Theory, Knowledge, History* (University of California Press 2005)
Cortés, JD, *Essays on Catholicism, Liberalism, and Socialism, Considered in Their Fundamental Principles*, W. McDonald (ed.), (Gill & Son 1879)
Coulson, NJ, *The History of Islamic Law* (EUP 1964)
Coursier, H, *The International Red Cross* (ICRC 1961)
Craven, MCR, *The International Covenant on Economic, Social and Cultural Rights* (Oxford University Press 1998)
Crawford, J, (ed.), *Rights of Peoples* (Clarendon Press 1992)
Crawford, J, Pellet, A and Olleson, S, *The Law of International Responsibility* (Oxford University Press 2010)
Crawford, J, *The International Law Commission's Articles on State Responsibility: Introduction, Text and Commentaries* (Cambridge University Press 2002)
Crémieux-Brilhac, JL and Picard, JF, (eds.), *Henri Laugier en son siecle* (CHRS Editions 1995)
Cryer, R, *Prosecuting International Crimes: Selectivity in the International Criminal Law Regime* (Cambridge University Press 2005)
Cryer, R, Friman, H, Robinson, D and Wilmshurst, E, *An Introduction to International Criminal Law and Procedure* (3rd ed., Cambridge University Press 2014)
Cruft, R, Liao, SM and Renzo, M, (eds.), *Philosophical Foundations of Human Rights* (Oxford University Press 2014)
Curran, CE, *Catholic Social Teaching, 1891–Present* (GUP 2002)
D'Aspremont, J and Besson, S, *The Oxford Handbook of the Sources of International Law* (Oxford University Press 2017)
Daly, E, *Dignity Rights* (UPennP 2012)
Danilenko, GM, *Law-Making in the International Community* (Martinus Nijhoff 1993)
Darcy, S and Powderly, J, (eds.), *Judicial Creativity at the International Criminal Tribunals* (Oxford University Press 2010)
Davis, DB, *The Problem of Slavery in the Age of Revolution 1770–1823* (Oxford University Press 1999)
De Hoogh, A, *Obligations Erga Omnes and International Crimes* (Martinus Nijhoff 1996)
De la Chapelle, P, *La Déclaration universelle des droits de l'homme et le catholicisme* (LGDJ 1967)
De Maeyer, J and Viaene, V, (eds.), *World Views and Worldly Wisdom - Visions et expériences du monde: Religion, Ideology and Politics, 1750–2000* (LUP 2016)
De Schutter, O, *International Human Rights Law* (2nd ed., Cambridge University Press 2014)
Debes, R (ed.), *Dignity. A History* (Oxford University Press 2017)
Delmas-Marty, M, *Trois défis pour un droit mondial* (Seuil 1998)

Delmas-Marty, M, *Vers un droit commun de l'humanité* (Les éditions Textuel 1996)
Devoto, G, *Avviamento alla etimologia italiana. Dizionario etimologico* (Le Monnier 1967)
Díaz, AP, *Los trabajos preparatorios de la Declaración Americana de los Derechos y Deberes del Hombre y el origen remoto de la Corte Interamericana* (Instituto de Investigaciones Jurídicas UNAM 2017)
Dinstein, Y, (ed.), *International Law at a Time of Perplexity: Essays in Honour of Shabtai Rosenne* (Martinus Nijhoff 1989)
Dinstein, Y, *The Conduct of Hostilities under the Law of International Armed Conflict* (Cambridge University Press 2004)
Donnedieu de Vabres, H, *Introduction à l'étude du droit pénal international: essai d'histoire et de critique sur la compétence criminelle dans les rapports avec l'étranger* (Sirey 1922)
Donnedieu De Vabres, H, *Les Principles Modernes Du Droit Penal International* (Sirey 1928)
Douzinas, C, *Human Rights and Empire: The Political Philosophy of Cosmopolitanism* (Routledge–Cavendish 2007)
Draper, GIAD, *The Red Cross Conventions* (Stevens & Sons 1958)
Drost, PN, *The Crime of State*, vol. II: Genocide (AW Sythoff 1959)
Dunant, H, *Un Souvenir de Solférino* (Jules-Guillaume Fick 1862)
Duprè, C, *The Age of Dignity, Human Rights and Constitutionalism in Europe* (Bloomsbury 2015)
Dupuy, PM and Viñuales, JE, *International Environmental Law* (Cambridge University Press 2018)
Dupuy, RJ, *L'humanité dans l'imaginaire des nations, conférences, essais et leçons du Collège de France* (Julliard 1991)
Düwell, M, Braarvig, J, Brownsword, R, Van Steenbergen, N, Mieth, D and Düring, D, *The Cambridge Handbook of Human Dignity: Interdisciplinary Perspectives* (Cambridge University Press 2014)
Dworkin, R, *Justice for Hedgehogs* (Harvard University Press 2011)
Dworkin, R, *Life's Dominion: An Argument about Abortion, Euthanasia and Individual Freedom* (Vintage Books 1994)
Dworkin, R, *Taking Rights Seriously* (Harvard University Press 1977)
Fernandez, J and Pacreau, X, *Statut de Rome de la Cour pénale internationale. Commentaire article par article*, 2 tomes (Pedone 2012)
Filmer, R, Sir, *Patriarcha and Other Writings*, J Sommerville (ed.) (Cambridge University Press 1991)
Fink, C, *Defending the Rights of Others: The Great Powers, The Jews, and International Minority Protection, 1878–1938* (Cambridge University Press 2004)
Finnis, J, *Aquinas. Moral, Political, and Legal Theory* (Oxford University Press 1998)
Finnis, J, *Natural Law and Natural Rights* (Oxford University Press 1980)
Fleck, D and Bothe, M (eds), *The Handbook of International Humanitarian Law* (3rd ed., Oxford University Press 2013)
Fortin, K, *The Accountability of Armed Groups under Human Rights Law* (Oxford University Press 2017)
Franck, TM, *The Power of Legitimacy among Nations* (Oxford University Press 1990)

Franklin, JH, *Jean Bodin and the Rise of Absolutist Theory* (Cambridge University Press 1973)
Gaeta, P, Viñuales, JE and Zappalá, S, *Cassese's International Law* (3rd ed., Oxford University Press 2020)
Gaeta, P, (ed.), *The UN Genocide Convention. A Commentary* (Oxford University Press 2009)
Gatrell, P, *A Whole Empire Walking: Refugees in Russia during World War I* (IUP 1999)
Gattini, A Garciandia, R and Webb, P, *Human Dignity and International Law* (Brill 2020)
Gentile, G, *Il pensiero italiano del Rinascimento* (1940) (3rd ed., Le Lettere 2003)
Gihl, T, *International Legislation. An Essay on Changes in International Law and in International Legal Situations* (Oxford University Press 1937)
Gildersleeve, VC, *Many a Good Crusade: Memoirs of Virginia Gildersleeve* (Macmillan 1954)
Ginsburg, T and Dixon, R (eds), *Comparative Constitutional Law* (Edward Elgar 2011)
Ginsburgs, G and Kudriavtsev, VN, (eds.), *The Nuremberg Trial and International Law* (Kluwer Academic Publishers 1990)
Glendon, MA, *A World Made New. Eleanor Roosevelt and the Universal Declaration of Human Rights* (Random House 2001)
Gousseff, C, *L'exil Russe. La Fabrique de réfugié apatride 1920–1928* (CNRS Editions 2011)
Greenberg, M, *Some Postulates of Biblical Criminal Law* (Yehezkel Kaufmann Jubilee Volume 1960)
Grewe, WG, (ed.), *Fontes Historiae Iuris Gentium 1815–1945. Sources Relating to the History of the Law of Nations* (De Gruyter 1988)
Grewe, WG, *The Epochs of International Law* (De Gruyter 2000)
Grosseteste, R, *Ethica Nicomachea*, Libri I–III ('recensio pura'), RA Gauthier (ed.) (Turnhout: Aristoteles Latinus 1972)
Grotius, H, *The Rights of War and Peace*, R Tuck transl. (Oxford University Press 2005)
Guelle, J, *La guerre continentale et les personnes* (Librairie Militaire De J. Domaine 1881)
Guelle, J, *Precis Des Lois de La Guerre Sur Terre* (Pedone Lauriel 1884)
Haggenmacher, P, *Grotius et la doctrine de la guerre juste* (Graduate Institute 1983)
Harding, A, *Medieval Law and the Foundations of the State* (Oxford University Press 2002)
Hathaway, JC, *The Law of Refugee Status* (Cambridge University Press 2014)
Heller, A, *Renaissance Man* (Routledge & Kegan Paul 1967)
Hensel, HM, (ed.), *The Legitimate Use of Military Force, The Just War Tradition and the Customary Law of Armed Conflict* (Routledge 2008)
Henzelin, M, *Le Principe de l'Universalité en Droit Pénal International: Droit et Obligation pour les États de Poursuivre et Juger selon le Principe de l'Universalité* (Bruylant 2000)
Hepburn, AC, (ed.), *Minorities and History* (Edward Arnold 1978)
Herczegh, G, *General Principles of Law and the International Legal Order* (Akadémiai Kiadó 1969)
Hersch, J, *Le droit d'etre un homme, Recueil de textes préparé sous la direction de Jeanne Hersch* (UNESCO 1968)

Hexter, JH, *The Vision of Politics on the Eve of the Reformation: More, Machiavelli, and Seyssel* (Basic Books 1973)
Higgins, AP *The Hague Peace Conferences and Other International Conferences Concerning The Laws And Usages of War Texts Of Conventions With Commentaries* (Cambridge University Press 1909)
Higgins, R, *Problems and Process* (Oxford University Press 1994)
Higgins, R, *Themes and Theories: Selected Essays, Speeches, and Writings in International Law* (Oxford University Press 2009)
Hiitonen, E, *La compétence de l'Organisation Internationale du Travail* (Rousseau & Cie 1929)
Hill, TE, Jr., *Dignity And Practical Reason In Kant's Moral Theory* (Cornell University Press 1992)
Hobbins, AJ, (ed.), *On the Edge of Greatness. The Diaries of John Humphrey, First Director of the United Nations Division of Human Rights, 1948–49* (McGill University Press 1994)
Hoffmann, SL, (ed.), *Human Rights in the Twentieth Century* (Cambridge University Press 2011)
Holborn, LW, *The International Refugee Organization: A Specialized Agency of the United Nations: Its History and Work, 1946–1952* (Oxford University Press 1956)
Holls, FW, *The Peace Conference at The Hague* (Macmillan 1900)
Höpfl, H, *Jesuit Political Thought: The Society of Jesus and the State, c.1540–1630* (Cambridge University Press 2004)
Horne, J, (ed.), *Vers la guerre totale: le tournant de 1914–1915* (Tallandier 2010)
Howland, D, *International Law and Japanese Sovereignty* (Palgrave Macmillan 2016)
Huber, M, *The Good Samaritan: Reflections on the Gospel and Work in the Red Cross* (Gollancz 1945)
Huber, M, *The Red Cross: Principles and Problems* (ICRC 1941)
Hugh, T, *The Slave Trade: The Story of the Atlantic Slave Trade, 1440–1870* (Simon & Schuster 1997)
Humphrey, JP, *Human Rights and the United Nations: a Great Adventure* (Transnational 1984)
Iriye, A, Goedde, P and Hitchcock, WI, (eds), *The Human Rights Revolution* (Oxford University Press 2012)
Jennings, R, and Watts, A, (eds), *Oppenheim's International Law* (9th ed., Oxford University Press 2008)
Jensen, SLB, *The Making of International Human Rights: The 1960s, Decolonization, and the Reconstruction of Global Values* (Cambridge University Press 2016)
Jeßberger F and Geneuss J (eds), *Why Punish Perpetrators of Mass Atrocities?: Purposes of Punishment in International Criminal Law* (Cambridge University Press 2020)
Jessup, P, *A Modern Law of Nations* (Macmillan 1948)
Johansen, B, *Contingency in a Sacred Law: Legal and Ethical Norms in the Muslim Fiqh* (Brill 1999)
Kalmo, H, and Skinner, Q (eds), *Sovereignty in Fragments* (Cambridge University Press 2010)
Kamali, MH, *Freedom of Expression in Islam* (Islamic Texts Society 1997)
Kamali, MH, *Human Dignity in Islam* (International Institute of Advanced Islamic Studies Malaysia 2007)

Kaufman, P et al (eds), *Humiliation, Degradation, Dehumanization: Human Dignity Violated* (Springer 2010)

Kévonian, D, *Réfugiés et diplomatie humanitaire* (Publications de la Sorbonne 2004)

Kolb, R, *Good Faith in International Law* (Bloomsbury 2017)

Koskenniemi, M, *The Gentle Civilizer of Nations, The Rise and Fall of International Law 1870–1960* (Cambridge University Press 2001)

Kretzmer, D and Klein, E (eds), *The Concept of Human Dignity in Human Rights Discourse* (Brill 2002)

Larsen, KM, Cooper, CG and Nystuen, G, *Searching for a 'Principle of Humanity' in International Humanitarian Law* (Cambridge University Press 2013)

Lattanzi, F and Schabas, WA (eds), *Essays on the Rome Statute of the International Criminal Court*, Vol. I (Il Sirente 1999)

Lauren, PG, *The Evolution of International Human Rights* (UPP 1998)

Lauterpacht, H, *An International Bill of the Rights of Man* (Cambridge University Press 1945)

Lauterpacht, H, *International Law and Human Rights* (Stevens & Sons 1950)

Lauterpacht, H, *Private Law Sources and Analogies of International Law* (Lawbook Exchange 1927)

Lauterpacht, H, *The Development of International Law by the International Court* (Stevens & Sons 1958)

Lawrence, TJ, *Les principes de droit international* (5th. ed., transl. J Dumas and A de La Pradelle, Oxford University Press 1920)

Le Bris, C, *L'humanité saisie par le Droit International Public* (LGDJ 2012)

Lee, RS, (ed.), *The International Criminal Court. The Making of the Rome Statute* (Kluwer Law International 1999)

Lemkin, R, *Axis Rule in Occupied Europe* (Carnegie Endowment for International Peace, 1944)

Lemkin, R, *Les actes constituant un danger général considerés comme delits de droit des gens* (Pedone 1933)

Levack, BP, *The Civil Lawyers in England 1603–1641: A Political Study* (Oxford University Press 1973)

Link, AS, *The Papers of Woodrow Wilson*, Vol. 58 (PUP 1966–1994)

Liulevicius, VG, *War Land on the Eastern Front: Culture, National Identity, and German Occupation in World War I* (Cambridge University Press 2000)

Magnard, P, *Actes du Colloque tenu à la Sorbonne, November 1992* (Champion 1995)

Malik, C, *The Problems of Coexistence* (Northwestern University Press 1955)

Malpas, J and Lickiss, N, (eds), *Perspectives on Human Dignity: A Conversation* (Springer 2007)

Margalit, A, *The Decent Society* (Harvard University Press 1998)

Margalit, A, *The Decent Society*, trans. N Goldblum, (Harvard University Press 1998)

Maritain, J, *Man and the State* (University of California Press 1951)

Maritain, J, *The Person and the Common Good*, trans. JJ Fitzgerald (UNDP 1947)

Marrus, M, *The Unwanted: European Refugees in the Twentieth Century* (Oxford University Press 1985)

Martens, FF, *Traité de droit international*, trans. Albert Leo (Librairie Marescq ainé 1883–1887)

Martin, FF, Schnably, SJ, Wilson, R, Simon, J and Tushnet, M, *International Human Rights and Humanitarian Law: Treaties, Cases and Analysis* (Cambridge University Press 2006)

Martinez, JS, *The Slave Trade and the Origins of International Human Rights Law* (Oxford University Press 2012)

Maurer, B, *Le principe de respect de la dignité humaine et la Convention Europeéene des Droits de l'Homme* (La Documentation Française 1999)

Mazower, M, *Governing the World: The History of an Idea, 1815 to the Present* (Penguin 2013)

Mazower, M, *No Enchanted Palace: The End of Empire and the Ideological Origins of the United Nations* (PUP 2009)

McCormack, TLH and Simpson, GJ, (eds), *The Law of War Crimes, National and International Approaches* (Kluwer Law International 1997)

McCoubrey H, *International Humanitarian Law: The Regulation of Armed Conflicts* (Dartmouth 1990)

McCrudden, C, (ed.), *Understanding Human Dignity* (Oxford University Press 2013)

McDougal, MS, Lasswell, HD and Chen, L, *Human Rights and World Public Order* (Yale University Press 1977)

McDougal, MS and Lasswell, HD, *Jurisprudence for a Free Society: Studies in Law, Science and Policy* (Martinus Nijhoff 1992)

McGlynn, C and Munro, V, *Rethinking Rape Law* (Routledge 2010)

McTurnan Kahin, G, *The Asian-African Conference* (Cornell University Press 1956)

Mérignhac, A, *De la sanction des infractions au droit des gens commises au cours de la guerre européenne, par les Empires du Centre* (Pedone 1917)

Meron, T, *Bloody Constraint: War and Chivalry in Shakespeare* (Oxford University Press 1998)

Meron, T, *Henry's Wars and Shakespeare's Laws: Perspectives on the Law of War in the Later Middle Ages* (Oxford University Press 1993)

Meron, T, *Human Rights in International Law* (Oxford University Press 1984)

Meron, T, *Human Rights Law-Making in the United Nations* (Oxford University Press 1986)

Meron, T, *The Humanization of International Law* (Martinus Nijhoff 2006)

Meron, T, *War Crimes Law Comes of Age* (Oxford University Press 1998)

Merriell, DJ, *To the Image of The Trinity: A Study in the Development of Aquinas' Teaching* (Pontifical Institute of Mediaeval Studies 1990)

Mettraux, G, *International Crimes and the ad Hoc Tribunals* (Oxford University Press 2005)

Meyer, MJ and Parent, WA, (eds), *The Constitution of Rights: Human Dignity and American Values* (Cornell University Press 1992)

Meyrowitz, H, *La Repression par les tribunaux allemands des crimes contre l'humanité et l'appartenance à une organisation criminelle en application de la loi n° 10 du Conseil de Contrôle allié* (LGDP 1961)

Miller, DH, *The Drafting of the Covenant*, vol. 2, (G.P. Putnam's sons 1928)

Millot, A, *Les Mandats internationaux*, (Émile Larose, Libraire-Editeur 1924)

Moeckli, D, Shah, S and Sivakumaran, S, (eds), *International Human Rights Law* (2nd ed., Oxford University Press 2014)

Moir, L, *The Law of Internal Armed Conflict* (Cambridge University Press 2002)

Monod, JC, *La querelle de la secularisation, de Hegel à Blumenberg* (Librarie Philosophique J. Vrin 2002)
Morelle, C and Jakob, P, *Henri Laugier. Un esprit sans frontières* (Bruylant 1997)
Morsink, J, *The Universal Declaration of Human Rights: Origins, Drafting, and Intent* (UPP 1999)
Moskowitz, M, *The Policies and Dynamics of Human Rights* (Oceana 1968)
Moyn, S, *Christian Human Rights* (University of Pennsylvania Press 2015)
Moyn, S, *Human Rights and the Uses of History* (Verso 2014)
Moyn, S, *The Last Utopia: Human Rights in History* (Harvard University Press 2010)
Moynier, G, *Essai sur les caracteres generaux des lois de la guerre* (Eggiman, C&Cie 1895)
Næss, A, *Ecology, Community, Lifestyle* (D. Rothenberg, trans.) (Cambridge University Press 1989)
Nersessian, DL, *Genocide and Political Groups* (Oxford University Press 2010)
Nivet, P, *La France occupée, 1914–1918* (Armand Colin 2011)
Noiriel, G, *La tyrannie du national: le droit d'asile en Europe (1793–1993)* (Calmann-Lévy 1991)
Normand, R and Zaidi, S, *Human Rights at the UN: The Political History of Universal Justice* (IUP 2008)
Norwood, SH, *The Third Reich in the Ivory Tower: Complicity and Conflict on American Campuses* (Cambridge University Press 2009)
Nowak, M, Birk, M and Monina,G, (eds.), *The United Nations Convention Against Torture: A Commentary* (2nd ed., Oxford University Press 2019)
Nowak, M, *UN Covenant on Civil and Political Rights: CCPR Commentary* (2nd ed., NP Engel 2005)
Nouwen, S, *Complementarity in the Line of Fire: The Catalysing Effect of the International Criminal Court in Uganda and Sudan* (Cambridge University Press 2013)
Nozick, R, *Anarchy, State and Utopia* (Oxford University Press 1974)
O'Brien, DJ and Shannon, TA (eds), *Catholic Social Thought: The Documentary Heritage* (Orbis Books 1992)
O'Malley, JW, *What Happened at Vatican II* (Harvard University Press 2010)
Oakes, J, *Slavery and Freedom: An Interpretation of the Old South* (Alfred A. Knopf 1990)
Ohlin, JD, (ed.), *Theoretical Boundaries of Armed Conflict and Human Rights* (Cambridge University Press 2016)
Orakhelashvili, A, *Peremptory Norms in International Law* (Oxford University Press 2006)
Pagden, A and Lawrance, J, (eds), *Francisco de Vitoria: Political Writings* (Cambridge University Press 1992)
Parlett, K, *The Individual in the International Legal System* (Cambridge University Press 2011)
Pascal, B, *Pensées*, transl. R Ariew (Hackett 2004)
Passelecq, G and Suchecky, B, *The Hidden Encyclical of Pius XI*, trans. S Rendall (Harcourt, Brace 1997)
Paulsson, J, *The Idea of Arbitration* (Oxford University Press 2013)
Peczenick, A, *On Law and Reason* (Springer 2008)

Pedersen, S, *The Guardians: The League of Nations and the Crisis of Empire* (Oxford University Press 2015)
Pellegrino, ED, et al (eds), *Human Dignity and Bioethics* (Notre Dame Press 2009)
Pentzopoulos, D, *The Balkan Exchange of Minorities and its Impact upon Greece* (Mouton 1962)
Peters, A, *Beyond Human Rights. The Legal Status of the Individual in International Law* (Cambridge University Press 2016)
Phelan, E, *Albert Thomas et la création du B.I.T.* (Grasset 1936)
Pictet, J, et al (eds), *The Geneva Conventions of 12 August 1949: Commentary*, Vol. I, Convention for the Amelioration of the Condition of the Wounded and Sick in Armies in the Field (ICRC 1952)
Pictet, J, et al (eds), *The Geneva Conventions of 12 August 1949: Commentary*, Vol. III, Third Geneva Convention relative to the treatment of prisoners of war (ICRC 1960)
Pictet, J, et al, (eds), *The Geneva Conventions of 12 August 1949: Commentary*, Vol. IV, Geneva Convention relative to the Protection of Civilian Persons in Time of War (ICRC 1958)
Pictet, J, et al, *The Geneva Conventions of 12 August 1949: Commentary*, Vol. II, Geneva Convention for the Amelioration of the Condition of Wounded, Sick and Shipwrecked Members of Armed Forces at Sea (ICRC 1960)
Poggi, G, *The Development of the Modern State: A Sociological Introduction* (Hutchinson 1978)
Politi, M and Nesi, G, (eds), *The Rome Statute of the International Criminal Court* (Routledge 2001)
Politis, N, *Les nouvelles tendances du droit international* (Librairie Hachette 1927)
Portmann, R, *Legal Personality in International Law* (Cambridge University Press 2010)
Poustogarov, FV, *Au Service de la Paix: Frédéric de Martens et les Conférences Internationales de la Paix de 1899 et 1907* (University of Geneva 1999)
Provost, R, *International Human Rights and Humanitarian Law* (Cambridge University Press 2002)
Quataert, JH, *Advocating Dignity: Human Rights Mobilizations in Global Politics* (UPennPress 2009)
Ragazzi, M, *The Concept of International Obligations Erga Omnes* (Oxford University Press 1997);
Rakover, N, *Human Dignity in Jewish Law* (Library of Jewish Law 1998)
Ratner, SR, Abrams, JS and Bischoff, J, *Accountability for Human Rights Atrocities in International Law* (3rd ed., Oxford University Press 2009)
Rawls, J, *A Theory of Justice* (Oxford University Press 1971)
Réale, É, *Le régime des passeports et la Société des Nations* (Rousseau 1930)
Recchia, S and Urbinati, N, (ed.), *A Cosmopolitanism of Nations: Giuseppe Mazzini's Writings on Democracy, Nation Building, and International Relations* (Princeton University Press 2009)
Rehman, J, *International Human Rights Law* (2nd ed., Pearson 2010)
Reus-Smit, C, *Individual Rights and the Making of the International System* (Cambridge University Press 2013)
Reuter, P, *Droit International Public* (6th ed., Presses Universitaires de France 1983)

Richards, R, *The Species Problem: A Philosophical Analysis* (Cambridge University Press 2010)
Ripstein, A, *Force and Freedom: Kant's Legal and Political Philosophy* (Harvard University Press 2009)
Robinson, D, 'Defining Crimes Against Humanity at the Rome Conference' [1999] 93 AJIL 43
Robinson, J, *Human Rights and Fundamental Freedoms* (Institute of Jewish Affairs 1946)
Robinson, N, *The Genocide Convention. A Commentary* (World Jewish Congress 1960)
Robinson, N, *The Universal Declaration of Human Rights* (Institute of Jewish Affairs 1958)
Rodenhäuser, T, *Organizing Rebellion* (Oxford University Press 2018)
Rodgers, G, et al., *The ILO and the Quest for Social Justice, 1919—2009* (ILO 2009)
Rodley, NS, *The Treatment of Prisoners under International Law* (2nd ed., Oxford University Press 1999)
Rolston, H, *Environmental Ethics: Duties to and Values in the Natural World* (TUP 1988)
Romulo, CP, *The Meaning of Bandung* (North Carolina University Press 1956)
Rosen, R, *Dignity: Its History and Meaning* (Harvard University Press 2012)
Rotberg, R, (ed.), *When States Fail: Causes and Consequences* (Princeton University Press 2004)
Rotenstreich, N, *Man and his Dignity* (Magnes Press, Hebrew University 1983)
Rotondi, G, *Leges Publicae Populi Romani* (Società editrice libraria 1912)
Rousseau, Ch, *Principes généraux du Droit international public*, vol. I (Pédone 1944)
Russell, RD, *A History of The United Nations Charter: The Role of the United States 1940–1945* (Brookings 1958)
Sadat LN, (ed.), *Forging a Convention for Crimes Against Humanity* (Cambridge University Press 2011)
Safferling, C and Conze, E, (eds), *The Genocide Convention Sixty Years after its Adoption* (Asser Press 2010)
Safferling, C, *International Criminal Procedure* (Oxford University Press 2003)
Sanajaoba, N, (ed.), *A Manual of International Humanitarian Laws* (Regency 2004)
Sandoz, Y, Swinarski, C and Zimmermann, B, (eds), *Commentary on the Additional Protocols of 8 June 1977 to the Geneva Conventions of 12 August 1949* (Geneva, 1987)
Sangiovanni, A, *Humanity Without Dignity: Moral Equality, Respect, and Human Rights* (Harvard University Press 2017)
Sarat, A, (ed.), *Knowing the Suffering of Others: Legal Perspectives on Pain and Its Meanings* (University of Alberta Press 2014)
Sawyer, R, *Slavery in the Twentieth Century* (Routledge & Kegan Paul ed. 1986)
Saxon, D, (ed.), *International Humanitarian Law and the Changing Technology of War* (Martinus Nijhoff 2013)
Scelle, G, *Précis de droit des gens* (Sirey 1932)
Schabas, WA and Bernaz, N, (eds), *Routledge Handbook of International Criminal Law* (Routledge 2011)
Schabas, WA, *Cambridge Companion to International Criminal Law* (Cambridge University Press 2016)

Schabas, WA, *Genocide in International Law* (2nd ed., Cambridge University Press 2009), 17
Schabas, WA, *The European Convention on Human Rights: A Commentary* (Oxford University Press 2015)
Schabas, WA, *The International Criminal Court: A Commentary on the Rome Statute*, Oxford Commentaries on International Law (2nd ed., Oxford University Press 2016)
Schabas, WA, *The Trial of the Kaiser* (Oxford University Press 2018)
Schabas, WA, *The UN International Criminal Tribunals. The Former Yugoslavia* (Cambridge University Press 2006)
Schaper, BW, *Albert Thomas: trente ans de réformisme social* (Van Gorcum 1959)
Schefgel, J, *L'Apatridie des réfugiés russes* (Éditions Godde 1934)
Scheler, M, *Formalism in Ethics and Non-formal Ethics of Values: A New Attempt toward the Foundation of an Ethical Personalism* (trans. M. S. Frings and R. L. Funk, Northwestern University Press 1973)
Schindler, D and Toman, J, *The Laws of Armed Conflicts* (4th ed., Martinus Nijhoff 2004)
Schopenhauer, A, *The Basis of Morality*, trans. and intro. AB Bullock, (Dover 2005)
Schrijver, N, *Sovereignty over Natural Resources: Balancing Rights and Duties* (Cambridge University Press 1997)
Schuck, MJ and Crowley-Buck, J, (eds), *Democracy, Culture, Catholicism: Voices from Four Continents* (Firenze University Press 2015)
Schwarzenberger, G, *The Dynamics of International Law* (Professional Books, Milton, 1976)
Schwebel, SM, *General Principles of Law and International Due Process: Principles and Norms Applicable* (Oxford University Press 2017)
Schwelb, E, *Human Rights and the International Community. The Roots and Growth of the Universal Declaration of Human Rights, 1948-1963* (Quadrangle Books 1964)
Searle, JR, *Speech Acts: An Essay in the Philosophy of Language* (Cambridge University Press 1969);
Shaw, M, *International Law* (8th ed., Cambridge University Press 2018)
Sheehan, J, *Where Have All the Soldiers Gone? The Transformation of Modern Europe* (Houghton Mifflin 2008)
Sheeran, S and Rodley, N, (eds), *Routledge Handbook of International Human Rights Law* (Routledge 2013)
Shelton, D, *Oxford Handbook of International Human Rights Law* (Oxford University Press 2013)
Simma, B, Khan, DE, Nolte, G, Paulus, A and Wessendorf, N, (eds), *The Charter of the United Nations, A Commentary*, Vol. I-III, (3rd ed., Oxford University Press 2012)
Simpson, AWB, *Human Rights and the End of Empire: Britain and the Genesis of the European Convention* (Oxford University Press 2004)
Skinner, Q, *The Foundations of Modern Political Thought* (Cambridge University Press 1978)
Skran, CM, *Refugees in Inter-War Europe: The Emergence of a Regime* (Clarendon Press 1995)
Slotte, P and Halme-Tuomisaari, M, (eds), *Revisiting the Origins of Human Rights* (Cambridge University Press 2015)
Smith, DC, *H.G. Wells: Desperately Mortal: A Biography* (Yale University Press 1986)

Sommerville, J, (ed.), *King James VI and I, Political Writings* (Cambridge University Press 1994)
Sommerville, J, *Royalists and Patriots: Politics and Ideology in England 1603–1640* (2nd ed., Routledge 1999)
Ssenyonjo, M, *Economic, Social and Cultural Rights in International Law* (Hart 2009)
Stahn, C, (ed.), *The Law and Practice of the International Criminal Court* (Oxford University Press 2015)
Starck, C, *Constitutionalism, Universalism and Democracy: A Comparative Analysis* (Nomos 1999)
Steiner, H, Alston, P and Goodman, R, *International Human Rights in Context* (3rd ed., Oxford University Press 2008)
Steiner, Z, *The Lights that Failed: European International History, 1919–1933* (Oxford University Press 2005)
Stone, J, *International Guarantees of Minority Rights* (Oxford University Press 1932)
Stribis, I, *La manifestation des lacunes en droit international* (Athènes 2009)
Swinarski, C, (ed.), *Studies and Essays on International Humanitarian Law and Red Cross Principles in Honour of Jean Pictet* (Martinus Nijhoff 1984)
Tams, C and Sloan, J, *The Development of International Law by the International Court of Justice* (Oxford University Press 2013)
Tams, C, *Enforcing Obligations Erga Omnes in International Law* (Cambridge University Press 2005)
Tasioulas, J, (ed.), *The Cambridge Companion to the Philosophy of Law* (Cambridge University Press 2020)
Ternon, Y, *L'État criminel, les Génocides au XX siècle* (Seuil 1995)
Testart, A, *Des dons et des dieux. Anthropologie religieuse et sociologie comparative* (Errance 2006)
Thomas, A, *L'Organisation Internationale du Travail et la première année de son activité* (ILO 1921)
Tomuschat, C and JM Thouvenin (eds), *The Fundamental Rules of the International Legal Order: Jus cogens and Obligations Erga omnes* (Martinus Nijhoff 2006)
Tomuschat, C, *Human Rights: Between Idealism and Realism* (3rd ed., Oxford University Press 2014)
Torpey, JC, *The Invention of the Passport: Surveillance, Citizenship, and the State, Cambridge Studies in Law and Society* (Cambridge University Press 2000)
Traer, R, *Faith in Human Rights: Support in Religious Traditions for a Global Struggle* (GUP 1991)
Triepel, H, *Droit international et droit interne* (Panthéon–Assas ed 2010)
Triffterer, O, (ed.), *Commentary on the Rome Statute of the International Criminal Court* (2nd ed., Hart 2008)
Trinkaus, C, *In Our Image and Likeness: Humanity And Divinity in Italian Humanist Thought* (UND Press 1995)
Tuck, R, *Natural Rights Theories* (Cambridge University Press 1979)
UNESCO, *Human Rights: Comments and Interpretations* (UNESCO, Greenwood Press 1949)
UNESCO, *International Dimensions of Humanitarian Law*, Henry-Dunant Institute (UNESCO, Martinus Nijhoff 1988)
Upthegrove, CL, *Empire by Mandate* (Bookman Associates 1954)

Van der Wilt, HG, et al. (eds), *The Genocide Convention: The Legacy of 60 Years* (Martinus Nijhoff 2012)
Vincent, A, *Theories of the State* (Oxford University Press 1987)
Vincenti, U, *Diritti e dignità umana* (Laterza 2009)
Vindry, N, *L'Apatridie (absence de nationalité)* (Vadon 1925)
Virally, M, *Le droit international en devenir: Essais écrits au fil des ans* (Graduate Institute 1990)
Vohrah, LC, et al. (eds), *Man's Inhumanity to Man* (Kluwer Law International 2003)
Von Wright, GH, *Norm and Action: A Logical Enquiry* (Routledge & Kegan Paul 1963)
Waldron, J, (ed.), *Theories of Rights* (Oxford University Press 1984)
Waldron, J, *Dignity, Rank and Rights*, M. Dan–Cohen (ed.), (Oxford University Press 2012)
Walworth, A, *Wilson and His Peacemakers* (Norton 1986)
Watenpaugh, KD, *Bread from Stones: The Middle East and the Making of Modern Humanitarianism* (University of California Press 2015)
Watt, L, *Pope Pius XII on World Order* (Catholic Social Guild 1940)
Weatherall, T, *Jus Cogens: International Law and Social Contract* (Cambridge University Press 2015)
Weil, P, *Qu'est-ce qu'un Français? Histoire de la nationalité française depuis la Révolution* (Grasset 2002)
Werle, G, Jessberger, F, *Principles of International Criminal Law* (3rd ed., Oxford University Press 2014)
Werle, G, *Principles of International Criminal Law* (T.M.C. Asser Press 2005)
Whelan, D, *Indivisible Human Rights. A History* (University of Pennsylvania Press 2010)
Wilson, W, *The Public Papers of Woodrow Wilson: War and Peace, War and Peace*, vol II, RS Baker and WE Dodd (eds) (Harper & Brothers, 1926)
Winter, J and Prost, A, *René Cassin and Human Rights from the Great War to the Universal Declaration* (Cambridge University Press 2013)
Wolfrum, R, (ed.), *United Nations: Law, Policies and Practice* (Springer 1995)
Wright, Q, *Mandates under the League of Nations* (University of California Press 1930)
Zagrebelsky, G, *Intorno alla legge. Il diritto come dimensione del vivere comune* (Einaudi 2009)
Zahar, A and Sluiter, G, *International Criminal Law* (Oxford University Press 2008)
Zegveld, L, *Accountability of Armed Opposition Groups in International Law* (Cambridge University Press 2002)
Zimmermann, A, Dörschner, J and Machts, F, (eds), *The 1951 Convention Relating to the Status of Refugees and Its 1967 Protocol* (Oxford University Press 2011)
Zimmermann, R, *The Law of Obligations: Roman Foundations of the Civilian Tradition* (Oxford University Press 1996)

JOURNAL ARTICLES

Abi-Saab, G, 'The Uses of Article 19' [1999] 10 *EJIL* 339–351
Akehurst, M, 'Reprisals by Third States' [1970] 44 *BYIL* 1

Alston, P, 'Does the Past Matter? On the Origins of Human Rights' [2013] 126(7) *HLR* 2043–2081

Ambos, K, 'Toward a Universal System of Crime: Comments on George Fletcher's Grammar of Criminal Law' [2007] 28 *CardozoL.Rev.* 2647

Andorno, R, 'Human Dignity and Human Rights as a Common Ground for a Global Bioethics' [2009] 34(3) *J Med Philos* 223–240

Andorno, R, 'The Paradoxical Notion of Human Dignity' [2001] 5(2)*Rivista Internazionale di Filosofia del Diritto* 151–168

Anghie, A, 'Colonialism and the Birth of International Institutions: Sovereignty, Economy, and the Mandate System of the League of Nations' [2001] 34 *NYUJIL&P* 513

Audinet, E, 'Le retrait des naturalisations accordées aux anciens sujets de puissances en guerre avec la France' [1915] 42 *JDI* 129–140

Bagaric, M and Allan, J, 'The Vacuous Concept of Dignity' [2006] 5(2) *JHR* 257–270

Baldwin, G, 'Reason of State and English Parliaments, 1610–42' [2004] 25 *HPT* 620–641

Bales, K and Robbins, PT, 'No One Shall be Held in Slavery or Servitude: A Critical Analysis of International Slavery Agreements' [2001] 2 *HRR* 18–45

Barrett, J, 'Dignatio and the Human Body' [2005] 21(4) *SAJHR* 525–546

Bassiouni, MC, 'Enslavement as an International Crime' [1991] 23 *NYJIL&P* 445

Bassiouni, MC, 'From Versailles to Rwanda in Seventy-Five Years: The Need to Establish a Permanent International Criminal Court' [1997] 10 *Harv HRJ* 11–62

Bassiouni, MC, 'Universal Jurisdiction for International Crimes' [2001] 42 *VJIL* 81

Bassiouni, MC, 'World War I, *The War to End All Wars* and the Birth of a Handicapped International Criminal Justice System' [2002] 30 *DJIL&P* 244

Bassiouni, MC and Badr, GM, 'The Shari'a: Sources, Interpretation, and Rule Making' [2002] 1 *UCLA JINEL* 135

Beck, RJ, 'Britain and the 1933 Refugee Convention: National or State Sovereignty?' [1999] 11(4) *IJRL* 597–624

Becker, JJ, 'Albert Thomas d'un siècle à l'autre. Bilan de l'expérience de guerre' [2008] 2 *Les Cahiers de l'Irice* 2

Beitz, CR, 'Human Dignity in the Theory of Human Rights: Nothing But a Phrase?' [2009] 41(3) *PhilosPublicAff* 259–290

Benvenisti, E, 'Human Dignity in Combat: The Duty to Spare Enemy Civilians' [2006] 39 *ILR* 81

Bianchi, A, 'Ferrini v Federal Republic of Germany' [2005] 99 *AJIL* 242

Bianchi, A, 'Human Rights and the Magic of Jus Cogens' [2008] 19(3) *EJIL* 491–508

Bianchi, A, 'Immunity v. Human Rights: the Pinochet Case' [1999] 10 *EJIL* 237–277

Borgwardt, E, 'When You State a Moral Principle, You Are Stuck with It: The 1941 Atlantic Charter as a Human Rights Instrument' [2006] 46 *VJIL* 501

Buergenthal, T, 'The Evolving International Human Rights System' [2006] 100(4) *AJIL* 783–807

Burgers, JH, 'The Road to San Francisco: The Revival of the Human Rights Idea in the Twentieth Century' [1992] 14 *HRQ* 447

Burke, R, 'The Compelling Dialogue of Freedom, Human Rights at the Bandung Conference' [2006] 28(4) *HRQ* 947–965

Carozza, PG, 'From Conquest to Constitutions: Retrieving a Latin American Tradition of the Idea of Human Rights' [2003] 25 *HRQ* 281

Cassese, A, 'The Martens Clause: Half a Loaf or Simply Pie in the Sky?' [2000] 11 *EJIL* 187

Cassin, R, 'Quelques souvenirs sur la Déclaration Universelle de 1948' [1968] 1 *Revue de droit contemporain* 10

Chetail, V, 'Sovereignty and Migration in the Doctrine of the Law of Nations: An Intellectual History of Hospitality from Vitoria to Vattel' [2017] 27(4) *EJIL* 901–922

Christenson, GA, 'Jus Cogens: Guarding Interests Fundamental to International Society' [1987] 28 *VaJIntlL* 645

Ciampi, A, 'The Italian Court of Cassation Asserts Civil Jurisdiction over Germany in a Criminal Case Relating to the Second World War: The Civitella Case' [2009] 7 *JICJ* 597–615

Conklin, AL, 'Colonialism and Human Rights: A Contradiction in Terms? The Case of France and West Africa, 1895–1914' [1998] 103(2) *AHR* 419–442

Coupland, R and Herby, P, 'Review of the Legality of Weapons: A New Approach, the SIrUS Project' [1999] 835 *IRRC* 583–592

Coupland, R, 'Humanity: What Is It and How Does It Influence International Law?' [2001] 844 *IRRC* 969–990

Crawford, J, 'Revising the Draft Articles on State Responsibility' [1999] 10 *EJIL* 435–460

De Sena, P and De Vittor, F, 'State Immunity and Human Rights: The Italian Supreme Court Decision on the Ferrini Case' [2005] 19 *EJIL* 89–112

Delmas-Marty, M, 'Le crime contre l'humanité, les droits de l'homme et l'irréductible humain' [1994] 3 *RSC* 477

Dickinson, E, 'The New Law of Nations' [1925–1926] 32 *WVLQ* 4

Dinstein, Y, 'International Criminal Law' [1985] 20 *ILR* 206

Donnelly, J, 'Human Rights and Human Dignity: An Analytic Critique of Non-Western Conceptions of Human Rights' [1982] 76(2) *AmPolSciRev* 303–316

Doswald-Beck, L and Vité, S, 'International Humanitarian Law and Human Rights Law' [1993] 293 *IRRC* 94

Doswald–Beck, L, 'International Humanitarian Law and the Advisory Opinion of the International Court of Justice on the Legality of the Threat or Use of Nuclear Weapons' [1997] 316 *IRRC* 35

Draper, GIAD, 'The Ethical and Juridical Status of Constraints in War' [1972] 55 *Military Law Review* (Department of the Army Pamphlet 1972) 169

Dupré, C, 'Unlocking Human Dignity: Towards a Theory for the 21st Century' [2009] 3 (2) *EHRLR* 190–205

Dupuy, PM, 'L'obligation en droit international' [2000] 44 *Archives de philosophie du droit*

Dupuy, PM, 'Quarante ans de codification du droit de la responsabilité des etats: un bilan' [2003] 107 *RGDIP* 305

Dworkin, R, 'The Model of Rules' [1967] 35 *UChiLRev* 14

Eckel, J, 'Human Rights and Decolonization: New Perspectives and Open Questions' [2010] 1 *Humanity:IJHR*, Fall, 111–135

Englard, I, 'Human Dignity: From Antiquity to Modern Israel's Constitutional Framework' [2000] *CLR* 21

Feldman, D, 'Human Dignity as a legal value', Part I–II [1999–2000] *PL* 682–702

Fink, C, 'Minority Rights as an International Question' [2000] 9(3) *ContempEurHist* 385–400

Fox, H, 'State Responsibility and Tort Proceedings against a Foreign State in Municipal Courts' [1989] 20 *NYIL* 3–34
Friedmann, W, 'The Uses of "General Principles" in the Development of International Law' [1963] 57 *AJIL* 279–299
Gaeta, P, 'Does President Al Bashir Enjoy Immunity from Arrest?' [2009] 7 *JICJ* 315–332
Gasser, HP, 'International Humanitarian Law and Human Rights Law in Non-International Armed Conflict: Joint Venture or Mutual Exclusion?' [2002] 45 *GYIL* 149
Gattini, A, 'War Crimes and State Immunity in the Ferrini Decision' [2005] 2 *JICJ* 224–242
Gerber, P, Kyriakakis, J and O'Byrne, K, 'General Comment 16 on State Obligations Regarding the Impact of the Business Sector on Children's Rights: What Is Its Standing, Meaning and Effect?' [2013] 14 *MJIL* 93–129
Glendon, MA, 'The Forgotten Crucible: The Latin American Influence on the Universal Human Rights Idea' [2003] 16 *HHRJ* 27–39
Goodwin-Gill, GS, 'The Right to Seek Asylum: Interception at Sea and the Principle of Non-Refoulement'(2011) 23 *IJRL* 3
Gross, AM, 'Human Proportions: Are Human Rights the Emperor's New Clothes of the International Law of Occupation?' [2007] 18 *EJIL* 1
Gutteridge, JAC, 'The Geneva Conventions of 1949' [1949] 26 *BYIL* 294
Harvey, DA, 'Lost Children or Enemy Aliens? Classifying the Population of Alsace after the First World War' [1999] 34 *JCH* 537–554
Hathaway, JC, 'The Evolution of Refugee Status in International Law: 1920–1950' [1984] 33(2) *ICLQ* 348
Henckaerts, JM, 'The Grave Breaches Regime as Customary International Law' [2009] 7 *JICJ* 683
Henkin, L, 'Human Rights (1985–1990)' [1995] 2 MPEPIL
Henkin, L, 'The United Nations and Human Rights' [1965] 19(3) *IO* 504–517
Heyns, C, 'Autonomous Weapons in Armed Conflict and the Right to a Dignified Life: An African Perspective' [2017] 33(1) *SAJHR* 46–71
Higgins, R, 'Reality and Hope and International Human Rights: A Critique' [1981] 9(5) *HofstraLRev* 1–15
Higgins, R, 'Recent Developments in the Law of Sovereign Immunity in the United Kingdom' [1977] 71(3) *AJIL* 423–437
Hobbins, AJ, 'John Peters Humphrey and the Genesis of the Universal Declaration of Human Rights' [1999] 9 *JOrSt* 24–41
Hobbins, AJ, 'René Cassin and the Daughter of Time: The First Draft of the Universal Declaration of Human Rights' [1989] 2 *Fontanus* 7–26
Hohfeld, WN, 'Fundamental Legal Conceptions as Applied to Judicial Reasoning' [1913] 23 *YLJ* 16–59
Hörnle, T and Kremnitzer, M, 'Human Dignity as a Protected Interest in Criminal Law' [2013] 44 *Isr. L. Rev* 143–167
Humphrey, JP, "International Protection of Human Rights", The Annals of the American Academy of Political and Social Science' [1948] 255 *Foreign Policies and Relations of the United States* 15–21
Hwang, P, 'Defining Crimes Against Humanity in the Rome Statute of the International Criminal Court' [1998] 22 *FILJ* 457

Jessberger, F and Powell, C, 'Prosecuting Pinochet in South Africa: Implementing the Rome Statute of the International Criminal Court' [2001] 14 *SAJCJ* 344

Kaleck, W, 'From Pinochet to Rumsfeld: Universal Jurisdiction in Europe 1998–2008' [2009] 30 *MJIL* 927

Kelman, HC, 'The Conditions, Criteria, and Dialectics of Human Dignity – A Transnational Perspective' [1977] 21 *ISQ* 529–552

Kévonian, D, 'Question des réfugiés, droits de l'homme: éléments d'une convergence pendant l'entre-deux-guerres' [2003] 72 *Matériaux pour l'histoire de notre temps*, 40–49

Kolb, R, 'Aspects historiques de la relation entre le droit international humanitaire et les droits de l'homme' [1999] 37 *CYIL* 57

Kolb, R, 'Principles as Sources of International Law (With Special Reference to Good Faith)' [2006] 53(1) *NILR* 1

Kolnai, A, 'Dignity' [1976] 51 *Philosophy* 197

Kreicker, H, 'National Prosecution of Genocide from a Comparative Perspective' [2005] 5 *ICL Review* 313

Kress, C, 'Versailles-Nuremberg-the Hague: Germany and International Criminal Law' [2006] 40 *IL* 15

Krill de Capello, HH, 'The Creation of the United Nations Educational, Scientific, and Cultural Organization' [1970] 24(1) *IO* 1–30

Kunz, JL, 'The United Nations Convention on Genocide' [1949] 43 *AJIL* 738

Lagodny, O, 'Human Dignity and Its Impact on German Substantive Criminal Law and Criminal Procedure' [1999] 33 *Isr. L. Rev.* 575

Lauterpacht, E, 'The Legal Irrelevance of the "State of War"' [1968] 62 *ASIL Proc* 58

Lauterpacht, H, 'The Universal Declaration of Human Rights' [1948] 25 *BYIL* 354–381

Le Moli, G, 'Autonomy and Accountability of the UN in Peacekeeping Operations: The Case of the Central African Republic' [2017] 20 *UNYB* 213–238

Le Moli, G, 'Three Circles of Dignity' [2019] 11 *JHRP* 1–13

Le Moli, G and Viñuales, JE, 'Today as Yesterday? Unilateral Coercive Measures and Human Dignity' [2019] *Chinese JIL* 18(2) 437–447

Lee, E, 'The Declaration of Philadelphia: Retrospect and Prospect' [1994] 133(4) *ILR* 467–485

Lee, MYK, 'Universal Human Dignity: Some Reflections in the Asian Context' [2008] 3 (1) *AsJCL* 1–33

Lee, RS, 'The Rwanda Tribunal' [1996] 9 *LJIL* 37

Lemkin, R, 'Genocide as a Crime under International Law' [1947] 41(1) *AJIL* 145–151

Lemkin, R, 'Genocide' [1946] 15(2) *American Scholar* 227–230

Lippman, M, 'Islamic Criminal Law and Procedures: Religious Fundamentalism v. Modern Law' [1989] 12(1) *BCICLR* 56

Luban, D, 'Human Dignity, Humiliation and Torture' [2009] 19 *Kennedy Institute of Ethics Journal* 211–230

Macklin, R, 'Dignity Is a Useless Concept' [2013] 327(7429) *BMJ* 1419–1420

Matz, N, 'Civilization and the Mandate System under the League of Nations' [2005] 9 (1) *UNYB* 47–95

McAuliffe deGuzman, M, 'The Road from Rome, The Developing Law of Crimes Against Humanity' [2000] 22 *HRQ* 335

McClelland, J, 'The Review of Weapons in accordance with Article 36 of Additional Protocol 1' [2003] 850 *IRRC* 397–415

McCrudden, C, 'Human Dignity and Judicial Interpretation of Human Rights' [2008] 19(4) *EJIL* 655, 655–724
McDougal MS and Lasswell, HD, 'The Identification and Appraisal of Diverse Systems of Public Order' [1959] 53(1) *AJIL* 1–29
McGreevy, JT, 'Catholics, History, and Conscience' [2009] *VLR* 54
Meron, T, 'Francis Lieber's Code and Principles of Humanity' [1998] 36 *ColumJTransnatlL* 269
Meron, T, 'The Humanization of Humanitarian Law' [2000] 94 *AJIL* 239
Meron, T, 'The Martens Clause, Principles of Humanity and Dictates of Public Conscience' [2000] 94 *AJIL* 78
Meron, T, 'War Crimes in Yugoslavia and the Development of International Law' [1994] 88 *AJIL* 78
Meyrovitz, H, 'The Principle of Superfluous Injury or Unnecessary Suffering' [1994] 299 *IRRC* 98
Misner, P, 'The Predecessors of "Rerum Novarum" Within Catholicism' [1991] 49 *Review of Social Economy* 4, Centennial of 'Rerum Novarum' and Semicentennial of the Association, 444–464
Monod, JC, 'What's New in Our Current "International Secularism"?' [2012] 25(1) *LJIL* 67–72
Morsink, J, 'World War Two and the Universal Declaration' [1993] 15 *Human Rights Quarterly* 357–405
Pellet, A, 'Can a State Commit a Crime? Definitely, Yes!' [1999] 10(2) *EJIL* 425–434
Pellet, A, 'The New Draft Articles of the International Law Commission on the Responsibility of States for Internationally Wrongful Acts: A Requiem for States' Crime?' [2001] 32 *NethYIL* 55
Poustogarov, VV, 'The Martens Clause in International Law' [1999] 1 *JHIL* 125–135
Pratt, V and Viñuales, JE, 'Rétroactivité et non-rétroactivité en droit international: essai de clarification conceptuelle à partir de l'éxpérience du Procès de Nuremberg' [2013] 59 *Annuaire français de droit international* 327–358
Provost, R, 'Reciprocity in Human Rights and Humanitarian Law' [1994] 65 *BYIL* 383
Rassam, AY, 'Contemporary Forms of Slavery and the Evolution of the Prohibition of Slavery and the Slave Trade Under Customary International Law' [1999] 39 *VJIL* 303
Reisman, M, 'Application of Humanitarian Law in Non–International Armed Conflicts, Remarks by W. Michael Reisman' [1991] 85 *ASIL Proc* 83
Reisman, M and Silk, J, 'Which Law Applies to the Afghan Conflict' [1988] 82 *AJIL* 465
Resnick, J and Chi-hye Suk, J, 'Adding Insult to Injury: Questioning the Role of Dignity in Conceptions of Sovereignty' [2003] 55 *SLR* 1921–1962
Rikhof, J, 'Hate Speech and ICL: The Mugesera Decision by the Supreme Court of Canada' [2005] 3 *JICJ* 1121–1133
Roberts, K, 'The Contribution of the ICTY to the Grave Breaches Regime' [2009] 7 *JICJ* 743
Rodenhäuser, T, 'Human Rights Obligations of Non-State Armed Groups in Other Situations of Violence: The Syria Example' [2012] 3 *IHLS* 263
Rolston, H, 'Is There an Ecological Ethic? [1975] 85(2)*Ethics* 93–109
Romulo, CP, 'On Natural Law and International Law' [1949] 35(8) *Va.L.Rev* 1052
Root, E, 'Francis Lieber' [1913] 7 *AJIL* 453–469

Routley, R, 'Is There a Need for a New, an Environmental Ethic?' [1973] 1 *Proceedings of the 15th World Congress of Philosophy* 205–210

Ruiz Miguel, C, 'Human Dignity: History of an Idea' [2002] 50 *Jahrbuch des öffentlichen Rechts* 281

Sachariew, K, 'State Responsibility for Multilateral Treaty Violations: Identifying the Injured State and Its Legal Status' [1998] 35 *NILR* 273–289

Sadat, LN, 'Crimes Against Humanity in the Modern Age' [2013] 107 *AJIL* 334

Sajoo, AB, 'Islam and Human Rights: Congruence or Dichotomy?' [1990] 4 *TICLJ* 23–34

Scelle, G, 'Une ère juridique nouvelle,' *La paix par le droit* (July–August 1919),

Schabas, WA, 'Genocide Trials and Gacaca Courts' [200] 3 *JICJ* 879

Schachter, O, 'Human Dignity as a Normative Concept' [1983] 77 *AJIL* 848

Schwelb, E, 'Some Aspects of International Jus Cogens as Formulated by the International Law Commission' [1967] 61 *AJIL* 946

Sensen, O, 'Human Dignity in Historical Perspective: The Contemporary and Traditional Paradigms' [2011] 10 *EJPT* 71

Senturk, R, 'Adamiyyah and 'Ismah: The Contested Relationship between Humanity and Human Rights in the Classical Islamic Law' [2002] 8 *TKIS* 39–70

Senturk, R, 'Sociology of Rights: I Am Therefore I Have Rights: Human Rights in Islam Between Universalistic and Communalistic Perspectives' [2005] 2(1) *MWJHR* 1

Shultziner, D, 'A Jewish Conception of Human Dignity: Philosophy and its Ethical Implications for Israeli Supreme Court Decisions' [2006] 34 *JReliEthi* 663

Shultziner, D and Rabinovici, I, 'Human Dignity, Self-Worth, and Humiliation: A Comparative Legal–Psychological Approach Psychology' [2012] 18(1) *PubPoly&L* 105–143

Sicilianos, LA, 'The Classification of Obligations and the Multilateral Dimension of the Relations of International Responsibility' [2002] 13 *EJIL* 1127–1145

Simma, B, 'Universality of International Law from the Perspective of a Practitioner' [2009] 20(2) *EJIL* 265–297

Simma, B and Paulus, AL, 'The Responsibility of Individuals for Human Rights Abuses in Internal Conflicts: A Positivist View' [1999] 93 *AJIL* 302

Simpson, AWB, 'Britain and the European Convention' [2001] 34(3) *CornILJ* 523–553

Simpson, B, 'Self-Determination, Human Rights and the End of Empire in the 1970s' [2013] 4(2) *Humanity: IJHR*, 239–260

Siordet, F, 'La Conférence diplomatique de Genève' [1949] 31 *RICR* 475

Szpak, A, 'National, Ethnic, Racial, and Religious Groups Protected against Genocide in the Jurisprudence of the ad hoc International Criminal Tribunals' [2012] 23 *EJIL* 155

Thomas, A, 'Justice sociale et paix universelle. Réflexions sur un texte' [1924] 6 *La Revue de Paris* 241–261

Thomas, A, 'Organisation Internationale du Travail: origine, développement, avenir' [1921] 1 *RIT* 1

Tschirkovitch, S, 'Les nouvelles Conventions internationales de Genève relatives à la protection des victimes de la guerre du 12 août 1949' [1950] 54 *RGDIP* 97

Verdross, A, 'Les principes généraux du droit applicables aux rapports internationaux' [1938] 45 RGDIP 44

Vernon, R, 'What is Crime against Humanity?' [2002] 10 *JPP* 231–49

Viñuales, JE, 'Cartographies imaginaires: Observations sur la portee juridique du concept de "régime spécial" en droit international' [2013] 140 *JDI* (Clunet) 405
Waltz, S, 'Reclaiming and Rebuilding the History of the Universal Declaration of Human Rights' [2002] 23(3) *Third World Quarterly* 437–448 Waldron, J, 'How Law Protects Dignity' [2012] 71(1) *CLJ* 200–222
Wartel, E, 'Humanitarians and their Moral Stance in War: The Underlying Values' [2009] 91 *IRRC* 779–802
Weis, P, 'The International Protection of Refugees' [1954] 48(2) *AJIL* 194
Werle, G and Burghardt, B, 'Do Crimes Against Humanity Require the Participation of a State or a "State-Like" Organization?' [2012] 10 *JICJ* 1151
Williams, G, 'The Definition of Crime' [1955] 8 *Current Legal Problems* 107
Wippman, D, 'The Evolution and Implementation of Minority Rights' [1997] 66 *FLR* 597
Wyler, E, 'From "State Crime" to "Responsibility to Serious Breaches for Obligations of Peremptory Norms of General International Law"' [2002] 13(5) *EJIL* 1147–1160
Zahra, T, 'The Minority Problem: National Classification in the French and Czechoslovak Borderlands' [2008] 17 *CEH* 137–165

HAGUE ACADEMY COURSES

Besson, S, 'La due diligence en droit international' [2020] 409 RCADI
Cançado Trindade, AA, 'International Law for Humankind: Towards a New Jus Gentium' [2005] 317 RCADI
Cassin, R, 'La declaration universelle et la mise en oeuvre des droits de l'homme' [1951] 79 RCADI
Chacko, CJ, 'India's Contribution to the Field of International Law Concepts' [1958] 93 RCADI
Crawford, J, 'Multilateral Rights and Obligations in International Law' [2006] 319 RCADI
Draper, GIAD, 'The Geneva Conventions of 1949' [1965] 114 RCADI
Dupuy, PM, 'L'unité de l'ordre juridique international – Cours général de droit international public' [2002] 297 RCADI
Fenwick, CG, 'The Progress of International Law during the Last Forty Years' [1951] 79 RCADI
Fitzmaurice, G, 'The General Principles of International Law, Considered from the Standpoint of the Rule of Law' [1957] 92 RCADI
Frowein, A, 'Reactions by not Directly Affected States to Breaches of International Law' [1994] 248 RCADI 396
Graven, J, 'Les crimes contre l'humanité' [1950] 76 RCADI
Guggenheim, P, 'Les principes de Droit international public' [1952] 80 RCADI
Jennings, RY, 'General Course on Principles of International Law' [1967] 121 RCADI

Kaeckenbeeck, G, 'La Charte de San-Francisco dans ses rapports avec le droit international' [1948] 70 RCADI

Kalshoven, F, 'Arms, Armaments and International Law' [1985] 191 RCADI

Lagarde, P, 'La réciprocité en droit international privé' [1977] 154 RCADI

Lauterpacht, H, 'The International Protection of Human Rights' [1947] 70 RCADI

Mazzeschi, P, 'Responsabilité de l'Etat pour violation des obligations positives relatives aux droits de l'homme' [2008] 333 RCADI

Meron, T, 'International Law in the Age of Human Rights' [2003] 301 RCADI

Pictet, J, 'La Croix-Rouge et les Conventions de Genève' [1950] 76 RCADI

Politis, N, 'Le problème des limitations de la souveraineté et la théorie de l'abus des droits dans les rapports internationaux' [1925] 6 RCADI

Reuter, P, 'Principes de Droit international public' [1961] 103 RCADI

Rolin, H, 'Les principes de Droit international public' [1950] 77 RCADI

Röling, BVA, 'The Law of War and the National Jurisdiction since 1945' [1960] 100 RCADI

Rosenne, S, 'The Perplexities of Modern International Law' [2001] 291 RCADI

Rousseau, Ch, 'Principes de Droit international public' [1958] 93 RCADI

Schindler, D, 'The Different Types of Armed Conflicts According to the Geneva Coventions and Protocols' [1972] 163 RCADI

Schwarzenberger, G, 'The Fundamental Principles of International Law' [1955] 87 RCADI

Simma, B, 'From Bilateralism to Community Interest' [1994] 250 RCADI

Sorensen, M, 'Principes de Droit international public' [1960] 101 RCADI

Vichniac, M, 'Le statut international des apatrides' [1933] 43 RCADI

Virally, M, 'Le principe de réciprocité dans le droit international contemporain' [1967] 122 RCADI

Watts, A, 'The Legal Position in International Law of Heads of States, Head of Governments and Foreign Ministers' [1994] 247 RCADI

Index

For EU product safety concerns, contact us at Calle de José Abascal, 56–1°, 28003 Madrid, Spain or eugpsr@cambridge.org.

www.ingramcontent.com/pod-product-compliance
Ingram Content Group UK Ltd.
Pitfield, Milton Keynes, MK11 3LW, UK
UKHW020651180726
473384UK00011B/553

9781009045711